MEN OF ARMOR:
THE HISTORY OF B COMPANY, 756TH
TANK BATTALION IN WORLD WAR II

MEN OF ARMOR:
THE HISTORY OF B COMPANY, 756TH TANK BATTALION IN WORLD WAR II

Part I: Beginnings, North Africa, and Italy

JEFF DANBY

CASEMATE

Philadelphia & Oxford

Published in the United States of America and Great Britain in 2021 by
CASEMATE PUBLISHERS
1950 Lawrence Road, Havertown, PA 19083, USA
and
The Old Music Hall, 106–108 Cowley Road, Oxford OX4 1JE, UK

Hardback Edition: ISBN 978-1-63624-013-8
Digital Edition: ISBN 978-1-63624-014-5

A CIP record for this book is available from the British Library

Printed and bound in the United States of America by Sheridan

Typeset by Lapiz Digital Services

For a complete list of Casemate titles, please contact:

CASEMATE PUBLISHERS (US)
Telephone (610) 853-9131
Fax (610) 853-9146
Email: casemate@casematepublishers.com
www.casematepublishers.com

CASEMATE PUBLISHERS (UK)
Telephone (01865) 241249
Email: casemate-uk@casematepublishers.co.uk
www.casematepublishers.co.uk

Front cover image: Sgt Richter and fellow B Company tankers crowd around a captured German tank in Tunisia. (Arthur Richter)

To all the fine men who served in
B Company of the 756th Tank Battalion
During World War II,
Especially those forty-seven tankers
Who made the ultimate sacrifice.

"Courage is fear holding on a minute longer."
—George S. Patton

"Experience: that most brutal of teachers.
But you learn, my God do you learn."
—C. S. Lewis

"Sweat saves blood, blood saves lives, and brains save both."
—Erwin Rommel

"Victory belongs to the most persevering."
—Napoleon Bonaparte

"War is hell."
—William Tecumseh Sherman

Contents

List of Maps   ix
Dedication   xi
Introduction: *The Research Behind* Men of Armor   xv

              The Setting   1
Chapter 1   Origins: June 1940 to June 1941   13
Chapter 2   Formation: June 1941 to December 1941   26
Chapter 3   Preparing for a New Kind of War: December 1941
              to May 1942   42
Chapter 4   California and a Captaincy: May 1942 to January 1943   56
Chapter 5   North African Foothold: January 1943 to February 1943   74
Chapter 6   Border Watchers: February 1943 to May 1943   86
Chapter 7   Tunisia: April 1943   100
Chapter 8   Bizerte Bystanders: May 1943 to 15 September 1943   115
Chapter 9   Italy: 16 September 1943 to 22 November 1943   130
Chapter 10   Reorganized: 23 November 1943 to 10 January 1944   150
Chapter 11   The Gates of Hell: 11 January 1944 to 21 January 1944   163
Chapter 12   The Rapido River: 21 January 1944 to 26 January 1944   178
Chapter 13   Attack: 27 January 1944   200
Chapter 14   Bridgehead: Evening 27 January 1944 to 29 January 1944   223
Chapter 15   Caira: Evening 29 January 1944 to 30 January 1944   243
Chapter 16   The Barracks: 31 January 1944 to 1 February 1944   255
              Wilkinson's Odyssey: Part One   273

Appendix 1   Glossary, Phonetic Alphabet, and Military Clock   276
Appendix 2   U.S. Army Grades (Officers and Enlisted) of World War II   279
Appendix 3   U.S. Army Organization of WWII Combat Infantry Units   281
Appendix 4   B Company, 756th Tank Battalion (L) Roster of 1 June 1941   282
Appendix 5   B Company, 756th Tank Battalion Roster from 10 January
              to 27 January 1944   284

Appendix 6   Table of Organization for U.S. Army Tank Company
              (Light), March 1942   286
Appendix 7   Table of Organization for U.S. Army Tank Company
              (Medium), September 1943   287
Appendix 8   Vehicle Chart for U.S. Army Tank Battalion (Medium),
              September 1943   288
Appendix 9   Table of Organization for U.S. Army Tank Battalion
              (Medium), 1943   289
Appendix 10   756th Tank Battalion (L) Cadre Orders, June 1941   291
Appendix 11   B Company 756th Tank Battalion, 1 June 1941
              Morning Report   293
Appendix 12   B Company, 756th Tank Battalion, Record of Events,
              December 1941   294
Appendix 13   756th Arrival at Cassino Document   295
Appendix 14   Yellow Orders from 756th HQ for 27 January 1944   296
Appendix 15   29 January 1944 B Company Morning Reports   297

Special Acknowledgments   298
Bibliography   300
Endnotes   309
Index   363

List of Maps

1. Expansion of Axis Power in Europe, 1941 — xviii
2. The Continental United States, 1941 — 12
3. Western Washington State, 1941 — 25
4. California, 1942 — 41
5. North Africa, 1943 — 73
6. Tunisia, April 1943 — 99
7. Southern Italy (Looking Northward), 1 October 1943 — 129
8. B Company, 756th Tank Battalion, in Southern Italy, 17 September 1943–23 February 1944 — 149
9. Approaching Cassino Through the Mignano Gap, Mid-January 1944 — 162
10. Cassino Region Battle Lines, 20 January 1944 — 173
11. 36th Infantry Division Attack on the Gari/Rapido, 20–21 January 1944 — 177
12. Locating Potential Tank Trails Across the Rapido, 24 January 1944 — 189
13. Wilkinson's Attack, 1pm, 27 January 1944 — 218
14. Crossing the Rapido, 4pm, 29 January 1944 — 240
15. Composite View of Barracks Area (Facing North), February 1944 (Photo) — 254
16. Cassino Area Map, 1944 — 272

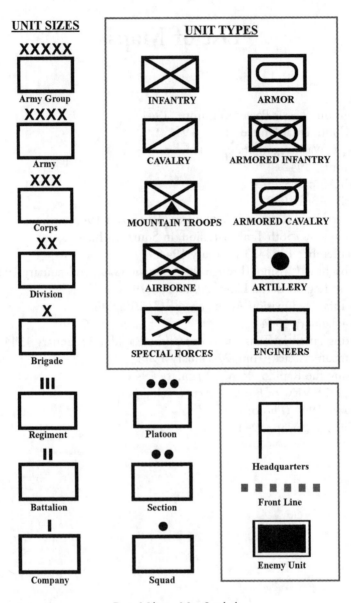

Basic Military Map Symbols

Dedication

Forty-seven men died in combat while serving in B Company—including my own grandfather. Surviving B Company tankers insisted the war's true "heroes" were their crewmates who did not return home. This work is dedicated to them:

Pvt John F. Bacha
Sgt Harold M. Behymer
2nd Lt Winston L. Blythe
Pvt Robert A. Bohland
T/5 William R. Boyer
Pvt Charles R. Brewer
Pvt Paul N. Cardullo
Pfc Frank Carmello
Pfc Charles W. Connor
Sgt Melville E. Corson
1st Lt George A. Current
1st Lt Edgar R. Danby
Cpl John W. Davis
Pvt Dual F. Dishner
Pvt Ascencion Esparza
S/Sgt Chester L. Estkowski
Sgt Leonard D. Froneberger
Pfc Michael Gautieri
2nd Lt Wayne B. Henry
Pvt Charles R. Johns
Pvt Burdette W. Kinney
Sgt Luther A. Kinsworthy
Pfc Verner L. Kreitlow
Pvt Merlin A. Kudick

Cpl Donald E. LaDue
1st Lt Verus M. Langham
Pvt Ruben B. Mapes
Pfc John D. Mekus
2nd Lt Anthony F. Melfi
Sgt Frank W. Mielcarski
2nd Lt Andrew D. Orient
Pfc David J. Orris
Cpl William T. Payne
Pvt William F. Pennetta
T/5 Paul A. Saale
Sgt Frank M. Schafer
T/4 Reuben C. Schipper
S/Sgt Hamilton A. Smith
Pvt Walter F. Smith
T/5 Leak H. Smitherman
Sgt Walter C. Taylor
Cpl Paul P. Tirpak
Cpl Steve Vargo
T/4 Bernard C. Wammes
T/4 Joe K. Wright
Sgt Eugene K. Wunderlich
Cpl Ervin E. Zentz

To thoroughly research this company's history, I obtained copies of the "Individual Deceased Personnel Files" (IDPFs) for each man. These are better described as their "Graves Registration" files, chronicling the search, retrieval, and burial of their earthly remains. IDPF is a cold, bureaucratic acronym that masks pure horror within their aged, yellowed pages. The fading type on mimeographed forms and hand-scrawled notes along the margins reveal tragic details of real lives snuffed out in ghastly ways. In some files, skeletal charts show half a body missing. One learns, along with the medical examiner, what happens when a human being encounters a *Panzerfaust* blast. Several files include the testimony of French villagers who reverently removed chunks of charred flesh and bone from shattered American tanks and buried these unknown foreign liberators in their own local cemeteries. Graves Registration arrived months—sometimes years—later to finally reclaim those remains. To help in the identification, surviving crewmates were often asked to complete affidavits describing how they had been splattered with the blood, muscle, and brain matter of their friends; to relive the terror of fleeing fiery tanks while listening helplessly to the screams of comrades being roasted alive. This is truly the stuff of nightmares.

Even so, these gory details pale next to the despair and anguish expressed by surviving family members in their correspondence to various U.S. government agencies. Nearly every file contains these letters, and each one screams of huge holes ripped into the lives of countless people: Mothers, fathers, wives, sweethearts, sons, daughters, friends, and colleagues left bewildered, devastated, and scarred forever over the loss of their men. Beautifully penned letters cling to faint hopes of a bureaucratic error—that a dead son, brother, or fiancé might still be alive in some prisoner of war camp somewhere. Grieving mothers pleaded for their sons' remains to be returned home quickly just so they could be close to them. Such requests were usually honored but took several years to fulfill. In some cases, nothing could be returned because nothing was ever recovered. Some wrote to President Truman in frustration—hoping he could perform the impossible. Others asked only for a photograph of their loved one's overseas gravesite because they could never earn the means to travel the great distances themselves. Wives requested personal effects, hoping the return of a wedding ring, engraved watch, or cherished bracelet would reunite them in some way with their dead lover. Many times, such items couldn't be returned because they had perished along with the tanker, or were so badly damaged, burned, or plastered in blood as to be deemed "unsuitable" for repatriation. Paternalistic U.S. government policies generally prohibited the return of items testifying to violent deaths. Nevertheless, in most cases *some* personal effects—usually camp items, clothing, or B-trains footlockers—were eventually returned to family.[1]

I hate those files. They are emotional torture to read. Yet I believe each man would want you to know *exactly* what happened to them in clearest detail. Perhaps when enough of us view combat realistically and honestly, such fiascos won't keep happening over and over again. There is nothing glamorous, glorious, or entertaining about war.

These forty-seven fallen men hailed from twenty-three different states—representing nearly half the continental United States. Seven joined from Ohio alone. Their average age was twenty-six. The oldest was thirty-four and the youngest only eighteen. They forfeited promising, bright futures and their unfulfilled contributions to humanity will never be known. When one considers that these forty-seven were but a tiny percentage of some *sixty million lives* extinguished in World War II, it seems ludicrous to characterize that war in terms of winners and losers—although it remains fashionable and romantic to do so. *Both sides* lost in that war. One can only truthfully claim the "winners" may have lost a bit less than the "losers." One cannot sift meticulously through forty-seven U.S. government IDPFs and conclude otherwise.

Two B Company survivors also deserve special recognition: Charles M. Wilkinson and David D. Redle, the two company commanders who led combat operations. Their recollections and contributions comprise a substantial share of this narrative, and a comprehensive unit history simply could not have been written without them. I came to know both men quite well—Dave much more so than Charles—but only because Charles passed away in 2009, just as I was beginning to assemble material for this work. Charles's voice carries on, however, in his fine memoirs and a highly-detailed war diary he left to the world, which his family so graciously shared with me. Charles was a sensitive, articulate writer with a keen eye, an adventurer's spirit, and a rare devotion to honest self-assessment. He was also a steadfast, thoughtful company commander; a tall, lean Texan rancher who inspired many by always setting an even-handed, courageous example.

Dave didn't keep a wartime diary. He had no need of one because he was blessed with an extraordinary memory. I tested his recollections against the unit records, journals, and other primary source documents many, many times. Very rarely was he wrong and when he was, it was over some trivial detail—such as being off by a day when recalling the arrival of a new platoon leader or mistakenly believing that one of his dairy farming tankers came from Wisconsin rather than Michigan. In terms of the action, however, Dave remembered everything with vivid, cinematic clarity. I have no doubt that his shrewd attention to every last detail helped Dave protect his men and survive the war. Dave was a soldier's officer with "a lion's heart"—as an admiring fellow officer succinctly described him.[2] He earned the undying respect and admiration of everyone associated with him—officers and enlisted men alike—and led his company through nearly-impossible missions with a practical hand, razor-sharp intellect, and an unpretentious disposition.

Both Charles and Dave were young men shouldered with the crushing responsibility of leading a hundred men and seventeen 32-ton tanks into combat. In 1941, they were untested Army reserve officers fresh out of college, barely in their twenties and assigned to a fledgling unit without tanks in a new service branch lacking any established doctrine. From 1943 through 1945, both men commanded this remarkable tank company through some of the war's harshest and bloodiest battles. They were incredibly adept and courageous officers, completely dedicated to their men and to the success of their mission. Perhaps they were products of a different era, but I don't think so. Both men were proud of their unique service—but at the same time they viewed themselves as quite ordinary. Dave once told me "you would do the same" had I faced the same hellish conditions under which he struggled. I don't believe he meant me *personally*; he meant we *all* have the capability to handle far more than we think. Therein is the entire message of this multi-volume history: *Each of us* has the untapped talents and latent capacity to endure extreme hardship and solve seemingly insurmountable problems. Look to these men as proof and inspiration.

The wartime lessons learned by Dave, Charles, and all the other tankers of B Company, 756th Tank Battalion, are life's lessons learned. If they could defeat what a terrible World War threw at them, then you and I can certainly overcome what life tosses our way. Always keep your wits and your faith. Every big problem can be broken down into smaller ones and solved one segment at a time. Focus on the immediate task at hand and attend to the needs of those around you, and you can overcome almost any obstacle with time. Don't fret over the things you can't control, and don't make excuses for failing to correct the things you can. You will never overcome a challenge if you lie down and quit. If you die striving, so be it. There's no better way to live and no better way to meet your end. Death finds us all at some point so there is no sense in wasting time by worrying about it.

Persevere.

Introduction:
The Research Behind *Men of Armor*

My dad was two days shy of his eighth birthday when the war claimed his father. The U.S. Army never gave the circumstances—only that 1st Lt Edgar R. Danby died in battle on 27 August 1944, somewhere in southern France while serving in B Company of the 756th Tank Battalion. Because Edgar shares a common grave with two crewmates at the Zachary Taylor National Cemetery in Louisville, Kentucky, my family assumed something catastrophic happened to his Sherman tank—the result, perhaps, of an artillery shell blast or from striking a mine. Edgar's wife, Maxine, was too distraught and preoccupied with raising my father and his younger brother to investigate. Edgar's father, Septimus, wrote letters to the U.S. Army seeking assurances his beloved son did not suffer. The Army always responded but could never provide those assurances. In time, Septimus gave up the effort and lived out his remaining days as a grieving parent left to ponder. His deep religious faith brought him some solace.

Like many, I grew up in the aftermath of World War II also pondering. Edgar's Army photos hung on our family room wall beside cartoon paintings given to him by French soldiers he trained while serving as an armor instructor with the Fifth Army Invasion Training Center near Oran, Algeria. I remember being six years old and wondering what happened to him. The question always nagged at me, but I grew older not knowing where to look for answers or if it was even wise to start digging. Edgar's violent death was still a very painful memory for my grandmother, father, and uncle.

Marrying and raising a young family changed my complacent attitude. I suddenly felt a responsibility—really, an *obligation*—to preserve Edgar's memory in a meaningful way for my children. He was a brilliant professional musician with a bright career ahead of him. He kept volunteering for combat even though the Army kept giving him opportunities to avoid it. A couple of old photos and anonymous paintings did not do his sacrifice justice. On the fifty-sixth anniversary of his death, 27 August 2000, I posted one of those desperate "looking for someone who knew my grandfather" messages on the Society of the Third Infantry Division website. Two days later Karl Kincaid responded. Karl served in B Company of the 756th Tank Battalion but arrived as a replacement several months after Edgar's death. Nevertheless, he put me in touch with David Redle, Edgar's commanding officer. I will never forget how nervous I was making that first phone call to Dave and how gracious he was relaying all the crucial details my family had never been told. Edgar's death was instant. He did not suffer. A German tank ambushed him near Allan, France. My next call was to my dad, and then my grandmother. Both were equally stunned and grateful.

My appetite for knowledge was only whetted. Who was with him? Why were they in Allan? Who were they fighting? Every answer yielded ten new tantalizing questions and I soon became adept at tracking down sources. I wrote, called, and interviewed every associated living veteran I could find. I meticulously documented everything they told me. I became involved with the 756th Tank Battalion Association—serving as roster secretary, attending annual reunions before their retirement in 2010, and setting up and maintaining their website (www.756tank.com). That early research into my grandfather's small role in the battle for Allan, France, led to the book *Day of the Panzer* (Casemate Publishing, 2008), but the process yielded even more fascinating information beyond the limited scope of that work. Obviously, I had to write another book—this one detailing the history of B Company, 756th Tank Battalion over the *entire* war.

For the next few years, I toiled to recover the documentary record of the company—which was scattered everywhere. Even as I started writing in 2014, I never stopped searching.

Most surviving 756th Tank Battalion's unit records are housed at the National Archives in College Park, Maryland. Photos and film can be found there as well. The company "Morning Reports" are kept at the National Personnel Records Center in St Louis, Missouri. Trips involving many days of culling and copying were required at both places. The 756th Tank Battalion was attached to many different "parent" outfits during the war. Those unit records had to be researched and copied as well. I also made a trip to the U.S. Army War College in Carlisle, Pennsylvania, to copy manuscript materials. The IDPF Graves Registration files are now housed under the U.S. Army Human Resources Command at Fort Knox, Kentucky. These can only be obtained through formal Freedom of Information Act requests. You can only ask for a few at a time and a year may pass before you receive them. It took several years to collect the nearly fifty I needed.

Fortunately, much can also be found online. The National Archives has a search section on their website. With practice and patience, one can find prisoner of war records, enlistment records and more. Fort Leavenworth's Combined Arms Research Library (CARL) has a magnificent searchable digital collection that only expands with time—so I am constantly rechecking their website. One can find rare unit records, manuscripts, official unit histories, books, etc., all in PDF form—impossible to obtain otherwise. I simply can't praise CARL enough. Ancestry.com, Newspapers.com, and Findagrave.com also became invaluable sources. There are also many online university libraries featuring searchable electronic collections of yearbooks, U.S. Army maps, and Signal Corps photos. Whenever I needed a used or out-of-print book, I generally found it at Alibris.com or Abebooks.com—maybe not the first time, but by checking back a few months later. Again, online research requires patience, creativity, and dogged determination. Nothing easy is ever given to you—but if you keep on panning through the muck, eventually you uncover gold.

Because of my twenty-year connection with the 756th Tank Battalion Association, I have a ready network of veterans' families I can call upon to help. They have provided me with invaluable photos, diaries, memoirs, and interviews of their dads, granddads, or uncles who served in the outfit but have since passed away. If I needed personal details of veterans with no past connections to the Association, I reached out to hometown newspapers, VFW Halls, American Legion Posts, and genealogy societies. Sometimes they helped me locate veterans' families. Sometimes not. Not all searches end in success.

I did not hesitate to contact historical societies in key towns in Europe where the 756th fought. As a result, I've made wonderful friends with other historians, researchers, and authors in Germany, France, Italy, Netherlands, Switzerland, and New Zealand. Here's my highest advice to anyone researching WWII: Help your fellow travelers. If you can assist someone in their research, take the time and do so. Even if they can't repay you in kind, somebody someplace else will help you when you can't repay them in kind. Yes, I know this is called "good karma"—but it's 100% true. Sometimes, unexpectedly wonderful things happen. Just last year, my filmmaker friend, Ron Lowther, discovered the long-lost B Company unit journal gathering dust in the attic of the Eisenhower Presidential Library. I looked high and low for that journal many years ago and gave up on the assumption the U.S. Army disposed of it in the 1950s. I didn't find that journal. Ron did—by accident—simply because I helped him and he knew about my work.

It's strange this needs to be said, but cooperation is so much better than conflict.

EXPANSION
of AXIS POWER
in EUROPE
December 1941

The Setting

An average young American man living somewhere within the immense continental expanse of 1930s America worried little about European squabbles. As the Great Depression dragged on from one year into

British Mark I Tank (1916)

the next, simply making ends meet became his chief challenge. Seeking a job, keeping a job, or acquiring the skills to land a job were his overarching ambitions. Many toiled as farmhands, factory laborers, clerks, or shopkeepers. Others apprenticed long hours toward a skilled trade. Those with professional aims studied for college degrees. Miserable economy aside, the United States remained the world's leading manufacturer—hungry for a new generation of engineers, chemists, and business managers. Naturally, young men desire more from life than just a steady paycheck, so remaining concerns gravitated toward finding wives, raising families, buying cozy homes, driving sleek new cars, or finding leisure time for life's simple pleasures such as camping, fishing, or sandlot baseball. These were the modest aims of many in 1930s America. A long grueling tour through Europe did not factor into those plans—certainly not the claustrophobic, austere, and terrifying trials of life inside a tank.

Every evening, the mahogany radio in the family living room warmed to a soft orange glow and the Art Deco speaker grill oscillated a crackling myriad of voices delivering news and entertainment from near and far: Japan invades Manchuria. Prohibition is repealed to the joy of many. An enigmatic and charismatic figure named Adolf Hitler is named Chancellor of Germany. The magnificent Hoover Dam is dedicated. Fascist Italy invades Abyssinia. Jessie Owens wins four gold medals at the 1936 Olympics. A civil war erupts and consumes Spain. Max Schmeling knocks out Joe Louis for the World Heavyweight title. A huge dust storm ravages the Plain States. Pioneering aviator Amelia Earhart mysteriously disappears somewhere over the Pacific. Japan sinks an American gunboat, the USS *Panay*, in the Yangtze River. A resurgent Germany absorbs Austria and then Czechoslovakia. Joe Louis pummels Max Schmeling to regain the World Heavyweight title. A hurricane slams into New England. A radio play by Orson Welles panics some Americans over fictional Martian invaders. What was real or imaginary, threatening or entertaining was not always easy to discern—especially against the backdrop bustle of more pressing personal concerns.

Most of those radio reports and newsprint stories took place "out there" well beyond the familiar environs of a farm, town, or city. Local life, though economically challenged, marched on as it always had. And despite the growing turmoil around the world, few had any reason to believe such faraway events could ever directly affect America.

The radio and the transatlantic cable may have brought instant news, but Europe could have just as easily been located on the moon. Commercial airline service floundered in its absolute infancy. There were no jet planes. A propeller seaplane journey across the Atlantic was a hair-raising twenty-nine-hour ordeal through low altitude turbulence buffeting travelers about inside a noisy cabin. Few did it, wanted to do it, or could even afford to do it. Transatlantic Zeppelins offered three or four days of quieter and more relaxing travel, but flights—also unaffordable for most—were few and far between. When the *Hindenburg* exploded in a massive fireball at Lakehurst, New Jersey, on 6 May 1937, all transatlantic Zeppelin services effectively ceased. In order to travel to and from Europe, most people had to journey by sea—consuming a full week's worth of time aboard the newest and fastest ocean liners. Older steamships took even longer.

The temperament of the American people was steadfastly anti-war—and for understandable reasons. The "Great War" experience of 1914–18 planted an indelible disgust deep inside the American psyche. Few had any desire to repeat that disaster. The lives of 116,000 young American men were lost in that futile effort, with hundreds of thousands of others gassed, maimed, or left suffering from what was, at the time, indelicately called "shell shock." The war was astonishingly brutal, destructive, and bloody. In total, seventeen million were killed—mostly young European men. Worse, four meat-grinding years of unceasing trench warfare did little to resolve the underlying causes—the petty bickering between aristocrats and officials, the corrupting power of central banks, the national jealousies, and economic colonial rivalries. Most Americans had little appetite for entanglement in another mess like that.

The 1920 presidential election marked a thorough repudiation of that war and of Wilsonian foreign interventionism. The public chose "a return to normalcy,"[1] rejected President Wilson's grandiose "League of Nations" project and concentrated instead on creating wealth in the form of faster automobiles, soaring gothic skyscrapers, and a vast array of consumer wonder products. In fact, "war" became so unpopular that a series of international treaties in the early 1920s scrapped much of the world's armies and navies.[2] By 1928, even war itself was outlawed.[3] Naïve in retrospect, perhaps, but at the time, these agreements were viewed as pioneering triumphs of diplomacy. So fervent burned the anti-war sentiment that throughout the 1920s, U.S. silver dollars were minted with "PEACE" stamped boldly below an expectant eagle gazing toward a bright sunrise. A branch of olive leaves lay clutched in its talons, but noticeably absent were the familiar arrows. Major hostilities still raged here and there around the world: Russia and China were embroiled in civil wars. Mussolini seized power in Italy. Ireland was in revolt. Mexico was in revolt. Dozens of smaller conflicts also smoldered throughout the decade—ranging from labor spats over wages, to unending border tiffs and unquenchable nationalistic independence movements. The U.S., however, refrained from most of these disputes militarily and hummed along just fine—confirming for many that a policy of neutrality worked best.

The collapse of the markets in 1929 and subsequent global depression in the 1930s certainly dampened American optimism, but not the anti-war zeal. Although some lone voices—such as Winston Churchill of Great Britain—expressed grave concerns over the burgeoning confidence of Nazi Germany and the imperial intentions of a rising Japan, they were considered alarmist, extremist, or irrational opinions at the time. The 1919 Treaty of Versailles straight-jacketed Germany both economically and militarily—so severely that the German Mark had vaporized into a hyperinflationary ether by 1923. Famed British economist John Maynard Keynes wrote a world bestselling book in 1919 criticizing the treaty as overly harsh and self-defeating.[4] Keynes feared European disaster. The U.S. never signed the Treaty of Versailles out of similar concerns, but instead made separate peace with Germany in 1920. Three years later, news stories of starving Germans pushing wheelbarrows full of cash to purchase sawdust-leaven bread certainly confirmed Keynes's warnings. In time, many Europeans came to regret the terms of the treaty, and international enforcement softened considerably.

By the time Hitler consolidated power in the mid-1930s and started reconstituting and modernizing the German military, the treaty was essentially dead. France and Great Britain did not want to risk renewed conflict with Germany, and Hitler skillfully exploited this sentiment throughout the '30s. Part of his success, no doubt, is owed to his adversaries' political paralysis stemming from "Treaty of Versailles guilt." The United States had little reason to oppose German rearmament, especially since the build-up seemed to go hand in hand with Germany's welcome economic resurgence and confidence. American banks and large corporations such as Standard Oil and the Ford Motor Company had bet heavily on German industry throughout the '20s and began seeing hefty returns on that investment. Millions of Americans of German ancestry maintained some fondness for their mother country and found little to admire in the decadence, incompetence, and social turmoil characteristic of the 1920s Weimar era. Starry-eyed journalists, academics, and government elites became increasingly enamored over centralized state-planning schemes and openly *admired* the outward industrial accomplishments showcased by strongmen such as Hitler, Stalin, and Mussolini. Many glowing articles were written about these suspect figures—by a press all too eager to overlook their flaws. Other strategic thinkers feared the expansionist designs of the Soviet Communism brand in particular and regarded a revived Germany as a functional counterbalance to Stalin. Charles Lindbergh, the American icon who piloted the first non-stop, solo transatlantic airplane voyage in 1927, was an invited guest of Nazi Germany for several official visits in the mid-1930s.[5] Upon returning to the U.S., Lindbergh quite publicly declared that war with Germany would be foolhardy and disastrous. Ambassador Joe Kennedy, a prominent Democrat, and Senator Robert

Taft, a prominent Republican, agreed. President Franklin Roosevelt won re-election in 1936 by pledging vociferously to keep America out of European affairs.

Americans took great comfort in their geography. The country was buttressed by two immense oceans on either flank, a vast frozen artic wasteland to the north and an assortment of weak countries to the south, swept relatively clear of European and Asian interference under decades of Monroe Doctrine enforcement.[6] This was why "Fortress America" and "America First" political movements naturally attracted so many adherents at the time. The expansionary designs of Nazi Germany and Imperial Japan were locally focused and limited by the technology of the times. The United States lay thousands of miles away—well beyond any realistic military danger. No nation possessed bomber aircraft that could fly more than a few hundred miles. Intercontinental bombers existed only on the pages of dime store science magazines—in futuristic, imaginative illustrations alongside flying cars, monorail sky tubes, and Flash Gordon-style rocket ships and ray guns. Aircraft carriers were controversial naval experiments, untested in battle, and the subject of endless debate among senior military planners.

At the end of the Great War, aviation proponent Colonel William "Billy" Mitchell argued that battleships would be rendered obsolete because of airplanes. Mitchell envisioned coastal air forces repulsing enemy navies with revolutionary ease. From this radical proposition, Mitchell and other aviation visionaries pitched the ideas of floating airfields or "aircraft carriers." The War Department was intrigued and Mitchell demonstrated through live exercises that a few ordinary biplanes could drop cheap bombs and sink big expensive ships. The sacrificial targets, however, were old, decommissioned battleships and decrepit cruisers sitting dead in the water with nobody on deck returning fire upon the slow, wobbly attackers. The Navy conducted their own aviation bombardment tests and arrived, not surprisingly, at quite different conclusions. Subsequent trials held jointly by Mitchell and the Navy degenerated into turf fights over the ground rules before erupting into contentious publicity battles covered by a fascinated national press. The Navy claimed planes could be shot down well before they flew within bombing range. Air war proponents insisted the opposite and demonstrated through live-fire exercises the extreme difficulty for surface artillery to shoot down even the slowest planes moving across the sky. Battleship believers scoffed at the idea of aircraft carriers in general—criticizing their vulnerability and over-dependency on the protection of attendant packs of destroyers. All those extra ships consumed precious funds at a time when military budgets were paper thin. The debate raged on for years.

One thing was for certain: No one *really knew* if the big-gun battleships would remain sovereigns of the sea or if carrier planes would ultimately render them obsolete. Only a shooting war could end that argument. It was a controversy that few Americans outside stuffy War Department offices even cared about—save for any resulting cost overruns to an already tight military budget. In the end, the Navy compromised and purchased a few carriers to go along with their traditional fleet of battleships. Even as late as 1938, only sixteen escort-class or fleet-class sized aircraft carriers patrolled the oceans of the world.[7] Five belonged to the U.S., five others to the British, and one to France. Japan had six, and the Germans were about to launch their one and only flat-top, the *Graf Zeppelin*. So, of the handful of aircraft carriers floating among their entourages of support vessels, most were commanded by officers loyal to or friendly with the United States.

While the Navy argued battleships versus carriers, the Army debated horses versus tanks. To the few Americans who even paid attention to military matters, the tank was an odd contraption. Unlike the sleek, sweating, graceful horse, the tank was a cold, metallic, clumsy hulk—part bulldozer, part Brink's truck, and part pillbox. As a weapon, the tank had only recently debuted on the battlefield and registered a rather mixed record. For centuries, land warfare had been fought as lines of infantry, maneuvering and firing across large battlefields with archers or cannon artillery supporting from the rear. When a crack formed in an opposing line, horse-mounted cavalry was unleashed upon the breach—often causing the enemy to break ranks. Good timing resulted in a rout—and often victory. This simple, ancient method proved tried and true for centuries. The advent of the machine gun (MG), however, positioned generously throughout static trenches beyond minefields and rows of barbed wire during the Great War, turned battlefield convention upside down. Waves of horse cavalry could not break a trench stalemate. Artillery barrages, aerial bombardments, poison gas attacks, and suicidal infantry charges also failed to gain more than a few hundred yards of muddy ground against the ferocious, ceaseless bite of MG spray. And any measly gains were usually lost to enemy counterattacks the following day. Military planners exhausted all attempts at conventional solutions to break the impasse and began looking toward "wonder weapons" for salvation. This is how the tank was born.

Conceived in secret and tested independently by both British and French developers, the first tanks were rushed to the front in September 1916. The British officially dubbed these new contraptions "land ships" and even assigned "His Majesty's Ship" (H.M.S.-L.) designations to each one.[8] The first land ship model was rather unimaginatively called a "Mark I." The name "tank" originated because, during manufacture, British hulls were intentionally mislabeled "water carriers" to obscure their true purpose.[9] For better or worse, the phony name stuck. The French, who reliably assign more glamorous sounding names to novel advancements, called their creation a *char canon*, *char mitrailleuse*, or *char d'assaut*—which translate as "cannon chariot," "machine-gun chariot," and "attack chariot" respectively, or simply *char* (chariot) for short.

The British first threw their Mark I tanks against stubborn German emplacements at the Battle of the Somme on 15 September 1916.[10] The results proved lackluster—yet promising. Several of the thirty-two attacking tanks advanced deep enough to wreak havoc among the German trenches but withdrew due to lack of support.[11] In subsequent days, the tanks charged and withdrew again and again, reaping results enticing enough for the British to order a thousand more new land ships by month's end. The British Mark I tanks used in these early actions were hulking, rhomboidal-shaped boxes of riveted iron, with a pair of caterpillar tracks rotating around the entire hull. Cannons, MGs, and vision slits bristled along both sides. They were obnoxiously loud, vibrated like the dickens, and spewed smoke like flaming oil pots. They crept painfully slowly, broke down often, and easily succumbed to artillery bursts. Their stuffy interiors were under-ventilated and members of the eight-man crews passed out often from breathing their own engine exhaust and ammunition fumes. In order to communicate with headquarters (HQ), carrier pigeons were dispatched from a tiny rooftop door. Despite the drawbacks, the first tanks could traverse churned earth where horses and infantrymen failed, and so improved models, Mark II through VII, soon joined the fight. In the end, over 2,000 of these tank models entered service.

The French also experimented with sending big boxy tanks bashing about the Great War's killing fields but decided early on to take the concept in a different direction—concentrating, instead, on building smaller, lighter machines designed to "swarm" the enemy in sheer numbers. The result was the Renault FT tank. The FT required only a two-man crew: a driver and a gunner. The caterpillar tracks were placed outside the hull and set lower to allow the driver a better field of vision. A curved skid protruded off the rear to prevent the tank from flipping over on its back while crossing trenches. The truly revolutionary feature of the FT, however, was a fully rotating cannon or MG turret placed top and center upon the rest of the chassis. This innovation would become a fixture to every successful tank design ever since. Though much smaller in size, the FT was barely faster than the heftier British Mark tanks—clocking a whopping five miles per hour (MPH).[12] The FT did not reach the battlefield in large numbers until May of 1918—entering a phase in the war where elaborate trench defenses began collapsing and troop maneuver regained prominence. Although slow, under these more open battlefield conditions, the FTs proved they could, indeed, "swarm" defenses.

American doughboys joined the Great War in the summer of 1917 but brought no tanks of their own. The War Department hadn't developed anything of this kind for mass production, so the French provided the U.S. Army with the necessary FTs and the operational training. American tankers of the 1st Provisional Tank Brigade fired their first shots at Saint-Mihiel on 12 September 1918, near the war's end.[13] The brigade commander was one Lieutenant Colonel (Lt Col) George S. Patton Jr., a 32-year-old West Point cavalry officer. The Americans performed about as well as their mechanically unreliable FTs would allow. More importantly, they gained combat experience in armor. Another U.S. Army officer also fighting at Saint-Mihiel was Major Adna Chaffee. Chaffee commanded the infantrymen fighting alongside the tanks. Both Chaffee and Patton would be forever changed by their Great War experiences and observations in armor employment.

The Germans were latecomers to the Great War tank race. Their contribution, called an A7V *Sturmpanzerwagen* ("Storm Armor Wagon"), did not reach the battlefield until March of 1918.[14] The A7V was basically a tall, iron, rectangular monster boxed around a caterpillar tractor. A crew of eighteen crammed inside the unwieldy thing—manning a 57mm gun and several MGs while controlling overall operation. Its twin Daimler engines nudged the A7V up to eight MPH, but the overall design was downright awful. The hull sat too high and tipped over easily. The tracks could not cross a trench more than six feet wide without becoming hopelessly wedged. Only twenty were ever built. The Germans found a far cheaper way to employ armor was to recycle captured British tanks with black and white crosses painted on them. The only lasting contribution the A7V made to war was to introduce the word *panzer* into the military lexicon.

The Great War ended mercifully in armistice on 11 November 1918. During the '20s and early '30s, the British, French, Americans, Russians, Italians, and other nations tested a wide variety of tank designs both large and small. But, by and large, tank development remained a low-key, low-budget, backburner endeavor. The Germans, however, grew particularly fascinated with the idea of fast-moving armored troops and conducted secret experiments in violation of the Treaty of Versailles. One German officer who saw the revolutionary potential of tanks was Colonel Heinz Guderian. One could say that Guderian was to armor what Billy Mitchell was to planes, but Guderian also embraced the revolutionary potential of air power as well. In his 1936 book, *Achtung - Panzer!*, Guderian proposed tank forces organized into large armored divisions spearheading fully motorized infantry under close air support. He argued that infantry advances could be freed of the walking speed limitations of men and amplified severalfold by the motor speed of their vehicles. Concentrated attacks would then become fast, deep, and disorienting—disrupting the supply lines, organization, and morale far behind enemy lines. Reconnaissance planes and dive bombers would augment the shock of the attack. In what amounted to military heresy at the time, Guderian argued that tanks should not support infantry but that the infantry should support tanks! One key ingredient to Guderian's vision was the use of radio coordination for real-time command and control. Gone was archaic, time-consuming, and unreliable carrier pigeon messaging. Gone were rudimentary hand signals or colored flags restricting plodding tank formations to narrow line-of-sight operations. Guderian proposed *blitzkrieg* or "lightning war." Guderian's theories were not well received by most of his contemporaries, but military officers have always been a very conservative and traditional bunch. Guderian's ideas, however, attracted the enthusiastic support of the one man at the time that really mattered: Adolf Hitler. The conquest-minded German chancellor gave Guderian the green light to transform his ideas into reality.[15]

While the Germans organized their panzer divisions, U.S. Army planners dithered over the role and purpose of tanks. Some officers saw it as just another infantry support weapon and advocated for a few large, slow-moving pillboxes armed with cannons. Others saw tanks fulfilling limited cavalry applications and advocated for light, fast vehicles armed with MGs. Still, others regarded tanks as exotic toys and complete wastes of time, effort, and money. The remainder sat out the argument and scratched their heads.

During the 1920s, Colonel Adna Chaffee, presaging Guderian, emerged as an aggressive, vocal proponent for a motorized or "mechanized" Army. In 1931, the War Department assigned Chaffee to the 1st Cavalry Division to test his ideas. Because Chaffee proposed the obsolescence of the venerable horse, he ran into steadfast resistance from old troopers scattered among Army command. Over the next seven years, Chaffee secured barely enough funds to purchase the requisite number of light tanks and trucks to put wheels under one brigade's worth (two regiments) of troops. Chaffee's newborn baby was the 7th Cavalry Brigade (Mechanized). As of 1938, the U.S. Army could claim just this *one brigade* as its modern motorized showpiece. That same year, the United States fielded *zero* fully armored divisions, brigades, or even regiments. The sum total of American armor amounted to only a few spare companies of light and medium tanks assigned piecemeal to infantry divisions and National Guard units spread all over the country. The regular Army did, however, maintain a robust cavalry branch comprising *twelve* horse-mounted regiments, with the National Guard supporting another *seventeen* horse-mounted regiments.[16]

The British and French, growing increasingly anxious over the steady build-up in German armor, incorporated light, medium, and even "heavy" tanks into their armies by the late '30s. The French, in particular, built up their armor stocks so quickly that by 1940, *3,000* tanks had been spread out behind their lavish 200-mile-long Maginot Line network of defensive fortifications.[17] Unlike their German counterparts, however, few French tanks featured dependable inter-tank radio communications.[18] This basic omission would later prove disastrous.

By the late '30s, the news broadcast over American airwaves grew more disturbing and ominous. Unfortunately, these overseas reports were not fictional radio plays staged by Orson Welles. In November 1938, shocking anti-Jewish violence erupted across Germany and Austria in what became known as *Kristallnacht*, or the "Night of the Broken Glass." Tens of thousands of Jews were subsequently rounded up and sent to concentration camps. In May of 1939, Germany and Italy announced an "Iron Pact" military alliance. A few months later, in August 1939, Germany and the Soviet Union signed a non-aggression pact. This agreement shocked the world as both nations were hitherto considered bitter mortal adversaries. That same summer, Hitler accelerated his demands for the return of all Polish territory lost in the Great War Armistice. However, the mustachioed Austrian's tirades for effect, charm offensives, and Versailles victimhood blustering no longer yielded diplomatic traction. The French and British had exhausted their sympathies to even listen. Both nations warned, instead, that a German attack on Poland would trigger automatic war with them as well. They were serious this time, but Hitler did not believe them or even care. Insanity reigned and another disastrous European war seemed all but inevitable. Belgium mobilized. The Netherlands mobilized. Poland mustered what they could of an outdated, mostly reservist army relying upon magnificent horse cavalry and several hundred obsolete 1920s model tanks. Regrettably, their defensive preparations had been woefully delayed because of French and British fears that Polish mobilization might "provoke" Hitler.[19]

Then, on 1 September 1939, Hitler pulled the trigger—using the excuse of a staged border "attack" by German soldiers masquerading as Poles as pretext.[20] Fifty-two German divisions poured into western Poland to avenge this "Polish" incursion, making a complete mockery of what little substance remained of Prime Minister Chamberlain's 1938 Munich Agreement and of anybody who continued advocating peace. Six of the attacking outfits were Guderian's new panzer divisions comprising 2,500 modern tanks,[21] rolling with infantry and supporting attack planes in one giant sweeping pincer formation—as he so brazenly proposed only three years earlier. The operation devoured half the nation in less than a month. Midway through the operation, the Soviet Army attacked from the east, capturing the remainder of the country and wiping Poland completely off the Wilsonian map. This scandalous partitioning had been secretly prearranged by both powers in August through the German-Soviet non-Aggression pact. Though the German invasion was not "blitzkrieg" in the true Guderian sense, this terrifying new word soon rolled from the lips of millions around the world.[22]

After the feeding frenzy in the east subsided, everything in Europe stopped again. The continent sat for seven months deadlocked in a "phony war" where essentially nothing happened. Britain imposed a naval blockade in the North Sea. The French and Germans hastily amassed forces along their common border and a bizarre stare-down ensued. Troops on both sides directed music, propaganda, and witty schoolboy insults at each other—highlighting the patent absurdity of the standoff. Sardonic humorists labeled the situation a *sitzkreig*—meaning "sitting war" in German. On 9 April 1940, Germany moved to occupy Denmark and Norway to ensure critical shipments of iron ore from neutral Sweden and deny the British of potential naval bases and airfields. The operation was successfully concluded in only three weeks.

On 10 May, Hitler unleashed Guderian's panzer divisions a second time. This attack featured no staged pretext for propaganda purposes. Hitler wanted simply to conquer and humiliate France. The first casualty of the attack was Neville Chamberlain's political career. The lanky idealist resigned the same day, ceding the office of Prime Minister to a man many considered a hopeless crank only a few years earlier. Winston Churchill's hour arrived to stride upon the world stage.

Modern, industrial France was not rural Poland. At the time, the French fielded the strongest, best-trained, and best-equipped army in the world. They employed the same number of tanks and more artillery pieces than their German rivals.[23] As a consequence, nearly every conventional military expert at the time expected the German attack to devolve quickly into a repeat stalemate of the Great War, contesting the very same battlefields. But the Germans did not execute a conventional attack. Instead, they circumvented the vaunted Maginot Line and cut straight through the Netherlands at breakneck speed. This drew British and French forces northward and enabled the main German thrust to slash through the Ardennes, trapping astonished Allied forces along the coast. The Germans then tore through the rear of French and British lines in a mad dash toward Paris. The panzers behaved like wolf packs with radios. They hunted and killed their technically superior French *char* counterparts one by one with ruthless efficiency. The outrageous success of the invasion sent shockwaves around the world, shaking the U.S. government and War Department down to its granite foundations. Slack-jawed brass in Washington, D.C., watched helplessly as mighty France was bisected, strangled, and vanquished in under six weeks. This time, sweeping panzer *armies* led the charge in true *blitzkrieg* fashion. British Expeditionary Forces barely escaped annihilation by stuffing aboard a hodgepodge emergency flotilla comprising all available seaworthy vessels dispatched cross-channel from England to Dunkerque, France. Stunned veterans of the Great War retreated to their island homeland in utter humiliation—symbolically emasculated by ditching their guns, tanks, trucks, and artillery on French beaches while clambering for safety. Much of what they abandoned was factory-new equipment.

Back in the United States, long and distinguished military careers were suddenly over. Young lieutenant colonels became generals overnight. The only time the word "horse" was heard again in a War Department office was when one of those new generals yelled "horseshit!" to some naysayer—which happened often. The Army wanted tanks, men, rifles, trucks, and artillery pieces, and plenty fast. Plans were immediately drawn to create American mechanized armor divisions modeled after Guderian's fearsome panzer divisions. With France gone, fears swirled though D.C. over the fate of Britain and, to a lesser extent, the colonial ambitions of Imperial Japan in the Far East. The U.S. government dreaded, above all, a dystopian future where America was left alone to fight while more virulent German and Japanese armies and navies closed in over both oceans. Under such a nightmarish scenario, "Fortress America" would not be a nation of refuge, but a nation under siege. The American public, greatly rattled as well, wanted to modernize the Army and Navy rapidly but continued drawing the line at direct foreign involvement. Nevertheless, a growing chorus of interventionist voices advocated for increased material support of Britain. If Britain fell, they argued, little hope endured of ever rolling back the German conquest of Europe. Sending American boys overseas, however, remained completely out of the question. The ghosts of the Great War still haunted the political landscape as deeply as the daunting materiel and staffing shortages haunted the Army.

The U.S. Army possessed only 240 tanks when Germany invaded Poland in September 1939.[24] Most were of the outdated "light" variety. These were basically small, boxy tractors riveted together with thin armor, mounted upon caterpillar tracks, and equipped with only a MG or two. Poland deployed 475 similar models when they were invaded.[25] They amounted to little more than moving practice targets for Guderian's superior panzers. Poland put a million men on the battlefield—all highly motivated to defend their homeland,[26] and even they could not stop the better-equipped 1.5-million-man German invading army.[27] During this same time period, the U.S. Army boasted only 174,000 active-duty members.[28] American troop strength was less than *one-fifth* of the size of Poland's Army and ranked *nineteenth* overall! in the world. Even the Portuguese Army was larger.[29] By the time Germany invaded France in the Spring of 1940, U.S. Army numbers had inched up to 210,000 soldiers—of which only a paltry 75,000 could be dispatched anywhere in a crisis.[30] The sad reality was that even if the U.S. government wanted to aid France at the time, it had little to offer. When Germany conquered France and smashed the proud nation's *three-million-man* army, capturing thousands of new tanks and artillery pieces in the process, few could deny the woeful state of the American military. To regain any relevancy whatsoever, the U.S. Army had to modernize from a horse cavalry operation *overnight*, produce tanks not yet designed and multiply in size many times over. The task was gargantuan, and time was not on America's side.

By June 1940, the average young American male became quite concerned over events in Europe. He had certainly heard of Germany's fearsome panzers and knew something of the U.S. Army's small and ineffective tank force. He did not know, however, of plans being drawn in Washington, D.C., to place him inside some sort of American tank sent to confront those mighty German panzers. This loud, unwieldy iron box will then become a spartan home for him and several other nervous strangers drawn from around the country. Together, they will travel overseas to lands he never asked to visit. They will have no time to bathe and will reek of gasoline, cordite, and body odor for weeks on end. They will struggle to survive in cramped, uncomfortable and suffocating interiors during boiling hot summers and icy cold winters. They will fight in deafening, disorienting, and terrifying battles. The thick steel plate surrounding them will offer some protection from bullets—and yet attract the relentless deadly ire of larger caliber enemy guns. When hit, the hull will either clang like the interior of an enormous bell if they are lucky, or burst open as a violent flash of molten steel and fire if they are not. Some will be horribly wounded inside them. Some will perish inside them. Some will scramble out burning hatches but by the grace of God.

The following is the true story of the trials, the tragedy, and the triumph of the men from just one American tank company during that epic nightmare known as World War II ....

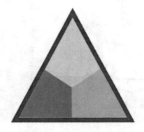

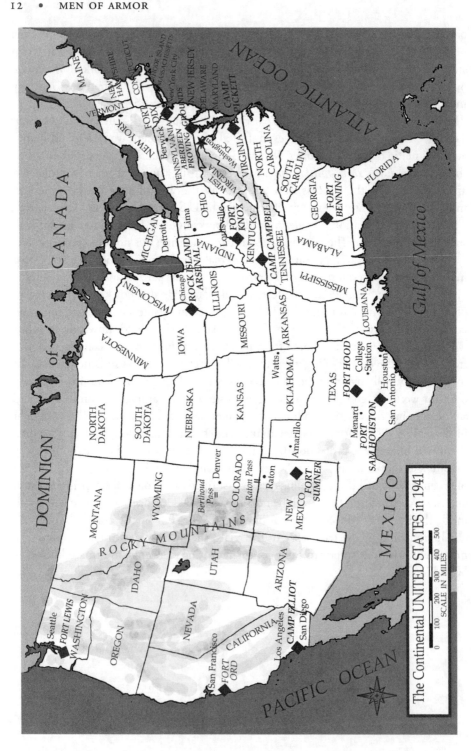

The Continental UNITED STATES in 1941

SCALE IN MILES
0   100   200   300   400   500

CHAPTER I

Origins: June 1940 to June 1941

A scorching June sun beat down upon the beige brick buildings and parched straw lawns of College Station, Texas. After four years of intense study, Charles M. Wilkinson walked briskly across the Texas Agricultural and Mechanical (A&M) campus with his prized academic degree in one hand while wiping brow sweat with

Renault FT-17 (1917)

the other. Graduation, however, was not yet complete. That evening, under cooler conditions, he would don a starch-ironed Reserve Officer Training Corps (ROTC) cadet uniform and attend a second ceremony to receive his commission as a second lieutenant (2nd Lt) in the United States Army Reserve. Most men of the Class of 1940 would also attend—as ROTC training was required of all physically qualified students at the college. Wilkinson was a young Texan intensely interested in all subjects—the sciences, the arts, military matters, and especially current events. His four-year undergraduate curriculum exposed him to many astonishing things, but nothing compared to what he witnessed unfolding in the world beyond campus. The international landscape of 1940 was quite different from that of his first day of college back in 1936. In fact, at that very moment, German troops rolled triumphantly through the streets of a vanquished and dumfounded Paris. The news cast a pall over what should have otherwise been a day of exhilaration for Wilkinson and his fellow graduates.[1]

In a somber, formal ceremony that evening, Wilkinson watched as each of his classmates received reserve officer commissions from the Commandant of Cadets, one after the other. The process took considerable time, with hundreds filing slowly across the stage dressed in West Point-style khakis and brown riding boots. The tall calfskin boots were a distinctively Texan enhancement to the uniform.[2] Wilkinson wondered what the future held for each of them. Some were good friends, and most others he knew by name or face. Upon reflection, the ROTC experience had been thorough, challenging, and enjoyable. But as an independent-minded son of a Texas ranching family, Wilkinson was not raised to blindly follow orders. He bristled over some of the ROTC's more nonsensical rules and found delight, from time to time, in testing the limits of discipline. Now, he hoped the program's regimentation properly prepared him and his classmates for whatever trials lay ahead. When Wilkinson's turn came to receive his papers, a "Certificate of Eligibility" was handed to him instead of a formal commission, but the difference was a mere technicality. Wilkinson remained a few months shy of twenty-one and U.S. Army regulations required this delay until his birthday in October, at which time his formal commission would arrive by mail. Nevertheless, Wilkinson walked out of the ceremony feeling like he had accomplished something very special.

That summer, Wilkinson returned home to his family's Menard cattle ranch to work long days in the dry Texas heat and ponder his near-term future. When time allowed, he followed world developments with continued astonishment. France and Germany signed a formal armistice on 24 June. Marshal Pétain's new government moved to Vichy on 2 July; British forces attacked and sank much of the French Navy soon after. President Roosevelt signed a law authorizing the rapid expansion of both the Atlantic and Pacific fleets. Germany began heavy aerial attacks on Great Britain in mid-August, pounding the island nation without mercy well into September. Everyone feared an expected cross-channel German invasion. The British reeled from the blows but endured—thanks to the gallantry of the Royal Air Force. The world, it seemed, was spinning rapidly out of control.

After a long summer of contentious debate, Congress passed the Selective Training and Service Act.[3] Roosevelt signed the bill into law on 16 September 1940 and the nation's first ever peacetime "draft" became reality. The law authorized Army troop strength upwards from 210,000 to 1.4 million and required one year of service from conscripts.[4] That same autumn also featured a presidential election with Roosevelt vying for an unprecedented third term. His opponent, Wendell Wilkie, a political novice, criticized Roosevelt's neutrality policy as being too passive and disengaged. Regardless of the election outcome, Wilkinson grew increasingly convinced he was destined for active duty in the U.S. Army. To maintain some control over his fate, he decided to volunteer, rather than register for the draft and risk drawing a poor assignment. Wilkinson also reasoned that putting an early foot in the door meant better prospects of earning a higher rank and thereby surviving hostilities—should the United States ever become embroiled in war. Within days of his 7 October birthday, Wilkinson's formal "Certificate of Capacity" arrived by mail and the new second lieutenant headed promptly to San Antonio to complete his volunteer papers at the Fourth Army HQ. Then he returned to the family ranch and lingered. The presidential election came and went with the public, skittish over putting a political newcomer in office, overwhelmingly re-electing President Roosevelt.

A few weeks later, Wilkinson's formal orders arrived. He was instructed to go to Fort Sam Houston in San Antonio for a final physical examination and then to report for duty at Fort Knox, Kentucky, on 20 March 1941. He learned of a new "armored" division being formed and was invited to join this exciting outfit. Wilkinson recognized the names of several fellow Texas A&M classmates listed on the same orders. It was comforting to know he was not being thrown in with a group of complete strangers. The assignment seemed cutting-edge and challenging. The new American Armored Force service branch had only been instituted in June of 1940—immediately after the Fall of France—and appeared to offer exactly the kinds of opportunities for adventure and advancement that Wilkinson longed to experience.

When the "Day of Judgment" arrived, Wilkinson—a lean, 6' 1" tall, lifelong rancher—easily passed his physical exam. He returned home, packed, said goodbyes to family and friends and was soon rail-bound for Kentucky. After a few days of travel, punctuated by countless station stops, he arrived at last at Fort Knox. Hundreds of wide-eyed arrivals just like him stepped down from the rail coaches and poured out onto the post platform. Chatty, nervous excitement filled the air.

Though situated seemingly in the middle of rural nowhere, Fort Knox teemed with khaki and olive drab activity. The surrounding terrain of forest-checkered fields and rolling meadows dissolved gently into a serene blue-gray horizon. Stately deciduous trees stood barren after winter's bite, but their branches abounded with emergent buds, and the cool, faint, and reassuring ozone scents of an impending spring drifted in over the random breezes rolling in from the west. The post itself showcased a variety of eclectic architecture. Majestic old red brick barracks and administrative offices lined wide streets, interspersed with newer, gleaming Art Deco-style buildings. Several white-spired cupolas and an inspiring flagpole rose above the rooftops. Above it all towered two enormous water reservoirs painted in bold, bright red-and-white checkered patterns to ward away wayward aircraft. On the outskirts, dozens and dozens of gleaming white wooden barracks, in varying stages of construction, sprouted up across acres and acres of freshly-graded soil. A mini-army of trucks and earth-moving equipment hummed constantly around these new creations—leaving thick clouds of dust and exhaust suspended in the air. Uniformed men were seen everywhere, moving in all directions along roads, sidewalks, and up and down building steps. Many marched in tight platoon-sized formations or sauntered about in smaller groups. An occasional soldier hastily snaked his way through the masses, obviously late for some important business somewhere. Salutes were ubiquitous, automatic, and delivered with crisp snaps. Everyone and everything had purpose. And of course, there were the tanks. Not many, but Wilkinson recognized them immediately as the M1 light tanks commonly known as "combat cars" and issued to the cavalry. Their main gun was a .50-caliber MG. These old, riveted boxes would not be America's answer to Hitler's panzers. Better ones were rumored to be in the works.

Wilkinson's orders were to report directly to the Division Officers Training Center (DOTC) upon arrival, so he followed the posted signs and found himself fumbling along with others deciphering similar instructions. At the DOTC, the new officers were issued uniforms and basic equipment and given a brief orientation. The big surprise came when the sleeping assignments were revealed. Despite the new construction, barracks bunks and officers' quarters remained in short supply, so Wilkinson and his new classmates were told to sleep "under canvas." In other words, they would camp out on the hard ground in drafty tents exposed to the elements. There was a time when an officer's commission begot certain perks. At Fort Knox, a gold bar on the collar earned you the same flapping canvas roof as a buck private.

Much of the coursework at the DOTC was conducted by the newly created 1st Armored Division[5] and amounted to six weeks of "basic training" for officers. Wilkinson found some of the classes, such as map reading, rifle marksmanship, vehicle operation, and vehicle maintenance informative and even fun. Other obligations, such as physical fitness routines and the close-order drills, he considered real yawners. Basically, these courses rehashed the same ROTC material he absorbed during his final year at Texas A&M College. Still, Wilkinson understood why these exercises were necessary. In 1939, the Army modernized from old "square" unit formations to new "triangular" ones. This meant that nearly every level of the Army "lost" a unit. Squads, platoons, and companies previously arranged in units of four were now reduced to three, and the old drill manual had been completely revised. For officers a year or more older than Wilkinson, the new formations seemed confusing and awkward.[6] 2nd lieutenants accustomed to drilling platoons of four eight-man squads were now expected to maintain similar compact formations with three ten-man squads. The new math often didn't add up and the results of the first attempts at drilling ranged from painfully embarrassing to downright hilarious. Since Wilkinson had already acquired a year's experience drilling under the new system at Texas A&M, he often found himself coaching the older officers along. One of these guys was a square-jawed Oklahoman by the name of French Lewis.

2nd Lt Lewis was almost three years older than Wilkinson, standing about 5' 9" with a stocky, muscular build and short dark hair. He was a 1937 graduate of the University of Arkansas[7] with an ROTC commission and worked as a geologist for the Magnolia Oil Company in Louisiana before volunteering.[8] Lewis grew up in Watts, Oklahoma, along the Arkansas border.[9] Although a good four-hundred miles northeast of Menard, Texas, Watts was another tiny town well within "cattle country" battling through drought and the Great Depression with toil, sweat, and close family ties. Because of their similar backgrounds, the two men gravitated together and became fast friends. Wilkinson helped Lewis absorb the Army's new drill protocols, and Lewis brought to the friendship some unique skills of his own—most notably the ability to remain absolutely calm in the face of danger.

Weapons demonstrations were always favorite events for Wilkinson, Lewis, and their peers. One day, a DOTC instructor led the class out to a large field to explode an anti-tank (AT) mine. The mine—a large cast iron disk about 18" in diameter and

6" thick—was placed at the bottom of a shallow pit. After an obligatory lecture on the weapon's specifications and applications, the instructor affixed a wired blasting cap charge to the mine and covered everything over with loose soil. Next, he unraveled a big spool of detonation wire, walked about twenty-five yards out, and told the class of the 200 or so officers present to back away to roughly the same distance. As everyone shuffled to reposition themselves, the instructor's tone grew serious: "Now, when this thing goes off, there will be quite a bit of rocks and dirt thrown into the air and some of it will fall where we are standing. Don't try to run away from it," he cautioned. "Stand still, look up, and dodge the rocks and clods as they fall ...." Then he gave a brief countdown as the men covered their ears and watched intently. On cue, the mine exploded in a deafening whoosh—throwing a thick wall of dirt and debris skyward. Despite the instructor's warnings not to run, most men scrambled away in panic—including the instructor. Wilkinson's first instincts were to join them, but he hesitated when he saw that French Lewis hadn't so much as flinched. The two friends remained still, looked up, and easily side-stepped the rocks and clumped dirt raining down around them—just as the instructor advised. As the dust settled, the rest of the class returned gradually—including one particularly embarrassed instructor. Lewis explained matter-of-factly that he had been part of a seismograph crew that used dynamite daily. Large explosions were nothing new to him.[10]

One of the more engaging and informative classes at the DOTC covered the history of tank warfare and development.[11] The big British Mark tanks and smaller French FTs of the Great War were described, of course, as were the experiences of Lt Col George S. Patton Jr's 1st Provisional Tank Brigade. Lt Col Patton was responsible for training the very first American tankers at Bourg, France, in early 1918. Not only did he develop the first U.S. Army armor course syllabus and the earliest tank command tactics,[12] but he went on to lead them in battle later that same year. After the Great War, American tanks were either based heavily upon the designs or were direct copies of French FT and British Mark models. Even as late as 1932, the main American "heavy" battle tank was a British Mark VIII.[13] Except for wider tracks, the Mark VIII didn't appear much different than those first rhomboidal boxes of the Great War. Americans experimented with newer tank designs throughout the '20s, but with tight budget constraints nothing really progressed beyond the test models. Not until 1935 did a truly modern American tank, the M1, reach mass production—and even this design was based on an earlier British 6-ton Vickers light tank.[14]

The 8.5-ton M1 was created primarily to fulfill Colonel Adna Chaffee's experiments into mechanized cavalry. It was called a "combat car" to sidestep a federal law mandating infantry control of all tanks, but in reality M1s were light tanks.[15] A model nearly identical to the M1 called an "M2A1" was also produced for the infantry. Both versions were armed with MGs and built upon the same chassis. Only minor turret variations set them apart.[16] Both M1s and M2s were fast. Their

250 horsepower Continental engines caused them to buck when floored and they could top out at a brisk 45 MPH—nine times faster than Patton's pokey Renault FTs of the Great War. By the close of 1939, the Army had 431 M1s and M2s. In 1940, that number doubled to 790.[17] These riveted little speed demons comprised the bulk of the American tank force. They were the only tank types widely used at Fort Knox during the spring of 1941, and the ones in which Wilkinson, Lewis and hundreds of other armor officers learned the basics of gunnery, radio communications, and vehicle maintenance. The M1s and M2s were also obsolete—every last one of them. Recent combat experiences in the Spanish Civil War and during the German *blitzkrieg* showed that light tanks needed bigger guns and thicker armor. MGs and speedy engines were powerless against the latest generation of AT guns. The newest American light tank model, the "M3," seemed to address these shortcomings. On paper at least, the M3, armed with a 37mm cannon, appeared to be on par with German Panzer IIIs currently ravaging Europe. The problem was that mass production of the M3 light had only started the previous month (March of 1941). Chrysler landed a contract to build hundreds, but none yet had been shipped to Fort Knox.[18] The first ones were, instead, shipped to help the British fighting in North Africa under the Lend-Lease Agreement—also established in March 1941.[19]

American medium tank development, especially, had been woefully neglected. In the early and mid-1930s, eighteen assorted T4 medium tank models were built and tested,[20] but the largest cannon mounted on any T4 was only a 37mm gun. All T4s were maintained by the 67th Infantry Regiment at Fort Benning and comprised the *entire* American medium tank corps as late as 1939.[21] Along with this motley assembly of medium tank test models sat junkyards of hopelessly outdated Mark VIIIs rusting in rows at Fort Meade, Maryland, and Fort Benning, Georgia. All had been declared obsolete in 1935—yet still awaited the cutting torch.[22] A new M2 medium tank model was rushed into production during the summer of 1939, but as the first batch of eighteen rolled off a Rock Island Arsenal assembly line in Illinois, the evolving combat in Europe proved even this version was obsolete.[23] The M2 medium's 37mm guns were fine for light tanks but inadequate for a larger "main battle tank." A 75mm cannon was now necessary. To keep pace, an M3 medium tank was hastily designed and tested during the summer and autumn of 1940. The M3 medium looked similar to the M2 medium except for the addition of a short-barreled 75mm cannon poking inelegantly out from an oversized sponson tacked to the front right side of the hull. The added feature looked like a lazy engineer's afterthought. Because the cannon had very limited traverse capability, the entire tank needed to shift around to engage a moving target. A better design was delayed until American industry figured out how to engineer a fully rotational turret that could bear the weight and recoil of a 75mm gun.[24] Because the War Department believed *any* *tank* with a 75mm gun was better than no tank at all, the M3 medium was rushed into production just to field *something* to match the firepower of Germany's newest

Panzer IVs. Not unit April 1941, however, did the first M3 mediums roll out of American factories—and these were shipped for final testing trials to the Aberdeen Proving Grounds in Maryland.[25] Fort Knox recruits would have to wait to see them.[26] As for that properly gunned medium tank with a fully rotational turret, the Army hadn't even *designed* one yet. Planners had been too preoccupied with producing and rushing large quantities of stopgap M3 mediums to the British.[27]

The sad truth was that Wilkinson, Lewis, and their fellow DOTC classmates were training to command light and medium tanks that didn't yet exist, and they had no idea of the capabilities or limitations of such theoretical weapons. American aviators faced a similar predicament, but at least American aircraft design and unit organization was not as antiquated as American armor. Even so, it was not entirely clear that Americans would even fight the Germans anytime soon. No war had been declared between the two nations and hopes remained that Britain might hold out long enough for Germany to sue for peace. With no clear idea of what to expect, anybody associated with American armor seemed to "make it up" as they fumbled along.

The American Armor Force was officially created on 10 July 1940.[28] The infantry, cavalry, and artillery branches all traced proud lineages back to the nation's founding. In comparison, the "history" of the American Armor Branch boasted all of nine months. To engender some *esprit de corps* among the recruits, much was made of this very scant history nonetheless. Colonel Daniel Van Voorhis was identified as the "grandfather" of American armor for organizing the very first American mechanized unit at Fort Eustis, Virginia, in 1930.[29] The "father" of American armor was Major General (Maj Gen) Adna Chaffee, who happened to also be the current commander of the entire Armored Force at Fort Knox.[30] Van Voorhis remained active as well—as a major general commanding the Panama Canal Zone.[31] The pedigree of the new Armored Force was very limited indeed.

The prime driving force behind the American Armored Force, without question, was Adna Chaffee. All throughout the 1930s, he harped on about the merits of mechanization to the point where the War Department gave him funding just to go away. Chaffee organized the 7th Cavalry Brigade into a mechanized outfit and put his brainchild to a grand test in Louisiana in May 1940. There, 100,000 Army regulars and reservists assembled for war games between mechanized and traditional forces. Virtually every tank belonging to the U.S. Army was brought in for the experiment.[32] As luck would have it, the massive operation coincided with Germany's attack on France. While Guderian's panzers sliced through the Low Countries, Chaffee's 7th Cavalry Brigade and a provisional tank brigade joined forces and ripped through old Army formations exercise after exercise.[33] Both events near and far, confirmed the gospel Chaffee had been preaching for years: Motorized troops and armor owned the future. Two months later, Chaffee got his armored force and was given command of it. However, the years spent beating his head against countless oak doors in D.C. took a heavy toll on his health. Chaffee looked much older than his fifty-six years and terminal cancer now sapped him of vitality.[34] Sadly, Chaffee was a proud "father" who would never live to see his beloved child mature into adulthood. Despite his debilitating condition, Maj Gen Chaffee dedicated long hours at Fort Knox when not crisscrossing the continent and checking on the progress of the Army's newest tanks. He was determined to devote his remaining days on earth making sure his Armored Force started off successfully.

In just nine months, the Armored Force grew from absolutely nothing into a vast undertaking whereby Fort Knox churned out 200 specially-trained officers and 2,000 enlisted men every twelve weeks.[35] These figured quickly doubled, then tripled as summer passed and the Fort's accommodations expanded. Chaffee needed 70,000 Armored Force troops trained by the end of the year. His nine-fold goal increase was ambitious.[36] Fifty percent of all arriving enlisted men needed specialized training as drivers, radiomen, armorers, repairmen, etc.,[37] and the vast majority of officers were reservists like Wilkinson and Lewis with no familiarity with tanks whatsoever. Most of the regular Army officers assigned also lacked basic armor experience.[38] Nearly all the officers required further instruction in such armor-specific sub-specialties as maintenance, communications, tactics, etc. Training, of course, consumed lots of time.

In the meantime, new armored divisions and independent tank battalions sprouted up in forts and camps over the country—at least in name. In the summer of 1940, the 1st and 2nd Armored Divisions and the 70th Tank Battalion (Tk Bn) formed—but at less than half the troop strength needed for each unit to function. A combat-ready armored division was supposed to field roughly 12,000 men and 400 tanks.[39] Many months passed before their hollow rolls could be filled with the requisite personnel. In November of 1940, four more tank battalions formed by consolidating eighteen National Guard tank companies scattered across the country.[40] And as recently as 15 April 1941, the 3rd and 4th Armored Divisions were created in Louisiana and New York, respectively—but with only skeleton cadres.[41] Ten new General Headquarters (GHQ) tank battalions were also scheduled for launch in June 1941.[42] Each new battalion, though much smaller in size to a division, still required roughly 600 men and fifty tanks. These were daunting personnel and equipment challenges for Chaffee to meet. No wonder his health failed rapidly.

The new Armored Force offered very little in the form of practical tactical instruction. Chaffee summed up the general mission rather vaguely: "The role of the armored division is the conduct of highly mobile ground warfare, primarily offensive in character, by a self-sustaining unit of great power and mobility, composed of specially equipped troops of the required arms and services."[43] A 1940 War Department training circular offered little more in the way of specifics: "The primary role of an armored force is offensive operation against vital objectives in rear of the hostile main battle positions, usually reached by a penetration of a weak portion of the front, or by the encirclement of an open flank."[44] Various missions were defined as follows: " ... a rapid seizure of a critical area, an enveloping or encircling movement, a push through a gap in the enemy line, an exploitation or a penetration of the enemy line, a physical overrunning and pursuit of fleeing troops … or forming a spearhead for a breakthrough against a weak spot in the hostile line."[45] These were dull, basic restatements of the main theses to Guderian's *Achtung - Panzer!*—offering no specifics for how companies, platoons, or individual tanks should operate within such a broad context. For guidance and inspiration, the experiences of the old horse cavalry were borrowed upon heavily.

In a departure from their equestrian origins, however, the men of the new Armor Force wore a special patch on their sleeves: a triangular insignia subdivided into three equal areas of yellow, blue, and red. Yellow was symbolic for cavalry, blue for infantry, and red for artillery. This represented the Army's concept of a Holy Trinity: the three traditional battlefield branches unified as one, with none dominating the others and each bringing something unique, yet essential, to the whole. Centered within the triangle were stitched black tank treads, a cannon and a red bolt of lightning. The symbolism was obvious: maneuver, firepower, and shock. Great care was taken to assure that equal numbers of officers were drawn from the three traditional branches—again, so that no old branch would come to dominate the new. All new officer transferees discarded their old branch lapel pins for new insignia: the gold profile of an old British Mark VIII tank. Enlisted men displayed the same silhouette but affixed to gold buttons. The Army intended for the special patch and collar insignia to instill a common purpose and an elite status into the men—even as they lacked equipment, training, and direction. But in their overzealousness to create this unique identity, the Army pushed the recruits to adopt the nickname "armoraiders."[46] The clumsy term never caught on with anybody. Instead, these new men of armor referred to themselves simply as "tankers."

Throughout the DOTC training, Wilkinson and his tanker classmates fully expected assignments with the 2nd Armored Division where they could expand the foundational knowledge Chaffee's instructors drilled into them. The 2nd Armored had been stationed at Fort Benning a full nine months—yet still lacked the necessary personnel. Maj Gen George S. Patton Jr. formally assumed duties as divisional commander on 4 April 1941, and the new officers beamed at the prospect of serving under a living legend.[47] However, as their six-week stint with the DOTC drew to a close, the soon-to-be graduates gathered for a general assembly. There, the formation of five new GHQ independent tank battalions was announced. These new units would be seeded at various places all around the country beginning 1 June—a date less than a month away. An appeal followed for volunteers to cadre each new outfit. One of these new battalions—the 76th Tank Battalion (L)—would be stationed in Washington State. The 76th Tank Battalion (L) was designated a "light" tank outfit—hence the added "(L)" behind the unit name. The prospect intrigued Wilkinson, not because of light tanks but for the opportunity to build a smaller unit from the ground up. The challenge appealed to his independent and ambitious nature. With armor his established specialty, he preferred to land in a unit where he could really shine. He had also heard often of the beauty of the Pacific Northwest and wanted to see it for himself. French Lewis was also fascinated by the potential, and so both men decided to volunteer together for the 76th. Several other DOTC classmates joined as well. A few days later, the 76th was re-designated as the 756th Tank Battalion (L), and the cadre of officer volunteers became "756ers."[48]

As the DOTC training concluded a few days later, the officers of the new 756th met at the officers' club for a "get acquainted" gathering. Drinks flowed, and lively conversations subsequently swirled among the young reservists and few older regular Army officers in attendance. The new battalion commander was Lt Col Severne S. MacLaughlin, a stately officer in his late 40s who rose through the enlisted ranks of the Michigan National Guard to earn a battlefield commission during the Great War.[49] He was also wounded in action.[50] MacLaughlin, a tall, thin, stylish, and well-spoken figure drew the instant respect and admiration of all his fellow officers.[51] His large round wire spectacles, trim gray hair, and dark chevron mustache bestowed him with a professorial and fatherly air.[52] In fact, he had served as an instructor in military tactics at Western Maryland College from 1934 to 1939.[53] He was the perfect man to lead the young cadre. Another regular Army officer, and the only West Point graduate in the group, was 30-year-old Captain Harry W. Sweeting.[54] Sweeting, also tall—but topped with short, dark hair and fine facial features—kept a spry athletic physique. The bright, self-assured, and talkative New Yorker was slated to be the new battalion supply officer (S-4).[55] Wilkinson's acquaintance and fellow Texas A&M graduate, 2nd Lt Foster Carroll Smith, also joined the 756th. "Blanco" Smith played professional baseball in the International League prior to joining the service. Captain Sweeting had trouble telling Wilkinson and Smith apart, and at one point he asked the two officers to identify themselves before the rest of the gathering. Sweeting's mix-up flattered Wilkinson, as Smith had been a very popular athlete at Texas A&M.[56] Several other friends from DOTC class also joined the 756th and Wilkinson left the meeting feeling the battalion was off to a fine start and that he made the right decision.

The DOTC wrapped up on 20 May 1941 and formal transfer orders were issued reassigning the new 756th cadre from Fort Knox to Fort Lewis.[57] All enlisted men and any officers without automobiles were required to make the 2,200-mile journey by troop train. Officers with cars received individual travel orders. A few days before departing, Captain Sweeting's car was stolen and his orders were recut, appointing him as troop train commander. However, just as the battalion prepared for departure, the local sheriff's office located Sweeting's missing car some thirty miles away in Louisville. At this point, Sweeting's orders could not be amended, but he was allowed to amend those of a fellow officer. As a consequence, the captain asked Wilkinson if he would drive his recovered car to Washington State. Wilkinson happily accepted—particularly upon learning he could take up to eleven days to complete the journey.

The longer travel time allowed Wilkinson to swing down to Texas before resuming on to Seattle. The trip from Fort Knox to Menard required only two days—earning Wilkinson several free days to relax and visit his folks and his three younger brothers and sister while enjoying the late spring weather on the homestead.[58] When the time came to finally leave, his grandmother and aunt fried a large batch of chicken and packed a picnic basket full of home-cooked goodies for Charles to take along. The delicious feast would last him three full days. Never before had Wilkinson traveled west of Texas, so he looked upon the rest of the journey as an adventure.

He departed north to Amarillo, Texas, then swung westward toward Raton, New Mexico. Ahead in the distance he noticed an immense cloud looming across much of the horizon. The ominous sight alarmed Wilkinson so much that he stopped the car along the roadside and stepped out to study it more carefully. After a few moments, he sheepishly realized he was only gazing upon the Sangre de Cristo mountain range. He forgave himself for overreacting and returned behind the wheel to drive on. In time, he swung northward along a narrow gravel road snaking through the Raton Pass into Colorado—yet all the while the menacing beauty of that distant range kept him marveling out of his left window. After all, Wilkinson had never even seen snow-peaked mountains before.

The war raging in Europe seemed like those mountains: disturbing, dangerous, but still distant. Might those overseas troubles also fade in Wilkinson's side mirror and allow him to resume a normal life and blissful future? The recent reports from Europe were not encouraging. The Germans had overrun Yugoslavia and Greece and wrested Crete away from the British. German panzers under the command of *Generalleutnant* Erwin Rommel routed British forces across North Africa in battle after battle. The only bright news came with the sinking of the newly-launched 50,000-ton German battleship *Bismarck*—dispatched by Royal Navy seaplanes to the bottom of the icy Atlantic. But even this British victory was a draw of sorts—as the *Bismarck* had previously sunk the older H.M.S *Hood* with a single shot to the stern magazine—killing or drowning 1,400 sailors in the span of only a few moments. The ugly truth was that Britain kept reeling from blow after blow. Perhaps an unprepared U.S. Army might soon be rushed overseas to the rescue. Perhaps it wasn't the distant mountains that caused Wilkinson to halt and calm his fears.

Wilkinson stopped to rest for the evening and then resumed travel the next morning—reaching Denver in only a few hours. He turned west and headed toward a far more spectacular mountain chain—the Rockies. This time, those snow-peaked mountains no longer brought him apprehension, because they were no longer unknowns, and a thin ribbon of asphalt showed the way through. As that road carried Wilkinson higher and higher, that seemingly insurmountable, monolithic ridgeline turned into a series of small peaks, valleys, and tight turns to be negotiated and conquered one after the other. At 11,000 feet, the weather chilled and the alpine air thinned making breathing difficult. Wilkinson was threading through the famed

Berthoud Pass. Once crested, he coasted an exhilarating thirteen miles down the opposite side. More ups and downs, twists and turns followed in the hours and days ahead. At times, the way through was narrow and treacherous with deadly drop-offs at either side, but Wilkinson embraced every road challenge one right after the other. Life was, after all, one grand adventure.

Over the next few days, Wilkinson enjoyed the gift of open road freedom and marveled at the untamed majesty of the American Northwest. Through moody mountain ranges, heady primordial forests, hushed valleys, meandering rivers, and unspoiled meadows of Colorado, Utah, Idaho, Oregon, and finally Washington State—all the result of happenstance military orders in a car belonging to someone else. The final stretch of the journey from Portland to Fort Lewis, Wilkinson thought, featured the most breathtaking scenery of all. America was a beautiful nation and he felt proud to wear a uniform representing it. During the final hours of the long journey, the distant hazy cone of Mount St Helens appeared as his occasional companion out the right passenger window, but as he swung northeast through Centralia and skirted past Olympia, the snow-crested peak of Mount Rainier loomed larger as a landscape fixture—rising above immense forests and fields as he neared Fort Lewis. He turned into the log and stone gateway entrance of his new post—constructed to commemorate a pioneering past which hadn't really ended. After being waved through, Wilkinson was convinced more than ever that he had made a great decision.[59]

Mount Rainier still lay some forty miles in the distance, but on clear days its massive square white top and attendant clouds dominated the post's skyline. Five-thousand miles beyond Rainer lay the turmoil of Europe. Mountains would figure prominently in the destinies of Wilkinson and the 756th Tank Battalion. Although none could know it at that time, they will cross literal mountains and move figurative ones in the months to come. At times, their mission will seem impossible, and the sheer cliffs, hairpin turns, and cavernous valleys along the way will present daunting challenges demanding unrelenting and thankless toil. Many will be lost along the way.

CHAPTER 2

Formation: June 1941 to December 1941

M1 "Combat Car" (1936)

Wilkinson drove slowly through Fort Lewis passing dozens and dozens of cookie-cutter Cape Cod homes, four-story red brick administrative buildings, orderly rows of long white barracks, and pine trees—lots of dark green pine trees. The damp air hung thick with the rich oxygenated aroma of nearby forests. Shiny civilian cars of every make and color were parked here and there—giving the sprawling post, on first glance, a relaxed civilian feel. The further he ventured into the heart of the installation, however, the more he could see a hive thriving with Army activity. Fort Lewis was, after all, home to the U.S. Fourth Army and the IX Corps comprising some 45,000 soldiers and 3,300 vehicles.[1] Many troops were members of the 41st and 3rd Infantry Divisions (Inf Div). On the outskirts, rows and rows of tents had been erected in open fields—just like at Fort Knox. Evidently, Fort Lewis also swarmed with more soldiers than bunks.

Infantrymen bearing bulky backpacks, wearing khaki ankle gaiters and World War I British-style Brodie helmets trudged about in long lines. They wore blue denim shirts and trousers—reserving their olive drab (OD) and khaki uniforms for parades or barracks duties.[2] Everyone gleamed with sweat and appeared somewhat haggard—but happy, otherwise, to return to camp after enduring grueling morning conditioning marches. On flat athletic fields, soldiers wearing peaked garrison caps and carrying 1903 model Springfield rifles marched around in tight rectangular formations as crusty sergeants barked after them. On more distant grounds, "Old Glory" shimmered and colorful guidons fluttered nobly above mounted troops of the 115th Cavalry Regiment pressing their steeds into thundering clods of moist dirt and turf. Long, green staff cars and canvas-covered trucks sporting big, round fenders motored about on Army business. Other trucks towed small artillery cannons or trailers crammed with supplies. Here and there, the long guns of the 205th Coast

Artillery's anti-aircraft (AA) batteries sat like silent sentinels atop wide spiderlike legs, barrels pointing skyward. Even a few old M1 and M2 combat cars from the 194th Tank Battalion could be seen—parked near white service buildings with open garages and mechanics leisurely ambling about. The 194th had been organized and assigned to Fort Lewis only three months earlier. The 752nd Tank Battalion (Medium) under the command of Lt Col Glen H. Anderson was also being organized at Fort Lewis at the same time as the 756th.[3] These three battalions were the only tank outfits assigned to the post—in fact, in the entire Pacific Northwest—but only the 194th had tanks.[4]

Due to the post's vastness, it took some time for Wilkinson to reach the tiny section where the 756th had been assigned. To his relief, the battalion had secured barracks space and he would not have to sleep "under canvas" for the time being. Wilkinson located the battalion headquarters inside a single-story white wood building. He reported for duty and discovered that he had been assigned as a platoon leader in B Company (Co). The other two platoon leaders were his DOTC classmates and friends, 2nd Lt French Lewis and 2nd Lt Blanco Smith.[5] He couldn't imagine a more perfect outcome.

The new company commander was Captain Dwight Terry—a tall, square-shouldered Texan with a deep booming voice who never lacked a cup of corrosively brewed coffee at the corner of his desk.[6] Terry, a 1932 graduate of Texas A&M,[7] came from Fort Knox by way of the 1st Armored Division. He had also served a stint as company commander in the Civilian Conservation Corps—Roosevelt's New Deal work program organized along military lines.[8] Terry assumed command of B Company on 2 June.[9] Wilkinson found his new captain sipping his thick coffee inside the B Company HQ in another white wood building nearby. After checking in, Wilkinson tracked down Captain Sweeting to reunite him with his car. Sweeting was pleased to see both man and car in top shape. Finally, Wilkinson hunted down yet another long, white wood building. This one was designated as the Bachelor Officers' Quarters (BOQ) for the 756th. The accommodations seemed austere but comfortable. Wilkinson found his room and unpacked quickly, then set out to find the rest of his new company. He discovered most of the enlisted men were attending classes, while others worked on their physical conditioning.

Wilkinson caught up with Lewis and Smith just as they completed organizing the company roles. This task boiled down to matching men to jobs outlined in the Table of Organization (T/O). Lewis, Smith, and most enlisted men arrived at Fort Lewis by train on 3 June. Since Wilkinson arrived a week later,[10] he missed a lion's share of this organizational work. By this time, most positions had been assigned to those seemingly best suited for them. Only twenty-three men in the entire company were regular Army professionals. The rest were conscripts brought in to complete one year of service under the 1940 Selective Service Act.[11] The toughest challenge for Lewis and Smith was determining which draftee best filled a particular role based upon his civilian work experience. In some cases, a match was clear. For example, Private (Pvt) Morris B. Thompson, a 26-year-old who managed a gas and service station in Idaho, made the ideal maintenance section sergeant.[12] An auto mechanic was a natural for tank mechanic, a truck driver for tank driver, and a bookkeeper for company clerk or supply assistant, etc. However, a number of conscripts showed no experiences matching a specific role. These leftover "basics" received tank crewmen assignments or were put in the kitchen—whether they wanted the job or not. Some had to learn complicated skills they had never even considered before—such as gunnery. Certainly, not everybody's preferences could be accommodated. In total, over one hundred enlisted men were matched to company positions ranging from the tank crews, to maintenance, mess, clerical, and supply.

Naturally, leadership roles went to the senior regular Army enlisted men with lengthy service records. Sergeant (Sgt) Ralph Robbins, nearing retirement age, was appointed company first sergeant (1st Sgt). His position, also known as "Top Kick" in Army parlance, made him responsible for the overall discipline of the enlisted men. Robbins's Army career started before the Great War and included service on General John J. Pershing's famous chase of Pancho Villa across Mexico.[13] Robbins was small in stature but a firm and even-handed disciplinarian.[14] His colorful and sharp sense of humor made him a popular figure,[15] but his twenty-five plus years of military experience bestowed him living legend status among the young men of the company. Three other regular Army veterans: Sgt Jack Hogan, Sgt Edward A. Shields, and Sgt Carl T. Crawford, all recent stateside returnees after completing lengthy duty tours in China and the Philippines, were assigned the three platoon sergeant positions and promoted to the rank of staff sergeant (S/Sgt).[16]

Each of the five company officers adopted special responsibilities as well. Lewis was put in charge of the mess and Wilkinson drew supply duties.[17] No sooner had Lewis learned his way around the kitchen, however, when he was transferred on 17 June to HQ Company to take command of the reconnaissance platoon.[18] A few weeks later on 9 June, Lt Smith also transferred to HQ Company—leaving Captain Terry and Lt Wilkinson as the only two assigned officers in B Company. Two other officers were brought in to fill platoon leader vacancies, but their "attachment" was only temporary—until more permanent officers could be secured.[19] As summer passed, Wilkinson and Terry got to know each other very well. Wilkinson learned Terry was quite content working behind a desk handling the administrative side of command, while Terry saw Wilkinson as the motivated outdoorsman itching for the next challenge. This personal understanding would serve Wilkinson well in the near future. An eminently decent man, Captain Terry nevertheless insisted on one peculiar rule: His officers and sergeants had to sport slim, trimmed mustaches like his, so Wilkinson and all the company's non-commissioned officers (NCOs) obliged.[20] At the end of July, both Smith and Lewis returned to B Company, but each had been promoted to first lieutenant (1st Lt) in the meantime.[21] This advance in grade placed them above the T/O needs for the company, so their assignments were also intended as temporary.[22]

A third officer assigned to B Company but absent on detached service was 1st Lt David McSparron—the company's executive officer (XO). McSparron stayed at Fort Knox for additional coursework in tank maintenance and wasn't expected to join B Company until late summer. The company XO's job included the oversight of the upkeep and supply of all the company's tanks and motor vehicles—a responsibility that required roughly ten extra weeks of specialized technical training.[23] In truth, 1st Lt McSparron wasn't missed, because B Company was a tank outfit without any tanks. In fact, the entire battalion hadn't received a single tank. The War Department's Table of Organization and Equipment (T/O&E) required each of the 756th Tank Battalion's three gun companies ("A," "B," and "C") to field seventeen new M3 light tanks. However, no M3s were available or expected to arrive anytime soon. The same shortages applied to other weapons. In fact, the *only* weapons issued to the 756th Tank Battalion thus far were three .45-caliber Smith and Wesson revolvers—suitable only for use on the target range.[24]

The production run for M3 light tanks had just begun and there simply weren't enough older M1 or M2 light tanks to satisfy training demands all across the country. The 194th Tank Battalion received a few but could not share them. The 756th's turn would have to wait until later. Without the necessary equipment, B Company members passed their weekday hours indoors listening to classroom lectures, or outdoors participating in close-order drills, calisthenics, marches, or attending demonstrations. Participation to all events was mandatory and punishment for rule breaking ranged from kitchen duty to hand digging useless holes.[25] As a work-around to the problem of missing rifles, Captain Terry acquired several youth model BB guns along with some old ammo boxes and mouse traps. The mouse trap springs were affixed to ammo boxes and used to clasp a target paper. These targets were then set up in an outdoor firing range the men dubbed "Mousetrap Range."[26]

To grasp the basics to crewing a tank, the carpenter shop constructed simple wooden H-shaped frames out of 2" x 4" and 1" x 4" timbers. Each frame was built to the approximate length and width of a small tank. A "crew" of four men took positions at each corner inside the "H" and carried the frame around to simulate a moving tank.[27] The men started calling their crude stand-ins "H-tanks" and the satirical nickname stuck.[28] Outsiders found the sight of grown men strolling about the grounds of Fort Lewis pretending to maneuver inside make-believe tanks beyond amusing and the crews soon became targets of incessant verbal abuse from passing infantry units.[29] The unwelcome attention grated the nascent tankers, but they did gain valuable and practical experience rehearsing roles, crew communication, and platoon and company coordination tactics. For example, "drivers" learned to respond automatically to the "foot" signals from the tank commander "seated" behind him. The commander accomplished this by pressing his free hand on the back of the driver's shoulders. In a real tank, the commander would be seated above in the turret and use his feet to do the same. The crews also learned how to follow the voice commands of their tank commanders as well as the hand signals of the platoon leaders and the company commander. More importantly, everyone learned to recognize and utilize terrain features for concealment, protection, and tactical advantage, and how to move in support of each other through "fire and maneuver" drills.[30] The men even practiced at night as part of the experience.[31] The process was slow going and exhausting at times—especially on dreary, cold, and wet Washington mornings or blistering late-summer afternoons. As an added bonus, the men received some great aerobic conditioning—something no gasoline-powered engine could ever give them.

As the days passed, the men carried their H-tanks around with more emphasis on platoon and company formations. On occasion, the entire battalion mobilized for "battle." An objective was identified, scouted, and attacked. Mimicking the historic role of horse cavalry, the "tanks" charged with the necessary numerical strength and "speed" to overwhelm an enemy weak point. A light tank battalion, in theory, was expected to fight as a whole or as separate companies in support of infantry formations—but no one was exactly sure on the details. Opinion was split inside the War Department. Armored divisions were meant to attack on a grand scale—spearheading the main forces the same way Guderian's panzers cut through Poland and France. Some thought independent tank battalions should attack in a similar fashion, but on a smaller scale, in support of an infantry division. However, Lieutenant General (Lt Gen) Lesley J. McNair, a heavily influential artilleryman in the War Department, dismissed the entire Armored Force concept as misguided. He saw value in tanks but only as close infantry support weapons restricted to accomplishing narrow objectives—such as knocking out enemy MG nests and pillboxes. McNair firmly believed that tanks should *not* do battle against enemy tanks. He argued the necessary upgrade in armor and firepower would only slow the tanks down and make them less effective as infantry support weapons. Instead, McNair proposed that a more practical and economical way to neutralize enemy tanks was through the creation of a separate "tank destroyer force" organized around mobile artillery and charged with the mission to "seek, strike, and destroy" enemy armor—thus freeing tanks of the burden. McNair could not stop the formation of armored divisions altogether, but his tank destroyer idea won War Department approval. Thus, a new and separate tank destroyer branch formed, and American tank design aims shifted from battling other tanks toward meeting infantry support needs. McNair was also given overall command of the GHQ tank battalions—which were created to be dispatched wherever armor was needed on the battlefield. This "interchangeable parts" approach was another concept he advocated. In theory, GHQ tank battalions were supposed to have the flexibility to fight in larger ad hoc "tank groups," loaned out to armored divisions for added punch, or attached to infantry divisions as armor support.[32] In truth, the GHQ tank battalions were largely expected to support infantry divisions and fight where the foot soldier, not the tank, spearheaded the attack. The Armored Force instruction at Fort Knox, however, trained *all* tankers in the same methods—whether they were assigned to big armored divisions or small GHQ tank battalions. Tankers at Fort Knox who were taught in the combined arms ways of armored divisions and then sent to GHQ battalions, like the 756th (L), discovered the tank's battlefield role was far less clear. As a consequence, much GHQ training relied on improvisation, and the officers, again, borrowed heavily from old cavalry doctrine for guidance.[33]

The infantry division the 756th was being groomed to support was the 3rd Infantry Division. The 3rd Division earned the nickname "Rock of the Marne" during the Great War for holding rock solid during a ferocious German attack at the Second Battle of the Marne. In 1939–40, all Army units were reorganized and the 3rd Division shifted from a big "square" arrangement of four regiments to a leaner "triangular" configuration of three. These changes took a great deal of time and energy to implement. The three regiments in the newly reorganized 3rd Division were the 7th, the 15th, and the 30th Infantry Regiments (Inf Regt). Each regiment boasted long prestigious combat lineages going as far back as the War Between the States. The 7th Regiment's combat history went back even further: the War of 1812. A regiment comprised roughly 4,000 men organized into nine infantry companies, three "heavy weapons" companies, and an HQ company. All regimental companies were collectively organized into three battalions designated as the 1st, the 2nd, and the 3rd Battalions (Bn). In addition to the three infantry regiments, the 3rd Division also included four battalions of artillery, the 10th Engineer Battalion, the 3rd Medical Battalion, the 3rd Quartermaster Battalion, the 3rd Reconnaissance Troop, and the 3rd Signal Company.[34] Eventually, the 756th Tank Battalion (L) would be added as an "attached" unit, but that day would wait until enough real tanks arrived. H-tanks had no practical function in the 3rd Division's more realistic drills and maneuvers. For the time being, both units trained separately.

During July and August, the battalion received a smattering of equipment and a few vehicles in dribs and drabs. First, three Harley-Davidson motorcycles were delivered. A short time later, three half-track trucks arrived.[35] By summer's end, the battalion added two 2-½-ton trucks, a command car, an ambulance, and—finally, six old M1 and M2 light tanks.[36] This hodgepodge of vehicles didn't come close to fulfilling their T/O&E. A fully equipped tank battalion required fifty-one tanks organized into three companies of three platoons each. These six tanks represented only enough to equip one five-tank platoon—while leaving a spare. Instead of organizing them as a single platoon, however, two tanks were farmed to each gun company. That way, all the crews could rotate in turns, away from H-tank practice to become acquainted with the M1's features.

The M1 "combat car" was first introduced into the U.S. Army in 1935 for mechanized cavalry use. A little over 100 were built over the next two years—all rolling out of the Rock Island Arsenal in Illinois.[37] The M1 was fourteen feet long, eight feet wide, and fully tracked. The hull armor consisted of steel plating welded together in some places and riveted in others. Its armor was only five-eighths of an inch at the thickest—useful for stopping small arms fire, but little more. A single two-man turret on top was armed with a .50-caliber and a .30-caliber MG. The M2 light tank, built specifically for infantry support, appeared virtually identical to the M1. The only obvious difference was that the larger single two-man turret had been replaced with two side-by-side one-man turrets. One mini-turret housed a .50-caliber MG and the other, a .30-caliber MG. Because of these prominent twin features, the M2s were nicknamed "Mae Wests" after the American actress and sex symbol of the time. When the M1 and M2 combat cars were assigned to the new Armor Force they were renamed M1A2 (gas-powered) and M1A1 (diesel) accordingly.[38] Although the oldest M1 was scarcely five years old, it was already hopelessly outdated. As early as 1937, the Spanish Civil War proved that light tanks needed thicker armor and a 37mm cannon in order to remain combat effective. The M1 had neither, so by 1941 they were relegated to training vehicles. The M3 light tank with thicker armor and a 37mm cannon would ultimately find its way into the 756th.

The M1 crew consisted of four, with two sitting above in the turret and two down below in the front. In the Mae West variant, the two men on top sat in separate turrets next to each other. The commander sat on the vehicle's left side and manned the .50-caliber MG. Below him to the front was the driver. On the commander's right, another crewman manned a turret-mounted .30-caliber MG. On the driver's right, a fourth crewman manned a hull-mounted .30-caliber MG as "bow gunner" and also doubled as an assistant driver—in case the regular driver became incapacitated. The M1 was not equipped with radios or an intercom. All communication was accomplished the same way the 756ers rehearsed in H-tanks—through hand signals and signal flags between tanks and voice or foot signals within the tank. The M1s offered no cannon training whatsoever, but the crews did learn plenty about MGs. The chassis of the old M1 and the soon-to-be M3 light tank were essentially the same—right down to the vertical volute suspension system. This, at least, gave the drivers a sense of what to expect with the M3, and the crews learned how to function in cramped, uncomfortable, and loud conditions. A few weeks later, two more M1s arrived—giving the battalion a grand total of eight.[39] The additional tanks meant three or more M1s could now maneuver together, allowing the crews to practice platoon tactics. Since the M1 moved surprisingly fast—topping out well above their "official" 45 MPH specifications[40]—the tankers became adept at integrating cavalry principles into their tactics. The cavalry was, after all, centered around shock and speed—principles difficult to replicate when carting about wooden frames on foot. Over and over, the M1 crews practiced storming targets with blazing speed while laying down suppressive torrents of MG fire. The tankers nicknamed these exhilarating attack drills "cruising,"[41] and the tiresome jibing hollered from passing infantry units ended overnight.

By summer's end, the battalion started receiving another new vehicle in small numbers: a ¼-ton truck the tankers called a "peep." The infantry called this same vehicle a "jeep."[42] A handful of jeeps were already seen buzzing around Fort Lewis when the battalion first arrived—and always attracted the excitement and envy of onlookers. Now the 756th received some of their own. Each time a new one appeared, the battalion officers immediately claimed it for "testing."[43] The jeeps were then bounced over rough terrain, sloshed through creeks, and raced up and down nearby hills until the novelty wore off. Then the enlisted men took their turns with them. Eventually, the "testing" ended and the jeeps ended up serving their rather mundane T/O roles as officer transports or light-duty supply trucks.

The news from Europe during the summer of '41 continued to be alarming, depressing, and mostly negative. In June, the United States broke off diplomatic relations with Germany and Italy. A few days later, Germany launched a massive invasion of the Soviet Union codenamed Operation *Barbarossa*. Over 150 divisions fanned out and rolled across the steppes of Russia—including seventeen panzer divisions. The force comprised a total of over three-million men and 3,850 tanks.[44] Throughout the summer, the German Wehrmacht encircled, trapped, and collected surrendering Soviet armies one after the other—penetrating deep inside Russia and the Ukraine to a battle line 500 miles east of where they started. The invasion had the makings of a rout. Town after town, city after city fell before Germany's panzers—with the ultimate prizes of Leningrad and Moscow to the north and the Caucasus oil fields to the south within view. At the same time in Egypt, Rommel's panzers threatened to annihilate the British Eighth Army. It appeared the war in Europe might end before the U.S. Army could effectively modernize.

On 22 August, the "father" of the American Armored Force, Maj Gen Adna Chaffee succumbed to cancer—leaving his labor of love orphaned but in the capable hands of the young Maj Gen Jacob L. Devers. Devers inherited an Armored Force that was rapidly expanding. Preparations to add even more armored divisions and GHQ battalions spun into overdrive. In July, the first substantial shipment of some eighty-four M3 light tanks arrived in Egypt to help shore up the British North African effort—with more deliveries on the way.[45] The M3 lights were produced exclusively at the massive American Car and Foundry Company in Berwick, Pennsylvania.[46] By the end of summer, some 100 M3 medium tanks also started rolling out of five different assembly lines in the U.S. and Canada.[47] The assembly lines to both M3 types were just gearing up, too. One new Detroit Chrysler plant *alone* was expected to churn out 450 tanks each month beginning in September.[48]

That summer and autumn, groups of officers and enlisted men of the 756th rotated in and out of the battalion to become experts in their roles. Some remained at Fort Lewis to acquire cooking,[49] quarter mastering, or truck driving skills.[50] Others returned east to Fort Knox to attain more technical expertise in such matters as communication and maintenance. On 19 July, 1st Lt Lewis left for Fort Knox to attend a month-long gunnery course.[51] On 24 August, 1st Lt McSparron arrived from Fort Knox to finally assume his duties as B Company XO.[52] On 3 September, some eighteen B Company enlisted men began attending a formal two-week tank driving school.[53] In the meantime, Lt Col MacLaughin shuttled back and forth several times on battalion business to Fort Ord near San Francisco—laying the groundwork for future training.[54] In his absence, 42-year-old Major Jacob R. Moon took charge.[55]

Late in the summer, a call went out for 756th officers willing to transfer over to the 194th Tank Battalion (L). The 194th received some of the very first M3 light tanks and was preparing to ship to the Philippines.[56] Wilkinson was quite happy in the 756th but considered the opportunity too good to pass up, and so he cast his name for the job—one of only four who responded. He was not chosen, however. Two other volunteers landed the assignment, and the 194th set sail a few weeks later.[57] Wilkinson wasn't too terribly disappointed, but he still longed for greater challenges—especially with the halfway mark of his one-year Army reserve commitment nearing.

Originally, the service requirement for reserve officers like Wilkinson and Lewis was set for only one year. However, the U.S. government recently altered those service terms and the Army began notifying reserve officers that only half of them would return to civilian life with the other half "asked" to stay active a bit longer.[58] The deteriorating situation in Europe was the reason. At first, no one was quite sure who would be "asked" to remain. During the summer, President Roosevelt petitioned Congress to extend the terms of the Selective Service Act beyond the original one-year obligation for conscripts. The hotly debated issue touched off a national firestorm. On 12 August, Congress finally agreed to Roosevelt's request,[59] but the act barely passed the House of Representatives. A single vote was the difference. The official count stood at 203 to 202, but even that figure was disputed afterwards. Many draftees were understandably peeved over having their terms extended after the fact—especially early inductees who planned on returning home in October 1941. By the summer of 1941, 900,000 young men had been drafted through the lottery system, but none had yet served their full term.[60] By and large, the American public remained dead set against direct American military involvement overseas and were deeply suspicious of the motives behind the expanded draft. A nasty political backlash began to brew. A movement called "Over the Hill in October" (O.H.I.O.) sprung up in places around the country. Conscripts threatened to walk away after their original year of service expired, in defiance of the Congressional extension. October arrived but few dared to follow through. Griping about Army life was a time-honored American tradition; desertion was not.

On 2 October 1941, 2nd Lt A. P. Severson joined B Company as a new platoon leader.[61] 1st Lt Lewis returned from Fort Knox gunnery school,[62] but his assignment to B Company was only temporary. On 28 October, 2nd Lt David D. Redle arrived to fill the remaining platoon leader spot—giving B Company three again.[63] Redle grew up in Wyoming and had graduated from Creighton University earlier that summer with a chemistry degree and an ROTC commission. He stood about 5' 7" with a rail thin physique but was a rugged frontiersman in both mind and spirit. For many years, Redle's father ran a grocery store catering to rough and tumble ore miners working near Sheridan, Wyoming. Redle grew up in a large family with several older brothers, so he learned to become quite adept at survival on many levels.[64]

By this point in time, the battalion acquired enough hand-me-down M1s and Mae Wests to equip each of the three companies with seven or eight respectively. Though barely covering half the battalion's T/O requirements, the numbers were enough to retire the embarrassing H-tanks, and the battalion could finally participate in large-scale maneuvers with their 3rd Division infantry brethren. On Tuesday 21 October, the "largest tank maneuver ever held on the West Coast" thundered over five square miles of flat piney loam at the southern edge of Fort Lewis near Roy, Washington. The local newspapers announced the exercise beforehand so the locals would not be alarmed. This "all out test" pitted an attacking fifty-tank force comprising 756th light and 752nd medium tanks against defenders employing AT guns. No ammunition was fired, but "dummy" Molotov cocktails were utilized. Over 5,000 men participated in the mock battle while the 3rd Division commander, Maj Gen John P. Lucas, watched intently.[65] Four weeks later, on 18 November, the same forces scrimmaged again upon the same grounds—this time firing dummy ammunition.[66]

The 3rd Division was attached to the Navy/Marines Amphibious Corps Pacific Fleet for the purposes of practicing beach landings.[67] Rumors circulated that both 756th and the 3rd Division would relocate to Hawaii for more advanced training.[68] During November, the 756th tankers joined the 3rd Division at Henderson Inlet on Puget Sound to practice sea landings for the first time together. The work focused chiefly on moving men and equipment from ship to shore aboard open-decked LCP (landing craft, personnel) boats.[69] These small, 35-foot-long plywood vessels were not designed to carry vehicles or tanks, so the tankers' contributions were limited. During the same time frame, all B Company members journeyed by truck each morning to a pool in Tacoma to earn their swimming qualifications. Every man passed.[70] On 13 November, 1st Lt Lewis transferred to HQ Company to become the battalion reconnaissance officer.[71] That same day, Wilkinson temporarily joined HQ Company as a student maintenance officer.[72] The assignment was a clear sign he was being groomed for an XO position in the future.

On 1 December, a flatbed rail shipment of some forty half-tracks arrived for apportionment between the 756th and 752nd Tank Battalions.[73] The additional vehicles helped fill gaps in the T/Os to both outfits, but not where needed most: tanks.

Six months after arriving at Fort Lewis, the men of the 756th settled into the standard routine of garrison life. The coming and going of men in training, the physical fitness routines, the regular visits to the rifle and pistol ranges, the crew turns in the old M1s, the periodic parade reviews—all pulsed along at a comforting rhythm of sorts. On weekends, military life would pause briefly so the officers and troops could pursue their own interests, and many dated women from the local town. There were cinema films and football games to attend. There were humorous radio shows, epic boxing matches, swing music trends, and big band leaders to follow. The sting of the summer's draft extension wore off and some dared dream of returning home soon. Lt Wilkinson became so lulled by the routine, that on Saturday 6 December, he purchased a car just to explore the countryside beyond Fort Lewis during his remaining weekends with the battalion. He planned for that same car to eventually carry him back home to Texas. After proudly showing off his new wheels to the other officers at the BOQ, Wilkinson listened in on the radio as his alma mater, Texas A&M, beat Washington State by the score of 7–0 to close out a stellar football season record of nine wins with only one loss.[74] Life was very good indeed.

The morning of 7 December 1941 began as yet another lazy Sunday like countless others before. The weather was cool, gray, and drizzly—perfect for staying indoors and reading a good book or listening to another competitive football game on the radio. Wilkinson and his fellow 756th officers relaxed quietly in their rooms or gathered for hot coffee and idle chit-chat in the BOQ lounge at the end of the hall. Lt Lewis was half-listening to the programming on his small radio when an interrupting news bulletin jarred him to his feet. He bolted across the hall into Wilkinson's room exclaiming: "The Japs have attacked Pearl Harbor!"[75] The officers who were gathered in the BOQ lounge heard the same report on another radio. Slams followed and a few choice words reverberated down the hallway. One by one, bewildered young men emerged from their rooms to check on the commotion and join a growing gathering of shocked officers huddled around the lounge radio. A few more sketchy details were given, but nothing of substance. In exasperation, someone finally howled: "Where's that goddamn Navy?!"—having no clue that half the Pacific fleet was either sunk, capsized, or still burning near Ford Island at that very moment.[76]

2nd Lt Redle was the weekend duty officer, responsible for maintaining the battalion routine in absence of the commanding officer. Lt Col MacLaughlin lay bedridden and unavailable—convalescing in the hospital due to illness.[77] Major Moon was not immediately available either. Many of the officers and enlisted men had taken weekend passes to destinations all over Washington State and as far away as British Columbia and Oregon. Fortunately, Major Moon hadn't ventured too far from post and rushed back to the 756th HQ office around noon to relieve Redle—allowing him to return to B Company.[78] Moon's voice soon broke over the barracks' public address system calling upon all officers of the 756th to urgently report for duty and gather at the officers' mess.[79] The IX Corp HQ issued orders, as well, suspending all passes and requiring all personnel to return posthaste.[80] All afternoon, anxious men wearing civilian clothing arrived through the main gate by various means as Army vehicles buzzed and screamed about the fort. Many men didn't even know where "Pearl Harbor" was.[81]

Wilkinson, Redle, Lewis, and other available officers of the 756th changed into their service dress uniforms and hustled over to the officers' mess to meet Major Moon for an informal planning session. Drinks flowed to help ease the tension. By 1530 (military time), the officers formulated a "battle plan": All battalion men were to be personally prepared in four hours,[82] with every tank fueled and armed and the crews ready to move out at midnight.[83] Where they were going or what they were supposed to do, no one was quite sure—but the general goal was to reposition all tanks and crews somewhere away from the fort in case of attack. At 1600, a battalion formation was called to discover who remained missing. A motley collection of sorry soldiers gathered on the wet grounds outside the barracks as roll was called. Some stood in uniform, while the rest fidgeted awkwardly in civilian clothes. Shirt tails stuck out, hats were absent, and ties either hung askew or were missing altogether.[84] They certainly did not look like a military unit prepared for action. Throughout a foggy, rainy afternoon and evening, Fort Lewis continued to teem in organized panic with no one really knowing for certain what to do—only that preparations of some sort had to be made. At one point, everyone received gas masks with orders to carry them at all times. The Military Police (MP) fanned through neighboring towns rounding up any officers and soldiers who had not yet heard the news.[85]

Captain Terry arrived at camp around the time B Company began stocking and fueling their eight sorry M1s. Packing the ammunition took the most time. Each tank was armed with three or four MGs. However, most of the feeding belts hung empty with the ammunition sealed away in cans. A fully loaded M1 carried 10,000 rounds of .30-caliber and 8,000 rounds of .50-caliber rounds—and every single bullet had to be belt seated carefully by means of a hand cranked loader. The task dragged on well past midnight and didn't wrap up until 0600 on 8 December. Companies A and C muddled through the same process. By the time B Company tanks were finally stocked and ready, the clock read 0615. An exhausted Redle wandered back to the BOQ. Along the way, he saw 3rd Division men heading to morning Mass. As a devout Catholic, he felt obliged to join—especially in a time of national distress—and did not finally collapse on his BOQ bunk until 0730. After only one hour of sleep, he was awakened with new orders to "head out."[86]

By noon, all the men had gathered their equipment and camping materials together in the chilly rain and assembled outside the 756th garrison buildings. A half hour later, they rolled by motor column to a dispersal zone roughly two miles southeast of the fort.[87] As the bewildered men unpacked and set up camp in a wooded area, word spread like wildfire that Congress had formally declared war on

Japan.[88] More dismal news crackled over the radio: Wake Island had been attacked and the Midway Islands shelled. Japanese planes had also bombed Singapore and the Philippines. Wilkinson pondered the fate of the 194th Tank Battalion (L) recently sent to the Philippines.

The next day, Lt Col MacLaughlin finagled his way out of the hospital to reassume command of the 756th at their dispersal camp.[89] A heavy autumn travel schedule left him seriously ill, but his health had improved enough for duty.[90] On 10 December, rumors circulated over possible deployment destinations. How the 756th, only partially equipped with outdated tanks, could be sent anywhere was ignored during the swaps of wild conjecture. Ears remained glued to the radio—hoping to seize upon anything positive. Whenever an announcement broke telling of American forces fighting back somewhere in the Pacific, a hearty cheer filled the camp,[91] but everyone began feeling helpless just sitting in the rainy backwoods, and the dispersal orders seemed more and more pointless with each passing hour.

On 11 December, the battalion loaded and returned to Fort Lewis—arriving at their barracks around 1300. While unpacking their damp effects, a new alert sounded warning of an imminent attack. Some airplane pilot patrolling the coast of Washington reported seeing a "Japanese battle fleet" headed toward Seattle.[92] This sighting was taken seriously, and Fort Lewis erupted in a pandemonium even more frenzied than at the original news of Pearl Harbor. The 3rd Division troops hastily dispersed to defensive positions along the coast, and the 756th was ordered to defend the small town of Montesano near Grays Harbor with everything they had.[93] Presumably, this did not include the BB guns used at Mousetrap Range. While readying for the journey, more alarming news broke over the radio: Now Germany and Italy had declared war on the United States. Suddenly, America found itself in a two-front war against formidable enemies.

In late afternoon, 756th Tank Battalion (L) formed a convoy of trucks, jeeps, and vintage M1s for the sixty-mile journey to Montesano.[94] At 1730, in shivering drizzle, the convoy crept through the main gate and swung westward toward the coast. In the small towns and crossroads along the way, locals stared back with worried looks as the column passed. Civilians driving automobiles and delivery trucks weren't sure how to react. Some sped up. Some pulled over haphazardly to the shoulder, while others stopped unexpectedly in the road, becoming more hindrance than help. The roads were slick as nightfall rapidly descended. Captain Terry led the B Company section of the column and kept pressing the speed upwards. The tanks and vehicles were supposed to keep 300-yard intervals, but the road conditions were such that the task was virtually impossible, and the irregular accordion effect from the continual stopping then speeding again frayed the nerves of the anxious drivers. Lt Redle anchored the rear of the column. At one point, he glanced down at the speedometer to see his tank was barreling through the tiny town of McCleary at 55 MPH in complete darkness. One startled civilian driver in the oncoming lane slowed sharply as the column passed. To avoid a rear-end collision, the trailing car swerved toward S/Sgt Shields's tank. Shields's driver braked and jerked the tank hard right, clipping the car and crushing its trunk before skidding off the road. Miraculously, the car's driver was unhurt, but S/Sgt Shields's tank threw a track and overturned in a roadside ditch—pinning crewman Pvt Paul Jones's wrist against the hard ground.[95] Jones was eventually freed but his arm was left a mangled mess.[96]

2nd Lt Roger Fazendin had joined HQ Company the previous month[97] and rode in a truck full of enlisted men. He counted only three weapons among them: a revolver, a rifle, and a Thompson submachine gun. The 21-year-old Minnesotan wondered how they were supposed to defend the coast of Washington with so little.[98] Still, the men maintained surprisingly high spirits as they finally pulled into Montesano at 2230.[99] Lt Lewis's battalion recon platoon arrived first. Because of the darkness and late hour, Lewis asked local townsfolk for advice on the best location to set up camp. They suggested he take a secondary road north of town. When the battalion arrived at the site, they found the road acceptable but the surrounding terrain swampy and hilly. As a result, the entire battalion was forced to bivouac on the narrow road, and a chastened Lt Lewis learned to *never* entrust a civilian with an important military decision.[100]

After nightfall, the sky cleared enough to allow a cool silvery moon to appear. Several crates of Springfield 1903 bolt-action rifles arrived—all smeared liberally with Cosmoline grease after extended storage. Fazendin and his men unpacked the Great War relics in the middle of the street before the town's old courthouse. Few of the men knew how to handle the old rifles, so Fazendin provided a crash course on everything from loading and fastening slings to affixing bayonets under the scant, vacillating moonlight. Even with these additional rifles, approximately 200 of the 600 men in the battalion still remained weaponless.[101] Those without were instructed to "fight with their fists" if necessary.[102] Fazendin couldn't help but wonder if the 3rd Division and an underequipped, unprepared 756th Tank Battalion stretched so thin along the coastline represented but a "picket line" of resistance to any Japanese invaders.[103]

Once daylight arrived on 12 December, Wilkinson, Captain Terry, and several other battalion officers reconnoitered surrounding ground for a better campsite and more ideal terrain to employ tanks. From the coastline to Grays Harbor along the Chehalis River and areas in and around Montesano, they encountered ground too soft and swampy, with little room for maneuver.[104] Were the Japanese to land in the meantime, the tank crews were told to empty their MGs and trample them—"cruising around until they were killed."[105] Such instructions required no obvious tactics or coordination. These were orders to engage in a desperate free-for-all. The townsfolk, appreciative of military protection but also apprehensive over an invasion threat, made sure all the tankers were stocked with all the free coffee and donuts they could have wanted.[106]

Wilkinson, Terry, and the others finally found good ground close to the Pacific Ocean.[107] The site offered thick tree cover for tank concealment and solid soil to pitch tents and spread bedrolls.[108] The battalion promptly moved to the location, set up a new camp, then waited and watched an empty sea.

The Japanese Invasion fleet never appeared. Reconnaissance planes fanned out all along the Pacific coast, but never found a thing. In the end, everyone concluded the spotting pilot misinterpreted a series of cloud shadows or wave squalls for Admiral Yamamoto's secret armada.

During the afternoon of Saturday 13 December, the tired men of the 756th packed and headed back to Fort Lewis. The cold journey took two and a half hours without stopping.[109] Lt Wilkinson, Corporal (Cpl) Art Richter, and two others rode quietly together in the same tank—privately contemplating the entire affair.[110] Cpl Richter was originally from Nebraska but played collegiate football and graduated from Washington University. The tall, athletic redhead did not appreciate seeing his fellow Americans put through such distress.[111] The operation did little—except to show the men they were completely unprepared to handle a foreign invasion. Frustrated and angry, Wilkinson dismissed the entire event as "an exercise in futility."[112] At least, Wilkinson reasoned, the unit gained some experience living in pup tents and running a field kitchen out in the elements.[113] The fleeting thought provided little consolation.

Everyone seethed over the Japanese sneak attack on Pearl Harbor and wanted revenge. The tankers now wanted modern tanks and an even chance to fight. Gone was the idle talk among the officers and men about serving their requisite time and returning to civilian life. Gone were the newspaper debates over neutrality and intervention. A quaint and innocent era slipped away forever in the space of six incredible days.

Every man knew he was "in for the duration."

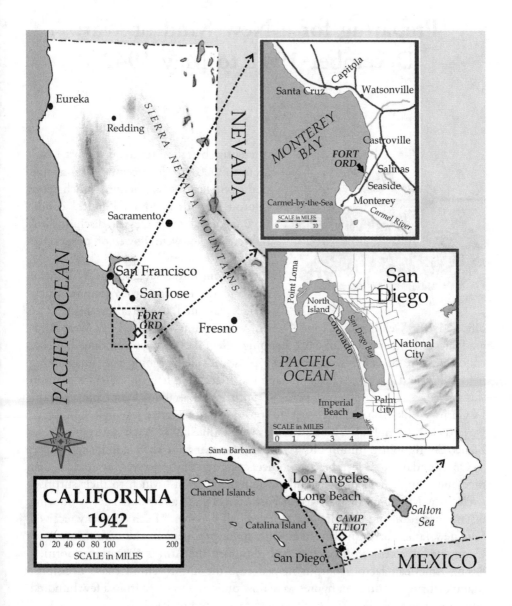

CALIFORNIA
1942

0 20 40 60 80 100   200
SCALE in MILES

CHAPTER 3

Preparing for a New Kind of War: December 1941 to May 1942

M3 Light Tank (1941)

The entire battalion returned to Fort Lewis around 2000 on 13 December.[1] From that point on, garrison life became much more rigorous and demanding. Physical conditioning kicked into high gear, discipline was tighter, and few were allowed off post except on official business.[2]

Not long after settling in, Wilkinson drove to the bus station to retrieve a new officer assigned to Battalion HQ.[3] The officer, 1st Lt Welborn G. "Tom" Dolvin, was a young Class of 1939 West Point graduate arriving by way of Fort Benning, Georgia.[4] Notwithstanding his elite education, the Siloam, Georgia, native possessed an easygoing and unassuming personality, and the two officers became fast friends.[5] A few days later, Wilkinson was moved to HQ Company so serve as 756th Tank Battalion's liaison officer to the IX Corps.[6] Wilkinson did not covet this position and regretted leaving B Company. Nevertheless, he embraced his new duties with enthusiasm.[7] A few days later, 1st Lt Blanco Smith, joined him in HQ Company—making the change more agreeable.[8]

On Monday 18 December, the officers of the 756th received assurances that their full complement of light tanks would arrive soon.[9] Much to their surprise, twelve new M3 light tanks arrived at Fort Lewis by rail a few days later —drawing instant attraction and boosting the morale of all the men.[10] Each company received four new tanks for immediate use, with more promised in the coming weeks.[11] Undoubtedly, recent world events had reshuffled the Army's allocation priorities. Rising American factory output helped ease the angst behind those decisions. Manufacturing production figures were now projected to surge from a few hundred tanks to an astronomical *2,400 per month* by the end of 1942.[12]

A crew of four operated the M3 light along with its state-of-the-art 37mm cannon and set of five MGs. One MG projected from the hull at the assistant driver position.

Two others protruded from side hull sponsons near the mid-front, manned by the two turret crewmen. A fifth MG was mounted atop the rear edge of the octagonal shaped turret, where the 37mm cannon was also housed. The turret featured a total of three pistol ports cut into the sides and rear for additional protection. The M3's hull was constructed of riveted plating—but offered better protection to the crew. The steel was thickest at the front at 1.75" and measured a robust 1" on the sides. The added armor raised the overall weight to thirteen tons—causing the M3 to move somewhat slower than the M1. Nevertheless, the M3 exhibited surprising pep on account of its 250 horsepower Continental radial gasoline-powered engine. Although officially rated with a top speed of 36 MPH,[13] on flat, hard surfaces it proved much faster. The new turret was more cramped and sat higher on the chassis—a design drawback. This gave the tank a taller profile and made defilade maneuvering more difficult. One significant improvement, however, was an enlarged rear idler wheel set lower to the ground—giving the chassis better ride stability and a more accurate firing platform.[14] The rear idler wheels on the old M1s and M2s set too high off the back and caused the tank to seesaw wildly after firing guns or crossing obstacles. The greatest improvement, however, was that the M3 featured a crew intercom and radio system for communicating with other tanks.[15] Together, these new features made the M3 light America's first truly modern tank and provided the tankers of the 756th with an immediate sense of pride and importance.

Wilkinson longed to climb in one but couldn't—since he was now trapped in HQ, basically running daily messages back and forth between Lt Col MacLaughlin and the XI Corps staff. Ever since the new tanks arrived, Wilkinson's passion for liaison work dwindled away. He made inquiries about transferring back to B Company but was rejected each time.[16] On 24 December, even more M3 lights arrived, and Wilkinson watched forlornly as they were unloaded from the train and driven to the 756th barracks. He now yearned to find *some way* of getting back into B Company.[17] A few days before, Congress expanded Selective Service Registration to include all males aged 19 to 65.[18] Recruitment offices around the country flooded with volunteers. Everyone everywhere seemed to be gearing up, mobilizing, and *doing*, while Wilkinson sat trapped in an administrative cul-de-sac.

That evening, another West Coast alert sounded, but Fort Lewis had become more accustomed to handling them. As part of the response, a platoon of five tanks from B Company was dispatched to the Boeing aircraft plant in Seattle out of concerns Japanese paratroopers might attack the factory.[19] The rest of the company continued with scheduled training—which involved ferrying tanks and crews in ship-to-shore exercises with 3rd Division troops in Puget Sound.[20] The debarkations had not yet developed into full-blown amphibious landings, but they were building up to that.

Wilkinson stayed up into the early morning hours of Christmas Day with Lewis and several other night owls, discussing weighty subjects such as philosophy, death, and the afterlife.[21] The next morning, Wilkinson awoke and realized he was spending his first Christmas ever away from home. With the gloomy thoughts from the previous night's conversation still weighing heavily on his mind, he dressed warmly and headed over to church wondering if this would be the last Christmas for him and many of his fellow tankers.[22] He finally shook off the melancholy and ended up attending the officers' club for an afternoon and evening mixer. There he met up with friends and a local girl he had been dating casually and danced both the night and his troubles away.[23]

The final days of 1941 brought extremely cold weather to Washington State and unbearable boredom for Lt Wilkinson. A liaison officer led a lonely life, indeed, in a garrison setting. On 27 December, the B Company platoon that had been dispatched earlier to Seattle returned.[24] In the meantime, more M3 lights arrived in dribs and drabs—bringing the overall battalion count up to a respectable total of forty new and eight old tanks.[25] On 30 December, all the tanks in the battalion thundered and roared in large-scale evening maneuvers and Wilkinson found his enthusiasm rekindled. Afterwards, he, Captain Terry, and Lts Lewis and Smith stayed up well past midnight avidly reviewing and critiquing the day's demonstration.[26]

The next day—New Year's Eve—Wilkinson tried to finish reading a book on tank history but found himself too mentally distracted and set the work aside. The news of the new World War, the personnel shuffling within the battalion, and his desire for greater challenges all weighed heavily on his mind. In Europe, Germany appeared on the cusp of total victory deep inside the Soviet Union. A bitter Russian winter, however, stalled the drive just shy of Moscow and Soviet forces used the opportunity to counterattack. In North Africa, the British staved off defeat in Egypt and began pushing Rommel's forces back toward Libya. The influx of new American-made tanks helped turn the tide. The war in the Pacific, however, continued unfolding badly for the United States. In the Philippines, some 2,000 American troops along with the M3 lights of the 192nd and 194th Tank Battalion barely held out against Japanese invaders a hundred times greater in strength and numbers.[27] Wilkinson recalled volunteering to transfer to the 194th only a few months earlier and pondered the fate of the officers selected over him. Many 756th tankers believed they were destined for the Philippines as reinforcements—perhaps leaving in only a matter of days.[28] No official orders bolstered this belief, but the speedy deliveries of M3s, the sudden ship-to-shore training, and the fact the 756th was only one of two GHQ light tank battalions available on the West Coast[29] made deployment seem imminent. In recent days, Wilkinson heard rumors that 1st Lt McSparron would transfer to HQ soon, leaving the B Company XO position vacant. Wilkinson coveted the position. Although his friend Dolvin, the West Pointer, was the rumored replacement, Wilkinson resolved to make his best pitch for the spot.

That evening, Wilkinson headed to the officers' club with French Lewis and a group of his closest friends. For the next few hours, the young lieutenants ditched their worries to enjoy a few drinks and the company of some beautiful girls. As midnight ushered in the 1942 New Year, they laughed, danced, and had a few drinks more.[30]

* * *

The first light of the New Year was not welcomed kindly by many recovering in the BOQ. Fortunately, the day's schedule was light, allowing those hungover to either sleep off the loud night's aftereffects or fuel up leisurely on strong coffee to restore function. Later that day, Wilkinson happened upon Captain Terry at the officers' club and the two engaged in a long productive conversation. Terry divulged that not only was the company's XO position available, but a platoon leader spot would be opening as well. Wilkinson told the captain of his strong desire to return to B Company and presented his best case on why the transfer made sense. Even so, he left the club believing Dolvin was a lock for the XO position and another lieutenant by the name of Williams would receive the platoon leader spot.[31] Three days later, however, Wilkinson learned the platoon leader position was his.[32] As expected, 1st Lt Dolvin made XO. McSparron and 2nd Lt Robert Kremer transferred over to HQ Company with new roles.[33] Wilkinson was beside himself with excitement.[34]

The only loose end in the swap involved coverage for the company's immediate tank maintenance responsibilities. Dolvin lacked the formal training but Wilkinson could boast of a few weeks of "student maintenance officer" experience. Still brimming with enthusiasm over the transfer, Wilkinson offered to pull double duty as 1st Platoon leader *and* maintenance officer until Dolvin learned his way around the shop. Captain Terry graciously accepted the offer.[35]

By this time, B Company had secured a full complement of seventeen tanks. On 6 January, all tanks and crews spent the day maneuvering over the cold, wintery terrain around Fort Lewis. For the first time ever, the entire company operated as one. Over the next few days, each of the three platoons drilled repeatedly on field tactics, navigation, map reading, and gunnery while negotiating through snow and ice.[36] New tank drivers received additional training. After each successful exercise, crew confidence and company morale ratcheted ever higher. Every evening, Wilkinson toiled late assuring every tank was properly maintained and fully stocked ahead of the next day's events. The double duty proved exhausting, but Wilkinson always collapsed in bed afterwards feeling he held the finest job in the Army.[37] Best of all, he and Dolvin worked together wonderfully.[38]

After a weekend of welcome rest, the company returned to the fields on Monday without missing a beat—this time, range testing the sponson guns of the M3 lights.[39] Training shifted mid-week to debarking operations with the 3rd Division and wrapped up on Friday with vehicle inspections—a test Wilkinson worked very diligently to pass.[40] That same evening, Wilkinson learned B Company had been selected to send one tank platoon on an intriguing assignment. This extended training involved "joint landings" with 3rd Division troops on "an island." Captain Terry was going and Wilkinson assumed Lt Dolvin would be the platoon leader chosen. Prime assignments like these generally went to officers on the fast career tracks. Lt Col MacLaughlin called an officers meeting to discuss the details. As he began speaking, Captain Terry slipped a small, folded note over to Wilkinson. Confused momentarily, Wilkinson flipped the paper open and quietly read the handwriting. His jaw dropped in disbelief. "Dolvin is not going on the maneuvers," Terry had written. "You and I are going."[41] Wilkinson knew this was reward for his hard work and initiative.

More details emerged the following day. The destination was an island near San Diego.[42] Wilkinson would command the 1st Platoon throughout the exercises, and his five tank commanders were S/Sgt Carl Crawford, Sgt John Reid, Sgt James Haspel, Sgt James MacFadden, and Cpl Ithel R. Adlard—all capable and dependable NCOs. The new M3s were not going, but five of the best M1s still assigned to the battalion were.[43] Captain Terry would travel along as an observer. The remainder of the afternoon and the following day were spent preparing for the journey.[44]

In the early evening hours of Tuesday 20 January, Lt Col MacLaughlin asked Wilkinson to assemble the five 1st Platoon crews and tanks on Fort Lewis's main drill field for a pep talk and send off. "Not only the eyes of Texas but the eyes of the entire Armored Force are going to be on you during this training," MacLaughlin declared. "And Lt Wilkinson will have to answer to me if you don't do a good job of it."[45] Wilkinson had no doubt that they would be successful.[46] At midnight, Wilkinson's platoon drove to Tacoma and parked near the attack transport, USS *Zeilin* (AP9), docked flush along a harbor pier. The following day, everything was loaded and secured deep inside the 500-foot-long ship's hold.[47] As Wilkinson and the commander of the 2nd Battalion Landing Team of the 7th Infantry Regiment discussed final preparations, some eight-hundred men filed aboard.[48]

At 0800 on Saturday 24 January, the USS *Zeilin* dropped its moorings, eased out of Tacoma Harbor and sailed into Puget Sound. To the starboard, the long gray wharfs and warehouses of Seattle slowly slipped by. On the portside, the magnificent Olympic Mountains shimmered under the midday sun while the *Zeilin* threaded the Strait of Juan de Fuca and slipped, at last, into the open sea.[49] Immediately, the untamed swells of the Pacific see-sawed the old ship while the bow swung southward. Before departure, Wilkinson insisted the ship's cargo master re-secure his five tanks and was now glad he did so. At 1500, the *Zeilin* rendezvoused with four oil tankers and a destroyer. The next morning, the small convoy lost sight of land and the swells grew heavier. Many soldiers grew seasick, but Wilkinson remained unaffected. At 1730, the ship's lights were blacked out for fear of Japanese submarines known to be lurking in the area. The threat of torpedoes unnerved the men, but there was nothing one could do but block out the fears and try to sleep.[50] By Tuesday, the sea calmed considerably, and warmer breezes grazed over the decks. Some officers took to basking shirtless topside. At one point, a relaxed sunbather quipped loudly "Ain't war hell?"[51] That evening, the last of the oil tankers dropped out of the convoy, leaving the steadily zig-zagging destroyer as the *Zeilin's* sole companion. The ships stopped briefly to refuel at San Pedro on Thursday morning, but no one was allowed to debark. The next day, they traced along a serene southern California coast, arrived at San Diego and moored in harbor by 1830. The men, however, weren't allowed to debark until the next morning—and only in small groups with valid passes.

Monday came, then Tuesday, and finally Wednesday passed—yet nothing much happened. The Navy, apparently, was still training the lighter boat crews and wasn't ready to start the landing exercises.[52] In the meantime, Wilkinson and the infantry officers held planning sessions. They learned training entailed full-blown amphibious landings at "North Island" on the tip of the Coronado Peninsula across from San Diego. The pristine, undeveloped white beaches there were property of the U.S. Navy and offered a good facsimile of every South Pacific island already taken by the Japanese.[53] Such exercises were new for the Army.[54] The officers were not given a guidebook on beach landing tanks alongside troops, so many details had to be fleshed out by the seat of the pants. The infantry officers proposed the tanks accompany the first assault wave, but Wilkinson insisted the third wave made a better choice to allow the engineers time to clear beach mines and obstacles. His suggestion, however, was overruled.[55] More debate followed over operational details, but once settled, the officers had little else to do but play card games.

The minds of Wilkinson's men numbed from living like sailors stuffed within the *Zeilin's* humid, claustrophobic bowels. The boredom from eating Navy beans every breakfast and the hours spent each day wiping down the tank ammunition to prevent salt air corrosion taxed their patience.[56] When shore leave passes finally found their pockets, the men escaped to town in small rotating groups aboard water taxis to take full advantage of the freedom.[57] A few went too far: Pvts Kelleher and Cogdill ended up stone drunk guests of the local MPs. After the episode, Wilkinson organized exercise sessions, football games, and chaperoned visits to San Diego shows for his men while ashore. By Wednesday, they even tired of shore leave and longed for the landing exercises to commence. One discouraging rumor circulated that they wouldn't train at all and would return to Fort Lewis instead.[58]

Finally, on Thursday 5 February, one crew from Wilkinson's platoon made their first amphibious landing. Roughly 300 yards off from North Island, Sgt McFadden's tank was lifted from the *Zeilin's* cargo hold and then lowered delicately toward the small open hold of an LCVP (Landing Craft, Vehicles & Personnel) pulled alongside.[59] Because of the action of the waves, the most critical part of the operation involved this transfer. The moment the wave peaked; the tank had to be released by the ship's crane onto the floor of the bobbing LCVP. For responsibility reasons, Wilkinson had to give the drop order. Any misjudgment could result in damage or loss of the tank, the LCVP, or worse—injury or death to someone aboard.[60]

Wilkinson's timing was perfect. The crews clambered down cargo netting draped down toward the LCVP and waited for the next high wave crest to leap the rest of the way.[61] Once everyone was safely boarded, the LCVP with tank and crew motored toward the landing zone, beached near shore and lowered the front door ramp into shallow surf. The crew then waited for a receding wave before driving down into knee-deep water and proceeding up onto the dry shore. At the same time, other LCVPs nearby dropped their ramps and disgorged storming infantry in a similar fashion.[62] The exercise was repeated twice with near perfect precision. Sgt McFadden received a mild admonishment for not waiting for the ramp door to completely drop before driving onto it.[63] The criticism was quite minor—given the fact that he had never done such a crazy thing before.

The next day, all five tanks of the 1st Platoon participated in the landings—again achieving complete success. That evening, the tanks remained ashore while Wilkinson and the five crews returned triumphantly to the *Zeilin* by motor launch.[64] Although the Marines were well practiced in such operations, Wilkinson privately celebrated his conviction that his crews were the first to ever land Army tanks on a beach in this manner.[65] In 1940, the 3rd Division practiced similar shore landings at Monterey, but no tanks were involved.[66] No doubt, eyes as high as the War Department observed the tanks in action that day and Wilkinson's crews had performed magnificently.

On Friday 6 February, the infantry landed on a different beach of North Island. No tanks took part, but Wilkinson tagged along as an observer. This time tragedy struck, and Wilkinson watched in horror as a large wave flipped a small motor launch near the beach—killing an infantryman aboard.[67] The freakish accident cast a heavy gloom over the rest of the day's activities. The incident served as a stark reminder that even practice exercises were fraught with unexpected dangers.[68]

Over the weekend, a few of Wilkinson's men enjoying shore leave tangled with some sailors who didn't appreciate the celebratory style of Army types.[69] Nothing terrible happened, but Wilkinson's involvement was required and he began wondering if some of his men possessed the maturity to serve as dependable soldiers.

On Monday, the landings resumed with the tanks participating once again. This time, practice locations involving heavier surf, and steeper beaches were selected for the drills. At times, Wilkinson and his crews received hefty soakings, but in all attempts his crews successfully reached shore with the infantry. At mid-week, Wilkinson boarded an LCVP with an infantry major and sought out new landing sites. One of Wilkinson's tanks and crew was brought along to make any test runs. At one particular location, the major kept pressuring Wilkinson to dispatch his crew where the water was clearly too deep, but Wilkinson steadfastly refused. The infantry officer was relentless in his demands. Finally, Wilkinson agreed—but only if the major took full responsibility for the tank *and* drove it himself.[70] Given those conditions, the major decided they should continue searching for a more promising place.[71] They did find one: at Imperial Beach, on the mainland but further to the south.

The next morning, 12 February, the 2nd Battalion, 7th Infantry Regiment, and Wilkinson's tank platoon loaded aboard the landing craft and headed for Imperial Beach. This particular beach presented much more of a challenge with higher surf and steeper sandbanks. The landings were, again, successful—but tainted by a second tragedy. This time, a Navy officer was killed by a loose surfboat near the beach. That very same officer had accompanied Wilkinson and the infantry major on an LCVP tour the prior day.[72]

Later that evening, Wilkinson reconnoitered another nearby beach with a Colonel Reagan, a Marine officer. Reagan had just returned from Pearl Harbor and confided to Wilkinson that six battleships had been heavily damaged at Pearl Harbor—not just the two publicly acknowledged. He also revealed that many other Navy vessels had been damaged as well.[73] These insider details stunned Wilkinson and caused him to wonder privately if all this training was in vain.

The infantry and tanks successfully landed again the next day, but Wilkinson did not see much value to additional practice and believed they would return soon to Fort Lewis. Captain Terry, who had observed each day's activities from the infantry command ship, told Wilkinson that Lt Dolvin would be bringing Lt Severson's 2nd Platoon to San Diego for training in the coming days.[74]

On Monday, the infantry planned to expand the landings the following day to include a simulated attack inland lasting several days. This added challenge rekindled Wilkinson's enthusiasm. The Tuesday landings on Imperial Beach succeeded without a hitch, with the infantry and tanks pressing a mile eastward through scrubland brush. They stopped near Palm City, set up camp for the evening and ate cold rations before falling asleep under the stars. At dawn the next morning, they pressed the "attack" deeper inland across tougher terrain of steep hills and ravines. For the first time, the tanks and infantry coordinated movements over an extended time period and everything flowed surprisingly well.

The combined-arms force encountered a very large hill, and the infantry commander, Lt Col Peter T. Wolfe,[75] encouraged his 500-man battalion to "take" the hillcrest with the support of the tanks. The infantry advanced partway up one side, cutting pathways through several rows of barbed-wire fence they encountered during the ascent. The tanks then formed a line and advanced alongside Wolfe's men until the highest point was "conquered." Everyone celebrated the victory for a few moments before descending and cutting new pathways through the fences. Once the exercise was over, Lt Col Wolfe gathered all the officers and men atop a small rise nearby for a critique session. Suddenly, Wilkinson heard a commotion behind him and turned to see a grizzled old rancher approaching on horseback, rifle locked squarely across his lap. With a face red with anger, the gray rancher loudly and boldly demanded the names of those responsible for cutting his fences. Wolfe's young staff officers dashed over to try and settle the man down. The entire time, everyone assumed they were maneuvering on government property when, in actuality, they had invaded a man's ranch. Wilkinson felt ashamed over his involvement—especially since he was a cattleman himself. At the same time, he deeply admired the man for his willingness to risk life and limb defending his livelihood—even though he was outgunned 500 to one. This was no exercise or a game to him. If anyone's heart brimmed with a righteous and undaunted American fighting spirit, it was that rancher. In the end Wolfe's staff promised to immediately send engineers to repair the fence damage. This pledge calmed the rancher down considerably.[76] Wilkinson would reflect on that old man's bravery afterwards for quite some time.

* * *

Wilkinson and his men expected to continue practicing beach landings, but were diverted instead to Camp Elliot, a Marine base north of San Diego, where they camped for several weeks in a state of limbo. To make good use of the time, Wilkinson created his own training program that included convoy and night driving practice.[77]

In the meantime, Lt Dolvin brought the 2nd Platoon from Fort Lewis via flatcar train. When they arrived in San Diego on 11 February, they loaded aboard the attack transport, USS *Harris* (AP8), and began the same amphibious training Wilkinson's platoon completed.[78] The 15th and 30th Regiments of the 3rd Division replaced the 7th Regiment for these new sets of exercises.[79] Captain Terry continued observing from the *Zeilin*. In the meantime, Wilkinson's men were told their next destination would be Fort Ord near San Francisco, but the wait dragged on.[80] To keep his platoon focused, Wilkinson urged more challenging training. During one exercise, two tanks collided so violently they bent their drive sprockets. Fortunately, no one was seriously hurt.[81] Another time, while on night driving maneuvers where tank commanders practiced using flashlights to communicate with one another, several tanks mired in mud, and Wilkinson almost flipped his own tank.[82] The men also tested mud grouser attachments to the tank treads but found them of little value.[83] The tankers craved live-fire practice on a nearby gunnery range, but Wilkinson could not secure permission from the Marines to do so. Frustrated over the delays, Wilkinson met with Terry on the *Zeilin* for news on the rumored move to Fort Ord. Instead, Terry said they might be returning to Fort Lewis after all.[84] In the meantime, a Japanese submarine shelled the coast of Santa Barbara for a good twenty minutes. Either the news of this attack or Terry pulling some backroom strings finally landed Wilkinson's men the firing range practice they coveted.[85] Afterwards, to keep his men from going completely stir crazy at Camp Elliot, Wilkinson led his platoon on a 115-mile road march aboard five tanks and three trucks. The journey took them high into the snow-capped Laguna Mountains. From there, they could see the Salton Sea in the distance.[86]

Finally, on 6 March, Wilkinson's platoon returned to the *Zeilin* and loaded up.[87] They practiced a few more beach landings before transferring over to a new attack transport, the USS *President Jackson* (AP37). Neither Terry nor Dolvin seemed to know where they were headed next.[88] But on 17 March, the *Jackson* steamed out of San Diego harbor along with the *Zeilin*, a destroyer, and a submarine. The small convoy headed north and stopped at Monterey. The *Zeilin* remained and all the infantry troops, and Captain Terry and Lt Dolvin debarked. The *Jackson*, however, continued north carrying Wilkinson and his platoon, with the destroyer and a blimp serving as escorts.[89] As the only Army officer remaining aboard, Wilkinson was given the colonel's private stateroom as his personal cabin.[90] The accommodations were wonderful, but the voyage was absolutely terrifying. A severe storm struck, tossing the ship about so violently that many times the propellers spun out of the foaming waves and into the open air. The blimp and destroyer scurried away at the first sign of trouble, leaving the *Jackson* alone— "taking a chance" a ship's officer wryly put it. Wilkinson happened to remember that this was the *very day* his original orders said he was supposed to go home.[91] At times, the battered ship creaked and groaned as if about to split in two. One of the *Jackson*'s forward lifeboats broke loose and bashed helplessly against the hull. In the chaos, an unfortunate sailor broke his leg and many in Wilkinson's platoon became violently seasick. One of the tankers was so fraught with anxiety that Wilkinson put him under guard for fear he might jump overboard.[92] The nightmarish journey lasted four full days before the storm's wrath finally subsided by Friday evening. Somehow the *Jackson* held together.

The next morning, 21 March, the snow-covered peaks of the Olympics appeared in the distance and the men actually cheered in relief. The *Jackson* steamed into the placid waters of Puget Sound and docked in Tacoma at 1500. The men debarked but left the tanks aboard. They climbed into trucks and traveled back to Fort Lewis and their familiar barracks. Upon arriving, Wilkinson walked directly over to the officers' club for a calming drink. He was surprised to see Lt Dolvin already there. Dolvin remarked that both he and Captain Terry had just arrived from Monterey after a taking nice relaxing train ride. He also reported that B Company would soon be packing for Fort Ord after all. Wilkinson shook his head in disbelief and ordered another drink.[93]

* * *

The next morning, Wilkinson's five M1s were unloaded from the *Jackson*, driven back to Fort Lewis, and parked in the company garrison area as if they had never departed.[94] The following morning, Monday 23 March, the old tanks were turned over to Ordnance and replaced with five new M3 lights. Wilkinson's men found it difficult to watch the old rust buckets drive away. They had been through a lot together. Captain Terry told Wilkinson he was so impressed by his performance in San Diego that he was recommending him for promotion to B Company XO. The position would soon be vacant, as Dolvin was leaving for Air Observers School as part of his own promotion to Battalion HQ.[95] That same day, Lt Col MacLaughlin called Wilkinson into his office and handed him a glowing Letter of Commendation composed and signed by the 7th Regiment commander. Wilkinson had never seen MacLaughlin so pleased.[96]

Much had changed in the 756th during the two months Wilkinson was away. Major Moon received a promotion to lieutenant colonel and transferred to Fort Knox.[97] MacLaughlin spent less and less time in the battalion preparing for his next assignment: command of the 3rd Tank Group. Other officers had departed to cadre new outfits or make room for promotions from within. The enlisted men also saw a great deal of turnover and reshuffling. Privates became sergeants and sergeants became privates without hesitation, according to maturity, dependability, and job performance. The battalion continually shed underperforming or excess personnel to allow companies, platoons, and individual tank crews to be forged into disciplined, effective teams.[98]

B Company experienced several changes with key enlisted personnel assignments. Army regulations forced 1st Sgt Robbins into retirement and S/Sgt Jack Hogan became the new "Top Kick."[99] Hogan was a swarthy, handsome man of mixed Irish and Mexican heritage.[100] In his mid-thirties and nearing twenty years of Army service, he had mastered all the ins and outs of Army life and made an obvious choice for the company's top enlisted man and chief disciplinarian.[101] He was also tough and fair without being mean. Like Captain Terry, Hogan famously guzzled a form of coffee that would knock down most men. His method was to brew five tablespoons of course grounds in a tin cup and swallow the thick mud straight.[102] Over the past months, the company's supply records had degenerated into an irreconcilable mess, leaving Lt Dolvin to sort out the books. The company's original supply sergeant, Sgt Elvis H. Lewis, was a decent old army type but ill-suited for record keeping. Dolvin forced Lewis to transfer out of the company and promoted Private First Class (Pfc) Gene B. Shirley to supply sergeant.[103]

Whereas, Sgt Lewis proved to be a poor bookkeeper, Mess Sgt James H. Blackwell proved to be *too good* of a cook. He began the job weighing 160 pounds. Nine months later, he tipped the scales at 240 pounds and could no longer squeeze into *any size* OD uniform issued by supply. The portly Blackwell was sternly warned to lose weight or he would be replaced as well.[104]

While the 1st and 2nd Platoons trained away in San Diego, Lt Redle's 3rd Platoon continued training rigorously in and around Fort Lewis. Part of the work included driving through a tank obstacle course while the crews wore full gas masks. They also received some amphibious training as well—just locally. Every day, a different tank would drive to Boston Harbor on Puget Sound and load aboard an LCM (Landing Craft, Mechanized)—a small vessel capable of carrying a single tank. From there, the LCM would make a two-hour journey to McNeil Island where the tank crew could practice several beach landings over the span of four hours before returning to Boston Harbor. The day after the 1st and 2nd Platoons returned from San Diego, Lt Severson's 2nd Platoon crew took a turn at Boston Harbor. As the LCM waited to pick them up, the props churned open a large pit in the soft sands just below the water's surface. Later in the afternoon when the LCM returned, the rising tide fooled the coxswain into believing he had cleared the trouble spot and found shallow water. When Severson's M3 debarked, however, it plunged like a 13-ton rock into the murky pit—completely disappearing in a gurgling rush of air bubbles. Severson and his crew, fortunately, escaped the hatches and swam to safety. B Company's tank retriever was sent to pull the sunken M3 from the pit, but when the crew tried attaching a winch to nearby utility poles, the timbers bowed under the strain. Lt Col MacLaughlin arrived to survey the situation and decided reluctantly to abandon the tank and report it as a training loss to the Army. After MacLaughlin departed, Sgt Shirley—B Company's new supply sergeant—discreetly suggested to Captain Terry that all missing material from Sgt Lewis's supply records should be included in the loss report. Terry agreed to the scheme. When the itemized loss statement reached Captain Sweeting's desk for his signature, the battalion supply officer raised an eyebrow and grumbled that B Company must have lost "a battleship." Nevertheless, he endorsed the report and submitted it onward. Surprisingly, nobody up the chain questioned the inflated charges, and B Company's muddled supply books were miraculously reconciled from that day forward.[105]

With Wilkinson's 1st Platoon and Severson's 2nd Platoon back at Fort Lewis, B Company resumed training as a full unit. In late March, the entire battalion drove all the way to Mount Rainier for extended maneuvers.[106] Part of the exercises included coordinating gunfire from multiple moving tanks upon multiple moving targets. At one point during the complicated drill, B Company's tanks received fire after accidentally entering the wrong area. Thankfully, nobody was injured, but Wilkinson received a long chewing out from Captain Sweeting for "driving recklessly."[107] During the road march back to Fort Lewis, Sweeting chewed him out again—this time because his platoon was "driving too cautiously." The second round of criticism seemed overly harsh. Later, after discussing the matter with Dolvin over drinks at the officers' club, Wilkinson felt better about the situation.[108] Sweeting was probably making sure Wilkinson's recent accolades weren't going to his head, that's all.

The tank training continued into April with the men hearing constant rumors about moving to Fort Ord "soon." But with each fresh round of gossip, the departure date kept being pushed later and later.[109] On April 3rd, 2nd Lt Fazendin moved from HQ to B Company to shadow Wilkinson and assume command of his platoon once Wilkinson's promotion to XO was made official.[110] In anticipation of the rumored Fort Ord move, the men collected spare parts and stockpiled every empty box and crate they could scrounge.[111] B Company tanks ran grenade courses[112] and concentrated on improving platoon tactics at a nearby range they called "the golf course." Sweeting received a promotion to major and his celebration party ended with him, Wilkinson, and Lewis engaged in a friendly ceremonial shoving match.[113]

At mid-month, Captain Terry told Wilkinson the battalion may not go to Fort Ord after all. Exhausted of the endless tail-chasing gossip, Wilkinson resolved from that point forward to never speculate over unit events or moves until they actually happened.[114] It was harder to maintain a similar policy over the war news. In the Pacific, U.S. forces at Bataan and Corregidor recently succumbed to the Japanese. What little remained of the battered 192nd and 194th Tank Battalions (L) was forced to surrender. With the Philippines now lost, talk ceased of the 756th being sent to save anyone. 2nd Lt Ray Treadwell of HQ Company, freshly returned from Fort Knox training, spoke of pessimism running rampant among the officers out east. Many feared the U.S. would be forced out of the war before any effective military response could even be marshaled.[115] In the meantime, the tankers could only focus on their training and wait. At least the weather in Washington State had turned warm, clear, and pleasant—a sharp contrast to the awful realities taking place in other lands around the world.[116]

On 21 April, B Company practiced a dawn attack. The mission was successful, but some equipment and tools were lost during the exercise.[117] Both Severson's and Redle's platoons performed well, but Fazendin's platoon exceeded expectations.[118] Two days later, the battalion practiced attacking as a full unit.[119] On Thursday 23 April, Major Sweeting led the battalion on another long road march to Mount Rainier that culminated in a prolonged combat simulation in the deep woods.[120] When the battalion returned to Fort Lewis the following day, Wilkinson's promotion to XO was made official and Dolvin moved over to the HQ staff.[121] As new B Company XO, Wilkinson was strongly encouraged by Major Sweeting to attend an upcoming tank mechanics course at Fort Knox. The commitment required several weeks away and Wilkinson hated leaving the company, but he knew Sweeting's recommendation made sense.[122] Before he could plan his trip east, however, the Fort Ord transfer was suddenly on again—but with B Company listed as the only unit of the 756th involved. This time the orders were concrete and immediate—not gossip—and extended to outside units as well. In fact, the *entire* 3rd Division received similar instructions to move to Fort Ord between 28 April and 5 May.[123]

On Monday 27 April, B Company's tanks and half-tracks were loaded on flat cars and secured with rolls of barbed wire. A boxcar was also stuffed full with supplementary equipment.[124] That same evening, the train shunted forward and rolled slowly toward California.[125] The men packed their bags, jammed the remaining company vehicles full of gear, and formed a convoy that departed Wednesday morning.[126] The men themselves boarded a troop train. Because Wilkinson and Terry had personal cars, they were allowed to leave a day later.[127] The move represented a permanent change of station for B Company. The remainder of the battalion was told to prepare to join them sometime in the near future.[128]

Wilkinson drove out the main gate of Fort Lewis at 1030 on 30 April, knowing this was probably the last time he would ever see the place. He was going to miss it. Wilkinson hated goodbyes, so he didn't utter a word to a soul before departing. He simply loaded his possessions, settled behind the wheel, and began driving.[129]

Ahead of him awaited a new job, a new post, and a new adventure in a tank outfit with an unclear future in a world gone mad. Wilkinson couldn't be happier.

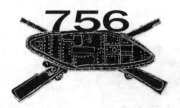

CHAPTER 4

California and a Captaincy: May 1942 to January 1943

M2 Half-Track Truck (1940)

Wilkinson's drive to Fort Ord lasted three days and covered 900 miles, but the entire journey was an eye feast of stunning scenery—from lush, pristine Oregon forests of deep green to untamed, windswept California coastlines of ocean blue. The B Company truck convoy arrived ahead of him but the troop train wasn't expected until the following day.[1] Fort Ord seemed as big as Fort Lewis but equipped with more modern accommodations. Noticeably absent were shade trees. Hundreds of new white, two-story barracks arranged in compact grids baked under the unfiltered California sun. Most buildings looked less than a year old and still carried the aroma of freshly cut lumber and drying paint. The fort's breathtaking panoramic view of Monterey Bay teased of the relaxing allure of a vacation brochure, but the activity on post was strictly army business. As the first of many 3rd Division trucks, troops, and equipment trickled into camp, an energizing "calm before the storm" feeling gained momentum. Wilkinson took advantage of his early arrival to take a quick drive along the coast to "reconnoiter" the tiny towns of Monterey and Carmel-by-the-Sea. After spying a few good eating establishments and hang outs, he returned to post for much-needed rest.[2]

Wilkinson's men arrived in force and in good spirits on Monday, 4 May. They unpacked with gusto, turned in their wool OD uniforms for lighter cotton khakis, and took up residence in their assigned barracks.[3] The next morning, the flatcar train from Fort Lewis arrived and one long, sweltering day was spent unloading the tanks, half-tracks, and boxcars chock-full of equipment.[4] Wilkinson became sidetracked into resolving a minor SNAFU where the fort staff had failed to assign B Company a maintenance shop. After a short bureaucratic scramble, he secured an empty building with no door lock and a dirt floor—deficiencies he quickly disregarded when he learned that the place also had its own private gas pump.[5]

With the shop situation resolved, Wilkinson searched the nearby countryside for terrain suitable for tank training, but found little—except for a small, rugged spot populated with far too many trees. The crews tested the area on Thursday, but the tanks took a real beating and the site was abandoned.[6] Eventually, more suitable and permanent training grounds were discovered among sandy hills further to the east.[7]

For the next few weeks, as the 3rd Division arrived, settled in, and organized itself, B Company trained mostly on its own. With Captain Terry preferring to remain office-bound attending to the administrative side of command, much of the company's operational duties fell to Wilkinson. The daily schedule, the training details, and all vehicle maintenance became Wilkinson's world. He relished the independence and cherished Terry's trust.[8] One rather unusual duty was given to him: the institution of an "internal counter-espionage program." Evidently, the U.S. government believed foreign subterfuge and domestic disloyalty represented a serious enough threat that trusted soldiers were asked to gather any suspicious names. Wilkinson was told to select three reliable enlisted men who would watch for trouble and report back to him. He chose his three platoon sergeants. The four men met secretly to briefly discuss the program and then returned to company business.[9]

Wilkinson delegated much of the training duties to his three platoon leaders: Severson, Redle, and Fazendin. Fazendin took responsibility for setting up a new gunnery range—a task he tackled with great passion.[10] Wilkinson developed a strong liking for Fazendin. The tall, cleft-chinned Minnesotan was always enthusiastic, and direct, and there was nothing he wasn't willing to do.[11] At times, a bit of an impulsive, non-conformist streak also slipped through, showing Wilkinson that the lanky, young lieutenant was an original thinker.

Since 3rd Division troops had not fully settled in, B Company was assigned to help train a cavalry troop (company) from the 107th Cavalry Regiment.[12] The 107th had been ordered to convert from horses to a fully mechanized outfit, and B Company's bittersweet job involved training these proud horsemen how to drive tanks. The troopers still retained their horses and struggled with letting go of the strong emotional bonds forged between men and beasts after years of working and camping together. The troop commander, Captain Crandall, was thoroughly disgusted over the order.[13] Nevertheless, the troopers behaved like consummate professionals, and after only five days of instruction mastered the basics of tank driving. The training resulted in only one minor accident—surprisingly less than what Wilkinson had first feared.[14] After much coaxing, Wilkinson finally convinced the troop XO to allow him to borrow a pair of the troop's horses. Once the training wrapped up on a Saturday afternoon, the captain, Wilkinson, and Lt Severson enjoyed a long, nostalgic ride together down a wide, sandy beach south of the fort.[15] Both riders recognized that a long, glorious era in military history had come to a sad end.

During the same time, Fazendin continued perfecting his gunnery range and revising the firing schedule. The 71st Air Observation Squadron was supposed to participate in some coordination tests with B Company but kept postponing appointments—raising Fazendin's angst and causing his temper to periodically flare.[16] At one point, Wilkinson had to step in and diplomatically smooth out the situation.[17] The trials finally commenced and were meant to coordinate air observation above with friendly tank action below. Though promising in concept, the tests failed in practice because planes high in the air could not locate the "enemy" AT guns on the ground.[18] In the end, B Company concluded the best way to locate enemy positions was still through trained eyes on the ground.

One day, several MPs appeared presenting arrest orders from the Federal Bureau of Investigation for an enlisted B Company man named Cardenas.[19] The MPs claimed Cardenas, a Spanish-born immigrant, served in Franco's fascist armed forces during the Spanish Civil War. The suspect was located, questioned, and escorted away—never to return to the company. The incident unsettled Wilkinson because the man's arrest did not result from the internal counter-espionage program he had been tasked with instituting only a few weeks earlier.[20] Cardenas had never mentioned a word to anybody about this past.

Another foreign-born B Company man named Pvt Kelleher boasted so often about his past that nobody believed him. The older, balding Irishman uttered many outlandish claims—including membership in the notorious Irish Republican Army. Few paid any attention to Kelleher's assertions given his blasé work attitude and proclivity for going AWOL (absent without leave) in epic style. Evidently, nobody in the government considered him much of a threat anyway. Although Kelleher was not an alcoholic in the clinical sense, every so often he would vanish, booze himself full of brawling bravado, and end up invariably in the custody of some local MP unit. His last drunken bout had occurred during amphibious training with Wilkinson's platoon in San Diego. In the months since, Kelleher seemed to have his act under control. Though not much of a soldier, he did manage to stay out of trouble, report for duty each day, and put in the minimum. On a personal level, Wilkinson rather liked the guy. Kelleher could be irritating a times but was generally harmless, congenial, and even amusing. Then, on 18 May, Kelleher disappeared again—this time for five full days.[21] On the 25th, Captain Terry called Wilkinson into his office to report Kelleher had been recovered by MPs in an inebriated stupor and tossed in a San Jose jail.[22] Wilkinson drove out to retrieve the Irishman and found him disheveled and roughed up but delighted to tears over being "rescued." When the two returned to Fort Ord, Captain Terry—far less entertained by Kelleher's shenanigans—ordered Wilkinson to convene a special summary court to mete out an appropriate punishment. To his credit, Kelleher made no excuses upon hearing the charges: "Oh, I did it, Shir …" he shrugged ruefully. Wilkinson sentenced him to thirty days confinement at the Fort Ord stockade but, before dismissing him, expressed his personal regrets for having to send him away. "Oh, that's all right, Shir," Kelleher replied. "You've saved my life lots of times." Wilkinson never saved Kelleher's life. His hungover mind had either confused his lieutenant for someone else or conjured up some new figment in an imaginary past.[23] Kelleher served his time but after the episode really had no future in B Company.

As May drew to a close, B Company trained again with the 107th Cavalry Troop.[24] At the same time, Wilkinson was given the assignment of drafting a new T/O for an amphibious tank company.[25] He was stunned over the realization he was probably the only officer in the entire Army at the time experienced enough in amphibious tank operations to create such a table. Though honored, Wilkinson quickly tired of the project after being repeatedly pressed for revisions.[26] If anything, Wilkinson learned he was not cut out for deskwork.

Around the same time, a new West Coast alert was issued to all American service personnel—reminding everybody at beautiful, sunny Fort Ord of the new World War. An enormous Japanese task force had been detected leaving naval bases for destinations unknown in the eastern Pacific.[27] The Fort Ord commanders treated the threat so seriously that 3rd Division troops relocated to dispersal camps during the night of 29–30 May.[28] In sharp contrast to the Fort Lewis alerts issued during a cold, damp Washington winter, this new one had the men camping under stars in a balmy, pleasant California spring. Unlike the earlier alerts, this Japanese threat turned out to be very real. Five days later, an epic naval battle ensued north of Hawaii off Midway Island. This time, the U.S. Navy exacted satisfying revenge for their battleship losses at Pearl Harbor—using Colonel Billy Mitchell's innovative air power principles. In a matter of hours, four Japanese aircraft carriers were deep-sixed with the loss of only one American carrier. A Japanese feint, further north toward Alaska, landed troops on two Aleutian Islands but the bulk of the task force withdrew, bloodied and humiliated. With the exception of the earlier Doolittle "hit-and-run" air raid on Tokyo, this stunning American victory represented the first bit of positive war news in a long time and injected a much-needed boost in morale to everyone at Fort Ord.

As camp activities intensified in anticipation of a resumption of amphibious training with the 3rd Division, Wilkinson received his XO training orders. On the morning of 4 June, an overly cheery 1st Sgt Hogan greeted him in the B Company HQ office. "Pack up!" the seasoned sergeant beamed. Wilkinson's orders were to drive to Fort Knox immediately and attend an eight-week tank maintenance class. Wilkinson knew the program was necessary to fulfill his duties as the company XO, so the assignment wasn't entirely unexpected. The timing, however, caught him off guard. What's more, he had to begin driving that *very day* to arrive in Kentucky in time for the new session—leaving him little time to pack.[29] Four days later, Wilkinson sat down in an austere Fort Knox classroom at 0515 for his first lesson. During his third morning attending class, Wilkinson received another shock when he was pulled aside and sworn in as a first lieutenant.[30] The swift promotion ceremony left him barely enough time to exchange his gold bar for a silver one before dashing off to attend another class.

The coursework ranged from highly engaging to downright boring. Class days were long, featuring copious information jammed into very little time. Quizzes and exams came in rapid succession: M3 suspension systems,[31] power trains, electrical systems, fuel-air systems, diagnosing dead engines,[32] etc. Students also untangled instructor-crafted "Plumber's Nightmares" to earn passing grades.[33] Wilkinson felt fortunate he could rely on field knowledge to help him decode some of the more esoteric details. After all, books and diagrams had limits. The best instruction, he found, came from "hands-on" shop work. There was no better way to understand a tank engine than to take one apart and put it back together again.

Wilkinson spent his scant leisure time during evenings and weekends with 2nd Lt Edwin B. Olson and 1st Lt Robert Dean—fellow 756th officers attending Fort Knox classes at the same time. Dean, of A Company, also muddled through tank maintenance. Olson, a C Company platoon leader, was enrolled in the communication school.[34] The tall, bright North Dakotan was obviously being groomed for a battalion staff position. With B Company rehearsing with the 3rd Division at Fort Ord, but the rest of the battalion still maneuvering around Fort Lewis, the men swapped six weeks' worth of missing chatter. On 15 June, 2nd Lt Fazendin also arrived for enrollment in another Fort Knox class—bringing with him the freshest and juiciest battalion gossip. Several key 756th officers had received promotions: MacLaughlin had made full colonel and had left to command the 3rd Tank Group. Although Major Ralph Alexander had been promoted to lieutenant colonel and put in charge of the battalion,[35] Major Sweeting actually ran the show.[36] Dolvin had made captain and was currently serving on the battalion staff. Severson, now a first lieutenant, had assumed duties as acting B Company XO. About a dozen other officers had also received promotions. One name noticeably missing from the list was Captain Terry.[37] Wilkinson felt badly over his commanding officer (CO) being passed up. Terry was a fine, competent officer who always had the best interests of his men at heart and deserved recognition for his hard work. However, Wilkinson sensed mounting tension between Terry and Sweeting and believed this recent snub probably had something to do with it.

The classes dragged into July, and with the slow passing of each long day, Wilkinson found himself missing B Company more and more. He received a general letter from Captain Terry inquiring about promotion news and other battalion business.[38] Reading between the lines, Wilkinson perceived his CO was deeply disappointed. Lt Redle also sent a letter detailing B Company's activities at length, which Wilkinson devoured with great interest. Redle reported the company had finished an intensive five-week training session with the 107th Cavalry and had also participated in a demonstration involving the crossing of trenches and other obstacles.[39] To help sell war bonds, one tank was put on temporary display in the nearby town of Watsonville, and the entire company rolled past a crowd of cheering thousands in the Monterey 4th of July parade.[40] Finally, Redle passed along how Terry had instituted some changes in the maintenance crew that had unintentionally affected company morale.[41] This last tidbit of information bothered Wilkinson. He detected a troublesome pattern emerging and his 8 August graduation date could not come fast enough.

Wilkinson's coursework shifted to live engines, light tank maintenance, and motorcycles. In between courses, the men watched training films chronicling the German invasions of Crete and Russia.[42] The news in Europe had turned grim again. A resurgent Rommel was marching and routing the British back into Egypt, while the German Wehrmacht launched a series of ambitious new offensives deep inside Russia.[43] Not surprisingly, the latest buzz had the 756th training next in the desert. Wilkinson loved being "in the know" but had learned long ago to avoid overinvesting in the rumor mill.[44]

Wilkinson spent his free time away from class on blind dates, movie outings, and restaurant jaunts to Louisville with Dean, Olson, and Fazendin. Lt Dean graduated in mid-July and returned to the battalion as the new maintenance officer. He wrote back to tell Wilkinson that the entire battalion would relocate from Fort Lewis to join B Company at Fort Ord on August 1st. This move represented a "permanent change in station."[45] Major Sweeting had become the new battalion CO after Lt Col Alexander transferred to command the 743rd Tank Battalion (L), recently activated at Fort Lewis.[46]

Sweeting's rise to battalion commander was an impressive accomplishment. Although a proud West Point graduate of 1933, Sweeting did not come from a military or privileged background. Everything Sweeting gained in his life came through his own hard work. His mother died when he was very young, and his family moved regularly. Originally from Portland, Oregon, but raised mostly in Moosic, Pennsylvania, and Rochester, New York,[47] Sweeting's father and grandfather toiled away countless hours as brick masons. As a consequence, the boy was raised by a mentor uncle who encouraged him to read books on military topics. The subject inspired his young mind, unleashed a creative imagination, and instilled within him boundless confidence and initiative.[48] He landed an appointment to the United States Military Academy (USMA), not through personal connections but by winning a highly competitive examination. Once at West Point, he thrived as a solid academic student and excelled as an expert rifleman and engaging storyteller.[49] Upon graduation and commission, Sweeting served with the 2nd Infantry Division at Fort Wayne, Detroit, where "after four years using the last of the oldest equipment in the Army," Sweeting quipped later, "we moved to Benning."[50] At Fort Benning, Georgia, Sweeting was introduced to tanks and fell in love. For the next two years he mastered all requisite coursework, then served with the 66th Light Tank Battalion at Fort Meade and with the 2nd Armored Division.[51] Sweeting found his niche in armor and a ticket to greater glory.

Lt Dean also reported that French Lewis had made captain and was put in charge of HQ Company.[52] Although Lewis beat Wilkinson to the coveted captaincy that all young lieutenants dream of landing, Wilkinson couldn't have been happier for his close friend.

8 August finally arrived. The demanding course was well worth the time, but Wilkinson felt relieved classroom life was finally over.[53] In fact, as soon as the

graduation ceremony ended in the early evening, he set out immediately for the West Coast.[54] He was allowed ten full days to make the journey by car.[55] Though anxious to return to Fort Ord, he felt obliged to drop by his family's Menard homestead for a short visit. Upon arrival, his folks, his grandmother, three younger brothers and sister,[56] as well as local friends and neighbors treated him like royalty. For the next several days, Wilkinson feasted on home cooking, beat the heat by dunking in the old swimming hole, and relaxed by taking long horseback rides.[57] Feeling somewhat melancholy the day before he had to leave, Wilkinson wandered alone through the nearby hills and fields wondering if he was seeing his beloved home for the last time.[58]

On Friday 14 August, Wilkinson said goodbye to his Mom and Dad and resumed the journey west. He ran into a heavy rainstorm, and was forced to stop at Fort Sumner, New Mexico, before resuming the next morning.[59] The remainder of the trip featured hot, dry weather and relatively uneventful driving. Wilkinson pulled into Fort Ord at 2200 on Monday 17 August, but the only 756th member he could find was Captain Dolvin.[60] At the time, all companies were somewhere out on Monterey Bay preparing for amphibious practice landings with the 3rd Division.

The next morning, Wilkinson tried locating and joining B Company, but the tank crews had already been crammed aboard the Attack Cargo Ship USS *Almaack* (AKA-10) with a battalion from the 7th Regiment.[61] The *Almaack* had departed San Francisco two days earlier, swung out into the Pacific and was scheduled to arrive in Monterey Bay later that morning. Two other transports carried the remaining 7th Regiment battalions and tank crews of the 756th.[62] Not only was this operation enormous in breadth, but it was also quite perilous in execution. All troops and tanks were scheduled to load the landing craft and hit the beaches starting at 1100. Because of the extremely rough shoreline and chaotic surf inside the landing zone, the Navy originally balked at participating. At first, the sea commanders thought that naïve 3rd Division officers chose the dreadful location but learned later that the War Department selected it—and insisted the landings take place come hell or high water.[63] During the previous week's trial runs, three naval landing craft broke apart on approach. Fortunately, nobody drowned.[64] The full-scale landings incorporated a subsequent beach assault exercise. "Opposing" the invasion along the coast and immediately inland sat a battalion of the 30th Infantry Regiment "defenders."[65] Although no live fire was involved, pre-positioned umpires would declare the winners and losers of ensuing mock battles. The operation was a big deal indeed—the largest U.S. Army amphibious exercise yet.

Wilkinson located Captain Terry at an observation station and was immediately told to help prepare a nearby eucalyptus grove as B Company's main campsite once a beachhead was secured.[66] At 1100, Army Air Corps attack planes from San Diego screamed in fast and low along the beach, laying a smokescreen while simulating strafing runs. Across the pale blue horizon, two destroyers darted back and forth as three nearer transports dispelled tanks and swarms of infantry into Higgins boats and LCTs (landing craft, tanks) bobbing below. The distant destroyers weren't participating in the drill but patrolling the perimeter as guards against any possible Japanese submarines lurking in the area. The landings unfolded spectacularly well, and despite the heavy, unpredictable surf, everyone and everything arrived safely ashore and a solid beachhead was expeditiously established before nightfall.[67] The next morning, B Company joined a massive infantry attack inland against "Red Force." Employing clockwork efficiency, the tanks and troops successfully achieved their objectives and returned to camp that evening, tired but triumphant.[68] Over the next few days, B Company tanks participated in several smaller combat simulations and executed each without too much difficulty. The main question had been settled, however: The 3rd Division and 756th Tank Battalion (L) had mastered amphibious landings. The next big mystery was, where would they be sent?

Everyone in B Company assumed they were destined for the Pacific. The men had been encouraged to learn judo and experts arrived to train them.[69] A Japanese language class was also established earlier in the summer and each company committed one enlisted man for instruction. B Company sent Sgt Ithel "Dick" Adlard as their representative. He made a natural choice as he had already learned Chinese prior to the war.[70] Adlard had been studying botany in China when Japan invaded in the late 1930s. He personally witnessed and even *filmed* a number of Japanese atrocities committed against civilians. At one point, he was asked to show his smuggled movies to the men of the 756th. Several reels showed Japanese soldiers using Chinese women and children for bayonet practice, and a few tankers fainted upon seeing the gruesome footage.[71]

American Marines fought bitterly in the Solomon Islands after making their own amphibious landings earlier in the month. Many speculated the 756th would soon join them. Wilkinson, however, remained unconvinced. A large-scale raid at Dieppe, France—involving mostly Canadian and British but also some American forces—took place on 19 August. Although the attack failed, Wilkinson sensed the incident signaled a second front in Europe might open very soon.[72] Long ago, Wilkinson gave up trying to outguess the War Department, but he did conclude that somebody higher up wanted them practicing rough surf landings for good reason. To him, the environment suggested a destination other than soft, sandy Pacific islands.

Wilkinson's immediate concerns centered on the restoration of company morale—which had degraded considerably in his absence.[73] His top priority was to restore discipline within the maintenance section. At first, Captain Terry resisted Wilkinson's suggestions, but he relented and allowed his XO to take appropriate charge of the crew.[74] Privately, Terry divulged his belief to Wilkinson that he was being forced out of the battalion soon anyway. Wilkinson wondered if his CO's pessimism contributed to the morale issues. During this same time, Major Sweeting approached Wilkinson about transferring to HQ Company. "There's a captaincy in it,"

Sweeting promised. But Wilkinson politely turned down the enticing offer, explaining he still had much unfinished business in B Company. Surprisingly, Sweeting didn't press him further.[75] Sweeting could be a complex, political operator at times with aims and machinations not always easy to ascertain. Wilkinson considered it best to remain truthful and transparent when dealing with the ambitious young West Pointer. Above all, Sweeting did appreciate straight honesty from his officers.

On Friday, 28 August, B Company participated in yet another simulated beach landing yielding solid results. The exercise included two nighttime changes of bivouac followed by an attack operation in the morning.[76] The "problem" concluded the following afternoon and the men of B Company returned to camp dirty and haggard.[77] Wilkinson remained concerned over low morale and resolved, after a restful Sunday passed, some changes were needed to shake them out of their doldrums.[78] On Monday, Wilkinson told Fazendin to lead the entire company out to the firing range where they could fire guns and blow things up all day long. Gunnery was always a highly popular activity with tankers. The change seemed to be enough to restore smiles and everyone returned to camp that evening with better attitudes.[79] On Tuesday, 1 September, the full company made a ten-mile march out of camp and back. The maintenance crew replaced the tracks on thirteen tanks and completed the remaining four the following day.[80] These repairs were ordered ahead of another "problem" scheduled for the following day. This new exercise only involved the battalion and pitted A Company against B Company—putting intra-outfit bragging rights on the line. B Company's role was to protect the Battalion HQ while A Company attempted to "capture the flag."[81]

On Thursday, 3 September, the two companies jockeyed for position within a section of sandy hills designated "Area D." In an attempt to throw A Company off, B Company secretly moved in the dead of night to another location, but the ruse didn't fool anybody. Worse, A Company "commandos" managed to slip undetected into the Battalion HQ and stole Captain Dolvin's map along with Major Sweeting's pup tent.[82] The next morning, B Company mounted a surprise counterattack on A Company's camp—collecting "enemy" prisoners and vehicles left and right. Just as victory seemed assured, the time clock expired.[83] The operation was enormously fun for all, but battalion bragging rights were never fully settled.

That weekend, Wilkinson got word that the 3rd Division and 756th would remain at Fort Ord for only two more weeks and then depart to an unspecified destination. Because of recent travel patterns for many 3rd Division staff officers, the East Coast was suspected, with Virginia the prime candidate.[84] Wilkinson didn't have to wait long for confirmation. Starting Monday morning, events spun so quickly that there was scarcely time to think. B Company received official orders to pack immediately and prepare for departure within the week.[85] Adding greatly to the stress was the Army's insistence upon everyone being "combat ready."[86] On Tuesday, Wilkinson learned Captain Terry was transferring out and he was being considered as Terry's successor. On Thursday, while scuttling about in the middle of a fourth straight day of hectic packing, Wilkinson received official notification that he was B Company's new CO. Terry landed a transfer assignment to Fort Knox as an Armor School instructor in amphibious operations. Wilkinson could scarcely believe the news. Here he was, a 22-year-old already given command of an Army company.[87] He had no time to celebrate, however, due to preparations for a court martial case he was scheduled to preside over that very evening.[88] Friday was spent inventorying company property and cleaning the garrison buildings ahead of departure.[89] No one was allowed to pack personal property beyond pocket items, so Wilkinson scrambled to find someone to take possession of his car.[90] In the end, he convinced a local friend to drive it back to Texas for him. On Saturday, a quiet Captain Terry signed B Company over to Wilkinson and the transfer of command was made official. That evening, Wilkinson finally found the free time to properly celebrate his promotion by dining at a local restaurant with Captain Dolvin and a few others.[91]

The 756th Tank Battalion (L) departed Fort Ord on Monday 14 September aboard three separate trains taking three separate routes. Companies B, A, and most of HQ boarded a single train consisting of troop coaches at the fore followed by flatcars transporting most of the tanks.[92] The officers occupied the last coach before the first flatcar.[93] The train set out from Fort Ord and headed due south. The officers, of course, knew they would eventually turn east, but the enlisted men were not informed for security reasons. Many assumed they were San Diego bound to board some ship for the Pacific theater, but when the train reached Los Angeles and then swung eastward toward Arizona, the jittery "Jap hunting" bravado dissolved into perplexed stares, whispered obscenities, and head scratching speculation over the Army's reasoning for the judo and Japanese classes.

The weather was oppressively hot and the journey took nine days to complete. During blazing daylight hours, Wilkinson and the other officers played poker inside their stuffy coach with all windows open in hopes of catching any faint dusty breezes stirred by the hypnotic rocking motion of the train. After sundown, the officers slipped out onto the nearby flatcar to beat the heat over cigarettes and laughs. They called this gathering place their "observation car."[94] The train chugged through Yuma, El Paso, San Antonio, and New Orleans with the swelter never abating. Muggy Mississippi and Alabama followed before the train finally swung northward into more temperate climes—reaching Virginia by Tuesday, 22 September. As the train neared their final destination of Camp Pickett, news of some last-minute assignments and transfers filtered through the juddering coaches. Because 1st Lt Severson transferred out of the battalion to join a glider troop outfit prior to departure, Wilkinson appointed Lt Redle as new B Company XO.[95] To fill Redle's vacant platoon leader position, 2nd Lt Robert Kremer moved to B Company.[96]

As the train pulled into Camp Pickett, Wilkinson was underwhelmed by the post's primitive accommodations and activity that appeared surprisingly disorganized. The buildings were new constructions, but no sidewalks had yet been laid and autumn rains had transformed the grounds into vast plains of mire.[97] The other two trains carrying the remainder of the 756th arrived—as did other various troop trains spewing forth thousands of men, hundreds of vehicles and countless equipment crates belonging to the 3rd Division. Suddenly, the muddy little camp crawled of men and their machines and degenerated into one enormous slop hole. Even though the weather remained stiflingly hot, the men were issued heavy wool OD uniforms and forbidden to wear lighter khakis—adding a layer of roasting itchiness to their wet misery.[98] Each of the three tank companies were assigned to each of the three regiments of the 3rd Division. A Company went to the 7th, C Company to the 30th, and B Company to the 15th.[99] The 15th Infantry Regiment called themselves the "Can Do" Regiment. This short, rousing motto arose during a long stationing in China from 1912 to 1938. All units of the 3rd Division now belonged to a new corps-sized group known as "Task Force A" commanded by Maj Gen George S. Patton Jr. Wilkinson considered Patton's involvement as great news.[100]

The next day, B Company was told to prepare for a "loading and unloading" exercise with the 15th Regiment at a nearby port. Wilkinson figured their destination was Norfolk, seventy miles to the east, as it represented the nearest harbor.[101] Surprise news followed: The men were told to leave their M3s on the flatcars because the entire battalion would receive completely new tanks. The very next day, a full complement of factory-new M5 light tanks arrived. These upgrades were based on an M3 frame but enhanced with sleek welded hulls, smooth Hydra-Matic transmissions and gyroscopic controls assisting the main guns.[102] They appeared stunningly modern. The controls operated similarly, but everything else about them just *looked* so much better aesthetically—like exchanging an old Model A Ford for a new Cadillac. "They are sweet babies," Wilkinson grinned.[103] Everyone was so impressed, they seemed almost afraid to touch them. On Friday, when word spread that B Company's participation in the port exercise had been canceled, all anyone could think about was testing out the new M5s. The next morning, they finally got a chance to drive them, and the new transmission received rave reviews.[104] The entire week that followed was spent at the gunnery range, and the B Company crews exceeded their ammunition allowance by enthusiastically firing off their new guns.[105] Wilkinson wasn't concerned about the violation, as his men were becoming expert shots.

Lt Fazendin, whose curiosity was exceeded only by his impetuosity at times, itched to test the stopping power of the M5's armor. The side armor had been upgraded from one inch to one-and-a-quarter inches, and the added steel was supposed to be thick enough to deflect .50-caliber armor piercing (AP) rounds.[106] Fazendin wanted assurances of the claim. After all, he was expected to entrust his life to this new tank. As an experiment, he positioned an M5 downrange and ordered a battalion cook to rake the side hull with a burst of MG fire from a truck-mounted .50-caliber Browning M2. Several errant shots damaged two boogie wheels, so Fazendin requested replacement parts from battalion maintenance—which attracted the swift scrutiny of Major Sweeting. Upon hearing details of the incident, the angry battalion CO berated Fazendin with a long, stormy verbal lashing. Before dismissing him, however, Sweeting's demeanor calmed to ask the obvious question: "Did the rounds penetrate?" "No," Fazendin replied, suppressing a smirk. "They only went about two-thirds the way through."[107] Fazendin's unauthorized experiment drew the instant attention of his fellow tankers, who closely inspected the damage for themselves. The tank interior showed bulging dimples where the bullets hit, but the increased armor thickness did live up to the manufacturer's claims.[108]

Commencing 29 September, most 3rd Division troops combined with 756th Companies A and C to practice a complex loading and landing exercise called Operation *Quick*. All men, equipment, vehicles, and tanks boarded thirteen transport ships at Norfolk, proceeded north through Chesapeake Bay, and landed near Solomon's Island.[109] The operation lasted roughly a week before the participants reloaded and returned to Norfolk. Why B Company wasn't invited remained a mystery, and no one dared ask. The Army frowned upon such questions. To keep his disappointed men occupied, Wilkinson searched the surrounding area for effective training grounds but had to compromise on land hopelessly flat and swampy.[110] As a consequence, whenever the tanks went out to train, no less than four or five tanks participated—otherwise someone might not return. Oftentimes, three or four tanks were needed to pull free a single tank stuck in the local mire.[111]

Long days of gunnery practice and mucky maneuvers continued deep into October. Despite the training challenges and disappointing delays, B Company's morale hovered in the clouds. Many tankers now entered their sixteenth straight month of training and felt great pride in their accomplishments. The men literally started with next to nothing—no tanks and three barely serviceable revolvers. They improvised by purchasing hardware store BB guns to learn target practice. They endured non-stop ridicule from Fort Lewis infantrymen while lugging around wooden frames to simulate platoon formations. At times, the taunting grew so unbearable the men begged to train at night to be spared additional embarrassment.[112] They progressed from outdated hand-me-down M1s and M2 "Mae Wests" through respectable riveted M3 lights to Uncle Sam's newest and most modern light tank: an all welded M5. No infantryman laughed at them now. They tested the mechanical limits of each successive tank design and pushed beyond the mental and physical limits within themselves. They drilled clockwork teamwork as crews, platoons, and as a full company in all kinds of weather, over all types of terrain, and in all sorts of situations—forming deep interpersonal bonds in the process. They had been given no formal instruction manual, so they devised their own solutions to every new training challenge thrown their way. In truth, they taught *themselves* how to be tankers. None asked to fight in this new World War but all felt ready to take that fight anywhere in the world—and the faster they could tackle the nasty job, the faster they could resume the cherished civilian lives they left behind. This great hope motivated them all.

* * *

Around mid-month, the 3rd Division received orders to set sail before month's end. For obvious security reasons, a destination was not given. Then the real shocker came: Companies A and C of the 756th Tank Battalion (L) would join, but B Company, HQ, and Service Companies would remain stateside until later sea transport could be arranged. Apparently, the 15th Regiment's transport ship turned out smaller than expected and thus lacked the necessary cargo space to accommodate B Company's tanks.[113] The news felt like a hard kick to the gut, and B Company's morale took a palpable plunge. Up to that point, the company had no AWOL incidents since leaving Fort Ord.[114] After the announcement, however, many enlisted men seemed to lose interest in training. Some began showing up late for duty, or not all. On 21 October, eight men stayed out well beyond the permission times scribbled on their passes.[115] Wilkinson cracked down on the slacking—by busting some guys down to private, meting out unpleasant tasks to others, or denying future passes. In some cases, he convened a summary court—meaning HQ officers met to determine disciplinary sentences. To lift spirits and rekindle motivation, he altered the training program to include more time at the gunnery range. He designed complex drills where the crews coordinated fire via radio while moving and using the new gyrostabilizer. He demanded the men check and recheck the guns, radios, etc. for optimal efficiency.[116] He tried anything he could imagine to keep their minds occupied.

On 22 October, Wilkinson stood upon a stark cement pier at Hampton Roads, Virginia with several other officers watching as the gray transport ships carrying the 3rd Division and tank Companies A and C pulled up anchor and then steamed eastward out of the bay and into the open Atlantic. His good friends Captain Edwin "Cotton" Arnold and 1st Lt Olson—both C Company officers—boarded those ships heading for the unknown.[117] He had no idea where they were going. All M5 tanks belonging to A and C Companies had been waterproofed prior to loading. Clearly, they were hitting a beach somewhere. Was it a second front in France? Would they help the British fight Rommel in Libya? The speculation made Wilkinson feel unexpectedly empty. He longed to go with them.[118] B Company's absence from the operation made very little sense to him. A and C Companies could claim, at best, two weeks of amphibious training, whereas B Company exceeded that severalfold.[119] B Company was probably the best-trained tank company for amphibious operations in the entire U.S. Army—and yet they weren't invited. Many decisions of the Army simply made no sense.

One by one, the ships disappeared over the horizon. Wilkinson turned and headed back to Camp Pickett to design another four-week training schedule for his company—but even he found little enthusiasm for writing it.[120]

* * *

For the next six weeks, B Company continued training in and around Camp Pickett. Much time was spent at the gunnery range, but Wilkinson saw an alarming drop in performance and accuracy.[121] The men seemed to go through the motions. While firing on moving targets one day, Lt Fazendin accidentally dispatched a round near 1st Sgt Hogan's location. Hogan was unhurt but could have easily been killed.[122] The near tragedy shocked the company out of its funk and the crews became more careful and attentive thereafter.

Many HQ Company officers showed disappointment, as well, over being left behind. Moods turned sour. With A and C Companies gone, the level of "chicken shit" rule nitpicking increased, with B Company the target of every inspection imaginable. Captain Charles Allen, in particular, found some problem every single time he visited.[123] Lt Edward Mandel dropped by to examine tanks so often that the mechanics wondered if he suffered from an unnatural obsession.[124] Even Major Sweeting couldn't seem to leave B Company alone—with the kitchen crew the periodic focus of his wrath.[125]

AWOL issues continued to plague B Company. Most men never presented a problem, but a few repeat offenders kept giving Wilkinson fits. Four became so insubordinate they had to be fined and sentenced to time in the stockade.[126] One man, in particular, proved so far beyond redemption that Wilkinson removed him from the company entirely.[127]

On 8 November, the daily newspaper arrived and the men finally learned where their fellow tankers landed: Casablanca, Morocco.[128] Although details were scant, the reports declared the landings a success with Patton's forces actively subduing half-hearted French opposition in and around the North African port city. Nothing could be gleaned regarding A or C Company specifically, but the operation seemed to be rolling along well. The reason for the odd orders to wear wool OD clothing in camp was now clear: It was all a ruse to convince any possible spies that Patton's forces were heading to northern Europe and not Africa.[129]

A new officer, 2nd Lt Ralph Shaw, joined B Company as a platoon leader.[130] He replaced a Lt Finn, who served in the company for only a few weeks. Shaw was a short, red-haired fellow who worked as a reporter for a Louisville newspaper prior to the war.[131] He made a great first impression on Wilkinson in his entrance interview.[132]

A few days later, the company was ordered to pack and prepare to move to New York City—their designated port of embarkation.[133] Finally, life seemed to roll again. So eager were the men to escape Camp Pickett that all the tanks and equipment were crated in less than two days. Lt Redle and Technician 4th Class (T/4) Clyde Cogdill departed immediately for the docks of Staten Island to serve as the advance team.[134] On 24 November, the tanks and equipment—but no men—were loaded aboard a flatcar train and departed immediately.[135] Then, for the next several days everyone sat around their Camp Pickett barracks surrounded by packed duffle bags, staring out at the gloomy weather and wondering when they could leave too.[136] Nobody had definite answers. Thanksgiving came and went, with B Company feeling as if they had been relegated to the rearmost echelon in the U.S. Army.[137]

Finally, at 1530 on Friday 28 November, B Company, HQ, and Service Companies of the 756th Tank Battalion (L) boarded a troop train.[138] Everyone fully expected to end up at Staten Island, but at 0430 the train shunted to a dead stop outside of Fort Dix, New Jersey.[139] The men were instructed to grab their gear, de-train, and start walking to their new quarters. After trudging several miles through the snow in bitter cold darkness, the men arrived at their new post: a windswept field filled with empty flapping tents.[140] The accommodations proved worse than gloomy, muddy Camp Pickett. Even crueler, the men were told the flimsy tents would be their homes for several weeks. The boredom in the days to follow bordered on the unbearable. The men couldn't engage in any meaningful training because their tanks and equipment sat on a loading lot on Staten Island.[141] To keep the men moving and warm, with their minds focused on something other than the misery of sleeping "under canvas," Wilkinson jammed the daily schedule with road marches and conditioning drills. More chicken shit "showdown" inspections of personal gear followed as did mindless close-order drills.[142] One day, the entire battalion endured an inspection so niggling and excruciatingly long that everyone wanted to scream.[143] Such treatment was better suited for raw recruits—not highly trained tankers and company-grade officers. Through it all, the weather never warmed above freezing, and the men often cursed New Jersey as the "coldest place" they'd been assigned.[144]

To escape the daily tedium and bland field kitchen fare, the officers occasionally traveled to New York City to devour a decent steak or to take in nightclub life or a Broadway show. The enlisted men, however, were rarely offered similar opportunities. Local passes were issued, of course, and movies and other entertainment was also available on post, but the day-to-day drudgery proved too much for some to bear. Moods soured, tempers flared, and arguments abounded. On 7 December, of all dates, Wilkinson placed two enlisted men under arrest and confined them to quarters for repeatedly arguing with Lt Shaw.[145] One angry man ended up earning a trip to the Fort Dix stockade.[146] Then, Sgt Eugene Wunderlich engaged in a loud, public quarrel with Lt Fazendin—leaving Wilkinson no choice but to bust the otherwise even-tempered sergeant down to private and to reassign him to another platoon.[147] Fazendin's temperament, in particular, seemed to be grating on his men lately, but insubordination of this sort could not be tolerated. A snowstorm, dumping six inches of fresh snow, didn't help with morale either.[148] Fortunately, tempers cooled by mid-month as the men realized their officers were just as frustrated over the situation.

A new series of promotions crossed the battalion clerk's desk in the HQ tent. In most cases, the promotions were awarded to men bringing their grades in line with the work they were already doing. Redle and Kremer were both promoted to first lieutenant[149] and Dolvin, the battalion XO, made major.[150] On 9 December, Wilkinson stopped by the HQ tent on a routine errand. The 1st Sgt and company clerk snapped to attention and delivered crisp salutes. Puzzled by this sudden display of formality, Wilkinson walked over to his desk to find his own promotion orders sitting dead center. Placed at the bottom of the typewritten papers sat the shiny silver double bar "railroad tracks" insignia of a captain. Wilkinson had turned twenty-three only two months earlier, and this promotion warmed an otherwise dismal New Jersey winter. Two days later, Lewis, Dolvin, Sweeting, and the other officers in HQ threw a small party in his honor, featuring champagne, steaks, and lots of laughs. For a few hours, anyway, the revelry harkened back to a more carefree pre-war life at Fort Lewis.[151]

On 18 December, a group of six enlisted men arrived to fill out the B Company T/O as "basics"—in other words: duties to be determined later. These men, however, were not inexperienced recruits. In fact, all came straight from an infantry AT program at Camp Wheeler, Georgia. There, the men learned to exploit every weakness in a tank using weapons ranging from 37mm cannons to Molotov cocktails. By training's end, the men were convinced anyone volunteering for tank service had to be a certified lunatic. Army logic, of course, naturally dictated these new AT experts receive assignments somewhere as tank crewmen. When the men learned their destination was the 756th Tank Battalion (L), some chose AWOL instead.[152]

Christmas came and New Year's 1943 passed, but B Company remained trapped inside Fort Dix tents, huddled around glowing stoves while awaiting departure instructions. Several times, orders arrived to pack, but each time additional plans fell through without explanation. Finally, on 13 January, the three seemingly forgotten companies of the battalion were told to gather their belongings and march immediately to the train station. This time, the orders held and events moved very quickly afterwards. The men jammed into rail cars at 1330, arrived in Jersey City at 1730 and boarded a ferry for Staten Island at 2030.[153] The men debarked, lugging their heavy barracks bags for some distance, before reaching the USAT *Santa Elena* moored against an enormous concrete dock. The 600-foot-long ship had been built as an elegant passenger liner in 1933 and had only recently been converted into a troop transport. While filing slowly up the crowded gangway, someone jokingly noted the date was January 13th. Pvt Luther Kinsworthy, mortified by the superstitious significance, exclaimed loudly: "My God, we'll never get back to the United States!"

The men jammed the *Santa Elena's* decks while shuffling in fits and starts along a line snaking down steep stairs and into a maze of narrow hallways deep inside the ship's interior. The amenities, though cramped, were positively luxurious compared to the stingy canvas tents of Fort Dix, and the ship's blasting heat felt heavenly. The enlisted men found refuge in bunks stacked three high—but offering little space between rows aside from a narrow walkway. After languishing for seven weeks on a frozen field in New Jersey, nobody complained.

The officers' accommodations topside were embarrassingly elegant: uncrowded staterooms and dining halls featuring fine china, linen napkins, and tuxedoed waiters.[154] After locating their sleeping quarters, Wilkinson, Fazendin, and several HQ Company officers hovered outside along the deck rail as the *Santa Elena* dropped its moorings, and with the gentle caresses of doting tugs, slipped quietly through the dark waters of New York Bay. The blazing lights of a confident and vibrant New York City skyline sparkled and shimmered only a few miles to the north—presenting an audacious backdrop for a more reserved Statue of Liberty. Not a single skyscraper was blacked out and America's greatest city seemed to thumb a brash neogothic nose at the rest of the world. The stints of idle chit-chat faded to silence as the *Santa Elena* gained steam under its own power, splitting the dark sea into higher and longer ribbons of white foam. As chillier Atlantic air swirled past their wool coats and overseas caps, the officers stood quietly, lost in their private thoughts—watching their homeland fade into a bright smudge on the horizon.[155] With the *Santa Elena* now entering a war zone patrolled by notorious German U-boats, a pair of destroyers and the battleship USS *Texas* joined as dark silhouetted sentries off to both port and starboard. The mood turned serious.

As Captain Wilkinson turned to reclaim the warmth of his stateroom, he noticed 1st Lt David Redle smile and wave to him. Redle had been guarding the B Company's tanks and crated materiel on Staten Island all this time. Before departure, Redle also made certain every piece of company property was safely secured deep inside the *Santa Elena*'s enormous hold. Right then, Wilkinson realized he had not seen nor spoken to his own XO in over two months.[156] Never once did he wonder, worry, or enquire about Redle's performance. He didn't have to. Whatever Wilkinson entrusted to Redle was in the best of hands.

U.S. 3rd Infantry Division

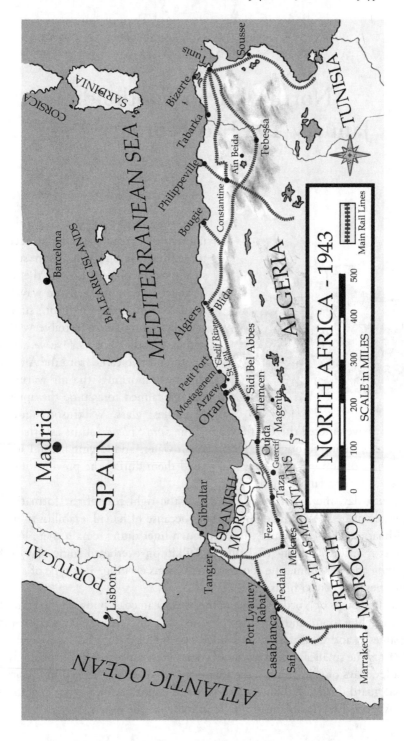

CHAPTER 5

North African Foothold: January 1943 to February 1943

M5A1 Light Tank (1942)

The first night at sea was relatively uneventful. Fazendin and Redle succumbed to seasickness but Wilkinson stayed as steady as an old cowboy in the saddle.[1] Strangely, the motion of the waves never bothered him a bit. Wilkinson's stateroom, though roomy and comfortable, was shared with seven other officers. Five were from the 756th and two came from the Air Corps.[2] The next morning, the air warmed and the sea calmed to assume the appearance of endless glass. Wilkinson figured the liner must have entered the Gulf Stream.[3] The *Santa Elena* and its escorts sailed at a steady clip, slicing through the placid cobalt waters and leaving behind sparkling wakes. Ships of all types and sizes had joined them during the previous night and jockeyed to form a large convoy.

The next day, the *Santa Elena* rotated to the right rear of the formation—an undesirable place known as "coffin corner" because of its vulnerability to hit-and-run U-boat attacks. Fortunately, the overladen liner didn't remain there long. The very next morning, Sunday 17 January, Wilkinson overheard some Navy officers whispering about a submarine spotted the previous evening. This type of rumor he thought best to keep to himself.

Sprawling maps of North Africa and the Moroccan coast hung off pushpins in the officers' briefing room, and Wilkinson learned that the 7th and 30th Regiments and Companies A and C of the 756th landed not at Casablanca but some eight miles northeast at the smaller coastal town of Fedala.[4] Resistance proved surprisingly light. After a few days of skirmishing, the infantry and tanks bivouacked in the area and assumed guard duties. Wilkinson also received confirmation of the obvious: Their ship was headed to Casablanca to be reunited with the others.

Much shipboard activity centered on giving inspections and enduring inspections.[5] Emergency exercises of every sort were held daily. Fire drills and abandon ship rehearsals required the participation of everyone aboard.[6] When not crammed together for some muster drill, the enlisted men packed together below decks—barely able to move without rudely poking into someone else. The sea roughened steadily and many men became violently seasick. The bunks and corridors soon reeked of both vomit and disinfectant. Few men could shower, so the thick musky punch of body odor and sweat also joined in offending the nostrils. By day four, most B Company men found their sea legs—with the exception of S/Sgt Morris Thompson who remained hopelessly nauseous.[7] The enlisted men were allowed to bump about the bowels of the vessel and even venture topside for fresh air and ocean views—provided they remained on designated decks. Even so, one could never fully escape the crush of the crowd.[8] For distraction and entertainment, Hollywood movies flickered away each night well into the early morning hours. The theater areas, like everywhere else, were always packed to capacity.[9]

The fifth day at sea marked the halfway mark of the voyage. The ocean air cooled markedly and the officers retreated into the ship's warm interior to pass away the time playing poker and bridge. Small amounts of cash and large egos were always involved. Wilkinson joined in the games—more to escape his restless boredom than any desire for material gain. He missed the daily papers and keeping abreast of the latest news on the war mostly.[10] A pep letter from President Roosevelt circulated among the officers above and was read aloud to the troops below. The president's words, though long on fighting spirit, were disappointingly short on war details.[11]

Without question, the Navy beat the Army in landing the best cooks for the war effort. The food served in the officers' mess was always exceptional. Each appetizing course rivaled the finest fare served in New York restaurants. The menu featured sirloin steaks, filet mignon, cherry pie, ice cream, etc.[12] Even the beverages offered tasted outstanding and were accessible to the officers at all hours. Wilkinson often scoffed at posh tea-drinking types, but to his amusement, he acquired the sipping habit while fidgeting about the *Santa Elena*.[13] The disparity in treatment between the men above and the men below, however, began weighing on him. To eat or drink, the enlisted men endured long chow lines in crowded corridors. By the time a man finally ate he had to practically jump over to the end of another long line for his next meal. Worse, fresh water supplies below started running low. Wilkinson was made aware of the problem when one of his sergeants, laden with a dozen clattering empty canteens, emerged from a stairwell and asked him for help. Wilkinson escorted the sergeant up to the officers' deck and showed him a drinking fountain where he could fill the canteens. An officer from another unit strolling by chastised Wilkinson:

"You shouldn't do that, or we may run out of water for the officers ..." he scowled.

"Good. Then maybe somebody will do something about the water supply," Wilkinson shot back.[14]

Wilkinson resolved that his men would no longer suffer alone, so he drafted a rotation whereby at least one B Company officer would remain below with the men at all times.[15]

The sea turned particularly violent on Wednesday, 20 January—so tempestuous at times, that fine china in the officers' mess often slid and shattered across the floor. Perhaps King Neptune was letting the officers know his sympathies lie with those unwashed masses in steerage. Thursday was Wilkinson's turn below, and although he sensed the beginnings of the flu, he joined his cramped men wedged among stacked bunks and stuffed duffle bags. Surprisingly, he found their spirits sky high. In fact, B Company morale hadn't been this good in a long time.[16] Happily, he had misjudged them. The difficulties aboard ship hadn't beaten them down but instead drew them closer. With no officers present, the sergeants and other natural leaders stepped forward to keep the company loose and focused. Jokes flew and friendships grew. Wilkinson delighted over seeing them pull together into such a close-knit bunch. Every good officer aspired for this kind of brotherhood to blossom under his command. It was a quality essential for pulling them through whatever uncertainties lay ahead. After sharing several hours of idle chit-chat, Wilkinson returned to the opulence above but left knowing his men possessed something finer than all perks found on the officers' decks.

The convoy spent the better part of Friday steaming around in large holding circles until a broken-down freighter could be repaired.[17] Once the convoy resumed eastward, rumors circulated over the expected arrival times at Casablanca. Some insisted Monday. Others argued Tuesday. As no explicit orders had been handed down, Wilkinson saw no point in adding to idle speculation—although he was often asked.[18] Rather, he joined a rip-roaring poker game and walked away sixteen dollars richer—with most of the winnings coming at the expense of Major Sweeting. The windfall represented a sweet measure of vengeance.[19] Lately, Sweeting had been tossing a few barbed comments Wilkinson's way that were unjustified. Whether the major's veiled insults represented some real change of attitude or were just a new series of intrigues in Sweeting's mind games, Wilkinson didn't know and he wasn't about to fret over them either. He had been in the Army long enough to learn that trying to outguess the motives or machinations of someone further up the command chain was a complete waste of time. Better to focus on the job and allow extraneous matters to dissipate—they almost always did.

On Monday, 25 January, at 1310, the first sliver of land appeared in the hazy distance. Hordes of welcoming seagulls darted and danced over the approaching ships—performing an acrobatic commotion in a whirlwind cacophony of shrieks and squeals.[20] As the *Santa Elena* and convoy companions neared, the gray land mass swelled to reveal sandy browns, dim patches of olive, and a mosaic hint of buildings. In time, a patchwork of alabaster resolved into a picturesque Casablanca, and the ocean transformed from deep crystal blue to dark murky green with the approaching shoreline.[21] As the sun set, the *Santa Elena* navigated gingerly against gentle briny breezes caressing the harbor entrance. The exotic city showcased an odd mix of exotic medieval Arabic and elegant contemporary French architecture and appeared relatively unscathed from battle. The harbor, however, remained an absolute mess from the Allied attack two-and-a-half months earlier. Several French warships and freighters lay sunk at their moorings—ripped open in places by violent bomb blasts. Some had even rolled completely over on their sides as if embarrassed by the events. The beautiful and enormous French battleship *Jean Bart* was the largest victim—sunk upright in harbor mud next to a long concrete wharf lined with shattered warehouses. Its ultramodern, gray hull sat in silent indignation as passing wakes of lesser ships lapped along the partially-submerged main deck.

The *Santa Elena* docked at dusk in a vacant space along the same wharf, but no one was allowed to debark until after 2100. When B Company's turn finally arrived, the men gathered their heavy packs along dimly lit corridors and shuffled at a snail's space toward a crowded, narrow staircase. A sole egress was approached by first forming a tight single row and then ascending steps through a small doorway at the top. Soldiers clanking ahead of B Company struggled to get through the tight hatch one man at a time—and the process was taking forever. Seeing this bottleneck, Wilkinson asked 1st Sgt Hogan to send two of the company's strongest men forward. Moments later, a pair of big Polish-Americans, Technician 5th Class (T/5) Paul T. Tirpak and T/5 Edward J. Sadowski, squeezed their way to the front of the line.[22] Both men were tank drivers, strong as oxen and stood at least six feet tall. Tirpak, from Cleveland, played semi-professional basketball before the war and never lacked a twirling football in his hands or a cheery attitude in his heart.[23] Sadowski was a quiet, muscle-armed Pennsylvania steel worker who swam rivers just for the hell of it.[24] As B Company ascended the stairs, Tirpak and Sadowski, posted outside either side of the narrow hatch, yanked each man through by the shoulders—equipment and all. As soon as one victim cleared, they immediately grabbed the next, and in clockwork fashion all 100 B Company men reached topside in record time. So efficient were Tirpak and Sadowski that Wilkinson told Hogan to put their names at the top of the list for the next round of passes.[25]

Next, the men filed down a long gangplank onto the concrete pier—thrilled to stride upon solid ground and move about freely again.[26] They gathered briefly for a head count and then started marching through the outskirts of the small city, taking in the unfamiliar sights, sounds, and smells of a completely foreign continent.[27] After twelve days living like livestock in a stale ship's hold, the world seemed new again. The warm air's bite was crisp and salty, carrying the fleeting odors of diesel exhaust, animal dung, and cooking fires. Every breath teased of adventure. Though the hour was late, thin swarthy citizens continued walking about the dimly lit streets. One extremely tall, slender black woman ambled through—towering over everybody, including Tirpak and Sadowski. The men gazed wide-eyed and speechless as she passed among them with oblivious bearing. After marching two-and-a-half miles, B Company reached a grassy hillside roughly a quarter mile from the ocean. They spread out across the treeless slope, unfurled their bedrolls, and fashioned shelter halves into tents.[28] HQ Company and Service Company joined soon after and guards were posted at the perimeter according to assignments drawn up earlier. Lulled by the rhythmic serenading of the nearby surf, the young Americans settled down to sleep their first night as foreigners.[29]

The next morning, everyone awoke to air so surprisingly chilly and moisture laden that sheets of dew formed on the insides of the tents and dripped down like soft rain upon their cozy bedrolls.[30] Once the sun emerged above the sandy hills to the east, however, an intense and oppressive heat took hold. By mid-morning, the sun burned so hot that the soaked bedrolls and tents had dried to a crisp again. The day was spent continuing with camp construction. Major Sweeting put B Company in charge of erecting mess tents and organizing the kitchen. Until this project was completed, the men dined on canned C-rations.[31] Other men drew the task of digging a latrine trench opposite camp roughly 300 yards beyond the road.[32] Because the location could be easily seen by everyone milling about on the hill, however, few took care of their personal business until after nightfall. Eventually, canvas curtains were tacked up on wooden frames to give the men some level of privacy.[33]

That afternoon, Captain Arnold of C Company paid a visit to his late-arriving compatriots. Like Wilkinson, Captain Arnold was a tall Texan and proud Texas A&M graduate (1939). He hailed from the prairie town of Greenville, was the son of a successful oil engineer, and had anchored his State Championship high school football team as star center.[34] Growing up, he was always called "Cotton" on account of his fuzzy blonde hair. The apt nickname never left him no matter where he went. Lt Olson also dropped in, and both officers eagerly regaled their friends with every detail of what they missed.

The landings at Fedala commenced in the predawn hours of 8 November 1942.[35] The surf churned wildly—creating hazards worse than the rehearsals at Monterey. Frightening mishaps resulted. Several landing craft wedged upon jagged reefs. The coxswains piloting other boats became disoriented by dark, unfamiliar surroundings and motored off in wrong directions. Some reached shore but beached too early. Several tanks swamped in the rough surf while attempting to disembark the LCMs. Fortunately, no crewmen drowned.[36] Despite these missteps, both A and C Companies landed in force at Fedala around 0500 and supported the 7th and 30th Regiments respectively.[37] French forces offered sporadic resistance—heavy in some places while non-existent in others. As dawn broke, the Americans braved the chattering of MGs and the booming of coastal guns to storm past the beach homes into town. A few buzzing French aircraft bombed the others as they scrambled across the beach.[38] The invasion force had plastered American flags everywhere—pinned to every soldier's shoulder, flown from every radio antenna, and painted on the sides of every vehicle—all with the hope of dissuading the French from firing upon their historic allies. In some cases, the gambit worked, but in others it had no effect whatsoever.

The surprise landings caught the defenders off guard and Fedala fell relatively quickly. However, the subsequent push toward Casablanca sixteen miles southwest involved another forty-eight hours of fits-and-starts clashing.[39] The delays came more as a consequence of concurrent political negotiations than anything else. By 11 November, a general armistice was finally achieved. Casablanca surrendered and most of the fighting ceased.[40] In some cases, isolated French units, unaware of the truce, battled on. Only one man from the 756th Tank Battalion was lost: Pfc Anthony M. Lierl. The 29-year-old Ohioan drowned during the evening of 10 November when an LCM carrying the truck and kitchen crew from A Company capsized in the rough surf.[41] His body was found two days later floating along shore. Lierl's loss earned him the tragic distinction as the first 756er to die in the line of duty. Amazingly, no other battalion member perished or even suffered serious wounds during this dangerous operation. In fact, the only other casualty was an A Company private who sustained superficial facial flash burns from the recoil of his own 37mm gun.[42] The 3rd Division on the whole, however, suffered sixty-six killed and over 200 wounded.[43] As the armistice took root, both A and C Companies set up camp at the Casablanca airport and assumed guard duties. The assignment lasted roughly three weeks before a new camp was established just south of Fedala.[44]

1st Lt Ed Olson, platoon leader in C Company, recounted surviving one long, hair-raising adventure aboard an LCM motoring around blindly in the darkness. The night began inauspiciously when his platoon topped off the charges to their tank batteries with small gasoline-powered "Johnny" motors.[45] The ship's poorly ventilated hold allowed a build-up of carbon monoxide fumes that made Olson's men so ill, they had to halt and be helped topside for fresh air. They recovered and were reunited with their M5s as each was loaded by crane into separate LCMs bobbing along the ship's waterline. The first LCMs, crammed with tanks or troops, circled repeatedly on the nearby sea—but soon became disoriented waiting for the others. All attack ships operated under strict blackout conditions, so no shipboard lights served as reference points. The sky was also heavily overcast, and all Fedala's lights had been shut off by the town's French defenders, making the shoreline impossible to discern.[46] The coxswain piloting Olson's LCM complained he could not get a clear compass reading and blamed Olson's steel tank for causing his magnetic needle to move erratically. When the predetermined moment arrived for the boats to turn toward Fedala, the coxswain made his best guess and opened up the throttle. Ten minutes ticked away. Then twenty minutes passed … but no shoreline appeared. Suddenly, the dark cutting silhouette of an American destroyer loomed over the waves nearby. Olson had mastered Morse code the previous summer at the Fort

Knox Communications School and signaled to the destroyer by flashlight that they needed help. The destroyer slowed to allow the disoriented LCM to pull alongside and receive vocal directions. The coxswain was shocked to learn he chose a bearing straight for the open sea—180 degrees opposite of where he was supposed to go. By the time Olson's LCM finally reached shore, dawn broke and everyone else had already been there an hour.

The LCM landing itself, however, was perfectly executed. The coxswain eased up gently to the beach and lowered the front gate. Olson's crew bounced the M5 onto wet sand without ever touching the surf. As his crew stopped to remove all waterproofing apparatus from the engine compartment, Olson set out on foot to locate the rest of his platoon. Further down the shoreline he saw another M5 tank trapped in the sand. The crew appeared to be attempting to extricate it with the tank's pioneer tools. Olson slogged toward them to determine if they were his men. As he neared, he recognized 2nd Lt Donald Gourley on his hands and knees feverishly scooping sand away from around a sunken tread. Gourley was an A Company platoon leader. Nearby, a tall American stood in wool ODs with his back turned surveying other activity along the beach.

Olson slipped past the lone helmeted man shouting: "Well Gourley, this is a hell of a place to throw a track!"

The figure reeled around sharply and bellowed into Olson's ear: "Who are you? *What* are you that you don't salute me when you come alongside me!?"

The young lieutenant turned to face the blazing blue eyes of Maj Gen George S. Patton Jr. Olson nervously saluted as the general let loose a second barrage of questions. He wanted to know what Olson was doing, the extent of his mission, what he planned to do next. Then he launched into a long lecture about proper military courtesy. When Patton finally stopped for a response, Olson explained himself as best as he could behind wide eyes and with a mouth full of cotton. Really, he simply wanted to find the rest of his platoon. Realizing this, the old general's voice softened to a fatherlier tone. He pointed to another M5 further down the beach skewed upon some jagged rocks.

"Now Lieutenant, might that be one of your tanks?"

Olson gave Patton his best parting salute, while assuring the general he would find out immediately and then trotted off to check. As he approached, Olson discerned that the hopelessly lodged tank displayed Company A markings—not his company. Olson looked around briefly for the crew but found no one in sight. Unwilling to waste more time, he backtracked toward his own tank and crew. Fearing another embarrassing encounter with the gruff general, he tracked high along the dunes and bluffs, wandered behind a row of cottages, and then slipped between two bungalows to regain access to the beach. As he brushed alongside a porch, he was startled to see a man sitting in a chair scarcely an arm's length away. His feet, propped high on the rail, were decked in magnificent cavalry boots. Olson looked up into the figure's face and locked eyes. It was Patton ... *again*. This time, the young lieutenant saluted very swiftly and the slightly amused general nodded.

"Was it your tank?" Patton queried.

"No, Sir!" Olson stammered while scampering down the beach—trying to put as much distance as possible between him and his intimidating commanding general.

Olson found Gourley again, still working to free his tank from the sand. A jeep pulled up to them and the driver offered his assistance. The two young officers climbed aboard and asked for help finding the other missing tanks. At that very moment, a French fighter plane appeared low over the beach. The wing dipped and the engine screamed straight toward them. Its sudden appearance drew sheer panic from the three men bunched in the jeep. "Strafer!" Gourley yelled. In a mad scramble to evacuate, the officers' legs entangled and both men collapsed in one pathetic heap, hanging halfway over the rear tire. The plane roared straight overhead without firing a shot. The pilot must have harbored pro-American sentiments, as he could have very easily killed all three of them with a short burst from his MGs.

Olson finally found the rest of his platoon later that morning. They had been assigned to support the 30th Regiment holding the north flank of Fedala. At the same time, the 7th Regiment and tanks of A Company advanced southwest toward Casablanca. Olson's mission turned out to be rather uneventful in the days that followed—certainly when compared to that crazy first morning.[47]

Although B Company had been scratched from the initial Operation *Torch* landings, they still remained the most experienced of all 756th companies in amphibious landings. Nevertheless, the A and C Company officers enjoyed mercilessly teasing their newly-arrived battalion mates with the nickname: "gang-plankers"—because they arrived via dock instead of beach.[48] The ribbing was easy to handle, but a third straight month without tanks bordered on absurdity. Casablanca harbor had since become jammed with more Allied ships than wharf space, and until B Company's tanks and equipment could be unloaded, the frustrated tankers found little to do except make camp improvements. They erected wooden frames of varying shapes and sizes to help beef up their tents, and the hillside took on the appearance of a shanty town rather than a temporary campsite.[49] Slit trenches, deep enough to shield a prone man, were dug adjacent to each tent in the unlikely event of attack.[50] With Rommel's legendary army fighting well over a thousand miles away beyond a forbidding Sahara Desert, deeper foxholes seemed superfluous. Better B rations replaced the canned C-rations the men had been eating.[51] B rations, although still packaged foods, were prepared by the field kitchen and tasted much more appetizing.

On 27 January the men could finally enjoy showers. Many had not been able to adequately bathe aboard the *Santa Elena*. Camp life had become routine enough that Wilkinson, Fazendin, and Shaw strolled down to Casablanca to take in the many strange sights and sounds. Along the way they passed friendly French Marines and colonial troops—smiling, nodding men against whom their fellow tankers and 3rd

Division troops battled only a few weeks earlier. The three young officers wandered a labyrinth of bustling streets lined with sun-bleached buildings veiled in the dusty haze of human activity—but featuring few motor vehicles. Only a handful of older model cars belched about the small city.[52] Most natives relied on horses or horse-drawn wagons for transportation. Even the taxis consisted of modest horse-drawn carts.[53] Everywhere, in the hot air hung the pungent odors of animal dung and unbathed humans.[54] A leather-skinned local named "Charlie" offered to serve as a guide and interpreter for a nominal price, and the three Americans accepted. As part of the tour, Charlie ushered the trio around the "Old Medina" marketplace—a raucous plaza circus of street vendors selling products of every sort. Wilkinson marveled at the inexpensive selection of belts, sandals, and other quality goods. Exotic fruits and foods were offered everywhere, and a wide range of cooking aromas helped to mask the smells of the unwashed crowd.[55] The merchants were every bit as pushy as the beggars—particularly upon the appearance of Americans. The locals coveted cigarettes, not money. Two large juicy oranges could be exchanged for a pack of unfiltered Camels.[56] French troops also circulated among the stands and carts without attracting the same fawning vendor attention.[57] Perhaps Americans represented easier prey. The three officers found the whole experience quite amusing—particularly the theatrics involved in give-and-take bartering.[58] Later, Charlie took them to experience—of all things—a tumultuous Jewish wedding where Wilkinson ended up receiving kisses on both cheeks by a bearded Arab![59] As a beautiful, bloated, amber sun descended into the Atlantic, the three settled into a promising restaurant called the Petit Pancet in the hope of capping off their daylong excursion with an exquisite dinner. The food, unfortunately, was not up to par with the fine meals served aboard the *Santa Elena*.[60]

Back at camp, the men of B Company learned they had been assigned temporary dock work as guards and stevedores.[61] With the rotation set to begin almost immediately, Wilkinson hastily drew up shift schedules and assigned himself as the first duty officer. The job seemed straightforward at first, but the logistics proved rather complicated. S/Sgt Crawford sorted out much of the details, and the first duty shift, beginning at 1600, 1 February, commenced without a hitch.[62] The work itself was boring and rote—basically amounting to pacing out predetermined routes while watching for thieves or saboteurs.[63] The Arabs unloading the cargo were destitute and labored away wearing little more than ragged loincloths. Although their temptation to steal may have been high, they possessed no pockets or sleeves in which to conceal anything. If the tankers did witness any suspicious activity among the dock workers, they were not permitted to intervene themselves but told to alert an overseer—who would then investigate and usually beat the accused.[64] French Morocco was truly half a world away from Middle America.

On 2 February, additional vessels arrived from the same convoy and weighed anchor just outside of port. One ship contained all of B Company's tanks and equipment.[65] Unfortunately, wharf gridlock had grown so severe that any happy reunion was still days away. In the meantime, the men paced out their dull guard rotations—scrambling only when the occasional klaxon blared warning of an imminent air raid. No enemy planes, of course, ever appeared.[66]

Wilkinson used his free time to catch up on reading and answering a large batch of personal mail recently delivered to his tent. Due to sea travel, everyone's mail had been delayed several weeks. News from home was not lighthearted for the captain. A good friend by the name of Gene Davis had died over Germany while serving as a bombardier in the Air Force.[67] To shift his mind away from the tragic news, he flipped on the company radio and tuned into some German propaganda broadcasts. The enemy's stories and features were generally corny and unconvincing but oddly entertaining.[68]

To keep the men from going out of their minds with boredom, Wilkinson filled their time away from dock duty with road marches and conditioning drills.[69] On 5 February, two B Company tanks, nicknamed "Balls O' Fire" and "Buccaneer," finally arrived in camp. These were the first B Company tanks the men had seen since November. The rest of company's tanks rolled in the following day—sending morale sky high.[70] The tankers, however, weren't permitted to touch them until the battalion maintenance officer thoroughly inspected each one. That process took another two days.[71]

The port duties continued into the middle of the month, with guard shifts as boring and uneventful as ever. For some reason, the authorities always seemed to fear saboteurs might strike, but none ever did.[72] Perhaps these concerns resulted more from the general news than from any specific threat. The Russians had seized the offensive in the Caucasus, while the British and late-arriving Americans pushed Rommel back into Tunisia in a series of skirmishes and runs. None of this, of course, was reported in the German propaganda radio shows that Wilkinson monitored.[73] Fears of neutral Spain joining the German cause also circulated in Allied leadership circles. If Spain flipped, then Spanish Morocco, lying only 175 miles northeast of Casablanca, would suddenly become enemy territory. This rumor, in particular, kept the officers from feeling too complacent.

After a month in Morocco and with their familiar tanks again parked nearby, camp activities returned to the mundane. When not marching or guarding docks, the enlisted men rolled dice or organized pick-up games of baseball or football. 1st Sgt Hogan even bought a bicycle to scoot around better.[74] In some cases, the daily routine dipped into carelessness. Pvt Myron Eckerly mishandled a .45-caliber pistol, shot a hole through his own left hand, and ended up in the hospital. He was not expected back for a full month.[75] Normally trivial issues suddenly warranted Wilkinson's intervention: Fazendin's 1st Platoon grew rowdy and had to be reined in; Another unit complained of T/4 Roy Burdette speeding around in a jeep; T/5s Louis A. Laliberty, Bates, Randolph H. Perdue, and Morris missed a guard duty shift and had to be reduced in grade; Morris took his punishment especially hard and required Wilkinson's fatherly reassurance.[76] Lt Shaw added to a growing track record of pushing the wrong buttons of the wrong people. This time, something he uttered upset the normally good-humored Lt Kremer, and Wilkinson had to intervene to smooth out the dispute. Such pettiness sent Wilkinson retreating into his diary to list all the normal things he missed in life: "newspapers, my own radio, good whiskey, a date with a nice girl, and American civilians."[77] After the sanity breather, he concluded his company needed a similar attitude adjustment with a complete change of scenery for a day. On 15 February, he led his men on a road march all the way to Fedala and back. Fedala was a much cleaner city than Casablanca. At the very least, everybody's nostrils would be given a fresh start.[78]

A few days later, Wilkinson learned that 19 February would be the company's last day of guard duty. The good news couldn't have come soon enough. Another troop ship convoy was scheduled to arrive that afternoon and the new chumps debarking would have the crappy job passed on to them.[79] This influx of fresh troops also meant the 756th had to relocate to make room for them. In advance of the move, Sweeting received a promotion to lieutenant colonel.[80]

With harbor guard responsibilities now off their backs, Company B behaved more like a tank outfit again. On 20 February, Wilkinson sent out two of his three platoons on a road march aboard their tanks.[81] The next morning the men were told to prepare for a major move in as little as four days. The destination: Port Lyautey, sixty miles to the northeast.[82] Companies A and C had already settled into the new camp, but the remainder of the battalion—HQ and Service Company—still waited for their vehicles and equipment to disembark.[83] In between packing preparations, Wilkinson kept his men conditioned and the tanks rolling—leaving no time for anyone to obsess further over trivial matters.[84]

At 0600 on Sunday 21 February, a hard rain pummeled B Company's hillside camp and persisted until early afternoon—leaving everything utterly soaked and the slit trenches overflowing with coffee-brown runoff.[85] The men toiled through the soggy mess, organizing, packing, and loading the vehicles. Two days later, the camp was torn down.[86] At 0800 on 24 February, B Company and the HQ and Service Companies—finally reunited with their vehicles—formed a convoy, pulled away from the foundational remnants of their seaside camp, and headed north.

B Company departed the Casablanca area with an unofficial new member. During B Company's stay, the camp always attracted vendors or beggars. Usually, they were shooed off by the guards. But two local destitute siblings simply could not be turned away. Sgt Donald L. Pennington, in particular, looked after them like a big brother.[87] Their names were Johnny and Sara Fatima. Johnny appeared to be seven or eight years old and Sara about five. Both were orphans, filthy and undernourished with heads so heavily lice-infested that their scalps moved. The Knoxville, Tennessee, native fashioned a stall out of spare shelter halves so the two children could privately bathe with soap and scrub their hair every day.[88] After a few weeks, both were free of lice. Pennington always made certain the two received proper food and clothing each day. During their stay, Johnny, in particular, bonded with several tank crews. The kids reminded the men of younger brothers and sisters back home. When the time came to leave, Sara chose to remain with area friends, but Johnny felt his new family was among these kind Americans and thus hitched a ride with one of the B Company tank crews.[89]

The column snaked through Fedala, then rumbled beyond Rabat—passing through placid pastures and sparse scrubland inhabited with only plump cacti and lazy grazing camels.[90] The weather was clear and the azure Atlantic was never too far off on the left.[91] The journey covered ninety miles—punctuated by a one-hour lunch break and a few quick stops to monitor vehicle condition. Long road marches were tough on tanks—especially in high heat—so the engines and tracks required frequent inspection. By 1500, the seventeen M5 lights, three half-tracks, three trucks, and two jeeps comprising B Company's convoy pulled into a camp roughly nine miles southeast of Port Lyautey.[92] The site had been selected earlier by A and C Companies and happened to be inside a large cork forest called the "Forêt de Mamora."[93] Cork bark harvested from these beautiful stately oaks was used to produce wine bottle stoppers. The sprawling trees provided both tactical concealment and refreshing shade for the tanks and crews, and the forest was large enough to ideally disperse the entire battalion properly over a large area. All in all, it proved to be a perfect bivouac site, and the battalion reunited for the first time since their expectant days at Camp Pickett.[94]

Flag of Free France

CHAPTER 6

Border Watchers: February 1943 to May 1943

Wilkinson and Sweeting had arrived at Port Lyautey the prior day, as part of the advance detail. The purpose of the trip was not only to inspect the new bivouac but to scout out ideal terrain for an upcoming joint exercise scheduled with French forces. Once the remainder of the battalion arrived, B Company was dispatched immediately to the field for a dress rehearsal of the "problem."[1] A "problem" was Army jargon for an exercise designed to meet a particular training objective.[2] In this instance, the exercises were quite extensive—aimed toward integrating American tanks with French infantry. Should the Spanish suddenly join the Axis and attack from the north across the Spanish–Moroccan border, the 756th had to be prepared to work with infantry from either the U.S. 3rd Division or French regiments.

For tanks to be successful, German armor mastermind Heinz Guderian identified three essential ingredients: favorable terrain, the element of surprise, and employment *en masse*.[3] Therefore, "problems" usually involved mobilizing tanks into striking formations. Companies and platoons rolled forward in lines, wedges, inverted wedges, slanted lines ("echelon right" and "echelon left"), or columns—depending on field conditions. When advancing toward enemy positions, terrain always dictated which formation worked best. Tanks generally avoided cresting hills or ridges. To do so exposed the tank's thinly armored underside to AT fire. Instead, tanks circumvented the heights, choosing instead to maneuver within foliage or along berms, walls, and buildings affording protection and concealment. This practice was known as "defilade," and competent platoon leaders and tank sergeants were expected to recognize and exploit favorable defilade conditions—particularly in defensive situations.

While crossing flat, open ground, tanks attacked as wedges. This allowed all guns to be brought to bear upon enemy targets. If forced to crest a hill or move through covering smoke, the formation shifted into a broad line, allowing all tanks to appear at once and thus deny the enemy the ability to pick off each emerging tank one at a time. Tankers also drilled to move together in bounds. Sometimes this occurred as a larger force springing forth and halting in successive stages and other times with individual tanks advancing in "leapfrog" fashion. In all situations, stationary tanks *always* covered the movement of others. Companies moved as companies and platoons moved as platoons. If a platoon was forced to operate alone then a section of two or three tanks covered the advance of the other section of two or three tanks. The absolute worst way tanks could attack was along a narrow column because only the lead tank could fire on the enemy—whereas multiple enemy gun positions could strike the lead tank.[4] For this same reason, a tank never attacked alone. No "problem" ever contemplated a lone tank venturing forth to "neutralize such-and-such position." The thought was as absurd as ordering an individual infantryman to attack without the covering support of his squad mates.[5]

Tanks did not operate in vacuums. They served as but one component in one large, complex front-line infantry operation integrating reconnaissance, engineering, chemical smoke, mortars, artillery, and logistics. When all parts joined together for a rehearsal, a "problem" quickly developed into a major undertaking—particularly when most troops involved spoke only French. Fortunately, B Company had several French speakers, most notably Communications Sgt Daniel Pompey and tank driver T/5 Louis A. Laliberty.[6] The company relied on their interpretation skills and a simplified set of hand signals in order to communicate.

With the first round of joint maneuvers scheduled to commence the following day, Wilkinson obtained some local maps and spent the afternoon scrutinizing the practice area on foot.[7] B Company was assigned to the defending force, so Wilkinson looked for any and all ideal attack routes. Once identified, his next concern was to locate suitable defilade defensive positions nearby. As Wilkinson surveyed the parched and gently rolling scrubland, an older Arab local with a sun-weathered face approached offering his assistance. The august, leathery man said he had once served in the French Army and was quite familiar with maps and military concepts. He cautioned that the countryside had undergone recent changes and marked those problem areas on Wilkinson's maps. Afterwards, he invited Wilkinson to his hut for a hospitality meal. Wilkinson graciously accepted and the two sat down inside a cozy, austere room while the man's wife served an appetizing plate of couscous and goat's milk. Although outside temperatures hovered around ninety degrees, Wilkinson ate the fresh but unrefrigerated offering and realized he was not only a U.S. Army officer but an American ambassador as well.[8]

The joint exercises unfolded in stages over three straight days.[9] In many instances, live fire was used, so conditions often became quite dangerous. Particular emphasis centered around radio coordination between all elements.[10] Maj Gen Patton even stopped by for a stretch, field glasses in hand, to observe the spectacle. His dour visage certainly kept everyone focused.[11]

The conditions were hot and arid, but the worst problem was the dust. It lay everywhere and infiltrated everything. Every time the tanks moved, they kicked up big billowing clouds of the stuff.[12] Not only did the rising reddish-brown plumes give away tank positions, but the powdery sand permeated every nook and cranny on machine and man. The crewmen sweated constantly and moist dirt caked into many uncomfortable places. Even tightened goggles couldn't prevent the abrasive dust from irritating the eyes—setting in motion a vicious cycle of flowing tears and stinging sweat.[13] Fine grit coated the engines and crew compartments, clogging filters and obscuring the instruments. As a consequence, two tanks developed engine trouble while operating deep in the field. Four hours passed before the maintenance crew could even find them. One crew teetered upon panic because they failed to practice water conservation and exhausted their potable water.[14]

The other tank's engine was declared a total loss because unfiltered dust somehow got sucked straight into the cylinders. Upon hearing of this, Sweeting became livid and vowed to personally charge the tank commander, Sgt Hamilton A. Smith, the full costs for a replacement motor. Under Army rules, Sweeting *could* do so if Hamilton was, indeed, negligent. Captain Wilkinson and Sgt Morris Thompson closely inspected the ruined engine and discovered a hose had been misconnected—improperly bypassing the air filter. Maintenance procedure required Ordnance to first guarantee an engine and for battalion maintenance to certify that guarantee before releasing a tank to a crew.[15] Wilkinson successfully argued this point to Sweeting, and Sgt Hamilton was cleared of any wrongdoing. In the end, Ordnance took the blame and accepted the charges.[16]

At the conclusion of the exercises, the French officers of the Port Lyautey regiment invited their American officer counterparts to a formal dinner lasting most of the afternoon. The officers of the 756th arrived at 1130 as a French military band, elegantly dressed in light blue and white uniforms, blared out lively music. The Americans entered the mess hall together, attracted quick and courteous greetings, but were swiftly separated and ushered off to various tables. The seating assignments were intended to foster new friendships. Lt Redle sat with three complete strangers—none of whom spoke English. With a few broken words and lots of hand gestures, the men carried on a conversation of sorts. Redle learned that two officers were French infantrymen and the other, a pilot. Redle also discovered the pilot hadn't flown in months because the Germans didn't trust him.[17] Because of the arrival and ongoing deluge of well-equipped Americans, the pilot felt confident and eager he would return to the skies soon.

Every half-hour or so, a French mess sergeant appeared before the seated crowd and broke into song detailing the virtues and features of the upcoming course. If the officers approved of what they heard, they cheered. If not, they booed. Over the next three hours, all servings were selected in this manner—yielding such delicacies as pink, sweet wine, couscous, tangerines, and champagne.[18] When the fairytale banquet finally concluded, the enchanted officers of the 756th returned to their dusty bivouac plebian lives of track grease, sump pits, and a new set of typhus shots.[19]

Wearied over hearing another round of trivial complaints, Captain Wilkinson instituted a new company rule: "If you complain, then you fix it." Lt Fazendin viewed this new policy as his personal invitation to make improvements—and one glaring problem he intended to rectify was the lack of decent beds for the enlisted men. The officers slept comfortably on cots while everybody else had to lie in the sand. Rear echelon supply sergeants were always in the market for "battlefield souvenirs"—foreign helmets, knives, handguns, medals, and other interesting military accessories. German militaria, in particular, drew top barter. Fazendin knew exactly where to find the stuff and thus organized an exchange for a batch of new U.S. Army issue cots. A few hours later, he triumphantly motored into camp carrying a truckload of canvas beds to divvy out and share among the men.[20] When Lt Col Sweeting learned of the deal, he made Fazendin take everything back.[21] In terms of maintaining some semblance of authorized bivouac decorum, cots were quite tame when compared to the old rusting bicycles, live hens, and growing piles of assorted junk, mementos, and local oddities other members of the battalion collected, swapped, and displayed.

Sweeting's problem wasn't the cots—it was that Fazendin procured them. Ever since the battalion's last days in California, Sweeting's attitude soured on the rangy, free-spirited lieutenant. Approximately a week before leaving Fort Ord, Fazendin's fiancée traveled down from Minnesota so the two could marry in Catholic Mass. Lt Redle served as Best Man and Captain Terry escorted the young bride down the aisle.[22] Exhibiting utter political naivety, Fazendin forgot to invite his battalion commander. Sweeting was so upset—and spiteful—over the perceived slight, he sent Fazendin to Camp Pickett with the advance detail—depriving the newlywed officer of several precious days to enjoy his new wife.[23] Fazendin didn't rehabilitate himself a few months later when he test-fired .50-caliber bullets into the side of a new M5. Captain Wilkinson had recently put in a glowing promotion recommendation for Fazendin. In Wilkinson's eyes, the lieutenant's organizational skills and accomplishments were exceptional. Sweeting responded by calling Wilkinson in and giving him an earful. At first, Wilkinson thought his lieutenant colonel was describing a completely different officer.

Fazendin was a man of action. When he thought of an idea, he simply went ahead and did it.[24] He was always thinking and so, consequently, he was always acting. In this respect, Fazendin mirrored a strong trait in Sweeting's own personality. Perhaps that's what really irked the West Pointer above everything else.

* * *

The maneuvers with the French continued into early March. For several days, heavy rain washed through the area. Every time the tanks parked, the crews were ordered to dig foxholes in the sopping wet mud—over and over again.[25] By 4 March, the rains had ended and so had the joint training. Despite the hardships—or *because* of them—the extended field training proved an invaluable experience.[26] The battalion returned to camp to clean up, service the vehicles, and attend closing demonstrations and seminars such as "how to remove and evacuate wounded men from tanks."[27]

The non-stop training marathon proved so thoroughly exhausting that some men slept through morning "Reveille." Displeased, Sweeting decreed that henceforth anyone missing their company's morning bugle call would not be fed the rest of the day. The problem stopped immediately.[28] B Company's bugler was tank driver T/4 Alfred Mancini. Prior to the war, Mancini had been a big band trumpeter in New York.[29] He played so clearly and beautifully, nobody in B Company wanted to miss Reveille at the start of day or "Taps" at close.[30] In between duties, Mancini entertained his fellow tankers by hooting out upbeat modern music numbers—earning the flattering nickname "Boogie Woogie Bugle Boy from Company B," after the popular song title.[31]

On 7 March, Sweeting gathered the company commanders together for a reconnaissance trip north to the Spanish–Moroccan border. The higher ups still harbored fears Spain might ally with Germany. As a consequence, Sweeting thought his captains should visit the desert borderline for themselves.[32] The officers returned later in the day but none the wiser.

On 12 March, however, the new 3rd Division commander, Maj Gen Lucian Truscott, and his Chief of Staff, Colonel Don E. Carleton, visited to lecture all battalion officers on their observations in Tunisia. Both men voiced strong opinions and pulled no punches. They said American troops had fought poorly on the other side of the desert.[33] In fact, when compared to German and British combat performance to date, U.S. Army conduct proved downright embarrassing. Truscott provided some distressing details about American debacles he witnessed firsthand at Sidi Bou Zid and Kasserine—yet emphasized that the Germans were no "supermen." They applied basic warfare principles with force and daring—achieving victories as a result.[34] Americans must do the same, he concluded. The scowling, gravel-voiced general's frankness left the battalion officers with plenty to ponder about their own combat readiness—much of which could not be immediately answered.[35] For the time being, the 3rd Division, the 756th Tank Battalion, and their French associates sat trapped in a holding pattern until more troops arrived from the States.

In the meantime, bivouac life under the cork oaks settled into a kind of "suburban" lifestyle for the tankers. The crews spread out roughly fifty yards from each another—living in framed tent "houses" beneath shady trees with scrubby grass "yards" and an M5 parked nearby. Each residence featured some motley collection of crates or drums serving as "porch chairs." In the evening, neighbors visited neighbors, and the gently competing strains of strumming guitars and melancholy harmonicas carried over the cooling breezes. It was a nostalgic time for swapping stories about home, the wonders of women past and present, and of aspirations for the future.

Arab vendors arrived daily outside the bivouac offering oranges, grapefruits, almonds, live chickens, and game cocks for trade.[36] They rarely walked away without a sale. On a few occasions, the visitors weren't looking to profit from mutual exchange but the opportunity to steal something. The tankers had to remain vigilant—especially those walking guard shifts. One time, Sgt Pennington was pacing the perimeter while B Company were settled in for a communal lunch near the kitchen. Suddenly, the diners heard Pennington yell "HALT!" followed by the quick, loud cracks of gunfire. The men rushed to find Pennington standing with his .45-caliber pistol drawn. A short distance away, an Arab teen writhed around on the ground, clutching his stomach in agony. Strewn about him lay the contents of a tanker's stolen barracks bag. Several associates of the gasping teen fled camp with a second bag. By sheer happenstance, both bags belonged to Pennington.[37] Captain Anthony M. "Doc" Sarno, the battalion surgeon, was promptly summoned to help save the kid but could do nothing except keep the boy comfortable as he passed away.

The next day, Pennington and Supply Sgt Shirley trekked all the way to the 3rd Division's supply depot in Rabat to replace the stolen items.[38] In another weird coincidence, they encountered a young Arab male wearing makeshift pants fashioned by cutting two holes in the bottom of a new U.S. Army barracks bag. On the man's backside was stenciled the task force number and the name "Sgt Donald Pennington." The two stunned NCOs alerted the nearest French gendarme, and the Arab was arrested. The police raided his nearby village and discovered several truckloads of stolen American military items.[39] Pennington's string of strange encounters ended up bringing down an elaborate theft ring.

The days of March 1943 rolled by as the 756th Tank Battalion border watched and awaited their next assignment. The tankers, once again, found themselves in a listless state of limbo. A new popular diversion swept through the bivouac: cock fighting. If dice or cards failed to entice the betting man into cracking open his wallet, a pair of angry roosters clashing about in a ring succeeded. The ancient sport was strangely mesmerizing for many and never failed to draw a passionate crowed. 1st Sgt Hogan always stood nearby to keep the matches fair and civil.[40]

Hens were also popular, and many crews kept them as pets outside their tents to gobble up nuisance bugs and transform the raw protein into fresh eggs. Some tankers didn't know the first thing about raising chickens but bought them anyway. Cpl Irving Shapiro, a small, funny Jewish kid from the heart of New York City, now serving as B Company's mail clerk, bought both a hen and rooster and became distressed and genuinely perplexed when they kept fluttering up into a tree near his tent. He thought chickens were supposed to live on the ground and thus tried tethering them. They kept getting free regardless. Shapiro's hen had a habit of wandering into the B Company officers' tent to lay her eggs. For some reason, she preferred depositing her gifts upon Fazendin's cot rather than with Shapiro. Keeping in spirit with Wilkinson's new company directive for "fixing problems," Fazendin simply claimed the eggs as his own, then fried them up and ate heartily.[41]

A few fresh eggs were not enough to overcome the dietary monotony of canned B- and C-rations. The company came to hate stew and hash—even when prepared well by the kitchen. In response, the officers and enlisted men established a voluntary fund to purchase fresh food for regular Sunday banquets. These became known as "company fund parties" and proved great morale boosters.[42] Wilkinson, 1st Sgt Hogan, and Mess Sgt Adlard organized each event the same way any field training "problem" was approached: Everyone in the company received a specific role. A team traveled to Rabat to purchase live chickens, potatoes, French bread, and wine. T/5 Laliberty served as interpreter. The maintenance section butchered the chickens, and each platoon helped with other kitchen duties. When the time came to sit down to dinner, each man received half a roast chicken, a heap of fried potatoes, French bread, and a cup of wine.[43] For several Sundays straight, the popular event was repeated. Sweeting, Captain Oscar Long, and other officers and NCOs from the battalion HQ were also invited and usually attended.[44] One weekend, a 200-pound hog was slaughtered and barbecued on a spit. On another, Wilkinson procured a huge 190-gallon barrel of dry dinner wine from the French military and set it up outside the officers' tent.[45]

After one particularly satisfying Sunday feast on 14 March, the battalion officers attended a poker party in Wilkinson's pyramidal tent.[46] Most B Company men were half buzzed on wine and stuffed with chicken to the point of lethargy. The officer on guard burst into Wilkinson's tent with an announcement that immediately broke up festivities: The battalion was ordered to send three officers and fifty men to cadre a new outfit called the "2637th Trucking Company" in Casablanca.[47] The group had only twenty-four hours to report for duty. 1st Sgt Hogan mustered the company and gave the notice—and the news was not received very well.[48] After everything they'd been through together, nobody wanted to be transferred. Wilkinson and Hogan were only given the evening to choose one officer and ten enlisted men from B Company to send away. The officer choice was not difficult. Over time, Lt Shaw had proven he couldn't seem to get along with anybody.[49] The choice in men, however, proved the toughest decision in Wilkinson's command thus far.[50] Most malcontents, delinquents, and "eight-ball" screw-ups—like Kelleher, the binge-drinking Irishman—had long since been weeded out of the company. With things running so smoothly, Wilkinson and Hogan found it very difficult to part with anybody. In the end, they reluctantly listed Shaw and only eight other B Company men—but the battalion signed off on the recommendations.

The next morning, the company mustered into formation with the men standing and fidgeting nervously while the list was read aloud.[51] Lt Shaw seemed quite happy to hear of his transfer. One by one, each of the eight enlisted men were called forward—many visibly broken up over being selected.[52] One young private listed wanted in the worst way to become a tank crewman but was too overweight and could never seem to shed enough girth to even squeeze through a tank hatch. An otherwise good-natured kid, Wilkinson struggled to find a suitable role for him in the company. When this young man's name was called, he didn't act at all surprised but stepped forward with a look of resignation. Some teased him with chants of "Eight-ball! Eight-ball! Eight-ball," but the big, heavyset private shrugged by quipping back: "Hell, I ain't no eight-ball, I'm a *sixteen*-ball!"[53]

The nine new truckers packed their gear and departed B Company. To put the whole unpleasant episode behind them as quickly as possible, Wilkinson sent the entire company out to the 37mm gunnery range to vent off nervous energy. Fazendin led the exercise—delivering what Wilkinson thought was the best instruction he had seen in a long time.[54]

The 3rd Division began packing for a move to Algeria, and Wilkinson heard rumors of the 756th leaving soon for Tunisia.[55] Lt Col Sweeting didn't know if the change of station rumors were true but could provide confirmation of other changes in the works—including some officer reshuffling within the battalion. Soon after, Captain French Lewis received command of A Company, Lt Olson landed battalion adjutant (S-1) responsibilities, and several other officers earned promotions as well—including Fazendin.[56] Wilkinson was pleased his persistence had paid off and Sweeting had finally made Fazendin a first lieutenant.[57] Although the lieutenant colonel could be stubborn and overly opinionated at times, he was not irrational. Wilkinson made some changes in B Company as well: Sgt Wunderlich took charge of Wilkinson's tank, and Mancini was promoted to sergeant and given his own tank command. Unfortunately, the Army put a stop to B Company's Sunday banquets by prohibiting all open market purchases. Similar dinners had gained popularity with other units, and the Army claimed local farm animals were becoming scarce.[58]

B Company continued range work in both daylight and evening conditions.[59] After concluding a long, satisfying day blasting away targets on 22 March, Wilkinson kicked back in the B Company officers' tent to tune into German propaganda on the radio. With Tunisia on his mind of late, he listened intently for the enemy's take on the situation. He knew of British forces pressing from the east and Americans pushing from the west and got a big chuckle out of the fact that not a shred of this was mentioned in the broadcast. Suddenly, Lt Redle burst into the tent and announced that several 756th officers and NCOs had been selected as Tunisia battlefield observers. Wilkinson, Captain Long, 1st Sgt Hogan, and S/Sgt Crawford were on the list.[60] Wilkinson rushed to Long's tent and learned the group was scheduled to leave in only two days. Also listed were Sgt James L. Harris of A Company, S/Sgt William Fodor of C Company, and S/Sgt Norman C. Fuller from Service Company.[61] On 24 March, Wilkinson, Long, and four very excited and energized NCOs packed and departed upon first light. After nearly two years of training, waiting, and training some more, a few 756ers, anyway, would finally witness actual combat action up close and personal. Granted, A and C Company crews fired a few shots in anger while landing at Fedala, but nobody actually believed they had "seen war."

Upon Captain Wilkinson's departure, 1st Lt Redle assumed command of B Company,[62] and Sgt Richter temporarily shouldered the duties of 1st Sgt Hogan. That same day, the 756th Tank Battalion was transferred over to the command of the II Corps HQ, indicating even bigger moves were imminent.[63] The tankers' rumor mill buzzed under an assumption Tunisia was next on their itinerary. On 4 April, 2nd Lt John Winlock joined B Company from the 2nd Replacement Depot as Lt Shaw's replacement.[64] In civilian life, Winlock served as a deputy sheriff in Harlan County, Kentucky. He was not only personable but hilarious, and his clever wit made him instantly popular with everyone in the battalion.

A few days later, formal orders arrived sending the 756th to Oran, Algeria, 400 miles to the east. The tankers loaded their tanks and half-tracks onto small French flatcars in Port Lyautey—securing the caterpillar tracks with 6" x 6" wedges to prevent the vehicles from shaking loose as they rocked along the narrow-gauge railroad.[65] Camp was torn down, and a motor convoy comprising all the battalion's wheeled vehicles departed the cork forest at 0700, 10 April.[66] Twenty B Company men accompanied the road column.[67] The remaining B Company tankers—three officers and eighty-four enlisted men—climbed aboard the train. In addition to the flatcars, B Company was allotted three German-made "forty and eight" boxcars—so named because each was rated to carry either forty men or eight horses.[68] The tank crews took up residence on the flatcars to guard their tanks. As a result, B Company's cooks, clerks, mechanics, and basics enjoyed plenty of open space inside the three boxcars.

At 0100, 11 April, the train shunted out of Port Lyautey and rolled deep into the Moroccan night. A few hours later, as the first serene rays of dawn broke into a blue-pink sky, the crews cut open C-ration cans and enjoyed breakfast with bright green, beautifully cultivated fields sliding by. But for the sight of young Arab children herding cattle, the crews could have convinced themselves they were enjoying a leisurely tour through the fertile heartland of America.[69] They passed through the junction towns of Meknes and Fes during the day and chugged toward Taza, with a bloated orange sun now setting to their rear, bringing down a cool cloak of darkness.[70] During one late-night stop, five boxcars filled with French Legionnaires were inserted between the B Company boxcars and flatcars.[71] As the train continued on into the blackness, the cars started to jerk and lurch. The air turned uncomfortably cold and the steam engine labored and groaned. Morning broke, revealing breathtaking misty vistas of rugged brown mountains and forest green valleys. The route now tracked through treacherous terrain along the northern edge of the Atlas Mountains, and the narrow ribbon ahead looked like the twin rails on a Coney Island rollercoaster. Seeing this, the crews congratulated themselves for taking extra care in securing the tanks prior to departure.[72] The men cut open cold C-rations again and tried dining without spilling breakfast all over themselves. Most extraneous items had been abandoned in the cork forest—the crates and can "chairs," the bicycles, and the chickens. Sgt Mancini, however, hid his hen in a box crate nest inside his M5, where she roosted atop twenty-one eggs. Mancini's crew secured their tank so well not a single egg cracked during the mountain journey and later out popped twenty-one peeping chicks.[73] In the late afternoon, a lone American B-25 flew low and slow over the train as if greeting the tankers' arrival to Algeria.[74] The roaring engines reverberated through the nearby hills and faded to a low groan as the glinting hull veered away to some unknown destination. The terrain grew flatter and drier, punctuated with sparser vegetation, and then the sun finally set—ending another long day that had been mercilessly hot.

The French Legionnaires in an adjacent boxcar freely shared canteens of dry wine with several B Company basics. The French were long accustomed to drinking wine daily and could handle the stimulative effects without behaving like fools. Americans could not. Three new B Company replacements brought in only a week before: Pfc Lotka U. Kupriance, Pvt Abe C. Beal, and Pvt Paul N. Cardullo, grew louder and more boisterous after every swig.[75] Soon, a contentious argument erupted over each man's ancestry. Kupriance was of Russian descent whereas Beal and Cardullo were German and Italian, respectively. At first, Kupriance and Beal ridiculed Cardullo by calling the Italians lousy fighters. Then Beal and Cardullo blasted Kupriance's Russians as unreliable communists. Finally, Cardullo and Kupriance blamed Beal because Germany started the whole war. The silly quarrel flared so fiercely that Redle and Richter, overhearing from the next boxcar over, feared the three might resort to physical blows. As soon as the train pulled to a brief stop, Richter bolted back to the trio's boxcar, poured their remaining wine over the side, and rejoined Redle before the train lurched forward again. A little while later, as the train slowed to a crawl, Richter noticed a French civilian jogging alongside, selling several wine bottles to the same three clowns. For a second time, the acting first sergeant dashed back to their boxcar and dumped out their booze. To end the drinking and stupid arguing once and for all, Richter informed the three drunken debaters they would be digging kitchen sumps once the company reached their destination.[76]

At 0400, 13 April, the train arrived at the Mediterranean port city of Oran. In a cool predawn, heavily laden with salt vapor rolling off the nearby sea, all tanks and equipment were unloaded by a railyard crew well practiced in moving promptly and efficiently. With the first rays of sunlight glinting and flickering through boxcar slats and crane lattices, the drowsy tankers formed a convoy and departed for Arzew—twenty-five miles further east along the coast.[77] On the way, they rendezvoused with the battalion motor column driving up from St Leu. The column had arrived the previous day and the vehicles were still caked with thick dust after a sweltering three-day journey.[78] On a treeless, rocky, and windswept hill outside of Arzew, the 756th made their new home—with companies, platoons, and individual tank crews staking out tiny plots of ocean view territory.[79] They were certainly not alone. The entire 3rd Division, comprising some 12,000 men and hundreds of vehicles, sprawled like a small tent city over adjacent slopes and ridges.[80] That evening, the timeless Mediterranean nearby murmured out an ancient hypnotic lullaby—harkening back to the tankers' first evening on the outskirts of Casablanca.[81] Even after living several months in Africa, the men still felt like wide-eyed strangers in a strange land.

Talk of Tunisia waned after the officers counseled the men that the North Africa campaign was winding down and the storied German Afrika Korps about to be crushed out of existence. The battalion prepared for their next operation—another probable amphibious landing somewhere in the Mediterranean. The coastal areas around Oran and Arzew served as training grounds for the Fifth Army Invasion Training Center (FAITC). The FAITC prepared Allied units for amphibious landings and beachhead expansion operations. Many drills used live fire to acclimate trainees to the actual sounds and hazards of combat. Since the FAITC's formation earlier in 1943, about a dozen units, ranging from individual companies to full battalions, received intensive instruction under the program. Now, the FAITC staff and facilities had expanded to train entire divisions at one time. The 3rd Division was their first. Training commenced on 22 March with a schedule lasting roughly a month. The 756th would receive a "refresher" near the end, and then the 2nd Armored Division and the 1st Infantry Division would rotate in.[82]

In the meantime, the 756th awaited their turn, and over the next two weeks B Company settled back into a familiar camp routine.[83] The men beat the heat by taking quick dips into the Mediterranean—a welcome and refreshing daily ritual. The mosquitos of Arzew, on the other hand, were unwelcome and unrefreshing annoyances. At sundown, abundant hordes arose like swirling mists from the thick grasses. With voracious bloodthirstiness, these tiny beasts left behind scores of itchy welts upon the unwary. Their salivary ducts also carried malaria—a fatiguing blood parasite causing "yellow jaundice" that could sideline a man for months. To escape these buzzing clouds, the men slept at night under fine mesh nets. Local lizards feasted upon them like candy, so nearly everybody kept pet chameleons tethered to their tents—everyone except Lt Winlock, who harbored a deep phobia for all reptilian creatures.[84] As a practical joke one day, Lt Kremer tied a chameleon to Winlock's mess gear dangling from a nail outside the kitchen and watched with wicked glee as the cringing Kentuckian futilely tossed rocks from a distance, fruitlessly trying to shoo the tiny lizard away.[85] The former police officer Winlock, a notorious practical joker himself, finally begged a passerby to rescue his mess kit.

The locals seemed better kempt and more cultured than those of French Morocco, and the surrounding lands were more beautiful and better cultivated.[86] Theft no longer posed a serious concern, so the tankers naturally felt more at ease in their new surroundings. Rotating passes were issued to nearby Oran for the men to experience the restaurants, cafes, movie houses, and Red Cross shows.[87] The sprawling outskirts of Oran smoked and steamed with all the features of a modern, thriving industrial metropolis and the noisy port teemed with trucks, troops, and transports ships at all hours. The city center showcased a relatively clean, contemporary European-style commercial district served by electric streetcars and wide avenues bordered with terraced residences and manicured palm gardens. The inhabitants represented a mixture of many cultures: Arabs, Berbers, French, Spaniards, and Jews. However, most signs were written in French. Beautiful women populated the shops and streets—from French civilians to American nurses—bustling on business or sashaying about in colorful sundresses and stylish hats, Red Cross light blue and whites, or Army khakis tailored to flatter the female form. Just the sight of a pretty woman brought untold joys to many American servicemen on pass. A particular girl wasn't the reason. It was the idea she represented. She signified visible proof of a promising and peaceful civilian life beyond stifling, contradictory demands of Army life and the irrational reality of another World War. The faster that war could be won, the quicker a more carefree life in the United States could be reclaimed.

Maj Gen Truscott wanted the war won yesterday and resolved to whip his 3rd Division into the toughest, fittest fighting force in the world. Toward that end, he incorporated a grueling march into the division's FAITC training regimen his exhausted troops came to curse as the "Truscott Trot." The march required 3rd Division soldiers to cover thirty miles in an eight-hour period—carrying full combat packs averaging sixty pounds each. To achieve this, a 5 MPH pace was maintained the first hour, a 4 MPH pace in the second and third hours, and a 3.5 MPH pace the remainder of the way.[88] Those failing the standard were washed out—presumably as replacements in a less demanding infantry division.[89] As a support unit assigned to the 3rd Division, 756th Tank Battalion tankers were also required to complete the "Truscott Trot" but under less strenuous conditions: no heavy infantry packs to carry. On days when the 756th participated in the thirty-mile circuit, Major Dolvin wryly penned "Tank Appreciation Course" on the battalion's master schedule.[90]

As April drew to a close, the 756th finally practiced beach landing refresher runs under what the FAITC labeled "Intensive Amphibious Training."[91] At 1000, 27 April, all the tanks and half-tracks of A, B, HQ, and Service Companies loaded aboard two 327-feet long LSTs (landing ship, tank) and slipped out onto the sapphire Mediterranean. At roughly 500 yards from shore, the gray boxy vessels dropped anchor to allow the rest of the mock task force vessels to assemble. The tankers then spent a quiet evening "at sea" before the LSTs' loud twin diesels started up again the following morning. The little armada skirted twenty-five miles of coastline displaying breathtaking geographical extremes—from fertile farms and pristine beaches to craggy cliffs and colossal sand dunes.[92] Finally, the ships arrived at the mouth of the Oued Chelif River to await construction of a prefabricated pontoon jetty jutting out from the beach.[93] The next day at 1500, B Company's LST eased up to the completed dock, opened an enormous prow and dispelled all the tanks and crews in a neat, orderly fashion.[94] This debarking method proved much easier than going through the hassle of waterproofing tanks for deposit in uncertain surf. At the same time, Landing Craft, Infantry (LCI) ships anchored closer to the beach and dropped off streams of 3rd Division infantrymen into waist-deep water.[95] Once ashore, the tanks and troops advanced inland along the riverbank, simulated an attack, and set up camp for the evening.[96]

Thus, was the extent of the 756th Tank Battalion's participation in "intensive" amphibious operations under the FAITC. For the next few days, the tankers sat sweating under camouflage tents wondering how they ended up taking such a giant training step backward.[97] On 1 May, the battalion hosted a demonstration featuring such head-drooping tedium as the "Challenges of Standing Guard," and "The Right and Wrong Ways of Driving Tanks." The communal frustration was palpable,[98] and the tankers began identifying with the beautiful girl who no one ever asked to dance.

On 5 May, Captain Wilkinson and the others arrived in camp and spilled down off a dusty truck after witnessing five weeks of front-line combat. They appeared haggard from the long journey but eager, nonetheless, to share firsthand observations and details to what the battalion had missed in Tunisia. Echoing Truscott's warnings from two months earlier, their conclusions were alarming and sobering: The Germans are tough fighters and combat is unfathomably brutal. Nobody is as prepared as they think they are ....

U.S. II Corps

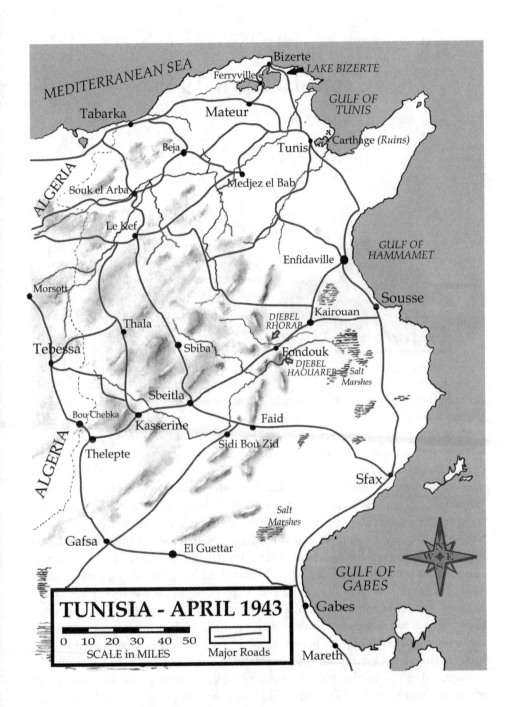

MEDITERRANEAN SEA

Bizerte
LAKE BIZERTE

Ferryville

*GULF OF
TUNIS*

Tabarka

Mateur

Carthage *(Ruins)*

Beja

Tunis

ALGERIA

Souk el Arba

Medjez el Bab

Le Kef

Enfidaville

*GULF OF
HAMMAMET*

Morsott

Sousse

Thala

*DJEBEL
RHORAB*

Kairouan

Tebessa

Sbiba

Fondouk

*DJEBEL
HAOUAREB*

*Salt
Marshes*

Sbeitla

Bou Chebka

Kasserine

Faid

Thelepte

Sidi Bou Zid

Sfax

*Salt
Marshes*

Gafsa

El Guettar

*GULF OF
GABES*

TUNISIA - APRIL 1943

0   10   20   30   40   50
SCALE in MILES   Major Roads

Gabes

Mareth

CHAPTER 7

Tunisia: April 1943

M3 Medium Tank (1942)

Wilkinson's Tunisian adventure began 24 March at 1030 aboard a jeep anchoring a truck column departing Port Lyautey in the pouring rain.[1] The long trek eastward would have been intolerable if not for the company of his good friend Captain Oscar Long.[2] Long was a fellow Texan and Texas A&M graduate (1938)—so both men already shared much in common.[3] Long was direct, unpretentious, and never one to pull a punch when a punch was needed. Though no giant, what he lacked in stature, he more than made up in sheer feistiness—particularly when confronting a grave injustice. When the remainder of the battalion prepared to ship out from New York in January, the tanks and trucks sat stored on a muddy lot under the care of an Army supply outfit. Most vehicles ended up sinking in six inches of muck and then froze in place under the blast of winter. Many batteries also went dead because charge levels were not properly maintained. When the time came to return the vehicles to the battalion and move them to the loading docks, the yard crews carelessly used winches to yank them free—shearing the track links and shredding rubber treads in the process. Upon seeing the damage, Long went absolutely ballistic. He stormed up to a group of astonished supply personnel and, with a Texas-sized voice employing some colorful adjectives, reminded them that *they all* got to go home to *their* wives every evening, but *he* was about to ship out and may never see *his* new wife again. In closing, Long blared he was *not* leaving the United States to fight in ruined equipment and that *they* would fix the damage to his satisfaction. They did. They were forced to steal batteries from some nearby Air Corps vehicles to finish the job, but they *did* fix the damage.[4] Therein was the main reason why Lt Col Sweeting put Long in charge of the battalion's Service Company. With the relentless pluck of a bulldog, he got things done. In that capacity, Captain Long was dispatched to Tunisia to learn all the ways desert combat put mechanical strains on tanks and vehicles.

The truck convoy pulled into Guercif at midnight—after 200 miles of bouncy travel. Wilkinson and Long, drenched and shivering, spent the night sleeping in the 30th Regiment's officers' club.[5] The next day, the convoy continued on to Tlemcen, Algeria—again after enduring another incessant driving rain.[6] On day three, the convoy pulled into Arzew on the Mediterranean, still soaking. Wilkinson and Long took some time to observe elements of the 15th Regiment training at the FAITC before settling in for the evening.[7]

The next day, Wilkinson, Long, and the four NCOs traveled to Bilda, near Algiers, enduring a fourth straight day of showers. Wilkinson's cousin was stationed in Algiers, engaged in diplomatic work for the U.S. government. Long seemed skeptical when Wilkinson told him of this familial connection. Nevertheless, the two hitched a ride and located an unremarkable five-story city building serving as the American consulate. A petite, blond female received them at the door—genuinely overjoyed upon recognizing "Charles." The young woman was Wilkinson's cousin—a State Department official named Nell Russell. A few years older than Wilkinson, Nell spoke fluent French and was heavily immersed in the upper machinations of regional diplomacy. She could not share much of her time but instructed her housekeeper to prepare a hearty meal for the two travelers and make her spare bedroom available to them for the evening.[8] The two officers dried out, rested, and returned to Bilda the next morning. By day five, the rain had finally lifted just as the six men reached Constantine to spend the night camped on the side of a hill. The next day, 30 March, they proceeded southeast to Ain Beida, closer to Tunisia, where they learned of their observation assignment with the 751st Tank Battalion.[9] The 751st was a medium tank outfit equipped with M3 Lees and attached to the 34th "Red Bull" Infantry Division under the command of Maj Gen Charles W. Ryder. The 34th Division was formed out of National Guard units from Minnesota, Iowa, and North Dakota and was the very first American infantry division to ship to Europe.[10] That evening, the six 756ers reached the bivouac of the 751st—only six miles shy of the main line of resistance. Everywhere, the dark business of combat operations was apparent—the streams of rumbling supply trucks, the sandbagged depots of ordnance and fuel, and the unnerving presence of greater numbers of ambulances. Artillery rumbled constantly in the distance. Everybody moved with stoic urgency and the usual buzz of lighthearted camp banter was noticeably absent.

In the early evening, the 756ers met briefly with Lt Col Louis A. Hammack, CO of the 751st Tank Battalion. The 40-year-old Hammack presented an impressive bearing and congenial temperament but was otherwise preoccupied with more pressing matters.[11] After the short introduction, the six observers filtered among strangers, erected their pup tents, and prepared for a restless sleep while ack-ack bursts flickered like lightning across the eastern horizon.[12]

The next morning, Thursday 1 April, they awoke to the screams of tan, gull-winged German Stuka dive bombers preying upon a nearby town. As Wilkinson, Long, and the others watched in grim wonder, a swarm of escort ME109 fighters swept in to protect their slower brethren as they dropped deadly payloads and swooped skyward. One ME109 flew directly over the 751st bivouac—gray razor wings flashing large black and white cross insignia while thundering through, scarcely thirty feet above the tents, vehicles, and astonished American soldiers.[13] Wilkinson could clearly see the pilot's face calmly sizing them up as if enjoying a relaxing Sunday drive. A mess sergeant scrambled atop a nearby truck and pitched a .50-caliber MG skyward. He squeezed off a chattering rebuttal, but his bullet spray was as late as it was ineffective. The brazen intruder disappeared unscathed beyond a nearby rise, leaving behind a blast of billowing brown dust. After the incident, Wilkinson and Long decided to widen their slit trench and dig their pup tent a bit deeper into the desert.[14]

Later, a brisk dry desert wind kicked up and persisted well into the next day.[15] Dust and sand worked its way into everything. Despite the blustery conditions, Wilkinson and Long joined Major Wendell Langdon, XO for the 751st Tank Battalion, to examine 34th Division front-line positions a few miles away.[16] A German attack was expected, but nothing happened and the visit turned out to be more instructional than eventful. The wind abated and the day resumed to the usual hot, stifling, and oppressive. Each night, however, temperatures plummeted into teeth chattering chilliness—reminding Wilkinson of how someone once succinctly described Africa as the "cold continent with a hot sun."[17]

The Germans didn't attack, but the 34th Division and the 751st Tank Battalion prepared an offensive of their own. The plan was to seize a key chunk of Tunisian desert known as the Fondouk Pass—a mountain gap they had attempted to conquer a few days earlier, but failed. With the disastrous and embarrassing lessons of Sidi Bou Zid and Kasserine still stinging, American soldiers and tankers itched with determination to prove their battle worthiness. As latecomers to desert warfare, the U.S. Army was put on a steep learning curve and under tremendous pressure to adapt and succeed in very little time.

The seesaw war in North Africa had been raging for over three years. The conflict began in June 1940 with an Italian declaration of war. Soon after, British forces repelled Italian territorial advances into Egypt—driving them deep into Libya to the west. In what would become a perpetual habit, the Germans came to the rescue of their hapless Italian allies in February 1941 by landing reinforcement forces under the command of *Generalleutnant* Erwin Rommel at Tripoli. Rommel's Afrika Korps then proceeded to drive the British all the way back into Egypt to where, by May of that same year, both sides ended up so exhausted they had to pause to replenish fuel, materiel, and men.

The wide-open expanse of scrubland and desert made an ideal canvas upon which generals could paint feints and flanking maneuvers with sweeping motorized

Cadet Harry W. Sweeting. *(1933 Howitzer, USMA Digital Collections)*

Cadet Welborn G. Dolvin. *(1939 Howitzer, USMA Digital Collections)*

Edwin Y. Arnold, 1939 (ROTC). *(Cushing Memorial Library and Archives, Texas A&M University)*

Oscar S. Long, 1938 (ROTC). *(Cushing Memorial Library and Archives, Texas A&M University)*

French G. Lewis (ROTC). *(University of Arkansas Razorback, 1937)*

Charles M. Wilkinson, 1939 (ROTC). *(Cushing Memorial Library and Archives, Texas A&M University)*

David D. Redle (ROTC). *(Creighton University Bluejay, 1941)*

Main gate at Fort Lewis, 1941. (*French G. Lewis*)

Above Captain Terry and Lt "Blanco" Smith, Fort Lewis, 1941. The battalion barracks are in the background. (*David D. Redle*)

Left June 1941 photo (cropped) of original officers to the 756th Tank Battalion: (1) 2nd Lt Charles Wilkinson, (2) Captain Dwight Terry, (3) Lt Col Severne MacLaughlin, (4) Captain Harry Sweeting, (5) 2nd Lt French Lewis, (6) Maj Jacob Moon. (*French G. Lewis*)

756ers carry an "H-tank." (*U.S. Army Armor and Cavalry Collection*)

Captain Sweeting driving a new jeep. The tankers called these versatile vehicles "peeps." (*French G. Lewis*)

T/4 Roy Kosanke (right) and Sgt Haskell Oliver (left) in Class A service uniforms near a beautiful 1940 Packard with 1942 Washington State plates. (*Haskell O. Oliver*)

Above A mechanic from B Company works on the bogie wheels of a M1 at Fort Lewis. (*U.S. Army Armor and Cavalry Collection*)

Left Lt French Lewis shows off his Thompson machine gun shooting skills on the small-arms range at Fort Lewis. (*French G. Lewis*)

756th Tank Battalion (L) area at Fort Lewis 1941. (*David D. Redle*)

756th tankers practice in old M1 "combat cars." (*David D. Redle*)

Lt Redle, 1942. (*David D. Redle*)

Lt Severson drives an M1 at Fort Lewis, 1941. (*David D. Redle*)

Above Avettant, Cogdill, Sprattler—three men with three different destinies. (*U.S. Army Armor and Cavalry Collection*)

Right Lt Fazendin uses hand signals to lead his platoon. (*David D. Redle*)

Lt Fazendin drives, 1942. (*David D. Redle*)

Kosanke and Cogdill, Fort Lewis. (*U.S. Army Armor and Cavalry Collection*)

Lt Wilkinson. (*David D. Redle*)   Lt Redle at Fort Ord, California. (*David D. Redle*)

Lt French Lewis stands proudly before a new M3 in 1942. (*French G. Lewis*)

The 756th Tank Battalion (L) lined up for a group photo at Fort Ord, 1942. (*Family of S/Sgt Frank A. Deputy*)

Lt Ed Olson and M5 tanks from C Company prepare to debark from Newport News, Virginia, October 1942. (*Library of Virginia*)

Aftermath of the invasion at Fedala Beach shows plenty of discarded equipment, vehicles, and damaged landing craft. 756th Companies A and C landed here on 8 November 1942. (*U.S. Army*)

An M5 cruises down the streets of Casablanca shortly after the truce was declared. This tank may be from C Company of the 756th or from the 67th Armored Regiment. Unit designation on the hull was obscured prior to publication. (*U.S. Army*)

756th Tank Battalion (L) crews at campsites with their M5s in a cork forest near Port Lyautey, French Morocco, February 1943. (*Donald G. Shonka*)

Left Congested, hazy Algiers and harbor as seen from the hills to the west. (*U.S. Army*)

Above Captured German 88s. (*U.S. Army*)

Left M3 medium tank moving in the North African desert. The M3's high profile provided a tall target for German AT gunners. (*U.S. Army*)

The confident tankers of B Company, 756th Tank Battalion, crowd near Sgt Richter (center, standing with hand on hip) around a captured German tank. This photo was likely taken in Tunisia before the unit departed for southern Italy. (*Arthur Richter*)

formations. North Africa allowed Guderian's vision of warfare to be tested without trees, rivers, or cities complicating the process. Tanks played the roles of chessboard queens and an arms race of sorts broke out between the British and Germans whereby each side tried to outdo the other in the quality, quantity, and employment of armor. A series of attack/counterattack cycles left the deserts of eastern Libya and western Egypt littered with hundreds upon hundreds of burned-out tanks, half-track, trucks, and gun positions—without either side finding the necessary traction to deliver a *coup de grâce*. This stalemate persisted through the long summer of 1941. These were the same months the 756th Tank Battalion formed at Fort Lewis but was deprived of tanks. Its light tanks were delivered instead to British forces trying to gain the upper hand over Rommel in Egypt. The British finally gained preeminence in November of 1941 and chased the Afrika Korps all the way back to the Gulf of Sirte. Rommel, however, did not earn the nickname "Desert Fox" without reason. The crafty German general counterattacked with a series of flanking maneuvers and forced the British to retreat so deep into Egypt that by June of 1942, Churchill feared losing the Suez Canal. Had Rommel been properly supplied by his German High Command, this likely would have happened, and a vital Allied supply route to the Far East would have been severed. At that time, however, the Germans threw virtually everything they had into the Russian campaign, and Rommel's pleadings on behalf of the Afrika Korps were largely ignored.

The British held out at El Alamein and counterattacked that autumn. But without requisite supplies from Germany and with captured British materiel running low, the Afrika Korps fell back into a series of tactical retreats—conceding all previous gains in Egyptian and Libyan territory. When Operation *Torch* successfully opened the floodgates for Allied troops to pour into Casablanca, Oran, and Algiers in late 1942, Rommel (now a Field Marshal) had little choice but to retreat deeper into Tunisia and form a redoubt as two mighty armies closed in on his flanks. Though placed in a daunting situation, this did not mean the Germans were weak. In fact, Germans proved most dangerous when their backs were to a wall.

The first Americans to cross into Tunisia did so under the command of Maj Gen Lloyd Fredendall of the U.S. II Corps. The II Corps comprised American troops arriving at Oran and Algiers in November 1942 as part of the Operation *Torch* landings. These forces combined to join with the British First Army pressing into Tunisia from the west. Fredendall's men were tasked with holding the front's southern flank by establishing defenses in key mountain passes throughout the area.[18] The Americans acted like naïve newcomers—overconfident in their technology and superabundance of materiel, while neglecting sound military practices. This lax attitude began at the top. Fredendall foolishly scattered his forces along a broad front rather than concentrating them at critical points so one group could support the other should trouble arise.[19] Worse, he never bothered to inspect his emplacements firsthand—preferring, instead, to trust maps over the observations of his own officers in the field. His troops were still inexperienced, and, although, after landing they prevailed in short skirmishes against French troops with wavering loyalties, they had yet to face a highly motivated, professional German army—tempered and honed after more than two years of desert combat. These were the ingredients of a developing disaster.

The Germans did not wait long to test the mettle of their newcomer "Ami" adversaries.[20] On 14 February 1943, Rommel sent 140 panzers slicing through American positions at Sidi Bou Zid. The surprise breach drew in reinforcements from the U.S. 1st Armored Division—exactly what the Germans hoped would happen. German AT guns, skillfully hidden nearby, promptly knocked out forty-six brand new American M4 medium tanks fumbling around in the open—wiping out, in essence, an entire battalion in only a few hours.[21] American forces withdrew in panic to the Kasserine Pass, where they were again outmaneuvered and trounced by their German pursuers a few days later. Thousands of fresh American troops fell prisoner, entire artillery batteries were captured, and thousands of tons of materiel burned under pillars of thick black smoke rising high over the desert. The usual "fog of war" deteriorated so rapidly into such a confusing and demoralizing rout, that one American airfield commander misinterpreted the explosion of a distant ammunition dump as a withdrawal signal and ordered all his planes destroyed.[22] British forces from the north had to be rushed down to buttress the situation. They succeeded but were left wondering if Americans were for them what the Italians had been for the Germans.

The Germans concluded from numerous prisoner of war (PW) interviews that "Ami" hearts really weren't in the war. Intelligence reports trickled up to the German High Command told of the latest doughboys joining the war out of boredom or misguided senses of adventure. American soldiers were dismissed as slack thrill seekers unwilling to fight when conditions turned sour. Hitler felt validated. He always viewed Americans as lazy decadent playboys anyway—not "tough people" like Europeans of peasant stock, accustomed to hardships and deprivation.[23]

To their credit, the U.S. Army made no excuses for the poor performance. Everything ranging from the training, tactics, and coordination of units to the personal performance of commanders underwent swift and ruthless "lessons learned" scrutiny. Failing practices were altered or ended. Officers and NCOs from outside units—such as the 756th Tank Battalion—rotated through as battlefield observers to avoid repeating deadly mistakes. Failing commanders were dismissed. Fredendall was replaced and the II Corps revamped under the more aggressive and competent "hands-on" leadership of Maj Gen George S. Patton, Jr. The corps' three divisions—the 1st and 34th Infantry and 1st Armored Divisions—took the offensive in mid-March. The Americans won a tough battle at El Guettar, regaining some confidence, but failed to breakthrough to the Mediterranean as planned. The Fondouk Pass stood in the way.

If Fondouk could be taken, all German forces still battling southeast would be forced to consolidate north or face annihilation.[24] The objective presented a supreme tactical challenge because of terrain heavily favoring the defenders. The pass lay roughly three and a half miles to the northeast beyond wide, open ground, flanked by a long chain of mountains extending southward called Djebel Haouareb. The north side of the pass was anchored by another tall mountain named Djebel Rhorab. German observation posts and concealed high-caliber guns lined the sides of both mountains, providing the spotters and crews with sweeping views of the entire western plain. Countless German mortar, MG, and smaller caliber AT emplacements had been blasted in the cliff rock and fortified with timber and steel beams. The desert floor along each mountain's base had also been lined with long rows of barbed wire and lethal minefields.[25] Artillery alone could not neutralize these positions. Only infantrymen could subdue them—provided they could get close enough.

The first attack on Fondouk commencing at dawn, 27 March, was intended primarily as a distraction. Patton wanted the 34th Division to pressure the Pass's southern flank to draw German forces in from other areas.[26] One particular section of the long Haouareb range was thought to be lightly defended, so the 34th Division maintained hopes they might actually succeed in taking the area.[27] As soon as the two lead regiments—the 135th and the 168th—started advancing, however, German artillery began blasting.[28] The infantry managed to crawl through the withering barrage only to be shellacked by mortar and MG fire a few hundred yards shy of the range. An arduous battle raged for three days. Elements of the 168th Infantry Regiment were able to partially climb Haouareb's steep base but found German defenses impossible to overcome. Confusion and fatigue took a toll. By midnight, 31 March, the two attacking regiments were ordered to pull back a full two miles under covering artillery and MG fire where they could safely reorganize. In satisfying Patton's modest orders to "make a lot of noise," the 34th Division paid a steep price of over 500 dead or wounded men.[29] The only saving grace from the frustrating affair was that a clearer sense of the strength and location of German mountainside positions had been gained.[30] The attackers also discovered tank support was ineffective beyond a certain point because the terrain became impassable to anything but foot soldiers.[31]

Wilkinson and the other 756ers arrived as plans solidified ahead of a second attack—this time, the pass itself was the objective, and committed Allied troop strength was three times what the 34th Division had employed during their ill-fated attempt.[32] On 4 April, the 34th Division was attached to the British IX Corps—putting the Americans completely under British control.[33] The new plan included British forces attacking the rear of Rhorab (north of the pass), with tanks from the British 6th Armoured Division targeting the pass at a later stage. Once the pass was breached, those same tanks could pour through virtually unopposed to capture the key crossroads town of Kairouan twenty-five miles east. The fall of Kairouan would certainly force all remaining German troops to flee northward.

Astonishingly, the plan called for the 34th Division to repeat the *very same attack* on the south side of the pass that had failed the prior week.

In the meantime, the Germans that were burrowed into the southern Haouareb range used the interlude to resupply positions, adjust defenses, and tap reinforcements. One grave concern the 34th Division commanders voiced over the plan was that German gun positions on Rhorab would not be silenced until later in the operation. This meant 34th Division troops would endure the full wrath of German guns from *both* mountains when they jumped off again. The British insisted on the timetable nevertheless. Maj Gen Charles W. Ryder, commanding the 34th, was incredulous. Many of his men purchased additional U.S. government life insurance when they learned of the orders.[34] As a concession, Ryder was promised additional artillery support and even an aerial bombardment prior to his men jumping off, but this brought him little solace.

On Monday, 5 April, Wilkinson and Long accompanied Lt Col Hammack and others on a thorough field reconnaissance of ground between 34th Division positions and German-held Haouareb.[35] The 751st was held in reserve during the first attack and subsequently provided with little more than sketchy infantry reports upon which to prepare.[36] From various vantage points, the tank officers scoured the terrain with sweaty field glasses in search of all advantages, concerns, and dangers. Every now and then, they warily scanned toward German hill positions two miles away. No doubt, somebody somewhere was staring straight back at them. The officers saw little opportunity for a defilade approach. With German eyes sitting roughly 200 feet above the desert floor, the defenders commanded a clear field of view of anything coming their way. The terrain was too level. Although dotted with clumped brush, a few groves of trees, and several dry creeks or "wadis" crisscrossing here and there—nothing could hide an approaching tank column. One stream bed, blessed with flowing water, seemed to offer promise, but further investigation revealed it also too flat and shallow to provide meaningful concealment. Worse, spinning treads were sure to kick up dust as they moved—leaving little doubt that armor accompanied the infantry attack.[37]

Hammack greatly feared AT guns. Just one well-placed German AT gun could disrupt his entire advance. The Germans were sinister experts at disguising AT guns to appear as the most innocuous land features: sand dunes, cacti, haystacks, bushes, trees, logs, or rock piles.[38] They even hid their deadly guns inside mud huts and tossed Arab garb over uniforms—allowing the crews to come and go freely without drawing suspicion.[39] The Germans seemed to particularly enjoy baiting Allied tankers into AT traps by dangling juicy targets openly downrange. One mischievously effective trick was to parade around several light tanks just beyond the effective fire of Allied guns. Many impatient and inexperienced tankers took off toward the enticing bait, only to perish inside carefully crafted kill zones.[40] Consequently, Hammack's officers studied the terrain with painstaking, almost obsessive, attention. Literally *anything* could be a disguised AT gun and *anywhere* could be a scrupulously constructed tank trap.

Without a doubt, the most fearsome German AT gun was the terrifying "88." An 88 originally served as an AA flak gun. It fired one 22-pound, 88mm shell at a blistering 3,700 feet a second—providing the vertical kinetic punch necessary to bring down high altitude bombers.[41] When the same gun was leveled horizontally upon enemy tanks, the results wrought pure devastation. No Allied tank had frontal armor thick enough to withstand an 88mm round fired from under 2,500 yards away. Even at that distance, a heavy AP slug spinning out from the long barrel of an 88 could easily penetrate over four inches of solid steel armor.[42] When positively identified, an 88 position usually drew the instant wrath of Allied troops. The Germans even used *this* to their advantage by constructing AT traps offering the 88 itself as bait. In such cases, smaller sized AT guns would be concealed in front and along the flanks of 88 positions—configured to knock out any Allied tanks maneuvering to engage the 88 they were "allowed" to see. Other 88s might also be positioned nearby for the same purpose.[43] As a result, Allied tankers learned through bitter experience that the first 88 gun to fire was often a lure and should not be engaged immediately.[44] Just listening to Hammack and his associates size up the situation provided an invaluable education to Wilkinson and the others—one that no Fort Knox class, War Department circular, or training "problem" could ever match.

The 751st Tank Battalion fought in M3 "Lee" medium tanks. The M3 mediums carried six or seven-man crews and featured a hull-mounted 75mm gun with limited traverse capability. A fully rotating 37mm turret sat on top. The tank weighed thirty tons with a top speed of 24 MPH.[45] Introduced to North Africa with the British in early 1942, the M3's appearance helped tip the desert war in favor of the Allies. The engine was more reliable, and the 75mm gun packed far more wallop than British tanks could deliver at the time.[46] The M3 withstood a lot of combat abuse, and its armor absorbed much of what the German Army fired at them—save for the dreaded 88. Over 6,000 M3 mediums had been built since introduction—most churned off from Detroit's hastily converted automobile assembly lines.[47] Production ended, however, in December 1942, and the same factories retooled into building new M4 mediums with fully rotating 75mm guns.

In the hours leading up to the attack, activity at the 751st's dusty bivouac kicked into high gear. Despite the hectic material preparations, the officers found time to meet over meals and discuss final battle plans. The operation was set to commence in the predawn hours of 8 April. The 135th Infantry Regiment would move from the south along a wadi running parallel to the Haouareb range at roughly 5,000 yards. The 133rd Infantry Regiment would follow. Once the troops were positioned, an artillery barrage and aerial bombardment would pummel the range to allow the men to attack. The tanks would delay their support until the infantry called them forward.

Wilkinson and Long joined several artillery observers at an observation post (OP) positioned on the side of a nearby hill. In the cool desert darkness, they waited and watched for a telltale flare from the 3rd Battalion, 135th, signaling that the attack line was set. At 0630, that lone flare rocketed high above the desert floor, and the 34th Division artillery immediately opened up with deafening fury. For two straight hours, violent flashes illuminated across the mountainside, sending jagged rocks flying and dust clouds swirling skyward. A relentless thunder rolled over the arid plain as a warm, beautiful sun glided up slowly from behind the pummeled range into a serene blue sky. For the grand finale, Allied bombers were supposed to lumber in overhead and strike the hill at 0830, but the planes never appeared. By 0900, the barrage had lifted and the infantry emerged from their wadi positions to meet the chatter of MGs and dull thumping of mortar bursts. The long artillery barrage seemed to have had no effect whatsoever. The advance moved painstakingly slowly and persisted well into the afternoon, as the men could use only precious brush clumps, cacti, or shallow sandy hummocks for concealment while inching forward.[48] Every now and then, some unlucky infantry man crumpled over, wounded or dead from a gunshot or shrapnel—leaving those around him to wonder if they might fall next. At one point, the men forded a shallow creek lined with gently waving grass and beautiful crimson poppies. After crossing, German reaction grew so severe that the advance faltered within 1,500 yards of Haouareb.[49] To reinvigorate the attack, tanks of the 751st were called forth, but the Germans responded with an artillery barrage—pre-registered to rain down upon the very place. As a result, the Americans were forced to hastily dig slit trenches and hunker down.[50] The tanks tried carrying the fight forward for a while but eventually withdrew for crucial servicing—leaving behind seven knocked out brethren. Some tanks shed tracks after frantically maneuvering to avoid artillery bracketing and were subsequently abandoned; others burned after absorbing lethal German AT hits.[51]

At dusk, the British unleashed another tank attack wave sweeping in from the northwest. Wilkinson and Long watched from their OP as long, boxy Churchill tanks rolled in fits and starts toward the pass—spitting fire from their main cannons and arcing tracer fire from MGs. Swarms of ant-like infantry accompanied them.[52] German reaction was swift and severe, and the Brits' drive also stalled, once several Churchill tanks began to sizzle and burst into flames under the gray twilight. At dawn, 9 April, Wilkinson awoke to find the British position basically unchanged from the previous evening. Those same attacking Churchills sat motionless and smoldering upon the plain, with the Germans still confidently controlling the gap. At first light, the plucky British renewed their attack only to be swamped again in a hail of mortar and AT fire. As a result, three more Churchills exploded and burned, and the advance stalled yet again.[53]

In the late afternoon, Wilkinson and Long descended from the OP to visit the 34th Division's rallying point. There, they discovered that at least nine tanks had been destroyed during the British attacks. When combined with earlier 751st losses, total Allied tank losses stood at sixteen—an entire company. As evening approached on 9 April, German control of Fondouk Pass endured. Their grip, however, was about to become severely tested on the flanks. After night fell, with a low moon setting in the west, the 1st Battalion of the 168th Regiment quietly infiltrated German positions on Haouareb—taking 130 prisoners and capturing several AT guns in a brilliant surprise attack.[54] To the north, the British also took Rhorab and another 100 prisoners as well. With both flanks suddenly under Allied control, British tanks stormed quickly through the gap, and Fondouk Pass finally fell.

The next morning, conditions were safe enough to visit the battlefield. Wilkinson, Long, 1st Sgt Hogan, and the others cautiously walked about, studying one captured German 88 position in particular. The gun showed severe blast damage from a high-explosive round. Two dead Germans lay nearby. Wilkinson ignored their shrapnel-riddled bodies. Positioned near the shattered gun sat the silent hulks of two knocked out M3s. Both came from the 751st Tank Battalion, with one successfully overrunning the position in what appeared to be a desperate charge. That tank was knocked out but hadn't burned. Wilkinson and the others walked over to inspect it more closely. At that very moment, medics were in the process of removing the mangled remains of three dead crewmen from the interior. A dead lieutenant drooped halfway out the top of the 37mm turret. Wilkinson and Long recognized him as a very popular and respected officer they had dined with only a few nights earlier.[55] Now, half the man's head was missing from his lifeless body. Shocked to the core, both Long and Wilkinson looked at each other with the same thought: "This is for real!"[56]

The other M3 was punctured through with several AT holes and completely burned out. Hatches had been thrown opened haphazardly, and shattered ammunition lay strewn about the perimeter. A crewman also lay dead in the nearby sand with a swarm of desert flies already descending upon him. Wilkinson climbed onto the front of the tank to study the AT penetration holes in greater detail. Something smelled of burnt meat. A moment's curiosity caused him to peer down inside the driver's hatch. The driver was still there, hunched against the blackened interior and burned beyond all recognition. His handless arms had contracted upward from the intense heat and his roasted flesh split open in places to reveal yellowed bone and boiled body fat. The gruesome sight sickened Wilkinson instantly and he promptly slid down from the hull—trying to erase the horrible image from his mind. There was nothing more he wanted to see at this site.[57]

The 756ers departed the American wreckage and proceeded toward the pass to inspect the positions of two more abandoned 88s. After looking over the captured guns, the men started venturing further. Off in the distance, a tall British NCO waved his arms frantically as they neared:

"Careful! It's all mined, don' cha know!" he hollered.

The six continued walking forward, but very gingerly, until they encountered a trip wire leading to a live "potato masher" German grenade. At that point, they decided they had seen enough and turned back toward to camp. The two-day battle claimed the lives of eleven 751st tankers—two of them officers. Another seven American tankers remained missing and unaccounted for. British tank losses were even worse. All in all, *fifty-two* Allied tanks lay strewn about the approaches and the interior of the Pass—casualties of mines, artillery, and the dreaded 88s.[58]

The next day, Wilkinson, Long and the others traveled through Fondouk Pass to witness the British advance on Kairouan. The attackers moved fast but suffered losses nevertheless under three separate German aerial bombings. One British tank the 756ers passed had sustained a direct hit during one of those attacks, killing four of the crew. A few Stukas, however, could not stave off the inevitable. As expected, German forces hastily vacated the southeastern plains to stay ahead of the British Eighth Army pressing in from the east and the collapse of Fondouk Pass to the west.[59] Kairouan was secured by 11 April and the key Mediterranean port city of Sousse fell to Allied forces the very next day.[60] On the road between cities, Wilkinson and Long passed long lines of disarmed and dispirited German prisoners being marched away from the front.

On Tuesday, 13 April, the six observers were so exhausted from their experiences they spent most of the day sleeping in camp.[61] The next morning, they hitched a ride on a truck headed to Sousse. Along the way, a strikingly calm British NCO standing alongside the road flagged them down to warn of a German sniper taking pot shots further ahead. His nonchalant advice was to simply speed through. The driver floored the accelerator and passed the stretch without incident.[62] Upon arriving at Sousse, they found a city heavily damaged from multiple bombings. Every building bore battle scars of some sort and many had been reduced to rubble. Rommel's forces had tried establishing a hasty defensive line there but failed, and now British Eighth Army troops poured through heading north. The Brits' morale was sky high. After battling the Germans for nearly three long years, cheery veterans of the North Africa campaign boasted openly of "giving the Germans a sample of Dunkirk."[63]

On 15 April, the 756th observers backtracked by truck toward Kairouan where they hoped to link up again with the 751st Tank Battalion. They came upon a broken-down British tank at the side of the desolate, dusty road and a frustrated crew attempting repairs. Seeing this, the men of the 756th asked the truck driver to stop nearby. They piled out and asked the British crew if they could help. At that very moment, one crewman shouted, "Dive Bomber!" and the low hum of an engine soaring high overhead broke into a whining crescendo. Wilkinson and the others scrambled away, running as far into the desert as possible before throwing themselves flat against the dirt. The British crew joined the rush—except for one dogged man. The sole hold-out, apparently tired of running countless other times, muttered a few obscenities and kept working on the tank. The Stuka's perfectly delivered payload struck through the turret before erupting—ripping the tank from the inside out in one terrific explosion and swallowing the stubborn crewman in a massive gust of flames and jagged tank parts. As the German plane engine faded off in the horizon and bits of smoldering wreckage tumbled to a halt in the surrounding scrubland, the stunned witnesses sat in momentary silence. Then, one by one, the British survivors quietly stood up, walked toward the burning hull and began collecting the body parts of their dead friend now blown about the perimeter. "Here's Tommy's hand," one proclaimed with disquieting frankness while retrieving a severed limb still blushed with fading life.[64] Believing it best to leave the crew in mourning, the men of the 756th returned to their truck—peppered with shrapnel holes but otherwise roadworthy—and continued on their way.

They arrived where the 751st was supposed to be but had since moved on. After spending the rest of the evening pursuing conflicting leads, they gave up searching and settled in for the night at Tebessa, Algeria.[65] The next morning, they backtracked toward Bou Chebka on the Tunisian border and finally located the 751st bivouacked serenely in a pine forest. The unit had been pulled away from the front and not expected to return to action anytime soon. With no further combat to observe, the 756ers focused on returning to their own unit. The 751st tried releasing them, but II Corps HQ refused to sign off on the transfer—claiming the assignment was "indefinite" and that Wilkinson and the others needed to "observe" the 751st for at least two more weeks.[66] The fact there was little to "observe" except officers playing poker, men washing clothes, or old Hollywood movies flickering after dark meant nothing to the paper pushers further up the chain.[67]

The next morning, Wilkinson caught a ride to Tebessa for a minor errand. There, he encountered remnants of the 752nd Tank Battalion—an old nemesis of the 756th. Nobody was really sure how or why the bad blood had started between them, but the rivalry smoldered the entire time both units trained at Fort Lewis. Despite those murky tensions, Wilkinson befriended one of the 752nd officers. When he discovered the unit was in town, he tried looking up this old acquaintance but discovered most of the original officers were gone. The unit had been devastated during the North Africa campaign—some from battle attrition but mostly because men and equipment were slowly siphoned away to replenish the rolls of other decimated armor units.[68] Only a small Fort Lewis remnant remained. In fact, the 752nd Tank Battalion existed on paper only. The leftovers were reconstituted as the "2642nd Replacement Depot" awaiting reassignment.[69] With self-effacing humor, the few familiar faces told Wilkinson that they had become "The North Africa Branch, Armor School."[70]

Another monotonous week dragged by for the 756th men in limbo "observing" at the 751st bivouac. On Friday, 23 April, the 751st moved from Bou Chebka to Morsott twenty-five miles north of Tebessa, with Wilkinson and the other 756ers in tow.[71] The first night brought a washout, leaving everyone soaking wet and wretched. Wilkinson learned the U.S. 1st Armored Division was also camped nearby, so the next day he sought out several officers he knew who were assigned to that outfit. He was particularly interested in talking to anyone who had experienced desert combat from inside light tanks. All his observations with the 751st were of medium tanks in action—both British and American versions. From what he could tell, light tanks had been relegated to minor support roles or were not being committed at all. Over the past three years, AT guns had become much larger with greater firing ranges. A "heavy" AT gun in 1940 was the 47mm. Now, with more powerful 75mm, 76mm, and 88mm AT guns dominating the battlefield, any tank equipped with a gun smaller than a 75mm performed from a severe disadvantage.[72] The M5 light's biggest gun was only a 37mm. Wilkinson feared the 756th's fifty-four M5 lights might already be obsolete before ever seeing action. After a few conversations, though, he felt somewhat reassured light tanks still filled a combat role.[73]

Wilkinson wondered when the 756th would finally get their chance to fight the Germans. He knew that his unit had moved from Port Lyautey to Arzew in his absence.[74] That journey put them 300 miles closer—but still 500 miles away from the action. The war in Tunisia was winding down with weeks—perhaps only days—remaining. Rommel's forces sat boxed into the northeastern corner of the territory, with the Mediterranean at their backs and no hope of escape. On all sides, Allied forces squeezed in on them like a vice. Wilkinson wondered if the 756th had time to even make the journey to Tunisia while the Afrika Korps still existed. Regardless of the near future, the young captain now just wanted to be back with his company.

The six-week assignment to Tunisia was well worth the time—yielding some practical and invaluable lessons. The unforgiving battlefield revealed very quickly what worked and what did not. Certain theoretical textbook assumptions regarding armor employment had been completely tossed out the window. For example, tank commanders in combat never "buttoned up" their hatches because they couldn't properly monitor events around them.[75] A tiny hatch periscope simply did not provide an adequate field of vision. Also, *all* tank crewmembers—not just the commander—had to help identify targets and remain vigilant to all other threats. Five sets of eyes worked much better than one.[76] Because casualties were inevitable, every crewman needed a functional understanding of his comrades' roles and the confidence to assume another's job at a moment's notice.[77] It was imperative, too, that *everyone* learned to use a compass, read a map, and navigate at night.[78] Finally, the six 756th observers discovered that training was a never-ending process and one could never have "too much" gunnery practice.[79]

Regarding the keys to successful combat leadership, one longstanding military truism remained the same: The best officers led from the front. Enlisted men demonstrated far more willingness to face danger when an officer moved out ahead of them. Platoon leaders, especially, had to set good examples. In those times when a tank platoon was divided into two sections, the platoon leader should always lead the foremost section. Good officers also refrained from overbearing behavior. One unmistakable cultural trend was a growing sense of egalitarianism among the ranks. In the past, an officer could issue an order and expect blind obedience. The modern citizen soldier, however, was often literate, inquisitive, and independent minded. He needed to know *why* he was being asked to undertake a specific action. Although battlefield conditions didn't always allow the luxury of relaxed and thorough explanations, tank officers were still encouraged to explain mission objectives to their tank commanders whenever possible. This way, the men were more apt to "buy in" to the task and perform at higher levels—simply because they understood the details and the aims.[80]

Tunisia yielded several other useful tips as well. For example, ricochet bursting was very effective. This was accomplished by setting a high explosive (HE) charge on short delay and then firing the round several yards short of the target. The projectile would bounce, burst over a position, and deliver up to five times the blast effect than was otherwise accomplished by hitting the spot directly.[81] This tactic proved especially useful against stubborn foxhole positions and even above the open hatches of German armor. In battle, Allied tankers learned to be leery of German tanks playing "possum" after being hit. Many times, German tank crews would play dead only to fire again once combat conditions returned to their favor.[82] A good rule of thumb was to keep blasting a German tank until it burned.[83] Lessons like these were very easy to disseminate among the 756th tank crews training in Arzew.

April neared to a close, but still no transfer orders arrived releasing the men back to the 756th. Wilkinson, Long, and the other four NCOs became so frustrated over the situation that they decided to take action. Wilkinson volunteered to travel the eighty miles west to Tabarka where the II Corps HQ was located and untangle the reasons behind the delay. The next morning, 30 April, he boarded a truck headed in that direction. After a long, uncomfortable ride, he arrived at the Corps HQ and met with the adjutant—who did some sleuth work and located the missing orders for Wilkinson and the others. They had been cut six days earlier—but misplaced due to a "failure of communication." Recognizing the error, the adjutant cut new orders on the spot, signed them, and handed them straight over to Wilkinson. The truck ride back to the 751st bivouac was another eighty miles of bone-jarring bumpiness, but Wilkinson felt like he had hit a game-winning home run the entire way. When he arrived waving the new orders, his fellow 756ers felt that way as well.

The next morning, the six men packed their belongings and boarded a hot, dusty French passenger train departing Tebessa for Constantine, Algeria. Most passengers were local Arab civilians, so the American tankers felt like the lonely foreigners they were.[84] Constantine itself was built along a magnificent river gorge. The small city had also become the temporary home of a number of Allied support units. The men happened upon an American general who noticed their armor insignia and struck up a conversation. When the general learned of their unit attachment, he informed them the 3rd Division had just been ordered from Arzew to Tunisia to help finish off Germans forces still holding out around Tunis.[85] In fact, the 3rd Division was expected to arrive in Constantine in less than two days.[86] This surprise news drew their immediate excitement. After double checking his pocket papers, however, the general cautioned that the 756th Tank Battalion was not listed on the same travel orders. As far as he could tell, the unit would remain in Arzew—indefinitely. Disheartened, Wilkinson, Long, and the others could not help wondering if they were being excluded because of their light tanks.[87]

The next morning, the disappointed tankers hitchhiked to an airport twenty miles outside of Constantine. After waiting a day, they piled aboard a packed C-47 to weather a bumpy flight to Algiers. After another twenty-four-hour delay, the group boarded a second plane heading westward—touching down at 1730 at the La Senia Aerodrome outside of Oran. A truck from the 756th awaited them as they landed, and the tired men climbed in the back. An hour later, they pulled into the battalion HQ bivouac at St Leu. Sweeting and many familiar faces warmly welcomed them as they arrived.[88] With the 3rd Division now gone, the 756th Tank Battalion (L) found themselves with no infantry unit to support and an uncertain future, but the six Tunisian combat observers were grateful to finally be home.

U.S. 34th Infantry Division

CHAPTER 8

Bizerte Bystanders: May 1943 to 15 September 1943

On 7 May, the 756th Tank Battalion (L) was formally detached from the 3rd Division and attached to the I Armored Corps.[1] Without a "parent" infantry division with which to train, an independent tank battalion essentially became an orphan. The situation was beyond concerning. Nobody wanted to end up like the 752nd—cannibalized by other tank units down to a handful of replacements.[2]

Wilkinson, Long, and the four NCOs relished their roles as the temporary stars of the outfit. Sweeting, Dolvin, and everyone down the ranks wanted to hear of their experiences and observations. For several days, the six Tunisian combat observers recounted the same stories and lessons learned over and over to anyone who asked.

The Battalion HQ moved thirty-two miles from St Leu to rejoin the other tank companies camped along the Chelif River after LST landing exercises.[3] The weather was beautiful, the roads clear, and the Mediterranean views as stunning as ever. The reunited battalion formed a new bivouac on a hilly, treeless area among vineyards and well-cultivated farms.[4] The location was not too far away from Pont du Chelif—a critical bridge spanning the Chelif River, but the nearest town of any size was Mostaganem, situated several miles southwest along the coast. The battalion vacated the Arzew area to make room for new units arriving for FAITC training. This new camp near the river was only temporary until those wearing shoulder stars up the chain figured out what to do next with the outfit.

To keep busy, the men washed the tanks and repainted new desert camouflage schemes on their hulls.[5] To hide their handiwork from any prying German planes, camouflage nets were strung above each one. To stay physically fit, the men participated in daily calisthenics, bayonet drills, and short marches ending with long refreshing swims in the Mediterranean.[6] Friendly boxing matches were arranged pitting officer against officer and enlisted man against enlisted man.[7] To guard against heat stroke, Sweeting ordered everybody to cut one pair of khaki slacks into shorts.[8] A steep hill towered next to the campsite, and the companies took turns running to the summit each morning immediately after calisthenics.[9] The two best B Company runners were Lt Redle and Sgt Daniel Pompey, the communications sergeant. At thirty-six years, Pompey was one of the oldest men in the company,[10] but he was also in extraordinary physical shape and absolutely relished beating his younger rivals to the hilltop—especially the athletic ones.[11] Prior to the war, the dark mustachioed Californian worked as a government fish inspector in San Francisco and always told amusing, colorful stories of his wild and varied life before landing his patronage job.[12] Pompey's only cross-county competition was Redle, and the two eagerly raced past everyone in their private competition to better the other. After a few days watching the races, Wilkinson decided to use their rivalry to the company's advantage. He instructed Pompey to lead the company up the hill, but he put Redle at the rear. He then announced that whoever Redle passed would receive an extra duty. Three or four heavier-set guys in the company always ended up huffing and puffing near the back. Redle kept them moving but never had the heart to actually pass them.[13]

The battalion set up gunnery ranges and drilled using everything from .45-caliber pistols and Tommy guns to the M5s' 37mm main guns.[14] To keep his men focused, Wilkinson offered various prizes for shooting accuracy.[15] On 9 May, Major Dolvin, Sgt Richter, and several other NCOs were sent to Tunisia as battlefield observers, but the last German hold-out cities of Tunis and Bizerte fell the day before—leaving Dolvin and Richter with nothing to observe except 100,000 prisoners being processed.[16] When the men returned, they described the whole scene as "hectic."[17] Camp life had also been hectic for Wilkinson after his own return from Tunisia—so much so, he wasn't able to call the entire company together until 13 May to formally relate his own battlefield observations.[18]

Despite the robust training and conditioning schedule, Lt Col Sweeting was unsatisfied with progress—especially regarding physical fitness. Perhaps the "Truscott Trot" inspired him, or perhaps Wilkinson and Long's Tunisian observations troubled him, but the young West Pointer decided his well-practiced tankers should become top notch athletes as well. On 16 May, Sweeting arranged for the battalion to move another twenty-two miles east to Petit Port, a tiny settlement on the Mediterranean coast.[19] The men immediately fell in love with the picturesque location. Majestic, aromatic cedar trees covered the nearby hills and a tranquil azure sea lapped along pristine beaches. The location seemed more of a resort than a military camp.[20] Every morning, Sweeting ordered the men to run two miles through thick surf sand before taking exhausting cross-country hikes through neighboring hills. MG and tank gunnery practice was held every day on the beach—and after many hours, raw sunburns peeled into dark tans. To cool down, the men swam every day—sometimes for up to ten hours at a stretch.[21] T/5 Ed Sadowski especially enjoyed the activity.

Each company formed beach volleyball teams and scheduled spirited matches against each other.[22] B Company's team, anchored by T/5 Paul Tirpak and Sgt Charles Graffagnini proved unbeatable. The tall, thin 23-year-old Graffagnini had been an all-star basketball player previously in his native Louisiana.[23]

In terms of morale, Sweeting's relocation of the battalion to Petit Port was a stroke of genius. The men worked long, hard hours but felt relaxed the entire time, as if on holiday.[24] Even a lecture about enemy mines was strangely soothing when taught upon a beautiful beach.[25] The only one who suffered seemed to be the poor Catholic Army chaplain who traveled sixty miles from Oran every Sunday to hold Mass for the men.[26]

During the few blocks of idle time—usually late evenings—the men shared their greatest hopes and deepest fears. Sometimes they spoke of professional or vocational aspirations. Other times they talked of girlfriends or wives and their fears of losing them. With the North Africa campaign now over, speculation swirled over where they might go next and how long the conflict would last.[27] Everyone simply wanted to fight, win the war quickly, and return home.[28] T/5 Tirpak, one of the lucky guys with a doting sweetheart at home, emerged as the company's eternal optimist. When conversation turned glum, the big Clevelander always proclaimed brightly:

"The war's going to end tomorrow and we'll be home the day after that!"[29]

If physical strength and the power of conviction was all that was needed to make that happen, then Tirpak was the first soldier anyone would call upon.

The battalion maintenance crews struggled with mechanical issues demanding ongoing attention. Most M5s had already logged over 1,000 miles of service and required extensive overhauls.[30] At the very least, every single tread pad had to be unbolted, removed, turned over, and bolted back again to assure even rubber wear.[31] The M5's quirky Cadillac engines needed regular synchronization to prevent shifting problems,[32] and a finicky electrical busbar and a weak thrust washer in the transmission caused untold headaches for the mechanics—making them scrounge around constantly for replacement parts.[33]

With the men's physical conditioning program running in high gear, the kitchen crew also scurried about in search of supplemental calories—especially in the form of flour and meat. The battalion could not convince the Army to increase their food allotment, but this did not prevent the kitchen from securing added provisions through creative methods. The company generally received an overallotment of Army gasoline, so Mess Sgt Adlard and 1st Sgt Hogan contacted a nearby infantry unit over-stocked with flour and baking soda but starving for fuel. One five-gallon can of gas yielded twenty-five pounds of flour. Half the company's pancakes were provided by swapping gas for grain. Wilkinson was kept out of the loop. There was nothing unethical about trading supplies with other units, but such activities were considered improper for officers, so the NCOs organized the swaps while leaving the officers uninformed. At the same time, officers learned not to ask—especially when thick fresh beef mysteriously appeared on plates being served out of the B Company kitchen. One evening, 1st Sgt Hogan, T/5 Roy Anderson, and Montana rancher Sgt Ray Colley knocked a local cow in the head with a ball-peen hammer. Whose cow it was, they never said. But in the still of the night, they quietly butchered the beast, buried the innards in a slit trench, and gave the rest to the B Company kitchen.[34] Hunger did, indeed, drive young men to extremes, but a bland diet and an unsympathetic Army quartermaster also bore some responsibility.

On 17 May, the beachcombing battalion received a reminder they were still part of a war. Urgent orders arrived instructing the 756th to paint all vehicles with fresh stars and appropriate tactical markings, crate up any extraneous materiel, and prepare for imminent ship transport.[35] Then, as usual, nothing happened. The battalion sat and waited for a several days. During the dead of night on 21 May, a swarm of planes passed overhead. The hum of the engines sounded oddly different from the usual Allied flyovers. The next morning the battalion learned Oran had been hit by German bombers. Even though the battalion lingered at Petit Port, all recent signs screamed of something big in the works. The amphibious refresher training at Arzew, the high gear physical conditioning, the recent "ship movement" orders, and now the German aerial attack—all pointed to some impending new operation.

During the last week of May, Sweeting sent the battalion tanks tearing through the nearby hills practicing complicated tactical problems. Each company took turns "battling" tanks from the other two companies. Sweeting was so pleased with the results, he threw a lavish beach party afterwards complete with wine and fresh lemonade.[36] On 31 May, a seasoned British officer visited the battalion and lectured the men on what to expect and what to do if captured by the enemy. His talk was spellbinding and informative—but also hair-raising and sobering.[37] The men considered his appearance as another clue the battalion was heading into battle.

For many stationed in the area, Tuesday, 1 June 1943 began as just another sweltering Algerian morning. For the 756th, however, the day marked the beginning of a third year of service—with many battalion veterans yet to see any combat at all. Lt Col Sweeting grew edgy over their latest movement delays and sent the companies off into the hills again for more tactical training. This time, he was far more critical in his evaluations—particularly regarding position strength. The new round of maneuvers lasted until Saturday morning when orders finally arrived directing the battalion to move out on Monday at dawn.[38] The training promptly ended and the men quickly packed before taking one last dip in the Mediterranean.[39] Atabrine, the bitter anti-malarial drug was administered to everyone orally, inducing roiling nausea in some.[40] Even those severely sickened by the side-effects were ordered to keep taking it daily.[41]

At 0700 on 7 June, the 756th left its seaside paradise and backtracked toward Oran via convoy. Instead of turning north into the city, however, the battalion was directed to head south, deep into the desert. Along the way, I Armored Corps commander Maj Gen George S. Patton Jr. dispassionately watched them thundering by. The change in course was unexpected and puzzling—somewhat reminiscent of the move from California to Virginia a year before. The men were reassured this desert diversion was all part of Patton's plan.[42] At least they had not been forgotten.

After traveling a hot and dusty 133 miles, most tanks, trucks, and half-tracks pulled into a new battalion bivouac around 2000 at Magenta—an isolated Arab town roughly thirty-five miles south-southwest of Sidi-Bel-Abbès and ninety miles from Oran.[43] Several tanks broke down along the way—overly stressed from the high heat—and maintenance crews remained behind working busily to get them moving again.

The new camp was established at the northern edge of the Sahara, situated in a sandy grassland valley plain bracketed with hills peppered with sparse vegetation. Many grand, old pine trees adorned the valley, and Wilkinson found the setting curiously pleasant.[44] Perhaps the semi-arid climate reminded him of central Texas. Soon after arrival, approximately 120 battalion men fell ill from food poisoning— likely the result of a dinner stop in Sidi-Bel-Abbès. Most sat sidelined for twenty-four hours.[45] Those unaffected prepared camp the following day, and by Wednesday, everyone was thrown right back into the thick of training.[46] A flag signal class and radio classes were added to the program,[47] and newcomers received a crash course in vehicle maintenance.[48] Dancing kites soared high over the desert floor and the tankers practiced shooting them down with turret-mounted .50-caliber anti-aircraft MGs.[49]

The days were oppressively hot—far drier and stifling than any other place the men had camped. The horrific midday heat led to an altered training schedule allowing for several hours of afternoon rest. The lost time was recovered by extending field exercises into late-night hours—when the air became much cooler. As a result, old movie showings were delayed until midnight.[50] Fresh water was so valuable that clothing had to be hand washed in gasoline.[51]

The flies were dreadful. They swarmed, pestered, and nipped constantly and refused to be shooed away. The only way to stop them was to kill them.[52] Evening mosquitos were just as aggressive. Sleep netting was an absolute must. During afternoon naps, the men tied back their tent flaps in hopes of capturing the occasional breeze but the netting always stayed in place. Lt Fazendin was not much of a nap taker, whereas his fellow B Company officers guarded their midday sleep jealously. Fazendin was also an avid harmonica player and had recently purchased an ocarina. During those quiet Magenta siestas, he unsuccessfully attempted to master the small flute-like instrument—over and over and over again. To finally get him to stop, Redle and Kremer dipped the mouthpiece into a dissolved Atabrine solution when the lieutenant briefly stepped out of the officers' tent, and then returned to their cots and pretended to sleep. Fazendin returned and sounded two notes before the bitter taste caused him to spit out a few choice words of disgust.[53] Redle and Kremer clenched their pillows to keep from laughing out loud.

To correct a glaring U.S. Army training deficiency, map reading and the use of polar coordinates were taught to all battalion members.[54] Polar coordinates are a method of determining an exact location by measuring distance and using a reference angle on the 360-degree horizon. More importantly, everyone learned how to use a compass. Wilkinson put Fazendin in charge of the compass class for B Company, and the innovative lieutenant designed an elaborate wilderness course. The route twisted and turned over several rugged miles and had to be navigated at night. At the finish line sat several parked supply trucks. Fazendin figured that if he divided up teams of mixed ranks, the higher ranks would end up doing all the work and the lower ranks would learn nothing. To avoid this, compass teams were chosen with only sergeants on one team, corporals on another, etc. The remaining teams comprised either privates first class or privates. At midnight, the teams were driven around the course in closed canvas trucks in ways intended to disorient them and then dropped off in the middle of nowhere. Each team had to navigate to the finish line within a set time. The higher enlisted ranks succeeded without difficulty, as did most of the lower ranks. Two teams of privates, however, got lost. One straggled over the finish line well past the deadline, and the other never showed up. At 0900 the following day, Battalion HQ received a phone call from an artillery unit. The missing team had wandered into their bivouac some fifteen miles away.[55]

Wilkinson was very pleased with Fazendin's compass course work and even more impressed with his growth as a leader. Earlier on in his career, the energetic lieutenant had tended to push his rank—consequently irritating many of the enlisted men he led.[56] Now, his men absolutely loved him. To his fellow officers, he was "Faz," but his platoon affectionately nicknamed him "Wild Thing" because he was willing to do or try almost anything.[57] Wilkinson was also impressed with Lt Winlock, who had joined only recently, while Wilkinson was traveling in Tunisia. The former deputy sheriff may have dreaded lizards, but he feared little else and never missed an opportunity to unleash his wicked sense of humor.[58] Fazendin, Winlock, Redle, and Kremer ran the B Company platoons like clockwork, but the duty roster never stayed set for long. A tank company always ebbed and flowed with personnel changes—either temporary or permanent. Lt Kremer was sent to the I Armored Corps logistics school and several enlisted men transferred out to other battalion roles or to take advantage of plum promotion opportunities.[59] To fill the new company vacancies, on 16 June a new officer, 2nd Lt Roland V. Hunter, arrived with fourteen enlisted replacements.[60] All were integrated into crews or given other company roles. Roughly a week later, four of the recent transferees were sent away on temporary duty serving as MPs with the Corps HQ.[61]

In late June, the battalion's focus shifted away from assimilating replacements to designing more rugged field training exercises for the tanks. On 29 June, the camp was tossed into a tizzy over rumors that enemy parachutists might try sabotaging their tanks. Guard duties doubled, but nobody unwelcome ever dropped in.[62] By early July, particular emphasis was placed on live gunnery practice. Everything was fired—from carbine rifles and Tommy guns to the 37mm cannon and a new secret shoulder-fired AT rocket nicknamed a "bazooka."[63] Tracer ammunition use was strictly prohibited on account of the dry conditions and dangers of igniting uncontrollable brush fires.[64] At Fort Ord in the summer of '42, a B Company platoon accidentally started a brush fire while on maneuvers. A *single* .30-caliber tracer round was the culprit. The red marker paint had worn off the tip after repeated wiping to remove moisture and was consequently missed during inspection. To contain the fire, the platoon hastily drove the tanks in circles around the growing conflagration. It eventually burned itself out, but Captain Terry later received a thorough upbraiding by the post commander over the incident.[65]

On 9 July, the battalion participated in an enormous training maneuver involving several other Army units. The exercise kicked off in the dead of night—beginning with a long convoy trip under blackout conditions. In a good omen, not a single vehicle broke down along the way.[66] A "battle" commenced at sunrise in a desolate, parched valley and unfolded over the entire day. The battalion pulled back from the operation late in the afternoon to service the tanks. Everything and everyone ended up plastered in dust, but the battalion received glowing reviews from the group commander.[67] The men and tanks returned to their Magenta bivouac early in the afternoon of 10 July to clean and rest. There, they learned Allied forces had invaded Sicily and were battling at that very moment.[68] They also discovered the I Armored Corps had since been re-designated as the Seventh Army. The Seventh Army, under Patton's command, had hit the southern coast of Sicily in the first attack wave. The 3rd Division had taken part in the beach assault. The news stung, as the 756th had obviously been passed over as participants. Some tankers held out hope their tanks might join once a beachhead was secured, but the next day the battalion was instead put under the command of the U.S. Fifth Army.[69] Three days after that, the battalion prepared for another major move—causing talk of Sicily to flare all over again.[70] Wilkinson received an advance map of the convoy route, however, and it clearly showed a destination of Bizerte, Tunisia.[71]

The latest news felt like another kick to the crotch. Puzzled battalion officers inquired up the command chain and were told, in essence, that the Sicilian operation already employed plenty of tanks—negating the need for any more.[72] The 2nd Armored Division, and the 753rd and 70th Tank Battalions got that call, but the 756th was passed up.[73] The explanation was difficult to swallow for tankers still waiting to fight after two full years of training. Some men wondered if their day would ever come.

On 18 July, the 756th began a marathon 876-mile overland journey to the port city of Bizerte.[74] The wheeled vehicles formed a long convoy—setting out at 0600. The tanks were secured upon rail flatbeds with most of the personnel dispersed among the coach cars of five different trains.[75] The motor convoy trip required four straight days upon road conditions ranging from fair to poor.[76] On the last leg of the journey, the tired travelers passed scores of bombed-out tanks, twisted truck chassis, shattered guns, and even entire derelict trains burned out and left to rust and bleach in the harsh elements.[77] The convoy halted at 1600 hours on 21 July in a prescribed staging area three miles south of Bizerte.[78] The vacant hillside location sat approximately a mile from Lake Bizerte—not far from the harbor channel linking the lake to the Mediterranean.[79] The views were stunning. Over a thousand ships could be seen anchored about upon the waters, with military units of all types camped everywhere along the rim of the fifty-square-mile lake.[80] The earliest arrivals spent the remainder of the day digging sumps, setting up the kitchen, and preparing camp for the influx of their comrades.[81] The others arrived in dribs and drabs over the next few days, with the last train arriving on 28 July.[82]

Wilkinson rode in the motor convoy with eighteen other B Company men. When the rest of B Company arrived later by train, he was disappointed to discover Lt Hunter had behaved very poorly in his absence. First, the company's newest officer illegally sold a carbine for sixty dollars to a sergeant in Magenta. Then Hunter and two enlisted men, Sgt James H. Gilkerson and T/5 Randolph H. Perdue, tasked with loading and securing the tanks on the flatbed cars. While on the job, Hunter drank himself to a point where he could no longer stand and left the other two to finish. Embarrassed, Gilkerson and Perdue rolled their sodden lieutenant under a tank until he sobered up. When Hunter finally woke, the day was late and they were all hungry. Hunter located a boxcar stacked with canned goods and made Perdue climb through some broken slats to steal a couple boxes. British guards patrolling the railyard observed the pilfering and arrested all three of them. Hunter misrepresented himself as a colonel and bluffed the guards into returning them to their unit.[83] The guards released them but not without a full report eventually landing on Sweeting's field desk in Bizerte. Sweeting's first instinct was to court martial Hunter,[84] but he decided instead to transfer him to Service Company for a fresh start and a chance at rehabilitation.[85]

As the battalion settled into their newest hillside home and sorted through such personnel problems, Sicily's capital of Palermo fell to 3rd Division troops.[86] Three days later, 25 July, Italy's Grand Fascist Council removed and arrested Mussolini to form a new government. Ultimately, Marshal Pietro Badoglio took charge.[87] In the days that followed, massive flying formations featuring hundreds of Allied planes rumbled over the skies of Bizerte toward Sicily.[88] The men of the 756th could only wonder what horror awaited those on the receiving end.

The battalion received a large shipment of tank treads, and the maintenance crews worked round the clock replacing worn out tracks.[89] For some reason, the Army wanted all the national star markings changed from white to yellow.[90] At the end of a feverish few days of cleaning, wiping, repairing, and repainting, all tanks and vehicles were lined up for Sweeting's inspection and the lieutenant colonel walked away satisfied.[91]

Fazendin learned by V-mail that he was the proud new father of a baby daughter.[92] In honor of the news, Fazendin found his bed short sheeted when he tried going to sleep that night. None of the officers owned up to the prank, but Winlock's involvement was strongly suspected.[93]

Once camp was settled, Wilkinson and Captain Lewis traveled southeast to Tunis to study captured German equipment and survey battle damage.[94] During the journey, they stopped to walk the ruins of ancient Carthage—leveled by the Romans in 146 BC.[95] They found the stone foundations completely deserted. No officials, no visitors, no locals, not even a caretaker could be seen anywhere. Lewis was an avid, lifelong student of history. Over the many months of their friendship, Wilkinson and he spent long hours discussing and comparing the past to current events. Now, like their centurion predecessors, the two American captains strolled the windswept ruins of the ancient city, talking terrain and tactics and imagining the epic battles that once raged around them. Toward the end of the excursion, Lewis reached down and pocketed a small chunk of fluted marble to send home as a souvenir.[96] Wilkinson raised an eyebrow and gently admonished his longtime friend for the petty theft.

"Hell," Lewis rationalized. "The folks back in Watts have never seen anything like this!"[97]

* * *

On 7 August 1943, Armed Forces radio announced a yellow alert. Twenty-eight enemy medium bombers had been seen departing Sardinia and were expected to strike Bizerte around 2200. Sure enough, at 2200, the planes appeared. The first ones skirted along the lake rim at top speed, dropping flares. Dozens of searchlights flashed on throughout the area—crisscrossing the sky suddenly with tight sweeping pillared beams of light. Then, the bulk of the German bomber force roared in from all directions, and the heavens filled with strobing ack-ack and swaying tracer fountains of MG fire emanating from every Allied unit stationed in the area. Warships, armed merchant vessels, ground artillery batteries, and AA units all joined a firework display a hundred times more spectacular than the grandest Fourth of July celebration. One by one, outgunned German planes sparkled and burst into flaming comets—spinning down in the lake or disappearing as a flash in the nearby desert. The few survivors of the lethal gauntlet sped off—only to be pursued and intercepted by British night fighter aircraft. The attack was a complete and utter failure. The next morning, Axis Sally of German propaganda radio—in her customarily taunting, yet alluring voice—announced the same attack had resulted in the sinking of three Allied ships with the loss of only two planes.[98] Local listeners found her claims hilarious.

On several other nights the Germans tried similar strikes but never hit much of anything. During one attack, though, they did manage to ignite a small ammunition depot near the lake, killing twenty mules belonging to the French Army.[99] That was their most productive night. Nevertheless, Axis Sally continued broadcasting outlandish claims of Bizerte's destruction beneath conquering German bombers—much to the amusement of the unscathed Allied troops stationed there.[100]

In mid-August, a number of 756ers fell victim to malaria—despite their daily ingesting of the unpalatable Atabrine tablets. Lt Col Sweeting, Major Dolvin, and several other battalion HQ officers were so badly stricken they required hospitalization. Captain Arnold took temporary battalion command and Captain Long served as his acting XO. Then, Fazendin fell ill on 10 August and was transferred to the 53rd Station Hospital. Wilkinson felt fluey as well but remained on duty.[101] The next day, the battalion moved south to Ferryville on the opposite side of the lake. The place featured less flies, less of a crowd, and was not nearly as windy as their previous hill nearer to Bizerte.[102]

During the evenings of 15 and 16 August, German planes attempted more suicidal attacks on Bizerte Harbor—resulting in the usual spectacle of sweeping searchlights, bursting ack-ack, and the flaming, cartwheeling fuselages of doomed gray bombers. This time, spent shrapnel from the attack tumbled about the 756th bivouac but nobody was hurt and nothing damaged.[103]

The next day, news spread of the 3rd Division's capture of Messina. The fall of the port city meant Sicily had completely succumbed to the Allies.[104] Wilkinson learned that the truck company the 756th had helped to cadre earlier in the year served with distinction during the Sicilian campaign. Several members even received Bronze and Silver Stars for valor.[105] Sadly, one man that B Company had sent, T/5 Edd Crabtree, was killed and another, Sgt Isaac Shind, was seriously wounded while serving with the unit.[106] One would think service with a truck company was much *safer* than a tank company, but not necessarily in war.

The men of the 756th celebrated the Sicilian victory by trucking to Bizerte and packing alongside thousands of other GIs for a live show featuring Bob Hope and Francis Langford.[107] The mood was buoyant and electric. The troops may not have directly participated in the Sicilian campaign, but everyone belonged on the same Allied team.

The battalion returned to the ceaseless routine of physical conditioning and field training. A volleyball tournament against neighboring units was arranged, and B Company's team again proved unbeatable—winning ten straight games and taking the series.[108] Fazendin returned from the hospital in time to lead his platoon for battalion maneuvers in the nearby desert.[109] Tragedy struck on 27 August, when one of the assault-gun platoon vehicles overturned during a dawn attack simulation. A young private named Chapman was crushed.[110] His death marked only the second fatality the battalion had experienced since formation.

For some time, Captain Long had suffered from severe stomach ulcers and he finally had to be admitted to the hospital.[111] If the small fiery Texan couldn't recover within thirty days, then he would be forced to return to the States.[112] Long desperately wanted to avoid this fate—at least, until the war was finished. Both

Sweeting and Dolvin returned to their battalion posts, but Dolvin rotated out on separate duty (SD) with the Fifth Army. With Long and Dolvin both absent, Sweeting promoted Wilkinson temporarily to acting Battalion S-3 on 29 August.[113] The job put Wilkinson third in command over the entire battalion—a remarkable achievement for a humble 23-year-old ROTC officer raised on a dusty Texas ranch. In Wilkinson's absence, Redle took charge of B Company.[114]

Wilkinson's new position gave him an unfamiliar "bird's-eye" view of the field exercises. Instead of a company officer participant, he now played the role of field officer judge. A and B Companies engaged in a seesaw series of simulated attacks against one another, but Redle had trouble maintaining his platoon formations. Fazendin's platoon appeared particularly undisciplined throughout the drills.[115] Perhaps the tall lieutenant was still suffering from the lethargic effects of malaria.

Sweeting remained weak after his bout with malaria, but his spirit was more restless than ever. The war news made him edgy and impatient. On 3 September, the British Eighth Army jumped from Sicily across the narrow Strait of Messina and onto the Italian boot tip. The five-mile water crossing was basically unopposed. Every day, waves of Allied bombers departing from North Africa and Sicily pounded further and further up the Italian peninsula. Germany was also getting hammered daily by vast aerial armadas dispatched from England as massive Soviet armies steamrolled in from the east. The rumor mill spun into overdrive on where the Allied troops might strike next. Some thought Italy. Others thought France.[116] Sweeting simply wanted to know if the 756th fit into *any* plan.

On 4 September, the anxious lieutenant colonel told Wilkinson he was dispatching him to Mostaganem to learn what he could directly from the Fifth Army HQ. The next morning, Wilkinson boarded an older C-47 at the Sidi Ahmed airport to endure a 400-mile coast-hugging flight to Algiers.[117] The second leg of the flight didn't leave until the following morning, so Wilkinson stopped by the American consulate again to visit his cousin Nell. This time, she invited him to dinner. A quiet courier was present wearing a leather attaché case attached to his wrist via a light-weight chain. The solemn man never took his eyes off the case. After dinner, the man departed. Nell asked Wilkinson if he wanted to know the contents of the briefcase but swore him to the strictest of secrecy. Of course, Wilkinson agreed.

"He had the terms for surrender for the Italian Army and will be flying to Washington with them tomorrow,"[118] she revealed in very hushed tones. "Even the courier doesn't know it."

Nell went on to divulge that Russia had very nearly signed a separate peace agreement with Germany only a few weeks earlier.[119] Wilkinson wasn't sure what to make of these stunning revelations, as he had grown accustomed to ignoring gossip and taking each day as it came. These claims, however, came straight from the mouth of a U.S. State Department official who happened to be his cousin. In any event, he had to keep all details to himself—no matter what he thought of them.

On 7 September, Wilkinson took a flight from Algiers at 1030, arrived at La Senia, and hitchhiked his way to Mostaganem. He reached the Fifth Army HQ at 1630—arriving with barely enough time to track down the officers Sweeting sent him to see.[120] Unfortunately, he learned nothing other than that the 756th Tank Battalion was *not even listed* on the Order of Battle for the next operation.[121] Wilkinson spent the next few days nosing around desks and asking more questions, but he uncovered little else. While trolling about the Red Cross officers' club in Oran on 8 September, he stopped dead in his tracks upon seeing a large newly posted notice:

"Italy Surrenders – Unconditionally, 5:30 Today. Eisenhower and Badaglio have signed the Armistice."

What Nell had revealed to him turned out to be completely true. Wilkinson grabbed a nearby newspaper and also read of Allied bombers striking Naples the night before.[122] The next day, while visiting a recuperating Captain Long in the 21st General Hospital,[123] news whirled of surprise Fifth Army landings at Salerno Beach south of Naples. Wilkinson flew back to the 756th on September 11—arriving at their Ferryville camp around dusk. Unfortunately, he could tell little more to Sweeting than what had already been reported in the newspapers.[124] Once again, the 756th sat as sidelined bystanders while yet another massive amphibious Allied operation unfolded in the Mediterranean.

The tankers spent the next few days range firing their 37mm main guns while digesting the latest reports. The Fifth Army seemed to be having a rough time establishing a beachhead.[125] The 36th "Texas" Infantry Division attacked toward the coastal town of Paestum and was nearly driven back into the sea by an unexpectedly large presence of German armor in the area.[126] For several breathless hours, the entire operation seemed to hang by a shoestring. Wilkinson knew a number of officers in the 36th Division and would have probably ended up in that unit had he not been selected for armor. He could not help but worry for his friends.

On the morning of 14 September, Wilkinson and Lewis drove to Bizerte Harbor to visit Major Dolvin assigned temporarily at the port HQ. Dolvin's SD work involved organizing sea transport of Army reinforcements for the Salerno beachhead. As the three men visited, the port commander entered the office and notified Dolvin of two available LSTs with enough space to transport an entire tank battalion. He asked if Dolvin knew of any tank outfit prepared to depart immediately. A slow smirk crossed the major's lips and he gestured over toward Wilkinson:

"Well, here's the battalion S-3 of the 756th ...."

He turned and looked squarely at his stunned friend while raising an eyebrow.

"What about it, Captain Wilkinson?"

Wilkinson felt the entire weight of the battalion on his shoulders. This momentous decision was *his* to make. Although he knew of a few battalion men down with malaria and of several tanks currently being serviced, the answer was obvious. He turned to inform the port commander that the 756th would load later that afternoon. The commander acknowledged and told him to notify Lt Col Sweeting immediately.

When Wilkinson told Sweeting, he was taken aback by his battalion commander's reaction. Sweeting was angry. Perhaps he was upset because *he* was not the one who had made the decision. At any rate, Wilkinson had acted properly within his role as battalion operations officer when making the call. Dolvin certainly agreed, and a narrow opportunity window allowed no time for deliberations. News of the move spread like wildfire among the tankers, and the bivouac erupted into a bustling hive of preparations. Tents were immediately stricken and camouflage netting pulled down and packed away.[127] The men were ordered to dispose of all things extraneous. Crates, chickens, and months' worth of precious booty of every shape and size had to be discarded, deserted, or donated to nearby units. Those carrying large wads of cash hurriedly deposited them for safekeeping into Army accounts. Some had amassed huge winnings after months of poker playing and crap shooting. Sgt Graffagnini frugally forwarded all but a paltry $10 of his monthly Army paycheck to his wife and young child back home, but to everyone's astonishment, the crafty gambler deposited an astounding $5,000 in cash winnings before loading up in Bizerte Harbor.[128]

Sweeting's bitterness swiftly dissolved, and the West Pointer turned completely gung-ho for action. Dolvin returned to duty as XO and Arnold was bumped back down to S-3. In turn, Wilkinson officially resumed command of B Company and oversaw his men laboring into the late hours packing, crating, fueling, and servicing. Before the break of dawn, an enormous convoy encompassing all the battalion's tanks, half-tracks, jeeps, and trucks rolled out of Ferryville to the docks of Bizerte where the massive prow doors of two ordinary LSTs sat agape, ready to receive them. B Company and Battalion HQ vehicles were directed toward LST #349. Each one was backed aboard, with most fully secured in under eight hours.[129] Only one maintenance half-track and a tank had to be left on the dock for lack of space. As a result, Sgt Richter, T/5 Tirpak, and seven other B Company members remained ashore awaiting later transport arrangements.[130]

By 2200 on 15 September, the two laden LSTs slipped silently out of Bizerte Harbor into a warm Mediterranean night to glide gently over dark undulating waves. Until both vessels released their moorings, the voyage was classified as "Destination Unknown," but once safely at sea the men received official confirmation that they were two days away from Salerno.[131] This time, no one was surprised. Most went to bed immediately—too exhausted to contemplate the full ramifications of these new orders. Wilkinson was one of them.[132]

At that very moment, a tenuous three-mile-deep beachhead in southern Italy flickered with the flaming wrecks of German panzers and Allied vehicles alike. Infantrymen and paratroopers tangled in private life-or-death struggles with German defenders holding the beach towns of Pasteum to the south, Salerno to the north, and all the high ground in between. Allied Navy destroyers skirted back and forth along the coastline like vigilant sentinels —serving as makeshift artillery while bombers pounded German positions just beyond the main line of resistance. Lightning-fast Luftwaffe fighters and aggravating Axis AA ground units counterstruck with methodical rage—threatening to shove the Allies back into the sea. In the meantime, the British Eighth Army raced overland from the southern tip of Italy with orders to bolster the U.S. Fifth Army's tenuous hold and bust open the beachhead.

Finally, the 756th Tank Battalion was heading into some real combat.

U.S. Fifth Army

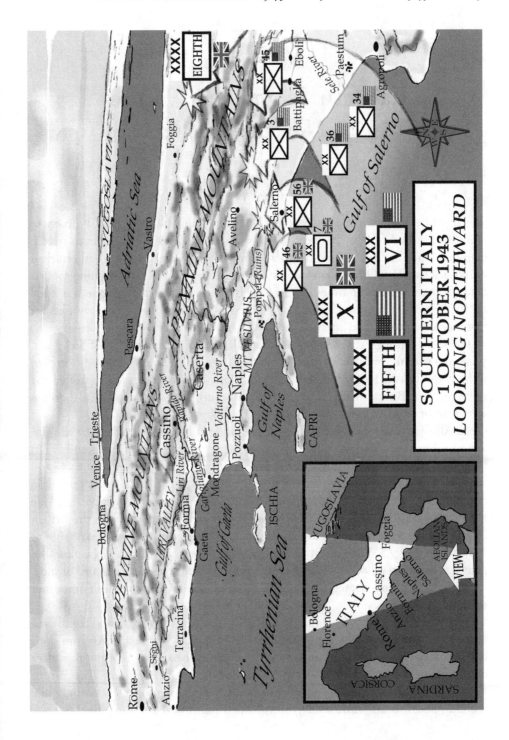

CHAPTER 9

Italy: 16 September 1943 to 22 November 1943

The first streaks of dawn showed clear skies and calm blue waters. The men of the 756th roused from a relatively restful slumber aboard the two LSTs to stretch cramped limbs and rub aching muscles. Some dropped down from tightly stacked bunks below decks. Others crawled out from familiar bedrolls after sleeping topside beneath the stars. By the time the sun fully broke over the sea, everyone was lined up for breakfast. They were not disappointed by the offering. The Navy had yet to serve any guest a bad meal—even lowly Army Joes. Throughout the day, the vessels sliced through calm, smooth waters along the northern edge of Sicily and presented magnificent views of the Aeolian Islands. The gentle voyage put the men in high spirits.[1] As 16 September drew to a close, 600 miles already separated the travelers from Bizerte. Despite an incredibly beautiful and peaceful day, the men were cautioned to expect a rough landing the following afternoon.[2]

An Allied invasion of Italy had been in the works for several months. The surprise announcement of a separate peace with the Italian government on 8 September did little to alter those plans. The planners correctly anticipated German forces would stay and fight—which is one reason why the British Eighth Army was ferried so quickly across the Strait of Messina on 3 September—to gain an important "toe hold" on the Italian peninsula. The Allies' master strategy called upon the British Eighth Army to aggressively push northward up the eastern Adriatic coast side of Italy, while the U.S. Fifth Army landed on the western side south of Naples. The plan was designed to swiftly flush German forces out of the southern third of Italy. As with most grand strategies, the smaller details seemed to play out smoother on paper.

The U.S. Fifth Army was commanded by Lt Gen Mark W. Clark and comprised two corps—the British X Corps and the U.S. VI Corps. The first units from both corps landed along a sixteen-mile stretch of sandy beach on Salerno Bay after midnight on 9 September in an operation codenamed "*Avalanche*." The British 46th and 56th Infantry Divisions hit the beaches near Salerno to the north, while the U.S. 36th "Texas" Infantry Division landed south near Paestum. To the shock of all, German panzers of the 16th Panzer Division unexpectedly prowled the area. Fortunately, the Germans were also caught off guard by fast-moving events. German commanders scrambled over news of the Italian surrender—developing hasty defenses and communication networks and had only begun to take control of Italian coastal fortifications in the region. The panzers led spirited but piecemeal counterattacks upon the 36th Division's beach positions—but spread enough chaos to cause the entire operation to teeter on debacle. U.S. Navy destroyers swept in close to shore, firing their deck guns and helped drive back the panzers.[3] Those brave actions by sea commanders and crews may have saved the day.

The U.S. 45th "Thunderbird" Infantry Division hastily debarked behind 36th Division positions—helping expand the beachhead deep enough that further German counterattacks on the 13th and 14th were more readily absorbed and repelled. Paratroopers from the 82nd Airborne Division were also dropped along the beachhead to reinforce scattered positions until landing craft depositing the first waves of attackers could fetch the 3rd Division from Sicily for added support. In the meantime, elements of the British Eighth Army were diverted from the Adriatic side of Italy to pressure German forces from the rear. This last development, to say the least, was highly embarrassing for U.S. Army staff officers still smarting from those earlier debacles in North Africa, and it was an indirect reason for the 756th Tank Battalion's hasty addition to the Order of Battle.

At noon on 17 September, the small convoy carrying the 756th caught sight of the Italian shoreline in the distance. The ships veered northward, keeping the coastline a safe distance to starboard until reaching the southern approach of Salerno Bay around 1700. Unsure of what they would encounter, hearts raced as all eyes strained to discern every detail in the distance. Countless troop ships and transport vessels hovered about the waters at various angles—some seemingly at rest while others slowly jockeyed around to new positions. Those displaying low waterlines and packed holds patiently awaited turns to approach the beach and disgorge their heaving contents. Countless men milled about restlessly along their railed decks. Other vessels rode high and empty atop buffeting waves away from the scene—steaming back to Sicily or North Africa to fetch more men and supplies. Impatient Navy destroyers cruised up and down the coastline as gray patrol craft buzzed about them like busy bees. Every so often, the destroyers' guns barked fire and the reverberations rolled like fuming thunder across the bay. Along the sandy shore, a long string of smoke pots churned out ground-hugging fog to obscure the bustling beach activity from German observation. Several large transports sat anchored in the surf, debarking streams of OD men and their weapons of war. To the relief of the late-arriving 756ers, no heavy battles seemed to be occurring at the time. At 1800, B Company's LST eased toward an open section of "Green Beach" near Paestum, but the vessel's draft proved too deep for debarkation in the area, and the helmsman was forced to reverse and wait for a deeper approach to become available.[4] At 2200, his turn finally came and, one by one, the tanks and crews landed amid the distant rhythmic booming of ack-ack guns.[5]

The night was moonlit blue and oddly serene. The Germans had withdrawn several miles from the beach to continue the fight on more favorable terms. Pockets of orange and yellow battle fires flickered both near and far, and the rude rows of war sounds never seemed too far away.[6] The groans of truck engines and acerbic smells of gasoline and diesel exhaust mixed in the evening air along with softer scents of moist vegetation, rich soil, and pastoral living.[7] The journey to the new bivouac traced along three miles of highway leading from the beach to a clearing roughly a mile outside of Paestum.[8] The convoy rolled slowly through the night, passing shifting silhouettes of ancient Roman architecture, stone walls, fields, and foliage. Even the mundane seemed ominous. Once the men arrived at their new bivouac, the tanks dispersed and the crews dug hasty foxholes.[9] Several dead Germans still lay about the area—cut down in a firefight only hours earlier. Their rumpled corpses were ignored—as if they might eventually get up and walk away so long as nobody looked their way.[10] With the jolting cracks of artillery and the intermittent chatter of not-so-distant MG firefights wailing like a twisted chorus around them, the men turned in for some restless sleep.[11] At 0300, the western shoreline erupted into a fearsome firework display reminiscent of Bizerte Harbor. The Germans chose the weary hour for an aerial attack, and every gun on every ship in the bay promptly saturated the skies with exploding ordnance.[12] Several stray AA shells burst about the battalion bivouac, but nobody was hurt. A few minutes later, the melee ended just as abruptly as it had begun, allowing the "peace" of night to return. The next morning, the men awoke to discover their bivouac situated in the middle of a large oil supply dump.[13] This revelation was extremely unsettling.

Another battalion motor convoy formed and promptly ventured several miles north to a new bivouac spot just four miles shy of the main battle line.[14] A Company dispersed beneath the covering foliage of an orange tree grove, while B Company positioned in a wooded draw nearby.[15] During the journey, the convoy passed a road curve with six or seven dead American soldiers strewn about like bloody ragdolls—all cut down in a recent firefight.[16] The gory sight came as a cold shock. The tankers were already battling jittery nerves and private doubts over heading into combat. Most had lost their appetites, while others vomited involuntarily from time to time over the stress.[17]

As B Company arrived at their new bivouac location, they found a half-track from Service Company broken down along a nearby roadside. While making repairs, the half-track crew had removed several land mines from their welded side brackets and carefully laid them out on the ground. Pvt Andrew M. Dick was driving the B Company's lead jeep with Sgt Pompey as his passenger. Dick slowed down to clear the half-track but failed to see the mines. When the jeep's left front tire struck one, the engine compartment ruptured in a deafening blast of shredded rubber and suspension parts. The hood burst upward, flipping the windshield completely over onto Dick and Pompey—showering both with shards of glass. Miraculously, other than a few minor scratches and bruises, neither man suffered any serious physical injuries. As the dust settled, Sgt Pompey calmly lifted the mangled windshield frame and extricated himself from the jeep's crumpled midsection—rising to his feet with one more story to add to his long repertoire of tales. Pvt Dick, however, was completely beside himself. B Company members jumped down from nearby vehicles to escort Dick away from the accident, but the young private remained so inconsolable and emotionally affected by the incident that he ultimately had to be medically evacuated.[18]

B Company spent the afternoon digging foxholes and concealing vehicles under shady trees in the wooded grove. German planes passed high overhead intermittently, giving the men the uneasy feeling they were being watched.[19] Meanwhile, back at the beach, the 3rd Division started debarking after making the short sea voyage from Sicily.[20] For once, the 756th actually *preceded* their old divisional attachment in an Order of Battle.

The 756th was formally attached to the "Thunderbird" 45th Division.[21] As a welcoming gesture, Lt Col Ralph Krieger of the 157th Infantry Regiment invited Lt Redle to ride with him to observe an Allied air attack upon front-line German positions near a road junction. Krieger personally ordered the strike as a demonstration to a larger group of officers on the effectiveness of ground–air coordination. The fighter-bombers were instructed to strafe and bomb east of the crossroads on both the north and south sides. As the officers gathered, the planes circled high overhead like hungry birds of prey. At the pre-appointed moment, they swooped down in tandem to begin the attack. To the horror of Krieger and the others, the planes struck south of the junction hitting areas on both the east and west sides. Half their payloads struck Allied troop positions. Disgusted, Krieger turned to Redle and vowed to never call for air support again.[22]

The next day, Sunday 19 September, the battalion's bivouac sites whirred in anticipation of combat. The tanks were serviced, loaded, and readied to fight alongside troops of the 45th Division.[23] During the previous evening, however, German forces withdrew further north—conceding twenty more miles of beachhead to the Allies.[24] The sizable retreat rendered the attack plans unnecessary and so the men stopped preparations and awaited their next movement orders.

The local Italians felt safe enough to emerge from their stone homes and cellar sanctuaries to greet their liberators. They appeared small and undernourished but curious and extremely friendly. Most of the Italian men sported dark mustaches—trimmed much the way American movies depicted them. It was hard to tell if art imitated life or the other way around. Although the locals basically wore rags and patches for clothing, they were too proud to beg. Surprisingly, many spoke English.[25] They reported that the day before the invasion, the Salerno area was free of Germans, but later that same evening an entire panzer division moved in—as if the Germans expected an attack.[26] Around this same time, a rumor floated through the U.S. Army Officer Corps of a 36th Division lieutenant colonel bragging openly in an Oran bar about Salerno landing plans. This "loose lips" incident reportedly took place several weeks before the operation commenced, and the officer was subsequently dismissed from the division.[27] What the Italian locals described seemed to provide some substance to the rumor.

On 20 September, advance units of the British Eighth Army arriving from the southeast linked up with the Salerno beachhead—explaining why the Germans had so easily conceded such a wide swath of territory the prior day. That same morning, at 0830, the 756th moved out in pursuit of them.[28] As they rolled, German and Allied planes performed a deadly aerial ballet high above. Several German ME109s broke free of their pursuers and attacked the empty orange grove just as the last A Company tanks vacated the bivouac.[29]

The journey to the battalion's new position was all of fifteen miles, but the road was so narrow and the traffic so thick moving in both directions, the trip took until 1300 to complete. Distressed civilians traveling on foot or pushing carts full of belongings made a mad haste to escape trouble, while American troops on foot or in vehicles made a mad haste to get into it. The new campsite was near the town of Eboli in the Italian interior, approximately ten miles from the beach, with the bordering terrain becoming more rugged and treacherous.[30] B Company was assigned to the 45th Division's Recon Troop as fire support.[31] The remainder of the 756th was attached to the 180th Infantry Regiment. The pleasant, partially wooded site had served as a German bivouac only a few days earlier and appeared almost move-in ready. A fresh stream ran through the middle of camp and the men were able to bathe and wash personal items upon settling in. After nightfall, the men lay awake listening to an unending duel between an American artillery unit to their rear and a German battery further north. Few could sleep, as rounds from both sides kept howling directly over camp.[32]

The next morning, T/5 Perdue had just finished digging a deeper foxhole when a wolf pack of growling Messerschmitts suddenly emerged above a nearby tree line—obviously aligning for a strafing run straight through the middle of the B Company bivouac. The 180-pound tank driver dove into his freshly dug pit only to be crushed immediately by something far heavier along his entire body. The sudden jolt knocked the breath out of him. As the planes passed, Perdue lifted his head high enough to witness bullet-pierced leaves sheared from nearby trees fluttering peacefully down in the glinting sunlight. Then, mere inches from his own nose, Perdue saw the broad beaming face of T/5 Tirpak. The 210-pounder failed to improve his own foxhole and chose to double up in Perdue's instead. The two men lay frozen in silence for a few more seconds—not daring to move until absolutely sure the terrifying German planes were gone. Finally, Tirpak lifted his muscular frame up and allowed Perdue to take a full breath again. The big athlete then stepped out of the hole and brushed some loose soil off from his OD coveralls.

"The war's going to end tomorrow and we'll be home the day after that!" He beamed, repeating his familiar mantra with jovial assurance.[33]

Nobody from B Company was hurt in the brief, violent aerial attack, but the encounter left many plenty scared.[34] Some deep and wondrous foxholes were excavated in earnest that evening as the company awaited their next orders. The following morning, Tuesday 21 September, the 2nd and 3rd Platoons were dispatched to the 45th Recon's bivouac approximately twelve miles east at Contursi. They were slowed again by roads clogged with the clashing two-way traffic of plodding refugees and hustling troops. At nightfall, both platoons fanned out with the troop to patrol heavily wooded hills flanking the ancient hilltop village.[35] That same evening, Sgt Richter and the nine other B Company men left behind in Bizerte rejoined the company, bringing with them the tank and maintenance half-track that could not be loaded on the earlier LST.[36] Captain Long, now recovered from his stomach ulcers, also rejoined the battalion.

On 22 September, Captain Wilkinson moved the remainder of B Company to Contursi to be closer to the action.[37] 2nd Platoon remained on patrol throughout day, but 3rd Platoon returned in the early morning hours and reported enduring German bombing and strafing several times during the past 24 hours. Fortunately, no one was hit or hurt.[38] The crews also reported how each attack suspiciously happened immediately after using the tank radios. The obvious conclusion was that the Germans were monitoring their signals and triangulating the platoon's position.[39] Word of this practice spread throughout the battalion and radios were used only sparingly afterwards.

Through ill luck, the new bivouac site was situated right in the middle of *another* long-distance artillery contest between American and German batteries. The grumbling tankers hastily dug a new series of foxholes before unrolling their bedrolls, slipping inside them, and covering their ears. The high explosive duel lasted all night long.[40]

The 45th Division pressed northward through the river valley running from Contursi to the town of Oliveto Citra, three miles away. Although the action took place at night, the fighting was no less vicious. B Company's 2nd Platoon supported the 45th Recon—probing the pitch darkness with great caution along hazardous narrow roads with steep, deadly drop-offs. C Company of the 756th directly supported the 180th Regiment's attack on Oliveto Citra itself. The medium tanks of the 191st Tank Battalion also participated. During the assault, one M5 from the 756th overturned and the tank commander was slightly injured.[41] Ironically, the battalion suffered more serious casualties back in the HQ area near the 180th Regiment's command post (CP). A German artillery attack that same afternoon wounded one 756th enlisted man and a second attack several hours later seriously wounded another.[42] A shell burst also destroyed one of the battalion's SCR-510 radios.[43]

Later that evening, 756th battalion surgeon "Doc" Sarno was called forward by the 45th Recon to aid a German soldier pinned beneath twisted railroad tracks uprooted during an earlier American artillery strike. To save the man from septic shock and certain death, Sarno was forced to amputate his leg. He performed the surgery and bandaged the man's stump—all within bullet range of German positions observing nearby. Once Sarno had finished, several Germans appeared waving the flag of the International Red Cross. As they stepped forward to retrieve their wounded comrade, Sarno gathered his instruments and walked back toward American lines.[44] After everyone returned safely to their respective sides, the local fighting kicked right back up as if nothing had happened.

The battle around Oliveto continued past daybreak with the infantry stalled by several well-defended German MG positions. When medium and light tanks were called forward to neutralize the nests, German AT guns positioned across the Sele River opened up on them. The fire appeared to come from hidden 88s, but German Mark IV medium tanks were also seen maneuvering among the thick foliage.[45] One M4 from the 191st was struck and caught fire and two others were damaged during the encounter. A light tank from C Company of the 756th overturned and a second one bogged down in the soft soil while jockeying into firing positions.[46] Eventually, the added pressure forced the Germans to retreat further up the valley and the Americans prevailed. The undamaged tanks withdrew for servicing. Afterwards, Lt Col Sweeting proudly noted in the official unit record of how this engagement was the 756th's first direct combat action in Italy.[47] Bragging rights, again, went to C Company.

That same day, 23 September, B Company's 2nd Platoon held up near Oliveto and waited for the rest of B Company the join them.[48] All local bridges had been blown by the retreating Germans—making the journey difficult and frustrating. The next day, camp was established across the Sele River and the usual round of foxhole digging and guard rotations followed.[49] The place was strikingly picturesque—offering ideal river swimming holes and cascading mountain waterfalls perfect for showering. The idyllic setting was disrupted that evening, however, by another overhead artillery duel that lasted all night long.[50] At this point, the men were either too tired or had grown so accustomed to the constant thundering bangs that they slept through the commotion. The combat nervousness also abated for many.[51] The stresses brought from constant vigilance remained, of course, but appetites returned and the tankers accepted this new "normal" life on the front line.

The 25th of September was spent servicing the tanks. Major Dolvin visited the B Company camp to inform Wilkinson that his company's attachment had shifted from the 45th Recon to the 157th Regiment. The new assignment required the tankers to move further up the Sele River toward Laviano. The company waited until after dark for travel—using the intermittent flashes from yet another all-night artillery duel to slowly navigate the treacherous terrain. As expected, gully bridges had been destroyed by the retreating Germans, and the serpentine road was pocked regularly with shell holes. Sgt Peter Chiarelli's tank slid into one crater and was unable to claw out without a tow. Other tank crews became disoriented, made wrong turns, and lost time reversing out of rocky predicaments.[52] The half-tracks of the maintenance section took a wrong side road and nearly drove into German territory before discovering their mistake and backtracking to safety.[53] Despite the delays and hazards, the company succeeded in covering the twelve-mile journey before dawn.

26 September was spent "sweating out" artillery barrages and making camp near Laviano. Later in the day, a swarm of local Italian kids "invaded the area" eager to greet the tall, clean foreigners from the "Land of Plenty," touch their big, strange machines, and score some candy or gum.[54] A heavy storm swept through the area that evening—persisting well into the next morning. The rain was the first the men had seen in four months and seemed to make up for all that lost time. By the time blue sky finally reappeared, everyone and everything was left thoroughly soaked.[55] The new day was spent wiping off the mud, drying out, and awaiting new orders.[56] Some of the local adults returned the kindness the men had shown their children by inviting them into their homes to share a family dinner.[57]

New orders never came. Apparently, the 157th Regiment had completed their mission without any need for B Company's tanks. Toward late afternoon of 28 September, B Company was formally relieved of the attachment and ordered to rejoin the battalion near Sant'Angelo dei Lombardi. The new destination lay another twelve miles to the northwest—a striking indication of how far the Germans had retreated in just the previous forty-eight hours. The entire route to S'Angelo snaked through mountainous terrain, however, and the actual road distance was more than double.

Pvt Abe Beal, now serving as an HQ messenger, had discovered just how treach-erous that route was earlier in the afternoon. Beal chauffeured Pvt Paul Ranspach on his motorcycle back to B Company in Laviano when the two arrived at a blown and twisted steel bridge. Ranspach dismounted and walked to a makeshift pedestrian bridge nearby. At the same time, Beal attempted a daredevil crossing along a narrow section of the bridge still linking both sides of the steep ravine. He lost control and both driver and machine plummeted over the side. Ranspach rushed to the cliff's edge to find Beal hanging precariously by his hands from telephone lines; the bike had smashed among the rocks fifty feet below. He helped Beal to safety and both men had to hitch a ride the rest of the way. The two finally arrived in camp at 1900—just in time to head back to S'Angelo all over again.[58]

As the company formed a convoy and set out at dusk, a cold front with thunder-storms rolled through the area, pummeling the column with driving sheets of rain. The deluge lasted much of the evening and scattered the company along twenty miles of roadway.[59] Without the lightning flashes serving as a driver's aid whereby the eyes could catch fleeting snapshots of dangerous washouts and bypassed bridges ahead, several tanks would have undoubtedly tumbled down deep ravines.[60] The journey was excruciatingly slow and left the men shivering wet. At one point, the tanks had to halt as an engineering team hastily constructed a bypass. While the crews watched and waited, an engineer working on the project was shot by a German sniper.[61] Then, as the column neared S'Angelo, each tank had to stop again to be painstakingly winched through a mountain pass in order to continue.[62]

By morning, only half the vehicles appeared at the new bivouac roughly three miles west of S'Angelo, situated along a rural road one-and-a-half miles southeast of Torella.[63] More company tanks arrived in dribs and drabs throughout the day.[64] The men tried cleaning the equipment and drying it out, but with mud knee deep in many places, the task proved impossible to complete.[65] The next day, 30 September, the last vehicles of B Company finally trickled into camp. These included the kitchen truck with crew and the supply section. To celebrate their return, Mess Sgt Adlard baked donuts and brewed steaming hot coffee for everyone, while S/Sgt Gene Shirley issued the men fresh sets of dry clothes.[66] Three B Company men sent to serve as temporary MPs in North Africa and Sicily also returned to the fold. They were Pfc Donald E. LaDue, Pvt Robert Osganian, and Pvt Clyde W. Guild.[67]

Pvt Guild was originally assigned to B Company while the unit desert trained at Magenta, Algeria. The 19-year-old had been drafted into the Army out of Wisconsin. Originally, Guild tried joining the Navy to follow his older brother but was rejected because he wore glasses. The Army happily snatched him up and shipped him overseas to join the 756th as a "basic." At the time, the battalion had no position for the wide-eyed teenager, so he was loaned out for a few months as an MP on detached duty. Now Guild had returned—just in time for a job opening. Wilkinson's jeep driver, Pvt Dick, remained unable to resume his driving duties after his earlier mine accident, so Wilkinson assigned Guild as his replacement.[68] The normally good humored and talkative kid was certainly up to the task but awestruck around commissioned officers and hopelessly tongue-tied whenever he drove his captain.[69]

The weather turned markedly chilly and north winds whipped down at punishing speeds from the nearby mountains as the battalion waited for its next round of orders. To pass the time, the officers played poker and fantan in flapping tents, while the enlisted men rolled dice. Many coughed and hacked from respiratory infections born out of the miserable, damp conditions. Some local Italian women helped with the laundry in exchange for C-rations.[70] More rain pummeled the camp on 2 and 3 October.[71] With little to do, Armed Forces radio became a daily focal point for many, and the war news seemed positive. The 34th Division had joined the Fifth Army push—shipped in from North Africa on 23 September.[72] Four American infantry divisions now slogged up the mountainous middle of Italy—the 34th, 36th, 45th, and 3rd Divisions—all under the command of the U.S. VI Corps and serving as the Fifth Army's right flank. The British X Corps and U.S. 82nd Airborne Division held the Fifth Army's left flank—fighting along the coast north of Salerno. At the time, the British X Corps had swung north of Monte Vesuvius to vie for the critical port city of Naples.[73] Meanwhile, the British Eighth Army battling up the far eastern side of Italy, secured the key hub city of Foggia. The advances on the Fifth Army side, however, had been slowed somewhat by German defensive preparations along the Volturno River, flowing roughly fifteen miles north of Naples. The cold, wet weather and treacherous terrain also worked to the defenders' advantage.[74]

Though the tankers couldn't plan for battle, they could still plan a decent home-cooked meal, and nothing broke the C-ration monotony better than a steaming batch of freshly fried chicken. The B Company men fanned out about town purchasing all the complementary necessities—potatoes, hams, and grapes, etc.[75] The threadbare natives didn't usually accept money—preferring clothing in general and shoes in particular as recompense for their meats and produce.[76] When all else failed, the locals could often be convinced into accepting unwanted Army C-ration cans as payment—but they did so more out of curiosity then any desire to escape their own repetitive diets. In the end, everyone walked away happy, and the chicken feast lasted several days.

By 7 October, the battalion finally received orders to move out. At 0330, Wilkinson arose from his bedroll and prepared to lead his company's convoy before realizing the day marked his 24th birthday. He had little time to ponder the significance and no time to celebrate. He did, however, allow himself a moment to make one private wish: to arrive safely home in Texas before his 25th birthday. The battalion set out at 0630 under slate-gray skies and misting rain. The journey westward toward Naples snaked along twenty miles of hilly roads—always slick and often muddy. They stopped to camp for the evening outside of Volturara Irpina, under the comforting cover of a stately old apple orchard.[77] When the men discovered dry straw in a nearby barn, they behaved as if they had struck pay dirt and eagerly stuffed armfuls of the extra bedding inside their tents.[78] The rain outside lasted all night long.

After servicing and fueling the vehicles the next morning, the battalion set out at 1145 for San Martino, another twenty-five miles to the northwest.[79] However, the rain-sodden roads degraded to a point of becoming virtually impassable. Many bridges had been destroyed earlier by the retreating Germans and their earthen bypasses washed out under the deluge. At one location, the column was delayed several hours as engineers repaired a damaged bridge.[80] At another, Sgt Hamilton A. Smith's tank suddenly spun off the road and threw a track. Sgt Louis J. Jarvis swerved to avoid a collision and overturned his own tank upon an embankment. Luckily, no one was hurt in the incident.[81] As a result of the jam up, Lt Redle's tank separated from the rest of the column and fell back—dragged along with other lagging units attempting to negotiate the same route.

The battalion finally reached San Martino later in the evening and set up camp at Cervinara, roughly two miles to the west.[82] The new bivouac included many friendly locals. The women enjoyed singing as they labored through their household chores and farming duties. Wilkinson found their voices beautiful and soothing and marveled at how they could serenade their way through the hardships and uncertainties of war. The next evening, Redle finally arrived from his long travel ordeal—and B Company was complete again.[83] A local lawyer invited Wilkinson in for a home-cooked dinner at the family table. The meal lasted three hours and featured five kinds of meat, spaghetti, grapes, apples, pie, wine, and brandy. The family was extremely hospitable and claimed to be anti-fascists, but Wilkinson had no way of knowing the truth.[84] His role was that of the gracious guest. He was, after all, an American ambassador as much as he was a U.S. Army officer.

From 11 to 17 October, the battalion waited patiently for additional instructions. B Company received a new upgraded M5A1 light tank, which Wilkinson promptly claimed as his own and took out to drive and test fire. Everything hummed like a charm.[85] The company test fired all their guns on 14 October with unintended and somewhat comical results. Upon hearing the ruckus, the locals scrambled for cover—mistakenly fearful of the Germans returning.[86] They had to be reassured repeatedly that all was well.

The weather grew increasingly chilly, and the crews switched to wearing combat jackets most of the time. With plenty of free time on their hands, the men took short sightseeing trips and commissioned a local photographer to take portrait photos. Wilkinson, 1st Sgt Hogan, and S/Sgt Crawford drove out to Naples one day but found nothing but destruction. The harbor, the docks, and most of the city's buildings were left in utter ruin from heavy fighting during the previous weeks. Everything appeared hopeless and grim. To the south, Monte Vesuvius spouted dark ash into the sky—underscoring the somber mood of the place. Wilkinson left Naples with the same thoughts he had while walking ancient Carthage: *This city must have been beautiful once.*[87]

During this same time, Fifth Army troops attacked aggressively along the Volturno and successfully crossed in multiple places—preventing the Germans from forming a defensive line and forcing them to retreat even further northward. On 17 October, the 756th was finally ordered to move again—nineteen miles northwest to Capitone.[88] The new location brought them to within three miles of the strategically key Volturno. For once, the journey progressed without incident, and aside from a finicky half-track motor, B Company suffered no other mechanical issues.[89] The countryside was as picturesque as the local Italians were celebratory. Many newly liberated civilians ran out to greet and shower the tankers with gifts of fruit as they passed through.[90]

On Monday 18 October, the battalion moved further northwest to an assembly area to prepare for the crossing of the Volturno River. The weather improved but the roads remained poor—mostly because of the unending crush of vehicles and troops funneling toward only one treadway pontoon bridge tethered by Army engineers across the river. B Company was called forward to cross at 1400. As Pvt Guild and Captain Wilkinson led the company column along a deeply rutted road toward the bridge approach, one of the half-tracks slid down into a ditch. The bridge's middle bowed downstream from the river's swift current and undulated like a caterpillar as each vehicle carefully traced the two narrow tracks lashed atop a series of giant inflatable rafts.[91] Fazendin bravely led the way on foot, directing the tank drivers with hand signals until all B Company vehicles had safely reached the other side.[92] As they started up a sharp zig-zag road on the opposite bank, however, two sharp blasts reverberated through the river valley from whence they just came.[93] A unit following theirs had accidentally struck two German mines on the riverbank.[94]

The entire battalion proceeded along a high winding road overlooking the scenic Volturno River Valley.[95] To the southwest of the village of Ruviano, they stopped and dispersed throughout a large, cultivated field.[96] With an unnerving and never-ending chaunt of artillery duels splitting the air, the tankers pitched tents and settled in for the evening. That same air, at least, was dry and unseasonably warm—bringing some respite.[97]

At 0330, Sweeting's voice roused Wilkinson from a deep sleep. The lieutenant colonel's tone was stern and sharp—urging the B Company commander to alert his men for battle and accompany him on reconnaissance. Within moments, B Company's camp was abuzz with adrenaline as men grabbed gear, piled into their tanks, and cranked cold engines back to life. Wilkinson jumped into Sweeting's jeep and sped off into the darkness toward the unmistakable chatter of small arms fire. As they neared the source, however, the ruckus dissipated and ceased altogether. A German contingent had attacked a local bridge but were driven back promptly by an American infantry unit stationed nearby. The short affair was over before Wilkinson's tanks could even engage.[98]

For the next three days, the 756th sat parked in familiar frustration as battles raged nearby to which they were not called on to participate. In the skies high above, planes dove and darted in strangely beautiful but deadly matches. On two occasions, the camp was thrown into high alert as German bombers blasted targets around them. The skies filled with ack-ack but none of the falling bombs ever threatened 756th positions. Another time, a wave of German planes swooped in so low over camp that the ground shook as they thundered through. A few tank crews managed to fire their turret-mounted .50-caliber MGs at them, but the planes screamed by so swiftly—intent on bombing targets on the other side of the mountain—to even notice the tracers at their tails.[99]

On 23 October, Pvt Guild drove Lt Redle and Pvt Ranspach on a jeep reconnaissance northward, bringing them to within a mile of the front lines. The slow journey meandered through ten miles of cheerless civilian destruction. They passed through Alvignano, Dragoni, and Alife—once ancient, beautiful pastoral valley towns blasted down to stone foundations by heavy fighting. The U.S. Army's 34th

"Red Bull" Infantry Division—the same outfit Captain Wilkinson had observed at the Fondouk Pass—led the fight through the area. As the trio neared the front, they passed a knocked out German Mark IV tank and a dead American soldier lying near a road bypass.[100] The fighting was fierce and the Allied infantry paid dearly for every mile gained, but Redle could clearly see why the 756th was not being called forward. The terrain offered little room for tank maneuver. The hills on both sides were too steep and the valley roads too narrow for any vehicular movement except in single file. Although the weather had warmed into a pleasant Indian summer, the heavy rains from the previous week still gushed down from the heights to pool as glassy ponds all over the battlefield—making the ground far too soft for anything but boot soles.[101]

Sweeting ordered each company to send several men to the front for a day. If his men could not fight directly, he thought close-range observation of infantry operations would serve them well as an educational experience. Wilkinson called for volunteers and, surprisingly, had no trouble filling the B Company quota. The men returned twenty-four hours later, dead silent and ashen faced. One of the volunteers was 20-year Army veteran and world-traveler 1st Sgt Hogan. When Wilkinson asked his normally upbeat and even-keeled sergeant how he liked life as a combat infantryman, Hogan somberly replied: "Captain, every one of those guys ought to get the Medal of Honor."[102]

On 25 October, the 756th was issued a new set of movement orders. This time, each of the three tank companies were dispatched in three entirely different directions. C Company and the Battalion HQ were assigned in support the 45th Division near Alife.[103] A Company was given the job of guarding the Fifth Army HQ at Caserta ten miles to the southwest, and B Company was assigned to guard the VI Corps HQ in nearby Caiazzo.[104] Although the guard assignments were considered "gravy" by many, Wilkinson was not pleased and complained his men had been reduced to "dog robbers" for Maj Gen Lucas.[105] ("Dog robber" was Army slang for a lackey junior officer given work his superior didn't want to do.) Good job or bad, Wilkinson had no choice but to accept the new role. At 1600, B Company made the short two-mile journey southeast to Caiazzo to begin work as armored security.[106] The next day, Wilkinson and Sweeting disbursed the tanks out to ideal defensive positions among rolling hills northeast of town and developed reaction plans should any German raiding party suddenly appear.[107] The 1st and 2nd Platoons were placed as roadblock outposts on the northern perimeter, with the 3rd Platoon and Company CP positioned a few hundred yards away from Maj Gen John P. Lucas's own CP.[108] The likelihood of a German ground attack this far from the front lines was remote but couldn't be completely discounted either.[109] The VI Corps CP still sat within range of German artillery, however, so tank crews were strongly cautioned to use the radio very sparingly to prevent the enemy from "fixing" target locations via radio compass triangulation.[110]

The crews settled into their mundane roadblock assignments and waited. Bored silly, Wilkinson, Redle, and Winlock passed the hours playing endless fantan games. In time, Fazendin talked of transferring over to Service Company to find more challenging work. One of the officers in the supply section wasn't performing up to par and rumors had him on his way out.[111] Wilkinson didn't want to lose Fazendin but wouldn't hold the energetic go-getter back from pursuing his ambitions either.

After a few days of doing nothing, Wilkinson asked Pvt Guild to drive him to Pompeii to see the excavated ruins of the ancient Roman city.[112] The twenty-five-mile jeep journey south crossed territory safely under Allied control; however, the heavens were always in doubt. As the two bounced along in silence, Wilkinson glanced skyward often —constantly watching for trouble. He remembered well the pinpoint precision of the Stuka dive bomber pilots in Tunisia. Pvt Guild, on the other hand, seemed more intimidated by his captain than German planes. The normally chatty and jovial jeep driver clammed up around Wilkinson—who always maintained a proper and professional bearing. During the journey, Wilkinson spotted a formation of planes approaching in the distance and directed Guild to pull over to the side. As the formation passed high overhead Wilkinson muttered aloud: "I wonder who those are …." Guild, seeing an opportunity to break the ice with a joke, remarked: "Those are B2s!" Wilkinson paused momentarily with a bewildered look. Nobody possessed such a plane. He turned slowly to face the young private, now eager to deliver the punchline. "What do you mean 'B2'?" Wilkinson queried. "B2 damn bad if they're not ours!" Guild smiled triumphantly. Wilkinson returned a stern look at Guild that made him think he might be destined for MP duty in Sicily again.[113] The joke may have bombed, but the remainder of the excursion unfolded without incident and the tour of Pompeii was magnificent.[114]

By 1 November, the front lines had shifted far enough north, the VI Corps CP moved up to Dragoni to maintain pace. B Company followed along with them, departing Caiazzo at 0500 and establishing a new series of roadblocks around the Corps CP by noon.[115] During this same time, A Company remained on guard at the Fifth Army HQ at Caserta and C Company continued their attachment with the 45th Division.[116] Some civilians living near B Company's 1st Platoon area told the tankers of eight Germans hiding in a cave in the nearby western hills—so the men went to investigate. They found the cavern and evidence of campers once living there, but no Germans.[117] Though the search was a fruitless sideshow, the exercise made the men feel they were still part of a war.

The entire month of October passed with the 756th involved in no combat operation whatsoever.[118] The inactivity transformed Lt Col Sweeting into a restless busybody. Not all his men were tank crewmen guarding generals or manning dull rear echelon roadblocks. To keep these others busy, Sweeting organized an ad hoc "pioneer platoon" and ordered the assigned members to learn how to build makeshift bridges, earthen bypasses, and such. In time, the group became proficient enough to assist the local engineers in their projects.[119]

Sweeting had a tendency to overcome his own boredom by engaging in what his officers came to call "personal reconnaissance." These were unprompted trips to the front lines—usually with nebulous or unnecessary aims. Irritatingly, the thrill-seeking lieutenant colonel often dragged his company commanders along with him. On one occasion, Wilkinson received the invitation. At the time, American and German infantrymen engaged in a brutal slugfest along rugged slopes leading to Venafro, fifteen miles to the northwest. The Germans' preferred method for defending hills was to allow the Allies to capture the front side and then pin down the attackers by holding the crest. The tactic was highly effective because the Germans could keep their high-ground positions well-supplied from the rear without being observed. Allied artillery and mortar couldn't break the impasse, because the hill crest sat in the way. Any round arcing over the top either exploded harmlessly above or downhill of the defenders' rear slope foxholes.

Sweeting took Wilkinson to one such hill under assault by American infantry. Although control of the summit remained hotly contested—as evidenced by the chatter of small arms and thumping of mortar—Sweeting insisted on scaling it to study German positions on the opposite side. Progress came at a snail's pace by inching over sharp stone on raw knees and tender bellies. As dusk fell, Sweeting finally abandoned the effort by stating the obvious: "We're going to get our heads shot off if we keep going any longer, so let's find a place to spend the night." They located a sheep fold built from boulders nearby, then squeezed inside atop dry manure for an uncomfortable sleep. Before dawn broke, they set out for home. On the way down, an apprehensive 34th Division sentry confronted them with a challenge question. Since the answer changed each evening and both men missed the update, several tense moments followed. In the end, they convinced the guard of their friendly origins and were allowed to pass.[120] Wilkinson learned little from the whole experience—other than his battalion CO reveled in taking unnecessary risks.

On 4 November, Wilkinson visited C Company's CP to learn if they had seen any action while supporting the 45th Division. They hadn't. Even though 45th Division troops battled to take the key valley town of Venafro, no tanks were called forward.[121] Later that day, Venafro fell and everyone to the rear was ordered to advance northward again. Wilkinson discovered the corps CP was relocating to Prata Sannita. With the weather turning colder and white snow starting to appear on the gray mountain peaks to the east, he set out to locate a choice company CP location before other units beat him to the punch.[122] He found the perfect place inside an old castle atop a hill in Lower Prata—claiming one room, in particular, featuring a massive, majestic fireplace.[123] On 10 November, B Company completed the ten-mile journey to their new home.[124] The platoons dispersed nearby forming roadblocks again and a cozy CP was established inside the castle.[125] To block window light from being seen by German observers and to protect against artillery shrapnel, all glass was boarded up. To keep warm, a fire was kept burning in the hearth.[126]

The castle was over a thousand years old, built in three sections atop a hill. The B Company CP was located in the upper portion. The middle section had fallen into disrepair and was uninhabitable—but still passable by walking a network of planks. The lower section housed an orphanage under the care of eight local nuns. Naturally, the men shared their candy, gum, and other sweet treats with the children. The nuns offered to hand wash the B Company laundry *gratis* but Wilkinson insisted the sisters receive payment for their labor.[127] According to the nuns, the castle was originally built in AD 800 by a wealthy count and countess, but when their son committed suicide, the distraught parents willed the castle to the church. The local parish had maintained the place ever since.[128] The antiquity fascinated the American guests. No town in the United States featured buildings this old. The village, too, appeared ageless. The ancient stone homes clustered around the castle were packed so tightly, the roads could not accommodate vehicles—only pedestrians. A quarter of a mile away lay the larger medieval town of Prata, where the corps CP was located and also the local Catholic church.[129]

Armistice Day, 11 November, had been an American national holiday since 1919—intended to forever commemorate the end of "The War to End All Wars." Wilkinson was not yet born when the so-called "Great War" concluded, but he knew of its horrors from the history books and stories of old timers who had fought in it. The irony of the anniversary did not escape him and put nobody he knew in any celebratory mood. The Great War had since become "World War I," and to find out where the 756th Tank Battalion fit in the current "World War II," Wilkinson drove to the battalion's new HQ, roughly six miles south of Venafro.[130] He discovered C Company Commander, 1st Lt Gourley, had been hit by shrapnel in his left forearm and evacuated. This happened when Sweeting took Gourley and Captain Arnold on one of his "personal reconnaissance" missions to evaluate the high ground north of Venafro. As a result, the three were caught in a German mortar barrage.[131] The episode left Sweeting's senior officers quietly fuming.[132] Many saw little reason for tank officers to nose about an active battlefield too steep and treacherous for tanks—such terrain was solely the domain of infantrymen.

The territory north of Venafro was protected by a long triple-crowned ridge, with more perilous peaks and ridges beyond—one small section of the 750-mile-long Apennine mountain range running the entire "spine" of the Italian peninsula. Infantrymen of the 45th Division prepared to attack just that one small ridge in hopes of forcing a general German retreat in another area a few miles to the southwest. There, the U.S. 3rd Division fought on the VI Corps' left flank inside a valley corridor known as the "Mignano Gap." This valley led straight to Monte Cassino ten miles to the northwest. Due to Monte Cassino's strategic importance, the Germans fiercely contested the Allied advance every step of the way. On both sides of the narrow valley, the terrain was so steep and rugged only pack mules could haul supplies up or bring the wounded and dead down. The fighting was especially brutal on two sharp hills rising like hurdles in the middle of the Mignano Gap: Monte Rotundo and Monte Lungo. For ten days in early November, the 3rd Division paid a heavy cost seizing those hills in combat reminiscent of the Great War— close, intimate, and brutal. Progress was measured in increments of only a few yards and gained by clawing across steep rock. Blood flowed freely on both sides. Light tanks, which provided some value in limited reconnaissance roles, were of no use at all.[133] Medium tanks, at least, could be called forward occasionally to fire a few HE 75mm shells into hillside targets—but only from safe distances. When Monte Rotundo finally fell in mid-November, the rolls were so decimated, depleted, and exhausted that the 3rd Division was pulled off the line. The 36th Division carried the fight forward through Monte Lungo and into the next town of San Pietro.

At the Battalion HQ, Wilkinson heard a rumor for the first time that the 756th was next in line to be upgraded from light to medium tanks. Wilkinson was always wary of rumors but this one he believed. Clearly, rapid technological advances on the battlefield had rendered light tanks obsolete for most roles. They now lacked both the armor and firepower necessary to function as main battle tanks. Wilkinson hoped if and when that reorganization happened, Redle would be rewarded with his own company to command.[134] No timeframe came with the rumor. As usual, one could only wait and see.

On 14 November, Fazendin transferred to Service Company as the battalion's new transportation officer.[135] The officer he replaced, 2nd Lt Moultrie Patten, had been unable to keep up with the demands of the job. Patten transferred temporarily for training to B Company but was ultimately destined for C Company. Wilkinson hated to lose Fazendin but certainly sympathized with his desires for new challenges and adventures.[136]

The weather turned colder and foggier, and then rain returned with a vengeance.[137] Road washouts around Prata separated the 2nd and 3rd Platoon roadblocks from the rest of the company and no supplies or mail could be delivered for several days.[138] The Volturno River swelled into foaming rapids, washing away those delicate pontoon bridges the engineers had so carefully built—thus preventing Lt Patten from reporting for duty until 16 November. The B Company HQ staff sat isolated inside the dark castle, monitoring battalion events by phone while comfortably toasting beside a roaring fireplace.[139] Nearby, batteries of U.S. Army 155mm "Long Tom" artillery thundered away at all hours.[140] Rumors kicked into high gear over the battalion's expected reorganization.[141] S/Sgt Crawford was ordered to attend 75mm gun training, and Sweeting confidently predicted that the battalion's new M4s would arrive by mid-December.[142]

The steady pounding rain lasted until 18 November, when the sun re-emerged in golden glory, and the clouds promptly dissipated as though nothing had ever happened.[143] The roads, however, became muddy rut-ways. On 19 November, Major Dolvin braved his way through the countryside to visit each company. During his stopover at B Company's castle, he reported the Battalion HQ positioned south of Venafro had been receiving steady shelling from German artillery. During an attack at 0930 that very morning, shrapnel struck and killed Pfc Melvin W. Nicholson of the recon platoon.[144] The ongoing harassment left the men so edgy that one sergeant thought he smelled poison gas and sounded the alarm—sending everyone in HQ scrambling for their masks. They discovered later that the strange odor had come from an open box of moth balls.[145]

The next day, Wilkinson ventured out by jeep to check on his roadblock crews and then proceeded further north to the Battalion HQ to file the company supply reports. German artillery fell so heavily during his drive that he decided to take a different route back to B Company. The alternate road turned out so terribly rutted and muddy that he nearly didn't make it back.[146] Although the skies stayed clear and blue, a few more days of sunshine were needed to dry out the area enough to allow for even basic vehicular traffic.

On Sunday 21 November, Lt Redle walked down from the castle to attend noon Mass in nearby Prata. Lt Fazendin promised to meet him there, as the two friends attended Mass together regularly. Fazendin failed to show. Redle thought his absence odd but assumed the battalion's newest transportation officer was simply buried in work.

Late afternoon the next day, Wilkinson and Sgt Pompey were playing a game of chess in the castle CP. The captain had just finished defeating his crafty communication sergeant for the first time ever, when the telephone rang.[147] Pompey answered and handed the receiver to Wilkinson. It was an artillery officer calling to inquire if B Company was missing a lieutenant. "No," Wilkinson replied. A few moments later, the officer called back and asked if Wilkinson was absolutely sure. Wilkinson felt confident that Redle, Winlock, Kremer, and Patten were either relaxing in the castle or attending to their roadblock platoons nearby, assured the caller of this and then hung up. The two calls, however, left him unsettled. After a few moments, Wilkinson called over to the battalion and learned Fazendin had been missing since noon, Sunday.[148] He put the battalion immediately in touch with the artillery officer.

Fazendin was found dazed, dehydrated, and nearly dead along the road overlooking the Volturno River. Thirty hours earlier, he and S/Sgt John M. Mulraney had traveled by jeep to Prata to attend Mass with Lt Redle. Along the way, Fazendin caught a glimpse of a pile of river gravel he believed would make a promising source of pothole filler, so he directed Mulraney to drive off the road and down the steep embankment for a closer look.[149] The jeep struck a German mine—killing Mulraney outright. Fazendin was thrown clear by the blast but suffered horrendous back injuries. Unable to walk, and too far from the road for anyone to hear his cries, the lieutenant clawed inch by agonizing inch up 300 yards of steep riverbank. His excruciating ordeal lasted all evening and well into the next day. Not until 1700 was his blast-bruised body discovered by an artillery officer riding by in another jeep. Fazendin was so delirious and wracked with pain, he could only repeat weakly: "B Company, 756th Tank Battalion."[150]

The popular "Wild Thing" lieutenant impulsively chased after a creative solution and briefly overlooked the potential for danger—as he was inclined to do. Now he was left struggling for his life inside an evacuation hospital. The incident served as a stark, cautionary warning to everybody.

U.S. 45th Infantry Division

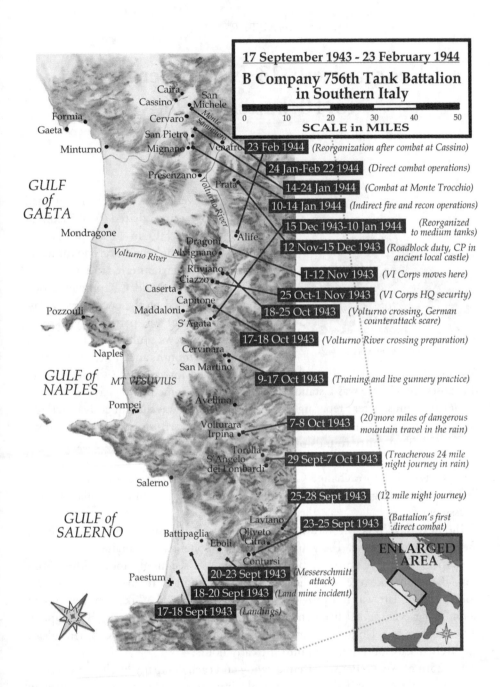

17 September 1943 - 23 February 1944

B Company 756th Tank Battalion in Southern Italy

SCALE in MILES
0   10   20   30   40   50

23 Feb 1944 *(Reorganization after combat at Cassino)*

24 Jan-Feb 22 1944 *(Direct combat operations)*

14-24 Jan 1944 *(Combat at Monte Trocchio)*

10-14 Jan 1944 *(Indirect fire and recon operations)*

15 Dec 1943-10 Jan 1944 *(Reorganized to medium tanks)*

12 Nov-15 Dec 1943 *(Roadblock duty, CP in ancient local castle)*

1-12 Nov 1943 *(VI Corps moves here)*

25 Oct-1 Nov 1943 *(VI Corps HQ security)*

18-25 Oct 1943 *(Volturno crossing, German counterattack scare)*

17-18 Oct 1943 *(Volturno River crossing preparation)*

9-17 Oct 1943 *(Training and live gunnery practice)*

7-8 Oct 1943 *(20 more miles of dangerous mountain travel in the rain)*

29 Sept-7 Oct 1943 *(Treacherous 24 mile night journey in rain)*

25-28 Sept 1943 *(12 mile night journey)*

23-25 Sept 1943 *(Battalion's first direct combat)*

20-23 Sept 1943 *(Messerschmitt attack)*

18-20 Sept 1943 *(Land mine incident)*

17-18 Sept 1943 *(Landings)*

GULF of GAETA

GULF of NAPLES

GULF of SALERNO

MT VESUVIUS

Volturno River

Monte Sammucro

Caira
Cassino
San Michele
Cervaro
San Pietro
Mignano
Venafro
Formia
Gaeta
Minturno
Presenzano
Prata
Mondragone
Dragoni
Alvignano
Alife
Ruviano
Ciazzo
Caserta
Capitone
Maddaloni
S'Agata
Pozzouli
Naples
Cervinara
San Martino
Avellino
Pompei
Volturara Irpina
Torella
S'Angelo dei Lombardi
Salerno
Laviano
Oliveto Citra
Battipaglia
Eboli
Contursi
Paestum

ENLARGED AREA

CHAPTER 10

Reorganized: 23 November 1943 to 10 January 1944

M4 Medium Tank (1942)

On 23 November, a somewhat subdued Lt Col Sweeting visited Wilkinson at B Company's HQ in Lower Prata. He reported Fazendin's condition had turned so dire he had since transferred to a full-service hospital. He also said C Company's bivouac was shelled by the enemy every day. This harassment was particularly irksome because the crews couldn't fire back. After nearly a full month's attachment to the 45th Division, the frustrated tankers had yet to be called forward on a single mission. The closest they came was a standby order to engage some pesky German MGs in the northern hills. After preparing, however, the request was subsequently canceled.[1] Another time, the Battalion HQ's three M8 75mm self-propelled "assault gun" howitzers lobbed thirty rounds of HE on a distant building—but the crews never heard if their contributions were successful.[2] Sweeting requested authorization from the 45th Division to exchange C Company for B Company as a morale booster. That way, the beleaguered men could receive some respite from the regular artillery harassment.[3]

The next day, Sweeting returned—but this time in buoyed spirits, clutching a bottle of sparkling wine. The young lieutenant colonel hadn't obtained permission to swap C with B Company, but the matter was seemingly moot: The 756th Tank Battalion had received official approval to upgrade to medium tanks. The reorganization date was not provided, but Sweeting assured Wilkinson it would be "soon." That evening, all five company commanders gathered by the B Company castle fireplace to celebrate the news and toss around personnel reassignment ideas. The lively discussion lasted well into the early hours.

The 25th of November was Thanksgiving and each company kitchen prepared a feast with real turkey and all the traditional trimmings.[4] The next day, the company commanders met again around the B Company fireplace for further planning. Instead of three gun companies, a medium tank battalion expanded to four: three with M4 medium tanks (A, B, and C) and one with M5 lights (D)—so the composition of the new D Company, in particular, was hotly debated.[5] Wilkinson lobbied hard for Redle as the new CO but was eventually overruled in favor of 1st Lt Kenneth S. Nelson. B Company Lts Kremer and Patten would report as platoon leaders, and Sgt Richter was made the new first sergeant. Thirteen other B Company members were also selected to fill out additional roles.[6] The other companies made similar personnel concessions. The next day, the new roster was made public. As expected, many of those transferred were not pleased, but all complaints fell on deaf ears.[7]

On 1 December, the 756th was relieved of all prior assignments and attached to the 2nd Tank Group. Each company remained in place, however, until formal relocation orders arrived. More details circulated around the battalion over Fazendin's condition. Without a doubt, the lieutenant was very lucky to be alive. He was stable but heading home in a full-body cast and facing a long and painful recovery ahead of him. The explosion had compressed his spine a full one-and-a-half inches. He was expected to remain immobilized for an entire year until his back was "stretched" to where he could function again.[8]

That same day, the B Company tank crews still manning the roadblocks around the VI Corps HQ watched waves of Allied planes passing overhead all day long. At the same time, American artillery batteries pounded ferociously upon German positions further north.[9] Apparently, something big was happening up that way.

The first two weeks of December came and went without any changes for the 756th. B Company remained headquartered inside the old castle with platoons dispersed on the outskirts. The guard duty assignments had long since become tedious and dull. The second anniversary of the attack on Pearl Harbor passed without observance or fanfare, and drenching rains fell intermittently.[10] Big news broke over Armed Forces radio about a surprise meeting between Roosevelt, Churchill, and Stalin in Tehran, Iran. The three world leaders resolved to maintain a strong alliance and hammer Germany from all sides until it was utterly crushed.

During those same early weeks of December, the 36th Division fought bitterly in the Mignano Gap to take the far slope of Monte Lungo and nearby village of San Pietro. The combat was some of the most intense to date in the battle for southern Italy. The Germans fought tenaciously to hold the village—hoping to buy as much time as possible until far more elaborate defenses were constructed further north at Cassino. On 16 December, San Pietro finally fell, but with the horrendous cost of 1,200 dead, wounded, or missing "Texas" Division infantrymen.[11] The village was so heavily bombarded in the weeks leading up to capture, the 36th Division basically captured a denuded hillside with gray stone rubble piles. Little recognizable remained of any tree or building.

The employment of tanks was dreadful during the engagement—resulting in foolish and unnecessary losses. Company "A" of the 753rd Tank Battalion was all but wiped out after being ordered to attack along a narrow mountain road in a futile attempt to gain ground above the town. The road offered little defilade opportunity and no room for maneuver. The Germans simply watched as the first tanks of the M4 column passed and then casually picked off the middle tanks with a hidden AT gun. The surviving tanks then struck mines and consequently blocked their brethren from retreating, causing the attack to stall into debacle.[12]

On 13 December, the 2nd and 3rd Platoons of B Company were relieved of their dull roadblock duties by medium tanks of the 755th Tank Battalion. For the first time in over a month, B Company was physically together again.[13] The next day, Major Dolvin dropped in with welcome news of the battalion's orders to move to Sant'Agata de' Goti (S'Agata) the next morning. There, they would reorganize.

At 0700 on 15 December, the entire battalion pulled back from the front. The journey south covered fifty miles and passed by way of Alife, Dragoni, Caiazzo, Caserta, and Maddaloni.[14] The weather was cold and clear, and road conditions were fair at best.[15] A reconstructed Volturno River pontoon bridge was crossed again after backtracking through Caiazzo. Because S'Agata was only eighteen miles northeast of Naples, the journey felt as though the clock had been rolled backward two months. Nevertheless, the new bivouac proved an ideal location for tank training—with choices of flat fields, rolling terrain, and challenging hills nearby. The village itself was a quiet, rustic, and picturesque farming community of limestone and red tiled roofed buildings. Many old homes and shops had been built atop an ancient fortress wall running along a deep river ravine. The bivouac was spread over an open field a few hundred yards west of town.[16] General Orders #107 issued by the Fifth Army HQ allotted the battalion only twenty-seven days to complete the transformation. At one minute after midnight, the 756th Tank Battalion (L) officially became a medium tank outfit and the countdown clock began ticking.[17]

The first five days were spent turning in the M5 lights, receiving and processing the M4 mediums, integrating roughly a hundred new replacement personnel, organizing the new D Company, and reshuffling crews. Because an M4 required five crew members to the M5's four, every single tank crew was affected.[18]

B Company received its first five M4s on 16 December. The company also welcomed twelve replacements and two new officers that same day. Wilkinson sat in his pyramidal tent shelling pecans mailed from his family in Texas when the new officers reported for duty. He asked Redle ahead of time to quietly observe each new officer as he interviewed them separately. Wilkinson continued to crack open and eat pecans as he evaluated his subject's responses—hoping this informal behavior would put the new officer at ease. His questions, however, were never chummy or personal—but probing, pointed, and businesslike. And his very last challenge was always same: "Lieutenant, are you ready to lead a platoon in combat tomorrow?" 2nd

Lt Wayne B. Henry, a 28-year-old 6' 4" blond from Illinois, was impressive—exuding confidence and competency from start to finish. The other officer, 2nd Lt William G. Leger, struggled with his answers and seemed to lack similar character traits. Wilkinson asked his XO afterwards for his impressions and Redle agreed. Perhaps, both men rationalized, Leger was simply nervous.[19]

By 18 December, B Company acquired their full complement of seventeen M4 tanks. The platoons were reorganized, replacements integrated, and new crew assignments completed. The same held true for the rest of the battalion.[20] In three short days, the battalion transitioned from fifty-one light tanks to fifty-one medium tanks and seventeen light tanks. The Battalion HQ's smaller 75mm M8 self-propelled howitzers were also swapped for six larger self-propelled 105mm M7 "Priest" assault guns, and overall personnel numbers swelled from thirty-three officers and 627 men to forty-two officers and 732 men.[21] Reorganization had been accomplished in less than seventy-two hours—a feat unthinkable in the earlier Fort Lewis days.[22] Sweeting was particularly proud his battalion had pulled off the lightning-quick transformation without a single enlisted man receiving a grade demotion or cut in pay. In fact, many men received promotions because of the addition of D Company.[23] A few "surplus" members transferred to the 6th Personnel Center where they could be matched to other units without a loss in grade or pay.[24]

The M4s received, unfortunately, were not in the best of condition, and so the maintenance crews had plenty of work cut out for them.[25] As B Company's XO, 1st Lt Redle's first order of business was to inventory the new tanks and create a log book for each one. The serial number cast upon every chassis, transmission, main gun, MG, etc., had to be located, charted, and tracked. The company's new maintenance records clerk was Cpl Anthony Notoroberto—a young Italian New Yorker admired for his saintly devotion to the care of his ill mother.[26] Both he and Redle spent the entire afternoon crawling around the interiors, undercarriages, and motor compartments of the M4s—creating meticulous records. Once the task was completed, Notoroberto asked Redle if he could study all seventeen books over the evening. Redle thought his request was bizarre, but he agreed. The next morning, Notoroberto handed over the books and asked Redle to "quiz" him on the numbers. To Redle's amazement the dark-haired, bushy-eyebrowed[27] corporal had not only memorized every single entry but could correctly cross-reference each one to the tank's War Department number, company number, or assigned commander. He failed to miss a single one of Redle's challenges.[28] Later, Redle learned Notoroberto had worked in the numbers racket in civilian life. Even though the NYC police hauled him in numerous times, they could never convict him of any wrongdoing because he never wrote anything down.[29]

Every company kitchen operated in full swing and the battalion received authorization to prepare Class A rations for the men. These freshly cooked meals tasted like a heavenly banquet compared to the bland C, K, D, or "Five-in-One" canned field rations consumed while at the front. Under the reorganization, B Company's new mess sergeant became S/Sgt Ray Colley—a trim Montana cowboy.[30] Colley made it his personal point of honor that nobody walked away hungry after any of his meals. With so many leftovers available, the local children—many dressed in little more than dirty rags—began arriving, seeking table scraps. S'Agata appeared beautiful outwardly, but the inhabitants were dirt poor.[31] The Americans, of course, happily shared their surplus. Many kids sang songs to show their appreciation. One local 14-year-old boy, in particular, was blessed with an exceptionally beautiful tenor voice ringing out over all the rest.[32] Sgt Louis J. Jarvis and Sgt Mancini, both accomplished musicians in civilian life, kept giving the boy extra food just to keep him singing.[33] In no time, the throng of children crowding around the mess grew into a nuisance. To keep control of the situation, Wilkinson told S/Sgt Colley to build a rope corral and line up the children inside each day, ranging from smallest to tallest. Kitchen helper Pvt Bernard Shue gathered together a bunch of empty one-gallon cans, attached wire bails as handles and passed them out to the kids to use as buckets.[34] Each day, after the tankers finished eating, they walked over to the line and divvied out the leftovers. Wilkinson's rule was simple: Any disorder and nobody eats. The children dutifully waited their turns, and as a result, few ever walked away without something.[35] Usually, Colley's crew cooked up so much food the children often took additional servings home to appreciative families.[36]

On 19 December, B Company received an extra officer: 2nd Lt John J. Czajkowski from Chicago. Wilkinson held his customary interview and thought the new lieutenant a good fit. The company continued with the work of reorganizing, training the new arrivals, and preparing the equipment. Morale shot sky high in anticipation over taking the new M4s out into the field.[37]

The M4s delivered to the 756th consisted of two model types: an M4 with an angled welded hull and an M4A1 with a rounded cast hull. The British nicknamed both types "Shermans," but American tankers always referred to them as either "M4s" or "mediums." Each weighed a respectable thirty-two tons with an armored steel thickness measuring two inches at the front and one-and-a-half inches on the sides. The M4 was the only American medium tank featuring a fully rotational 75mm cannon turret. This main gun was, by far, the M4's best feature. By early 1944, battlefield advances demanded an infantry support tank delivering large, high-explosive rounds at close range. The M5 light tank's 37mm gun was too weak. It fired a 3-pound M63 round sending a projectile downrange weighing only about a pound-and-a-half with roughly one-and-a-half ounces of TNT explosive.[38] The 75mm gun, on the other hand, fired a 19-pound M48 round dispatching a *15-pound* projectile with about a *pound-and-a half* of TNT.[39] It was like comparing a firecracker to a stick of dynamite. The 75mm main gun was also outfitted with a rudimentary gyrostabilizer. When engaged, this revolutionary device helped keep the gun elevation level while the tank was in motion.[40] The M4 gunner could traverse the gun a full

360 degrees by using either the slow, familiar hand wheel or by turning a pistol grip handle engaging an electric/hydraulic motor. The power traverse was one magnificent feature providing the M4 with a distinct battlefield advantage—the ability to whirl the gun around on target much faster than any German tank.[41]

Both tank models were powered by Wright Whirlwind R-975 9-cylinder radial engines. Originally designed for aircraft, the noisy motor was rated a hefty 400 horsepower and propelled the M4 up to 30 MPH over flat roadways.[42] Not surprisingly, putting a high-speed airplane engine inside a slow-moving tank led to some performance quirks. Oftentimes the engine had to be hand cranked up to forty times before starting.[43] Drivers also had to monitor the engine RPMs (revolutions per minute) while idling—otherwise the piston cylinders fouled of carbon and wore out prematurely.

Another new feature of the M4 was an azimuth dial added at the gunner's station. When combined with maps and firing tables, this instrument allowed the M4 to participate in indirect firing situations—similar to traditional artillery cannons.[44] Indirect fire techniques were new skills the 756th tank crews were expected to acquire during their short reorganization period.

A five-man crew manned the M4. The driver and bow gunner sat at their usual stations down front—entering and exiting through narrow oval roof hatches directly above their seats. The bow gunner station also had an emergency escape hatch cut into the floor behind his seat.

The turret crew positions were reconfigured. The gunner's station remained on the right side but the commander was now positioned behind him. A loader or "cannoneer" sat on the left side of the main gun and was responsible for inserting rounds into the breech. The task required speed, strength, and precision in noxious, cramped, and deafening conditions. Each round measured roughly three inches in diameter, twenty-four inches in length and weighed nearly twenty pounds. The breech block opened and closed automatically whenever rounds were seated and fired—meaning fingers could easily be severed or hands crushed if mistimed. The most common rounds used during combat were HE, armor piercing (AP or "shot"), and white phosphorous ("smoke"). HE was effective against most targets. Shot was a non-explosive steel slug designed to punch through enemy armor like a bullet. Smoke was used to mark distant targets or create smoke screens to mask tactical movement.

With a dedicated loader now added to the turret crew, the commander devoted his full attention to directing his crew's actions and monitoring the battlefield for dangers and targets. Whenever a target was identified, the commander instructed the gunner to traverse the turret accordingly and called out the appropriate round for the loader to use. With experience, loaders anticipated which rounds to have ready based on the type of target the commander identified. The commander verbally coached the gunner onto a mark by lining up a rough steel sight located outside his turret hatch with a steel vane welded on the turret above the gunner's telescopic sight.

Once the gunner confirmed the target in his telescopic gun sight, the commander estimated the distance, and the gunner adjusted the gun elevation to that range. At that point, the gun was ready to fire. A coaxial .30-caliber MG was also available to the gunner to engage and destroy targets. Crews strived for speed and efficiency during training. Obviously, the quicker a threat could be identified and destroyed, the better the chances for success and survival.

Should the unthinkable happen and the M4 was hit first, the turret crew suffered a terrible disadvantage: Only one hatch provided an exit for all three crew members. The loader faced the worst prospects for survival. To escape his station, he had to squeeze under the gun to reach the commander's position where the turret hatch was located. Because he had the furthest to go, he generally had to wait as the two others escaped ahead of him—and those few seconds were often all that was needed for the interior of an M4 to erupt into a raging inferno.

The commander communicated to his crew by flipping an intercom switch on the radio board behind him and then speaking into a handheld microphone. All tank members wore leather football-style crash helmets equipped with headphones to hear his instructions. When combat conditions became too noisy or the closed-circuit intercom failed, the five-man crew resorted to shouting or hand pressure signals to carry out the mission. Though a primitive and far less efficient way to operate, the crews still trained for that possibility.

To receive radio instructions from the platoon commander or platoon sergeant in another tank, the commander switched off the intercom system and turned on the platoon radio. All tanks were equipped with FM radio receivers for hearing commands, but only the platoon leader and the platoon sergeant's tanks were equipped with FM transmitters for sending orders.[45] FM radios were notoriously finicky and lacked a wide broadcast range—perhaps only ten or twenty miles under the best conditions. They did, however, allow for communication while on the move. The heavy clanking metal parts of an M4 in motion wreaked havoc with AM radio signals, so FM was a better choice.[46] Complicating matters, the infantry preferred AM radio bands, so the tanks and infantry could never communicate directly via radio with one another. This led to operational delays and the reliance on a cumbersome system whereby liaison personnel passed messages around inside battalion or regimental CPs.

The very first M4s were rushed to the British fighting in North Africa in September 1942.[47] The M4 gained instant popularity with British crews because of the cannon's far more potent 75mm HE round. The tank's thicker frontal armor also deflected many projectiles fired from German 37mm guns—the most common AT caliber at the time. Bigger rounds at closer ranges could still penetrate the M4, but such guns were not yet commonplace. After two years of combat, however, high velocity 75mm, 76mm, and 88mm guns became the dominant AT threats, and wary M4 crews learned to stay further and further away from these types of guns. German panzer firepower also began surpassing the M4's 75mm gun over this same timeframe. A German medium PzKw IV ("Mark IV") with 75mm cannon presented an even match, but the 45-ton Panther with a high velocity 75mm gun and the 60-ton Tiger with its deadly 88mm became veritable M4 killers. To survive an encounter with either, American tankers had to utilize the speed and maneuver of their tanks to try and hit their superior German counterparts in the sides or rear—or simply avoid them altogether and pass the problem off to tank destroyer or artillery units. Although the M4 remained an excellent infantry support weapon, by early 1944 virtually every type of German AT gun—whether towed, self-propelled, or armored—held a firepower advantage. And despite mounting M4 losses, the U.S. government developed no serious plans to replace it with something better gunned or more heavily armored.

At the outbreak of the war, U.S. Army doctrine set by Lt Gen Leslie McNair, an artillery officer, insisted that medium tanks should not directly engage enemy tanks. To fill that role, McNair created a separate force of self-propelled AT guns dubbed "Tank Destroyers" (TDs). In theory, the concept sounded marvelous, but in practice—an unworkable travesty. TDs were equipped with more powerful guns but were not as heavily armored as the M4. To accommodate the longer recoil from their bigger guns and dissipate cordite fumes more quickly, TDs required open top turrets. This left the gun crews vulnerable to everything ranging from airburst artillery to hand grenades or small arms fire—and even rainstorms. Because of this, TDs dared not go in the close-combat areas where the M4s operated—preferring instead to hang back at safer distances. TD crews struggled, however, to hit enemy tanks while operating several hundred yards to the rear—which frustrated the M4 crews and supporting infantry, who could see the panzers but dared not directly engage them. This asinine dilemma could have easily been avoided by simply delivering a better medium tank with a more powerful gun to *all* crews. Nevertheless, the War Department clung stubbornly to McNair's discredited "separate branch" armor theory and both M4 and TD crews paid dearly with their lives by fighting in such a handicapped manner.

Another shortcoming of the M4 was its narrow tracks. The tank would easily bog down in the sand, mud, or soft soil—places where German tanks with wider tracks easily crossed.[48] And although the M4's lower profile was a welcome improvement over the M3 medium, the M4 still sat higher than a German Mark IV and other comparable mediums tanks such as the Russian T-34. This higher profile made the M4 harder to conceal while seeking defilade.

The great triumph of the M4 was not the gun or design—but the wonder of American mass production. By late 1943, American factories churned out tens of thousands, with tens of thousands more on the way. Production of the M4A1 was authorized on 5 September 1941,[49] and the first models rolled out of Lima Locomotive Works in Ohio in February 1942.[50] By December 1943, 6,281 of the M4A1 version *alone* had been built. Other model types—6,848 M4s, 7,499 M4A4s—and roughly 6,000 M4A2s, had also been manufactured over the same time period.[51] By way of comparison, German industry produced approximately 5,000 PzKw IVs, 2,000 Panthers, and 800 Tigers over the same timeframe.[52] Therefore, American medium tank production outpaced the Germans on the order of four or five to one. German factories had no hope of closing this gap—especially when American planes, also churned out by the thousands, constantly kept bombing them.

The American production "miracle" should have been no surprise to Germany. In *Achtung - Panzer!*, a book Hitler enthusiastically championed, Heinz Guderian noted that American factories accounted for 77.2 percent of all the world's vehicles in 1936, whereas Germany accounted for only 4.8 percent.[53] The father of the *blitzkrieg* himself recognized U.S. industry already produced vehicles on the order of *sixteen times* that of Germany. Perhaps, if Hitler had heeded Guderian's math, he might have thought twice about rashly declaring war on the U.S. three years later. Hitler's right-hand man, the rotund and braggadocious Field Marshal Goering, once flippantly dismissed American industrial potential outright by remarking: "Americans cannot build airplanes. They are very good at refrigerators and razor blades."[54] Goering often made outrageous and idiotic boasts. Unfortunately, tens of millions of lives were snuffed out, maimed, or disrupted as a result of them.

By late 1943, Hitler habitually threw purple rages over equipment shortages before his generals, while Goering ducked from bunker to bunker, hoping to avoid waves of American bombers. At the same time, ports in Allied Europe and on liberated South Pacific islands overflowed with factory-new stockpiles of American aircraft, tanks, trucks, munitions, and all manner of supplies—pulled from the cavernous holds of thousands of American transport vessels streaming across oceans aggressively patrolled by a burgeoning American navy. The full spectrum of the industrial might and innovative spirit of the American economy was now directed toward winning the war—which is also why there is no excuse for American tankers and TD crews being forced to continue fighting inside tanks inferior to what the Germans—or even the Russians—could produce.[55]

* * *

Field training for the 756th Tank Battalion commenced on 20 December. The crews drove the M4s around for extended times and became accustomed to their size, power, and maneuvering capabilities. The daily field work was combined with daily classwork. The courses contained a whirlwind of information both old and new. The large group of replacements received a special three-day orientation course encompassing basic soldiering, calisthenics, military courtesy and discipline, Articles of War, bivouac and convoy security, guard duty, battalion organization and history, and the mission of tanks. The new men also learned how to identify mines and booby traps, how to protect against air attacks, and proper first echelon (front line) vehicle maintenance. As an added bonus, the men received the Army's official views on sexual hygiene—always guaranteed to elicit snickers and groans.[56] American soldiers everywhere were already fed up with being inspected, poked, prodded, and dusted as a result of the Army's "short arm" obsession.[57]

Doc Sarno taught refresher courses on First Aid and protection against chemical attacks, and 1st Lt Olson taught a class on radio communications. The tank crews brushed up on their .30- and .50-caliber MG firing skills on the range. The M4's instrumentation and the 75mm's gyrostabilizer were closely examined and the main gun was also range fired. Crews used familiar fire order and adjustment procedures practiced countless times on the M5's smaller 37mm for line-of-sight targeting, but new indirect fire protocols presented the biggest learning challenges. This new approach relied not on visual identification and range estimation for targeting, but on mathematical tables and azimuth readings. The Army insisted the tank crews spend a great deal of effort mastering this technique. At the same time, the mechanics poured through the M4 manuals, while the battalion's newest drivers practiced their skills by grinding through the gears of tanks, half-tracks, trucks, and jeeps. Finally, everybody was rounded out with refreshers on tank tactics at the company, platoon, and section levels.[58]

The rains returned on 22 December, adding a limb-numbing layer of misery to field training and range fire exercises. Despite the damp chill, the crews excelled. Wilkinson was forced, however, to reprimand T/5 Laliberty for drinking wine while on duty. The battalion took Christmas Day off to enjoy a warm meal of turkey, cherry pie, fruits, and nuts.[59] Few were allowed to leave camp though. Nearby Naples had been declared off limits due to an outbreak of typhoid fever.[60]

Training resumed 26 December—the rain let up but left behind the coldest day to date.[61] The crews dispersed across frigid fields to begin the indirect firing they studied so intently in class. On 27 December, B Company members Pvts Merle E. Brooks and Ford T. Draeger staggered back to duty after taking an unauthorized Christmas extension. Wilkinson rewarded the two celebrants with hard work detail.

The indirect firing practice continued through the 28th and 29th, but the crews and platoon leaders found the work difficult and confusing. Fortunately, B Company's newest lieutenant, 2nd Lt John Czajkowski was trained in artillery gunnery and brought everyone up to speed.[62] During this same time period, the tanks returned to bivouac every evening and the maintenance crews welded additional gun shield plating around the new telescopic sights and painted camouflage patterns on their hulls.[63] On 30 December, the crews returned to direct fire practice using the 75mm gun and also the .30-caliber and .50-caliber MGs. By the end of the day, Wilkinson sensed a major page had turned. The men began showing familiarity with, and great pride in, their new tanks.[64] A sad pall fell over camp, however, when the crews returned from the field to discover an A Company member named Adams had died in an accidental fall. The tanker's body had been located two days after he slipped off a blown bridge near S'Agata.[65]

New Year's Day 1944 ushered in a hard wind and driving rain so wicked that large trees toppled over, pup tents hopelessly thrashed and pyramidal tents collapsed—Wilkinson's included. The next day, the sky cleared and a calm, mellow sun emerged, helping dry things out quickly.[66] Sweeting spent the afternoon touring each company, giving a scripted pep talk called "A Desire to Close with the Enemy," and observing the training in progress.[67] The crews returned to the direct fire range in the early morning of 3 January—maneuvering over frost-covered ground and thick, dank air generating an unshakable chill all day long. Italian weather was maddingly volatile. Those suffering from chronic sinus problems or aching joints cursed the wild barometric pressure swings.

On 4 January, the Armed Forces Radio Service reported that Soviet armies had pushed to the Polish border—in essence, rolling back all of Operation *Barbarrosa*. That evening, Wilkinson joined his company officers Winlock, Czajkowski, Leger, and Henry in a friendly game of poker.[68] Only Redle was missing from the table. The next day, Sweeting led a class on direct fire but became so mixed up his lecture was unintentionally comical, and the officers struggled to suppress grins and giggles.[69] The tankers returned to indirect fire practice on the 6th. The exercises progressed smoothly, until Lt Czajkowski crushed his hand in his 75mm gun's recoil and had to go to hospital.[70] On 7 January, the indirect fire continued with the target range extended out to 8,000 yards. At those distances, the crews discovered the firing charts started to falter. Smoke rounds, for example, no longer fell as the tables predicted. The gunners and commanders also had a difficult time observing the results—even through binoculars and telescopic gun sights. In the end, they discovered the only practical way to engage targets so far away was to mark them first with smoke rounds.

The intense field training concluded on 8 January. Throughout the entire training period, Sgt Roland L. Buys and Sgt Gilkerson were forced to endure two mechanical nightmares for tanks. Only at the end, were these wrecks finally exchanged for better models with Ordnance.[71] The battalion's communications officer, 1st Lt Olson, received a promotion to captain—much to the congratulatory delight of his fellow officers.[72] A few other loose ends dealing with supply and record keeping were also rectified, and the twenty-one-day training marathon came to an official close. The men were very pleased with the performance of the M4's 75mm gun and felt confident of its battle worthiness. Many wished they had been given such a powerful gun much, much sooner.

For once, the 756th didn't have to wait long for a change of station instructions. The next day, 9 January, orders were cut by the Fifth Army for the Army's newest medium tank battalion to advance into the Mignano Gap.[73] At one minute after midnight on 10 January, the 756th was officially detached from the U.S. VI Corps and attached to the 1st Tank Group of the II Corps.[74] The 1st Tank Group provided a regimental-level armor command layer for the corps—facilitating the flexible employment of independent tank battalions. For all practical purposes, though, the 756th was dispatched to the front lines in support of the 34th Division.[75] The company commanders arose before dawn, scarfed down quick meals and shots of coffee, then climbed atop cold jeep seats and set out for chaotic battle lines further north.[76] The rest of the battalion was scheduled to follow later that evening under a cloak of darkness. Once the advance detail arrived, the officers were to find their new bivouac locations and immediately reconnoiter the hell awaiting them beyond the shattered stone ruins of Mignano and San Pietro and the scarred, blood-soaked hills of Monte Lungo and Rotundo.

U.S. VI Corps

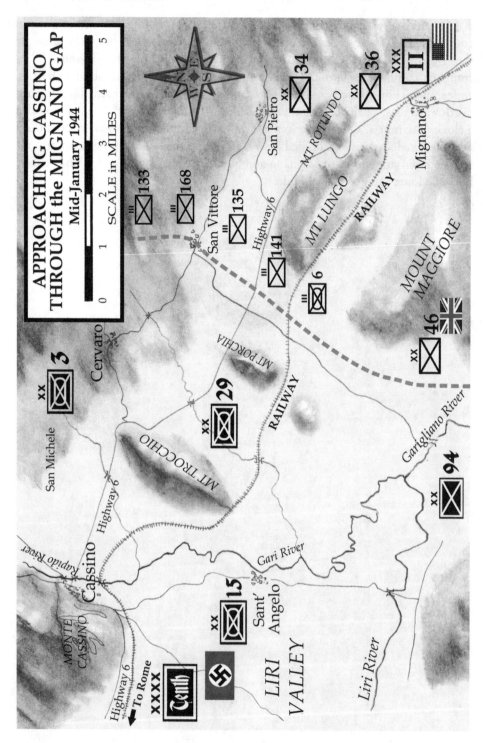

APPROACHING CASSINO
THROUGH the MIGNANO GAP
Mid-January 1944

SCALE in MILES
0 1 2 3 4 5

CHAPTER 11

The Gates of Hell: 11 January 1944 to 21 January 1944

On the moonless night of 10 January, a long convoy of medium tanks and trucks from the 756th Tank Battalion rumbled sixty miles northward to join the 34th Division at the front. The air was foggy and cold, and the journey was slow and laborious over roads hard surfaced but unpredictably slippery from condensation.[1] The M4's brake pads were notorious for slickening in wet conditions, but the drivers had become well accustomed to the challenges of the Italian countryside and grateful just to be spared another round of heavy rains.[2] The crews remained alert, but pensive and quiet—each man struggling to subdue his own unwelcome thoughts and private apprehensions. The dry-mouth anxiety felt similar to those very first hours on the beachhead near Pasteum.

The column crossed the Volturno River—skirting past silent, shadowy ruins of farmhouses and splintered trees. The horizon ahead flickered with the sporadic flashing of artillery, and a low muffled thunder underscored the menacing but mesmerizing display. As the tanks advanced deeper through the maw of the Mignano Valley, the spectacle swelled in sound, violence, and wrath. Two miles shy of Monte Rotundo, the unnerving cacophony completely enveloped them. Spread over the surrounding valley floor, American howitzers pounded out a deafening symphony of malice. The high granite mountains on either side served as a natural amphitheater—making every muzzle blast sound like ten. Ears numbed from the unrelenting, dissonant assault. Eyes struggled to focus through the strobe effect, and conversation was nearly impossible. A swirling haze of acrid cordite hung low in the cool air like sulfur oozing from the Netherworld. The 756th had truly arrived at the "Gates of Hell."

The tanks and trucks filed past the devastated village of Mignano as the strobing artillery illuminated the rubble like some demented movie projector. Each company was then separated from the main column and directed into adjacent fields to assume their seats in the "Devil's orchestra." B Company pulled into an area roughly 200 yards northeast of Mignano.[3] The new bivouac sat next to a dug-in artillery battery of 155mm Long Toms. The big guns roared with bone-jarring ferocity, sending concussive waves buffeting through B Company's camp so forcefully that a man would be knocked down if caught walking mid-stride.[4] Nearby, another battery of smaller 105mm howitzers also popped away with unceasing intemperance. B Company's campsite was heavily scarred with shell craters from battles past, but the location also offered protective foxholes—some of which were elaborately constructed by previous occupants and reinforced with thick roofs of timber and soil. The 36th Division had inhabited the same grounds only days before. Before that, the 3rd Division had called the place home. And before that, some unknown German unit had excavated the original burrows and trenches. Discarded tins, scraps of litter, and spent ammunition cartridges mixed in with the muddied soil. None of the previous tenants had shown any interest in housekeeping.

Amidst the sporadic racket of these noisy neighbors, Captain Wilkinson directed his M4s to spots he personally selected earlier so his crews could join in indirect firing operations if ordered. Once parked, the crews erected pup tents or took up residence in nearby foxholes. Lt Redle and his crew chose to unroll their bedrolls on open ground midway between their tank and a foxhole in order to retreat to either place quickly in an emergency. Despite the horrendous din, many tankers attempted sleep. Others stayed awake and tried reading or playing cards inside their tents, but the blast concussions kept extinguishing their candles and they soon quit in frustration and turned in as well.[5] In time, the artillery barrage slowed and then ceased altogether—but well past midnight.

When dawn broke, the four tank companies commanders, Captains Wilkinson and Lewis and Lts David Loeb and Nelson, drove three miles northwest to Monte Porchia—passing between Monte Rotundo and Monte Lungo, dodging shell craters and encountering all manner of vehicular wreckage along the way.[6] Because B Company had been assigned to guard the flanks of the 600-foot-high hill, Wilkinson brought his three platoon leaders along: Lts Winlock, Henry, and Leger.[7] Monte Porchia had just been captured by Task Force Allen after a brutal five-day fight. Scores of dead American and German soldiers remained scattered all over the rocky slope.[8] At first glance, one might have believed the prone figures were merely resting after a long, hard night. Occasional cool breezes would rustle clothing flaps or woolen sleeves—creating the illusion the wearers were stirring to life. Closer scrutiny, however, revealed missing limbs and blood saturated uniforms dried to a rusty brown. Some figures were no longer recognizable as human beings and perished in ways too horrific to contemplate—so one didn't. The eyes and minds of the living had to stay focused on matters of the living.

Task Force Allen, comprising units from the 1st Armored Division, had been so badly battered during the ordeal that the 34th Division was directed to continue their mission. The 756th officers slowly and methodically ascended the frigid slopes on foot. From the barren summit, they studied Monte Trocchio a mile further to the northwest. The long, gray granite ridge was the 34th's next objective. It stood twice as high as Monte Porchia but had a much longer and wider base—appearing like the scaly gray back of some huge prehistoric beast bursting up through the valley floor. In the distance beyond and to the left lay the strategically vital Liri Valley. This wide fertile bowl led directly to Rome some sixty miles further northwest. On the right, guarding the valley's entrance stood a 1,500-foot-high mountain parapet known as Monte Cassino.[9] A magnificent Benedictine abbey capped its southernmost edge. Even from five miles away, the ancient building's tall yellow-white walls sparkled in the morning sun with serene, tantalizing beauty.[10] On the valley floor directly beneath the abbey lay the town of Cassino. Certainly, at that very moment the Germans were feverishly completing a monster network of defenses along that same steep ridge and throughout the town. They would not concede this critical gateway without another bitter fight. Monte Cassino, however, was a problem for another day. The tank officers' immediate concerns were two-fold: Identify the most effective ways of supporting the upcoming infantry attack on Monte Trocchio and develop defenses for Monte Porchia against any possible German counterattack. After examining the terrain and discussing their observations with one another, the officers returned to bivouac later in the day to await further developments.

At the same time, the 34th Division advanced toward the small farming town of Cervaro roughly a mile northeast of Monte Trocchio. The artillery pounding the night before had been directed upon that ill-fated town as a prelude to this very attack.[11] Evidently, the operation was proceeding well, as no tank support had been requested.

The 34th Division first moved into the Mignano Gap in mid-December to relieve the 36th Division, exhausted after a meat-grinding battle to take the town of San Pietro and nearby Monte Lungo.[12] Allied progress up the narrow valley had been excruciatingly slow because the Germans used the same effective defensive tactic repeatedly: Secure the high mountains on both flanks and then select a crucial valley hill or town to hold the center. The Allies could not easily outflank or dislodge the defenders without paying an exorbitant price in lives, materiel, and time. Whenever the Germans were finally defeated, they simply fell back to another town and hill and repeated the same frustrating process all over again. Maj Gen Fred L. Walker, commanding the 36th Division, bitterly complained: "There is always another mountain pass beyond with Germans on it."[13] The tactic wore down entire Allied infantry divisions: The 3rd and 36th Division were burned out capturing Mignano, Monte Rotundo, Monte Lungo, and San Pietro, respectively. Next, Task Force Allen's troops were decimated taking Monte Porchia, and so the 34th Division and a rested and reorganized 36th Division assumed the lead. The 36th was ordered to press toward the southern half of Monte Trocchio,[14] while the 34th—still fresh after capturing San Vittore on 5 January—would take the hill's northern half and nearby town of Cervaro. These places presented the very last obstacles remaining in the Mignano Gap. Fortunately, three straight months of bitter fighting also left the Germans drained and battered, and they failed to fortify Cervaro as strongly as previous positions. As a result, by the end of 11 January, the town was successfully flanked and effectively sealed from receiving reinforcements.[15]

The morning of 12 January was bright, sunny, and beautiful. As the 168th Regiment of the 34th Division stormed the rubble-strewn streets of Cervaro,[16] an epic aerial battle unfurled high overhead. At one point, an American fighter plane burst into flames, spinning earthward. The pilot was able to bail out and parachute to safety near the 756th's camp—just as his doomed plane slammed into a nearby mountain.[17]

Cervaro fell with startling ease to the 168th, so B Company's mission shifted away from defending Monte Porchia to supporting infantry "mopping up" operations with indirect fire. Toward that end, Lt Col Sweeting and Captain Wilkinson scouted out firing positions southeast of town. Wilkinson was surprised to discover the landscape heavily cratered with shell holes. The devastation reminded him of grim battlefield photos he had seen in World War I history books.[18] By afternoon, however, the fire support plan had been canceled outright.[19]

Still in a reconnaissance mood, Wilkinson invited Lt Redle to return with him to the summit of Monte Porchia to study further the conditions around Monte Trocchio. While ascending the slopes, Wilkinson encountered a 36th Division captain who filled him in on additional details regarding the San Pietro battle a few weeks earlier. To his shock, Wilkinson learned that his good friend and fellow Texas A&M classmate, 1st Lt Charlie Hamner, had been killed in that fight.[20] By the time Wilkinson and Redle returned to their camp near Mignano later in the day, most of Cervaro had been cleared. Now, the 34th Division's focus shifted squarely upon the capture of Monte Trocchio.[21]

On the morning of 13 January, Lt Col Sweeting, Captain Wilkinson, and Lt Redle drove to the outskirts of Cervaro to scout out potential tank attack routes leading southwest toward Monte Trocchio. Sweeting choose B Company to support the infantry attack, but after surveying the situation told Wilkinson that he believed tanks wouldn't be able to cross Highway 6 due to heavy damage. The men parked the jeep and continued on foot toward the elongated mountain in search of alternative routes. Wilkinson and Sweeting set out in one direction, while Redle went another way to investigate an infantry report of a "bomb hole in a bridge." The morning had warmed to a balmy fifty-five degrees and the search was unexpectedly long. Redle, still attired in his winter tanker combat jacket and pants, began sweating profusely as he ducked, weaved, and scurried his way along the narrow ridge road. While approaching Cervaro, he came across a small stream flowing through an old culvert beneath the road. Nearby, a bomb blast had gouged out a sizable chunk of roadway. Surely, Redle thought, this was neither a "bridge" nor a "hole in the road"—and so he ventured on through the ruins of Cervaro. Roughly 200 yards beyond town, he passed several bedraggled American MG crews huddled behind rock piles and monitoring the quiet road ahead.

"Are you fellas in reserve?" Redle hollered.

"Yes ..." they grunted gruffly, and so Redle pressed on another several hundred yards—wondering now if the "bridge" was the figment of someone's imagination. He stole past a few more road bends before stopping at a small spring trickling over the road. He glanced up to see the sharp, gray slope of Monte Trocchio rising shockingly near and just above the tree line. Beyond its edge, Monte Cassino loomed only two miles further off in the distance. Crisper features to both the hilltop abbey and the sprawling town were clearly visible. At that very moment, a swarm of American B-25s raced into view and dropped a slew of bombs throughout Cassino, sending debris spinning skyward and thick clouds of dust billowing above the town's patchwork of orange tiled roofs. Awestruck, Redle watched the spectacle for a few minutes and decided he had probed far enough. As he turned to leave, the air cracked from several gun shots, and mortar rounds began bursting all around him. Realizing instantly that he had wandered into German territory, Redle dove into the roadside ditch and scrambled its entire length until reaching Cervaro. He arrived in the village's shattered center soaked, muddy, and gasping for air. Waiting for him were Sweeting and Wilkinson—eyebrows rising as he approached. Between breaths, Redle reported seeing the small culvert and bomb crater, but no bridge. When he described the extent of his search and of his close encounter with German gunfire, Sweeting burst out laughing. The lieutenant colonel recognized from infantry reports that Redle had strayed several hundred yards into enemy-held territory. Wilkinson stood mortified, but upon realizing his XO was otherwise unharmed, a smile of relief slowly crossed his face.

That same morning, Sgts Roland L. Buys and Hamilton A. Smith accompanied an infantry patrol reconnoitering a wider swath of terrain between Cervaro and Monte Trocchio.[22] As a result of the two sergeants' findings and the officers' field observations, only one B Company platoon was committed to the infantry's attack: Lt Winlock's 1st Platoon.[23] On the return trip to Mignano, the three officers stopped briefly to observe German prisoners being processed. Each one wore the thin black forearm band of the Herman Goering Division.[24]

The Long Toms and 105s positioned near B Company's bivouac fired steadily throughout the day and well into the evening—no doubt "softening up" Monte Trocchio ahead of the upcoming infantry assault. The men of B Company were becoming accustomed to the pounding racket. Shortly after midnight, however, Redle awoke to some heavy howling sounds that were clearly out of the ordinary. The Germans were returning counterbattery fire—sending high velocity flat-trajectory rounds whooshing directly over B Company's bivouac. The rounds snarled by before exploding into spark and flame against high ground a mile or so behind camp. After listening to a few passes, Redle deduced the trajectory as too low and fast to hit B Company, and so he turned over and attempted to fall back asleep. Moments later, the bivouac shuddered under a series of explosions. The Germans had ratcheted up the artillery duel by adding in higher arced "big stuff." The rude attack sent men diving immediately for foxholes or to the interiors and undercarriages of their M4s. Redle landed in the nearest foxhole and lay helplessly flat while another chain of explosions buffeted through camp. Over the clamor he heard some poor soul yelling "Medic! Medic!" Seconds later, *all* the big guns of the neighboring Long Tom battery responded—and the unified ferocity was *nothing* like the regular pounding the tankers had grown accustomed to hearing. One gun positioned near Redle's foxhole fired off rounds so rapidly he thought the muzzle would begin glowing red. Every time the long barrel bucked and belched fire, sheets of dirt and loose stone rained down upon him and other hapless B Company tankers that were huddled nearby. After a few minutes of this intense exchange, the Germans finally backed down and quit firing counterbattery. The Long Toms also fell silent and the vicious ten-minute duel concluded almost as abruptly as it had commenced.

Redle shook off the soil and rushed in the direction he had heard the earlier cries for help. The powder crew assigned to one of the Long Tom's had suffered a near miss. One enlisted man was slightly wounded and receiving medical attention as his crewmates excavated their buried equipment from the edge of a freshly cratered shell hole. Miraculously, nobody else was hurt.

A few hours later, dawn broke over the valley—allowing any damage sustained throughout the 756th bivouac to be more closely evaluated. A German shell had narrowly missed one of the HQ tanks, but the blast blew off both the engine's rear air filters. The medical half-track was found peppered through with dozens of shrapnel holes and the communication truck was blown completely apart. A pyramidal tent had also been shredded to pieces—soon after the occupants fled for cover. One man returned to find a 1-½-inch piece of shrapnel lodged in a boot upon which his head had rested only moments prior.[25] Luckily, no one from the 756th was killed outright, but three C Company men were left wounded—one of them seriously enough that he died three days later.[26]

The morning was again sunny and beautiful, and Wilkinson returned to Cervaro for a final reconnaissance.[27] After conferring with the officers of the 168th Regiment, he called upon 1st Lt Winlock to move the 1st Platoon forward into the town square by 0930 and prepare for battle. The attack commenced on schedule and proceeded with surprising speed. The infantry encountered little resistance—even as they methodically scaled the northeastern slopes of the mountain later in the afternoon.[28] At that point, Winlock's crews could not follow due to the steep pitch, but they did remain on the road providing fire support from a distance. Periodically, Winlock's crews were called upon to dispatch 75mm HE into suspected hillside pillboxes or discharge suppressive MG fire—allowing the infantry to flank and clear out the ridge one section at a time. During one engagement, Sgt Gilkerson attempted to maneuver his tank into a better firing position but threw both tracks and became hopelessly wedged against a granite ledge.[29] The drivers still grappling to understand the M4s limits, discovered the suspension system was prone to shedding the treads while reversing—even on mild grades with soft soil.[30] Gilkerson's crew dismounted to dig foxholes when German shelling started raining down around them. Pvt Cletus Offerman felt the ground shudder and was bowled over by a thick layer of churned soil. After extricating himself, he saw a hot, gleaming German artillery shell still smoking in a small pit near his feet. Miraculously, the round had failed to explode.[31]

Later in the afternoon, Wilkinson and Sweeting checked on the 1st Platoon's progress. Sweeting complimented Lt Winlock for selecting good defilade positions but cautioned his crews to wait until nightfall before withdrawing for servicing—particularly on account of the one disabled tank. Aside from the thrown tracks incident, B Company's first combat mission using M4 mediums was a great success. Certainly, two-and-a-half years of light tank training helped, but Wehrmacht master strategy also played a major role. Most Germans vacated the area—leaving behind only enough resistance on Monte Trocchio to cover their comrades' retreat to Monte Cassino. The Mignano Gap's last mountain may have fallen in an anticlimactic fashion, but as the exasperated Maj Gen Walker noted earlier, the Germans were always waiting on the next one.[32]

As instructed, Winlock's crews withdrew in the dead of night, taking Gilkerson's crew along with them. Lt Redle, Motor Sergeant Morris Thompson, and two mechanics piled into the T2 tank retriever and drove to Monte Trocchio to recover the disabled tank.[33] Upon reaching the location, Redle realized they were stopping only halfway down the same twisting road he had walked the previous morning.[34] As artillery burst sporadically around them, Technical Sergeant (T/Sgt) Thompson and the two mechanics worked frantically trying to reseat the thrown track back around the front drive sprocket. Because the 32-ton tank was askew and wedged against the steep granite ridge, the task proved virtually impossible. In desperation, Thompson yanked hard on a four-foot wrench handle as T/4 Roy R. Kosanke struggled to hold the head steady. Just then, an artillery round burst against nearby granite, sending the men scampering for cover. Kosanke tripped and Thompson stepped squarely on the fallen mechanic's hand. Kosanke's hand swelled up black and blue, but fortunately no bones were broken. Nevertheless, he needed immediate medical care and was sidelined for the evening.[35] Gilkerson's tank had to be abandoned until morning.[36]

Sunday, 16 January was spent restocking, refueling, and waiting. As American artillery batteries spread around Mignano pounded away on a series of new German targets laying beyond Monte Trocchio, Captain Wilkinson hovered about the 168th Regimental HQ with Lt Col Sweeting and Captain Arnold.[37] The 168th was being relieved by one of two sister regiments: the 135th.[38] The tank officers hoped to gain some idea of the 34th Division's next mission—but gleaned little. The next day, the battalion was ordered to move from Mignano to the vicinity of San Pietro five miles away.[39] At 0215, 18 January, the battalion rolled to their new bivouac under the usual cover of darkness. B Company took up positions upon sloped terrain three-quarters of a mile northwest of the devastated village.[40] All of San Pietro's ancient stone buildings sat as silent rubble piles after months of fierce ground combat and furious artillery dueling—and that sparring had still not ceased. The night before, some thirty men camped upon the same slope were wounded by yet another flurry of German shells.

Wilkinson noticed that a large hillside grove of olive trees had somehow managed to escape the carnage, and so he directed his crews to use their canopies as cover and to disperse across the gentle grade. The sickening odors of decomposing flesh wafted in waves over the cool night breeze. The place reeked of death but, at least, seemed relatively quiet. No noisy artillery batteries were positioned nearby. When morning broke, the tankers could finally see the source of the horrible stench: Scores of dead American and German soldiers were strewn about further up the hillside.[41] The area remained heavily mined so Graves Registration could not retrieve the month-old corpses without the aid of mine-clearing engineers.[42] Those teams, however, were too busy fighting and could not be freed for the job.

Beyond Monte Trocchio, the Germans settled behind their elaborate defenses at Cassino. This fortification network extended across the Liri Valley to the Tyrrhenian coast and then up and over the high Apennines and back down to the Adriatic. The slugfest up the Mignano Gap, lasting two-and-a-half months, was used by the Germans to buy precious time completing this one-hundred-mile-long "wall." The Germans called their masterwork the "Gustav Line" and intended to hold it forever. The British Eighth Army was responsible for attacking along the more rugged end of the Gustav Line on the eastern side of the Italian peninsula. The U.S. Fifth Army, however, was tasked with breaking through on the western side and gaining access into the strategically vital Liri Valley.

The Fifth Army's zone was subdivided into three sections. On the left, the British X Corps pressed along a twelve-mile section running from the sea into the Liri River. The U.S. II Corps—with the 36th and 34th Divisions at the fore—was responsible for attacking along a narrower six-mile-wide middle section where Cassino was located, and the French Expeditionary Corps held several miles of front along the Fifth Army's mountainous right flank. Without a doubt, the fortunes of the Fifth Army hinged on the capture of Cassino and the old abbey situated on the heights overlooking the valley. Even the most inexperienced infantry officer given a topographical map and pair of binoculars would conclude that an army holding Monte Cassino controlled the entire Liri Valley. One could not enter the valley without taking that mountain first. With rugged terrain flanking Monte Cassino to the right, and deep rapidly flowing rivers crisscrossing the lowlands to the left, the point could not be easily bypassed nor approached without sustaining horrendous losses. For years, Italian officers studied the location as an ideal natural fortress—virtually impregnable to an attacking army.[43]

The Benedictine abbey dated back to the founding of Christendom as the last vestiges of the Roman Empire crumbled into tragic ruin. For 1,500 years, the 660-foot-long redoubt stood as an island of peaceful spiritual contemplation, while countless regional wars flared and were forgotten, plagues waxed and waned, and new states emerged and then disintegrated all across Europe.[44] Over the centuries, generations of dedicated monks living behind the abbey's twelve-foot-thick walls dodged the occasional earthquake or barbarian sacking to amass the finest art, literature, and scholarly texts generated by Western civilization.[45] Monte Cassino quite literally housed the soul of Europe, and now two mighty armies sought control of it. The Geneva Convention Treaties, signed by all governments fielding those armies, prohibited the abbey's use for purposes of war. Although the old redoubt offered a tempting and ideal OP, German field commanders swore they would respect the site's neutrality.[46] The Americans and British were skeptical. German officials—particularly National Socialists—possessed a poor track record for trustworthiness.

In reality, the abbey wasn't the only ideal location the Germans could choose to watch Allied forces pouring in from the Mignano Gap. Many other nearby places offered observation points just as suitable, if not better. In fact, the long series of craggy heights rising all the way up to snow-capped Monte Caira five miles to the northwest provided innumerable caves, crevices, and smaller ridgelines from which to secretly scrutinize the valley below.

As soon as the U.S. Fifth Army broke out of Salerno in September 1943, the Germans started working intensively on their Gustav Line. For centuries, the town of Cassino had thrived as a peaceful and prosperous regional market hub, but by November 1943, the Germans had evacuated most of the 25,000 inhabitants—at times, on pain of whips and clubs—to begin converting the old town into a veritable fortress.[47] Over 44,000 Todt engineers poured into the area—transforming scores of village basements and outlying farmhouses into bunkers fortified with thick timber, crushed gravel, concrete, and steel— built to withstand even direct artillery blows.[48] The engineers also blasted out countless caves and hollows into the hard granite ridge behind and to the north of town. Inside each, they positioned MGs, mortars, and gun turrets with unobstructed fields of fire covering every approach leading to the Rapido and artillery OPs possessing panoramic views of the Mignano Gap. In a final touch of artistic deviousness, everything was disguised to appear as mundane civilian structures or innocent natural features.[49]

The Rapido River runs down from the high Apennines, flows past Cassino to become the Gari and then joins the Liri River to form the Garigliano. The Rapido is not particularly broad or normally treacherous, but the water levels do rise and fall with seasonal storms. Heavy snows and torrential rains upstream can temporarily transform the Rapido into a muddy, brimming ribbon of floodwaters. Countless weather cycles over millennia have carved a channel with high banks and an irregular riverbed where even low placid waters can conceal dangerous boulders, muck bars, pits, and drop-offs. Because of this, the Rapido River offers an ideal natural "moat" for any defender wishing to hold the high ground beyond. The Germans not only recognized this quality—but improved upon it—by sowing thick minefields throughout the farmland along both banks. Tree saplings and thickets of brush flourishing along the banks and already providing effective screens were left alone, but areas where vegetation hindered observation or the employment of MG "killing zones" were axed down, piled into long barrier rows and laced with razor-sharp concertina wire. For added unpleasantness, booby-trapped "potato masher" grenades were sprinkled throughout the twisted, withering branches.

Several miles downstream, where the Rapido/Gari merged to form the wider Garigliano, the 46th Division of the British X Corps attacked on 19 January in an attempt to gain a firm foothold into the southern edge of the Liri Valley. The Brits established a weak bridgehead but little else.[50] The German responded with such ferocity that the pinned and beleaguered British troops couldn't lift their heads above the riverbank without inviting a hail of bullets, mortar, and artillery.

Pressure shifted to the U.S. II Corps holding the Fifth Army's midsection to attempt the next river crossing. If they succeeded, the II Corps' next objective was the capture of Monte Castellone—a 771-meter-high rocky peak rising over the jagged massif a full two miles northwest of Cassino.[51] That distance equated to only a few inches on a military planner's map, but these were the toughest two miles in all of Italy at the time. The responsibility for capturing that territory fell upon the shoulders of Lt Gen Mark Clark of the Fifth Army and then cascaded into the arms of Maj Gen Geoffrey Keyes of the II Corps and Maj Gens Charles Ryder and Fred Walker of the 34th and 36th Divisions respectively. It then filtered further down into the laps of the regimental colonels, battalion lieutenant colonels and majors, before finally landing at the feet of the individual company captains and platoon lieutenants—all of whom reconnoitered their stakes in the situation, made operational recommendations based upon gathered information that was generally scant and often contradictory, and then prayed to God their guesses were right once the attack commenced. Many times, those guesses were wrong and dreadful adjustments had to be made on the fly.

On 19 January, rumors abounded of the 88th Infantry Division soon joining the fight in Italy and of the 3rd and 45th Division preparing for another invasion elsewhere.[52] Lt Col Sweeting and his company commanders clearly understood the 34th and 36th Division would attack Cassino soon and that the 756th Tank Battalion would play some key role, but details remained sketchy. At the very least, the tank officers needed to locate suitable indirect firing positions to support the infantry. Toward that end, Captain Wilkinson drove to Cervaro to scout the terrain north of town. At the time, bedraggled Italian civilians trickled back into town, looking to salvage useful items from the broken plaster and stone rubble that had once been their homes. Others quietly made coffins.[53] As he parked the

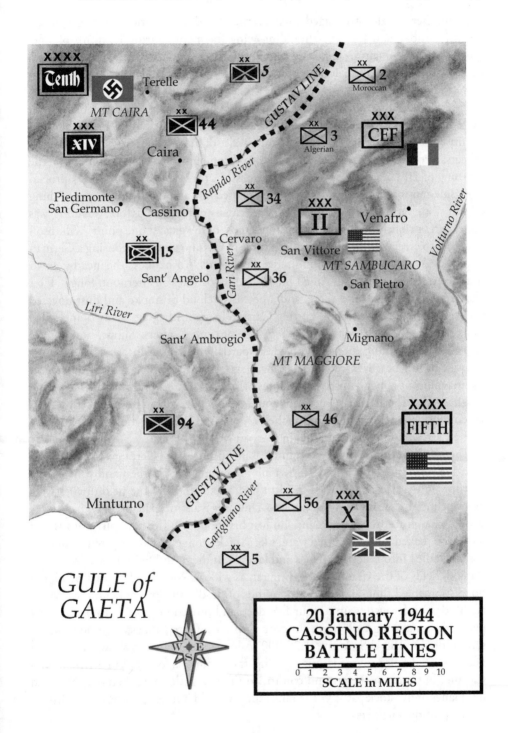

XXXX
Tenth

XX 5

XX 2
Moroccan

Terelle

MT CAIRA

XXX
XIV

XX 44

Caira

GUSTAV LINE

XX 3
Algerian

XXX
CEF

Rapido River

Piedimonte
San Germano

Cassino

XX 34

Cervaro

XXX
II

Venafro

Volturno River

XX 15

Gari River

San Vittore

MT SAMBUCARO

Sant' Angelo

XX 36

San Pietro

Liri River

Sant' Ambrogio

MT MAGGIORE

Mignano

XX 94

XX 46

XXXX
FIFTH

GUSTAV LINE

Garigliano River

Minturno

XX 56

XXX
X

XX 5

GULF of
GAETA

20 January 1944
CASSINO REGION
BATTLE LINES

0 1 2 3 4 5 6 7 8 9 10
SCALE in MILES

jeep, another aerial battle raged high overhead and an American fighter spiraled down in smoke and flames—shredding wing fragments during its death plunge. This time, no parachute appeared and the fuselage vanished in a fireball over a nearby ridge—taking the doomed pilot with it.[54] Perhaps the ground was the safer place to fight the war.

Later that evening, the 756th received their first tentative set of attack plans from the 34th Division HQ.[55] The battalion was also ordered to be prepared to fight on twenty-four-hours' notice.[56] Given a clearer sense of the mission, the 756th battalion officers, reconnaissance platoon members, and company commanders set out on the morning of 20 January to reconnoiter grounds northwest of Cervaro. They probed alongside cautious American infantrymen fanned out among the fields, establishing CPs in stone farmhouses vacated by the Germans only hours before. Scouting was done surreptitiously on foot and consumed most of the day. At one point, Wilkinson managed to creep within a few hundred yards of Cassino without arousing a German response. As the tankers reconnoitered fields and brush lines, the nearby town shuddered repeatedly under Allied hit-and-run air strikes all afternoon long.[57] Fires blazed in pockets here and there, and a pervasive cloud of smoke and dust hovered over the shattered townscape—casting Cassino in a ghostly gray. Many orange tiled roofs had been blown away—revealing skeletal timber rafters. Shops, homes, and apartments sustaining direct bomb blasts partially collapsed into cascading stone piles—clogging nearby streets and narrow alleyways. Perched high above the chaos sat the magnificent abbey—displaying scores of tiny gleaming windows in its towering pristine walls. The arriving Americans couldn't help but wonder if German observers sat comfortably behind those untouched ramparts at that very moment—laughing at their arrival and scrutinizing their every move.

The field scouting discovered an unpleasant surprise: The Germans had collapsed a bridge further up the Rapido—partially damming the riverbed and routing the overflow into adjacent lowlands to form hydra-like tendrils. The field ditches were overwhelmed by the fast-flowing waters—churning waist-deep in places with currents strong enough to drown the man who lost his footing.[58] The naturally porous and fertile soil soaked up the diverted water like a thick sponge. What the ground couldn't absorb pooled into mucky marshes and lakes.[59] At the 34th Division's section of the Rapido, fields of the viscous black mire ran as wide as 200 yards.[60] Worst of all, the flood submerged thousands upon thousands of deadly anti-personnel mines. Many lay hidden under waters up to four-feet deep and proved impossible to detect. Any plans for combining close tank support with an infantry attack were now put in serious doubt. The U.S. Army's 1:25,000 scale maps appeared to show a promising network of developed roads crisscrossing the ground between San Michele and Cassino, but eyes on the ground confirmed them as little more than deeply rutted farm lanes or livestock paths.[61] The tanks simply could not reach the Rapido without the help of the engineers.

The 756th needed an assembly area as close as possible to the action—where the tanks could be mustered, supplied, and readied for battle. The flooding greatly limited available choices. The best location turned out to be northwest of Cervaro, where the terrain gently sloped up from the Rapido toward the small farming hamlet of San Michele. The fields lying a mile west of the tiny crossroads town remained dry while offering clear panoramic views of the battlefield. The area also featured plenty of trees, brush and rippled landscape features allowing the tanks to provide fire support from a distance while maintaining defilade positions.

While the 756th and the 34th Division prepared their attack plans on Cassino, the 36th Division rushed to seize a section of the Rapido/Gari River near Sant' Angelo four miles to the south. Here, the diverted field waters replenished the riverbed with a vengeance. The bed was only twenty-five to fifty-feet wide, but the banks were eight-feet steep and the current flowed swiftly around twisting bends—swirling up to twelve-feet deep in some places. Fording was out of the question. Small boats had to be employed. The attack was hastily conceived in hopes of catching the Germans off guard so as to gain a firm foothold squarely in the center of the Liri Valley. If successful, an expanding bridgehead at Sant' Angelo might then be used to crowbar open the entire Gustav Line. The idea was a big gamble, but Lt Gen Clark believed the potential for payoff was worth the risk.

Despite the grave misgivings of the 36th Division commander, Maj Gen Walker, the attack commenced the evening of 20 January following a ferocious artillery barrage.[62] As the infantry fumbled forward through muddy minefields while toting heavy weapons *and* 13-foot-long boats weighing 400 pounds apiece,[63] the Germans of the 15th Panzer Grenadier Division slammed them pitilessly with mortars, MGs, and artillery.[64] The darkness provided no protection whatsoever. The Germans zeroed in on all river approaches beforehand, causing their swarms of shells to fall with devastating accuracy among the struggling Americans. Riflemen, BAR (Browning automatic rifle) men, and ammo bearers dove for cover or dropped dead trying.[65] Confusion ensued. The plywood hulls to many boats became riddled with shrapnel holes and were either discarded or sank immediately upon launch. Others still seaworthy enough to use were blown out of the water with their occupants swept away and drowned.[66] Of the 2,500 or so American troops who started the attack, perhaps only a few hundred managed to reach the opposite side—where they lay hopelessly pinned in place—soaking and shivering against the muddy riverbank. Many had to be withdrawn by the next morning.[67]

Lt Redle and other officers of the 756th monitored the battalion's AM radio—listening intently to the do-or-die drama unfolding in the 36th Division's sector.[68] All throughout 21 January, the 36th Division tried salvaging the feeble bridgehead with several seat-of-the-pants shoring-up operations—but to no avail. The element of surprise was lost, and the Germans exercised complete control of the situation. With too few troops across the river to provide covering protection, no vehicle-carrying

"Bailey" bridge could be assembled and secured by the engineers. Without those bridges, no tanks could reach the other side and clear the way for the arrival of reinforcements. The attack hopelessly stalled. The crowbar hit iron. On 22 January, the 36th Division abandoned the whole operation and withdrew anyone surviving along the far riverbank—leaving 143 confirmed dead, another 663 wounded, and 875 missing in action. This staggering loss of 1,681 men represented the fighting strength of two entire battalions—all sacrificed with absolutely nothing to show for it.[69]

The attack failed disastrously because preliminary reconnaissance was either faulty or skipped altogether.[70] Infantry officers were either too exhausted or too preoccupied with planning to lead patrols themselves. NCOs were given orders to conduct them instead. Human nature being such, the NCOs shied away from the necessary risks and reported areas clear that weren't properly probed. Once the main attack commenced, the pressure for success was so great that one battalion reported crossing the river when it really hadn't, and the other attacking battalions caught hell from above for not doing the same. The few infantrymen who did reach the opposite bank then wrongly assumed they benefited from flank support. Too many little errors compounded to the point where the entire operation unraveled. The only silver lining—albeit the thinnest thread—was that the epic failure left an indelible impression on the young officers of the 756th Tank Battalion. Captain Wilkinson, Lt Redle, and the others garnered all they could learn from the 36th Division's errors by monitoring radio communications, absorbing the official daily briefings, and heeding all the after-action scuttlebutt.[71]

They knew their turn was next, and they had not come this far to fail ....

U.S. 36th Infantry Division

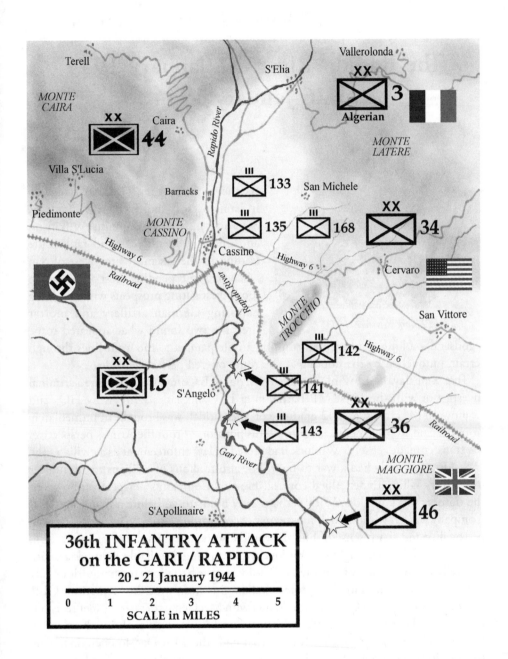

Terell

MONTE CAIRA

Caira

Villa S'Lucia

Piedimonte

MONTE CASSINO

Highway 6

Railroad

Barracks

Rapido River

S'Elia

Vallerolonda

Monte Latere

San Michele

Cassino

Highway 6

Cervaro

San Vittore

MONTE TROCCHIO

Highway 6

Rapido River

S'Angelo

Gari River

S'Apollinaire

MONTE MAGGIORE

Railroad

Algerian

**36th INFANTRY ATTACK
on the GARI / RAPIDO**
20 - 21 January 1944

0   1   2   3   4   5
SCALE in MILES

CHAPTER 12

The Rapido River: 21 January 1944 to 26 January 1944

T2 Tank Retriever (1943)

As the 36th Infantry Division struggled in vain to cross the river on 21 January, Sweeting instructed Captains Wilkinson and Lewis to identify a solid tank route leading to the assembly area west of San Michele. After spending most of the day on foot investigating prospects while dodging harassing German artillery and mortar fire,[1] the two found what appeared to be a godsend—a long, sunken road running a mile parallel to the front lines through terrain untouched by the flooding.[2] The route offered perfect defilade.

That same day, 1st Lt Winlock transferred out of B Company to become a criminal investigator with the 101st MP Battalion at Lt Gen Clark's Fifth Army HQ. 2nd Lt Howard M. Harley, a 1942 graduate of The Citidel, was brought in immediately from the 2nd Replacement Depot to fill his position.[3] From the Army's perspective, the transfer made sense, as Winlock had served in law enforcement as a civilian. The U.S. Army not only had a war to fight, but also millions of civilians to administer in territory falling under Allied control. From B Company's perspective, however, the transfer was a big loss. With perhaps only hours to go before a major battle, B Company was left without their most experienced platoon leader. Winlock's easygoing personality and sharp sense of humor would also be missed as a morale lifter. Still, his fellow officers made light of their loss by hammering the affable Kentuckian with farewell jokes of the same basic theme: Winlock—the battalion's most notorious lady charmer—had been drafted to protect Italian girls from oversexed American GIs![4]

Lt Col Sweeting and Captain Arnold met with Maj Gen Ryder to consider revisions to the 34th Division's attack plans.[5] The general insisted on tank involvement in the early phases of the attack.[6] Toward that end, the 34th Division's engineers set to work improving roads from Highway 6 into the upper Rapido Valley.[7] The basic battle plan utilized the classic triangular attack formation: Two of the 34th's three infantry regiments would strike side-by-side across the Rapido, with the remaining regiment held back in reserve. Within each attacking regiment, the pattern was repeated: Two battalions would strike while one battalion remained in reserve. Field conditions did not allow enough time to unspool the miles of telephone wire required to facilitate communications between infantry and tank commands. Therefore, liaison officers from the 756th would be dispatched with radio teams to coordinate instructions between the AM-based infantry and the FM-based tanks in the following manner: One tank officer would be assigned to each of the attacking infantry battalions and at each regimental CP. Lt Redle was selected to shadow the 2nd Battalion commander of the 133rd Regiment and relay his instructions by radio to the B Company platoon leaders.

The 34th Division's attack would commence along a two-mile section of the Rapido River north of the town. Basically, the challenge echoed conditions encountered nine months earlier at Fondouk Pass: The Allies needed to cross a flat river plain to capture a strategic pass on the left by clearing out German-held high ground on the right. Many smaller features beyond the Rapido had to be painstakingly studied before being approached. On the extreme left sat the town of Cassino with the abbey high on the ridge above. An ancient yellow stone castle with a soaring parapet capped another high, sharp hill immediately north of town. This hill was officially known as "193" from meter elevations listed on maps, but the Americans simply called it "Castle Hill." At the center of the 34th Division's attack zone, roughly a mile north of Cassino, lay a rowed cluster of single-story Italian military barracks. The grid of long modern buildings sat adjacent to a stately old farm called "Monte Villa"—and looked completely out-of-sorts with its idyllic rural surroundings. The thirty or so stark brick and cement buildings offered an ideal redoubt for German forces defending the river's west bank. Although many barrack roofs had been blown open from artillery and aerial bombardment, the unrelenting thrashing failed to penetrate numerous reinforced pillboxes concealed along the foundations.[8] Infantry would have to storm those positions. Maj Gen Ryder considered the barracks' capture critical to his division's overall battle plans. Once taken, his forces could then split along the ridge base: Half would move left on Cassino while the other half proceeded right toward the small town of Caira. The ultimate aim of the right flank was to take Monte Castellone, seal off Cassino from receiving reinforcements, and then move down upon the abbey through the highlands.[9]

The high ground between the barracks and Monte Castellone featured many challenging peaks, ridges, and high points. One lengthy ridge known locally as Colle Maiola ran up from Castle Hill and behind the barracks—with key elevations identified as "Hill 225" and "Hill 175" on the maps.[10] Approximately 100 yards to the right of the barracks sat a 156-meter-high conical mound, wryly dubbed "The Pimple" by the Americans.[11] Another high, rocky ridge behind The Pimple extended roughly a mile to the northwest before dropping down to the small valley village of Caira. This long, gray hill, dotted with scrub brush, stunted trees, and a few stone homes, was named "Hill 213"—also for its highest elevation point. Both hills appeared otherwise unremarkable—save for the knowledge that the Germans blasted and masked many gun positions into the sides of both hills.

In front of these forbidding granite masses lay a patchwork of farm fields leading down to the Rapido. The plain started out around 200 yards wide near the barracks and widened to roughly 1,000 yards nearer to Caira. A narrow ribbon of road hugged the base of The Pimple and Hill 213 leading from the barracks to Caira—skirting by an old walled cemetery along the way. The flatland between was dotted with modest stone farmhouses and crisscrossed by shallow irrigation ditches. The Germans cleared away much of the brush and trees, added extensive minefields and stitched row after row of barbed wire along the entire riverbank. For the infantry, the zone presented a daunting "no man's land." For the tanks, however, that same triangular patch of territory offered plenty of maneuvering space—and the anti-personnel mines, barbed wire, and shallow ditches could easily be trampled and neutralized beneath churning treads.

Before the tanks could cross, however, the infantry had to first establish a firm bridgehead on the far side. Until this was accomplished, the tanks could only provide limited support from defilade positions several hundred yards to the rear. If the infantry succeeded, Sweeting planned on A Company crossing first, followed by B Company. C company would continue offering fire support from the rear, while D Company's M5 light tanks patrolled as security along the flanks.[12] A greatest challenge facing the tank officers was finding suitable tank crossing sites. Once identified, the infantry and engineers would be alerted of those places.

The next day, 22 January, Captains Wilkinson, Lewis, and other 756th officers spent the morning and afternoon on foot surveying potential crossing sites north of the Monte Villa barracks. The task was dangerous and complicated. Nobody dared venture too close to the river because of the mines and muck. German observers followed their every move—periodically dispatching harassing mortar and artillery fire and sending the men scrambling. More probing reconnaissance would have to wait until after dark when the infantry could sneak armed patrols in a bit further.[13]

Astonishingly, many local Italian civilians continued working on nearby farms as they had for centuries. Women washed clothing on the banks of flowing streams. Children, thinly clad, toddled about barefoot as shells screamed overhead. Clusters of wretched refugees walked eastward into Allied territory carrying bundles of meager belongings while balancing baskets on their heads. Many appeared to be distressed families. Some suffered wounds from stray bullets or shell fragments, and American medics and doctors attended to them along with American troops.[14]

Late in the day, Wilkinson returned to his parked jeep to learn the U.S. 3rd Division and British forces had landed south of Rome at the coastal town of Anzio.[15]

The news raised Wilkinson's hopes that this new beachhead further north would ease the German grip on Cassino.[16] The development also explained why Lt Gen Clark had pushed so aggressively for the 36th Division's ill-fated river crossing effort two days earlier. Both operations launched simultaneously were supposed to divide German attention and rattle their military resolve over holding the Liri Valley.

In the dead of the night on 23 January, B Company's bivouac near San Pietro was rocked by an unusually heavy series of German artillery blasts. The tankers were dug in well and nobody was hurt by the barrage. After sunrise, Wilkinson returned to hiking the fields northwest of Cervaro—this time scouting out B Company's final tank positions in advance of the scheduled infantry attack the following evening.[17] The 133rd Regiment patrols from the previous night reported most brush and trees had been stripped from the river banks north of the barracks—providing the German defenders with clear "kill zones" for their MG crews. Anti-personnel mines seemed to be everywhere.[18] The patrols described the river level as low, but the current appeared swift and treacherous in places. The most promising tank crossing points appeared to be at a small stone bridge adjacent to the barracks complex and a longer cement bridge roughly 1,000 yards further north across from Caira among brush and pastureland. Mysteriously, the Germans had left both bridges intact—perhaps believing they were more useful to them in servicing their river defenses than they would ever be to the American forces stymied behind hundreds of yards of flooded fields.

Once the veil of darkness fell, new infantry patrols, employing the stealth of alley cats, fanned out to crack more German secrets. This was their last night to gather as much information as possible before the attack commenced the following evening. The Germans, unwilling to relinquish those secrets, stepped up patrols of their own along the same riverbanks. The tense valley echoed with the sporadic crackling of small arms, the rat-tat-tats of American Tommy guns, and short burps of German machine pistols as opposing teams surprised each other in the heart-pounding night. The anxiety escalated once artillery from both sides began lashing away at the rear positions of the other. The Germans introduced waves of Nebelwerfer "screaming meemie" rockets to top off the exchange.[19] The heated contest persisted the entire night, during which twenty rounds buffeted the A Company bivouac area. Again, the well-protected tankers remained unhurt with nothing damaged.[20]

During this unholy duel, Sweeting convened his company commanders to discuss and choose the best river crossing locations for the tanks.[21] Without question, the best prospects lay north of the barracks where the two bridges were situated.[22] The smaller bridge nearest the barracks, however, presented the most difficult approach. Wilkinson described the fields there and to the south as too wide and waterlogged to be crossed without extensive engineer work.[23] Captain Lewis reported better options further north. This area was also heavily flooded, but the riverbanks were lower and approaches appeared more promising—including several pathways leading to the second larger bridge further north. Whatever they decided, combat engineers had to be called in to build "corduroy" log roads first. In the end, Sweeting favored bypassing both bridges altogether and building a "tank trail" a few hundred yards north of the barracks heading straight to the river. If necessary, the engineers could blast down the banks to facilitate the tanks' crossing.[24] So confident was Sweeting in these plans that he vowed not to shave his face until Cassino fell.[25]

So confident were the Germans that nothing would breach their bristling Rapido defenses that they released captured 36th Division carrier pigeons to Allied lines with mischievous taunts. One rather humorous message read:

> You poor night watchmen, here is your pigeon No 2 back so that you won't starve. What do you plan in front of Cassino with your tin-can armor? Your captured syphilitic comrades have shown us the quality of the American solider. Your captains are too stupid to destroy secret orders before being captured. At the moment your troops south of Rome are getting a kick in the pants—you poor nose pickers. The Germans troops.[26]

On 24 January, while Allied planes dropped more somber leaflets upon Monte Cassino offering the German defenders a choice between "Stalingrad or Tunis,"[27] the tank crews struck their bivouac near San Pietro ahead of their final move to the new assembly area that evening. They were scheduled to arrive just as the infantry began the main attack. Sweeting and officers from the 1108th Engineer Group and the 234th Engineer Battalion met to discuss his river crossing ideas.[28] The day was misleadingly beautiful and unseasonable warm—a summerlike reprieve in the dead of winter.[29] Ragged civilians remaining in the area suspected something big was afoot. Many emerged from their homes and hiding places to watch and wave or shout words of encouragement to troops of all stations filtering on toward the Rapido Valley. Waiflike children, lightly clad and shoeless, in most cases, chased cheerily along—hoping for candy.[30] For those few hours, the young Americans basked in adulation generally reserved for championship teams entering stadiums—or perhaps doomed gladiators entering coliseums.

After the sun disappeared in the west, the tanks rolled down Highway 6, skirted the eastern edge of Monte Trocchio and emerged on the rim of the Rapido Valley. Like some sinister carnival show, the night's clouds flickered above from the irregular strobing of artillery. The heavy crack and boom sparring between American and German batteries rolled across the valley bowl like a long, heated argument between angry mountain gods. The darkness helped mask the arrival of the 756th tanks, but the Germans sensed their presence nonetheless and clawed at them with artillery. Highway 6 had long been well registered. One incoming round narrowly missed hitting an A Company tank, but the scorching blast set fire to the tarps, bedrolls, and camouflage netting secured to the back deck. The crew had to dismount and extinguish the blaze before dripping flames set the entire engine compartment on fire.[31] Other than that incident, all other tanks and crews passed through the gauntlet without harm.

While the tanks progressed deeper into the valley, every piece of American artillery in the area upsurged in intensity—blending as one endless disorienting blare.[32] The slopes of The Pimple and Hill 213 sparkled as if alive. Chains of brilliant red flashes popped across the granite to form a hellish kaleidoscope, and the valley floor quaked for miles around.[33] Undaunted, the Germans sent flares rocketing high over the battlefield, warning their own troops of imminent ground attack and depriving American infantry of the cloak of darkness.[34] The horrific Allied barrage lasted a full thirty minutes.[35] It seemed unbelievable that anyone on the receiving end could survive such an onslaught.

At 2200, the ground attack commenced.[36] The riflemen of the 135th and 133rd Regiments swept forward in scattered waves beginning roughly 1,000 yards[37] shy of the river, deftly crossing the first few hundred yards of field—ducking for cover whenever possible to escape the bright German flares and indiscriminate mortar fire. Communication wiremen raced about furiously unspooling rudimentary phone lines to keep the fast-moving CPs interconnected.[38] Then, everybody stopped to hunker down in anticipation of the next artillery barrage. After a few moments of eerie silence, the ground a few hundred yards ahead burst open sequentially as round after round of American artillery tossed blossoms of mud and sod spinning high into the cold night air. This new salvo was meant to subdue nearby German defenses and blast penetrating pathways through minefields and barbed wire. The Germans, however, craftily timed each volley and sent their own artillery raining down on the waiting American infantrymen at the same moment—in hopes the attack would stall from fear their own artillery was falling short of the intended targets.[39] The 34th Division veterans had encountered this old trick before. Few were fooled. The American barrage lifted and the infantry edged forward as planned. The cycle repeated two more times. Each time, the Germans showered the approaching line with heavier doses of mortar fire or thicker spray from MGs emanating from new and unexpected directions.[40]

The 135th Regiment advanced on the left, roughly a half-mile south of the barracks, hoping to cross the Rapido and seize the road leading south from the barracks into Cassino.[41] The 133rd Regiment attacked on the right, directly targeting the barracks and Hill 225. With capture of the barracks central to his division's battle plans, Maj Gen Ryder committed all three 133rd battalions to the effort—but with each battalion holding back one rifle company in reserve.[42] Ryder hoped the added troops would enable the 133rd to more swiftly subdue the barracks. After which, they would steamroll north to wipe out German gun positions dotting The Pimple and Hill 213—all before sunrise.[43] That was the plan, anyway.

The 1st and 3rd Battalions of the 133rd jumped off on schedule, but the 2nd Battalion was delayed a full thirty minutes on account of heavy German MG fire sweeping constantly over their section.[44] By midnight, all three battalions succeeded in closing to within a few hundred yards of the Rapido—and yet the drive stalled completely. The men discovered both sides of the narrow river thickly sown with minefields—all staked with polite "Minen" warning signs.[45] The rowed barriers of hacked brush, barbed wire, and booby-trapped grenades proved denser and more entangling than expected. Although the river approaches had been pockmarked with fresh artillery craters, the barrage failed to create any clear pathways through—and many blast-strewn mines remained intact and armed. Shell holes which normally provided some cover from enemy fire instead filled swiftly with frigid flood waters.[46] Infantrymen had to choose between getting soaked or getting shot at and shelled. Beyond the minefields, a knee-high wall of field stone and cement tracked along the eastern edge of the Rapido—serving as a dike in times when the river ran high.[47] Instead of keeping the river out of the fields, however, the wall now kept the flood water out of the river. The result was a bizarre, inverted situation where hundreds of yards of saturated stagnant muck pooled next to a river starved of water and trickling southward at eight feet below grade.[48]

The bravest men summoned the courage to press on, believing if they could reach the sunken riverbed, they could at least gain cover from the bursting mortar fire. They cautiously squirmed forward through the sucking mud—all the while probing gingerly for mines with trembling knife tips and numbed fingers.[49] Invariably some well-concealed German MG would sweep across their positions—forcing them to hug the ground and sending their comrades scrambling behind haystacks and clumped undergrowth or splashing into frigid water-filled ditches and shell holes. Every so often, a mine exploded somewhere in the night. The blast was sometimes followed by silence—other times by ghastly screams or fading groans.

In the meantime, the 756th tank column turned off Highway 6 and slowly snaked northward along rutted secondary roads and crooked field lanes toward the assembly area. Despite the engineers' best efforts, the route remained in appalling condition—even for tracked vehicles.[50] Each tank commander was issued a small luminescent radium disc to guide his driver through the dark while walking in front of the slow-moving tank.[51] Even this device could not prevent two light tanks and a medium tank from miring along a section of improvised roadway at a small stream crossing. This bottleneck halted the entire column for nearly three hours. Stones, logs, and anything else of substance was shoved under the tracks to free the tanks and provide footing for others to pass.[52] At 0200, the infantry called for tank support, but the tankers could not oblige. With the frustrating knowledge that their comrades-in-arms desperately needed assistance, the tankers redoubled their efforts to defeat the muddy creek.[53]

By 0345, A Company finally conquered the obstacle and B Company passed through as well.[54] The two companies achieved their respective assembly areas—farm fields roughly a mile due east of Monte Villa. A Company assumed the right flank and B Company pulled up on the left, roughly 300 yards northeast of the tiny hamlet of San Pasquale.[55] The remainder of the battalion was delayed, however, after the route subsequently degenerated into a rutted mess and the engineers feared they might not get their own repair equipment through. As a result, C and D Companies were forced to create makeshift assembly areas nearby and await a later time to proceed.[56]

The tankers who made it through found little time for rest. At 0500, two A Company tanks were called forward by the 133rd Regiment to trample fields heavily sown with two types of German anti-personnel mines: Schü mines and "Bouncing Bettys." Schü mines were designed to sever a man's foot, but Bouncing Bettys leaped to waist-level before exploding—spraying out 360 individual ball bearings capable of cutting down several men at once. Under the moving tracks of a mighty M4, however, both types popped off like harmless firecrackers. The tanks cleared a few new pathways for the infantry but could not advance beyond a certain point due to high floodwaters. Eventually, they drew back to firmer ground.[57] Another A Company platoon was called to provide fire support for infantrymen creeping closer to the Rapido.[58] Because tanks lacked night fighting instruments, any targeting after dark required bore sighting—in other words, gunners lined their shots by peering directly out of the gun barrels. After firing, however, the crews could not gauge a round's effectiveness and had to wait for the infantry to report results before making adjustments. The process was time consuming and not very effective.[59] Still, the infantry preferred even this cumbersome form of tank support to none at all, and so all three B Company platoons were called upon to place similar fire before the arrival of dawn.[60]

The sun flared over the horizon behind Monte Trocchio, ushering in a cool and crystal-clear 25 January morning. Atop Monte Cassino, the abbey shimmered in its usual glory against a serene blue sky.[61] The old fortress monastery seemed to have moved four times closer overnight. During lulls in gunfire, the sweet reprise of the Benedictine bells could be heard chiming in the distance—marking the steady passage of time from on high as they had for centuries.[62] Monks could sometimes be seen strolling obliviously about the entrance.[63] The thick, dewy air was laden with pungent mismatched aromas of rich loam and burnt cordite. The three battalions of the 133rd Regiment remained stymied in the extensive minefields.[64] Some riflemen managed to claw behind the cover of the low dike wall. Others managed to drop down into the deep river channel and scamper through the knee-deep water, only to hug against the opposite bank.[65] The vast majority, however, remained pinned along the river approaches—huddling and shivering in water-filled ditches and shell holes or trapped prone and vulnerable in wide-open mud flats. The dead and dying lay scattered everywhere.[66] Some of those killed lacked heads and hands—the gory result of Schü mines triggered while wriggling forward during the previous night.[67] A lion's share of the wounded were missing feet but could not be reached or helped. German mortar and artillery fire continued falling mercilessly upon them, and the medics—already overwhelmed with critical cases—could not reach them.[68] The few places where nighttime engineers marked pathways through the mines had been shredded from the relentless blasting,[69] and tape fragments wafted and tumbled across the mire as useless refuse. The infantry tried re-marking the paths with wads of toilet paper, but these also fluttered away with the brisk morning breezes.[70]

The 2nd Battalion, 133rd Regiment, was a unique unit alternately designated the "100th Infantry Battalion" and filled with mostly Japanese–American soldiers. The troops called themselves the "Puka" Battalion—a Japanese term for "two holes" referring to the double zeros in "100."[71] These young men were second generation "Nisei" children of parents and grandparents shamefully forced to relocate into detention camps back in the United States. Ironically, the Nisei Battalion chose "Remember Pearl Harbor" as their motto.[72] These were fiercely proud kids shouldered with hefty and undeserved cultural burdens. Rather than buckle under the pressure, they embraced their roles as underdogs and amassed a valiant battle record in both North Africa and southern Italy—earning the deep respect and admiration of their commanders and fellow countrymen. If a battalion was needed to cross the Rapido and root out tough German gun positions on the opposite bank, the Nisei boys were the first to be called. With that reputation for toughness, the 100th Battalion attacked along a segment of river a few hundred yards south of the barracks as the regiment's left flank, while the 1st and 3rd Battalions attacked further to the north.[73]

During the previous evening, the 100th Battalion struggled to overcome a small creek and thickly sown minefields. As of 0600, only a few Nisei troops had reached as far as the river channel.[74] With the arrival of dawn, German MG fire turned far more accurate and deadly. To squelch that fire and help the 100th advance, self-propelled howitzers of the 133rd's Cannon Company positioned near San Michele starting lobbing phosphorous smoke directly upon German positions.[75] The white-hot rounds fell atop German pillboxes but failed to diminish the enfilading MG fire. The bunkers were too heavily reinforced for the crews to even feel the heat. In fact, one smoke shell landed squarely in the doorway of one MG nest, but a short time later the gun fired right back up again.[76]

In the morning light, Lt Redle, his radio operator T/4 Carl Mras, and radio bearer Pvt Merle Brooks arrived at the 100th Battalion HQ, situated in a white stone house several hundred yards east of the action. The home was one of only a few in the area still supporting a roof. Redle was given orders to find the battalion commander and coordinate tank fire with his infantry, but the battalion commander—Major Casper Clough Jr.—was not there. Redle was told Clough could be found directing the attack at the battalion's forwardmost OP, so the three men guardedly set out toward the front lines. They found the young major from the Catskills of New York in the ruins of a second house sitting in a wide-open field only 300 yards from the river.[77] The roof had been completely blown away—leaving only the stone walls, and none taller than shoulder height.[78] Immediately ahead, the wrathful discharges and bursting of countless small arms, mortar, and MGs blended into a continuous clamor. Many of Clough's troops hugged the muddy ground in the fore—hoping to ride out the battering and advance a few more yards during the next lull. Others could be seen in the distance bravely marking minefields and wriggling forward in fits and starts under streaming bursts of MG spray. Clough lay flat upon a rubble pile next to a ruined wall—fixedly studying the battlefield through a set of field glasses. The gentle winds rolling down off the ridge shifted with capricious indifference, and Cannon Company's carefully laid smoke screen now drifted away from the German side and back over Clough's troops. Deprived of this precious cloak, the Nisei advance stalled again. A white-knuckled artillery liaison officer, with a field phone pressed hard against his ear, lay slouched in a nearby shell hole—calling out coordinates for a concentrated barrage from his rear batteries.[79] As he did so, Redle reported in to Clough and scampered for the cover of a nearby dip in the ground. At the same time, Mras and Brooks hastily unpacked the radio so Redle could call for fire from B Company tanks should Clough ask. Seconds later, the German pillbox positions beyond the river shuddered beneath a violent succession of 105mm artillery explosions. Dust, dirt, spattering mud, and pulverized granite billowed thick enough to temporarily shroud the ridgeline. In the hazy distance, Redle could see more of Clough's infantrymen struggling valiantly to scrabble past barbed wire and reach the far riverbank before the Germans recovered from the shelling.

The barrage lifted and an eerie silence fell over the battlefield for a moment or two. Voices could be heard coming from across the river. It was the Germans taunting their American adversaries with calls of "Help me, I'm hurt!" in broken English—hoping the ruse might draw some empathetic sucker out in the open where he could be cut down without mercy. Nobody fell for it.[80] The spiteful goading was answered with the cracks of rifles and bursting of MGs—and the wall of incessant noise quickly returned.

As the dust from the artillery attack settled, Redle and Clough scrutinized the far bank for the telltale flashes of MG positions. The base of Hill 225, 450 yards straight ahead, seemed to house several clusters—as did the barracks foundations on the right.[81] Once a target was positively identified, Redle radioed Lt Harley—commanding 1st Platoon tanks in defilade support positions approximately 1,000 yards to the rear.[82] Harley's gunner would then fire on the position and Redle would radio back any adjustments. Once a target was finally hit dead on, the other four tanks of Harley's platoon would join. When no targeting was in progress, Redle always shut the radio off to prevent the Germans from triangulating a fix on his signal.

1st Lt Young O. Kim, the 100th Battalion's intelligence officer (S-2) also lay prone among the ruins of the farmhouse scanning for German gun positions. To bait them into firing, Kim would periodically send one of his section men sprinting across a nearby field in a deadly game of "chicken." Oftentimes, a German MG crew would bite and chase after the man with bullet spray. He would then drop to a defilade ground position and crawl unobserved to safety. One of the company commanders near the river would then signal the gun's location so Redle could relay the information back to Lt Harley's platoon. The procedure continued all morning long, but the officers were never quite sure if they succeeded in knocking out a position for good. The Germans were proven masters at gun emplacement and had hidden so many in the area. Not only were ground positions on the opposite riverbank saturated with them, but bullet spray periodically rained down upon the Nisei troops from positions as high as 300 or even 500 feet further up the steep hillside.[83] All Redle and Clough's OP officers could do was to keep rooting out each position slowly and methodically until a point was reached where the infantry could storm them. When the Germans finally got a fix on Redle's radio signal, however, and began raining mortar down upon the shattered farmhouse, the game urgently changed to "kill before being killed."[84]

By noon, the 100th Battalion managed to work somewhere between one or two platoons over to the far riverbank. The exact number of men across was difficult to determine as everyone could only operate with their heads down. A handful men from the other two 133rd battalions further to the north persevered into similar positions: A few huddled along the river, with fewer still able to advance beyond.[85] The fire emanating from the barracks was brutal and the verbal pressure coming from the rear over establishing a bridgehead was equally as savage.[86] At 1245, Cannon Company laid down another thick smoke screen just beyond the river to inject some enthusiasm into a renewed assault wave.[87] As the white curtain formed, riflemen and engineers slithered over the bank to cut wire and clear mines.[88] Mine sweeping was much easier in daylight. One needed his *eyesight* along with bare hands and steady nerves to safely find and disarm a mine.[89]

Colonel Carley L. Marshall, CO of the 133rd Regiment,[90] sensed a breakthrough was imminent and hollered at his tank liaison for A Company tanks on the north flank to roll forward. Marshall's men *yearned* for a cavalry charge. Ideally, tanks should have accompanied the attack much earlier that morning.[91] Unfortunately, the armor still had no way of reaching the river.[92] All morning long, the engineers had worked like bees building a road of rowed logs extending some 400 yards to the river. Once completed, this corduroy road was supposed to enable A Co, 756th, to cross the river and crush the barracks pillboxes, but progress was constantly stalled by German artillery.[93] Then, by mid-morning, the log-laying teams encountered ground too sodden to even support the thick logs, so the effort was redirected toward constructing approaches to the north bridge leading to Caira instead.[94] When Lt Col Sweeting and Captain Lewis checked on the engineers' progress late in the morning, German artillery fell so heavily, the beleaguered engineers discussed working at night only.[95] Without a tank trail, the infantry could only depend on tank support from a distance.[96] Marshall's cavalry charge would have to wait.

The tankers tried moving closer. In the early afternoon, A Company tanks rolled out from their northern defilade positions and ventured as close to the flooded fields as they dared go. With clearer fire lanes, the crews could better target German

<u>Locating Potential Tank Trails Across the Rapido - 24 January 1944</u>

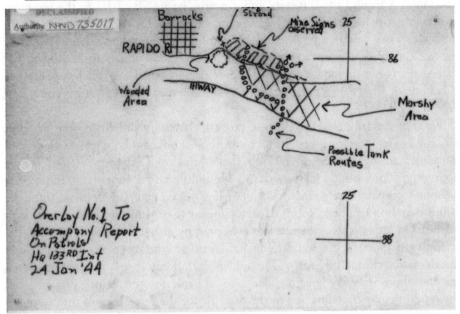

(Above) 24 January 1944 133rd Inf Regt hand drawn map of proposed tank routes across the Rapido based on patrol reports. Compare this to the 1944 1/25,000 map below of the same area. Right side is NORTH for both maps.

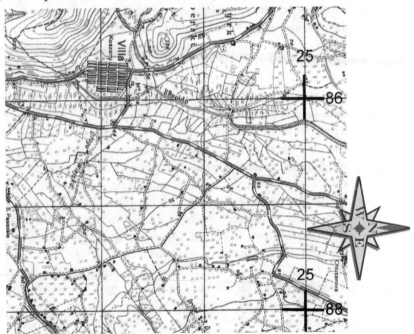

positions along the base of Hill 213—particularly a troublesome concentration of MGs in and around the cemetery and a nearby house. The MG in the house, at least, was permanently silenced.[97] In the meantime, C, D, and HQ Companies of the 756th Tank Battalion finally reached their final assembly areas after overcoming the rutted road problem of the previous night. The Germans saw them moving and shelled the column while it spread out over fields west of San Michele. Shrapnel killed one of the HQ jeep drivers as he frantically dug a foxhole at his company's new location.[98]

Word of the tank trail travails rose through the command chain. The II Corps promised to lend their own engineers to the project but could not release them until morning.[99] In the meantime, TDs from the 805th Tank Destroyer Battalion moved up into positions around Cervaro to provide additional fire support.[100] The 133rd's Cannon Company kept white smoke billowing over German positions. At 1400, the 100th Battalion launched a limited attack meant to expand the "bridgehead" a bit further. On a day where progress was measured by only a few yards at a time, the attack was deemed "successful."[101] The midday skies turned overcast and a cold, light drizzle misted through the air.[102] The sudden shift of barometric pressure prevented the phosphorous smoke hovering along the far bank from dissipating properly, and the resulting gray haze lingered in the dead air for the remainder of the afternoon —working more to the benefit of the German defenders than to anyone else. Hill 225, the barracks, The Pimple and Hill 213 took on the appearance of shrouded shadows, and it was no longer possible for the tankers or Cannon Company crews to see their targets. As a result, the infantry attack stalled yet again. For fear the Germans might take advantage of the lull and mount a counterattack, the gun crews continued firing blindly into known positions of previous targets.[103]

Mid-afternoon, Sweeting received a phone call from the 34th Division operations officer (G-3) requesting two sections of tanks be immediately dispatched toward Cassino via San Pasquale to gauge German reaction. The prior day, 2nd Lt Leger and Pfc Bernard Shue joined a 1st Battalion, 133rd, patrol investigating a small bridge spanning an irrigation ditch along that very route. The patrol returned with Leger reporting the bridge could not support tanks.[104] Sweeting wanted to test it regardless. One section of B Company tanks—led by Lt Leger with Sgts Haskell O. Oliver and Roland L. Buys following—set out down the one-lane road leading through San Pasquale to town.[105] As the trio reached to within 1,000 yards of Cassino, however, they were forced to halt upon discovering the small bridge completely blown.[106] Immediately, German artillery began raining down around them. With no way forward and nowhere to hide, the three tanks turned back.[107] Another C Company section was sent further southward toward Highway 6, but upon approach received dire warnings from nearby infantrymen of German AT guns lying in ambush further down the highway.[108] Ignoring the advice courted disaster, so the C Company tankers turned back as well. Perhaps the 34th Division staff hoped to find Germans vacating the city—or perhaps they thought a tank diversion east of town might draw enemy attention away from the barracks area to the north. Whatever the intent, neither probe accomplished much.[109]

At 1930, Sweeting met with the CO of B Co, 16th Armored Engineers Battalion. The two discussed progress on the northern tank trail and the prospect of adding another route a few hundred yards north of Cassino.[110] Afterward, Sweeting called together his company commanders at the 756th HQ assembly area to review plans for the following day: All crews were to be ready for battle. In the morning, A Company would dispatch two tanks to test the corduroy trail leading to the Caira bridge. If they could successfully cross, the rest of A Company would follow. B Company would support the crossing and then follow as well.[111] If the trail held out and the ground stayed firm, the 756th would blow through the stalemate along the Rapido.

By evening, the afternoon drizzle changed into a light rain, making even the high ground slippery. A misty shroud hung stubbornly over the valley, but Cannon Company continued striking previously registered targets across the river with regular HE howitzer fire.[112] All afternoon long, Clough's 100th Battalion OP positioned in the ruined farmhouse received a relentless pounding of German mortar and artillery.[113] By days' end, nearly all the twenty-six or so members of the battalion's communication and intelligence sections had suffered wounds—some seriously. Others had been killed. The artillery liaison team also sustained casualties—yet, somehow, Lt Redle and his two radiomen survived the ordeal unscathed. Major Clough, too, managed to escape the day unharmed.[114] Once the sun disappeared behind the ridge, the 27-year-old West Point graduate of 1939 dismissed Lt Redle until morning, and the three tankers set out for the relative safety of the rear—leaving Clough and his battered OP behind.[115] As they departed, the 34th Division's artillery batteries started pounding the ridge again. This time, the big booming 240mm and 8-inch guns from the corps artillery also joined the barrage. A few rounds fell short of their intended targets—exploding in the fields around and behind Clough's OP, and unnerving those remaining in the area who had expected some degree of respite. This "interdictory" artillery fire—meant to keep the Germans' heads down—was scheduled to fall all night long,[116] but those first stray rounds caused *everyone* to keep their heads down thereafter.

The pressures for success tumbling down the Allied command chain became a crushing weight at the lower levels. Maj Gen Keyes, II Corps CO, leaned heavily on Maj Gen Ryder to put his 34th Division troops across the Rapido.[117] Ryder, in turn, compelled Colonel Marshall of the 133rd Regiment to do the same. The dark-eyed colonel with a long, furrowed face and pencil thin mustache possessed a wide range of practical army experience—all gained without the benefit of a West Point appointment.[118] The 40-year-old Virginian's career began as a humble private during World War I, but he rose quickly through the enlisted ranks to artillery sergeant and received an infantry commission soon after the armistice.[119] For the next twenty years, Marshall amassed an impressive officer résumé by attending specialized schools ranging from infantry command and tank employment to general staff operation and with the acceptance of weighty assignments at faraway stations such as China and the Philippines.[120] At Fondouk Pass on 9 April 1943, Marshall's masterful leadership of the 1st Bn, 133rd, during the attack on Djebel Haouareb led to his Distinguished Service Cross award and eventual promotion to regimental commander.[121] On first glance, Marshall's tightly curled and immaculately waxed mustache combined with his trademark southern hospitality gave an impression of a quaint dandy, but if Marshall had learned anything during his long and varied Army career it was the importance of giving and accepting orders without hesitation.

Late in the evening, Marshall called Clough via field phone and told him he now wanted the 100th Battalion's reserve company to attack at dawn. At first, Clough pretended not to hear the order. An attack in broad daylight was clearly suicidal. But when Marshall brought Lt Col Eugene L. Moseley into the conference-line discussion, both Clough and Moseley began protesting the order. The 36-year-old Moseley commanded the 1st Battalion to the right of Clough. Moseley was a 1929 graduate of West Point with impeccable leadership experience and credentials as well.[122] Marshall wanted Moseley's reserve company to also attack at dawn, but Moseley was dead set against it. The more vehemently he raised his objections, the more adamant Marshall grew that his order be followed. Moseley finally relented but warned Marshall he would not order his men to attack without personally leading the charge.

Clough had already received the Silver Star for combat valor at the Battle of Mateur during the North Africa campaign while serving with the 26th Infantry Regiment (1st Inf Div). He also fought at Oran, Gafsa, and the Kasserine Pass. He knew battle and showed no fear for his personal safety.[123] Clough's bravery won him command of the 100th Battalion in early December 1943,[124] and he developed such unshakable admiration for the fighting spirit of the Nisei troops placed in his trust that he simply could not bring himself to order such magnificent men on a mission with virtually no chance of success.[125] In the 1939 USMA yearbook, Clough's classmates saluted "Cappy" as "a placid soul who has learned to take in stride the trials that beset a cadet."[126] Cappy tried placidly reasoning further with Marshall, but his regimental commander promptly cut him short and relieved him of his command. Stunned speechless, a shaken, tearful Clough walked slowly though the darkness back to 133rd Regiment CP to face an uncertain future.[127]

Colonel Marshall dispatched his S-3, Major George Dewey, to the 100th Battalion OP to assume command. However, once Dewey arrived and took stock of the situation, he immediately contacted Marshall to voice similar concerns and recommended Clough's restoration. Marshall refused his own operations officer's advice. Dewey also resolved he could not give such a bleak attack order from the rear and ventured out into the night in search of a better jump-off point along the river dike.[128] On the way, a member of Dewey's party accidentally stepped on a Bouncing Betty along a section of trail where the tape had been torn away. The mine leaped up from the ground—exploding into a blinding burst spiked with ball bearings. One man was killed instantly and the battalion's XO, Major Jack Johnson, fell mortally wounded. Dewey was blown into the mud with both legs mangled and badly bleeding. With dawn but a few hours away, Dewey had to be evacuated and Major Clough was placed back in command.[129] The controversial attack had not even commenced yet, and already the regiment had lost its XO and S-3.

At 0645, Captain Lewis met with the combat engineers near the north bridge to review work on the corduroy road. Again, German artillery harassment lasting all night long had severely hampered progress. Lewis ordered A Company forward to test a way through nevertheless. The first tank got as far as the Caira bridge approach and promptly slid down into the mud—with tilted tracks churning helplessly in the slick slime. The second tank tried maneuvering around the first and also became hopelessly mired. None of the other tanks could pass the bottleneck and were forced to reverse out.[130] Obviously, the engineers had more work to do.

Lt Redle and radiomen Mras and Brooks set out from the B Company assembly area for Clough's OP—plodding along the same path they had taken the previous day. Almost immediately, German mortar rounds began popping all around them, and yet the men continued forward. Evidently, the Germans had zeroed in the route overnight. Another group of soldiers walking barely twenty yards ahead of Redle's group sustained a direct hit. An officer was killed and several others were knocked down, seriously wounded. Redle and his radio crew pressed on.[131] They neared the shattered farmhouse, already under a relentless rain of exploding mortar and raking MG fire. As Pvt Brooks clambered for cover, he lost his footing and fell seated up atop a small rise. A long burst of MG fire peeled across the nearby ground—missing the stunned radio bearer by mere inches and splattering his ODs with sticky mud and clumps of rich Italian topsoil. Brooks rolled off the mound and scrambled behind a ruined cement pillar—where he remained hopelessly pinned for several hours. Mras found refuge in the same shell hole of the previous day, but Redle ended up leaping into a latrine trench. Although, his situation was extremely unpleasant, he determined relocation would be more dangerous.

Despite the protests from his battalion commanders, Colonel Marshall's dawn attack was in motion.[132] The morning started with good visibility but a low-hanging haze had descended over the entire valley—making target identification difficult.[133] Approximately 180 men from the 100th Battalion's B Company waited in muddy ditches, swales, and shell holes near the OP for the attack order that Clough dreaded giving. The 133rd's Cannon Company and mortars of the 2nd Chemical Weapons Battalion[134] lobbed in countless rounds of phosphorous smoke canisters along the riverbed to help fortify a temporary wall of cloud. Clough gave the green light. His troops began crawling forward on their stomachs to marked lanes leading through minefields to the river channel. As they crept in fits and starts, German MGs fired blindly at them through the long, thick white smoke. Suddenly, the shifting winds split open the protective veil—the worst thing that could happen and at the worst possible time. Immediately, German artillery rained down upon the exposed men—causing some to jump up instinctively and run into the mine fields where they were either killed outright or fell maimed and dying after setting off indiscriminate blasts.[135] Those keeping their composure embraced the soil and endured and prayed. Cannon Company tried laying more smoke rounds in along the river, but the wind proved too strong for any misting cover to hold.[136] The attack collapsed just as Clough had feared.

Clough's OP continued getting rocked under periodic mortar fire. During one brief lull, Pvt Brooks bounded for the relative safety of one of the ruined farmhouse's roofless rooms. During another mortar wave, however, a round exploded in the room dead center—throwing him violently against a stone wall. Ashen and dazed, but otherwise unharmed, Brooks staggered out into the open where a flurry of MG bullets sent him diving behind another ruined wall. In that same short morning, Brooks had survived three close brushes with death.[137] Luck either favored him or was about to run out.

Another gust of shells exploded directly behind the ruined house, striking down officers and enlisted men who had hitherto remained unscathed. This perfectly registered barrage left even the OP's most seasoned combat veterans dazed and shaken. Some of the unharmed sat up, grinning foolishly—not knowing what else to do. Others froze face down for fear of seeing the aftermath. Lt Redle lay unhurt in a shell hole, took a deep breath and called out "Who got hit?" One teenaged rifleman raised a bloody hand. Another soldier hit in the back fidgeted silently as a comrade poured sulfa powder into his wounds. Another young soldier lying in a nearby ditch didn't respond at all. A medic examined him to discover a single tiny mortar sliver had pierced his heart—killing him instantly.[138]

A war correspondent from the Los Angeles Times named Tom Treanor crawled up to the OP at dawn to share the miseries of a combat infantrymen all day long. When circumstances allowed, he interviewed whoever was near—taking great care to always scrawl the name and hometown of each soldier in his notebook.[139] Treanor's gutsy presence assured the beleaguered men that, at least, some word of their hardships would reach home.

Despite the morning's terrible start, Major Clough implored his surviving company commanders and platoon leaders by phone and radio to keep the attack moving. "You've got to push!" He kept pleading.[140] His men responded as best as possible. Some even succeeded in crawling several yards beyond the riverbank. However, the effort was flagging, and the German response was simply too broad and robust to regenerate any momentum.[141] The 100th Battalion neared exhaustion.

In the meantime, on the 133rd Regiment's far right flank to the north of the barracks, Lt Col Moseley personally led the 1st Battalion's charge over the riverbank—as he vowed to Colonel Marshall he would do. Tragically, the instant he raised his head over the edge, a German bullet pierced him squarely through the forehead. Moseley's men watched in horror as their commander's head jerked back violently and his limp body tumbled into the shallow river. In anger, they let loose a long fusillade but the futile outburst gained them no territory and restored no life to an experienced and admired officer whose death was completely in vain.[142]

The German artillery harassment of the engineers trying to complete the tank route to the north bridge fell so heavy, work completely ceased. Although the earlier crossing attempt failed, the tanks continued supporting the infantry from a distance of 600 to 1,000 yards away. A Company concentrated fire on Hill 213 and the cemetery—taking great pains to avoid piercing trees in the foreground and showering American troops below with shrapnel.[143] At the same time, B Company pumped countless HE rounds throughout the barracks area.[144] One C Company platoon also moved into position to provide supporting fire for the 135th Regiment now attacking along the river bed south of the barracks.[145] At 1300, A Company tanks prepared for another crossing attempt —this time after moving to a stretch of road 500 yards parallel to the Rapido and running between the barracks and the north bridge.[146] Sweeting, shuttling back and forth in an M5 light tank,[147] encouraging the crews to try crossing anywhere along the half-mile section showing promising approaches and low river banks. At the same time, Wilkinson was alerted to position B Company to cover A Company's left flank, and the 756th HQ mortar platoon started lobbing suppressing fire into the side of Hill 213.[148] Captain Lewis's tanks began rolling off the asphalt road toward the Rapido. As expected, the ground was too soggy and the tanks bogged everywhere almost immediately. Thirty minutes later, five A company tanks remained so hopelessly mired the drivers stopped spinning their tracks for fear of burning out clutches. All others successfully backed out. None came close to even reaching the river.[149] A frustrated Sweeting directed Captain Lewis to give up the effort and return to supporting the infantry from afar. The crews trapped in the five stuck tanks were told to continue firing until expending all ammunition, then take their radio crystals, leave the tanks after dark, and walk back to the assembly area.[150]

At 1415, the phone rang at the 756th HQ in San Michele. The 34th G-3, again, wanted a section of tanks sent toward Cassino in the direction of Highway 6—this time for the purpose of drawing fire from German guns hidden in town. The mission was highly dangerous to say the least. S/Sgt William Fodor of C Company led a two-tank section with instructions to "jot down" the locations of any guns he could see shooting at him. As his section progressed down the narrow, bumpy country road toward town, the coal miner from West Virginia maintained radio contact with Major Dolvin, who closely monitored his progress from the 756th CP in San Michele.

"Is this as far as you want me to go?" Fodor asked.

The battalion XO answered: "Go ahead …."

Fodor's tanks probed deeper. Several times the staff sergeant repeated the question, but Dolvin always responded: "Go ahead …."

Finally, Dolvin asked: "Have you got to that blown bridge on the outskirts of town?"

"No" Fodor replied.

"Go ahead …" the major urged.

Then Dolvin heard the unmistakable crackle of explosions through the open radio channel. He snatched his binoculars and focused in on Fodor's location four miles to the southwest. A second slew of artillery shells burst around the staff sergeant's two plodding M4 tanks.

"Are you under fire?" Dolvin calmly inquired.

"God yes! It's all around me!" Fodor barked.

The Germans had smartly deduced Fodor's intentions and used indirect artillery fire emanating from behind the hills to avoid giving away their gun locations. Fodor's section pressed further toward the blown bridge, where they found some semblance of cover. From there they fired round after round into town without drawing any sort of counter-response. Eventually, Fodor's tanks withdrew, and the staff sergeant returned to HQ with an empty notebook. The Germans holding Cassino were far too experienced to fall for such amateur baiting tactics.[151]

Lt Wayne B. Henry and S/Sgt Carl T. Crawford of B Company's 2nd Platoon mounted their tanks to test the route beyond San Pasquale once again—this time, discovering the Germans had since established a hefty roadblock at the site of the blown bridge. With the way now barred, Henry and Crawford turned back, and Lt Leger and Cpl Henry E. Gohde set out on foot from B Company's assembly area in search of alternative ways of crossing the irrigation ditch.[152]

Even after all the day's frustrating failures and despite a pervasive haze obscuring the battlefield,[153] the tank commanders had developed a growing understanding of the infantry's needs and had learned how to hammer German positions with greater effectiveness and efficiency—even from long distances. So busy were the gun crews that, by evening, A Company had completely exhausted ammunition stocks. Any tanks not stuck in the mud withdrew back to the assembly area to obtain more supplies.[154] In a mad dash to satisfy demand, one Service Company truck plunged into a shell hole and the driver was crushed to death by ammunition sliding on top of him.[155]

Sweeting grew concerned the 133rd Regiment might achieve a breakthrough and his tanks would be empty when that critical moment arrived. At 1700, he directed Captain Wilkinson to slow B Company's fire rates in order to conserve ammunition. If the 133rd succeeded in crossing the river, B Company would then assume A Company's primary support role.[156] Sweeting also ordered three T2 tank retrievers to depart after dusk and recover the five stuck A Company tanks.[157]

Dusk arrived but no breakthrough ever occurred. Here and there, a few American troops established toeholds over the west bank, but those gains were purchased at great cost throughout the day and completely erased by evening. The Germans masterfully absorbed the heavy pounding from Allied tanks and artillery while shoving the attacking infantry back into the river—relying mostly on the barrels of their blistering MGs.[158] The 34th Division's two-day attack struck an immovable wall, and Maj Gen Ryder was the first to recognize plans had to change. The 133rd Regiment, on the whole, neared exhaustion, but the 100th Battalion, in particular—with over 300 Nisei troops now dead or wounded,[159] neared annihilation. As the day drew to a close, Ryder devised a new strategy of shifting the attack northward, whereby his reserve regiment, the 168th, would strike near the northern bridge leading over to Caira. Once across the Rapido, the regiment would split into two forces: one to take Caira north of Hill 213, with the remainder clearing out the hill itself while pressing down upon the barracks on the flank.[160] With pressure bearing down upon the barracks from two sides, German resolve was likely to crack and a way into Cassino could be blown open.[161] The key to Ryder's plan was tanks. To silence those infernal German MGs, tanks *had* to accompany the infantry across the river.[162] Ryder was fast becoming impressed with Sweeting's initiative and willingness to make things happen, and he gambled the young battalion commander wouldn't disappoint him.

After dark, the engineers resumed progress on the corduroy road, while Sweeting finalized his battalion attack plans for the following day. This time, B Company would join the infantry at the fore with rear fire support coming from A and C Companies working in concert with the battalion's mortars and assault guns.[163] Captain Arnold attended the 1830 planning meeting at the 168th Regiment CP. Sweeting joined about an hour later. The officers of the 168th, many of whom were hardened veterans of tough battles extending from the Mignano Gap all the way back to the Fondouk Pass, were optimistic of the plan's success—particularly with the addition of close tank support.[164] And with 1,500 engineers now toiling away in the immediate area, the officers adjourned feeling highly confident the tank routes would be ready by morning, as well.[165]

At 2020, Sweeting and Arnold returned to the 756th assembly area and called together the company commanders to discuss tactical details.[166] Sweeting had noticed earlier that the Germans had failed to clear a long row of trees bordering the river by the northern bridge. He instructed Wilkinson to use those trees to conceal B Company's approach and shield the tanks from potential AT fire.[167] The crafty lieutenant colonel also planned to use that same tree line to pull off a dawn feint: A Company would move toward the north bridge first, stop some distance away and fire aggressively as if preparing to attack. B Company would use the diversion to maneuver forward behind the tree line, after which A Company would withdraw. Sweeting hoped the ruse would fool the Germans into believing *all* the tanks had pulled back ahead of the infantry attack.[168]

In the meantime, Lt Redle and his radio crew hung tough at Major Clough's besieged OP, calling in tank fire from the rear whenever required. As dusk thickened into night, the coordination of supporting fire from B Company's tanks shifted from challenging to impossible. Anybody surviving the OP battering from the previous day was now either wounded or dead—with the exception of Redle, Mras, and Brooks.[169] The fact Brooks wasn't killed earlier was a miracle. Major Clough's left arm had been ripped open by mortar shrapnel and he'd also lost a few fingers from his right hand. Despite these nasty wounds, Clough steadfastly commanded his men—refusing medical attention, save for bandages hastily wrapped to inhibit the bleeding.[170] Over the course of two horrific days, Clough's proud 800-man Nisei Battalion had been reduced to scattered pockets of huddled troops spread along a few hundred yards of riverbank across from the barracks.[171] Many survivors suffered bloody left hands from repeatedly bashing the bolts of their mud-clogged M1 Garand rifles to keep them firing.[172] Clough's B Company, which jumped off earlier, vanished in the mire somewhere inside the 300 yards separating the OP from the Rapido.[173] Bodies, body parts, and discarded weapons littered the scene—cast about like refuse among coils of broken barbed wire, fluttering tape, water-filled shell holes, and exposed mines. And yet, the German mortar kept falling and the MGs kept firing unabated. A few B Company riflemen survived this torment by playing possum among the dead all day long. Under cover of night, these brave souls mustered the courage to lift themselves out of the mud and crawl up to join the others at the dike.[174] In a cruel twist of fate, orders came down from Regimental HQ soon after —withdrawing the 100th Battalion from the river and all the way back to the assembly area for reorganization.[175] War is, indeed, hell.

An exhausted and wounded but ever-defiant Major Clough dismissed Redle and his two radio men from their liaison duties and bid them a good night and good luck. Relieved—even astounded—to have survived a second full day of intense combat, the three exhausted tankers ambled back toward B Company's CP somewhere at the rear. While groping in the darkness along the same marked field trail on which they arrived, a new wave of mortar and artillery began bursting about them. This time, Pvt Brooks's luck finally ran out. A hot steel fragment ripped into the young radio bearer's back—collapsing him to the ground. Mras and Redle rushed to the stricken man's aid and found him alive and breathing, but unsure if he had suffered serious internal damage.[176]

After getting Brooks proper medical attention and seeing he was safely evacuated, Lt Redle stumbled into B Company's assembly area well past midnight. He looked so grimy, haggard, and drained that Wilkinson ordered him to get rest immediately and "follow the tracks" after awakening at sunrise.[177] Once the attack was underway, Wilkinson needed a fresh and alert second-in-command directing the company CP.[178] The tall, young captain gathered his platoon leaders and platoon sergeants together to pass along the plan basics: B Company would strike across the Rapido at 0730 the next morning,[179]and the men could expect only three hours of rest before a 0400 muster.

Over two and a half years had passed since B Company had first organized at Fort Lewis. During that time, the company participated in countless exercises as the new American Armored Force expanded rapidly through four generations of tanks. The men journeyed across thousands of miles by foot, track, and ship while learning to fire everything from BB guns to 75mm cannons with expert proficiency. They simulated attacks by sea and on land over all manner of terrain. They trained, drilled, and maneuvered as sections, platoons, companies, and as an entire battalion. They suffered through many false alarms and false starts and endured intervening tension, tedium, and dread. They experienced combat as observers and peripheral participants. Now, their day of judgment had finally arrived. B Company was about to assume center stage on the most brutal of battlefields and *lead* the attack while the world watched.

For some, this would be their last night in service of the company. For others, this would be their last night on earth.

U.S. 100th Infantry Battalion

CHAPTER 13

Attack: 27 January 1944

Captain Wilkinson's tank crews cranked their silent M4s to life in a cold, dead Italian night. One by one, the rotary engines sputtered, belched, and protested before acquiescing into low, impatient rumbling. At 0400, the sixteen olive drab giants formed a haphazard column[1] and slowly rolled from the assembly area into predawn gloom.[2] For a brief moment, Wilkinson considered waking Redle—just to be assured his XO would not miss the attack—but then quickly decided against it. Redle would be ready as he always was. Wilkinson took great pains to never overlook a detail, but he also drew a firm line over needless worry.

The column slowly snaked northward along the same sunken road Wilkinson and Lewis had scouted a few days earlier and selected for its textbook defilade.[3] They passed silent farm fields, brush lines, olive groves, and ancient stone homes—all silhouetted in pale, eerie starlight. The muted grays cloaked a scenic countryside pockmarked and scarred from recent shelling, but the terrifying sounds of a nearby war could not be concealed. The muffled thuds of artillery and mortar, and the prattling of automatic weapons in the distance heckled the coffee-fueled tankers.

Wilkinson's and S/Sgt Crawford's tanks led the column, with Lt Henry and the 2nd Platoon immediately following. Lt Leger's 3rd Platoon took up the middle and Lt Harley's 1st Platoon trailed to the rear.[4] After about a mile of travel, the column eased west onto a narrow lane of soft, muddy soil. The tanks bobbed along the rutted pathway at a snail's pace for a few hundred yards and halted near the makeshift log roadway constructed in haste by the engineers.[5] Lt Col Sweeting emerged and signaled for the B Company platoon leaders to dismount and venture forth on foot. The five officers trudged to where they could safely scrutinize the approaches of their planned river crossing point. However, the first rays of dawn revealed that the hastily built corduroy road ended well short of the small cement bridge spanning the Rapido, and what had been laid was an ugly mess. Instead of firm timbers, some sections had been laid using weaker wire matting with others completely submerged in standing water. In those places, hastily set stakes draped with tape marked the way through. After briefly discussing the conditions, the officers agreed to proceed and make the best of the situation. They returned to their platoons and waited as infantrymen filtered into the area. Satisfied B Company was prepared, Sweeting bounded over to his jeep and returned to his CP positioned near the sunken road.[6]

A glorious morning burst upon the valley with bright bands of yellow sunlight streaming across the B Company assembly area.[7] Redle and Mras roused from a deep sleep to find all the tanks gone. The two had slept so soundly they never heard the loud engines and clanking tracks departing some three hours earlier. As ordered, both men followed the tread marks up the sunken road until they located the 756th's forward CP. Redle reported for duty and Sweeting informed him the attack was imminent and to remain at the CP pending further instructions. As 34th Division batteries unleashed some 5,460 rounds[8] of heavy artillery upon German positions across the river, Redle and Mras dug a foxhole and waited. The hellish prelude lasted an entire hour.[9]

At 0700, the tanks of A Company brazenly spread out over high, open ground several hundred yards east of the bridge. All at once, they began firing salvos into German positions honeycombed all along Hill 213—repeating fire as quickly as the aching arms to each loader allowed. A large house and stone wall just to the left of the cemetery took a lion's share of the beating.[10] For a full fifteen minutes, Captain Lewis's crews made a complete show of their appearance—discharging over 1,000 rounds of 75mm HE. Each round had been preset on a delayed fuse to achieve maximum destruction upon penetration.[11] While A Company crews fired at will, the B Company column lurched forward one by one upon the corduroy road following S/Sgt Crawford's lead.[12] At the same time, the infantry from the 1st and 3rd Battalions of the 168th Regiment streamed forward on narrow footpaths marked with engineering tape.[13]

The row of B Company tanks crept delicately toward the tree-lined section of the Rapido where the bridge lay. The patchwork road of logs and mesh was narrow and undulated unexpectedly in the muck with the passing weight of each 32-ton tank—putting the skills of the drivers to an extreme test. An M4 had no steering wheel like a civilian car. Instead, two floor-mounted hand levers operated each track independently. When both levers were pushed forward, the tracks moved at equal speeds and when pulled back, the tracks braked. In order to steer, each lever was pushed and pulled relative to the other. Both hands controlled these without the benefit of power assist. The left foot operated a clutch pedal. When shifting through transmission gears, the left hand grasped both steering levers to momentarily free the right hand to move a side lever selecting five forward speeds and one reverse speed. The right foot controlled an accelerator pedal, but a throttle lever had to first be adjusted—again, with the right hand. The driver had very limited visibility—especially when lowered in "button up" mode and peering through a small hatch-mounted periscope. With the seat up and hatch open, his field of vision was only marginally better, and he had to often peer down to his left and watch the tachymeter so he didn't inadvertently stall the engine. Much of the driving was accomplished by "feel"—a combination of experience and intuition which allowed the driver to sense tread movement as if they were his own feet. The M4's narrow tracks slipped, shifted, and skidded constantly along the narrow corduroy road. When a driver felt his machine start to bog, he quickly shifted gears to prevent the tracks from digging in instead of moving forward.[14] And when a track slipped off the edge—which happened often—the driver had to rely on swift, steady hands to regain the roadway.

The head of the column cleared the end of the log pathway—reaching a muddy road roughly 100 yards short of the small bridge leading westward to Caira. As Wilkinson's tanks negotiated through the muck, A Company ceased firing and withdrew to higher ground near San Michele—exactly as Sweeting had planned.[15]

Lt Henry, S/Sgt Crawford, and the three other tanks of the 2nd Platoon split to the left—plodding toward the bridge with instructions to assume support positions along the approaches while the other two platoons passed. They crossed a small water-filled ditch and turned onto a gravel road. Wilkinson noticed Henry had turned too early and moved his own tank over to correct him. A frantic, mud-caked infantry wireman ran toward Wilkinson, waving his arms. He had just strung critical communication wire through the area. To avoid severing his lines, Wilkinson ordered the driver to pull off the road, and immediately, the tank bogged down into the soupy soil.[16]

Despite the wrong turn, Lt Henry's platoon arrived where they were supposed to, but when the lanky blond lieutenant tried maneuvering his tank through a huge puddle of standing water near the river's edge, it too became bogged. Realizing his situation was hopeless, Henry slid down from his turret hatch and splashed over to S/Sgt Crawford's tank. The sergeant's M4 was the only other platoon tank equipped with a two-way radio, so in order to stay in contact with Wilkinson and the battalion, Henry bumped Crawford from of his turret post. Crawford, in turn, took over the bow gunner's spot—just in case Henry were to swap tanks again later.[17] The displaced bow gunner lingered on the ground nearby and tried to stay out of harm's way.

German artillery and mortar fire started exploding around the fields near the bridge, sending the infantry scattering for cover. The 3rd Platoon led by Lt Leger approached the bridge by tracing along the narrow muddy road. Leger's driver, T/4 Jessie Rickerson, swerved slightly to avoid a large shell hole but ended up slipping over the road's edge. One track caught soft soil and sunk immediately into several inches of field mud. Rickerson pulled back fiercely on the steering levers to stop the swirling tread from sucking them down deeper. The tank hung in place. To rectify the situation, Lt Leger needed to dismount, walk to the front, and provide Rickerson with clear hand signals and verbal instructions, but the nearby bursting of artillery unnerved the new lieutenant. Instead, he attempted to direct his driver by peering out of his periscope under "buttoned up" turret hatches. Across the field, Wilkinson watched in disbelief as Leger's tank struggled blindly to regain the road. The rest of the 3rd Platoon idled helplessly behind him—completely bottlenecked until the only way forward could be cleared. Wilkinson grabbed his hand mike, switched to the company band, and hailed Leger over and over—but the lieutenant did not respond.[18] As Wilkinson feared, Leger's tank sunk further and became hopelessly stuck—trapping the nine remaining tanks behind him.[19]

Enraged, Wilkinson dismounted and ran over to Leger's tank—dodging muddy artillery blasts and risking hidden mines. He climbed up the tilted side, pounded on the turret and yelled repeatedly, but the panicked lieutenant refused to answer. Wilkinson dropped down to where he could more closely inspect the bogged track. The predicament was unnecessary and completely avoidable as Henry's platoon had successfully passed the same shell hole moments earlier. Leger's error in judgment now put the entire attack in jeopardy.[20] For a split second, Wilkinson second guessed his decision not to awaken Redle at 0400.[21] At this moment, he sorely needed Redle's experience and steadfastness.

The infantry of the 1st Bn, 168th, continued amassing nearby in greater numbers.[22] The men had been instructed not to jump off without tank support and now many anxious eyes watched to see what those trapped tanks would do next. Wilkinson decided his only option was to find an alternate way to move the remainder of his company up to the bridge. He ran to his own disabled tank to instruct Lts Henry and Harley of his plans via radio. Along the way, he encountered Sweeting, who rushed up to investigate after hearing Wilkinson's unheeded radio calls to Leger. The two men decided to walk to Lt Henry's platoon waiting near the bridge approaches, and to their surprise, discovered the lieutenant had already crossed the bridge on his own initiative. Through the small thicket of trees lining the riverbed, they observed two American tanks zipping back and forth over a field along the opposite bank—crushing rowed barbed wire and popping off Schü mines by the dozens.[23] A third tank slowly crossed the narrow cement bridge, preparing to join them. Infantrymen of A Co, 168th, huddled like baby ducklings behind the big, olive beast as it edged along.[24] Other riflemen had already crossed and clambered up the far riverbank. After three frustrating days of deadlock, the sight of tanks and troops moving beyond the Rapido was a beautiful one to behold. Sweeting was so pleased he turned to Wilkinson and said he would recommend Henry for a medal. By 0900, nearly three-quarters of A Co, 168th, was across but stymied by withering mortar and small arms fire. Several men were down after being maimed from mines.[25]

As another barrage of heavy German artillery exploded all around them, Sweeting and Wilkinson took cover beside the 2nd Platoon tank of Sgt Graffagnini—mired near the bridge in the same mud that had claimed Lt Henry's tank.[26] Between bursts, the two officers discussed ways of getting more tanks across. Suddenly, a deafening blast swept both men to the ground. Neither man was hurt, but an infantryman carrying a pack radio nearby took a chunk of shrapnel through the arm. His humerus bone was completely severed—leaving the rest of his arm dangling by a few strips of flesh and torn muscle. The stricken man's comrades rushed to his aid and hollered for medics. As the poor man lay in shock, another infantryman picked up his pack radio and continued carrying it forward.[27]

Wilkinson and Sweeting parted ways soon after.[28] The lieutenant colonel doubled back to relieve Leger as Wilkinson scouted an alternative crossing route for the 1st Platoon.[29] A flat field nearby held some promise. Wilkinson saw a rifle company skirting along the edge. He stopped the company commander, who reported the field was full of anti-personnel mines but thought the ground might be firm enough to support tanks. This wasn't an ideal way to choose a tank route but the infantry officer's hunch was all he had. Wilkinson raced back to where the 1st Platoon remained trapped behind Leger's tanks, spread out along the narrow gravel road. Lt Harley's tank was already hopelessly mired after attempting to pivot away from the bottleneck.[30] S/Sgt Haspel's tank had also attempted to turn around as well but slid halfway into a deep water-filled ditch. T/4 Rufus Marin, Haspel's short, popular tank driver of Mexican descent, bravely remained at his post, jostling steering levers while spinning rooster tails of mud in a valiant attempt to keep the tank from rolling completely onto its side.[31] The dirty water lapped up to within an inch of his open hatch before the engine swamped and sputtered into silence.[32] The Italian mud had now claimed a fifth victim from Wilkinson's sixteen-tank company.

The last M4 in line belonged to Idaho native Sgt Leland P. Campbell and was still perched upon a fairly substantial portion of road.[33] Wilkinson directed the 24-year-old Campbell to turn around and attempt to cross the open field toward the bridge. He then instructed the remaining 1st Platoon tanks to follow if Campbell succeeded.[34] To his partial amazement and relief, Campbell's tank easily traversed the field, churning thick dark soil and popping off anti-personnel mines like champagne corks. Wilkinson caught up with Campbell a few dozen yards shy of the bridge, scaled the turret and instructed the sergeant to take the bow gunner position.[35] The regular bow gunner, Pfc Joseph Cutrone, climbed on the deck behind the turret and held on.[36] Wilkinson would not risk any further command problems and resolved to lead the attack himself.[37] Because Sgt Campbell's tank was equipped with a radio receiver only, Wilkinson would have to swap positions with Lt Henry after his tank reached the opposite bank.

The bridge approach was already deeply rutted from the passage of just the first three tanks. The driver, T/5 Louis A. Laliberty, avoided the jumbled mess by bobbing gently over the only remaining section of passable ground—leaving a deep fresh set of furrows in the sodden soil.[38] Whoever attempted to follow would have an even worse time getting through. As Laliberty squared up to the narrow bridge and shifted into low gear, Wilkinson watched wearily ahead for the dreaded flash of an AT gun from somewhere beyond the river's tree-lined banks. If the Germans concealed any AT gun in the area, this was the most likely point to zero in the sights. The bridge was barely wide enough to accommodate the breadth of a tank and certainly not rated for the load.[39] A low stone wall lined one side of the bridge, and infantrymen who had been lying beside it for cover temporarily shifted to the wall's top to allow Wilkinson's M4 to creep past. Once clear of the abutments, Wilkinson directed Laliberty to kick up the throttle immediately and steer over to Lt Henry's position.

Surprisingly, the German response on the far bank was limited to only small arms fire and the occasional sweeps of MGs. The activity was enough to keep the attacking infantry flat but did nothing to prevent Lt Henry's tanks from merrily trampling the Germans' meticulously laid minefields and barbed-wire rows.[40] If an AT gun was present, the Germans seemed loath to reveal it.

Wilkinson's tank pulled to within shouting distance of Lt Henry's tank. Wilkinson suggested a swap, but Henry hollered that his transmitter was not working. Without a transmitter, an exchange was meaningless. The commanders agreed to communicate via hand signals and continue clearing paths for the infantry. The plan was passed along to Sgt Clyde F. Cogdill and Sgt Louis J. Jarvis commanding the other two tanks.[41] Bow gunner Pfc Cutrone was left without a station and crouched completely defenseless behind the turret, so Wilkinson dismissed the 27-year-old New Yorker—instructing him to make his way back to the company. Cutrone jumped off the rear deck and bounded back toward river—taking great pains to step only where the tanks had trod.[42]

The Germans had previously cleared all covering vegetation from the Rapido all the way to the base of Hill 213. This greatly enhanced the defenders view of the entire river from across 600 yards of flat fields.[43] Along the entire western riverbank they laid minefields running as deep as 300 yards. To give the American infantry any chance of reaching Hill 213, much had to be destroyed first by Wilkinson's crews.[44]

As the four lonely tanks rolled methodically back and forth over countless rows of razor-sharp concertina wire, Wilkinson caught sight of MG flashes several hundred yards away emanating from a stone house near the cemetery. The gun was one of several spitting intermittent harassing fire—enough to keep the gathering infantry pinned along the riverbank. Wilkinson called the attention of his gunner, Cpl Paul T. Tirpak, toward the target. The big athletic Ohioan rapidly wheeled the turret gun around, while loader Pvt John F. Bacha, another Ohioan, readied several HE rounds on the floor around his cramped station. One HE round was already in the breech ready to go. Tirpak saw another burst of flash in the lower window and fired the first round, hitting the house squarely and blasting stone and tile skyward. The smoking breech block swung open automatically and dropped a hot brass casing to the floor. As it clattered about, Bacha slammed a fresh round into the chamber. Tirpak fine-tuned the elevation and fired again—this time penetrating the interior and blowing jets of dust and flame from all windows. As a final measure, a third round was dispatched yielding similar results and the German MG never fired again.[45]

For the next two hours, under clear skies and air temperatures hovering at forty-five degrees,[46] the four B Company tanks freely roamed the fields east of

Caira —crushing the Germans' carefully laid obstacles.[47] So confident were the defenders that no American armor could cross the flood zone, they incorporated no AT guns and few AT mines into those defenses.[48] Some German MGs sprayed intermittently at any infantry attempting to creep past the riverbanks but many other positions sat quiet—for fear of being seen and silenced forever by Wilkinson's tanks.[49] Overmatched for the moment, the defenders chose to bide time until AT help could be summoned forward or the American tanks exhausted their fuel and ammo and retreated. To keep the American infantry pinned at the Rapido, however, the Germans concentrated artillery fire along the riverbanks—raining down everything from Nebelwerfer rockets, big 120mm and smaller mortar rounds on the gathering troops trying to filter toward the banks.[50] A single-engine Piper Cub plane dispatched by 34th Division artillery zig-zagged overhead frantically looking for German artillery sources, but the effort brought no immediate relief for the infantry pummeled to a standstill below.[51]

The 3rd Bn, 168th, had no choice but to hunker down in the cold mud among the trapped tanks near the bridge approach. Much of the 1st Bn, 168th, remained trapped along the Rapido as well. By 1040, one 3rd Battalion company managed to reach the riverbank, but the men were ordered to halt until Wilkinson's tanks had crushed more paths on the opposite side.[52] L Company, caught along the river approaches was hit hardest by the German artillery—with men falling dead or wounded at a shocking rate.[53] Cannon Company laid a smoke screen to enable L Company to withdraw back to a safer distance and avoid complete annihilation. This intervention succeeded.[54]

Perhaps had the infantry moved more aggressively and immediately followed after the four M4s had cleared the bridge, the initial attack might have been more successful. Two full battalions might have crossed before the Germans responded with artillery. This hesitancy may have been due to unfamiliarity. Many infantrymen were new to the regiment or new in their leadership roles. Many veterans had received promotions only the day before. Sgts became S/Sgts, Pfcs became Sgts, and Pvts became Pfcs. Although these were veterans hardened from months of combat, they were still young men tentative about their new leadership responsibilities.[55] Approximately half the men were replacements brought in to fill ranks depleted after the battle of San Pietro. Many of these men lacked combat experience in general and tank training in particular. Most balked at shadowing tanks too closely because they knew tanks attracted artillery and AT fire.[56] Yet tanks needed that close foot soldier security in order to protect *all* the infantry. Without riflemen nearby serving as extra eyes and ears, tanks were highly vulnerable to a wide variety of threats, ranging from AT guns to sticky bombs, grenades, or sniper shots.[57]

By late morning, the infantry attack completely stalled 200 yards west of the Rapido under heavy mortar, artillery, and small arms fire.[58] The only two companies across—A and B Companies of the 168th—were forced to dig in to survive. B Co,

168th, lost several officers and essentially sat paralyzed.[59] Wilkinson's tanks pressed further toward Hill 213, trampling additional wire obstacles and setting off more anti-personnel mines as they rolled.[60] About 100 yards from the base of the hill ran one long, continuous barbed-wire band approximately fifteen-yards high. Beyond it lay numerous MG nests—some placed in camouflaged steel pillboxes and others housed inside elaborate underground bunkers built into the hillside. A few stone homes and outbuildings nestled along the base also concealed MG nests. Whenever spotted, Wilkinson's crews hammered those nests without pity but discovered the lower firing guns were much harder to see than the higher ones.[61] Beyond the MG emplacements, lay a long brush pile of trees cleared from the slopes in order to create an extra barrier protecting the hill itself. And just below the crest of the hill was yet another band of double-apron wire.[62] There was so much to blast, trample, and destroy, that it was difficult to prioritize.

German 120mm fire fell unabated upon the men hunkered along the river. The lonely Cub still circled overhead hoping to gain a precise fix, but the spotter's best reading narrowed down the source to somewhere in a draw beyond Hill 213.[63] Enemy 240mm fire also fell heavy all morning long. These huge, earth-shaking howitzer rounds screamed in from somewhere beyond Sant' Angelo several miles to the south.[64]

Four tanks were not going to be enough to carry the day. Lt Col Sweeting could clearly see this—especially with the infantry stalled. All twelve remaining tanks of B Company, however, sat mired in the muck at the river approach. To maintain maximum pressure on the Germans across the river—Sweeting scurried from tank to tank directing the gunners to keep firing on targets, even while they worked on extricating their machines. Sgt Alfred Mancini's driver, T/5 John "Red" Senior tried walking his tank out of the muck by alternating back and forth on the track control sticks—jerking the tank violently from side to side. The technique failed to gain any traction whatsoever and so the crew finally gave up trying. During an artillery lull, Sweeting climbed on the back deck and directed Sgt Mancini to fire into a particular spot on Hill 213 where he suspected a German gun emplacement was hidden. In a flash, the spirited lieutenant colonel dropped down and ran off to deliver more of his hunches to other stalled tank crews.

Acting on Sweeting's advice, Cpl Alexander Huffman sent several rounds of HE directly into the location. Seconds later, the Germans dispatched several return volleys of their own HE. As soon as the first round exploded, Sgt Mancini immediately buttoned up. The remaining shells buffeted the tank violently and blew one track completely off the drive sprocket. An incoming round exploded squarely upon the front slope, making the interior clang like a bell. The crew were unhurt but their ears were left ringing for hours. After several long moments of relative calm, Mancini summoned up the courage to crack open the turret hatch and survey the damage. The radio antenna was nearly severed in two and left hanging. Anything not armored on the hull was peppered full of shrapnel holes—from ventilator covers to the pioneer tools.[65] Amazingly, T/5 Senior's steel helmet remained strapped to the front siren—but punched with so many holes, it looked like a cheese grater.[66]

After several trials, Sgt Graffagnini's crew freed their tank from the mud near the bridge, and Sweeting caught a glimpse of them moving. In his zeal to put more tanks across, the lieutenant colonel climbed into the turret and took command—displacing Graffagnini to the back deck. He settled in behind the gunner, Cpl Marvin E. King, grabbed the commander's headset and hand mike and checked to make sure the intercom switch was flipped. Sweeting then asked the driver, T/4 Randolph Perdue, if he thought he could ford the river just south of the bridge. The Indianan from Lafayette briefly surveyed the area from his driver's hatch.[67] Although the river had been partially dammed upstream, enough water flowed to make any crossing attempt risky.[68] The river looked about three-feet deep and twenty-feet wide, but the banks were not as high as most places. "We can try," Perdue replied. Gingerly, the 21-year-old driver maneuvered the tank through the field muck to the most promising section.[69] Once square, he shifted gears, gunned the throttle, and threw both steering levers forward. The tank lurched ahead, kicking up fountains of wet soil before pitching down into the river. An enormous wave splashed over the front slope drenching Perdue's face as he struggled to maintain even pressure on the controls. As the tank hit the far bank, the driver gunned the throttle again. The nose pitched upward and the treads clawed desperately into the loose dirt causing large sheets to crumble away. Without solid traction, the tank slid backward into the river. Frigid water washed over the back deck, soaking Graffagnini's pants and cascading into the engine vents. The batteries shorted out and the engine fell dead silent. After several seconds, Sweeting slammed down the hand mike in frustration, hoisted himself out of the tank and splashed back toward American-held territory in search of another venture.

Graffagnini slipped back into his dead tank. There was nothing his crew could do now except to stay in place as water slowly trickled into the driver's compartment. Leaving the tank was out of the question. One German tossing a single grenade through a hatch could easily destroy it. The battlefield offered no safer cover either. The ever-present cracking of small arms and popping of mortar convinced them of that. Nevertheless, the wait was unnerving and uncomfortable. At one point, a German infantryman emerged along the bank—momentarily crouched above them. Perdue grabbed his Tommy gun, shoved it out the driver's hatch, and sprayed a full magazine of .45-caliber ammunition in the intruder's general direction, but the German vanished well before the burst. A short time later, a second soldier was seen creeping along the same bank, but this one wore familiar tanker coveralls. Perdue recognized the lost American as Pfc Joseph Cutrone, the displaced bow gunner dismissed by Wilkinson after crossing the bridge. Perdue called him over to escape the exploding mortar and snapping bullets. While clambering up the front slope, Cutrone's helmet skidded into the water and he turned to retrieve it. "Forget it and get in here!" Perdue shouted. The young man sensibly scrambled to the safety of the interior.[70]

In the meantime, the tanks of Captain Wilkinson, Lt Henry, and Sgts Cogdill and Jarvis moved methodically toward the walled cemetery near the road to Caira. The old graveyard, protected by an elaborate minefield and barbed-wire fortifications, became their temporary focus.[71] After flattening several rows of razor wire, the tanks reached a gravel road running along the base of Hill 213. They fanned out, turned northwest toward Caira, and knocked out one especially irksome nest of MGs operating inside a two-story house.[72] At one point, Lt Henry's tank passed a stone pile. A solitary German soldier emerged from behind and took a rifle shot at Henry's head—but missed. Sgt Jarvis, trailing Henry's tank, immediately sent a burst of MG fire sparking against the nearby rocks. The startled German dropped his rifle and bolted for the safety of a nearby farmhouse. Jarvis's tank followed him with guns blazing, but the panicked German managed to disappear through the doorway. Undeterred, the sergeant sent four quick 75mm shells into the stone house, blowing out plaster and dust from the interior. Then for good measure, Jarvis directed his driver to circle around the house while he tossed several hand grenades through the windows.[73] The only way the German could have survived was if he reached some bunker hidden along the foundations. That mystery would have to be solved later by the infantry.

Sgt Jarvis's tank then proceeded approximately 300 yards north of the cemetery to flatten another barbed-wire field adjacent to a series of waist-high stumps the Germans had cut to form an AT barrier. Wire was strung between the stumps and booby-trapped with charges to stymie any attacking infantrymen.[74] After a few more minutes, Wilkinson noticed Jarvis's tank had stopped moving. Concerned, the captain directed Laliberty to drive over to Jarvis's position where he discovered the sergeant's tank had hit an AT mine. He and his crew were unhurt, but one track was blown completely off—leaving them hopelessly immobilized. Wilkinson instructed Jarvis to stay with the tank until dark and then crawl with his crew back to safety.[75]

By this time, Sweeting had all but given up on getting additional tanks across until the engineers could repair the road. All morning long, Colonel Mark M. Boatner, CO of the 168th Regiment, prodded Sweeting to send more tanks, but Sweeting could only promise to do his best to deliver.[76] During that same time, B Company's remaining tanks became so thoroughly bogged only the battalion's T2s had any hope of pulling them free, and the engineers could not start repairing the road until those tanks were cleared.[77] At 1120, Sweeting called the battalion maintenance crews forward to begin immediate retrieval—an extremely dangerous job because the winching crews had to work in broad daylight with German artillery exploding all around them. That same hour, Sweeting met with the engineers to discuss the prospect of building a second separate corduroy route toward the same bridge. Next, the restless lieutenant colonel focused on directing Wilkinson via radio on where to go and which targets to hit next.[78] Since Wilkinson had no transmitter, the captain couldn't suggest alternatives and moved as Sweeting instructed.

As noon approached, an anxious Maj Gen Ryder watched the battle from his Monte Trocchio OP in the east.[79] Lt Gen Mark Clark was only moments away from joining him to evaluate the attack's progress.[80] Ryder became gravely concerned the bogged tanks were not receiving top priority by his engineers and phoned his operations staff to insist adamantly: "We must get those tanks across."[81] At the same time, restless 34th Division support units kept phoning HQ for permission to move closer to the Caira bridge but were told to wait on account of German artillery falling so heavily all along the river.[82] At 1125, the division's artillery observation plane finally registered a clear fix on one of the Nebelwerfer locations and radioed back the coordinates for a prompt counterbattery response.[83]

By noon, L Co, 168th, reported they had finally crossed the river after regrouping and moving 500 yards further to the north.[84] A and C Companies, 168th, resumed their perilous advance across the flat, open ground toward Hill 213. Progress was painfully slow—due to relentless German artillery blasting. By 1225, the men phoned for a squad of engineers to assist them in clearing minefields so they could rescue wounded comrades and then recover the dead.[85] Infantrymen had not been trained to clear minefields and relied on either the engineers or tanks to clear pathways.[86] The engineers, however, were fully committed to restoring the tank road, so the 168th had to proceed without their assistance.

In the early afternoon, Lt Gen Mark Clark joined Ryder at the 34th Division's Monte Trocchio OP. Through binocular sets, the two generals impatiently studied and discussed the panoramic spectacle unfolding two miles to the west. On the 34th's northern flank, miserable riflemen clawed and crept haltingly toward Wilkinson's three moving tanks—still busily bulldozing back and forth atop razor wire defenses near the cemetery.[87] German artillery and mortars burst around them with the same unrelenting regularity they had since dawn—arbitrarily maiming or snuffing out the lives of unlucky infantrymen squirming through the forbidding fields between the Rapido and Hill 213.[88] At the south flank of the 34th Division's attack, one company from the 135th Regiment surprisingly breached the Rapido just to the south of the barracks—briefly securing a segment of road below Hill 175.[89] Without tanks, however, the gain was tenuous. To aid them, Sweeting directed 1st Lt Loeb of C Company to try moving tanks toward a narrow foot bridge just north of the barracks,[90] but Loeb's crews could find no ground firm enough to get them anywhere close to the position. With that option closed, Sweeting ordered Loeb to instead attempt a river crossing a full 1,000 yards north of Wilkinson's tanks. This area sat in the French zone of operation. Loeb tried that location as well but could find no suitable approaches there either.[91]

The French Expeditionary Corps (Corps Expéditionnaire Français, or CEF) under General Alphonse Juin held the Fifth Army's northernmost flank and was tasked with a dual mission of drawing German reserves in from the Liri Valley while preventing German reinforcements from sliding down the Gustav Line to shore up Cassino. The Fifth Army believed simultaneous pressure coming from the CEF in the mountains north as the 34th Division pushed on Cassino might prove enough to crack the overall German grip on the area.[92] This was the classic "broad front" strategy favored by senior American infantry officers—meant to disperse, engage, and exhaust the enemy everywhere at once.

On 25 January, CEF forces—including fearsome colonial troops of the Algerian 3rd and Moroccan 2nd Infantry Divisions—battled up the steep approaches of Monte Belvedere, five miles due north of Cassino.[93] Combat was bloody, fierce, and personal—and the agility and tenacity of the French colonials shocked even the experienced German mountain troops holding the northern flank.[94] On 26 January, the 915-meter-high summit of Belvedere fell and French forces dashed westward toward the mountain town of Terelle roughly a mile east of the snowy cap of Monte Caira.[95] Although CEF gains were fragile and won with great sacrifice, Juin believed his men had earned a golden opportunity to break through into the Liri Valley, five miles further west—thereby cutting Cassino completely off from the rear. A week earlier, the determined French general had pleaded with Lt Gen Clark to allow him to attack the northern town of Atina with the intention of striking westward to the Liri from that location. Clark had turned down his request.[96] Undeterred, Juin petitioned Clark persistently for reinforcements to beef up his northern attack, with the promise that Monte Cassino might be circumvented completely. Clark rebuffed him each time.[97] The American commander could not be dissuaded away from his more conservative and methodical "broad front" plan. In fairness, Clark had few units to spare and was also loath to change his carefully constructed plans on yet another gamble—particularly after the terrible mauling his 36th Division had suffered six days earlier along the banks of the Rapido.[98] In the end, the most Clark was willing to concede to Juin was an offer to move the 36th Division's only unmolested infantry regiment—the 142nd—into a support position between CEF and 34th Division sectors. This alone was not enough to put anybody in the Liri Valley but would certainly help shore up both the French and 34th Division's immediate designs on Caira and the highlands beyond. At noon, 27 January, the 142nd was temporarily attached to the 34th Division and started moving by truck and foot from Sant' Angelo.[99] By 1310, they closed in on a new assembly area near Sant' Elia, roughly two miles north of San Michele.[100]

With an eternal Italian sun glowing with oblivious optimism high above the carnage of mortals, Captain Wilkinson's three remaining tanks did their level best to carry out Clark's plans. They were ranging further and further toward Caira in search of more MGs to silence and wire to trample, when Sweeting's voice cracked in over Wilkinson's radio receiver. The battalion commander now wanted the crews to turn around and attack south instead.[101] Sweeting was gambling. Wilkinson's tanks had absolutely no infantry support, but he hoped their sudden appearance at the barracks might help the men of the 135th hold the road further south and even flush the Germans from the area. On this hunch alone, the three tanks reversed course and crawled in single file along the thin gravel road running the base of Hill 213.[102] Wilkinson led the drive with Lt Henry following and Sgt Cogdill bringing up the rear—each tank spaced roughly fifty yards from each other. Ammunition and fuel stocks dwindled, so greater care was given to target identification. From time to time, the small column stopped momentarily to blast away positions clearly concealing German MGs. They proceeded past The Pimple, sweeping so close along the granite foundation the commanders could have reached out and touched the steep hill as they passed. Immediately to his left, Wilkinson caught sight of an iron pillbox only a few dozen yards from the road. The position was so well camouflaged, none of the tank commanders noticed it until they passed behind it. "Iron Spider" pillboxes such as these were virtually impenetrable from the front—even from direct hits. The rear, however, was open and vulnerable. Rather than back up and destroy the position, Wilkinson decided to press ahead before returning later to blast it into oblivion.[103]

The gravel road gave way to narrow blacktop,[104] and The Pimple receded to reveal a deep draw on the right, a small cement bridge, and cluster of ruined homes. Two-hundred yards straight ahead lay the bombed-out ruins of the barracks. About thirty yards beyond the bridge to the left, lay muddy lowlands covered in haystacks and rowed barbed wire leading down to the river.[105] In the middle of the field lay at least *two* low-profile concrete bunkers housing multiple MG crews. These elongated emplacements had been the bane of the 135th Regiment for the past two days—responsible for wounding or killing dozens of Americans—perhaps even claiming Lt Col Moseley's life. From the back, however, these seemingly impregnable emplacements sat completely defenseless. One large, open rear doorway allowed for the easy access of German troops—and also American tank HE rounds. These were unbelievably ripe plums ready for picking. Wilkinson ordered T/5 Laliberty to roll ahead where they could place a clear shot into the rear of the furthest bunker.[106]

The nearby Germans seemed powerless to stop the intrusion and fell eerily quiet—the way crickets at night suddenly hush upon a stranger's trespass. Three American tanks had somehow slipped behind their elaborate chessboard defenses and threatened to clear out their back row. As hundreds of sets of American eyes watched through field glasses from beyond the Rapido, Wilkinson's tank bounded across the narrow concrete bridge and ventured far enough down the road to gain a clear shot.[107] Lt Henry's tank followed in support, crossed the bridge and halted momentarily beyond the abutments. The bunker sat well below the road grade—beyond the declination level for the main gun. To bring it to bear on the far bunker's rear doorway, Laliberty jack-knifed Wilkinson's tank atop the narrow road and walked the tracks partway down the graded embankment. Cpl Tirpak then zeroed the main gun upon the entrance and Wilkinson gave the fire order. With a brilliant orange flash and thunderous crack, the pillbox interior shook—followed immediately with the agonized screams of the dying. Thick smoke billowed from the doorway and gun-sight holes, and the cries fell silent.[108]

Wilkinson ordered Laliberty to back up onto the roadway to continue the hunt. Out of the corner of his left eye, the captain saw a German soldier in a running crouch diving for the cover of a haystack. The soldier carried a rifle-sized tube with what appeared to be a derby hat affixed on one end.[109] The weapon looked remarkably similar to a U.S. Army "bazooka" and Wilkinson instantly sensed trouble. "Traverse left!" the captain yelled to Tirpak seated below his waist. The big man cranked the turret around at a furious pace, but by hand—forgetting to utilize the much faster power traverse handle.[110] The fearless German emerged from behind the haystack, tube tucked firmly under his right armpit and pointed the "derby hat" directly at Wilkinson's turret.[111]

As Tirpak leveled the main gun upon the haystack, Wilkinson opened his mouth to give the "fire" order; but before he could, the entire tank jolted with a deafening bang. Searing heat flashed through the turret interior evaporating into trails of sparks and thick acrid smoke. Wilkinson was knocked back violently against the turret wall and collapsed halfway down the interior. Though stunned momentarily, he had the presence of mind to finish the "fire" order intended for Tirpak. The corporal, however, lay sprawled atop Wilkinson—completely unresponsive. Wilkinson struggled to pull himself free from the heavy weight of the gunner's brawny torso. He lifted his shoulders above Tirpak's limp head to where he could see straight into the man's face. Tirpak's eyes were rolled completely back in his head. His OD coveralls were blown wide open and his broad chest completely caved in—revealing a jellied mass of blood and shredded internals. Tirpak had absorbed the full force of a German *Panzerfaust* blast. Mercifully, his death was instant.[112]

At that same moment, Wilkinson saw the turret floor awhirl with flame. His ears still rang from concussive aftereffects, but he could clearly hear the loader, Pvt Bacha, screaming: "FIRE! OUT! OUT!!" Through thickening haze, Wilkinson saw T/5 Laliberty and Sgt Campbell hoist themselves up through the overhead hatches from their seats down below. For a split second, the captain was angry. He hadn't given the order to abandon the tank and he wasn't about to quit. The sentiment was powerful but fleeting. Wilkinson fast came to his senses, ripped off his headset and climbed over Tirpak's lifeless body into the bright crystal blue sky above the turret hatch to slide down the side of the doomed tank. As he did, he saw Laliberty and Campbell roll for the cover of the roadside ditch and rushed over to join them.[113]

The three men huddled in the shallow trench for several quiet seconds until their adrenaline-fueled lungs calmed to where they could again interact. They looked at each other blankly, unsure of what to do next. Laliberty and Crawford were fine physically, but Wilkinson's face was singed red from explosive flash burns. He also bled above the left eye from a spattering of tiny shrapnel wounds that had narrowly missed blinding him.[114]

Wilkinson suddenly realized someone was missing and broke the silence.

"Where's Bacha???" Wilkinson asked the others.

"He's a goner ..." Laliberty quietly answered while staring forward.

"I heard him shout after the explosion ..." Wilkinson countered while lurching up in hopes of rescuing the young crewman from the smoldering tank. Laliberty immediately yanked his captain back down into the ditch to give a more detailed explanation: When the tank was hit, Laliberty had looked up to Bacha's place in the turret basket behind him. The blast had split the 23-year-old Ohioan's abdomen wide open and his intestines were tumbling out.[115] Although the doomed man may have cried out for a few moments, his horrific wounds were clearly not survivable. Before Wilkinson could even formulate another response, the three men found themselves completely surrounded by Germans demanding their surrender. They hadn't been in the ditch more than thirty seconds.[116]

Seeing Wilkinson's M4 smoldering and the crew bailing, Sgt Cogdill and Lt Henry started backing their tanks away from the danger.[117] Cogdill's tank successfully retreated over the narrow bridge to escape behind The Pimple—owing to the adept driving of T/5 Joe K. Wright.[118] Lt Henry's tank, however, became lodged on the bridge's west abutment and began listing heavily to the right. The driver, T/4 Edward A. Avettant of New Orleans, Louisiana halted the track movement momentarily for fear the 32-ton machine might topple over into the twenty-feet-deep gully.[119] Lt Henry slipped out from the turret hatch and stepped gingerly across the tank's skewed back deck—looking for some way to direct Avettant free of the jam. Out of sheer nervous habit, the tall, thin lieutenant reached inside the breast pocket of his coveralls to fish for a cigarette and lighter while contemplating the situation. Before he could raise the flame and draw a puff of calming nicotine, a bullet from a German marksman hit him squarely in the head—killing him instantly.[120] Henry's body crumpled, slipped over the deck, and tumbled into the brush and loose stones of the ravine below.[121] A nearby German MG crew riddled the lieutenant's sprawled body with a swarm of bullets—just to be assured of the kill.[122]

For a few anxious moments, S/Sgt Crawford and the three others sat motionless inside the tank. Avettant again attempted walking the treads but the hull was too firmly lodged, and the tank wouldn't budge forward at all. Two quick deafening bangs shook the chassis. The Germans had fired two *Panzerfaust* rounds directly into the differential housing below the front slope. The crew compartment was not compromised but the transmission was now rendered completely inoperable. The four survivors decided to take their chances and vacate, but as soon as they emerged from the hatches, the Germans quickly surrounded them and forced surrender.[123]

S/Sgt Crawford and T/4 Avettant, along with gunner Cpl Charles H. Coleman and loader Pfc Hubert S. Shew, were searched, stripped of any weapons, and pooled with Wilkinson and his surviving crew.[124] The Germans did not seem to be the least bit concerned about prisoner interaction and the seven Americans spoke rather openly to one another. Wilkinson, still haunted at the thought of abandoning Bacha, asked S/Sgt Crawford if he had, by chance, seen the young loader escape. Crawford reported watching Bacha attempting to clear the turret hatch seconds after Wilkinson got out, but he faltered and fell back inside. That was the last he saw of him.[125] The old sergeant seemed more concerned with Wilkinson's injuries. The captain's face was now blistered and swelling to a deep red. With nothing protecting Wilkinson from the harsh sunlight and cold mountain air, Crawford handed him his own helmet and insisted that he wear it.[126]

Meanwhile, 1,000 yards away, B Company's mired tanks continued lending supporting fire to the infantry still creeping across the river. Through field glasses, several tank commanders and crewmen witnessed the capture of their comrades near the barracks but were powerless to do anything about it.[127] They had no way of knowing who lived or died—only that seven or eight of their friends appeared to have been captured. As of 1300 only Sgt Cogdill's tank remained active of the original four. Alone and without support, Cogdill slowly backed away from The Pimple and Hill 213, firing whenever necessary until all ammunition was nearly exhausted. Then, in an attempt to return home, he backed toward the river, keeping his frontal armor plate toward the Germans. As they neared the north bridge, however, the tank bogged in deep mud.[128] The 33-year-old tank commander from Chadron, Nebraska, and his crew decided to stay put until evening before abandoning the tank and returning to B Company.[129] In the meantime, they had several anxious hours to sit and speculate over what had happened to the others.

Once it was clear Wilkinson's tanks had been knocked out of action, Redle left the battalion CP and walked to the B Company CP his captain had established earlier that same morning. The post was close to the river inside a cramped and demolished building. Redle wondered if he would ever see the tall, lean Texan again.

By 1530, Colonel Boatner of the 168th believed he had delivered enough men across the Rapido to maintain a bridgehead for the evening. The combat engineers and Major Dolvin's maintenance teams focused exclusively on repairing the road and recovering the bogged tanks.[130] To speed up progress, light tanks from D Company delivered logs and culverts and provided some screening protection for the engineers from German artillery.[131] By 1610, two full companies of engineers were committed to resolving the bridge site problem, with four more companies on the way.[132]

In the late afternoon, the infantry of the 168th maintained two tenuous positions on the western Rapido riverbank. A and B Companies, 168th, held the flat fields southeast of the cemetery, with men still crawling in fits and starts toward the damaged walls and smashed mausoleums. Roughly 500 yards north of the Caira bridge, however, I and L Companies, 168th, were forced to withdraw temporarily due to high concentrations of German artillery and mortar falling on their positions.[133] The shelling rained so heavily that both companies nearly became disorganized. Cannon Company, again, had to lay smoke to facilitate the withdrawal.[134] Once back east of the river, I Company's commander ordered his men to dig in among the tanks trapped along the bridge approaches. L Company had become so rattled from the earlier pounding that many survivors rushed all the way back to the original assembly area to reorganize. The ground was pockmarked with huge, watery shell holes. Some of the panicked men tumbled into them and ended up discarding precious equipment in order to extricate themselves.[135] A short time later, however, K Company and remnants of I and L Company re-crossed the Rapido and recaptured their northern foothold.[136] German artillery could be ferocious when concentrated, but it couldn't fall everywhere at once. Because the enemy had to eventually shift its focus on to other areas of Allied activity, two platoons were even able to strike out toward Caira through fields technically in the French sector.[137]

In addition to fire support from the tanks stuck near the river, the infantry relied on tank destroyer fire from afar. TDs from the 805th Tank Destroyer Battalion blasted away on problem positions from the high ground further east. At one point they hammered a stubborn MG position until several shell-shocked Germans finally fled the crumbling house entirely.[138] C Co, 168th, was able to cross the Rapido, and by 1630, American infantry had closed in on the cemetery—an accomplishment made possible because of paths crushed earlier by Wilkinson's tanks.[139]

A German self-propelled (SP) AT gun emerged somewhere along the road bend heading down from Caira and fired at the B Company tanks mired along the tank trail to the bridge. Luckily, riverbank trees helped shield the trapped M4s from the stalker's deadly fire. The squat, gray machine's appearance was distressing proof that German armor had since moved into the area. However, the gutsy gun was forced to withdraw almost as quickly as it appeared due to the rapid response of 34th Division artillery counterbattery.[140] By late afternoon, several B Company tanks had been pulled free of the muck but still could not get across the Rapido.[141]

German artillery and mortar continued falling regularly near the bridge. The rounds originated from multiple locations—which made tracking their sources difficult. Some batteries appeared to be as close as Cassino's southern edge, but the heavier stuff screamed in from either Piedimonte San Germano, six miles west, or Atina eight miles north in the high Apennines.[142] Several times, the 34th Division HQ implored the II Corps to arrange air strikes upon those positions, but the Allied Air Force could not possibly accommodate all the requests pouring in from the various commands jammed within the region. Nevertheless, two bombing missions were arranged—both striking Piedimonte. The first bombs fell at 1100 and a follow-up wave struck at 1540.[143] No additional sorties could be arranged that afternoon, because of an unfolding German counterattack on French forces further north. As a consequence, all available bombers were diverted to strike the mountain village of Terelle.[144] The effectiveness of these bombing missions was always difficult to measure. Even when the pilots were certain they had scored direct hits, they often learned later they had wasted payloads striking elaborate dummy positions. The

Germans created decoy sites by removing the wheels from requisitioned Italian carts and affixing them to tree trunks cut to appear as long gun barrels. They would then throw superficial "camouflage" over the top of them and dig slit trenches nearby. Several times, Allied bombers fell for these deceptions.[145] The two air strikes on Piedimonte brought no reduction in the number of German shells falling on the men crawling through the mud along the Rapido. Not until early evening did the rate of German shelling show any noticeable drop.

With the day winding down, Lt Col Sweeting made arrangements to resume the attack once the roadway was clear. This time, C Company tanks would pass through B Company positions and take the lead. After meeting with Colonel Boatner of the 168th Regiment, however, both officers decided to delay attack plans until the 29th—hoping the extra day would buy the engineers the necessary time to fix the roads. As a result, the infantrymen holding ground across the Rapido were instructed to remain in place for the next forty hours.[146] As soon as Sweeting left the meeting, he phoned the G-3 of the 34th Division to request additional tanks. He was immediately promised an entire company from the 760th Tank Battalion would be promptly sent to him for temporary attachment to the 756th.[147] The surprisingly swift response demonstrated Maj Gen Ryder's high confidence in Sweeting's abilities.

By 1830, the 1st Bn, 168th, reported sending scouting parties west of the cemetery while others moved along the base of Hill 213. At the same time, A Company riflemen creeping south toward The Pimple[148] drew withering fire from the heights and halted.[149] The 3rd Bn, 168th, reported also having two companies probing cautiously toward Caira and encountering thick minefields and twisted wire.[150] At the same hour, the 2nd Bn, 168th, maintained reserve positions along the riverbanks.[151] As the sun set, however, the perimeter probing was halted and the infantry consolidated defensive lines northeast and southeast of the cemetery.[152]

The day's actions had been costly for both the 168th Regiment and the 756th Tank Battalion. Although the exact number of dead was unknown, dozens lay motionless among the cratered minefields. No one dared risk recovering them. These unfortunate souls were trapped not only in a physical "no man's land" but an administrative one as well. Technically, they were "missing in action," but a company first sergeant was always reluctant to record a duty status change unless certain. In the fog of war, a missing man might only be temporarily separated from his unit. Sometimes, a man believed dead by his comrades, turned up later alive. Therefore, until a soldier's remains were positively identified, his duty status was left unchanged—in other words, he remained "on duty." The total number of wounded was also difficult to determine because of a communication lag between overwhelmed aid stations and field hospitals. However, I and L Companies did report evacuating nearly *forty* men felled by shrapnel during the day.[153]

* * *

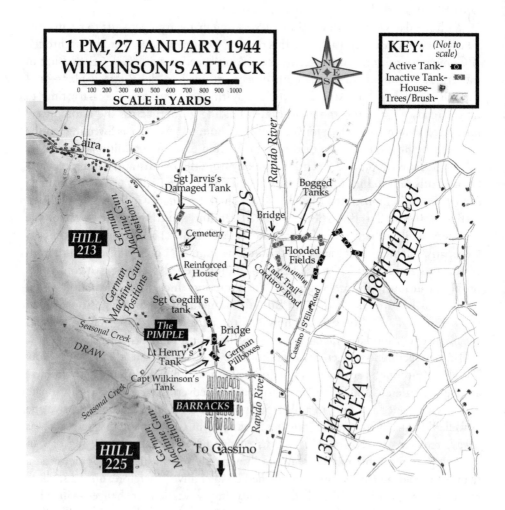

1 PM, 27 JANUARY 1944
WILKINSON'S ATTACK

0 100 200 300 400 500 600 700 800 900 1000

SCALE in YARDS

KEY: *(Not to scale)*
Active Tank-
Inactive Tank-
House-
Trees/Brush-

Caira

Rapido River

Sgt Jarvis's
Damaged Tank

Bogged
Tanks

Bridge

MINEFIELDS

HILL
213

German Machine Gun Positions

Cemetery

Flooded
Fields

Reinforced
House

"Tank Trail"
Corduroy Road

168th Inf Regt
AREA

Sgt Cogdill's
tank

Seasonal Creek

The
PIMPLE

Bridge

DRAW

Lt Henry's
Tank

German
Pillboxes

135th Inf Regt
AREA

Capt Wilkinson's
Tank

Seasonal Creek

BARRACKS

Rapido River

HILL
225

German Machine Gun Positions

To Cassino

A gloomy dusk settled upon the valley like a dreadful hangover. Behind German lines, the seven B Company captives were escorted away from the barracks to a camp several hundred yards upland. An English-speaking German tried interrogating the men, but T/4 Avettant pretended he couldn't understand a word—much to the frustration of his captor and private amusement of his fellow tankers.[154] Captain Wilkinson was separated from the enlisted men and also interrogated briefly.[155] He answered only the barest minimum and was subsequently turned over to two guards who escorted him up a long mountain trail. The rock and soil had been churned considerably from earlier American artillery blasts and Wilkinson noticed his guards appeared quite apprehensive and in a great hurry to pass through.

After plodding for what felt like hours, the three finally reached a small hamlet comprising several stone houses. From the abundance of phone wires strung through and bustle of men in *feldgrau* uniforms, Wilkinson surmised the location was a German CP. It was a very strange feeling indeed, to see his adversaries living and breathing the war. But he recognized the same tense expressions and the interminable "what the hell am I doing here" stares common to the faces of every soldier in every war.

A German officer greeted Wilkinson speaking superb English. Judging from the man's shoulder board insignia, Wilkinson figured he was a colonel or lieutenant colonel, and probably a battalion or regimental commander. The officer was calm and amiable, and asked Wilkinson a few general questions but did not press too hard for answers. He seemed more concerned about being a good host then an interrogator. After the short exchange, Wilkinson was put in a room with about thirty German regulars—all were heavily armed and preparing to move to the front after first getting a few hours of rest. Remarkably, Wilkinson was told to find an open space among them and to also get some sleep. Any attempt to seize a weapon and escape would have been suicide, of course, so Wilkinson did as he was told and gave in to his exhaustion. In the deep of the night, he was roused and placed aboard a truck with several other Allied prisoners—but none were from the 756th. The men sat silently and ruefully as the truck drove northward over a long, bumpy gravel road.[156] Time passed slowly, marked by the relentless drone of the engine and the irregular shuddering of the axle … and then the gravity of the situation finally hit Wilkinson. He was being driven further and further away from the war, the unit that was his home and the men who had been his family for the last two and a half years. He had become a lonely prisoner of war.

* * *

Redle's work at the forward CP was ceaseless and dizzying. The company seemed in utter chaos, and the XO had no free moment to reflect on Wilkinson's fate. His captain was unofficially considered "missing"—but so were many other B Company members. Redle spent much of the afternoon and evening just trying to determine who was where and how to get them home again. Most B Company tanks sat either half sunk in mud near the river or knocked out beyond it.[157] Every hour, the tanks with functioning transmitters radioed 1st Sgt Hogan at the battalion's San Michele CP to report on their statuses. As always, communication was kept at the barest minimum to avoid German compass triangulation. Already, several crews were being forced to sweat out petrifying German artillery barrages after their positions became compromised. Once darkness fell, Hogan started calling the crews home so they could finally enjoy food and rest.

S/Sgt Oric Johannesen, the tall, blond 3rd Platoon sergeant from Oregon,[158] found his tank the unwelcome target of some German flat-trajectory gun firing in the dark from somewhere beyond Hill 213.[159] After nervously enduring several near misses, Johannesen's crew finally gained a firm fix on the gun's location by bore sighting the flash and counting down the seconds before the shell arrived. They responded by sending four or five rounds of quick counterbattery, and the pesky German gun left them in peace.[160] Afterwards, Johannesen received orders from Hogan for his crew to abandon the tank until morning, so they promptly removed the radio crystals and started walking toward the rear. Along the way, they encountered an infantry major who ordered them to return. When they arrived at the tank, the major told Johannesen to restore the radio so he could call out. The big, athletic tanker tried warning him of the hazards, but the major wouldn't listen. The instant Johannesen turned the radio on and passed the hand mike to the officer, German artillery shells began exploding all over the place. The major promptly dropped the mike and shot off into the darkness like a frightened rabbit.[161] The barrage eventually lifted, and Johannesen and his crew disabled their radio a second time and resumed the long trek to the rear.

Sgt Graffagnini and his crew sat trapped and shivering all day inside their stalled tank parked in the middle of the Rapido River—bearing the pinging of small arms fire and buffeting of mortar and artillery. After Pfc Cutrone took refuge inside, the icy waters rose up to the knees of the men seated down front, and gasoline somehow seeped into the crew compartment. At one point, Cutrone absentmindedly pulled out a cigarette and flipped open a lighter. T/4 Perdue swiftly intervened before their suffering ended in a fiery disaster. Later, the loader, Pvt Gene Palumbo, cracked open the turret pistol port to steal a peek outside. At that very instant, a German shell exploded nearby, and the blast coming through the small, square opening knocked Palumbo against the gun breech. As darkness arrived and a short lull fell upon their little piece of the battlefield, Graffagnini suggested making their escape.[162] With cramped legs and stiff backs, the five men slipped into the frigid, waist-deep river water but were already so numbed they hardly felt any discomfort. After soaking for hours in the driver's seat, Perdue couldn't even feel his feet.[163] Once atop the east riverbank, the men separated. Sgt Graffagnini and Pfc Cutrone wandered back to B Company's CP,[164] but T/4 Perdue and Cpl King stayed to assist infantry medics evacuating the wounded by serving as litter bearers. The work was so exhausting, the two burrowed into a nearby haystack afterwards and immediately fell asleep.[165] Pvt Palumbo, shivering and alone, happened across a group of infantrymen and hunkered down with them for the evening.[166]

Many more B Company tank crews drifted into the B Company CP throughout the evening—each with their own tales of trepidation and survival. During their walk back, Sgt Mancini's crew had to jump in the mud to avoid one flurry of Nebelwerfer explosions. T/5 Senior wore the same badly battered helmet that had been clasped to the exterior of this tank all day long—drawing strange looks from everyone he passed. Though perforated with countless shrapnel holes, the driver figured wearing something was better than nothing at all.[167] Sgt Cogdill and crew reached the CP later that same evening, but Sgt Jarvis and crew had much further to travel. After smashing the radio crystals and disabling the main gun, the battle-weary tankers backtracked through pitch darkness from north of the cemetery all the way to the B Company camp—painstakingly retracing their own tread marks to avoid stepping on anti-personnel mines.[168]

After debriefing everyone as they arrived, Redle gained a much clearer picture of what had happened earlier that day.[169] Clearly, Wilkinson had been captured—as had most of his crew and those from Lt Henry's tank.[170] Redle picked up his field phone to report this grim conclusion to Sweeting. At first the busy lieutenant colonel couldn't be tracked down, and finally, when he eventually picked up the line, couldn't be made to believe the news. Redle had to repeatedly recount every eyewitness detail before Sweeting finally accepted that Wilkinson was gone. Then the line fell quiet for a long moment before Sweeting's voice crackled back through—informing Redle he was the new B Company commander. Redle acknowledged the appointment and the lieutenant colonel abruptly hung up. Every young lieutenant dreamed of one day commanding a company, but this promotion was unexpected and unwelcome and brought Redle no joy.[171] By midnight, the new B Company CO accounted for most of his remaining tank crews—safely returned to camp. Lt Col Sweeting, on the other hand, moved to other matters and buzzed on through the night with his usual unearthly energy—checking and rechecking the progress of the engineers and the tank retrievers.[172]

Lt Leger, the platoon leader relieved earlier for refusing to answer Wilkinson's calls, was sent to B Company's rear CP. His morning failures had left him bitter and surly—making him an unpleasant distraction to all within earshot. Even the normally mild-mannered 1st Sgt Hogan called Redle to complain he would "kill" Leger if he wasn't removed soon. Redle ordered Leger to join him at the forward CP, where the officer behaved much calmer.[173] Eventually, Redle assigned him as liaison to the 3rd Bn, 133rd Regiment.[174]

In the cold early morning hours, when little else remained for Redle to do except wait as the T2 crews recovered tanks throughout the night, the young lieutenant stepped a few yards away from his forward CP to find a place to sleep. Under some concrete steps leading to the stone remnants of a house leveled by artillery, he found a straw-lined space big enough to accommodate his slight frame. A rotting cat lay curled in a corner. Death seemed to find every nook and cranny of this battlefield. He grabbed the decomposing animal by a limb, tossed it outside, then squeezed inside to nestle upon the straw. With the flickering of artillery and wrathful sounds of war fluctuating around him, Redle took inventory of the day's events. He concluded Wilkinson's tanks—though successful at the onset—failed in their mission because they lacked necessary infantry support.[175] He reflected on the dangers of overconfidence. He strategized on how to scrutinize new platoon leaders in the future and spot early warning signs in their behavior. After considering a few more company matters, Redle set the war aside entirely, reached inside his pocket and pulled out his Rosary. Ever since his childhood, Redle ended every evening the same way: prayer. He prayed for his family, for the safety of his company, and for the strength and wisdom to carry out the heavy responsibilities as B Company Commander. Then Redle surrendered all his worldly concerns to God and fell asleep.[176]

Lt Fazendin once marveled that inside Redle's chest beat the "heart of a lion."[177] On the outside, he looked and acted nothing like a "king of the jungle." His OD coveralls hung rumpled and baggy off his thin frame. Whenever he pulled a steel pot over his leather tanker helmet, he had to twist it to one side to keep it from slipping off. Though slight in stature, Redle kept an exceedingly fit and hardy physique—capable of enduring physical hardships exhausting men twice his size. Though he was quiet, unassuming, and humble—he possessed a razor-sharp mind that processed and absorbed everything happening all around him at once. Though never a proselytizer, his religious faith was always sincere and anchored firmly upon granite.[178] He never fretted over past mistakes—choosing instead to learn from them and move on. He never worried about the future but set achievable goals and worked tirelessly to attain them—one tiny step at a time. He carried no regal pedigree and possessed no sense of entitlement. Relentless toil and study earned him a chemistry degree and a reserve officer commission from the University of Creighton in 1941.[179] Relentless toil and study also put him at the top of his ROTC class in military tactics and earned him an invitation into the new Armor Branch.[180] All his life, Redle simply scratched through every challenge tossed his way as the perennial underdog—and always triumphed in the end.

The 25-year-old Wyoming man's heart held, indeed, an enormous hidden reservoir of strength—powerful enough to carry many others along with him. Yes, 1st Lt David D. Redle was quite ready to lead B Company.

U.S. 168th Infantry Regiment

M5 tanks from A Company, 756th Tank Battalion, line up and await orders on a cold day in the Italian countryside. This photo was likely taken in late October 1943—just a few weeks before the battalion was reorganized with M4 medium tanks. (*Doyle Cody Collection*)

Above Pfc Clyde Guild of B Company takes a cigarette break atop a jeep. (*Clyde W. Guild*)

Left Lt Winlock, Captain Wilkinson, and Lt Fazendin pose in Italy wearing tanker coveralls and full combat gear. (*David D. Redle*)

Left Treadway bridge where the 756th crossed the Volturno River. (*U.S. Army*)

Below Venafro, Italy. A mule train carries ammunition into combat. The 756th Tank Battalion (L) saw limited action supporting the 45th Inf Div in this area before upgrading to a medium tank battalion in December 1943. (*U.S. Army*)

Pvt Gene Palumbo, Sgt Leland Campbell, and Cpl Paul Tirpak confidently pose next to an M4 tank. Location is believed to be the Mignano area in mid-January 1944. Two weeks later, one would be dead, another captured, and the third unable to ever return to tank duty. (*U.S. Army Armor and Cavalry Collection*)

The ruins of San Pietro. The trucks parked by the wall at the lower right are likely those of the 756th Tank Battalion. (*Doyle Cody Collection*)

Left Italian civilian refugees wait for transportation to an Allied refugee camp. This photo was taken at Acquafondata (five miles northwest of Cassino). (*National Archives, SC 186903*)

Lt Redle in combat coveralls, Italy 1944. (*David D. Redle*)

Left Troops of the 34th Infantry Division move cautiously through the rubble-strewn streets of Cervaro. (*U.S. Army*)

VIEW of CASSINO to the West from San Michele

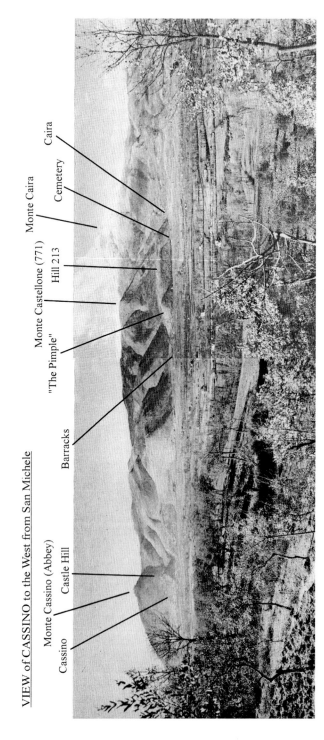

Cassino
Monte Cassino (Abbey)
Castle Hill
Barracks
"The Pimple"
Monte Castellone (771)
Hill 213
Monte Caira
Cemetery
Caira

From this high-ground vantage point at San Michele, Cassino lies three miles to the southwest, and "The Pimple" lies three miles due west. All the area between served as Allied staging ground and was subjected to near-constant German artillery bombardment. Tom Treanor, war correspondent for the *Los Angeles Times*, wrote in his 1 Feb 1944 "The Home Front" column: "The only saving grace for the men on the ground is that the Germans have so many targets to choose from that they can't possibly concentrate on just any one of them." Many Italian farming families remained in their homes and suffered alongside the troops. (*U.S. Army*)

View of Monte Caira (upper right), Cassino, and Highway 6 (lower left) from Monte Trocchio. This was Lt Gen Mark Clark's view of battlefield events during the morning of 27 January 1944. (*National Archives, SC 359290*)

View south toward Cassino from the approximate location of Col Marshall's 133rd Inf Regt CP. The abbey holds the high ground above the town. Just below and slightly to the right is "Castle Hill." Cassino itself lies below Castle Hill. The foreground soil appears to be churned by tank treads. (*National Archives, SC 359288*)

Left 1939 USMA Cadet Casper Clough. Major Clough developed deep admiration for the fighting spirit of the 100th Battalion (Nisei) troops he led at Cassino: "I know there are good combat units—parachutists, rangers, and special service forces—but I'll take the Hawaii soldiers of the 100th. We need more of them." (*1939 Howitzer, USMA Digital Collections*)

Right 2nd Lt Wayne B. Henry, commander of the first Allied tank to cross the Rapido River at the Battle of Cassino. His initiative on 27 January 1944 saved an ambitious attack that had stalled along the muddy eastern bank. (*Wayne B. Henry family*)

Lt Henry's doomed M4 from B Co, 756th, hangs abandoned after becoming ensnared atop a bridge abutment between The Pimple and the barracks. On the right there appears to be a German prisoner wearing a Red Cross armband and assisting a U.S. mine-clearing team. View is north. Photo taken 8 February 1944. (*National Archives, SC 187910*)

An M4 tank likely bogged near the Rapido River. Above it is the saddle between The Pimple (left) and Hill 213 (right). The foreground shows mud churned from countless treads and artillery shells. Trees have been reduced to twisted poles. (*U.S. Army*)

Left C Co, 756th, #14 tank is searched for salvageable equipment. Note how the jeep in the foreground has a wire cutter mounted on the front. (*Critical Past*)

Below B Co, 756th, tanks also trapped in the mud. Some were not extricated until after the war ended. (*U.S. Army*)

A platoon of tanks from C Company, 760th Tank Battalion, parked in defilade positions along "Sorrell's Skyway"—formed by draining the Rapido River. (*Critical Past*)

Sturmgeschütz III destroyed near the cemetery north of Cassino on 29 January 1944. This SP gun was likely responsible for knocking out four A Co, 756th, tanks—killing several tankers and wounding Captain French Lewis. (*Polish Institute and Sikorski Museum, London*)

CHAPTER 14

Bridgehead: Evening 27 January 1944 to 29 January 1944

Colonel Mark M. Boatner commanded the 168th Regiment with dogged fervor.[1] The 47-year-old, 1918 graduate of West Point came from a New Orleans family of antebellum roots and proud military lineage. He lived and breathed the Army with devout reverence. Though short in stature, the self-described "King of the Runts," was athletic, smart, and driven. At the start of the war, he switched his commission from engineers to infantry just to land a combat command. After receiving that command in North Africa, he was injured in a jeep accident—but hid the lingering pain of three broken ribs to avoid being replaced.[2] Now he was presented with the greatest challenge of his career: breaking through the multilayered defenses of the Gustav Line.

As darkness fell on 27 January, Boatner's men not only hoped to keep the fragile ground they held beyond the Rapido but to expand and take Hill 213 and The Pimple before morning. As A and B Companies of the 3rd Bn, 168th, consolidated defensively southeast of the cemetery, and elements of the 3rd Bn, 168th, did the same northeast of the cemetery,[3] C Company stealthily passed through the regiment's southeast positions to infiltrate German nighttime defenses.[4] As midnight passed, the C Company men crawled up the hillside relatively undetected. German artillery continued falling throughout the night—coming mostly from the southwest and increasing in frequency between 0100 to 0400.[5] The salvos, however, seemed more for harassment than as a response to anything the 168th was doing in particular.[6]

The lead elements of C Company eventually reached the top of Hill 213, but the company commander feared his gains were untenable and ordered his men to withdraw before dawn revealed their presence.[7] At 0300, 28 January, A Co, 168th, also attempted to advance on The Pimple but were detected and pinned down by concentrated spray from at least fifteen MGs.[8] The ruckus awoke other German MG crews along Hill 213, inciting them to fire indiscriminately on 3rd Bn, 168th, positions north of the cemetery—even though the Americans were well dug in 800 yards away and cloaked by complete darkness.[9] The Germans seemed determined to prove Hill 213 and The Pimple remained under their firm control. The long, tense evening finally gave way to the first flickers of a cold, gray dawn—with both sides still swapping gunfire from the same places they started at sundown.

The rising sun brought a welcome break from the high cloud cover, but lingering mist kept ground visibility fair at best.[10] To the immediate northeast of the 168th Regiment, the 142nd Regimental Combat Team (RCT) under the command of the 34th Division's assistant division commander, Brigadier General (Brig Gen) Frederic B. Butler, attempted their own dawn crossing of the Rapido.[11] The maneuver was designed to shore up a gap between 168th positions to the south and French forces further north. The 142nd RCT, alternately dubbed "Task Force Butler" (TFB), was an ad hoc unit built around the 142nd Infantry Regiment with attached armor, artillery, and recon units providing added muscle. The attack commenced along a narrow section of the river and was met promptly with heavy MG fire and a walled artillery response. The 3rd Bn, 142nd, leading the charge, became ensnared in intricate minefields and suffered the brunt of the beating—losing their CO and XO during the opening salvos and degrading into ever-worsening confusion thereafter. By 0700, the 3rd Battalion was forced to pull back completely and the entire attack was called off until the following day.[12]

At 0800, Maj Gen Ryder hailed Colonel Boatner by phone—hoping to hear better news but was told that Hill 213 was too heavily defended by MGs to take the prior night and artillery still fell too thick for the 168th to maneuver effectively by daylight. Boatner offered to attempt a noon attack but had little confidence in its success. In the end, the 168th's attack plans were also delayed another day. To dissuade the Germans from even thinking of counterattacking, Ryder next phoned his artillery declaring: "I want that hill pounded to hell."[13]

Most B Co, 756th, tanks sat silently where they were left the night before—scattered haphazardly across the watery bog as though some giant, angry child had cast them aside. Some lay tilted at forty-five-degree angles, others were pitched nose first into ditches with guns spun a kilter. Still others had rolled completely over onto their sides—sunk partway down into the unforgiving muck. Radio antennas were twisted and sheared, and pioneer tools were shattered or blown completely off the hulls. Some tanks had thrown tracks.[14] Several other M4s from A and C Companies also sat trapped in adjacent fields from prior failed attempts to breach the river. In all, the 756th reported a full fifty percent of their tanks were either stuck or out of service. Four or five had become waterlogged and were completely abandoned to Ordnance for future salvage.[15]

The crews left the tanks temporarily the night before to obtain rations and rest. After they departed, the infantry took up residence inside their cold, dark hulls—seeking some respite from the incessant bursting of German artillery and mortar.[16] The tall poplars along the river once concealing the tank approach from German view were being slowly shredded with every volley. All that remained of some were twisted, splintered trunks. With the sun fixed as a white disk in a gray sky behind Monte Trocchio, the B Company tank crews returned to reclaim their posts and perform as pillbox artillery for the scant infantry across the river.[17] All the while, the 756th's T2 tank retriever crews continued with the salvage efforts.

Great care, planning, and execution went into every recovery. A trapped tank could not be extricated without a firm foundation upon which to operate a winch or hitch a tow cable. Maneuvering a T2 into a suitable position was half the battle, as the unforgiving mud was only too eager to claim another victim. Worse, B Company's maintenance section, led by T/Sgt Morris B. Thompson, had to operate in full view of German observers concealed 600 yards away on Hill 213. Every time Thompson's men tried to hook a cable to a stricken hull, the Germans rained artillery down upon them—sending the mechanics scurrying back into the T2's interior. After a while, the T2 crew timed the number of seconds they had to accomplish the task before the Germans responded, and worked accordingly. Several trapped tanks had to be rolled completely over on their sides before they could be pulled free—which meant the mechanics had to time their work in stages and brave many artillery salvos just to finish one job.[18] This deadly game of cat and mouse continued all day long. Complicating the recovery was the fact that every tank pulled free also required repairs of some sort. Although the combat elements of the 756th were positioned around nearby San Michele, the "B-trains" service elements were stationed ten miles back near San Pietro—out of the range of most German artillery.[19] Critical tank parts had to then be trucked over congested roads harassed constantly by German artillery.

Lt Redle devoted his day to overseeing the recovery and tracking down a few B Company men who were still missing. Cpl King and T/5 Perdue stumbled into the B Company CP early in the morning after sleeping all night in the haystack, but Pvt Palumbo was nowhere to be found.[20] Redle ventured very cautiously out as far as the Rapido River in search of him and to also take stock of any changes on the battlefield. Men from 2nd Bn, 168th, hunkering along the banks, waiting in reserve, reacted to his appearance with guarded glances. Beyond the banks in the distance, the abandoned tanks of Sgts Cogdill and Jarvis sat motionless among forbidding rows of concertina wire. Until that ground could be secured, they would remain unrecoverable. He found no sign, however, of Pvt Palumbo. Artillery burst sporadically about and bullets snarled and snapped past his head. Nearby, a familiar figure waded through the knee-deep mud waters frantically running communication lines in advance of the next attack. Redle recognized the man as Captain Ed Olson and was shocked to discover another 756th member operating so close to the front.

"What the hell are you doing here?" Redle hollered. "Looking for a Purple Heart?"

"Hell NO!" Olson shot back sternly. The battalion's communications officer was in no jovial mood.[21]

After returning safely to his CP, Redle received a typed message from Lt Col Sweeting, signed at 1400 under his call sign "Sunray," advising that B Company be pulled from combat until the majority of the company's tanks were recovered and repaired. Sweeting also insisted that two men remain with each trapped tank at all times to guard against German sabotage—particularly at night.[22] Perhaps the battalion CO's orders were overly cautious, but Redle welcomed the extra time to reorganize his men. They needed it. He needed it.

* * *

Like a busy bee, Sweeting spent much of the day buzzing around the area preparing for the new attack. At 0700, he met in the field with S-3 Captain Arnold to review tank retrieval operations and progress on the engineers' road.[23] Major Dolvin, who was in charge of the overall tank recovery, made certain that any tank trapped on the roadway was cleared first.[24] A mini-army of 1,500 engineers now repaired the corduroy road and surveyed alternative crossing routes.[25] Everyone was keenly aware that Lt Gen Mark Clark had become personally interested in their efforts.[26] The bridge approach used by Wilkinson's tanks the day before was too saturated to restore without importing massive amounts of gravel.[27] One promising alternative was an old river ford just north of the narrow bridge. At that location, the engineers started dumping scavenged rocks and fill to form a raised pathway to the opposite bank.[28] Proper roadway materials remained in dreadfully short supply and the engineers lamented to Sweeting that the job could be completed quickly *if* they had the right supplies.[29] As a substitute for logs and Sommerfeld matting, the engineers scrounged chicken wire from supply dumps as far away as San Pietro.[30] The 150-foot long rolls of 42-inch-wide wire made for poor roadway material, but nothing better was available.[31]

To help in the effort, Sweeting diverted several of his tank crews away from infantry fire support duties for a time. He ordered them to blast round after round of HE at one particular spot of the riverbank until they excavated a ramp up the other side. After expending nearly 1,000 rounds, Sweeting finally gave up on the idea. The thick mud simply absorbed the shock of the blasts.[32]

At noon, C Company of the 760th Tank Battalion arrived in the 756th's assembly area for attachment.[33] The CO, 1st Lt Frederick L. Nelson, reported to Lt Col Sweeting for duty at 1400 and the two discussed attack plans for the following day.[34] C Co, 760th, would support the 756th's C and A Companies as they breached the river and serve as the battalion's reserve company. Essentially, they would assume B Company's role until Redle's men could reorganize. Nelson's men were already experienced combat veterans and well suited for the job. They had also been operating medium tanks much longer than the 756th, as the 760th started as a medium tank outfit in November 1941 and trained in Texas and Camp Pickett, Virginia before shipping out to Casablanca in 1943.[35] In early 1943, the 760th tankers parked in the same cork forests near where the 756th bivouacked—but unlike their recently converted medium tank counterparts, they enjoyed many more months of M4 training and thus developed deeper familiarity with their machines. The 760th saw its first heavy combat in the early days of January 1944 near Monte Rotundo and San Pietro.[36] C Company's previous CO fell wounded and the dark-haired, bushy-topped Nelson took command after only a few days at the front.[37] One week of battle was all that was required to transform an untested soldier into a veteran. Nelson's tankers now entered their fifth straight week of combat.

At 1800, Sweeting met with the COs of the 235th Engineering Battalion and B Company of the 16th Armored Engineers to discuss night construction plans. The engineers reported progress on two routes and the identification of a possible third. Both officers promised to continue updating Sweeting every two hours.[38]

At 1900, Sweeting convened a meeting of all his company commanders and the platoon leaders of the HQ assault guns and mortars to discuss the attack plan for the 29th: The 756th Tank Battalion and C Co, 760th, was fully attached to the 168th Regiment and would attack as an entire battalion.[39] A Co, 756th, would lead the assault at dawn, followed by C Co, 756th. Sweeting's tank would follow A Company, and Captain Arnold's tank would follow just ahead of C Company. C Co, 760th, would remain in reserve and both the assault-gun platoon and mortar platoon would be prepared to fire on call. The river would be breached in three potential places: the bridge, the ford to the north, and another possible location much further to the northeast—near the bridge the Germans dropped to partially divert the river.[40] The crossing would coincide with the infantry attack at 0730.[41] The actual tank crossing point would not be chosen until the last minute and would depend upon progress the engineers made during the night.[42] Once across, A Company would attack northwest toward Caira, and C Company would attack south toward the barracks.[43] The infantry of the 168th would take Hill 213 and The Pimple in the middle. Both hills were too steep for tank operation, so the infantry would have to scale them without close tank support.[44]

As the cool dreary day drew to a close, the tank crews continued hitting targets along the hazy ridgeline across the river at the request of the 168th infantry.[45] Despite dispatching hundreds of rounds, German positions around the cemetery and in the hills beyond the barracks remained stubbornly—almost inexplicably—active.[46]

Platoon leader 1st Lt Robert L. Gilman of A Co, 756th, and Captain Walker Sorrell of the engineers ventured a mile north-northeast into French territory to scout the potential third crossing site.[47] At the location, the Germans dropped a bridge low enough to inundate the southwestern fields without damming the river completely. The 24-year-old Sorrell noticed a dry streambed nearby and formulated a brilliant idea: Why not divert the river water *completely* into the old streambed? This would not only drain the flooded fields but might *also* transform the dry river into a sunken roadway for the tanks. Gilman and Sorrell returned at dusk to propose the audacious plan.[48] With the enthusiastic endorsement of their COs, work began at once.[49]

At 2200, Dolvin reported that all trapped B Company tanks had been pulled off the tank route.[50] This did not mean all tanks were recovered or even operational—only that the main route had been cleared in advance of the attack. At the close of day, the number of operational tanks at the 756th's disposal rose to thirty-eight—with thirty-three others undergoing repairs.[51] The number of men on duty, however, dropped. HQ Company had lost six men from artillery attacks throughout the day: One was killed with five others wounded and evacuated.[52] Two other battalion men were also wounded but stayed at their posts.[53]

With midnight approaching, the infantrymen of the 168th holding the fields west of the Rapido heard the ominous sounds of some heavy-tracked vehicle roaming nearby. They could not, however, get a fix on the location. The granite hills and cold moist air played tricks with the acoustics. After a few moments, the growling engine suddenly fell silent. An inquiring phone call was placed to the 756th HQ near San Michele, but the mystery tank was most certainly *not* from their outfit.[54]

In the meantime, the Germans used the lull in the action to bury the body of Lt Henry under a pile of rocks and loose gravel near his dead tank.[55] Henry's pockets were searched for any identification to help properly mark the grave. Everything was promptly returned. Nothing was pilfered—not even the brass second lieutenant bars on his bullet riddled combat jacket. Regular soldiers of the German Army showed remarkable respect for the dead officers of their Western Front adversaries. Curious and paradoxical conduct, to say the least, considering the five-year torrent of theft, death, and destruction their government had unleashed all across Europe. It is a tragic feature of all wars that the respects and honors lavished upon the dead are not extended to the living.

* * *

The early hours of 29 January were unusually quiet. All three regiments of the 34th Division reported little German activity, aside from intermittent MG fire emanating from the barracks and along the ridgeline running northwest of The Pimple.[56] At 0400, the German MG chatter stepped up briefly and ten scattered artillery rounds burst about the 168th area, but the display seemed nothing more than nervous fidgeting.[57] The Germans suspected the Americans were up to something. The previous day they had watched from the highlands as hordes of American engineers and a handful of tank recovery crews worked intently to pierce their carefully conceived Rapido defenses. The Germans could slow those efforts with harassing fire by daylight, but when darkness fell, they were rendered blind and powerless to halt that progress. Maj Gen Keyes of the II Corps had assigned all his engineers to help the 34th Division construct the attack routes, and the extra hands paid dividends.[58] At 0110, the engineers reported three tank crossings in place. Two were constructed near the Caira bridge: One was a bypass just to the south of the bridge, and the second was a ford just to the north. The third route was the ingenious idea proposed earlier by Captain Sorrell: The river was diverted at the downed bridge about a mile north-northeast and a dirt ramp was laid leading down into the drained riverbed.[59] In theory, this formed a long channel that would allow the tanks to move in defilade all the way down to the 168th jump-off point. The great unknown, however, was whether the riverbed was firm enough to support the weight of a passing tank column. Sorrell needed a pathfinder and so, in his slow Alabama drawl, he asked Sweeting:

"Can you take the chance of losing a light tank if we find you a way to get across?"

"I have so many bigger tanks stuck now," Sweeting shrugged, "that one light tank won't make a damn bit of difference."[60]

2nd Lt William H. Newman of D Company was summoned forward with an M5 light for the mission.

* * *

In the 0520 predawn darkness, 1st Lt David Loeb, CO of C Company, 756th, called his company leaders together for one last pep talk before his crews mounted for battle. With uncanny timing, German artillery burst about the assembly area—leaving two tankers dead and Loeb and six others sprawled about wounded on the ground.[61] Word of the incident spread like wildfire through the battalion. Sweeting ordered Loeb's XO, 2nd Lt Gordon E. Perkins,[62] to reorganize the company but the shock was too great and the time too short to be accomplished ahead of the scheduled attack.[63] Instead, Captain Lewis's A Company was told to lead and the newly attached C Co, 760th, would follow.[64]

At 0600, the tanks formed a column, with Sweeting and Arnold assuming positions near the middle. The column rolled toward a newly laid corduroy roadway leading to the first crossing point south of the bridge. As they departed, Maj Gen Ryder called for an update and was confidently assured the tanks were preparing to breach the Rapido in three places.[65] American artillery began pounding Hill 213 on schedule. German artillery batteries reciprocated and shells started exploding all along the marching route—showering the tanks with dirt and mud. In a bad omen, a high-velocity flat-trajectory gun of some sort joined the melee from the direction of the barracks.[66] More serious problems emerged. As the tank column snaked toward the log roads, the tankers saw that the new route to the south ended well short of the river, and the northern route was completely blocked by two trucks buried in mud up to their axels.[67] Sweeting sent a light tank ahead to test the southern route—only to discover the engineers had no time to bind the timbers together.[68] As the M5 barreled down the trembling track, logs were kicked up and tossed in every direction. Upon reaching the end, the light tank promptly sank in mud up to its sponsons.[69]

With the southern road left a jumbled and hopeless mess, A Company was forced to shift to the same northern route that had ensnared B Company two days earlier. Captain Lewis requested for a smoke screen laid west of the river to help conceal their move, but the request was denied when 34th Infantry artillerymen protested that their own observation efforts would be hampered.[70] The 3rd Platoon, commanded by S/Sgt James "Red" Harris of Texas, led the column.[71] Captain Lewis followed, with Lt Roland V. Hunter's 2nd Platoon behind him and Lt Robert L. Gilman's 1st Platoon bringing up the rear.[72] With German artillery harassing them as they rolled, the column turned onto the northern roadway at 0630. Lewis radioed Sweeting for instructions on how to handle the two trucks blocking the far end. Sweeting ordered him to crash through them.[73] This roadway was constructed far better than the first, although water in the roped off areas proved deeper than expected.[74] Even so, S/Sgt Harris's platoon was able to negotiate through to the end, ram the trucks aside and reach the ford north of the bridge.

The morning was crisp and clear—almost too beautiful for combat.[75] The artillery exploded ceaselessly along both sides of the river as American infantrymen and tank crews anxiously prepared to jump off.[76] At the same time, the remaining column of tanks from C Co, 760th, crawled slowly northward along the Cassino–Sant' Elia road toward the third attack route, but no one was really sure if the drained river idea would even work. Since the crossing site was located a mile north inside territory assigned to Juin's forces, the French were alerted so as not to mistaken Sweeting's approaching M4s for German panzers and begin firing at them.[77]

All three battalions of the 168th were committed to the attack, but the 2nd Battalion was given the far more difficult assignment of storming Hill 213—after first advancing 600 yards beyond the Rapido.[78] The task was virtually impossible without close tank support, and so the infantry remained very hesitant to move until the tanks moved first.

At 0700, S/Sgt Harris's tank gently dipped down into the shallow river and balanced along the reinforced ford. After gaining the opposite bank, he turned south and stopped beyond a small rock shack momentarily as Sgt Howard Harrison's tank splashed carefully along the same shallow ford. After scaling the bank, Harrison turned south to follow Harris.[79] More tanks followed: Sgt Raymond Galbraith, S/Sgt Thomas P. Ames, Captain Lewis, and finally Sgt Mack N. Corbitt. As each new tank joined, the column expanded southward—paralleling the river in fifty-yard intervals.[80] The seventh A Company tank attempting to cross, however, slid into the river—blocking the ford and preventing any remaining tanks from passing. Nothing the crew or the engineers immediately tried made the treads regain traction.[81]

In the meantime, Captain Lewis's six tanks rolled in a broad line slowly toward the cemetery. Two platoons of infantry from E Company, 168th, emerged from the riverbanks to follow but dropped for cover as soon as German MGs started spraying at them from the cemetery.[82] Lewis's tanks continued the slow advance—firing at the walls and crypts the Germans had modified into firebases.[83] After crossing 200 yards without incident, Lewis's tank suddenly shuddered with a violent clang. A German AP round clipped the turret's top rear—spraying spalls of liquefied steel inside and directly into the face and throat of the loader, Pvt Edward J. Dudzinski.[84] The 24-year-old dropped to the cramped floor of the turret basket as his horrified crewmates watched death vanquish his jerking, bleeding body. The radio behind Lewis was blown apart and shattered vacuum tubes popped and fizzled as Lewis desperately scanned the terrain ahead for the culprit.

S/Sgt Ames, in the tank to Lewis's left, saw a squat *Sturmgeschütz* III SP AT gun concealed near the cemetery and screamed into his mike: "Look out, Captain! Look out! He's right over there by the corner!"[85] But Lewis could not hear Ames's warning. A split second later, a second round perforated the front turret ring of Lewis's tank and passed completely through the interior—leaving a savage trail of sizzling shrapnel, sparks, and smoke. Lewis's gunner, Cpl Nazzario Martinez, was peppered with molten steel. His thigh, in particular, lay split wide open, bleeding profusely. Lewis sat momentarily stunned and also bled heavily from multiple wounds to one leg and both feet. The men should have been killed outright, but the gun breech deflected the brunt of the blast. Lewis shook off his immediate shock and called out the "abandon tank" order. Driver T/4 Edward R. Mize and bow gunner Sgt Glee H. Maude bailed out through the front hatches and scampered around to the rear. Lewis and Martinez next tumbled out of the smoking turret and rolled across the deck until dropping into the furrowed tracks at the rear.

As Lewis pulled himself up from the mud, he looked up in time to see S/Sgt Ames's nearby tank convulse under another sickening bang.[86] Seconds later, Sgt Galbraith's treads rocked back violently as flames jetted out of the turret. The forward hatches to both doomed tanks flew open and dazed men tumbled from ringing interiors. Galbraith was not one of them. In the distance, Sgt Harrison's tank also began smoking and burning. Lewis could scarcely believe the horror unfolding before his eyes. Other than Ames, nobody could seem to find the enemy gun, and Ames failed to hit it in time. In less than a minute, four of Lewis's tanks were gone. Men with whom he had trained intensively for months were now dead, dying, or clawing for survival and he was absolutely powerless to help them. Lewis's eyes fixed upon S/Sgt Harris's tank at the far south, advancing slowly with the turret traversing impatiently —seemingly waiting for the inevitable *coup de grâce*. At any moment, he expected to see it, too, erupt in flames. The rude shock of a cannon blast buffeted Lewis from behind. Thirty yards to his right, Sgt Corbitt's tank returned fire and destroyed the SP gun before it could finish off both he and Harris.[87]

The very instant Lewis's tank was knocked out, Sweeting's voice screamed over the battalion radio band for the remaining tanks to charge the German AT gun and shoot wildly. "Hell for leather!" he raged zealously. "If you don't get it then ram it!"[88] Such pleas smacked of suicide to the other tankers listening in. What if other AT guns lay hidden in the cemetery? The battalion commander seemed far too eager to gamble *their* lives away over his hunches. Sweeting's reckless ranting probably did more damage to battalion morale than the actual loss of Lewis's four tanks. Men needed to believe their COs would protect them—not treat them as disposable.

In contrast, Captain Lewis's heart bled for the welfare of his men. After his attack stalled and the German SP gun was destroyed, Lewis devoted himself completely to rescuing and saving as many of the wounded as possible. S/Sgt Ames pulled himself slowly out of his ruined tank, then rolled in agony over the back deck and onto the ground. The whole lower half of his body was a shredded bloody mess. Despite excruciating pain in both feet and the dangers from hidden land mines, Lewis hobbled across thirty yards of open field and dragged the shocked tank commander to the tank's rear to shield him from German sniping. Lewis then fashioned a makeshift sling by clasping their two pistol belts together. At a small stone shack near the river crossing point, survivors of the disaster congregated and rendered basic medical aid to one another. Lewis saw Sgt Maude dragging Cpl Martinez in that direction and decided to follow. He strapped Ames to his back and began crawling toward the others—making sure to remain in the tread marks for fear of mines. As he inched along, German bullets snapped past his ears and MG fire cut like invisible scythes across the high grass nearby. Halfway through the agonizing trek, Lewis decided to set Ames down and seek help carrying him. Sgt Corbitt noticed Lewis's struggles and reversed his tank to where his crew could safely retrieve the wounded staff sergeant, secure him to the front slope, and back up further to the shack.[89] As they did so, T/4 Leroy "Chief" Doolittle ran by headed in the same direction. The tank driver's arms were so horribly burned that sheets of skin slid off his hands. Nevertheless, Doolittle maintained the presence of mind to safely reach the others.

By now, over a dozen bloody and burned men congregated near the old stone building. Many sat or lay groaning and suffering from pain and shock. A few were wounded infantrymen, but most were tankers.[90] The first tanker wounded in the attack was T/4 Earl Hollon. Earlier, Hollon had been hit in the face with shrapnel as he drove his tank across the riverbed. Though bleeding profusely from multiple wounds and suffering from a shell fragment lodged in one eye, he refused to stop or change drivers to keep the route clear for the other tanks to follow. After his tank was knocked out shortly thereafter, Hollon insisted on helping his fellow wounded tankers reach the shed and would not stop until finally succumbing to blindness from his own wounds.[91] Only two medics were present—but all they could really do was apply tourniquets or compresses to slow bleeding, pack sulfa to prevent infection, or administer morphine to alleviate pain. No stretchers were available to evacuate the seriously wounded. Those who could walk were sent across the river with instructions to send for a doctor. Lewis refused to leave until all his men were evacuated first.[92] Six other A Company tankers, including Sgt Galbraith, remained unaccounted for—likely perished inside their burning tanks.[93]

Lt Col John L. Powers, a 29-year-old West Pointer commanding the 2nd Bn, 168th,[94] and Colonel Boatner deliberated over the infantry's next move. Only two tanks remained in support of the attack, with both "A" and "B" river crossing routes now blocked. No further tanks could cross until one of those routes was cleared. However, Boatner, an engineer by training, felt encouraged by progress reported by the T2 crews working on the problem.[95] With the day still young, both commanders agreed to temporarily suspend the attack until more tanks could join.[96]

By 0930, one route was cleared wide enough to squeeze two more A Company tanks through, but both promptly bogged after crossing.[97] With precious time now ticking away, Sweeting grew more convinced the "Route C" riverbed route starting near Sant' Elia might be his best—and perhaps *only*—attack option. He checked regularly on the progress of Lt Nelson's C Co, 760th, tank column heading northward but they had been slowed to a snail's pace.[98] The area had become extremely congested with French and TFB forces regrouping ahead of their own attack.[99] Traffic flow was strictly controlled, otherwise no one would be able to move at all. German artillery disruptions didn't help matters either.

In the meantime, infantry of the 168th still holding fields to the northeast and southeast of the cemetery decided upon venturing forth with caution.[100] The Germans laid smoke on Caira in the northwest, the barracks to the south and around the cemetery itself—trying to conceal the repositioning of their troops and SP guns to counter American movements.[101] Artillery shells burst sporadically about the crossroads north of the cemetery, and German mortar and MG resistance continued unabated. Despite these daunting conditions, one platoon from C Company seized considerable ground behind the cemetery.[102] Two platoons of F Company, 2nd Battalion, also stole across the river to assume positions near the tanks of S/Sgt Harris and Sgt Corbitt.[103] These two surviving tanks blasted constantly at German cemetery positions to aid the nearby infantry as they maneuvered. At 1130, E Company reported a third platoon had also successfully crossed river.[104]

By late morning, the capricious winds of southern Italy rolled fog and haze down from the highlands, blanketing the valley with low cloud cover. The development did not hamper ground operations, but wreaked havoc with counterbattery artillery and aerial observations. Air bombing support missions planned for 0900, 1000, and 1030 had to be canceled outright.[105]

At noon, Colonel Boatner reported his men were unable to overcome dense automatic fire coming from the cemetery, and more tanks were needed to proceed.[106] At 1255, the engineers declared the ford crossing had been cleared and was ready for testing again.[107] Another M4 rolled forward and crossed without any complications.[108] With the route now reopened, Sweeting earned a golden opportunity to shape the next phase of battle. Rather than send his tanks into combat in piecemeal fashion, he chose to build up his forces first. This way he could attack *en masse* for maximum shock value—the textbook way tanks were supposed to be employed. If another German SP gun sat hidden nearby, it had no hope of stopping them.

Such a large complex armor attack needed steadfast leadership. But with the loss of all three highly experienced 756th medium tank company commanders in less than two days,[109] and having no familiarity with Lt Nelson of the attached C Co, 760th, Sweeting decided his best option was to lead the assault himself. Major Dolvin, his trusted XO, was given charge of protecting Sweeting's left flank.

The new attack plans came together quickly—scheduled to commence at 1600. Sweeting could draw upon twenty-five operational medium tanks but preferred adding more to be assured of overwhelming firepower.[110] At 1425, he phoned Ryder and requested two more tank companies. His request was passed up to the II Corps, in control of the 1st Tank Group, but the corps would only promise to *try* securing them for him this time.[111] Even if the request was eventually granted, additional tanks could not possibly arrive ahead of the 1600 attack. Sweeting would have to proceed with what he had on hand, regardless.

At 1455, the infantrymen of the 168th relayed back a bit of good news: A second operational German SP gun—indeed hidden near the cemetery—had been destroyed.[112] No others appeared to be in the immediate area. Further south, however, at least one AT gun hidden in the barracks area fired harassing shots every so often. The gun was so well hidden that no muzzle flash could be seen and thus the TDs and tank crews positioned east of the Rapido could not knock it out. In the meantime, the two tanks of Sgts Harris and Corbitt began running woefully short on ammunition.[113]

Around the same time, Captain Sorrell and fellow engineer Lt Dallas Lynch climbed into Lt William H. Newman's M5 tank near the blown Sant' Elia bridge further to the northeast.[114] Newman tested his battalion radio link as driver T/4 Rene E. Cyr pushed the steering levers forward and eased all fifteen tons down upon the drained gravel. The bed felt firm, and the light tank clawed forward without difficultly. Three more locations along the mile-long route, however, had to be tested for clearance: two blown footbridges and a marked teller mine. The fallen footbridges had been dynamited earlier by Sorrell's men to create openings wide enough for tanks. The mine, however, had to be straddled.[115] Cyr adeptly passed through each obstacle without trouble, and Lt Newman radioed Sweeting of their success in coded messages. The final test was the departure point from the bed into the fields near the Caira bridge. Sorrell and Lynch dismounted to help direct Cyr in easing the M5 up the soft sod embankment. The sudden snap of German sniper bullets whizzing past Sorrell's thick army-issue eyeglasses sent the young officer scampering into a field ten yards away—as if shaking off angry bees. Alarmed, Lynch hollered "Brother, you had better get back here before you get blown up!" Sorrell halted and backtracked gingerly. By then Cyr had successfully emerged from the riverbed and both men scampered back within the protection of the M5's interior. Lt Newman clicked on his hand mike and gave the signal Sweeting longed to hear:

"Uncle George, come ahead."[116]

Just after 1600 hours, the sixteen M4 tanks of C Co, 760th, reached the river ramp near Sant' Elia, slipped down one at a time onto the wet gravel of the drained riverbed and began the journey south. As they snaked along cautiously between the sunken banks, smoke canisters dispatched from the 756th Tank Battalion's mortar platoon landed on the eastern bank—concealing them from German observation.[117] Once the column successfully negotiated past the two blown footbridges and the marked teller mine, they were home free. Upon hearing this, Lt Col Sweeting dropped down into the turret of HQ M4, *Hellcat* near Caira bridge,[118] secured the headsets of his leather helmet tightly against the sides of his scruffy week-old beard[119] and ordered his driver, T/5 Jack Brown,[120] to cross the river ford. *Hellcat* pitched forward down a deep earthen ramp before leveling onto the ford and gearing slowly forward.

Before *Hellcat* reached the opposite side, T/4 Ralph Donley[121] squeezed out of the bow gunner hatch and clambered up the muddy bank to direct Brown between some trees lining the opposite edge. As Hellcat cleared, Donley climbed back up to his hatch. In doing so, he unconsciously grabbed the gun barrel to steady himself—an amateur move strictly forbidden should the tube remain hot after excessive firing. At this moment, the barrel was still cold, but Donley knew it made no difference according to regulations. Sweeting scowled from the turret hatch five feet away, and Donley cringed on the expectation he was about to receive a first-class chewing out.

"Dooley … " Sweeting snapped—mispronouncing the 26-year-old Utahn's[122] name as he always did.

"Yes, Sir!" Donley responded.

"If you live through this, you will be famous …."

Donley was at a loss for an appropriate response. Sweeting's vivid imagination was already anticipating a place in the history books.

"I don't want to be famous … I want to *live* through it!" he stammered.

"You can't think of that!" Sweeting chided philosophically. "You can't think of *that!*"[123]

Donley slunk back down safely inside the forward hatch as *Hellcat* disappeared in the drifting mortar smoke and veered south along the river. The long trail of C Co, 760th, tanks successfully emerged at the same river point and followed behind.[124] At the same time, Major Dolvin led the remaining tanks of A and B companies across the river ford near the bridge.[125] B Company was able to lend four tanks to the effort: 2nd Lt John J. Czajkowski, now given charge of the 2nd Platoon, commanded one; Sgts Wunderlich, Smith, and Cogdill commanded the others.[126] In the span of only a few minutes, twenty-three tanks had crossed. They fanned out behind a swirling curtain of smoke all along the western bank and rolled forward slowly—emerging from the mist at once by 1640.[127] The sudden appearance of so many tanks stunned both the German and American infantry alike.[128]

Lt Col Sweeting clicked on his battalion radio transmitter and announced dramatically: "OK boys, we're across! Now let's get the bastards out!"

The broad wave of American armor lurched forward into higher gear, blasting clusters of HE into the hillside 600 yards away, exploding along the rock like a giant chain of firecrackers. At the same time, every MG spat fire—from the turret co-axials to the hull mounts. Streams of red tracer-laced .30-caliber swept to and fro like angry flames from dragons—crisscrossing high over the flat muddy fields to avoid hitting any American infantrymen while pummeling the hill base in a hail of lead. The tanks pressed on with triumphant confidence, crushing more segments of rowed barbed wire and setting off countless anti-personnel mines.[129] After a few moments, Sweeting stole a rearward glance at the battlefield and noticed a key element was missing.

He grabbed his radio mike and shouted: "What the hell's holding up the infantry?!"[130]

After being pinned down for so long, the American doughboys on the ground weren't sure what to do. The tank advance halted momentarily to await their appearance. Few dared rise—out of fear the stunned silent German MG and mortar crews might wake again and mow them down.[131]

"Jesus Christ, let's get these boys up. There's nothing here!" Sweeting hollered.

To prove it, Sweeting brazenly hopped out on top of his tank turret in plain view of everyone—and beckoned the infantry to follow. The crazy gesture worked, and dozens of infantrymen began rising from the fields and along the riverbank.[132] The advance continued, but this time with 2nd Bn, 168th, infantrymen storming ahead.[133] Fearing swift and fiery retribution from the tanks, the Germans responded with only a paltry smattering of MG and mortar resistance. Even German artillery went uncharacteristically silent.[134] Nevertheless, Sweeting ordered the 756th's mortar platoon to keep dropping smoke along the river to help conceal medics as they worked on evacuating the wounded infantry and Captain Lewis's tankers.[135]

With the German hold on the river permanently broken, the chief challenge of the Americans was to keep the attack coordinated while grabbing as much land as possible. The 168th was plagued, however, by serious communication challenges. Phone wires were constantly severed—by artillery blasts or from tank treads churning through, and every single platoon radio had become waterlogged and rendered unusable after their operators had crossed the Rapido earlier under intense fire.[136] Two artillery radios with extended ranges survived the river crossing only to be lost when their operators were cut down while moving through the fields. The only method remaining for Lt Col Powers to communicate with his forward line was through a solitary SCR-195 radio assigned to one of his heavy mortar platoons.[137]

Even so, Powers masterfully kept his entire infantry moving cohesively by using just that one link.

Radio use in the tanks was *always* confusing and problematic. In combat, the interior of an M4 was deafeningly loud and eardrums constantly rang. A tank commander frequently shouted an order several times via a closed-circuit intercom before his crew understood him in their headsets. To hear an incoming radio message, tank operations often halted completely.[138] The commander also had to remember to toggle a selector switch between intercom and radio functions. In the heat of battle this was a detail easy to overlook. Even Sweeting was prone to forget about the switch. Earlier, when the lieutenant colonel was bounding about the San Michele assembly area in his command tank, those monitoring the battalion radio band heard him repeating: "Left, Brown. Go left." Followed by: "Damn it, Brown! I said go left!" And finally: "BROWN!!! ... oops." Sweeting had forgotten to flip the radio to intercom and his driver hadn't heard a word—but the rest of the battalion certainly did.[139]

Another time, one of the tank platoon leaders lost in the thick of fire support operations absentmindedly shouted over his radio: "I'm out of ammunition, God damn it!"[140] Any Germans monitoring the battalion band would have found this detail particularly interesting. And the Germans were always listening in .... On occasion, they used their best American accents to issue phony orders over various U.S. Army bands. Simple phrases such as "Stop firing!" or "We are firing on our own men!" were intended to cause hesitation and breed confusion.[141] To avoid being duped, the tankers relied on call signs and code words, but the system often changed and the men would forget what certain words meant. Oftentimes, the tankers had no choice but to revert to plain instructions to get their point across.[142] As a result of all of this, the radio was used sparingly in battle and only when absolutely required—and tank commanders were constantly reminded to switch off the broadcast function when not in use.

Another great challenge for tankers was to avoid accidentally wounding or killing their own infantrymen. Fratricide was every tanker's deepest terror—especially during the chaos of battle. With the infantry now sweeping ahead of the advancing tanks, the bow gunners stopped firing their MGs for fear some infantryman might inadvertently dart into the spray. And despite the personal dangers, tank drivers drove with their heads halfway above their hatch covers to avoid accidentally crushing someone. Gunners restricted their main gun fire upon the same places where 34th Division artillery continued falling—high on Hill 213—to avoid accidentally decapitating their fellow countrymen moving about in the foreground.[143] Even so, Sweeting broke in several times over the radio—obsessively reminding his tanks crews not to shoot at any unidentified targets.[144] At one point, the infantry had closed in upon a ruined two-story house just beyond the cemetery. The tankers could clearly see soldiers vacating the upper floor but withheld fire until absolutely certain the escaping men were Germans.[145]

In the early evening, the cemetery finally fell to the 168th, and the steady pounding of Hill 213 by the artillery and tanks halted abruptly—signaling a new phase of battle had begun.[146] As the long, gray ridge again emerged from the dissipating dust and smoke, F and G Company passed through E Company positions to strike the very heart of the hill.[147] At the same time, Companies I and K hit the north edge,[148] while the 1st Battalion stormed the south end and The Pimple.[149] The fight now belonged to the infantry—carried forth at the squad level by men laying down suppressing fire while their comrades ascended and flanked, then dropped to lay suppressive fire enabling their squad mates to catch up. The tedious process was repeated over and over again. The tanks could not follow due to the steep gradient.[150]

Sweeting's tanks worked in scattered teams along the hill base, crushing over barbed wire and anti-personnel mines while waiting for assistance requests from the infantry.[151] Sometimes, those calls were for tanks to lay suppressive MG fire ahead of a particular infantry maneuver.[152] Other times, the tanks simply blasted away on an identified MG position or bunker hewn into the hillside granite.[153] The infantry cut through layers of wire and avoided countless mines during their assent. Direct resistance, however, was scant.[154] At 1850, with the infantry midway through the operation, a buoyant Sweeting coordinated plans with Major Dolvin for the resupply of tanks the following morning.[155] Over a thousand rounds of tank HE had been pumped into the hillside throughout the day.[156] The crews were also running low on .30-caliber ammunition, and each tank had nearly burned through all 160 gallons of fuel.

Many Germans recognized they had been bested and surrendered without much hassle. At dusk, as the American troops reached the hilltop, prisoner numbers swelled to where they had to be sent downhill bearing white flags, but with no guard escort.[157] Infantry companies A and C succeeded in taking the north slope of The Pimple, while B Company maintained a roadblock along the base as protection against a German counterattack from the barracks.[158] At 2040, to help solidify that roadblock position, the infantry called two tanks forward in the darkness to crush barbed wire and clear anti-personnel mines buried in the nearby fields.[159] Despite the visibility challenges, the two tanks accomplished the job without incident and returned a short time later.[160]

In an attempt to separate those Americans operating on the hillside from their brethren on the plain, German mortar and artillery began exploding along the hill base—right where the main skirt of concertina wire had been breached. The barrage proved ineffective.[161] After a while, the mortar attacks petered out, but the artillery continued to fall sporadically—yet amounted to little more than a nuisance.[162]

By 2200, Companies F and G consolidated their positions along the hilltop while collecting another round of prisoners.[163] They cut through a double-apron wire fence just below the hillcrest and captured an elaborate network of foxholes protected by thick overhead covers. Small signs were planted near each entrance with inscriptions: "G-23," "G-25," etc. The German engineers had such confidence in their defensive handiwork that each foxhole had been assigned a permanent address. Along the hilltop itself ran another band of double-apron wire,[164] protecting another elaborate network of dugouts serving as sleeping quarters.[165] Since these positions sat tucked along the opposite side of the hill, they had remained impervious to artillery—a classic German hill fortification. Many of those bunkers showed evidence of abandonment in haste.

Just before midnight arrived, a single flare rocketed up high over Hill 213—a triumphant signal that the American troops had reached their objective.[166] The brass stars observing a few miles east on Monte Trocchio sighed in collective relief. A few moments later, Maj Gen Ryder's buoyant voice crackled over Lt Col Sweeting's tank radio:

"Colonel, you have done a grand job, God bless you!"

Bending the rules of radio communications, Ryder recommended Sweeting pull his tanks back for resupply, but the 756th Tank Battalion CO declined:

"Sir, if it's all right, I would like to remain here and form a strong point against a counterattack."[167]

This was exactly the sort of aggressive spirit Ryder loved seeing in his battalion commanders, and the grateful general readily agreed.[168]

* * *

In the early hours of 30 January, the Americans held a fragile grip upon the half-mile-long eastern slope of Hill 213—from base to crest. During the assault, many areas had been bypassed to quickly secure the ridgeline. As a result, German troops unwilling to surrender without a fight remained hidden in isolated bunkers and well disguised dugouts on the hillside.[169] With the arrival of darkness, some chose to make their presence known—emerging briefly to toss grenades or pop off a few rifle shots before disappearing again—leaving the Americans cussing mad and in no mood to show mercy. Ryder ordered his men to hold the hill at all costs and patrol aggressively, so the night brought little sleep for anyone.[170] Every so often, the crack of a rifle or the burst of an MG would cut through the cold still air. Other times, a mine would flash in the darkness and disturbing cries for a medic would follow. The grief and consternation caused by the cursed mines never ceased.

Sweeting's tanks formed a strong point near the cemetery, settled in and awaited daybreak. An infantry detachment served as perimeter security.[171] In pitch darkness, there was not much a tank crew could do to help a busy infantry mopping up resistance on the nearby hill. In fact, tank movement had to be severely restricted for fear of crushing any American dead or the unconscious wounded still lying about the battlefield.[172]

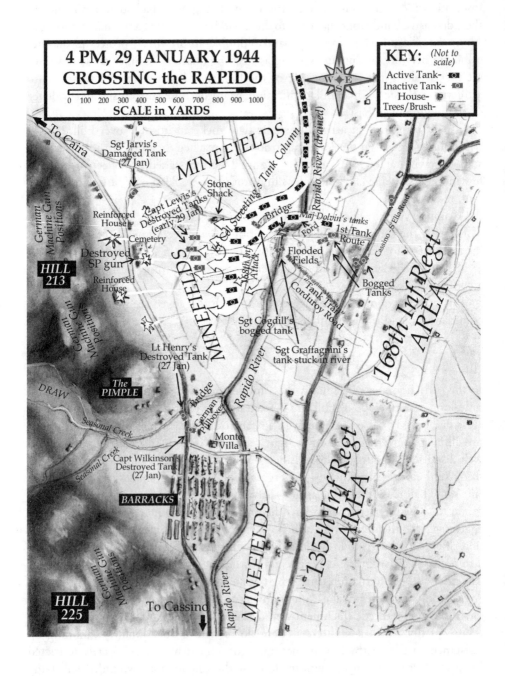

4 PM, 29 JANUARY 1944
CROSSING the RAPIDO

SCALE in YARDS
0 100 200 300 400 500 600 700 800 900 1000

KEY: *(Not to scale)*
Active Tank-
Inactive Tank-
House-
Trees/Brush-

To Caira

Sgt Jarvis's Damaged Tank (27 Jan)

MINEFIELDS

Col Sweeting's Tank Column

Rapido River (drained)

Stone Shack

Capt Lewis's Destroyed Tanks (early 29 Jan)

Reinforced House

Bridge

Maj Dolvin's tanks

Ford

1st Tank Route

Cemetery

German Machine Gun Positions

Destroyed SP gun

HILL 213

168th Inf Reg't AREA

Cassino–S'Ella Road

Reinforced House

168th Inf Attack

Flooded Fields

Bogged Tanks

German Gun Machine Positions

"Tank Trail"
Corduroy Road

Sgt Cogdill's bogged tank

MINEFIELDS

Sgt Graffagnini's tank stuck in river

Lt Henry's Destroyed Tank (27 Jan)

DRAW

The PIMPLE

Rapido River

Bridge

German Pillbox

Seasonal Creek

Monte Villa

Seasonal Creek

Capt Wilkinson's Destroyed Tank (27 Jan)

BARRACKS

135th Inf Reg't AREA

German Gun Machine Positions

HILL 225

To Cassino

Rapido River

MINEFIELDS

The Germans surrendered the cemetery hours before, but the grounds remained dangerous and forbidding. The two SP guns knocked out earlier sat smoldering near the cemetery walls but could not be approached for inspection until morning.[173] S-mines with trip wires were strung all around the place—set to explode at the slightest disturbance. Rows of anti-personnel mines and barbed wire stretched east along the road from the cemetery wall all the way around Hill 213 toward Caira. Next to the barbed wire, the Germans had laid four rows of AT Teller mines near the road junction leading back to the bridge. Sgt Jarvis's tank had hit one two days earlier and the abandoned hulk still sat in the mud among the others with a shattered track. The Germans had since scorched the interior to prevent its recovery.[174] Beyond the Teller mines lay two more elaborate rows of S-mines connected to trip wires strung six inches off the ground.[175]

The tankers marveled at the clever defenses the Germans concealed in and around the cemetery. Decoy dugouts installed near the cemetery wall had been positioned to draw American infantry to their deaths into a nearby minefield consisting of twenty-one triangular rows sown with scores of S-mines.[176] Many manned positions had stayed absolutely silent when Wilkinson's tanks had passed through two days earlier, and the captain and the other three tank commanders never noticed the dangers—even as they passed within a few yards of them. The German occupants had been extremely disciplined and never gave those positions away.[177] Several pillboxes were fashioned from reclaimed metal boilers four feet in diameter and seven-feet long. These were then flipped on end and sunk into the ground with only 18" protruding from the top. A slit was cut into this small, exposed section to allow an MG to fire from the inside.[178] Another concrete bunker was large enough to comfortably house close to thirty men. It was also well stocked and even equipped with bunks and heating.[179] An even bigger bunker was packed full of ammunition—including 9,000 rounds of MG ammo, 7,500 rounds of rifle ammo, 210 potato masher grenades, and nearly 100 rounds more of various rifle grenades.[180] Without question, the Germans intended to hold out a very long time, but the sudden appearance of so many American tanks in the late afternoon had changed their minds.

* * *

No doctor ever arrived to attend to the wounded tankers sprawled around the stone shed near the river. A lone surgeon working from a Red Cross half-track in the fields nearby had been too overwhelmed picking up other wounded infantryman to ever reach them.[181] Eventually, stretcher-bearing medics did appear to evacuate each stricken tanker one at a time back across the river. With the arrival of nightfall, the last one was finally carried away.[182] Captain Lewis refused any medical help for himself until everyone else was gone. Then, the mud-caked captain refused a spot on the last stretcher, insisting instead on hobbling alone back to the Battalion HQ to report directly on the day's events.[183] Major Dolvin didn't realize the severity of Lewis's wounds until the captain began fainting mid-sentence. Doc Sarno was summoned immediately. He discovered Lewis's boots filled with blood up to their tops and feared the captain might lose both feet from infection.[184] After cleaning and wrapping the wounds, Lewis was evacuated to the care of surgeons at the 300th General Hospital in Naples.[185] Only time would tell if the captain's feet could be saved.

In the meantime, A Company command passed temporarily to 1st Lt Walter L. Greene.[186] 1st Lt David Redle, who had been in charge of B Company for only two days, was now the longest serving CO of the 756th's three medium tank companies. Although Redle's company remained woefully short of operational tanks, the mechanics slowly brought the damaged ones back on line. The four B Company tanks participating in the day's attack ended up parked near the cemetery along with others from A Company and C Co, 760th. Several more B Company tanks prepared to join them in the morning.[187]

Lt Redle settled into his regular nighttime refuge beneath the broken concrete steps and, by candlelight, censored a batch of letters his men wished to mail home.[188] His nearest companions were Pfc Clyde Guild, bundled up in a pile of blankets a few feet away, and a very brave and stubborn Italian farming family nearby who continued eking out an existence among the shattered remains of their stone house. This was probably the last night he would need to sleep under those same stairs. He would rise before dawn and move permanently across the river.

After finishing the letters, Redle turned in. The night air hung damp and frigid, but Redle found dry warmth inside the thick Klondike sleeping bag his father had sent to him before the arrival of winter. The bag was superior to the canvas cover and thin wool blankets the U.S. Army issued to their officers,[189] and it served as a comforting reminder of a loving father back in Wyoming who prayed fervently for his safety and for three other Redle sons fighting across the globe.[190]

That love, those prayers, and a deep sense of duty kept Lt Redle calm and focused. However, in war, one could never be assured this was enough to succeed or survive.

German 44th Infantry Division

CHAPTER 15

Caira: Evening 29 January 1944 to 30 January 1944

Like some besieged pioneer wagon train crossing the Old West, Sweeting's tankers formed a strong point and arranged their guns outward so no foe could attack them from behind. Sweeting's great fear was of infiltrating German saboteurs sneaking up and destroying his turret guns or killing his crews by dropping potato masher grenades down gun barrels or through hatches. He ordered Brown and Donley to remain especially alert by keeping their heads completely above their front hatches. The night was as black as coal and the two men couldn't see a thing—except whenever 34th Division artillery batteries fired salvos further east. But that occasional flickering only cast fleeting shadows that tricked the eyes and tortured the mind into constantly choosing between the real and imagined. Though exhausted to the core, no one dared sleep.

Without warning, German artillery exploded about the area, causing heads to duck, mouths to cuss, and hatches to slam shut. The attack was vicious but short. During the pause, T/5 Brown vacated his driver's seat and slid down *Hellcat*'s front slope to aid a nearby infantryman writhing on the ground with shrapnel wounds. Once the stricken infantryman was evacuated, the young Oklahoman returned to his position but became gnawed with a sense of foreboding. Finally overwhelmed by it, Brown whispered over to Donley that they should lower their seats to protect their heads. Donley nodded in agreement. Quietly and deliberately, the two men made the lever adjustments in a way Sweeting would not hear them rustling. No sooner had they finished when a German shell burst directly off the front of the tank, spraying shrapnel up the front slope and completely blowing away the bow-gun baffle. The main barrel was left gouged so deeply that the rifled interior bulged and the entire gun was rendered operable.[1] Had their faces been out of the turret hatches as Sweeting ordered, both men would have been decapitated.

German shells continued falling sporadically throughout the night—making the resupply of tanks a heart-pounding terror. Because no truck or jeep had any hope of plowing through the mud, all supplies had to be transported on foot. Anyone available in the 756th—from cooks to truck drivers to mechanics—was recruited to cart heavy ammunition canisters and five-gallon fuel cans over dark, muddy trails—trudging across the Rapido and then along narrow demarked pathways leading through minefields until arriving at the tanks huddled near the cemetery.[2] After unburdening their aching arms, each man then walked back across the river to repeat the process all over again. Even so, the quantity of supplies moved during the night was barely enough to keep the tanks running the next morning.[3]

That same evening, the 133rd Regiment relieved 135th positions along the Rapido banks facing the barracks and road leading south to Cassino. The 135th had been fighting five straight days and sorely needed rest. Even so, it was a case of the exhausted being replaced by the depleted. The 133rd was still grappling through the process of reorganization after its brutal decimation two days earlier. The 133rd's 100th (Nisei) Battalion wasn't even combat capable. The 135th pulled back to serve as divisional reserve near San Michele at midnight, 30 January.[4]

The 1st and 2nd Battalions of the 168th continued clearing out stubborn German positions on Hill 213 and The Pimple. The 3rd Battalion, however, had been trapped for two days in wet, cold foxholes on both sides of the Rapido, in the French sector to the northeast.[5] Without direct tank support to help silence German MGs or open pathways through minefields, they simply could not move during daylight. With the arrival of darkness, however, the 3rd Battalion was able to fully cross the river to occupy positions on the northeast slope of Hill 213 and in adjacent fields.[6] I and K Companies held the hill while L Company protected the flanks and assisted French forces working through minefields north of them.[7] The 2nd Battalion continued combing across the middle of the hill and linked up with 3rd Battalion patrols along the crestline at around 0400.[8] To the south, the 1st Battalion captured much of The Pimple—but in methodical stages. At first, they encountered tangled wire arrays and vacated enemy positions but little armed resistance. Then, forty exhausted Germans surrendered without much fight.[9] As they pressed on, they captured dozens more prisoners scattered about in pockets—also seizing prized equipment and sizable amounts of ammunition.[10] At 0300, A Company infantrymen even captured a German-towed gun along with the crew—a true trophy![11] Most prisoners came from the 1st Company of the 132nd Grenadier Regiment, 44th Infantry Division.[12] They reported first occupying their hillside positions on the 13 January and spoke of receiving supplies via mule trains originating from Caira.[13] Others lied, claiming there was nothing in Caira at all.[14] With their supply lines now clearly severed, these isolated Germans chose surrender. German artillery, on the other hand, did not quit. Throughout the night, heavy rounds exploded sporadically—wounding several more men of the 2nd Bn, 168th. The blasts did nothing, however, to stop the Americans from consolidating their hold on both hills.[15]

An hour before daybreak, the Germans attempted a counterattack of sorts—undertaken principally by disorganized pockets of troops encircled and hoping to break out before the Americans completely sealed them off.[16] Essentially, the trapped Germans would emerge from their holes and bunkers to toss a few hand grenades or squeeze off a few rounds of rifle or MG fire. As soon as they received counter fire, they threw up their hands to surrender. It was an infuriating practice that tested the patience of the Americans on the receiving end—some of whom were killed or wounded needlessly. As dawn broke, Sweeting's tanks were called in to help mop up the mess. To oblige, he moved most of his tanks into a hollow tucked along the base of Hill 213, in order to protect the crews from German artillery and mortars as they operated. At the same time, one platoon was positioned to the north and another to the south—serving as flank protection.[17]

To lead the operation, Sweeting took command of another tank. At one point, the 756th CO observed a solitary grenade-bearing German emerge from a hole only fifty yards away—looking around intently for someone to kill. Sweeting ordered his gunner to quickly traverse the 75mm gun onto the man. When the German saw the big barrel swinging in his direction, he promptly surrendered—along with three others burrowed like moles inside the same hole. In a separate incident a short time later, two other Germans popped out from a different hillside hideout and froze upon seeing Sweeting's gun barrel trained upon them. A third German emerged from the same hole, prepared to chuck a hand grenade—but saw Sweeting's gun and also hesitated. Just as Sweeting was about to give the fire order, all three threw their hands up in surrender and narrowly avoided a fiery end.[18]

By mid-morning, Hill 213 resistance had been quashed enough for the Americans to declare the German "counterattack" over.[19] However, the 168th Regiment was reluctant to claim full control of the hill with Germans still popping out of holes unexpectedly. As a bright smudge of a sun rose over a cloud-shrouded Monte Trocchio, the ruined barracks erupted like an angry hornet nest. German rifles and MGs rattled away constantly—unnerving everybody. Sweeting grew concerned that the commotion might be a prelude to a true German counterattack and advised his tankers to stand prepared. Even so, he felt confident his crews could stop anything. As of 0840 that morning, Sweeting had twenty-six M4 tanks and one light M5 positioned across the river at his immediate disposal. Fourteen tanks were from the 756th and thirteen from C Co, 760th. Twenty-nine of the 756th's M4s were still unfit for service—either trapped in the mud or in need of repairs after extrication. Five operational mediums and thirteen light tanks remained under battalion control on the east side of the river. It was unwise tactically to shift all the tanks over to Hill 213—especially when resupply remained so problematic. Men on foot alone simply could not keep up with the material demands. Sweeting's tanks supporting the 168th operated satisfactorily but were unacceptably low on ammunition and gasoline. Major Dolvin, however, was formulating a dramatic plan to come to their rescue.[20]

* * *

Lts Redle and Harley set out before dawn in cool hanging fog and braved their way toward the cemetery across the river as Sweeting's tanks prepared to help the infantry quell the remaining German holdouts.[21] After surviving mud, minefields, and occasional German mortar bursts and sniper fire, the two officers found B Company's reconstituted 2nd Platoon idling near the cemetery.[22] The grounds nearby were a horror show. Not only were dead German soldiers and a few Americans splayed about, but many mausoleums had been blown open from battle and the decomposed remains of long dead Italian civilians were strewn all over the place.[23] The stench was unbearable.[24]

Before moving the tanks closer to the hill, Sweeting informed Redle that B Company's next mission would be to attack the barracks, so Redle cautiously proceeded southward on foot to survey the area—taking 1st Platoon leader 2nd Lt Harley along with him.[25] The two walked past infantrymen darting about and others carting supplies up the slope before encountering a few more silently manning the southernmost roadblock at the base of The Pimple. They slipped past them all, while hugging along the base of the cold granite rock to a point where Redle finally dared lift his head to peer south. The moment he did, he drew instant German rifle fire. He tried moving about and testing different vantage points, but the result was always the same: A torrent of enemy bullets forced him back. Realizing the futility of the situation, Redle and Harley finally withdrew.[26] At the very least, the two officers learned the barracks were well defended.

In the meantime, at the B Company HQ near San Michele, Pvt Gene Palumbo finally reappeared after being missing for three days. The haggard loader told 1st Sgt Hogan that he'd been fighting alongside the infantry the entire time.[27] Hogan had no way of verifying Palumbo's claim but was relieved to see him alive and well and able to rejoin his crew.[28]

* * *

The 168th infantry—particularly the men from Lt Col Powers's 2nd Battalion—grew exhausted from lack of sleep. Most had been fighting non-stop for more than twenty-four hours. Colonel Boatner was also deeply concerned about exposure on his flanks: Caira to the north and the barracks to the south. He relayed these concerns to Divisional HQ and was assured the 133rd would take care of the barracks. His men were to concentrate on capturing Caira with whomever Boatner could spare.[29]

Caira lay to the north, nestled inside a sloped valley between Hill 213 and the rising highlands where the French were targeting. Several German prisoners revealed that the tiny farming village housed their battalion HQ—making Caira a clear flank threat to any future American operations directed toward the barracks or Cassino. It was from Caira that the Germans had snuck down two *Sturmgeschütz* IIIs the previous evening—destroying several of Captain Lewis's tanks and halting 168th infantrymen for half a day. Further German control of Caira was simply unacceptable, but whether Colonel Boatner could muster enough men to take the town was an open question. No one from the 1st and 2nd Battalions could be spared. The troops were already overextended securing The Pimple and much of Hill 213. The three rifle companies of the 3rd Bn, 168th, holding the north section of Hill 213 and all fields to the east, were also overextended but not as sparsely. In the end, one platoon from Captain Anderson Q. Smith's K Company was pulled aside for the Caira mission.[30] The men would not attack alone, however. They would have tanks.

At 0800, Lt Col Sweeting hastily met with the 3rd Bn, 168th, HQ staff to consider the best attack options. 1st Lt Leo J. Trahan of the 2nd Platoon, C Co, 760th Tank Battalion, and Lt Kerner,[31] leader of the 1st Platoon, K Company, also attended. The officers settled upon a plan whereby Trahan's four tanks would lead while Kerner's platoon followed closely behind.[32] At full strength, an infantry platoon consisted of forty-eight riflemen and BAR men. Kerner's depleted "platoon," however, consisted of just eighteen haggard soldiers.[33]

At 0845, Lt Trahan's tanks set out very cautiously along the narrow road heading north from the cemetery—immediately crushing coils of barbed wire and setting off scores of anti-personnel mines. Lt Kerner rode along on the back deck of Trahan's tank so the two leaders could closely coordinate actions.[34] Kerner's infantry kept pace by crouching behind the rear tank for protection—taking great care to remain inside the tread tracks.[35] Thick bands of chemical mortar smoke hung in areas along the slope to the right as a result of ongoing Hill 213 "mopping up" operations, but an even denser blanket of fog started rolling down from the frigid highlands—cascading across the road just as Trahan's small column achieved a point where they could finally fire straight into the tiny town. After advancing nearly 300 yards from the cemetery without any issues, visibility was suddenly a grave concern.[36]

Up to that point, the Germans had remained absolutely silent.[37] Rifle shots abruptly cut the cool moist air and then the dreaded MGs started rattling. In an instant, Kerner's men found themselves locked in close-quartered combat inside a swirling bank of fog.[38] Following Lt Kerner's keen directions, the tanks gained the upper hand by dispatching HE rounds point blank into German positions nearby.[39] The winds shifted again and a German AT gun blasted—piercing one of Trahan's M4s and setting the hull ablaze. The frantic crew threw open the hatches in escape and one crewman was shot and seriously wounded by a German soldier lurking only a few yards away. The tank commander, Sgt Carley W. Biles, fuming with vengeance, chased the German through the fog and cut him to the ground with bursts from his Tommy gun.[40]

The thick haze shifted yet again along the base of Hill 213—giving Trahan's remaining tankers a quick glimpse of the location of the squat, gray SP gun responsible, as well as a second one parked nearby. A flurry of fire by Trahan's gunners followed—promptly knocking out both German guns.[41] Their defeat opened the way to Caira. At that same moment, the 142nd Regiment and French forces attacked though the fields a few hundred yards further north.[42] The sudden pressure from both forces so unnerved the Caira defenders that they readily capitulated upon the arrival of Kerner's riflemen and Trahan's tankers. Over a hundred Germans surrendered, including a command staff comprising five officers representing the 1st Battalion, 131st Grenadier Regiment (44th Infantry Division).[43] To help process them all, Captain Smith dispatched his 2nd Platoon, K Company, to Caira.[44] About twenty percent were non-Germans—Austrians, Czechs, or Poles—volunteers or draftees impressed into the Wehrmacht.[45] All were promptly disarmed and sent streaming back toward the cemetery. By 1130, Caira belonged to the Americans.[46] The operation was a stunning success, in large part because of excellent infantry–tank teamwork.[47] A short time later, Sweeting's voice exuberantly exclaimed over the radio: "We've got so many prisoners, we're giving them away! We hand them a white flag and tell them which way to go!"[48]

For the next hour, the small force continued collecting prisoners in and around Caira.[49] Kerner's riflemen and Trahan's tankers were astounded to find enormous bunkers constructed along the foundations of several stone homes. Each had been built to accommodate an entire platoon—generously equipped with heating, bunks, and full stocks of food and ammunition.[50] Kerner's point scouts observed Germans moving about on a hill to the southwest of Caira and behind Hill 213. Litter bearers were also seen collecting the remains of many dead. Fearing the French moving through to the north might mistake their American M4 tanks as the enemy, Lt Trahan asked that French forces to be alerted to their presence. The 34th Division G-3 relayed Trahan's concerns through their French liaison officer.[51] As Kerner's men attempted to fan out westward from Caira, however, they met stiff resistance and halted. Artillery and mortar were then called in to lay down a protective barrier.[52]

In the early part of the afternoon, several stray artillery shells exploded about the Caira area, but only the French seemed to be firing at the time. The 168th complained about the encroachment—but the French insisted the shelling was not from them.[53] A short time later, errant MG spray ricocheted among the stone walls where Trahan's tank crews were operating. The French, still attacking in the north, had introduced their own M4 tanks with all MGs blazing. Presumably, the loose lead came from them. Several more stray streams of bullets bounced about Caira, so Trahan ordered his tanks to find cover deeper inside town. By mid-afternoon, Trahan's tanks had nearly exhausted all ammunition, so Lt Col Sweeting ordered them to return to the cemetery area.[54]

* * *

While K Company swept through the opposition at Caira with relative ease, the 2nd Bn, 168th, continued rooting out some infuriating—almost irrational—pockets of resistance on fog-shrouded Hill 213.[55] Oftentimes, Powers's men resorted to shoving hand grenades down holes to force fanatical Germans burrowed below to finally quit.[56] One house near the hill base had been obliterated down to its foundations during earlier combat, but the Germans, holed in the basement, refused to capitulate until totally surrounded. When they finally did give up, the Americans discovered a foundation fitted with an interior concrete bunker and a surrounding buffer of crushed gravel. The house had sustained direct hits many times from tank fire—yet the subterranean pillbox remained completely unscathed. Several smaller iron pillboxes were also cleared—and each of these were so well disguised that a man had to practically stand on top of one to see it.[57] "There was no doubt the Germans intended to say there a long time," Sweeting apprised visiting reporter Hal Boyle of the *Associated Press*.[58] Sweeting was only repeating—albeit in sanitized language—what American infantrymen all over the area were muttering among themselves.

At 1100, the last vestiges of resistance on Hill 213 finally folded.[59] In the end, an astounding total of *eighty-six* separate German MG emplacements had been neutralized along the base of both Hill 213 and The Pimple—many blasted away by Sweeting's tanks.[60] At the hill's south end, the 1st Bn, 168th, tried edging their way around The Pimple to consolidate the regiment's left flank, but was driven back by withering small arms fire coming from the barracks.[61] Lt Col Sweeting ordered a two-tank section south to silence those German rifles and MGs, but the moment they rounded the road bend by The Pimple, an AT gun concealed deep inside the barracks ruins started firing at them. The M4s returned fire reflexively but could not determine the AT gun's location and pulled back before being destroyed.[62]

* * *

That same morning, Major Dolvin organized all sixteen remaining M5 tanks of D Company into a column and prepared to cross the Rapido.[63] Every nook and cranny inside each tank was crammed full of 75mm and .30-caliber ammunition and motor oil cans, and every deck was stacked with five-gallon cans full of gasoline—each tied, strapped, and lashed to the hulls in every way possible. At 0900, Dolvin informed Sweeting via radio that the loading was complete, and Sweeting ordered him to proceed immediately. With Dolvin commanding the lead tank,[64] the column crept northward before easing down into the sunken river channel and lumbering along the same defilade route Sweeting's tanks had traveled the prior afternoon. The sunken course had already been dubbed "Sorrell's Skyline Drive" by Allied war correspondents covering the action.[65] Spotty haze still rolling off the hills greatly helped shield the column's approach from German observation.[66]

At 1100, Dolvin's column emerged from the riverbed near the bridge and the old stone shack. German artillery greeted them as the first few tanks clawed up the banks—spraying grimy muck and causing spent shrapnel to clatter across their hulls. The German SP gun hidden in the barracks ruins also fired at them.[67] One crewman, Pfc Louis E. Cottonware of Vader, Washington,[68] was killed instantly by one round nearly scoring a direct hit on his moving tank.[69] As Cottonware's crewmates struggled to overcome the concussive effects, the young man's lifeless body crumpled beside them inside the tight crew compartment. He had been completely decapitated.[70] One of the tank commanders, Sgt Robert J. Holloway, was also clipped on the cheek by shrapnel.[71] Though bleeding profusely, he remained at his post.[72]

Seeing Dolvin's supply column under withering artillery assault, Lt Col Powers of the 2nd Bn, 168th, hastily radioed his 81mm mortar platoon to render assistance. Three minutes later, smoke rounds whistled overhead and exploded along the 600-yard route stretching from the river to Hill 213—completely shrouding the approaching tanks.[73] Amazingly, not a single M5 was lost during the journey.

Dolvin found Lt Col Sweeting waiting in his command tank fifty yards from the 2nd Bn, 168th, CP near the base of Hill 213. Despite a long night with little sleep, the 756th CO remained high on battle adrenaline and was exhilarated over the arrival of Dolvin's supply column.[74] As volleys of German mortar rounds burst about, the M5 crews quickly dismounted to unload supplies on the ground nearby. The crews moved with such haste—fumbling, bumping, and tripping over each other as they tossed gas, oil, and ammunition cans around—that they unintentionally looked like some improvised vaudeville comedy act.[75] After watching their frenzied activity for a while, one parched infantryman wedged inside a nearby slit trench raised his haggard, unshaven face and dolefully called to one of the feverish M5 crews:

"Did you bring water for us?"

The tankers looked sheepishly at one another. They'd completely overlooked the most basic supply of all![76]

Dolvin, Sweeting, and Captain Arnold congregated near Sweeting's tank. The battalion CO, still stoked on victory, spoke first of attacking the barracks as quickly as possible:

"Check with Marshall to be sure we have no troops south of the barracks," Sweeting directed Dolvin. "And if it would be possible to organize a Fodor mission down that way."[77]

The lieutenant colonel was suggesting, again, to offer S/Sgt Fodor up as bait—this time to smoke out the German SP guns lurking about the barracks.

While the three officers stood and conferred, some faraway German rifleman took irregular pot shots at them. They ignored his bullets pinging off the hull nearby and discussed plans for the remainder of the day.[78] Sweeting had already prepared the tank crews to guard against a German counterattack. When Lt Trahan's platoon was dispatched to Caira, the lieutenant colonel positioned the rest of his tanks defensively along the entire hill base—concealing them whenever possible. Three M4s were positioned near the smoldering *Sturmgeschütz* III at the cemetery. The rest were distributed under artillery-shredded trees or along the stone walls of shattered farmhouses.[79] Even though Dolvin's column restocked the tanks with sorely-needed supplies, after thirty-six straight hours of combat, crew fatigue became a concern.[80] Sweeting told Dolvin to return later that same afternoon with two platoons of light tanks and one platoon of medium tanks to allow C Co, 760th, to pull back across the river, rest the crews, and perform vehicle maintenance and any necessary repairs.[81]

At 1145, Dolvin and the column of empty M5s departed after successfully unloading all supplies in under thirty minutes.[82] German artillery harassed them during their entire drive back to the assembly area and the three M4s parked near the cemetery were also molested with several waves of Nebelwerfer rockets.[83] Fortunately, no other tankers were wounded.

Two-and-a-half hours later, the relief column of M5 lights and M4 mediums returned via the sunken riverbed. This time, Major Dolvin stayed behind, so the mission was led by 1st Lt Robert Kremer—recently promoted as D Company CO.[84] Most of the morning fog had since dissipated, so a smoke screen was maintained along the river to conceal the column's progress. Sweeting anticipated the German SP gun hiding in the barracks would try striking again and pre-positioned two M4s as lookouts near The Pimple road bend. At 1545, Kremer's column arose from the sunken river. As expected, the German SP gun opened fire—but proved impossible to locate. Kremer's tanks dashed to safety behind Hill 213 without losing anybody, but one of the SP's shots struck a disabled tank abandoned earlier along the supply route—setting it on fire.[85] Soon after, the SP gun went silent, and the two M4s stationed near The Pimple were called back in frustration.[86]

Sweeting briefed Kremer on the plans to relieve C Co, 760th, and put him in charge of perimeter security. By 1830 that evening, the exchange was completed and the 760th tankers prepared to return across the river after nightfall.[87] Kremer positioned his relief tanks in defensive positions covering both north and south approaches and established direct telephone lines to both Sweeting and Lt Col

Powers at the 2nd Bn, 168th, CP. In the meantime, Sweeting and Arnold met with Colonel Boatner to coordinate plans for the following day. The discussion centered on the barracks' challenges and ways of destroying the troublesome German SP gun.[88]

German artillery fell heavily over the area all evening long. No tanks sustained direct hits, but two—one light and one medium—were severely damaged in close calls. The M4 crew could not extinguish a gasoline fire ignited by one blast and had to abandon the tank and watch as flames completely engulfed it.[89]

With midnight approaching, the 168th continued collecting and processing a few straggling prisoners here and there. The Americans suspected these final holdouts were the ones most guilty of "doing the sniping" during the day.[90] The Germans launched a respectable counterattack from Monte Castellone around the mid-afternoon. Roughly 150 troops bounded down the slopes toward Caira, only to be promptly and violently repulsed. The survivors retreated, leaving thirty of their dead sprawled across the draw behind Hill 213.[91] German artillery stopped raining down upon 168th positions later that same evening[92] and the 133rd Regiment area south along the Rapido also fell silent.[93] As a consequence, 34th Division artillery activity relaxed considerably—this, after expending over 3,000 rounds of 105mm, 1,267 rounds of 155mm and sixty-five rounds of smoke on German positions registered by the infantry throughout the day.[94] Both sides seemed drained from the day's combat and desired respite.

The quick capture of Caira in the morning was an unexpected gift for the Americans. That same day, French forces further north had also found success—but after a troubled start eerily similar to Captain Lewis's ill-fated tank attack the prior day. In the early afternoon, a concealed German SP gun destroyed several French M4s advancing across the flat, open fields a mile north of the cemetery.[95] From Hill 213, thick, black smoke from the flaming wrecks could be seen rising above the battlefield. The advance faltered for a spell, but the French rallied, overwhelmed the gun position, and forced the Germans to concede the entire plain. By evening, French infantry and armor had pushed aggressively into the slopes north of Caira toward snow-peaked Monte Caira. At first, the 142nd RCT shadowed the advance—shoring up the flanks of the CEF on the right and the 34th Division on the left,[96] but as the French pressed higher into the rugged hills, the 142nd RCT rushed forward to fill a gap forming northwest of Caira. One recon troop from the 142nd was specifically tasked with aggressively patrolling and protecting the 34th Division's northern flank.[97] The injection of these troops created a battlefield salient—forcing the Germans behind Caira to retreat even further up into the hills.[98]

The backstory to the day's successes was enthusiastically pursued by Allied war correspondents darting among the CPs in San Michele. Although the press was prohibited from identifying units or divulging operational particulars, Army censors signed off on accounts celebrating "Sorrell's Skyline Drive," and a GI hero *du jour* was born. The young captain was pumped to provide every detail about his life. Where from? "Ozark, Alabama." College? "Mississippi State Junior College." Sports? "Football." Married? "No." Questions about his childhood, his mother, father, brothers, sister, aunts, and uncles followed … the Press wanted to know everything about him. That evening, typewriters clacked away by candlelight, and in the days that followed, newspaper headlines across the U.S. trumpeted everyman tributes such as: "*Captain Walker Byrd Sorrell Outwits Germans in Italy,*" "*Young Combat Engineer Solves Problem That Stumped Generals in Italy Drive,*" and "*Drawling Alabama Combat Engineer Broke Nazi Line.*" Each piece featured lengthy quotes from Sorrell describing all aspects of his impressive accomplishment, but his most endearing line read like a wacky Army recruitment pitch:

"You know, it doesn't take any engineering knowledge to be a combat engineer—it just takes a willing heart and a strong back and a weak mind."[99]

No doubt, the Army was pleased nonetheless, and Sorrell was recommended for the Distinguished Service Cross.[100]

With Caira firmly under control and the northern flank secured, 34th Division planners were free to pursue more aggressive plans for seizing the barracks and the town of Cassino further south. The fall of Caira also presented a tantalizing opportunity to a much faster "back door" capture of the Benedictine monastery through the highlands to the rear.[101] Whether the staff grade officers gathered on Monte Trocchio above or the field and company-grade officers huddled around candlelit maps in blacked out rooms of ruined farmhouses below had the imagination, time, and requisite materiel to exploit this latest opportunity was a great unknown.

The other great unknown was luck. Every battle plan relied on a certain degree of it. But fortunes, like the bitter winds rolling down off Monte Caira, seemed to shift on a whim.

U.S. 760th Tank Battalion

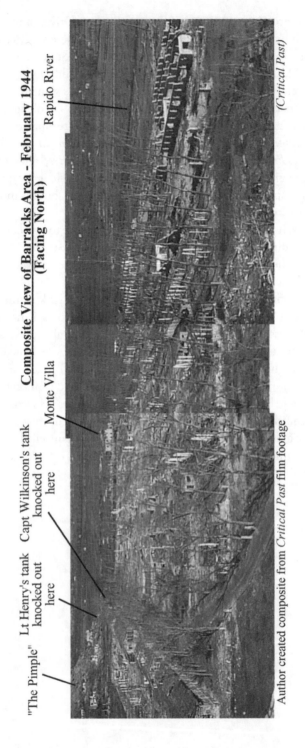

Composite View of Barracks Area - February 1944
(Facing North)

Rapido River

Monte Villa

Capt Wilkinson's tank knocked out here

Lt Henry's tank knocked out here

"The Pimple"

(*Critical Past*)

Author created composite from *Critical Past* film footage

CHAPTER 16

The Barracks: 31 January 1944 to 1 February 1944

The ruined Italian Army barracks compound remained the main obstacle to Allied plans for taking Cassino. Non-stop bombardment by American artillery batteries for many days had accomplished little—other than to reduce most of the long buildings into long rubble piles. Along the battered concrete foundations, stubborn German defenders carried on a spirited fight from countless well-concealed, reinforced positions and exhausted troops of the 2nd Battalion, 168th, holding Hill 213 and The Pimple bore the brunt of their wrath. Often, biting MG fire raked across the bald, rocky slope—preventing Powers's men from consolidating their hillside positions.[1] At other times, pesky German rifle sniping pinned the frustrated men flat against cold granite—unable to eat, sleep, or risk answering the call of nature—an action grimly dubbed "Operation Purple Heart."[2] And every time an M4 tried nosing around the bend along the base of The Pimple to quell the sniping, some invisible German SP gun concealed among the rubble would fire at the emergence point—forcing the American tanks to back off.[3] An impasse resulted, and the maddening harassment continued unabated.

With sunrise, temperatures rose to a rather balmy forty-eight degrees. For once, no capricious alpine breezes swept down from the massif, so a disquieting haze of fresh dew and acrid cordite smoke hovered like a low blanket over the valley.[4] The Germans attempted a counterattack of sorts at 0640 upon 1st Bn, 168th, positions along the south face of The Pimple. Some *landsers*[5] attacked by way of the barracks, but most filtered down through the rocky draw to the southwest—darting and shooting while bounding among the ravines and ruined hillside houses. A general alert spread swiftly to the other battalions, and the tank crews scrambled to their stations.[6] A few moments later, successive salvos of American artillery howled in overhead and burst into giant blossoms of dirt and gravel among the attackers—shattering German resolve. By 0715, the charge had completely dissipated and the uneasy status quo returned.[7]

In the meantime, the French solidified their hard-fought gains further north. On Marino Hill northeast of Caira, one particularly stubborn German hold-out had finally collapsed the previous evening, yielding dozens of prisoners.[8]

At 0950, troops of the 168th spotted a German SP gun scurrying north of Caira. A hastily organized infantry patrol and platoon of light tanks from D Co, 756th Tank Battalion, chased after it down a muddy gravel road. After tracking for a few hundred yards, the pursuers radioed that the SP gun had vanished into the wooded highlands.[9] The patrol was ordered, nevertheless, to keep probing northward until making contact with 142nd RCT forces.[10] At the time, the 142nd was only a mile north but advancing steadily along a narrow switchback road leading up through steep, rugged terrain to the ancient mountain village of Terelle.[11] German opposition in the area was virtually non-existent and even enemy artillery went uncharacteristically silent.[12] That vacuum drew 142nd RCT and French forces further into the rocky highlands northwest of Cassino—with hopes of seizing as much ground as possible before the Germans could regroup.[13] Not until the mid-afternoon did troops of the 142nd and French forces finally meet any meaningful German resistance again.[14]

The patrol from Caira hadn't traveled far when they encountered a small creek. The first M5 attempting to cross promptly sank in thick mud—blocking the rest of the tanks from passing.[15] The patrol pressed onward without tanks and also encountered little German opposition—so they kept moving.[16] Through the use of tow cables, the bogged tank was finally pulled free by early afternoon and the tankers located a more substantial crossing to rejoin the patrol. On Maj Gen Ryder's personal orders, four additional M5 lights were sent as reinforcements. By 1630, all nine M5s had successfully traversed the troublesome stream and rolled onward in search of the patrol.[17] By 1800, the tanks drove halfway up the dangerous switchback road but still hadn't reached them.[18] Guides from the 142nd were sent down to lead them the rest of the way.[19] Just before midnight, the M5s finally rendezvoused with the infantry patrol and 142nd RCT forces—having encountered little resistance the entire way.[20] At that same time, however, 142nd RCT patrols that had fanned out into the ravines only a half-mile northwest of Caira, ran into stiff opposition.[21] The Germans had seemingly fallen back to a consolidation line in the high ground.

* * *

Although 1st Lt Robert Kremer commanded D Co, 756th, he did not lead the nine M5s northward because Sweeting had put him in charge of tank security along Hill 213. Instead, one of Kremer's platoon leaders led that contact patrol to the 142nd RCT. With Lt Col Sweeting now pulled away and attending numerous planning meetings, all local responsibilities and challenges fell squarely upon Kremer's shoulders.

The 2nd Bn, 168th, grew increasingly concerned about finding some way to alleviate the ceaseless and aggravating small arms fire emanating from the barracks. By 1215, 168th CO Colonel Boatner became directly involved—proposing that a modest tank/infantry foray similar to the earlier one on Caira might put an end to the problem. Because of wider security concerns, Kremer could only spare two M4s and one M5 for the job. At 1300, a small contingent of infantry joined the idling tanks behind The Pimple and slowly inched toward the road bend. Kremer arranged for the 756th's mortar platoon to lay smoke ahead of the attack and the shroud of thick smoke formed perfectly—obscuring the small force just as it swung past the road bend to gain sight of the bridge where Lt Henry's abandoned M4 still hung, and the "no man's land" section of road where Captain Wilkinson's knocked-out tank sat askew.[22] Shifting winds, however, soon tore several holes in the fragile curtain, and the German SP gun fired from somewhere within the northwest section of the barracks. The lead M4 shuddered under a direct hit and started crackling and smoking.[23] Swiftly, the crew vacated though all three hatches just as the interior flashed into a swirling inferno. The two remaining tanks frantically tried pinpointing the German gun position but withdrew moments later for fear of meeting the same fate. With the tank support now gone, the infantry fell back as well and the mission ended with nothing accomplished.[24]

Lt Col Sweeting concluded earlier that any tank attack around The Pimple was likely to fail. The approach was too narrow. With a steep granite wall hugging the road to the west and broad, low, mucky fields east, the narrow roadway formed a natural bottleneck that could not be breached—so long as that SP gun remained hidden. Even with a smokescreen, the German gun crew had cleverly pre-registered the approach so they could fire blindly at the spot and still knock out approaching tanks. For an attack on the barracks from the north to succeed, any SP guns hidden among the ruins had to first be located, then destroyed or driven out. The best observations suggested that at least *two* SP guns lay lurking among the shattered buildings: one somewhere in the northwest section and another more to the southeast.[25]

Sweeting arranged for an entire company of M-10 TDs from the 776th Tank Destroyer Battalion to be attached to his battalion—all dedicated to finding those guns and knocking them out from a distance. Late that same afternoon, twelve TDs from C Co, 776th, moved into positions roughly a mile to the northeast.[26] From there, the five-man crews could study the barracks through spotting scopes and binoculars and also provide infantry fire support from afar whenever needed.[27] The idea worked better in theory. The TDs, also fully tracked, had to maneuver over the same mucky ground and rutted roads that bedeviled the M4s[28] and were thus limited in their choice of firing positions. What firm ground they could use did not allow for their three-inch flat-trajectory guns to cover all sections of the barracks. German artillery observers, too, monitored the arrival of M-10s with immense interest and did not spare them from harassment. Because the M-10s featured open-topped turrets that left the gun crews vulnerable to airbursts, the men often scattered for cover whenever artillery exploded about—which meant they weren't observing or firing their main guns.

At 1430, The 756th's attachment officially switched from the 168th to the 135th Regiment.[29] The change was a sign that the 34th Division's latest attack phase was taking shape. These plans called for the 168th to remain on Hill 213 in a "reserve" role, while the 135th massed and attacked westward from Caira.[30] To gather critical intelligence ahead of that attack, 168th patrols spent the remainder of the afternoon probing beyond Hill 213.[31] They observed pockets of Germans snaking trails on the lower slopes of Monte Castellone, half-a-mile to the west. In some places, Germans could be seen dug in, but in others they only seemed to mill about. One larger group of roughly fifteen were observed talking casually to an Italian woman outside her stone cottage.[32] Beyond these limited sightings, total German troop strength was difficult to ascertain. Nevertheless, these scant details were passed on to the 135th Regiment HQ staff.

The new attack plan also called for the 133rd Regiment to clear out the barracks before proceeding southward upon Cassino.[33] The 133rd, however, was nowhere close to full battle strength. The 100th (Nisei) Battalion was still so hollow after the previous week's combat losses that the survivors could only be counted on to hold territory—not capture it. The 1st and 3rd Battalions were also undermanned but considered combat capable. They would rely on close tank support to serve as a force multiplier.

Soon after sundown, the 133rd dispatched night patrols to gauge German reaction—tiptoeing past their own bloated dead to reach the drained riverbanks.[34] In some areas, the scouts attracted heavy MG fire, so the men halted and settled in place to serve as listening posts throughout the night.[35] Other locations drew no reaction at all—but minefields and barbed wire thwarted deeper investigation.[36] The barracks remained too active with small arms fire to be approached until much later in the evening. Even then, it was difficult to observe anything. A vehicle of some sort could be seen burning beyond the northwest corner of the compound—illuminating the surrounding ruins in pale, flickering yellow.[37] But the firelight was too dim to determine troop strength or reveal the locations of the SP guns. Quietly, L and K Companies of the 3rd Bn, 133rd, took up positions east and southeast of the barracks along the river. These were the same grounds their Nisei brethren had been so badly pummeled only days before. I Company settled into a reserve position a few hundred yards east. The 1st Bn, 133rd, positioned further to the south, closer to Cassino.[38] As midnight approached, the newly-arrived troops could hear several vehicles moving among the stone buildings and narrow streets,[39] but because of the persistent background rumbling of artillery they could not tell if the sounds originated from tanks or trucks.[40]

Lt Redle's battered B Company had been reconstituted to half-strength. Earlier in the day, four more of his tanks had crossed the river to join the four B Company M4s already stationed near the cemetery—doubling the total tanks he had available to eight.[41] One of the newly arriving tanks belonged to Redle, and the other three were commanded by Lt Howard M. Harley, Sgt Alfred Mancini, and Cpl Harold M. Behymer.[42] Six crews spent the day firing countless HE rounds into the barracks area. The other two B Company M4s assisted the infantry patrols probing west of Caira.[43] Lt Redle, Pfc Clyde Guild, and several others established a new forward CP inside a ruined farmhouse near Hill 213 and across the road from the cemetery. Judging from the bloodstains, bandages, and gory paraphernalia left behind, the white stone house appeared to have served as an aid station for German medics. Built along the foundation, however, sat a heavily armored pillbox. Redle was deeply impressed by the quality of the construction. The long, narrow room was dug down four feet below grade, outfitted with steel walls and a ceiling of five-inch-thick H-beams butted together with four feet of reinforced concrete poured on top. Two MG ports were situated at either end—providing a wide field of fire in the direction of the Rapido. But the most impressive feature of the room had been added by an American tank gunner: One of the narrow gun ports had been chipped wider from an extremely accurate 75mm tank round. The pillbox's fortress-like walls became a deathtrap instead. All the occupants inside were killed instantly by the resulting explosion. Their remains had been mostly removed, but the dried blood and bits of decaying flesh splattered over the walls testified to the extreme violence of the incident.[44] The pillbox would now provide refuge from German artillery for Redle's CP members—and hopefully *save* their lives.[45]

Sgt Pompey chose a long, stone shed behind the house to serve as B Company's new communication hub. After clearing away loose rubble and debris, Pompey unpacked his telephone equipment and started stringing lines.[46] With B Company now spread out over ten miles and operating with three separate command posts, communications became a supreme challenge. The rear CP was located in San Pietro far to the east—coordinating the activities of the "B-trains" kitchen, supply, and maintenance sections. The "A-trains" remainder of the company was located in the combat zone and split between two locations."[47] 1st Sgt Hogan headed the original combat CP near San Michele and directed the provisioning of the tanks and crews. Hogan also handled most administrative matters so Lt Redle could focus on battle operations.[48] Redle's new forward CP near Hill 213 would coordinate those operations with the infantry.

At 1130, Lt Col Sweeting, upon return to the battalion after a day jam-packed with planning meetings, called together Major Dolvin, Captain Arnold, Lt Redle, Lt Perkins of C Co, 756th, and Lt Nelson of C Co, 760th, to disseminate the division's attack plans for the following day.[49] The 756th had thirty-eight combat-ready tanks available, with twenty-six still undergoing repairs and seven lost to date. The attachment of C Co, 760th, and the recent addition of the 2nd Platoon, A Co, 760th, however, provided Sweeting with nineteen additional medium tanks.[50] In total, fifty-seven operational tanks could be called forth, if needed.

At dawn, the 756th Tank Battalion would support the infantry attack in two places. C Co, 760th, tanks would back the 135th Regiment push from Caira toward Monte Castellone on the division's right flank, and the 133rd would rush the barracks with the nearby support of Lt Dale F. Pride's 2nd Platoon of A Co, 760th, on the left flank.[51] During the night, three more B Company tanks, commanded by S/Sgt Johannesen, Sgt Buys, and Sgt Graffagnini, crossed the river to join Lt Redle's growing force—now swelled to eleven tanks.[52] Lt Redle's tanks would provide more distant fire support for the 133rd from the north.[53] Because the two hidden German SP guns represented such serious AT threats, the infantry would strike out initially toward the barracks attack without close tank support. In the meantime, Redle was instructed to work a section of tanks up into the draw behind Hill 213, where the crews might find a new vantage point from which to fire on the SP guns.[54] Whether tanks could even reach the area was an open question, as they had to first pass through Caira and then negotiate down long, winding, and rugged dirt lanes behind Hill 213.

Redle departed the meeting as German artillery violently buffeted through the area. For the past two days, the tanks had operated in relative safety along the base of Hill 213—tucked where German artillery had difficulty reaching them. But the Germans adapted and began sending higher-trajectory howitzer rounds that now exploded perilously close to the parked armor. In turn, Redle's crew adapted by repositioning their tank over a deep tread furrow to create a protected crawl space. The crew stayed inside the tank for their rest, but Redle unrolled his Klondike sleeping bag and squeezed underneath—looking to catch a few hours of uneasy sleep while keeping a quick egress in case of emergency.[55]

The deadly rain of artillery continued unabated for hours—hurling gusts of soil, stone, and clanging shrapnel against the thick steel hulls. A laden M5 from D Company had started resupplying Sgt Harrison's A Company M4 when the onslaught commenced, and both crews hastily retreated inside their respective tanks to ride out the firestorm. During one explosion, several gas cans lashed to the M5's rear deck were ripped open by shrapnel—unleashing a cascade of fuel down inside the engine compartment. The four-man crew cleared the hatches just as the rear deck erupted in a massive fireball. Sgt Harrison's crew hurriedly beckoned the homeless crew their way, and nine men somehow packed inside the M4's cramped interior. Moments later, Harrison's tank shuddered from a direct hit upon the loader's side of the turret. Sgt Harrison slumped over with multiple shrapnel wounds, and the loader, Pvt Albert T. Gober, suffered a horrific laceration to the waist. Several others were knocked out cold. As choking smoke flashed into furious fire, those still conscious frantically pulled their stricken comrades free from the flaming wreck and huddled against the cold granite rocks of Hill 213. The attack persisted all night long and nobody could be evacuated until morning. In the meantime, Harrison's severely wounded loader died of his wounds.[56]

Even though the day featured little in the way of offensive operations, the 756th lost several more key men. Two crewmen from A Company were killed outright.[57] Four others—a sergeant, two corporals, and a private first class—were wounded and evacuated.[58] All were experienced tankers and difficult to replace.[59]

* * *

By the early morning hours of 1 February, the German artillery had finally stopped but had failed to delay the Americans' attack preparations. Infantry combat followed a cycle similar to that of an archer plying a bow and arrow. The bow was drawn back slowly and fully while taking careful aim before releasing. Launch too soon and the attack might fail due to rushed preparedness. Wait too long and the attack might fail because overly-tensed troops lost their combat edge. Experienced combat leaders like Maj Gen Ryder were keenly attuned to this rhythm. With dawn breaking, the 52-year-old Kansan[60] bounded back and forth among various forward CPs positioned on both sides of the Rapido—making sure his troops were focused and no detail had been overlooked by his field commanders. At one point, the lanky, 6' 4" tall general met briefly with Sweeting in the morning mist as sniper bullets pinged off a nearby tank hull. After a few moments, Ryder strode away into the fog to check on the preparedness of another unit.[61]

Ryder's conscientious habits and studious approach to life had earned him the nickname "Doc" from his fellow cadets at West Point.[62] Those classmates were Dwight Eisenhower, Omar Bradley, and dozens of others, now fellow general officers prosecuting a modern war. The 1915 U.S. Military Academy graduating class was called the "Class the Stars Fell On," but Ryder saw no hint of glamor whatsoever in his chosen vocation.[63] For him, military life represented both a personal sacrifice and a higher calling—not unlike the austere lives of those Benedictine monks on nearby Monastery Hill.[64] Ryder embodied that same humility, that same drive for excellence, and that same unquenchable thirst for knowledge and meticulous attention to detail.[65]

Ryder hated desk work and never limited himself to the relative safety of some rear HQ.[66] Even after thirty years of service in the Army, he saw himself first and foremost as a common infantryman. He had acquired no haughty mannerisms or eccentricities. He wore a plain government-issued OD uniform with helmet, jacket, web belt, and field boots—devoid of any medals or ostentatious accessories. Only the twin silver stars pinned to his shirt indicated he shouldered additional responsibilities. Ryder's long, gaunt, and deeply furrowed face featured heavy eye bags and closely cropped silver hair—confirming that his stars had only fallen on him after years of bearing very heavy burdens. Depending on the situation, the mood in his light blue eyes could range from the serene and hopeful to arctic cold. Fresh out of West Point, Ryder served during World War I as a battalion commander and learned very early in his career that war was an appalling, brutal business. After surviving thirteen months through the unspeakable horrors of trench warfare and the insanity-inducing cadence of artillery, Ryder was nearly killed when an enemy shell burst near him while leading an attack during the Battle of Soissons in July 1918.[67] A piece of German shrapnel from that incident remained forever lodged near his heart—serving as a reminder to him on the fickleness of fate.[68] Decorated twice with the Distinguished Service Cross for bravery during that war,[69] Ryder possessed an authoritative infantry combat résumé few could match—or dare question.

Ryder took command of the 34th Infantry Division in June of 1942, soon after the unit's arrival in Ireland.[70] In February 1943, when the 168th Regiment was wiped out by German forces in the division's first true test of combat at Faïd Pass, Tunisia, Ryder was stung by criticism over the preparedness of his troops. Although the 168th was not under his command at the time, but under the control of Fredendall's II Corps HQ, Ryder was held responsible for their training.[71] Ryder considered the blame a personal challenge. He immediately dispatched a memo to all his officers urging a "flaming desire" be instilled in every infantryman "to close with the enemy with the rifle and the bayonet and kill him."[72] Ever since that incident, Ryder demanded his officers always set an aggressive example. And despite the personal dangers, the tall general circulated daily at the front lines to gather firsthand impressions, boost troop morale, and make certain that "offensive spirit" stayed with his officers.[73] And in times like this when a major attack was about to commence, Ryder aimed to be everywhere at once.

The 135th Regiment, under the command of Lt Col Robert W. Ward, had moved through Caira under cover of darkness—primed to attack Monte Castellone.[74] If successful, the 135th would then swing southward and capture the long-ridged plateau beyond Hill 213 leading down to Cassino called "Colle Maiola." The 133rd was ready to strike the barracks and seize the road leading south into Cassino. The 168th consolidated in reserve on Hill 213 and prepared to lend support wherever needed.[75] Sweeting's tanks prepared to spread out along the base of Hill 213 from Caira to The Pimple with instructions to put on a "big show."[76] Sweeting's men also pre-positioned 100 smoke pots to conceal any subsequent tank maneuvers —all set to ignite on a moment's notice.[77] M-10 TDs were also positioned on the opposite bank of the Rapido, and the remaining tanks of the 753rd and 760th Tank Battalions of the 1st Tank Group were scattered across ground in defilade positions a mile or two east of Cassino to provide added fire support.[78] Ryder wondered if his attack plans relied too heavily on the cooperation of infantry and tanks. Out of those concerns, he insisted the tankers know exactly where the infantry operated at all times and repeatedly emphasized the significance of diligent liaison work with all his field commanders.[79]

At 0630, as a lone German MG chattered away from somewhere amidst the barracks' rubble and with stray German artillery rounds bursting about the valley, Ryder pondered making last-minute adjustments to his strike plans.[80] A frigid fog blanketed the area—yielding exceptionally poor visibility. This change in weather made Ryder reach for his field phone.[81] He ordered the northern attack to jump off as scheduled from Caira, but his instincts told him to delay the tank show and southern attack by the 133rd.[82] He couldn't risk tank fire near moving infantry unless everyone could see each other.

The men of the 135th Regiment fanned out from Caira to become ghostly shadows in the quiet, thick, gray fog. After only a few steps, their faint forms disappeared altogether among coarse rocks, steep cliffs, and deep ravines to the south and west.[83] Like stalking mountain lions, the 3rd Battalion easily achieved their first objectives and began scaling the eastern face of Monte Castellone virtually unopposed.[84] For once, the thick fog worked against the defenders and the apathetic Germans were caught completely off guard by the sudden appearance of hundreds of Americans in their midst. The quick success of the 3rd Battalion allowed the 2nd Battalion to slip in quietly from behind to move upon Colle Maiola roughly one-and-a-half miles south of Caira and three-quarters of a mile west of The Pimple—also encountering little opposition.[85] By 0955, the 3rd Battalion reported that lead elements had scaled to within 200 yards of Monte Castellone's 771-meter-high top and hadn't encountered a single soul.[86] Amazingly, in less than three hours much of the rugged granite heights of Monte Castellone and Colle Maiola ceded to 135th Regiment control.[87] The attack was a stunning success—exceeding even the most optimistic expectations.

In the meantime, the same mountain fog spilled thickly along the valley floor and prevented the tanks of the 756th from maneuvering to their support positions effectively.[88] At 0620, Lt Redle's tanks departed the cemetery but required a full hour to safely travel half a mile south to The Pimple.[89] As they reached the place, the crews heard the barracks already seething with German MG and small arms fire. Much of the rage was directed upon 2nd Bn, 168th, positions tiered upon The Pimple's slopes.[90] Two of Redle's tanks—one under the command of S/Sgt Oric Johannesen[91]—attempted nosing around the hill base, but the German self-propelled AT gun crews heard the approaching engines and began firing at the emergence point in the road. Through the fog, the M4 crews blindly returned fire but were forced to withdraw—yet again—after no one could spot the SP's muzzle flashes.[92] Judging from the intensity of the German response, however, it appeared that *three* SP guns now skulked about the ruins.[93] The artillery of the 34th Division along with the mortar and assault-gun platoons of the 756th rained fire down upon their suspected positions, but failed to silence them.[94] They, too, were reduced to firing blindly through the mist.

By now, 168th CO Colonel Boatner was completely frustrated over the unending abuse his troops suffered from the incessant barracks gunfire. For four days, none of his men had been able to enjoy a moment's peace. As a result, no one could effectively rest, eat a decent meal, or even step away to relieve their bladders without putting their lives in jeopardy. Out of sheer exasperation, the former engineer snatched a field phone and carped bitterly to the II Corps HQ: "Jump in and clear the place out!"[95]

In the late morning, the beleaguered 2nd Bn, 168th, ensnared a lone German venturing out too far from the barracks. Through interrogation, the prisoner divulged that a rocket launching half-track and two towed howitzers were hidden among the ruins but claimed that he only knew of the presence of one SP gun.[96] Soon after, somebody thought they spotted the SP gun at the southeast corner of the barracks and American artillery began pounding away at the entire section.[97]

During this effort, the official attachment of the 756th Tank Battalion transferred from the 135th to the 133rd, and liaison officers swapped places to ensure proper coordination.[98] Maj Gen Ryder then ordered the 133rd to move one infantry company near The Pimple and commence the attack from there using the close support of the tanks of the 2nd Platoon, A Co, 760th, and more distant support from 756th tanks and TDs of the 776th.[99]

By noon, much of the valley fog had burned away to reveal partly cloudy skies. A thin persistent haze, however, limited visibility from greater distances—particularly affecting the artillery, TDs, and tanks holding support positions across the Rapido.[100] The improved conditions, however, were favorable enough to commence combined tank/infantry operations, and so the 133rd Regiment HQ contacted their mortar platoons to begin dropping smoke on the barracks ahead of the main attack.[101]

* * *

The 3rd Bn, 133rd, was given the daunting task of overpowering the barracks—under the leadership of a new officer who had never even seen combat. The 3rd Battalion's former CO, Lt Col Frank A. Reagan, was promoted to the Regimental HQ staff and a young Major Warren C. Chapman was brought in as his replacement.[102] Nine days earlier, Chapman sat at a comfortable desk in Washington, D.C., when unexpected orders arrived sending him halfway around the world to the 34th Division. The 28-year-old had graduated from the USMA's class of 1939 along with fellow classmates Casper Clough and Welborn "Tom" Dolvin.[103] If "stars" fell on Ryder's 1915 class, then "oak leaves" positively inundated the 456 members of the Class of 1939.[104] Many of these young men, all under thirty years of age, were made fast majors and lieutenant colonels and given the awesome responsibility of leading 800-man combat battalions. Normally, the job required twenty years of careful vetting and an exhaustive résumé of leadership assignments, but the staffing strains of World War II landed many recent USMA graduates in the role with as little as five years of experience. The "vetting" occurred on the battlefield. After spending a whirlwind seven days shuttling from plane to plane, Chapman finally arrived at the Gustav Line to discover if he would sink or swim. The Nevada City, California, native had been affectionately nicknamed "Buzz" by his USMA peers and lauded for guiding his "intermurder" football team through two consecutive championships.[105] Nobody at Cassino cared about any of this history, and a few hours were all "Buzz" was given to acclimate to combat life and interact with the battle-hardened captains, lieutenants, and sergeants who he was expected to lead. Naturally, they viewed their new CO with some level of suspicion.[106]

All three rifle companies in Chapman's battalion had lost key personnel during the previous week's fighting but still retained a healthy share of experienced combat leaders. Captain Wayne D. Fraizer, I Company's commander, was one of them. His men would strike first down from the north.[107] The five accompanying M4 tanks from A Company, 760th Tank Battalion, would delay movement until the SP gun was either destroyed or driven back.[108] L and K Companies would then sweep in from across the Rapido once I Company and the tanks had gained a solid foothold.

Fraizer's men finally jumped off at 1430, firing and maneuvering behind a thick wall of mortar smoke across 100 yards of open field until they reached the first barracks row in the northern most section of the ruins.[109] At 1500, scouts spotted an SP gun—a *Sturmgeschütz* III model—parked deep within the rubble on the western side.[110] The location was quickly passed on to the tanks and TDs monitoring from the perimeter, but nobody could gain a clear shot at it. Nevertheless, the German gun crew were spooked enough to fire up their engine and retreat deeper down the road. The concession was a huge one—allowing Lt Pride's M4s to skirt past The Pimple and gain better fire support positions as the infantry consolidated along the first barracks row.[111]

At 1515, I Company attempted to press deeper through the brick rubble and broken cement pillars of the first barracks row but became stymied by two German MGs and all manner of small arms. The *Sturmgeschütz* joined in and fired off four angry shots—but failed to dislodge Fraizer's men.[112] For the next hour, a stalemate ensued.

In the meantime, the two tanks commanded by Lt Howard M. Harley and Sgt Alfred Mancini, lumbered very slowly down a dirt path from Caira into the draw west of Hill 213, half a mile northwest of the barracks.[113] The two crews found a suitable vantage point to fire into the ruins but still couldn't gain a clear shot at the SP gun position. While maneuvering for a better angle, both tanks bogged in the soft soil and became trapped. Sgt Mancini's tank eventually pulled free, but Lt Harley's tank had to be stripped and abandoned. Both crews returned aboard Mancini's tank via Caira, bringing seven prisoners along with them.[114]

Near The Pimple, two B Company tanks awaited orders to storm into the barracks once the SP gun had been neutralized.[115] Lt Redle lay flat in the field about 100 yards east of The Pimple, analyzing the noisy infantry stalemate further south.[116] Unfortunately, the same mortar smoke protecting Fraizer's men also made the *Sturmgeschütz's* muzzle flash impossible to pinpoint.[117] Under such circumstances, Redle certainly could not order his tanks forward and often restricted their fire for fear of hitting friendly troops or Lt Pride's tanks shifting about in the haze. As a result, B Company's supporting fire was greatly hindered.

Thinner smoke drifted over the southern section of the barracks, so the tanks of the 753rd and 760th Tank Battalions positioned east of the Rapido enjoyed greater latitude, striking targets to the Germans' rear—most notably, several troublesome German MG positions sputtering away along the hillside roughly 100 yards south of the barracks.[118] At 1625, one lucky HE round ignited a hidden German fuel depot roughly 300 yards northwest of the barracks, billowing an orange fireball skyward.[119] As a massive fire ensued, I Company used the distraction to attack again—taking the remainder of the first barracks row and nineteen German prisoners.[120] A second SP gun, positioned further down the road from the first, fired heatedly at the deeper American incursion—this time inflicting casualties among Fraizer's men. German artillery followed—exploding in the fields just east of the barracks.[121] To consolidate these American gains, additional mortar smoke was called in. To the north, Redle's tanks maneuvered to try and strike at the two *Sturmgeschützes* sitting deep along the main road on the west side of the barracks, but the fresh smoke fell too densely to gain a clear shot at either one.[122] Out of frustration, the infantry lobbed mortar rounds at the irksome SP guns and angrily raked their squat hulls with MG fire. But as 1700 passed, the battle waned into yet another stalemate.[123]

With evening approaching, Lt Col Sweeting concluded that the infantry was unlikely to attack deeper inside the barracks and so advised Lt Redle to pull his tanks back, form strong points behind The Pimple, settle in for the night, and await further instructions.[124]

* * *

For much of the afternoon, the 34th Division staff were absorbed processing the details of the 135th Regiment's successful morning attack west of Hill 213. Nineteen Germans taken prisoner from the area provided some tantalizing intelligence. They claimed Monte Castellone had been abandoned the day before[125] and had heard of no plans to reinforce the position.[126] But with heavy fog encasing the craggy highlands all day long, the prisoners' claims were impossible to verify through observation alone.[127] As the 135th consolidated the days' gains, patrols were dispatched deep into the cool dense mists—well beyond the regimental perimeter. They returned later with reports that the Germans seemed to have vacated the entire area, indeed—leading to hopeful speculation that even the abbey, itself, had been abandoned.[128]

This stunning news prompted Ryder to instruct Lt Col Ward to attack southward the very next morning and take Point 706, Colle Sant' Angelo and Massa Albaneta.[129] The 135th's ultimate goal was the capture of "Snakeshead Ridge"—roughly half a mile northwest of the abbey.[130] If these objectives could be realized before the Germans could respond in force, then the 135th Regiment would earn the honor of "garrisoning" only a few hundred yards away from the ancient monastery's southwestern wall.[131] They would also be forever lauded for cracking the Gustav Wall and blowing the door wide open for Allied armies to spill into the Liri Valley. This tantalizing opportunity suddenly relegated the barracks struggle to a secondary affair.

Before the 135th could advance toward the abbey, however, it had to first consolidate its present position and establish supply lines to Caira. Also, it dared not attack again until the 142nd could be shifted down from the north to relieve the regiment from its current positions. Any premature move would leave the 135th's rear flank dangerously exposed. But for the 142nd to relieve the 135th, French forces, in turn, had to relieve 142nd positions. In short, for the 135th to meet Ryder's wishes, thousands of men and hundreds of tons of equipment had to reposition across several miles of mountainous terrain in very little time. For the remainder of the day, the phone lines at the II Corps HQ burned as anxious officers coordinated the formidable logistics behind such a move.

As if to remind the Allies that the highlands were still theirs, the Germans mounted a fierce counterattack at 1430 upon 3rd Battalion positions scattered along the eastern face of Monte Castellone. If the Germans had conceded the mountain, they certainly hadn't retreated very far away. The rushing wave of *feldgrau* uniforms was repulsed only with such great violence that, in the aftermath, fifty German corpses lay strewn about the foggy, barren slope. The shocking raid inflicted thirty-five casualties on the 3rd Battalion—including the capture of one officer and three enlisted men.[132]

Around the same time, German artillery fell heavily upon Caira and continued unabated for nearly two hours.[133] By late afternoon, the 1st Battalion moved into support positions behind the 2nd Battalion on Colle Maiola.[134] Its arrival freed F Company to probe several hundred yards further southwest and seize Hill 445—situated one-half mile north of Snakeshead Ridge. From there, additional patrols ventured another 500 yards south—returning at 1730 with a haul of eleven more prisoners.[135] The captives appeared to be a disparate bunch belonging to units ranging from the 90th Panzer Grenadier Division and the 33rd Engineering Battalion to the 15th Panzer Grenadier Division. The captives identified the town of Santa Lucia, three miles to the west, as an important command hub housing many German HQs. This crucial bit of intelligence was promptly forwarded to II Corps artillery.[136]

In the late afternoon, Maj Gen Ryder returned his attention to the barracks business and was not pleased with the progress. At 1800, the dissatisfied general phoned Colonel Marshall, CO of the 133rd, to question if one company was enough for the job. Marshall reiterated his belief that the added support of bazooka teams and tanks made I Company a force strong enough to complete the task. Ryder yielded, but suggested, nevertheless, that Marshall consider moving an additional infantry platoon up from the south. The final decision, of course, was Marshall's.

There would be no break until morning.

"We want to get that town so try to get that barracks cleaned up tonight." Ryder emphasized in closing.[137]

At that very moment, as dusk descended over the valley, I Company BAR men and riflemen holding ground in the first barracks row laid down a hail of suppressing fire—allowing a bazooka team to bound forward and attempt a clear shot at the closest SP gun parked on the road near the third row. Just as the team prepared to fire, however, the *Sturmgeschütz* crew started the engine and backed away from view. Moments later, 1st Bn, 133rd, troops positioned to the south and east of the Rapido heard the machine rumbling down the narrow blacktop road toward Cassino.[138] 34th Division artillery tried blasting at the squat vehicle as it raced away but were unable to register a direct hit.[139] Then, much to the frustration of all the Americans watching in the area, the SP gun vanished within the safety of the town's maze of yellow stone buildings.

The men of I Company strongly suspected a second SP gun still lurked in the vicinity of the first—but were hesitant to venture beyond the second barracks row without a workable plan to neutralize it. An infantryman might find protective cover in the rubble from bullet fire, but he was defenseless against HE blasts. Sweeting phoned Dolvin and ordered him to form a "tank hunting patrol" with the mission of sneaking in from the south and knocking out the *Sturmgeschütz* whenever it appeared or if it also attempted an escape toward Cassino.[140] Dolvin consulted the engineers of the 235th Engineers Battalion for advice on the best approach route and then arranged for guides from 1st Bn, 133rd, to direct a section of M4s to the location.[141] At 2000, Dolvin's tank patrol departed for a location roughly one-half mile south of the barracks and only 200 yards away from the road leading into town.[142] In the meantime, I Company began a night assault on the second barracks row.[143] The Germans responded with withering MG and mortar fire. The *Sturmgeschütz* also joined the fray but consistently fired over the attackers' heads—more intent, perhaps, on preventing supporting tanks or infantry from moving in as reinforcements. To improve visibility, the Germans arced up several illumination flares, and a spirited firefight raged among the disorienting, dancing shadows cast by the blazing white lights bobbing high in the cool night air.[144]

Fearing the second SP gun might escape to Cassino, Sweeting contacted the infantry and suggested hastily laying mines across the road and the dry riverbed south of the barracks. He proposed seeding a spot where the engineers had cut a pathway through minefields only a few days earlier and recommended the minelaying team comprise infantry, engineers, and tankers.[145] Sweeting's creative idea was every bit as ambitious as it was detailed and took nearly an hour to organize. By the time the team had assembled and ventured forth, a second vehicle was heard speeding down the road through the darkness. Shortly thereafter, the infantry fighting in the barracks reported the SP gun fire and chatter from at least one MG had suddenly ceased. Evidently, Sweeting's minelayers arrived too late. Sensing I Company had finally gained the advantage, Colonel Marshall ordered a reserve platoon to move up from the south and assist Fraizer's men.[146] His order came nearly three hours after Ryder had made the very same suggestion. Had these additional troops been committed much earlier, the extra firepower might have enabled the bazooka teams to move into position quicker and destroy both SP guns when first spotted.

As of 2120, I Company reported being on the move, halfway through the barracks compound. Only one MG continued firing at them as they bounded from cover to cover under the fading German flares. After three hours of fighting, the company suffered three dead and sixteen wounded—the loss of nearly half a platoon in combat strength.[147] At 2130, a 1st Bn, 133rd, mine-clearing party working along the dry Rapido in the dark watched wide-eyed as a German half-track barreled past them in another mad dash for Cassino.[148] This was the third motorized vehicle to escape along the same route and was solid evidence the Germans had conceded the barracks.[149] As a fresh series of German Nebelwerfer rockets shrieked and exploded along the Rapido River,[150] the engineering officer in charge of Sweeting's ad hoc minelaying party reported his team could not reach the road due to freshly lain German anti-personnel mines and heavy fire spraying from nearby bunkers. At this point, Sweeting believed all the barracks' SP guns had evaded his trap and saw little point in closing the barn doors after the horses had escaped. He dismissed the patrol for the evening[151] but with a nagging dread that those very same guns would be seen again ....

To flush out any remaining German *landsers* lingering about the south section of the barracks and dissuade them of any notion of a counterattack, the 3rd Bn, 133rd, called for a sustained artillery concentration roughly 400 yards south of the barracks. The 1st Bn, 133rd, drew back their mine-clearing parties from the area—allowing the barrage to commence and fall heavily for quite some time.[152] By 2330, the entire barrack compound had finally succumbed and 3rd Bn, 133rd, troops moved to establish outposts along the west. During the six-hour-long battle, fifty-four Germans had been taken prisoner.[153] As midnight approached, a calm of sorts descended over the area,[154] and the cold, grimy, and exhausted men of the 168th on Hill 213 could finally enjoy some unmolested sleep.

In the western highlands, the 135th Regiment waited on Monte Castellone and Colle Maiola for the 142nd relief to arrive that was very slow in coming. As late as

1800, the 142nd remained sidetracked mopping up pockets of German resistance four miles north on Massa Manna.[155] French forces had begun relieving them but were also delayed as a result of their own combat challenges.[156] By 2140, the first 142nd relief unit plodded southward but was still more than a mile away. In an effort to speed up the process, the 3rd Bn, 135th, dispatched patrols to locate them and guide them in.[157]

As the battle for the barracks wound down, Sweeting—charged with enthusiasm after attending the latest planning meetings with the Infantry COs—called together Dolvin, Arnold, Redle, and all other company commanders of the 756th and attached units to lay out the next day's mission. The new plan was detailed, comprehensive, and ambitious. A composite company comprising two platoons of four tanks and one platoon of three tanks would be formed from the B and C Company tanks parked near The Pimple.[158] This company would accompany the 3rd Bn, 133rd, at daybreak in an attack upon Cassino originating from the barracks.[159] An A Company platoon positioned roughly one-half mile northeast of Cassino would provide fire support, while the attack column rolled south. The position would also serve as Sweeting's OP, so he could personally direct and adjust the fire from the M4 platoon, along with the battalion's mortar and assault guns also positioned nearby.[160] If necessary, Sweeting could call upon TDs positioned north and northeast of the barracks for additional supporting fire.[161] Sweeting then turned to Redle and informed the young lieutenant he had the honor of leading the composite tank company attack on the town. If everything unfolded as planned, Cassino would fall under Allied control the same time tomorrow, and Redle would be the tank officer credited with leading the charge. Sweeting's appointment was a ringing endorsement of Redle's abilities.

The 756th Tank Battalion operated under tremendous strain. The battalion's "B-trains" service elements functioned a full ten miles east near San Pietro.[162] The battalion's HQ and forward support were two miles east at San Michele.[163] Thirty-six tanks were either stuck in the mud to the northeast, undergoing major repairs, or written off as complete battlefield losses. The remaining twenty-seven medium tanks still in service were scattered in a crescent across three miles of terrain stretching north of the barracks to the east of Cassino.[164] Many had been pushed beyond their maintenance requirements. Because roads remained impassable to truck traffic, only M5s could reliably haul supplies to the M4s operating near Hill 213. But with most of the battalion's M5s now pulled as support for the 142nd RCT's mountain drive three miles north, gas and ammo had to be carried, yet again, on foot by night.

Late that evening, the light tanks were released from their assignment with the 142nd RCT and began returning.[165] This development offered hope for the strained backs and sore feet trudging back and forth across the Rapido with supplies. The engineers reported great improvements to the original tank trail to the northeast and believed those enhancements would allow the tanks to return across the river the following day for overdue servicing and resupply.[166] No one held their breath on the news.

The battalion survived the day without loss of life, but two more officers succumbed to wounds: 2nd Lt John J. Czajkowski of B Co—recently returned—sustained another a hand injury,[167] and 1st Lt Ralph L. Hanson.[168] Lt Hanson, the battalion's assault-gun platoon leader, was knocked to the ground by German shrapnel while directing and adjusting his platoon's howitzer fire. The popular, handsome young lieutenant was evacuated to a field hospital, but the piercing wound to his back came within a hair's breadth of killing him outright.[169]

B Company was now down to only two officers. The battalion wasn't only running short on tanks but on good leaders as well. And with the enormous responsibility of the Cassino attack now placed squarely atop Lt Redle's shoulders, the pressures on him weren't only to succeed in this mission but to *survive* for the next.

U.S. 133rd Infantry Regiment

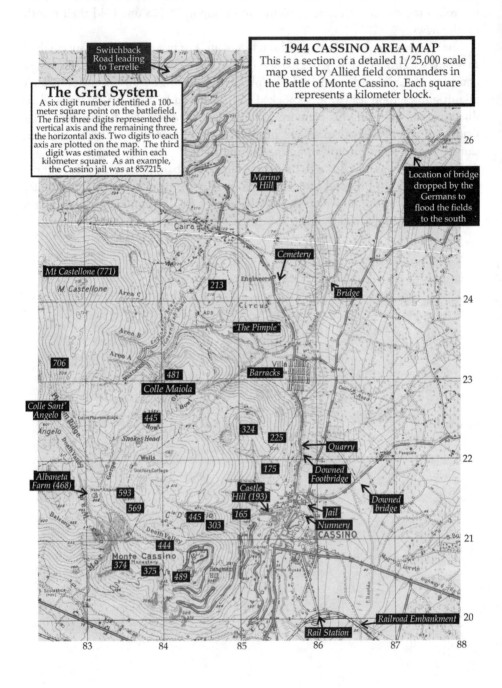

Switchback Road leading to Terrelle

1944 CASSINO AREA MAP
This is a section of a detailed 1/25,000 scale map used by Allied field commanders in the Battle of Monte Cassino. Each square represents a kilometer block.

The Grid System
A six digit number identified a 100-meter square point on the battlefield. The first three digits represented the vertical axis and the remaining three, the horizontal axis. Two digits to each axis are plotted on the map. The third digit was estimated within each kilometer square. As an example, the Cassino jail was at 857215.

Location of bridge dropped by the Germans to flood the fields to the south

Marino Hill

Caira

Cemetery

Engineers

Mt Castellone (771)

M. Castellone   Area C

213

Bridge

Circus

ADS

"The Pimple"

Area B

M. Villa

Area A

Villa

706

481

Barracks

Colle Maiola

Colle Sant' Angelo

445

Angelo

Snakes Head

324

225

Wells

Doctors Cottage

Quarry

175

Downed Footbridge

Albaneta Farm (468)

593

569

445   303

165

Castle Hill (193)

Jail

Downed bridge

444

Nunnery

CASSINO

Monte Cassino

374   375   489

Hangman Hill

Highway 6

Railroad Embankment

Rail Station

83   84   85   86   87   88

26   24   23   22   21   20

Wilkinson's Odyssey: Part One

After his capture at Cassino on 27 January 1944, the truck in which Captain Wilkinson was placed rode through the darkness for about an hour before arriving at a German field hospital. There, Wilkinson's facial burns were treated and bandaged, but a small piece of shrapnel lodged above his left eye could not be removed and was left in place. He was shown to a steel cot on the upper floor of a barracks and allowed to sleep until morning. Most others in the room were French-Algerian prisoners recuperating from light wounds. Wilkinson was the only American present—still dressed in his combat jumpsuit layered over his wool uniform. The helmet S/Sgt Crawford gave him to protect his burns, however, was confiscated. All prisoners were allowed to move about freely within the barracks, and the entire place appeared only lightly guarded.

A few nights later, Wilkinson and a group of prisoners were escorted to another truck. This one was equipped with a high canvas cover over the back deck but featured no tail gate—only a small canvas half door. Wilkinson was the last to enter and sat on a wooden chair near the back. When the truck began moving, he tested the door's latch and found it unlocked. He looked around but noticed no guard riding in back with the prisoners. A while later, as the truck slowed down to a rolling stop, Wilkinson lifted the latch and looked around to see if anyone was willing to join him, but there were no takers. He pushed the door open further and slipped out alone onto the pavement—fully expecting to set off some sort of commotion. Nothing happened. Then, as the truck rolled on obliviously in the darkness, Wilkinson dipped over to the road shoulder and darted off quietly into the Italian countryside—desperate to put as much distance between him and the road as possible.

The terrain was coarse—a supreme challenge to navigate without daylight. Oftentimes, he stumbled over rocks and through briars. Progress was slow and painful. At one point, he discovered a narrow livestock trail and followed it for a while. He stopped for a spell and attempted rest but found himself too wired for sleep and decided to resume roaming. He scarcely took ten more steps when an unexpected gruff voice speaking German challenged him. Evidently, Wilkinson had walked straight into the perimeter of a German bivouac. Astonished, the American captain mumbled something awkward and unintelligible. Then, the German guard stepped straight up to Wilkinson while holding his rifle across his chest and tried looking the American directly in the face. The guard noticed the bandage on Wilkinson's head and then saw the uniform. The pitch darkness concealed all the incriminating details. "Oh, Soldat!" the guard exclaimed and then politely waved him through. Wilkinson scurried on before the guard could ask him any further questions—disbelieving all the while he had dodged such a close call. From that point on, the escaped American tried moving with both greater speed and care.[1]

As a pale moon broke over the horizon, Wilkinson happened upon an old water well equipped with a bucket and pail. There, he was finally able to quench his parched throat. He passed through the ruins of an Ancient Roman amphitheater just as dawn broke. Two young civilian men had begun their morning work in a nearby orchard. Wilkinson approached them, showed them his uniform and communicated his hunger to them in his best broken Italian. The men politely shared their wine but had no food. He next encountered a rural family who took him in, fed him, and allowed him to sleep for the night. The next day he moved on to another family who did likewise. The locals always seemed willing to help but also feared German reprisal and never wanted to harbor him for long. Wilkinson didn't mind moving on as a fugitive. Though often hungry and cold, he found exhilaration in escaping captivity and from simply being *alive*. Though the running game was dangerous and unpredictable, it still unfolded like one grand adventure.[2] The itinerant life as a free man was far preferable to a dull one trapped in a prisoner of war camp.

Eventually, Wilkinson met up with partisans operating in the highlands above the town of Palestrina, twenty miles southeast of Rome. The group seemed somewhat suspicious of Wilkinson at first but soon accepted him, re-dressed his head wounds, and gave him a civilian coat and hat to put over his uniform. Several members were escaped Soviet soldiers who demonstrated shocking brutality in their methods. Wilkinson witnessed the Russians execute four captured German soldiers in cold blood. One of the victims, the only child of a widowed mother, begged for his life for her sake. He was cruelly mocked by the Russians and shot. The incident left Wilkinson stunned. After about a week, the partisans assigned a guide to Wilkinson with an alias of "Amerigo" to help return him to Allied lines. The pair started out on foot for Rome, subsisting off handouts from local farmers they met along the way. Their diet generally consisted of bread, goat's cheese, and red wine. Around mid-February, they met up with two British captains named David Moyle and David Buchanan.[3] They also wore civilian clothing over their uniforms. Both had been captured originally in North Africa and taken to a prisoner of war camp in northern Italy but escaped during the tumult following Mussolini's overthrow. They chose to head south. After comparing plans, Wilkinson decided to part from Amerigo—believing his chances of rejoining the 756th Tank Battalion were better by joining up with the two British captains.[4]

The three officers headed toward the Anzio beachhead, hoping for repatriation after an Allied breakout. Eventually they reached the hilltop town of Segni, approximately twenty miles northeast of Allied lines. The townspeople were sympathetic to their plight and arranged for the three to live in a primitive stone hut roughly a half-day's walk away in the mountains. A shepherd and his family were their only neighbors. Every few days, the townspeople sent a basket of provisions so the men would not starve. The three passed the long, dull hours playing bridge with a battered deck of cards one of the British officers kept in his pocket. After about two weeks, their benefactors escorted them on a long hike through the mountains south to show them the coastline. They gazed out from a snow-covered peak, serene and silent, breathing cool, crisp alpine air. In the panoramic distance, they could see Anzio and the blue Mediterranean. Toy-like ships hovered near shore as puffs of white phosphorous smoke hung above the tiny battlefield. Though remote, dangerous, and forbidding—everything appeared so eerily beautiful. There was, however, no way the men could reach the coast without crossing through several miles of territory teeming with German troops. After observing for roughly fifteen minutes, the small party headed back for Segni, and Wilkinson and the two British officers returned to their hut and waited.

A few nights later, Segni was inexplicably bombed in an Allied air attack. As a result, many townspeople were displaced, and the supply visits to the hut ended. Captain Buchanan departed on foot for town to check on the situation but did not return. Instead, two German soldiers came and recaptured Wilkinson as he relaxed unaware in the mountain hut. Only Moyle was able to escape. During the walk back, Wilkinson tried overtaking one of his captors but failed after a brief, violent struggle. Subdued, bloodied, and forced to walk with his hands over his head for nearly eight miles, Wilkinson was taken to a German bivouac housing roughly 200 men. The commander interviewed Wilkinson along with the two men who captured him. When the German captain learned that one of the men had taken Wilkinson's watch, he made him return it. That evening, Wilkinson was loaded into a Volkswagen sedan and taken to a small prisoner of war enclosure on the outskirts of Rome known as "The Movie Studio."[5] After six weeks of running and hiding in the Italian countryside, Wilkinson again became the guest of the Third Reich—this time for the remainder of the war.

Glossary, Phonetic Alphabet, and Military Clock

Term	Description
A-trains	The part of an army unit engaged in the combat area
Airburst	Artillery or mortar round intended to explode overhead
AP	Armor piercing
Assembly area	Area for final adjustments before battle, usually a mile or two from the front
AT gun	Anti-tank gun (towed or self-propelled)
AWOL	Absent without leave
B-trains	The part of an army unit supporting an army unit in combat but located away from combat
BAR	Browning automatic rifle
Bivouac	A temporary encampment without shelter
Bn	Battalion
BOQ	Bachelor Officers' Quarters
Caliber	Internal diameter of gun bore (expressed in inches or millimeters)
CO	Commanding officer
Co	Company
CP	Command post
Defilade	Arranging forces by using natural obstacles to avoid enemy fire
Div	Division
DOTC	Division Officers' Training Corps
Doughboy	Slang term used by tankers to describe an infantryman
DOW	Died of wounds
Echelon	The formation and maneuvering of troops in step-like fashion

EM	Enlisted man or men
G-2	Intelligence officer/section, division or Army level
G-3	Operations officer/section, division or Army level
GHQ	General headquarters
GO	General orders
H-hour	Start time of an operation
HE	High explosive
Howitzer	Artillery cannon that dispatches rounds on parabolic trajectories
HQ	Headquarters
Inf	Infantry
KIA	Killed in action
Landser	Common German infantryman or riflemen
LCI	Landing craft, infantry
LCM	Landing craft, mechanized
LCP	Landing craft, personnel
LCT	Landing craft, tank
LST	Landing ship, tank
LWA	Lightly wounded in action
MG	Machine gun
MIA	Missing in action
mm	Millimeter (25.4 mm equals 1 inch)
Mortar	Muzzle loading, low velocity artillery with a very short range
MP	Military police
MPH	Miles per hour
NCO	Non-commissioned officer
OD	Olive drab
Panzer	German word for tank or armor
Panzerfaust	"Tank fist" (German handheld AT rocket)
Pillbox	Small concrete structure housing an MG or AT gun
PW	Prisoner of war
RCT	Regimental combat team
Regt	Regiment
ROTC	Reserve Officers' Training Corps

RPM	Revolutions per minute
S-1	Personnel officer/section, battalion or regimental level
S-2	Intelligence officer/section, battalion or regimental level
S-3	Operations officer/section, battalion or regimental level
S-4	Logistics officer/section, battalion or regimental level
S/A	Small arms (refers to handheld rifles, pistols, and machine pistols)
SFW	Shell fragment wound
Shot	Tanker slang for armor piercing (AP) round
SNAFU	An acronym for "Situation Normal All F*cked Up"—an error
SP	Self-propelled (refers to a motorized AT gun—usually with caterpillar tracks)
Sv	Service
SWA	Severely wounded in action
T/O	Table of organization
T/O&E	Table of organization and equipment
TD	Tank destroyer
Tk	Tank
USMA	United States Military Academy at West Point, New York
WIA	Wounded in action
WP	White Phosphorus—used for marking or blinding a target
XO	Executive officer

WWII U.S. Army Phonetic Alphabet

ABLE	HOW	OBOE	VICTOR
BAKER	ITEM	PETER	WILLIAM
CHARLIE	JIG	QUEEN	X-RAY
DOG	KING	ROGER	YOKE
EASY	LOVE	SUGAR	ZEBRA
FOX	MIKE	TARE	
GEORGE	NAN	UNCLE	

MILITARY CLOCK

U.S. Army Grades (Officers and Enlisted) of World War II

Grade	Abbreviation*	Insignia
Officers		
General of the Army	-	✪
General	Gen	★★★★
Lieutenant General	Lt Gen	★★★
Major General	Maj Gen	★★
Brigadier General	Brig Gen	★
Colonel	Col	🦅
Lieutenant Colonel	Lt Col	✿ (Silver)
Major	Maj	✿ (Gold)
Captain	Capt	▯▯
First Lieutenant	1st Lt	▮ (Silver)
Second Lieutenant	2nd Lt	▮ (Gold)

Grade	Abbreviation*	Insignia
Warrant Officers		
Chief Warrant Officer	CWO	
Warrant Officer	WO	
Enlisted		
Master Sergeant	M/Sgt	
First Sergeant	1st Sgt	
Technical Sergeant	T/Sgt	
Staff Sergeant	S/Sgt	
Technician 3rd Class	T/3	
Sergeant	Sgt	
Technician 4th Class	T/4	
Corporal	Cpl	
Technician 5th Class	T/5	
Private First Class	Pfc	
Private	Pvt	(None)

*As recommended in War Department circular AR 850-150 (August 1943) and used in Morning Reports dated from 1941 through 1946. There was variance in some cases.

U.S. Army Organization of WWII Combat Infantry Units

(Largest to smallest)

Army Unit	Approximate Size/Description	Commanded by	Independent Medium Tank Battalion Equivalent
Army Group	2 or more armies	General	-
Army	2 to 5 corps	General	-
Corps	2 to 5 divisions	Lt Gen	-
Division	12,000 men in 3 regiments	Major General	-
Brigade	2 regiments	Brigadier General	-
Regiment	3,000 men in 3 battalions	Colonel	-
Battalion	900 men in 5 companies	Lieutenant Colonel	700 men in 6 Companies (4 tank companies)
Company	180 men in 4 platoons	Captain (1st Sergeant is the highest EM)	100 men in 17 tanks in 3 platoons
Platoon	48 men in 3 squads	2nd Lieutenant (Technical Sergeant is Platoon Sergeant)	25 men in 5 tanks (full strength) (Staff Sergeant is Platoon Sergeant)
Section/Patrol	2 or 3 squads		Section (2 or 3 tanks)
Squad	12 men	Staff Sergeant	Tank (4 or 5 crewmen)
Soldier	1 man		Tank crewman

B Company, 756th Tank Battalion (L)
Roster of 1 June 1941

Capt Dwight L. D. Terry
1st Lt David D. McSparron
2nd Lt French G. Lewis
2nd Lt Foster C. Smith
2nd Lt Charles M. Wilkinson

Sgt Carl T. Crawford
Sgt Jack Hogan
Sgt Ralph Robbins
Sgt Frank T. Eaton
Sgt Edward A. Shields
Sgt George A. Wooldridge
Cpl Lawrence Cowan
Pfc Edd A. Crabtree
Pfc Myron J. Eckerle
Pfc Dowell Hickey
Pfc Woodson Lawhorn
Pfc Raymond Lee
Pfc Elvis H. Lewis
Pfc James E. Marshall
Pfc Donald L. Pennington
Pvt Ithel R. Adlard
Pvt Marico Anderson
Pvt James H. Blackwell
Pvt Joe Branham
Pvt Bertie L. Bulen
Pvt Roy C. Burdette
Pvt Eugene F. Burgess
Pvt William J. Burns

Pvt Charles Burstein
Pvt Roland L. Buys
Pvt Frederick A. Calkins
Pvt Leland P. Campbell
Pvt John R. Carlson
Pvt Allen B. Carter
Pvt Clyde F. Cogdill
Pvt Raymond W. Colley
Pvt Earl W. Cunningham
Pvt Dennis J. Duffy
Pvt Bennett W. Edwards
Pvt Gerald T. Fennell
Pvt Verne W. Fisco
Pvt Franklin J. Fiss
Pvt James G. Haag
Pvt James E. Haspel
Pvt Quentin J. Hayden
Pvt Paul L. Hurlocker
Pvt Norman G. Jacobson
Pvt James F. James
Pvt Oric W. Johannesen
Pvt Paul M. Jones
Pvt Harold A. Jones
Pvt George B. Jones
Pvt Earl C. Kilgore
Pvt Luther A. Kinsworthy
Pvt Jared H. LaForge
Pvt Roy Lee
Pvt Robert M. Lillard

Pvt Frank C. Manak
Pvt Rufus P. Marin
Pvt Buster McClain
Pvt John C. McCoy
Pvt James D. P. McFadden
Pvt Ivan L. Mealer
Pvt James L. Middleton
Pvt George A. Montgomery
Pvt Arthur R. Morris
Pvt Noah R. Mudd
Pvt Alvin Nusz
Pvt John A. O'Malley
Pvt Haskell O. Oliver
Pvt Louis D. Olson
Pvt Robert Osganian
Pvt George T. Oviatt
Pvt Randolph H. Perdue
Pvt Daniel Pompey
Pvt Robert J. Pringle
Pvt Harris Ravetto
Pvt Henry A. Redinger
Pvt John K. Reid
Pvt Arthur F. Richter
Pvt Paul E. Robison
Pvt Loren G. Rosencrantz
Pvt William W. Schmidt
Pvt Merton W. Schultz
Pvt Clinton W. Seal

Pvt Gene B. Shirley
Pvt Bernard J. Simon
Pvt Onic E. Smeltzer
Pvt Hamilton A. Smith
Pvt Harold T. Sowers
Pvt Marvin A. Stradley
Pvt Arne Strand
Pvt Ray A. Taylor
Pvt Clifford J. Teek
Pvt Lester M. Thompson
Pvt Morris B. Thompson
Pvt Herman E. Thom
Pvt James R. Tisnado
Pvt Daniel J. Usher
Pvt Harvey J .Vaughan
Pvt William S. Villa
Pvt Cullen Ward
Pvt Lee E. Westbrook
Pvt Kenneth L. White
Pvt Thomas J. Williams
Pvt Alfred Winsett
Pvt John W. Womack
Pvt Terry E. Workman
Pvt Charles W. Wright
Pvt Joe K. Wright
Pvt Layfe Wright
Pvt Eugene K. Wunderlich
Pvt Edward J. Zyloney

B Company, 756th Tank Battalion Roster from 10 January to 27 January 1944

Source: B Company, 756th Tank Battalion, Morning Reports (MR) roster dated 15 Dec 1943 and subsequent MRs through 10 Jan 1944.

Capt Charles M. Wilkinson Jr.
1st Lt David D. Redle
2nd Lt John J. Czajkowski *(absent-injured)*
2nd Lt Wayne B. Henry
2nd Lt William G. Leger
2nd Lt John R. Winlock

1st/Sgt Jack Hogan
T/Sgt Morris B. Thompson
S/Sgt Raymond F. Colley
S/Sgt Carl T. Crawford
S/Sgt James B. Haspel
S/Sgt Oric Johannesen
S/Sgt Gene B. Shirley
Sgt Roland L. Buys
Sgt Leland P. Campbell
Sgt Clyde F. Cogdill
Sgt James B. Gilkerson
Sgt Charles J. Graffagnini
Sgt Louis J. Jarvis
Sgt Alfred W. Mancini Jr.
Sgt Haskell O. Oliver
Sgt Daniel Pompey
Sgt Hamilton A. Smith
Sgt Eugene Wunderlich
T/4 Edward A Avettant
T/4 Bertie L. Bulen
T/4 Roy C. Burdette
T/4 Oscar T. Crenshaw

T/4 Earl Cunningham
T/4 Luther M. Kinsworthy
T/4 Roy R. Kosanke
T/4 Rufus R. Marin
T/4 Carl A. Mras
T/4 Randolph Perdue
T/4 Jesse Rickerson Jr.
T/4 Werner Sprattler
T/4 Arno Strand
T/4 Armus Turtainen
Cpl Harold M. Behymer
Cpl Granger J. Butler
Cpl Charles H. Coleman
Cpl Joseph Cutrone
Cpl Robert B. Danner
Cpl Ed Farley
Cpl Henry E. Ghode
Cpl David L. Grate
Cpl Alexander L. Huffman
Cpl Marvin E. King
Cpl Frank T. Mielcarski
Cpl Eugene R. Rule
Cpl Ralph A. Rutzen
Cpl Henry J. Sanislow
Cpl Lloyd R. Stout
Cpl Paul T. Tirpak
Cpl Steve Vargo
T/5 Roy L. Anderson
T/5 John Dufalla

T/5 Edward D. Durham
T/5 Francis A. Fischer
T/5 Raymond S. Getz
T/5 Albert A. Jaksys
T/5 Louis A. Laliberty
T/5 Frank C. Manak
T/5 Anthony Notaroberto
T/5 Elbert Rainwater
T/5 John J. Roth
T/5 Edward J. Sadowski
T/5 John Senior
T/5 Irving Shapiro
T/5 Guy M. Sheffield
T/5 Edward Tomaszewski
T/5 Frank Ware
T/5 Joe K. Wright
Pfc Thomas M. Barber
Pfc William R. Boyer
Pfc Paul N. Cardullo
Pfc Gerald C. Chotin
Pfc Joseph Cutrone
Pfc Melville E. Corson
Pfc Leonard D. Froneberger Jr.
Pfc Clyde W. Guild
Pfc Earl C. Kilgore
Pfc Lotka U. Kupriance
Pfc Donald E. Ladue
Pfc George W. Minnick Jr.
Pfc David J. Orris
Pfc James W. Rupert
Pfc Hubert S. Shew
Pfc Bernard J. Shue
Pfc Leak H Smitherman.
Pfc Robert B. Thomas Jr.
Pvt John F. Bacha
Pvt Kevin F. Brennan
Pvt Merle E. Brooks
Pvt Thomas Corboy

Pvt Valentine Crowe
Pvt George C. Davis
Pvt Ford T. Draeger
Pvt Robert L. Duncan
Pvt Anton E. Fricke
Pvt Robert F. Gilbert
Pvt Hulon Long
Pvt Reuben Mapes
Pvt James W. Martin
Pvt Harold H. Matthies
Pvt Oscar W. McEntire
Pvt William J. McInrue
Pvt Delmar P. McIntyre
Pvt Nicholas P. Motto
Pvt Cletus J. Offerman
Pvt Gene Palumbo
Pvt Francis Payne
Pvt Reynold Peters
Pvt Eugene Radzikowski
Pvt Raymond R. Reid
Pvt Paul A. Saale
Pvt Edward C. Shea
Pvt Emil A. Tikkanen
Pvt Bernard C. Wammes
Pvt John Wessels

Changes as of 27 January 1944:

Departures:

2nd Lt John R. Winlock (transfer)
(21 Jan 44)

Arrivals:

2nd Lt Howard M. Harley (21 Jan 44)

Absentees:

Sgt James H. Gilkerson (sick) (22 Jan 44)
Pvt Merle E. Brooks (wounded)
(27 Jan 44)

Table of Organization for U.S. Army Tank Company (Light), March 1942

(5 Officers, 105 Enlisted Men Total)

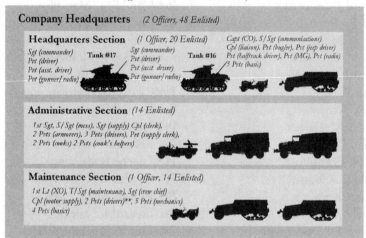

Company Headquarters *(2 Officers, 48 Enlisted)*

Headquarters Section *(1 Officer, 20 Enlisted)*

Sgt (commander)
Pvt (driver)
Pvt (asst. driver)
Pvt (gunner/radio)
Tank #17

Sgt (commander)
Pvt (driver)
Pvt (asst. driver)
Pvt (gunner/radio)
Tank #16

Capt (CO), S/Sgt (communications)
Cpl (liaison), Pvt (bugler), Pvt (jeep driver)
Pvt (halftrack driver), Pvt (MG), Pvt (radio)
5 Pvts (basic)

Administrative Section *(14 Enlisted)*

1st Sgt, S/Sgt (mess), Sgt (supply) Cpl (clerk),
2 Pvts (armorers), 3 Pvts (drivers), Pvt (supply clerk),
2 Pvts (cooks) 2 Pvts (cook's helpers)

Maintenance Section *(1 Officer, 14 Enlisted)*

1st Lt (XO), T/Sgt (maintenance), Sgt (crew chief)
Cpl (motor supply), 2 Pvts (drivers)**, 5 Pvts (mechanics)
4 Pvts (basics)

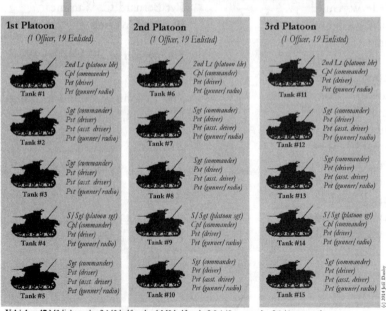

1st Platoon *(1 Officer, 19 Enlisted)*

2nd Lt (platoon ldr) / Cpl (commander) / Pvt (driver) / Pvt (gunner/radio) — **Tank #1**
Sgt (commander) / Pvt (driver) / Pvt (asst. driver) / Pvt (gunner/radio) — **Tank #2**
Sgt (commander) / Pvt (driver) / Pvt (asst. driver) / Pvt (gunner/radio) — **Tank #3**
S/Sgt (platoon sgt) / Cpl (commander) / Pvt (driver) / Pvt (gunner/radio) — **Tank #4**
Sgt (commander) / Pvt (driver) / Pvt (asst. driver) / Pvt (gunner/radio) — **Tank #5**

2nd Platoon *(1 Officer, 19 Enlisted)*

2nd Lt (platoon ldr) / Cpl (commander) / Pvt (driver) / Pvt (gunner/radio) — **Tank #6**
Sgt (commander) / Pvt (driver) / Pvt (asst. driver) / Pvt (gunner/radio) — **Tank #7**
Sgt (commander) / Pvt (driver) / Pvt (asst. driver) / Pvt (gunner/radio) — **Tank #8**
S/Sgt (platoon sgt) / Cpl (commander) / Pvt (driver) / Pvt (gunner/radio) — **Tank #9**
Sgt (commander) / Pvt (driver) / Pvt (asst. driver) / Pvt (gunner/radio) — **Tank #10**

3rd Platoon *(1 Officer, 19 Enlisted)*

2nd Lt (platoon ldr) / Cpl (commander) / Pvt (driver) / Pvt (gunner/radio) — **Tank #11**
Sgt (commander) / Pvt (driver) / Pvt (asst. driver) / Pvt (gunner/radio) — **Tank #12**
Sgt (commander) / Pvt (driver) / Pvt (asst. driver) / Pvt (gunner/radio) — **Tank #13**
S/Sgt (platoon sgt) / Cpl (commander) / Pvt (driver) / Pvt (gunner/radio) — **Tank #14**
Sgt (commander) / Pvt (driver) / Pvt (asst. driver) / Pvt (gunner/radio) — **Tank #15**

Vehicles: 17 M3 light tanks, **2** M3 halftracks, **1** M2 halftrack, **2** 2-1/2 ton trucks, **2** 1/4-ton trucks, **1** self-propelled anti-tank gun (unspecified).

NOTES: Self-propelled gun type and crew requirements are unspecified. It is also unclear why the Platoon Leader and Platoon Sergeant for each platoon is not also listed as the "commander." These were probably oversights at the time.

Source: War Department 1 March 1942 T/O & E 17-17

Table of Organization for U.S. Army Tank Company (Medium), September 1943

(5 Officers, 117 Enlisted Men Total)

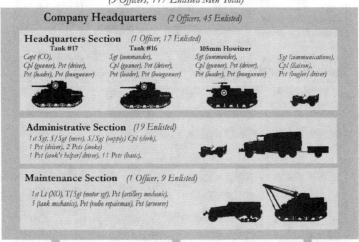

Company Headquarters *(2 Officers, 45 Enlisted)*

Headquarters Section *(1 Officer, 17 Enlisted)*

Tank #17	Tank #16	105mm Howitzer	
Capt (CO),	*Sgt (commander),*	*Sgt (commander),*	*Sgt (communications),*
Cpl (gunner), Prt (driver),	*Cpl (gunner), Prt (driver),*	*Cpl (gunner), Prt (driver),*	*Cpl (liaison),*
Prt (loader), Prt (bowgunner)	*Prt (loader), Prt (bowgunner)*	*Prt (loader), Prt (bowgunner)*	*Prt (bugler/driver)*

Administrative Section *(19 Enlisted)*

1st Sgt, S/Sgt (mess), S/Sgt (supply) Cpl (clerk),
1 Prt (driver), 2 Prts (cooks)
1 Prt (cook's helper/driver), 11 Prts (basic),

Maintenance Section *(1 Officer, 9 Enlisted)*

1st Lt (XO), T/Sgt (motor sgt), Prt (artillery mechanic),
5 (tank mechanics), Prt (radio repairman), Prt (armorer)

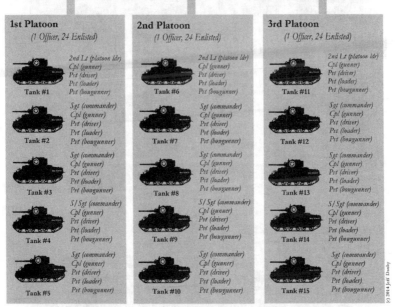

1st Platoon	2nd Platoon	3rd Platoon
(1 Officer, 24 Enlisted)	*(1 Officer, 24 Enlisted)*	*(1 Officer, 24 Enlisted)*

Tank #1 — *2nd Lt (platoon ldr), Cpl (gunner), Prt (driver), Prt (loader), Prt (bowgunner)*	**Tank #6** — *2nd Lt (platoon ldr), Cpl (gunner), Prt (driver), Prt (loader), Prt (bowgunner)*	**Tank #11** — *2nd Lt (platoon ldr), Cpl (gunner), Prt (driver), Prt (loader), Prt (bowgunner)*
Tank #2 — *Sgt (commander), Cpl (gunner), Prt (driver), Prt (loader), Prt (bowgunner)*	**Tank #7** — *Sgt (commander), Cpl (gunner), Prt (driver), Prt (loader), Prt (bowgunner)*	**Tank #12** — *Sgt (commander), Cpl (gunner), Prt (driver), Prt (loader), Prt (bowgunner)*
Tank #3 — *Sgt (commander), Cpl (gunner), Prt (driver), Prt (loader), Prt (bowgunner)*	**Tank #8** — *Sgt (commander), Cpl (gunner), Prt (driver), Prt (loader), Prt (bowgunner)*	**Tank #13** — *Sgt (commander), Cpl (gunner), Prt (driver), Prt (loader), Prt (bowgunner)*
Tank #4 — *S/Sgt (commander), Cpl (gunner), Prt (driver), Prt (loader), Prt (bowgunner)*	**Tank #9** — *S/Sgt (commander), Cpl (gunner), Prt (driver), Prt (loader), Prt (bowgunner)*	**Tank #14** — *S/Sgt (commander), Cpl (gunner), Prt (driver), Prt (loader), Prt (bowgunner)*
Tank #5 — *Sgt (commander), Cpl (gunner), Prt (driver), Prt (loader), Prt (bowgunner)*	**Tank #10** — *Sgt (commander), Cpl (gunner), Prt (driver), Prt (loader), Prt (bowgunner)*	**Tank #15** — *Sgt (commander), Cpl (gunner), Prt (driver), Prt (loader), Prt (bowgunner)*

Vehicles: **17** M4 medium tanks, **1** M7 Assault Gun with 105mm howitzer, **2** jeeps, **1** M3 halftrack, **1** 2-1/2 ton truck with trailer, **1** M32 tank recovery vehicle

NOTES: *With B Co./756th Tank Battalion, a T2 tank retriever was substituted for an M5. M4 tanks also included M4A1 cast hull models. M7 Assault Gun assigned to HQ Company AG Platoon. Prt grades listed allowed for a certain number of T/4 and T/5 specialists to be assigned at Company Commander's discretion.*

Source: War Department 15 September 1943 T/O & E 17 - 27

© 2014 Jeff Danby

Vehicle Chart for U.S. Army Tank Battalion (Medium), September 1943

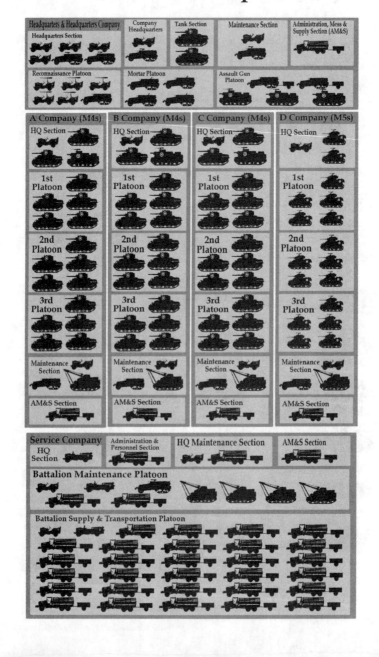

Table of Organization for U.S. Army Tank Battalion (Medium), 1943

U.S. ARMY MEDIUM TANK BATTALION Table of Organization & Equipment 17-25 (15 September 1943)*	Headquarters Company	Medium Tank Company "A"	Medium Tank Company "B"	Medium Tank Company "C"	Light Tank Company "D"	Service Company	Medical Detachment	Battalion TOTALS
Personnel:								
Officers	13	5	5	5	5	7	2	42
Enlisted Men	134	117	117	117	92	112	18	707
Tanks:								
M4 Medium Tank (75mm gun)	2	17	17	17	---	---	---	53
M4 Medium Tank (105mm howitzer)	3	1	1	1	---	---	---	6
M5 Light Tank (37mm gun)	---	---	---	---	17	---	---	17
Other Motorized Vehicles:								
¼-ton Truck (Jeep)	11	2	2	2	2	3	1	23
¾-ton Command Truck	---	---	---	---	---	1	---	1
¾-ton Weapons Carrier	---	---	---	---	---	1	---	1
2-½-ton Truck	1	1	1	1	1	34	---	39
M3 Half-track Ambulance	---	---	---	---	---	---	3	3

U.S. ARMY MEDIUM TANK BATTALION Table of Organization & Equipment 17-25 (15 September 1943)*	Headquarters Company	Medium Tank Company "A"	Medium Tank Company "B"	Medium Tank Company "C"	Light Tank Company "D"	Service Company	Medical Detachment	Battalion TOTALS
13 M3A1 Half-track Truck	8	1	1	1	1	1	---	13
M21 81mm Mortar Half-track	3	---	---	---	---	---	---	3
T5 Tank Recovery Vehicle	---	1	1	1	1	2	---	6
Heavy Wrecking Truck	---	---	---	---	---	2	---	2
Trailers:								
M10 Ammo Trailer	4	---	---	---	---	13	---	17
1-ton Trailer	2	1	1	1	1	20	1	27
Small Arms:								
.45-caliber Pistol	3	---	---	---	---	---	---	3
.45-caliber Submachine Gun	47	95	95	95	73	44	---	449
.30-caliber M1 Carbine Rifle	77	27	27	27	24	71	---	257
.30-caliber M1 Rifle	20	---	---	---	---	---	---	20
Heavy Arms:								
.30-caliber Light Machine Gun	3	1	1	1	1	11	---	18
.50-caliber M2 Heavy Machine Gun	5	2	2	2	3	12	---	26
2.36-inch Bazooka	12	3	3	3	2	12	---	35
81mm Mortar (unmounted)	---	1	1	1	1	2	---	6

Note: Some variances and substitutions occurred based on equipment availability.

756th Tank Battalion (L) Cadre Orders, June 1941

HEADQUARTERS ARMORED FORCE
Fort Knox, Kentucky

May 20, 1941

Special Orders)
          :
Number 140)   EXTRACT
         *   *   *

     12. Pursuant to authority contained in letter, War
Department, The Adjutant General's Office, Subject: Cadres
for the Armored Force, File: AG 320.2 (2-7-41) E-C,
February 21, 1941, the following named officers are relieved
from assignment and duty with the 1st Armored Division,
effective June 1, 1941, and are then assigned to units and
stations indicated after their respective names. They
proceed at the proper time, on or about the dates indicated,
to their new stations, for duty.

     756TH TANK BATTALION (L): GHQ RESERVE
     TO FORT LEWIS? WASHINGTON = JUNE2 1941.L

     Detached Service for eleven (11) days

     Captain Harold F. Thomas, O-227736
     Captain Dwight L.D. Terry, O-267460
     Captain Donald E. Mathes, O-165280
     Captain Abe Bock, O-255188
     Captain Vernon H. McKissick, O-259039
     Captain James M. Hamilton, Jr., O-252991
     Captain Robert C. Wakefield, O-238525
     ** *********************************
     ****
     ****

     First Lieutenant Clifton C. Andrues, O-322714
     Second Lieutenant Christian T. Den Ouden, O-350152
     Second Lieutenant Fred L. Schmidt, O-351009
     Second Lieutenant John E. Simkins,Jr., O-377420
     Second Lieutenant Edward S. Mandel, O-364927
     Second Lieutenant Clarence L. Slaysman, O-361381
     Second Lieutenant Charles B. Allen, O-345029
     Second Lieutenant Wade H. Anderson, O-364079
     Second Lieutenant William C. CarterJr., O-375852
     Second Lieutenant French G. Lewis, O-363587
     Second Lieutenant Foster Cl Smith, O-356180
     Second Lieutenant Ray Sl Treadwell, O-389764

Pa., 12, S/O #140, Hq. Armored Fore , Ft Knox, Ky.,cont'd.

Se   Second Lieutenant Charles McC. Wilkinson, Jr., O-399273
                        Second Lieutenant Howard A. Mahurin, O-399273
****
****

        The reavel directed is necessary in the mil-
itary service and will be on a troop movement basis. FD
1586 P 31-0624 A 0310-02; FD 1437 P 83-0600 A 0410-01;
QM 1622 P 54-0100-0284-1378-0701 A 0525-01 "D".
        Those officers whose presence with troops i s
not required are authorized to travel by privately owned
car with reimbursement as authorized in paragraph 1 i, AR
35-4820. In such case, detached service for the number of
days indicated above is authorized.
                *   *   *
                By command of Major General CHAFFEE:

                                SERENO E. BRETT,
                        Colonel, General Staff Corps,
                                Chief of Staff.
OFFICIAL:
        /s/ Madison Pearson,
        MADISON PEARSON,
        Leut. Colonel, A G.D.
        Adjutant General

                        "A TRUE EXTRACT COPY:"
                                George A. Moeller,
                                GEORGE A. MOELLER,
                        1st Lt., 69th Armored Regiment (M)
                                Asst. Adjutant.

B Company 756th Tank Battalion, 1 June 1941 Morning Report

Capt. Terry, 1st Lts Smith & McSparren asgd, DS enr to jn.; 2nd Lts Lewis & Wilkinson asgd, DS enr to jn.; XXX Sgt Robbins asgd, DS enr to jn.; Sgt Seaton asgd, abs sk Ft Knox, Ky.; Sgts. Crawford, Hogan, Shields,& Wooldridge asgd & jd.; Cpl Cowan asgd & jd.; Pvts 1cl Blackwell, Eckerle, Hayden, Lawhorn, Lee R., Lewis, Marshall & Pennington asgd & jd.; Pvts Anderson, Branham, Burgess, Haag, Haspel, Mudd & Perdue, asgd & jd.; Pvts 1cl Crabtree & Hickey asgd, DS A.F.S. Ft. Knox, Ky.; Pvt Burdette asgd, DS A.F.S. Ft. Knox, Ky.; Pvts (SS) Adlard, Bulen, Burns, Burstein, Buys, Calkins, Campbell, Carter, Carlson, Coghill, Colley, Cunningham, Duffy, Edwards, Fennell, Fisco, Fiss, Harlocker, Jacobson, James, Johannssen, Jones C.B., Jones H.A., Jones F.M., Kilgore, Kinsworthy, La Forge, Lee Roy, Lillard, Manak, Marin, Mc Clain, Mc Coy, Mc Fadden, Mealer, Middleton, Montgomery, Oliver, Redinger, Reid, Rosencrantz, Schmidt, Seal, Taylor, Thompson L.M., Thompson M.B., Thun, Usher, Westbrook, Williams, Winsett, Wright,L., Wright, J.K.& Wunderlich asgd & jd.; Pvts (SS) Morris, Muss, Olsen, O'Malley, Osganian, Oviatt, Pompey, Pringle, Ravotto, Richter, Robison, Schultz, Shirley, Simon, Smeltzer, Smith, Sowers, Stradler, Strand, Teel, Tisnado, Vaughan, Vilda, Ward, White, Womack, Workman, Wright,C.W.,&Zylaney asgd & on DS A.F.S. Ft. Knox, Ky.

B Company, 756th Tank Battalion, Record of Events, December 1941

STATION AND RECORD OF EVENTS

Dec. 1941

1-7 Usual garrison duties

7th Japan declared war. All 5 trucks of 756th used Co B at 3:30 PM. Armament and ammunition, tanks and ready to take field by midnight.

8th Co B took field at 3:00 PM in area near #5 17 with remainder of Bn (less Co C).

9th Co B remained in bivouac.

10th Co B remained in bivouac.

11th Co B constructed training measures in area 39. At noon ordered to So Bn at 1:00 PM, arrived in area 1:30 PM. 756th to Bn sub under X Army Corps at 5:00 AM Dec 11th. At 3 PM Bn alerted. Moved from area 6:00 PM. Bivouaced on outskirts of Montesano, Wash at 11:00 PM.

12th Moved bivouac about 3 miles East at 1:00 PM.

13th Left bivouac 5:00 PM, arrived Ft Lewis, Wn. 8:30 PM.

STATION AND RECORD OF EVENTS

13-14 Remained in Ft Lewis, Wn, garrison duties.

14 One Platoon Co. B. ordered to Seattle 4:30 PM, arrived and bivouaced outside Boeing Field at 7:00 AM. 5 Tanks and 43 E.M. 2 Officers, necessary truck and arms. Remainder of Co performed usual garrison duties.

25 Platoon remained in bivouac. Rest of Co did usual garrison duty.

26 Same as 25th.

27 Platoon left bivouac at 12:10 PM, arrived Ft Lewis 3:00 PM.

28-31 Usual garrison duties

756th Arrival at Cassino Document

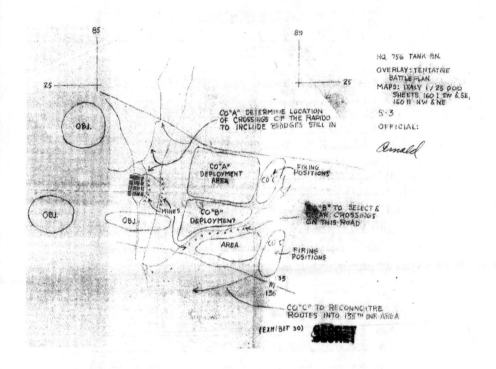

Yellow Orders from 756th HQ for 27 January 1944

Message 1 (page 1 of 2)

THESE SPACES FOR MESSAGE CENTER ONLY

TIME FILED — MSG CEN NO. — HOW SENT

MESSAGE (SUBMIT TO MESSAGE CENTER IN DUPLICATE) (CLASSIFICATION)

No. 1 (1 page of 2) DATE 27/1600A

To CAPT DAVIS

CROSSING MUST BE CONSTRUCTED TONIGHT TO GET ALL TANKS ACROSS. 235 BN WILL WORK ALSO. AM ATTEMPTING TO GET ALL PRE-

OFFICIAL DESIGNATION OF SENDER — TIME SIGNED

AUTHORIZED TO BE SENT IN CLEAR — SIGNATURE OF OFFICER — SIGNATURE AND GRADE OF WRITER

Message 1 (page 2 of 2)

THESE SPACES FOR MESSAGE CENTER ONLY

TIME FILED — MSG CEN NO. — HOW SENT

MESSAGE (SUBMIT TO MESSAGE CENTER IN DUPLICATE) (CLASSIFICATION)

No. 1 (page 2 of 2) DATE 27/16 A

To CAPT DAVIS

FABRICATED CORDUROY AVAILABLE. GENERAL CLARK IS VERY INTERESTED. DESTROY THIS MESSAGE.

SEAGULL 756th

OFFICIAL DESIGNATION OF SENDER — TIME SIGNED

AUTHORIZED TO BE SENT IN CLEAR (Exhibit #46) SIGNATURE OF OFFICER — SIGNATURE AND GRADE OF WRITER

29 January 1944 B Company Morning Reports

COMPANY MORNING REPORT ENDING 2400 29 January 194 4

STATION 1 mi W of S. Michele, Italy 10981 464

ORGANIZATION Co "B", 756th Tank Bn Inf

SERIAL NUMBER	NAME	GRADE	CODE
O-1015853	Czajkowski, John J. sk	2nd Lt	

Fr abs sk (ID) 36th Gen Hosp. to dy. 1030A.
as of 27 Jan/44. Not reld of duties upon
departure.

| O-399273 | Wilkinson, Jr. Charles M. | Capt | |
| O-1013942 | Henry, Wayne B. | 2nd Lt | |

Above two (2) O missing in action as of
27 Jan/44.

6255436	Crawford, Carl T.	S/Sgt	
39676367	Campbell, Leland P.	Sgt	
34150957	Avettant, Edward A.	T/4	
35029371	Coleman, Charles H.	Cpl	
35028693	Tirpak, Paul P.	Cpl	
31046421	Laliberty, Louis A.	T/5	
38044768	Shew, Hubert S.	Pfc	
35393730	Bacha, John F.	Pvt	

Above eight (8) EM missing in action as
of 27 Jan/44.

OFFICER STRENGTH	FLD O & CAPT		1ST LT		2D LT		W.O		FLT O	
	PRES	ABS'T	PRES	ABS'T	PRES	ABS'T	PRES	ABS'T	PRES	ABS'T
ASSIGNED										
ATTACHED UNASSIGNED										
ATTACHED FR OTHER ORGN										
TOTAL										

AVN CADET & ENLISTED STRENGTH	AVIATION CADETS		PRESENT FOR DUTY	PRESENT NOT FOR DY	ABSENT	PRESENT AND ABSENT
	PRESENT	ABSENT				
ASSIGNED						
ATTACHED UNASSIGNED						
ATTACHED FR OTHER ORGN						
TOTAL						

RATIONS
I ESTIMATED NUMBER OF RATIONS REQUIRED FOR — DAY OF WEEK / DATE — NUMBER
II MESS ATTENDANCE FOR DAY OF THIS REPORT — BREAKFAST DINNER SUPPER — TOTAL / AVERAGE
III MEN AUTHORIZED TO MESS SEPARATELY — MEN ATCHD FOR RATIONS O & OTHERS MESSED — MEN PRESENT / LESS / NET / PLUS — TOTAL

PAGE 1 OF 2 PAGES

SIGNATURE

...Y ...G REPORT ENDING 2400 29 January 194 4

STATION 1 mi W of S. Michele, Italy APO 464

ORGANIZATION Co "B", 756th Tank Bn Inf

SERIAL NUMBER	NAME	GRADE	CODE

RECORD OF EVENTS

Two (2) O and eight (8) EM, missing in action when two tanks became immobilized in
enemy territory after crossing Rapido
River on 27 January 1944.

OFFICER STRENGTH	FLD O & CAPT		1ST LT		2D LT		WO		FLT O	
	PRES	ABS'T	PRES	ABS'T	PRES	ACS'T	PRES	ABS'T	PRES	ABS'T
ASSIGNED			1		3					
ATTACHED UNASSIGNED										
ATTACHED FR OTHER ORGN										
TOTAL			1		3					

AVN CADET & ENLISTED STRENGTH	AVIATION CADETS		PRESENT FOR DUTY	PRESENT NOT FOR DY	ABSENT	PRESENT AND ABSENT
	PRESENT	ABSENT				
ASSIGNED			100		4	104
ATTACHED UNASSIGNED						
ATTACHED FR OTHER ORGN						
TOTAL			100		4	104

RATIONS
I ESTIMATED NUMBER OF RATIONS REQUIRED FOR — DAY OF WEEK Tuesday / DATE 1 February 1944 — NUMBER 104
II MESS ATTENDANCE FOR DAY OF THIS REPORT — BREAKFAST 104 DINNER 104 SUPPER 104 — TOTAL 312 / AVERAGE 104
III MEN AUTHORIZED TO MESS SEPARATELY — MEN ATCHD FOR RATIONS O & OTHERS MESSED 4 — MEN PRESENT 100 / LESS / NET 100 / PLUS 4 — TOTAL 104

PAGE 2 OF 2 PAGES

I CERTIFY THAT THIS MORNING REPORT IS CORRECT AND THAT RATION FIGURES IN PART IS REPRESENT AN ACTUAL COUNT AS REPORTED TO ME

SIGNATURE LEROY G. FINN, 1st Lt Inf

Special Acknowledgments

I would like to give special thanks to the following people for their contributions in making this ambitious history possible.

Melinda Woofter, my wife—for encouraging, listening, and exhibiting boundless patience.

Russell Danby-Jones, my father and retired high school history teacher of thirty-two years—for editing and proofreading.

A. Harding Ganz, professor emeritus of history, the Ohio State University—for mentoring, strategizing, proofreading, and editing. Harding was a tank platoon leader with the 4th Armored Division in the 1960s and is author of *Ghost Division: The 11th "Gespenster" Panzer Division and the German Armored Force in World War II* (Stackpole books, 2016).

Tim Stoy, USMA Class of 1981 and U.S. Army Lt Col (Ret)—for editing and proofreading. Tim is the current historian for the 15th Infantry Regiment and Society of the Third Infantry Division. He and his wife, Monika, work tirelessly dedicating World War II memorials all over Europe.

Ron Lowther, independent documentary filmmaker, Flying Lobster Productions—for sharing interviews, photos, documents, and ideas. Ron is developing a film documentary on the 756th Tank Battalion.

David A. Redle, son of David D. Redle, retired attorney and professor emeritus, University of Akron—for editing, proofreading, and posing many excellent questions that helped build a more detailed narrative.

Bernard "Bud" Fink, B Company combat veteran—for editing and clarifying. Bud came to 756th Tank Battalion as a 19-year-old tank gunner in early 1945. He only recently passed away and is terribly missed.

Victor "Tory" Failmezger, U.S. Navy Commander (Ret) and former Assistant Naval Attaché to Italy—for sharing his Italian maps and sources. Tory is the author of *American Knights: The Untold Story of the Men of the Legendary 601st Tank Destroyer Battalion.* (Osprey, 2015).

Susan Strange of Strange Research—for obtaining scans of many of the NARA unit journals, overlays, maps, and photos used in this project.

Sydney Soderberg, researcher—for obtaining copies of the long-lost B Company, 756th Tank Battalion, Unit Journal from the Eisenhower Library in Abeline, Kansas.

Dave Kerr, 191st Tank Battalion researcher—for sharing his many HQ scans of National Archives World War II photos.

Jeffrey Plowman, author of *The Battles for Monte Cassino* (After the Battle, 2011)—for proofing my draft and helping me obtain key photographs.

Bibliography

Published Books

Ankrum, Homer R. *Dogfaces Who Smiled Through Tears*. Lake Mills, Iowa: Graphic Publishing Company, 1988.

Atkinson, Rick. *An Army at Dawn: The War in North Africa, 1942–43*. New York, New York: Henry Holt and Company, LLC., 2002.

Barry, Steven Thomas. *Battalion Commanders at War: US Army Tactical Leadership in the Mediterranean Theater, 1942–1943*. Lawrence, Kansas: University Press of Kansas, 2013.

Bartholomew, E. *First World War Tanks*. Oxford, UK: Shire Publications Ltd., 2009.

Bierman, John, and Colin Smith. *War Without Hate: The Desert Campaign of 1940–1943*. New York: Penguin Books Ltd., 2004.

Bishop, Chris, and Chris McNabb, eds. *Campaigns of World War II Day by Day*. Hauppauge, New York: Barron's Educational Series, Inc., 2003.

Blumenson, Martin. *Salerno to Cassino*. Washington, D.C.: Center of Military History, U.S. Army, 1993.

Böhmler, Rudolf. *Monte Cassino: A German View*. Maximilian Verlag GmbH & Co, 1956. Reprint, South Yorkshire, UK: Pen and Sword Books, 2015.

Bond, Harold L. *Return to Cassino: A Memoir of the Fight for Rome*. Garden City, New York: Doubleday & Company, Inc. 1964.

Buell, Hal. *World War II Album*. New York, New York: Black Dog and Leventhal Publishers Inc., 2002.

Caddick-Adams, Peter. *Monte Cassino: Ten Armies in Hell*. New York, New York: Oxford University Press, 2012.

Camp, Brig Gen T. J. *Tankers in Tunisia*. Reprint, Honolulu, Hawaii: University Press of the Pacific, 2004.

Carruthers, Bob. *Panzer IV: The Workhorse of the Panzerwaffe*. South Yorkshire, UK: Pen and Sword Books, Ltd., 2013.

Chamberlain, Peter, and Chris Ellis. *The Sherman: An Illustrated History of the M4 Medium Tank*. New York, New York: Arco Publishing Company, Inc., 1978.

Cooke, Alistair. *Alistair Cooke's America*. New York: Alfred A. Knopf, Inc., 1973.

Duus, Masayo Umezawa. *Unlikely Liberators, The Men of the 100th and 442nd*. English Translation. Honolulu, Hawaii: University of Hawaii Press, 2006.

Fazendin, Roger. *The 756th Tank Battalion in the Battle of Monte Cassino, 1944*. Cave Creek, Arizona: Stories Unlimited, 1991. Reprint. Lincoln, Nebraska: iUniverse Inc., 1991.

Fletcher, David. *British Mark I Tank 1916*. Oxford, United Kingdom: Osprey Publishing, 2004.

Frieser, Karl-Heinz. *The Blitzkrieg Legend: The 1940 Campaign in the West*. Annapolis, Maryland: Naval Institute Press, 2005.

Froeschle, Helmuth O. *Our Story of the 760th Tank Battalion, WWII*. Reprint. Victoria, Canada: Trafford Publishing, 2007.

Ford, Ken. *Cassino 1944: Breaking the Gustav Line*. Oxford, UK: Osprey Publishing Ltd., 2004.

Forty, George. *US Army Handbook 1939–45*. New York, New York: Barnes and Noble Books, 1998.

Forty, Jonathan. *Tanks in Detail: M3-M3A1-M3A3 Stuart I–V*. Surrey, UK: Ian Allan Publishing, Ltd., 2002.

Forty, Simon, and Jonathan Forty. *Survivors: Battlefield Relics of WWII*. New York, New York: Chartwell Books, 2018.

Gillie, M. H. *Forging the Thunderbolt: History of the U.S. Army's Armored Forces, 1917–45*. The Military Service Publishing Company, 1947. Reprint, Mechanicsburg, Pennsylvania: Stackpole Books, 2006.

Gooderson, Ian. *Battles in Focus: Cassino*. London, UK: Brassey's, 2003.

Graham, Dominick. *Cassino: Battle Book No. 16*. New York, New York: Ballantine Books, Inc., 1970.

Green, Michael. *M4 Sherman: Combat and Development History of the Sherman Tank and All Sherman Variants*. Osceola, Wisconsin: Motorbooks International Publishers & Wholesalers, 1993.

Green, Michael, and James D. Brown. *M4 Sherman at War*. St Paul, Minnesota: MBI Publishing Co., 2007.

Guderian, Heinz. *Achtung – Panzer! The Development of Tank Warfare*. Translated by Christopher Duffy. Reprint, London, UK: Orion Books, Ltd., 1992.

Haygood, David. *Monte Cassino*. Garden City, New York: Double Day & Company, Inc, 1984.

Hearn, Chester G. *The American Soldier in World War II*. London, UK: Salamander Books, 2000.

Hougen, Lt. Col. John H. *The Story of the Famous 34th Infantry Division*. Reprint. Nashville, TN: The Battery Press, 1979.

Howe, George F. *Old Ironsides: The Battle History of the 1st Armored Division*. Washington, D.C.: Combat Forces Press, 1957; Reprint, Nashville, Tennessee: The Battery Press, 1979.

Howe, George F. *United States Army in World War II Mediterranean Theater of Operations: North Africa: Seizing the Initiative in the West*. Washington, D.C.: Office of the Chief of Military History, Department of the Army, 1957.

Huff, S/Sgt. Richard A., ed. *The Fighting 36th: A Pictorial History of the Texas Division in Combat*. Austin, Texas: 36th Division Association, 1945.

Hunnicutt, R. P. *Sherman: A History of the American Medium Tank*. Novato, California: Presidio Press, 1978. Reprint, Stamford, CT: Historical Archive Press, 1994.

Jackson, Julian. *The Fall of France: The Nazi Invasion of 1940*. Oxford, UK: Oxford University Press, 2003.

Lemons, Charles. *Organization and Markings of United States Armor Units 1918–1941*. Atglen, Pennsylvania: Schiffer Publishing Ltd., 2004.

Macksey, Kenneth. *Tank Tactics 1939–45*. Surrey, England: Almark Publishing Co. Ltd., 1976.

Macksey, Kenneth. *Tank vs Tank: The Illustrated Story of Armored Battlefield Conflict in the Twentieth Century*. London, UK: Barnes & Noble Books, 1999.

McGee, Addison. *He's in the Armored Force Now*. New York, New York: Robert M. McBride and Co., 1942.

McLean, Donald B., ed. *Company Officer's Handbook of the German Army*. Wickenburg, Arizona: Normount Technical Publications, 1975.

Parker, Matthew. *Monte Cassino: The Hardest-Fought Battle of World War II*. New York, New York: Doubleday, 2004.

Peek, Clifford H., ed. *Five Years, Five Countries, Five Campaigns: An Account of the One-Hundred-Forty-First Infantry in World War II*. Munich, Germany: F Bruckmann KG, 1945.

Pimlott, John. *The Historical Atlas of World War II*. New York, New York: Henry Holt and Company, Inc., 1995.

Plowman, Jeffrey, and Perry Rowe. *The Battles for Monte Cassino Then and Now*. Essex, UK: Battle of Britain International Ltd., 2011.

Prohme, Rupert. *History of 30th Infantry Regiment World War II*. Washington, D.C.: Infantry Journal Press, 1947.

Rector, Matthew D. *The United States Army at Fort Knox (Images of America)*. Chicago, Illinois: Arcadia Publishing, 2005.

Rottman, Gordon L. *Panzerfaust and Panzerschreck*. Oxford, UK: Osprey Publishing, 2014.

Sawicki, James A. *Tank Battalions of the U.S. Army*. Dumfries, Virginia: Wyvern Publications, 1983.

Sheppard, Ruth, ed. *The Tank Commander Pocket Manual 1939–1945*. Oxford, UK: Pool of London Press, 2016.

Smith, E.D., *The Battles for Monte Cassino*. New York, New York: Charles Scribner & Sons, 1975.

Smith, Lee Caraway. *A River Swift and Deadly: The 36th "Texas" Infantry Division at the Rapido River*. Austin, Texas: Eakin Press, 1989.

Stanton, Shelby L. *Order of Battle U.S. Army, World War II*. Novato, California: Presidio Press, 1984.

Taggart, Donald G. *The History of the Third Infantry Division in World War II*. Reprint, Nashville, Tennessee: The Battery Press, 1987.

Treanor, Tom. *One Damn Thing After Another*. Garden City, New York: Doubleday, Doran & Company, Inc., 1944.

United States Army. *752nd Tank Bn*. 1945. (PDF version downloaded from Bangor Public Library), World War Regimental Histories. Book 60. http://digicom.bpl.lib.me.us/ww_reg_his/60, accessed 20 April 2021.

Vollert, Verlag J. *Tankograd Technical Manual Series No 6013: U.S. WWII M5 & M5A1 Stuart Light Tanks*. Translated and edited by Michael Franz. Erlangen, Germany: Tankograd Publishing, 2008.

Wallace, Robert. *The Italian Campaign*. Morristown, New Jersey: Time-Life Books, Inc., 1978.

Wernick, Robert. *Blitzkrieg*. Alexandria, Virgina: Time-Life Books, 1977.

White, Nathan W. *From Fedala to Berchtesgaden: A History of the Seventh United States Infantry in WWII*. Providence, Rhode Island: Bickford Engraving & Electrotype Co., 1947.

Whitlock, Flint. *The Rock of Anzio: From Sicily to Dachau: A History of the U.S. 45th Infantry Division*. Boulder, Colorado: Westview Press, 1998.

Yeide, Harry. *The Infantry's Armor: The US Army's Separate Tank Battalions in World War II*. Mechanicsburg, Pennsylvania: Stackpole Books, 2010.

Zaloga, Steven J. *Early US Armor, Tanks 1916–40*. Oxford, UK: Osprey Publishing, 2017.

Zaloga, Steven J. *M3 & M5 Stuart Light Tank 1940–45*. Oxford, UK: Osprey Publishing, 1999.

Zaloga, Steven J. *M3 Lee/Grant Medium Tank 1941–45*. New York, New York: Osprey Publishing, 2005.

Zaloga, Steven J. *Sherman Medium Tank 1942–45*. Oxford, UK: Osprey Publishing, 2001.

Zaloga, Steven J. *US Field Artillery of World War II*. New York, New York: Osprey Publishing, 2007.

Zaloga, Steven J. *US Army Tank Crewman 1941–45, European Theater of Operations 1944–45*. Oxford, UK: Osprey Publishing, 2004.

Unpublished or Self-Published Books and Dissertations

Andrews, Maj Samuel R. *"Major General Charles Ryder: The Forging of a World War II Division Commander"* Monograph. School of Advanced Military Studies, United States Army Command and General Staff College, Fort Leavenworth, KS, 2014. (Electronic copy obtained through CARL)

Daskevich II, Colonel Anthony F. "Insights into Modularity 753rd Tank Battalion in World War II." USAWC Strategy Research Project, US Army War College, Carlisle Barracks, Pennsylvania, March 2008.

Esposito, Cheryl. *The 756th Tank Battalion in the European Theatre*. Privately printed, 1999.

Kosanke, Roy. "756th Tank Battalion Reunion Book." 756th Tank Battalion Association, late 1980s. Photo-scanned.

McMahon, Kevin. *In the Vicinity of Cairo, Italy: Letters Home from Lt. James E. McMahon during his service in World War II*. Privately printed, 2010.

Mudd, Lee. "History of the 756th Tank Battalion and the Development of the Tank-Infantry Team in World War II." Thesis, Johns Hopkins University, 2000.

Palumbo, Gene. *Load Kick Fire: Fighting with the 756th Tank Battalion, B Company, on the front lines during WWII.* Privately printed by the author, 2012.

Wilkinson, Richard F. *The Breakthrough Battalion: Battles of Company C of the 133rd Infantry Regiment, Tunisia and Italy 1943–1945.* Williamsburg, Virginia: by the author, 2005.

War Department Field Manuals, Training Manuals, Regulations, and Organizational Tables

Unless specified otherwise, all items listed below were published by the U.S. Government Printing Office in Washington, D.C., at time of release.

Armored Force Field Manual FM 17-10, Tactics and Technique, 7 March 1942.

Armored Force Field Manual FM 17-12, Tank Gunnery, 22 April 1943.

Armored Force Field Manual FM 17-30, Tank Platoon, 22 October 1942.

Armored Force Field Manual FM 17-32, Tank Company Light and Medium, 2 August 1942.

Armored Force Field Manual FM 17-33, Armored Battalion Light and Medium, 18 Sept 1942.

Army Regulations AR 850-150, Authorized Abbreviations and Symbols—13 November 1943 and 18 September 1944, with supplements.

Employment of Tanks with Infantry FM 17-36, War Department, 13 March 1944. Reprint. West Chester, Ohio: The Nafiziger Collection, Inc., 2000.

Recognition Pictorial Manual on Armored Vehicles FM 30-40, 3 November 1943.

Table of Organization No. 17-25, War Department, Washington, D.C., 15 September 1943, Medium Tank Battalion

Table of Organization No. 17-27, War Department, Washington, D.C., 1 March 1942, Medium Tank Company, Armored Regiment, or Tank Battalion, Medium.

Table of Organization No. 17-27, War Department, Washington, D.C., 15 September 1943, Medium Tank Company for Tank Battalion.

Table of Organization No. 18-27, War Department, Washington, D.C., 15 March 1944, Tank Destroyer Gun Company, Tank Destroyer Battalion, Self-Propelled.

Technical Manual TM 12-427, Military Occupational Classifications of Enlisted Personnel—12 July 1944.

Fort Benning Monographs

Obtained and downloaded as PDF files at: https://www.benning.army.mil/Library/Donovanpapers/wwii/index.html, accessed 20 April 2021.

Gray, Jr., 1st Lt Belfrad H., "The Crossing of the Rapido River and Occupation of Positions Above Cassino, Italy, by Company "I," 168th Infantry (34th Infantry Division) 27 January–15 February 1944 (Rome-Arno Campaign) (Personal Experience of a Squad Leader)." The Infantry School, Fort Benning, Georgia, Advanced Infantry Officers Course 1947–1948.

Luttrell, Captain James A., "The Operations of the 168th Infantry (34th Infantry Division) in the Rapido River Crossing, 28 January–10 February 1944. (Rome-Arno Campaign) (Personal Experience of a Cannon Company Commander)." The Infantry School, Fort Benning, Georgia, Advanced Infantry Officers Course 1948–1949.

Primary Source Official Documents, Reports, and Lists

National Archives and Records Administration (College Park, MD). Many original U.S. Army records, including WWII enlistment records and casualty lists are housed at this facility. A tiny amount of material has been digitized and is available for download online at: https://www.archives.gov/, accessed 20 April 2021.

34th Infantry Division, (Army Records Group 407, Boxes 8172 and 8173) for dates 23 January to 13 February 1944, includes the following materials:
Communications to the Fifth Army HQ, French CEF HQ, and II Corps HQ.
II Corps G-3 Reports, Counterbattery Reports.
34th Infantry Division G-3 Journal, G-3 Reports, G-2 Reports, Field Orders, and Messages.
34th Infantry Division Artillery S-3 Reports.
1st Tank Group S-3 Reports.
105th AA AW Battalion S-3 Reports.
109th Engineering Battalion S-3 Reports.
133rd Infantry Regiment S-3 Reports, Patrol Reports.
135th Infantry Regiment S-3 Reports.
168th Infantry Regiment S-3 Reports.
756th Tank Battalion S-3 Reports.
776th Tank Destroyer Battalion S-3 Reports.

756th Tank Battalion, (Army Records Group 407, Boxes 16769–16772): 1943 Unit History, 1944 Unit History, Commander's Narratives, Unit Journal, Rosters, Field Orders, and "Yellow" Orders.
Fifth Army Invasion Training Center (FAITC), (Records Group 407, box 2397): G-3 Report, History, 1943 Training Directive.

Records of World War II Prisoners of War, 1942–47, documenting the period 7 December 1941–19 November 1946 at National Archives website: https://aad.archives.gov/aad/series-list.jsp?cat=WR26, accessed 20 April 2021.
World War II Army Enlistment Records, documenting the period ca. 1938–46, at National Archives website: https://aad.archives.gov/aad/series-list.jsp?cat=WR26, accessed 20 April 2021.

National Personnel Records Center (St Louis, MO): Microfilm images of the "Morning Reports" to each U.S. Army company are kept at the NPRC. These are daily records of the location and basic activities of the company as well as any changes of duty status to all personnel assigned to the company: https://www.archives.gov/st-louis.

756th Tank Battalion, B Company: June 1941–February 1946 (May and June 1943 missing from NPRC), A, C, D, HQ, and Service Companies and Medical Detachment: 1941–44 (select dates).
133rd Infantry Regiment HQ Co: January 1944 (select dates).
168th Infantry Regiment, HQ Co, 2nd Bn HQ, 3rd Bn HQ, E, F, G, H, I, K, and L Cos: January 1944 (select dates).
760th Tank Battalion, C Co: February 1944 (complete month).

Dwight D. Eisenhower Library (Abilene, KS): U.S. Army: Unit Records, 1917–50, 756th Tank Battalion, Box 146.
B Company 756th Tank Battalion, Unit Journal, January–September 1944.

U.S. Army Human Resources Command (Fort Knox, KY): The U.S. Army HRC keeps the original "Graves Registration" Individual Deceased Personnel Files (IDPF) for all those U.S. Army members killed in action in World War II: www.hrc.army.mil, accessed 20 April 2021.

IDPFs for the following: John F. Bacha, Herman J. Bayless, Edward J. Dudinski, William Fodor, Raymond V. Galbraith, Wayne B. Henry, Jack Hogan, David J. Orris, Paul T. Tirpak, and Eugene Wunderlich.

American Battlefield Monuments Commission: American WWII overseas graves listing with the "American Battlefield Monuments Commission" at: http://www.abmc.gov/, accessed 20 April 2021.

U.S. Government Records at Ancestry.com:
Obtained through website subscription at: http://www.ancestry.com, accessed 20 April 2021.

Social Security Death Index.
United States Army WWII Draft Cards 1940–47.
United States Census for 1920, 1930, and 1940.
United States War Department, Press Releases and Related Records, 1942–45
United States World War II Hospital Admission Card Files, 1942–54.
United States Passport Applications 1795–1925.

College Yearbooks:
Accessed at www.ancestry.com: "US school yearbooks, 1880–2012."
Barton, Warren D., ed. *Longhorn.* College Station, TX: Texas A&M College, 1939.
Bird, Jimmy L., ed. *Razorback.* Fayetteville, AR: University of Arkansas, 1937.
Loveless, Sidney L., ed. *Longhorn.* College Station, TX: Texas A&M College, 1938.
Monaghan, William and Davis, William, eds. *The BlueJay.* Omaha, NE: Creighton University School of Journalism, 1941.

U.S. Army Registry of Officers:
Books downloaded in PDF form from: https://archive.org/, accessed 20 April 2021.
United States Army. *Official U.S. Army Register.* Washington, D.C.: War Department, The Adjutant General's Office, United States Government Printing Office. 1941, 1943, 1944, 1945, and 1946.

United States Military Library, digital collections:
Cadet class yearbooks accessed from: https://usma.libguides.com/welcome, accessed 20 April 2021.
Knapp, James B., ed. *Howitzer.* West Point, NY: United States Corps of Cadets, 1939.
Otto, S. E., ed. *Howitzer.* West Point, NY: United States Corps of Cadets, 1933.

Combined Arms Research Library (CARL): CARL is part of the U.S. Army's Combined Research Center. The purpose of CARL is to serve as an online resource to the General Staff College, but a vast number of historical documents and declassified material has been digitized and is available to the general public for online research and download. CARL is an extraordinary resource for WWII historians: https://usacac.army.mil/organizations/cace/carl/, accessed 20 April 2021.

Drake, Col Thomas D. *"Factual Account of Operations 168th Infantry, 34th Division, from 24 December 1942 to 17 February 1943"* After Action Report. 2 April 1945.
756th Tank Battalion "Reports of Action of the 751st Tank Battalion," 1943–45.

760th Tank Battalion "Operations in Italy, January 1944," "Operations in Italy, February 1944," and "Operation in Italy, May 1944," After Action Reports.

34th Infantry Division, Lessons Learned in Combat, November 7–8 1942 – September 1944. Italy, September 1944.

Members of the 34th Infantry Division, *The Story of the 34th Infantry Division: Louisiana to Pisa.* MTOUSA: Information and Education Section, 1945.

Walker, Maj Gen Fred L Walker, *"Comments on the Rapido River Crossing, January 1944,"* Library USA CGSC Ft Leavenworth KS, 1960.

United States Army, A Military Encyclopedia Based on Operations in the Italian Campaigns 1943–1945. G-3 Section, Headquarters 15th Army Group, 1945.

United States Army, *Fifth Army History, Part IV, Cassino and Anzio, 16 January 1944–13 March 1944.* Florence, Italy: L'Impronta Press, 1944.

United States Army. *Report of the New Weapons Board.* Washington, D.C.: Army Service Forces. 27 April 1944.

Primary Source Letters, Diaries, Memoirs, Photos, and Miscellaneous

Donley, Ralph. Wartime Diary dated from 1 January 1943 to 27 June 1945, (76 pages). Donley was a sergeant in the 756th Tk Bn HQ Co. (Photocopies provided to the author by Ralph Donley.)

Donley, Ralph. "Recollections," (5 pages). Written for the author and dated 8 March 2005.

Lewis, French. Personal papers, notes, news articles, memoirs, letters, military orders, and letters pertaining to the 756th Tank Battalion, (~2,100 pages). (Photocopies provided to the author by Grieg Lewis, son.)

Haspel, James E. Interview by Pamela G. Patrick on 18 September 1984, (6 pages). (Photocopies provided to the author by Haspel's family.)

Offerman, Dick. (Son of Cletus J. Offerman, B Company/756th Tank Battalion). "My Dad was a Tanker." Biography, letters, and photos, December 2005, (65 pages). (PDF version provided to the author.)

Olson, Edwin B. War Recollections, Early 2000s (12 pages). (Photocopies provided to author by Edwin B. Olson.)

Ranspach, Paul. Wartime diary dated from 15 September 1943 to 23 October 1945 and photos, (76 pages). Ranspach was a member of both B and D Companies, 756th Tank Battalion. (Photocopies provided to the author by the Ranspach family through the 756th Tank Battalion Association.)

Redle, David D. "B Company, 756th Tank Battalion Added Recollections" unpublished memoirs. (14 pages), written in the late 1990s. (Photocopies provided to the author by David D. Redle.)

Redle, David D. "B Company History" memoirs. (38 handwritten pages), 2004. (Presented to the author at interview 13 March 2004.)

Richter, Arthur F. "Arthur F. Richter's Experience in WWII" memoirs. (26 pages), 2007. (Photocopies provided to the author by Arthur F. Richter.)

Wilkinson, Charles M., Wartime Diary dated from 7 December 1941 to 23 January 1944, (414 pages). (Photocopies provided to the author by the Wilkinson family.)

Wilkinson, Charles M., Authored four personal unpublished memoirs covering his wartime service and experiences as a prisoner of war: "The Way It All Started." (25 pages) May 2004; "My Experiences in Italy, Part One." March, 2000 (11 pages); "My Experiences in Italy, Part Two." c. 2001, (17 pages); "A Guest of the Third Reich." November, 2002 (37 pages). (Photocopies of each provided to the author by Charles M. Wilkinson.)

Primary Source Interviews and Correspondence

756th Tank Battalion Veterans:
Includes letters, e-mails, phone conversations, personal interviews, photos, and documents shared with the author. Some books, diaries, and photos formally maintained by the 756th Tank Battalion Association are now in the possession of the U.S. Army Armor and Cavalry Collection in Fort Benning, Georgia.

B Company Veterans:
Roy Anderson, Clyde Guild, Alfred Mancini, Gene Palumbo, Randolph Perdue, David D. Redle, Arthur Richter, Henry J. Sanislow, Charles M. Wilkinson.
Other 756th Tank Battalion Veterans:
Jack Brown (HQ Co), Roy Collins (HQ Co), Jack Deenihan (A Co), Ralph Donley (HQ Co), Edwin B. Olson (C and HQ Co), French G. Lewis (A, B and HQ Cos), Mike Sudvary (A Co).

756th Veterans' Families and Friends:
Ed Brennan (son to Kevin F. Brennan, B Co), Dave Deputy (grandson of Frank Deputy, A Co), Earl L. Hanson (nephew to Ralph L. Hanson, A Co), family to James Haspel (B Co), family of Wayne B. Henry (B Co), Greig Lewis (son to French G. Lewis, A, B and HQ Cos), Dick Offerman (son of Cletus Offerman, B Co), Martha Ours, (daughter of Anthony F. Melfi, B Co), family to Haskell O. Oliver (B Co), family to Paul Ranspach (B and D Cos), Alfreda Sadowski (wife to Ed Sadowski, B Co.), Bob Shonka (son to Donald G. Shonka, A Co), Michael Thompson (son to Morris B. Thompson, B Co), family of Charles M. Wilkinson (B Co).

Motion Pictures and Photographs

"Abwehr eines US Bomberangriffes am 11. 01. 1944," German newsreel on air war around Monte Cassino, 1944, at: https://www.dailymotion.com/video/x4177bg, accessed 20 April 2021.
"Battle of San Pietro" by the War Department, 1945, at https://www.youtube.com/watch?v=1pAPOi-fAaQY, accessed 20 April 2021.
"Into the Jaws of Death, Battle of Fondouk, 8/9 April 1943," by Mick Holtby for the Queen's Royal Lancers Museum at: https://www.youtube.com/watch?v=OkoFfr6hgKw, accessed 20 April 2021.
Stock footage available at: www.criticalpast.com, accessed 20 April 2021:
"Battle of Monte Cassino, Italy, U.S. Troops on Mountainside …"
"Battle of Monte Cassino, Italy. Views of town and Abbey, as US troops prepare …"
"Scenes from the Battle of Monte Cassino, Italy, during World War II."
"Soldiers of 2nd New Zealand division at the Battle of Monte Cassino …"
"United States 5th Army Soldiers shell the town of Cassino, Italy during World War II."
"US Army units shell the town of Monte Cassino, Italy, during World War Two."

Internet Articles

"100th Infantry Battalion Veterans Education Center," "Keynote address by Young O. Kim" on 3 July 1982 at: http://www.100thbattalion.org/archives/puka-puka-parades/european-campaigns/keynote-address-by-young-o-kim/, accessed 20 April 2021.
133rd Inf Regt Commander's Narrative for January 1944 by Col Marshall, transcribed and posted by 34th Infantry Division Association at: http://www.34ida.org/history/133_narr_history.html (accessed 20 April 2021).

776th Tank Destroyer Battalion Unit Journal, 1 February 1944 (PDF scanned form obtained at: http://tankdestroyer.net/units/battalions700s/274-776th-tank-destroyer-battalion, accessed 20 April 2021).

Askey, Nigel. "Operation Barbarossa," "German Deployment Overview Fast-Facts": http://www.operationbarbarossa.net/german-forces-operation-barbarossa-june-july-1941/, accessed 20 April 2021.

Bernard, Lyle W. "Harry W. Sweeting, 1933" memorial: https://www.westpointaog.org/memorial-article?id=eac96987-faa1-4d3c-aa41-54bdefa047bc, accessed 20 April 2021.

"Charles W. Ryder, 1915" (West Point obituary), https://www.westpointaog.org/memorials, accessed 20 April 2021.

George S. Patton service summary at: https://en.wikipedia.org/wiki/Service_summary_of_George_S._Patton, accessed 20 April 2021.

Haze Gray and Underway World Aircraft Carrier Lists at: http://www.hazegray.org/navhist/carriers/, accessed 20 April 2021.

"History of the 107th Mechanized Cavalry" at: https://www.107thmechcavsqd.com/history-of-the-107th-mechanized-cavalry/, accessed 20 April 2021.

Texas A&M 1941 seasonal football record at: https://www.sports-reference.com/cfb/schools/texas-am/1941-schedule.html, accessed 20 April 2021.

"Texas A&M University Corps of Cadets" article, "Senior Boots" section at: http://en.wikipedia.org/wiki/Texas_A%26M_University_Corps_of_Cadets, accessed 20 April 2021.

"Unit Journal of Cannon Company, 133rd Infantry, January–March 1944" transcribed at: http://www.34infdiv.org/history/133cannon/4401.html, accessed 18 May 2015.

Endnotes

Dedication

1   "B-trains" refers to rear echelon service units. Non-essential personal property such as souvenirs, books, letters, extra clothing, etc., were stored away from the combat zone.

2   Roger Fazendin, *The 756th Tank Battalion in the Battle of Monte Cassino, 1944*, (Cave Creek, Arizona: Stories Unlimited, 1991; Reprint. Lincoln, Nebraska: iUniverse Inc., 1991.), xxxiv. (Reprint version cited throughout the book, unless otherwise noted.)

The Setting

1   President Warren G. Harding's winning campaign promise of 1920. Harding won 404 of the 535 electoral votes and 60 percent of the popular vote.

2   Washington Disarmament Conference.

3   Kellogg–Briand Pact of 1928 was signed at first by the United States, France, and Germany, and then later by Britain, Italy, Japan, China, the Soviet Union, and many other leading countries. In total, fifty-four nations committed. Ironically, the treaty is still in effect.

4   In his 1919 book, *The Economic Consequences of Peace*, John Maynard Keynes argued for a more equitable treaty allowing for an integrated European economy and criticized the Allies for violating the terms of the 1918 armistice.

5   Lindbergh lived in England from 1936 to 1939 and visited Germany several times to report on their aviation advances.

6   "Monroe Doctrine" foreign policy was established by U.S. President James Monroe in 1823 and opposed any further European colonization in North or South America.

7   Haze Gray & Underway World Aircraft Carrier Lists at http://www.hazegray.org/navhist/carriers/.

8   David Fletcher, *British Mark I Tank 1916* (Oxford, UK: Osprey Publishing. 2004), 9.

9   M. H. Gillie, *Forging the Thunderbolt* (The Military Service Publishing Company, 1947; reprint, Mechanicsburg, PA: Stackpole Books, 2006), 4.

10 Fletcher, *British Mark I Tank*, 21–22.

11 Ibid.

12 Kenneth Macksey, *Tank vs Tank* (London, UK: Barnes & Noble Books. 1999), 28.

13 Gillie, *Forging the Thunderbolt*, 12–13.

14 E. Bartholomew, *First World War Tanks* (Oxford, UK: Shire Publications Ltd., 2009), 22.

15 Kenneth Macksey, *Tank Tactics 1939–45* (Surrey, England: Almark Publishing Co. Ltd., 1976), 7–12. Guderian credited British Colonel J.F.C. Fuller for first developing the concept of massed armored forces cutting through the rear echelons of adversaries. Guderian built upon Fuller's ideas.

16 Shelby L. Stanton, *Order of Battle U.S. Army, World War II* (Novato, California: Presidio Press, 1984), 21.

17 Julian Jackson, *The Fall of France: The Nazi Invasion of 1940* (Oxford, UK: Oxford University Press, 2003), 13–14.

18 Karl-Heinz Frieser, *The Blitzkrieg Legend: The 1940 Campaign in the West* (Annapolis, MD: Naval Institute Press, 2005), 237–38.

19 Robert Wernick, *Blitzkrieg* (Alexandria, VA: Time-Life Books, 1977), 26.

20 Known as the "Gleiwitz incident."

21 John Pimlott, *The Historical Atlas of World War II* (New York, New York: Henry Holt and Company, Inc., 1995), 44.

22 Ibid. Although attack speed was emphasized, these six panzer divisions were not concentrated on a particular point but rather moved with the infantry as a whole.

23 Hal Buell, *World War II Album* (New York, New York: Black Dog and Leventhal Publishers Inc., 2002), 6.

24 Harry Yeide, *The Infantry's Armor: The U.S. Army's Separate Tank Battalions in World War II* (Mechanicsburg, Pennsylvania: Stackpole Books, 2010), 2.

25 Pimlot, *Historical Atlas of WWII*, 44.

26 Wernick, *Blitzkrieg*, 26.

27 Pimlot, *Historical Atlas of WWII*, 44.

28 George Forty, *U.S. Army Handbook 1939–45* (New York, NY: Barnes & Noble Books, 1998), 2–3.

29 Michael D. Hall, "Architect of Victory: George C. Marshall shaped the wartime US Army and advised President Franklin D. Roosevelt throughout World War II." *WWII History Magazine*, December 2013, 8.

30 Forty, *U.S. Army Handbook*, 3–4.

Chapter 1

1 Charles M. Wilkinson, personal memoirs titled "The Way It All Started," (25 pages), 2004, 1.

2 "Texas A&M University Corps of Cadets" article at http://en.wikipedia.org/wiki/Texas_A%26M_University_Corps_of_Cadets

3 Originally known as the Burke-Wadsworth Act.

4 Forty, *U.S. Army Handbook*, 5; Chester G. Hearn, *The American Soldier in World War II* (London, UK: Salamander Books, 2000), 8.

5 French G. Lewis hand-written autobiography and personal military papers. Technically, Wilkinson and Lewis were assigned to the 69th Armored Regiment of the 1st Armored Division.

6 Wilkinson, "The Way It All Started," 2.

7 Lewis personal papers: *Tulsa World News* article clipping, 22 June 1944, (page unknown).

8 Lewis, personal papers, undated autobiography.

9 Ibid., 31 January 1941 orders.

10 Wilkinson, "The Way It All Started," 2; Lewis, personal papers, undated autobiography.

11 Not from Wilkinson's recollections specifically, but inferred from the book by Captain Addison McGee, *He's in the Armored Force Now* (New York, New York: Robert M. McBride and Co., 1942), 149: McGee writes that every "new Armoraider learns about the history of the organization."

12 Charles Lemons, *Organization and Markings of United States Armor Units 1918–1941* (Atglen, Pennsylvania: Schiffer Publishing Ltd., 2004), 8.

13 Ibid., 40.

14 Steven J. Zaloga, *M3 & M5 Stuart Light Tank 1940–45* (Oxford, UK: Osprey Publishing, 1999), 4.

15 Gillie, *Forging the Thunderbolt*, 159; The Defense Act of 1920 required tanks to be assigned to the infantry.

16 Zaloga, *M3 & M5 Stuart Light Tank*, 4.

17 Ibid., 40.

18 Ibid., 8; Implied. Most tanks in the early production runs were sent to British forces.

19 Ibid.

20 R. P. Hunnicutt, *Sherman: A History of the American Medium Tank* (Novato, California: Presidio Press, 1978; reprint, Stamford, CT: Historical Archive Press, 1994), 27–29.

21 Lemons, *Organization and Markings*, 98–101.

22 Ibid., 69–70.

23 Hunnicutt, *Sherman*, 36.

24 Ibid., 47.

25 Ibid., 48–50.

26 Steven J. Zaloga, *M3 Lee/Grant Medium Tank 1941–45* (New York, NY: Osprey Publishing, 2005), production chart on page 14.

27 Hunnicutt, *Sherman*, 117–118; This would later become the M4 "Sherman." According to Hunnicutt, the design features were finalized at Aberdeen on 18 April 1941 and a plywood mock-up and test model were authorized the following month.

28 Created originally as a "service test" in order to avoid the red tape of obtaining congressional approval (Gillie, *Forging the Thunderbolt*, 163).

29 McGee, *He's in the Armored Force*, 149.

30 Ibid., 151.

31 Ibid.

32 Gillie, *Forging the Thunderbolt*, 157.

33 Yeide, *Infantry's Armor*, 2.

34 McGee, *He's in the Armored Force*, 151; Gillie, *Forging the Thunderbolt*, 196.

35 Gillie, *Forging the Thunderbolt*, 176.

36 Ibid., 180.

37 Ibid., 174.

38 Ibid., 193.

39 Ibid., 168.

40 Ibid., 188; these were the 191st, 192nd, 193rd, and 194th Tank Battalions.

41 Ibid., 192.

42 Ibid.; Yeide, *The Infantry's Armor*, 3.

43 Gillie, *Forging the Thunderbolt*, 165.

44 McGee, *He's in the Armored Force*, 180.

45 Ibid., 182.

46 This term is promoted throughout the 1942 book *He's in the Armored Force Now*, by Gillie.

47 George S. Patton service summary at: https://en.wikipedia.org/wiki/Service_summary_of_George_S._Patton.

48 James A. Sawicki, *Tank Battalions of the U.S. Army* (Dumfries, Virginia: Wyvern Publications, 1983), 331. Redesignation was 8 May 1941. Five new GHQ units were activated on 30 May 1941: the 752nd and 756th went to Fort Lewis; the 759th to Camp Bliss, the 754th to Pine Camp, NY; and the 757th to Fort Ord. "Fort Knox Gets $298,430 For Shops," *The Courier-Journal* (Louisville, Kentucky), 30 May 1941, 4.

49 Born 1894, according to his grave marker at Arlington National Cemetery (www.findagrave.com).

50 United States Army, *Official U.S. Army Register* (Washington, D.C.: War Department, The Adjutant General's Office, United States Government Printing Office, 1943), 554; *Army Register 1941*, 529; lists him as a Purple Heart recipient.

51 Edwin B. Olson, phone conversation, 9 January 2009.

52 Wilkinson, "The Way It All Started," 3.

53 "Col MacLaughlin Dies in Hospital" *The Evening Sun* (Hanover, Pennsylvania), 8 July 1964, 23–24.

54 "Harry W. Sweeting" was his official name. Sweeting graduated from the United States Military Academy (USMA) at West Point, New York, in 1933.

55 Original 756th roster for B Company; Lewis personal papers, *Army Register 1943*, 866; Sweeting was born in Oregon but his family moved to New York in his infancy according to his obituary "Harry W. Sweeting, 1933" written by Lyle W. Bernard at https://www.westpointaog.org/memorials.

56 Wilkinson, "The Way It All Started," 3.

57 This date is from Lewis's undated autobiography.

58 Wilkinson, letter to Redle dated 29 January 2001.

59 Wilkinson, "The Way It All Started," 3.

Chapter 2

1 *Fort Lewis Sentinel*, Vol 1, No. 2, 1941, 3. These were numbers given for a troop review held on 9 May 1941.

2 Ibid., 13.

3 Sawicki, *Tank Battalions of the U.S. Army*, 327; Lewis personal papers; "Tanks Arrive," *Spokane Chronicle* (Spokane, Washington), 3 June 1941, 2: The 752nd was formed with thirteen officers and 489 men, while the 756th (L) was formed with thirteen officers and 326 men.

4 Lemons, *Organization and Markings*, 152–154. As with the 756th, the 752nd did not receive their full T/O complement of tanks until early 1942. Only these three tank battalions are listed as stationed at Fort Lewis in 1941.

5 B Company, 756th Tank Battalion, Morning Reports, June 1941. WWII U.S. Army Morning Reports were daily reports filed by each company documenting basic activities and any changes of duty status to its members. The reports are preserved on microfilm at the National Personnel Records Center in St Louis, Missouri (https://www.archives.gov/st-louis).

6 David D. Redle interview, 13 March 2004; Arthur Richter, "Arthur F. Richter Experience in WWII" memoirs, 2007.

7 Arthur Richter letter, 12 January 2007, and memoirs; Wilkinson letter, 18 April 2005.

8 Wilkinson letter, 18 April 2005.

9 Wilkinson, "The Way It All Started," 4; B Co/756th Morning Reports, June 1941.

10 B Co/756th Morning Reports record Wilkinson joined on 10 June 1942.

11 B Co/756th Morning Reports, July 1942.

12 Michael Thompson (son of Morris B. Thompson) phone conversation, 5 October 2019.

13 Wilkinson, "The Way It All Started," 4; B Co/756th, Morning Reports, June 1941.

14 Richter e-mail, 12 June 2009.

15 Redle letter, 28 June 2009.

16 Wilkinson "The Way It All Started," 4; B Co/756th, Morning Reports, 24 June 1941; Richter letter, 12 January 2007; Richter memoirs; Richter e-mail, 12 June 2009.

17 B Co/756th Morning Reports, June 1941.

18 Ibid.; Lewis undated autobiography.

19 B Co/756th Morning Reports, June 1941, lists these two officers as "2nd Lts Packwood and Stucky atchd and jd" on 17 June. The B Co/756th Morning Reports, July 1941 records both transferred out on 19 July.

20 Redle letter, 7 June 2001.

21 B Co/756th Morning Reports, July 1941, entry for the 28th.

22 The Table of Organization allowed for five company officers: a captain, a first lieutenant (executive officer) and three second lieutenants (platoon leaders).

23 Wilkinson, "The Way It All Started," 4.

24 Lee Mudd, "History of the 756th Tank Battalion and the Development of the Tank-Infantry Team in World War II" (Thesis, Johns Hopkins University, 2000), 10: Mudd's source was French Lewis; Lewis personal papers.

25 Richter memoirs, and letter, 12 January 2007.

26 Lewis personal papers.

27 Mudd, "History 756th," 10.

28 The "H-tanks" were alternatively nicknamed "M2 by fours," Ralph Donley letter, 8 March 2005.

29 Lewis personal papers.

30 Richter memoirs, and letter, 12 January 2007.

31 Lewis personal papers.

32 Colonel Anthony F. Daskevich II, "Insights into Modularity 753rd Tank Battalion in World War II" (USAWC Strategy Research Project, U.S. Army War College, Carlisle Barracks, PA, March 2008), 4.

33 Redle letter, 2 March 2001.

34 Donald G. Taggart, *The History of the Third Infantry Division in World War II* (1946; reprint, Nashville, Tennessee: The Battery Press, 1987), 4.

35 Lewis personal papers (early 1990s notes for Fazendin book); Mudd, "History 756th," 10; Estimation on time. All vehicles listed were acquired by September.

36 Wilkinson "The Way It All Started," 4: Wilkinson describes a mix of M1 and M2 tanks. By this time, the troops called either model an M1.

37 Zaloga, *M3 & M5 Stuart Light Tank*, 40.

38 Steven J. Zaloga. *Early US Armor, Tanks 1916–40* (Oxford, UK: Osprey Publishing, 2017), 30–38.

39 Redle "B Company History" (38 pages) handwritten for the author and presented at our interview on 13 March 2004, 1.

40 The M1s could go as fast as 70 MPH under the right conditions according to Redle in an interview, 13 March 2004.

41   Redle "B Company History," 6.

42   The tankers consistently used the nickname "peep" during the war. To avoid confusing the modern reader, the author has adopted the more commonly-known "jeep" throughout the work.

43   Wilkinson ,"The Way It All Started," 4.

44   Nigel Askey, "Operation Barbarossa," "German Deployment Overview Fast-Facts" http://www.operation-barbarossa.net/german-forces-operation-barbarossa-june-july-1941/.

45   Zaloga, *M3 & M5 Stuart Light Tank*, 9.

46   Jonathan Forty, *Tanks in Detail: M3-M3A1-M3A3 Stuart I-V* (Surrey, UK: Ian Allan Publishing, Ltd., 2002), 12, 35.

47   Zaloga, *M3 Lee/Grant Medium Tank*, 14; "Tanks in Volume Production at Detroit" *Battle Creek Enquirer* (Battle Creek, Michigan), 28 August 1941, 20.

48   "The Washington Merry-Go-Round" *Poughkeepsie Journal* (Poughkeepsie, New York), 20 Aug 1941, 6.

49   "B&C" school was for "bakers and cooks."

50   B Co/756th Morning Reports, September 1941: various reports and lists.

51   HQ Co/756th Morning Reports, July 1941, entry for the 19th; Lewis personal papers and autobiography.

52   B Co/756th Morning Reports, August 1941, entry for the 24th.

53   Ibid., September 1941, entry for the 3rd, these men returned on the 20th.

54   HQ Co/756th Morning Reports, August 1941.

55   *Army Register 1945*, 662: Moon was born in Alabama in 1899 and graduated from the USMA in 1924.

56   Wilkinson, "The Way It All Started," 4. Although Wilkinson does not specify the battalion, only two were sent to the Philippines in early September: the 192nd and the 194th. It's reasonable to assume the 194th put out the officer request as the 194th was stationed at Fort Lewis.

57   Ibid.: Both officers were captured by the Japanese when the Philippines fell. Wilkinson believes both survived the war.

58   Ibid.

59   Forty, *U.S. Army Handbook*, 5.

60   Ibid. United States population at the time was 132 million.

61   B Co/756th Morning Reports, 2 October 1941.

62   B Co/756th Morning Reports, 20 October 1941; Lewis personal papers.

63   B Co/756th Morning Reports, 28 October 1941; HQ Co/756th Morning Reports, 24 October 1941. Lewis transferred back to HQ Company four days prior on the 28th.

64   Redle letter, 29 April 2003.

65   "Tank Battle Slated for Fort Lewis" *Statesman Journal* (Salem, Oregon), 21 October 1941, 1, 3.

66   "Maneuvers for Tank Troops" *The Capital Journal* (Salem, Oregon), 11 November 1941, 12.

67   Taggart, *Third Infantry Division*, 4.

68   Redle "B Company History," 6; Redle letter, 2 April 2000.

69   Taggart, *Third Infantry Division*, 4.

70   Redle "B Company History," 6.

71   B Co/756th Morning Reports, 13 November 1941; Lewis personal papers.

72   B Co/756th Morning Reports, 13 November 1941.

73   "Fort Lewis," *Statesman Journal* (Salem, Oregon), 2 December 1941, 12.

74   Charles M. Wilkinson began a personal diary on 7 December 1941, perhaps anticipating that he might serve a small part in history. He was right, and this book would not have been possible without his highly detailed notes and observations; Texas A&M 1941 seasonal football record at: https://www.sports-reference.com/cfb/schools/texas-am/1941-schedule.html.

75   Lewis, personal papers.

76   Wilkinson, "The Way it All Started," 5.

77   HQ Co/756th Morning Reports, 15 November 1941 and 9 December 1941. The Morning Reports do not specify if he suffered from illness or injury.

78   Redle, "B Company History," 2.

79   Lewis, personal papers.

80   Redle, "B Company History," 2.

81   Donley letter, 8 March 2005.

82   Wilkinson diary, 7 December 1941.

83   B Co/756th Morning Reports, 7 December 1941.

84   Donley letter, 8 March 2005.

85   Donley letter, 3 May 2008.

86   Redle, "B Company History," 3.

87   Wilkinson diary, 8 December 1941; HQ Co/756th Morning Reports, 8 December 1941.

88   Edwin B. Olson letter, 18 December 2006.

89   Morning Reports, HQ Co/756th, 15 November 1941 and 9 December 1941.

90   Speculative, however, the Morning Reports record MacLaughlin was in the hospital from 15 November to 9 December 1941 and had recently travelled to Georgia and California: Morning Reports, HQ Co/756th, 1, 4, and 9 November 1941.

91   Wilkinson diary, 10 December 1941.

92   Wilkinson, "The Way It All Started," 5.

93   HQ Co/756th Morning Reports, 11 December 1941.

94   Wilkinson diary, 11 December 1941.

95   Lewis, personal papers: Lewis recalls there were no casualties; but Redle says Jones eventually lost an arm: Redle "B Company History," 5.

96   Wilkinson diary, 11 December 1941: Wilkinson reports Jones's arm was broken. Interestingly, the B Company Morning Reports for December 1941 record that Jones reported back for duty on 16 December after being hospitalized since the 11th.

97   HQ Co/756th Morning Reports, 4 November 1941.

98   Roger A. Fazendin obituary.

99   HQ Co/756th Morning Reports, 11 December 1941.

100   Redle, "B Company History," 5; Lewis, personal papers.

101   Lewis, personal papers.

102   Ibid.

103   Fazendin, *756th at Cassino*, xx.

104   Wilkinson diary, 11 December 1941; Lewis personal papers.

105   Redle, "B Company History," 5.

106   Lewis, personal papers.

107   Wilkinson diary, 12 December 1941; Lewis, personal papers.

108   Lewis, personal papers.

109   Wilkinson diary, 13 December 1941.

110   Ibid., The others in Wilkinson's tank were Cpl Hickey (regular Army) and Pvt Hurlacker.

111   Redle phone conversation, November 2001; Richter interview, 13 February 2002.

112   Wilkinson, "The Way It All Started," 5.

113   Ibid.

Chapter 3

1   HQ Co/756th Morning Reports, 13 December 1941; B Co/756th Morning Reports, 13 December 1941.

2   Mudd, "History 756th," 12, citing Redle interview.

3   Wilkinson, "The Way It All Started," 5: Wilkinson specifically recalls picking up Dolvin after the Montesano incident and before becoming battalion liaison officer; The Morning Report for HQ Company, 3 Nov 1941, shows Dolvin was assigned first to the battalion. However, no entry records his arrival. The next reference for Dolvin has him assigned to B Company on 5 January 1941. It's likely that Dolvin was assigned to the 756th but did not physically arrive until Wilkinson picked him up on this later date.

4   Wilkinson, "The Way It All Started, 5; *Army Register 1945*, 255.

5   James B. Knapp, ed., *Howitzer* (West Point, NY: United States Corps of Cadets, 1939), 151.

6   HQ Co/756th Morning Reports, 17 December 1941.

7   Wilkinson diary, 16 December 1941.

8   B Co/756th Morning Reports, 22 December 1944.

9   Wilkinson diary, 18 December 1941.

10   Ibid., 23 December 1941.

11   Ibid.

12   "American Tank Output Raised" *Arizona Republic* (Phoenix, Arizona), 15 December 1941, 4.

13   Forty, *Tanks in Detail: M3-M3A1-M3A3 Stuart I-V*, 16.

14   Mudd, "History 756th," 12.

15   Forty, *Tanks in detail: M3-M3A1-M3A3 Stuart I-V,*16; SCR-210 radio (receiver) in all tanks and an SCR-245 (transmitter) in the command tanks.

16   Wilkinson diary, 24 December 1941.

17   Ibid.

18   Ibid.; 19 December 1941.

19   Lewis, personal papers; B Co/756th Morning Reports, 24 December 1941; Richter memoirs 2007.

20   Redle, "B Company History," 8.

21   Wilkinson diary, 24 December 1941.

22   Wilkinson's diary entries for 24 and 25 December shows Charles in an unusually somber and fatalistic mood with these two short comments: "Will it be the last?" (Regarding Christmas for himself) and "How many of us will not celebrate next Christmas?"

23   Wilkinson diary, 25 December 1941. The girl's name was Jean.

24   B Co/756th Morning Reports, 27 December 1941: Five tanks, several trucks, forty-three EMs, and two officers were involved.

25   Wilkinson diary, 1 January 1942.

26   Ibid., 30 December 1941.

27   Ibid., 31 December 1941: Wilkinson's figures.

28   Wilkinson diary, 26 and 31 December 1941.

29   194th Tk Bn (L) was in Washington State and the 757th Tk Bn (L) was at Fort Ord at this time according to Sawicki, *Tank Battalions of the U.S. Army*. Author cannot find evidence of any other light tank battalion on the West Coast during this time.

30   Wilkinson diary, 31 December 1941 and 1 January 1942.

31   Wilkinson diary, 2 January 1942.

32   HQ Co/756th Morning Reports, 3 January 1942; Wilkinson diary, 3 January 1942.

33   HQ Co/756th Morning Reports, 6 January 1942; B Co/756th Morning Reports, 6 January 1942.

34   Wilkinson diary, 3 January 1942: Wilkinson comments: "I don't know who was responsible for it, but I am grateful to whoever it was."

35   Wilkinson diary, 5 January 1942.

36   Mudd, "History 756th," 11.

37   Wilkinson diary, 6, 7, and 8 January 1942.

38   Ibid., 8 January 1942.

39   Ibid., 12 January 1942.

40   Ibid., 13 and15 January 1942: the two other officers involved in the landings were 1st Lt Oscar Long of A Company and 1st Lt Edwin Arnold of C Company. Wilkinson does not specify that the landings were coordinated with the 3rd Inf Div, but it's all but certain they were.

41   Wilkinson, "The Way It All Started," 5; Wilkinson diary, 16 January 1942.

42   Wilkinson diary, 18 January 1942.

43   Wilkinson, "The Way It All Started," 5. Wilkinson does not list Adlard in his memoirs, but the B Co/756th Morning Reports from January and March 1942 list him as the fifth NCO sent on these exercises.

44   Wilkinson diary, 20 January 1942.

45   Wilkinson, "The Way It All Started," 5.

46   Ibid.

47   Wilkinson diary, 21 January 1942.

48   B Co/756th Morning Reports, January 1942, 21 entry, and March 1942 records Wilkinson's 1st Platoon was attached to the 2nd Bn/7th Inf Regt landing team, However, Taggart, *Third Infantry Division*, 5, claims it was 1st Bn landing team. The twenty-five 1st Platoon men sent were Lt Wilkinson; S/Sgt Crawford; Sgts Haspel, Reid, and McFadden; Cpl Adlard; Pfcs Blackwell, Crabtree, H. A. Jones, Kilgore, Campbell, and

Colley; Pvts Sprattler, L. Wright, Burstein, Ravetto, Avettant, Cogdill, Henderson, Jarvis, Kelleher, Shew, Rickerson, Laliberty, and Ware. Some of these men were kitchen staff.

49   Wilkinson, "The Way It All Started," 6.

50   Wilkinson diary, 25 and 28 January 1942.

51   Wilkinson, "The Way It All Started," 6.

52   Wilkinson diary, 3 February 1942. Lighters were small boats used to transfer supplies and equipment from shore out to ships moored in the harbor.

53   Wilkinson, "The Way It All Started," 6.

54   Ibid.

55   Wilkinson diary, 30 January 1942.

56   Redle "B Company History," 7.

57   Richter, e-mail 12 June 2009.

58   Wilkinson diary, 31 January–4 February 1942.

59   Wilkinson's notes are unclear as to whether the *Zeilin* or another ship participated; Richter e-mail, 12 June 2009.

60   Redle, "B Company History,"10–11.

61   Wilkinson, "The Way It All Started," 6.

62   Ibid.

63   Wilkinson diary, 5 February 1942.

64   Wilkinson, "The Way It All Started," 6.

65   Ibid.; According to Yeide, *The Infantry's Armor*, 11, Company A of the 70th Tk Bn participated in secret amphibious landings with the 1st Inf Div on the United States East Coast during the summer of 1941. Wilkinson's diary entry for 2 February 1942 records: "Got a new battalion commander today, Major Salzman, who witnessed the First Division landings on the East Coast." Clearly, Wilkinson heard of these East Coast landings while in San Diego but might not have known all the details, or he simply forgot about the episode when he wrote his memoirs later. It is true, however, that the 756th participated in the very first army amphibious landings on the United States West Coast.

66   Mudd, "History 756th," 12.

67   Wilkinson diary, 6 February 1942. Wilkinson identifies the man as "H inf"—probably meaning an H Company member (H Company was the "heavy weapons" company of the 2nd Bn, 7th Inf Regt.)

68   Wilkinson, "The Way It All Started," 7.

69   Wilkinson diary, 8 February 1942.

70   Wilkinson, "The Way It All Started," 7.

71   Ibid.

72   In his diary entry for 12 February 1942, Wilkinson records the man's name as "Lieutenant Drews." He does not say how he was killed, only that death resulted from a "surfboat accident."

73   Ibid.

74   Wilkinson diary, 9 February 1942.

75   Wilkinson identifies him as "Col Wolfe." In the book by Nathan W. White, *From Fedala to Berchtesgaden: A History of the Seventh United States Infantry in WWII* (Providence, RI: Bickford Engraving & Electrotype Co., 1947), Lt Col Peter T. Wolfe is identified as the 7th Inf Regt commander at the time on page xx.

76   Wilkinson, "The Way It All Started," 7.

77   Ibid., 8.

78   B Co/756th Morning Reports, February 1941; HQ Co/756th of the 756th also participated.

79   Taggart, *Third Infantry Division*, 5.

80   Wilkinson diary, 19 February 1942.

81   Ibid., 23 February 1942.

82   Ibid., 25 February 1942.

83   Ibid., 24 February 1942. Grousers were traction attachments mounted to the outside of each tread link to create a wider track.

84   Ibid., 26 February–1 March 1942.

85   Ibid., 2 March 1942.

86   Ibid., 4 March 1942.

87   Ibid., 6 March 1942.
88   Ibid., 16 March 1942.
89   Ibid., 17 and 18 March 1942.
90   Wilkinson, "The Way It All Started," 9.
91   Wilkinson diary, 19 March 1942; Richter memoirs 2007.
92   Redle, "B Company History," 7: Redle originally identified Terry as putting Thompson under guard but Terry was not aboard. The officer had to be Wilkinson. Redle also thought the distressed man was Morris B. Thompson, but the Morning Reports show Thompson was not sent with Wilkinson's platoon at the time but remained at Fort Lewis. The true identity of the seasick man remains a mystery.
93   Wilkinson diary, 21 March 1942.
94   Wilkinson, "The Way It All Started," 9.
95   Wilkinson diary, 24 February 1942.
96   Wilkinson, "The Way It All Started," 9.
97   HQ Co/756th Morning Reports, January 1942.
98   Ibid.
99   B Co/756th Morning Reports, 25 March 1942.
100 Wilkinson letter, 31 May 2005.
101 Ibid. Hogan was born 10 September 1908 according to his IDPF.
102 Clyde Guild interview, 15 September 2006.
103 Redle letter, 28 June 2008; B Co/756th Morning Reports, 25 March 1942.
104 Redle letter, 28 June 2008; B Co/756th Morning Reports, 28 June 1941, shows both Lewis and Blackwell were appointed sergeants on the same day. Duties were not listed.
105 Redle, "B Company History," 9.
106 Wilkinson diary, 25 March 1942.
107 Ibid., 26 and 27 March 1942.
108 Ibid., 28 March 1942.
109 Wilkinson diary, 1 and 2 April 1942.
110 Ibid., 3 April 1942.
111 Ibid., 10 and 11 April 1942.
112 Ibid., 13 April 1942.
113 Ibid., 18 April 1942.
114 Ibid., 15 April 1942.
115 Ibid., 14 April 1942.
116 Ibid., 20 April 1942.
117 Ibid., 21 April 1942.
118 Ibid., 16 April 1942.
119 Ibid., 22 April 1942.
120 Ibid., 23 April 1942.
121 B Co/756th Morning Reports, 24 April 1942.
122 Wilkinson diary, 26 April 1942.
123 Taggart, Third Infantry Division, 6.
124 Wilkinson, "The Way It All Started," 9.
125 Wilkinson diary, 27 April 1942.
126 Ibid., 28 April 1942.
127 Ibid., 25 April 1942.
128 Wilkinson, "The Way It All Started," 10; HQ Co/756th Morning Reports, August 1942.
129 Wilkinson diary, 30 April 1942.

Chapter 4

1   Wilkinson diary, 1, 2, and 3 May 1942; Departed 1 May and arrived 3 May—a Sunday.
2   Ibid., 4 May 1942.

3   Redle letter, 25 January 2004.

4   Wilkinson diary, 5 May 1942.

5   Ibid., 6 May 1942.

6   Ibid., 7 May 1942.

7   Wilkinson, "The Way It All Started," 10.

8   Ibid.

9   Ibid.

10   Wilkinson diary, 11 May 1942.

11   Randolph Perdue phone conversation, 31 January 2004.

12   The 107th Cavalry Regiment was originally part of the Ohio National Guard prior to federalization; "History of the 107th Mechanized Cavalry" at https://www.107thmechcavsqd.com/history-of-the-107th-mechanized-cavalry/; According to Stanton, *Order of Battle US Army*, 317, after federalizing in March 1941, this unit relocated to Fort Ord, California on 24 December 1941,and was re-designated later as the 107th Cavalry Group and the 22nd and 107th Cavalry Recon Squadrons.

13   Wilkinson, "The Way It All Started," 11, Wilkinson writes he encountered Crandall again later at Oflag 64. This man was likely Maj Robert W. Crandall, USMA Class of 1939, who escaped captivity in early 1945 and was later killed in action in Italy on 25 April 1945 while commanding a battalion in the 473rd Inf Regt, 92nd Inf Div.

14   Wilkinson diary, 12 May 1942.

15   Wilkinson, "The Way It All Started," 11; Wilkinson diary, 16 May 1942: This ride took place on Saturday, May 16.

16   Unable to develop any further history on this unit.

17   Wilkinson diary, 13 and 14 May 1942.

18   Ibid., 21 May 1942.

19   First name is unknown. The Morning Reports at this time were handwritten and did not include first names.

20   Wilkinson, "The Way It All Started," 10. A clear reference is not provided in the Morning Reports. For security reasons, the incident may not have been recorded.

21   B Co/756th Morning Reports, 18 May 1942.

22   Ibid., 23 May 1942.

23   Wilkinson, "The Way It All Started," 10; B Co/756th Morning Reports, 26 May 1942.

24   Wilkinson diary, 25 May 1942.

25   Ibid., 26 May 1942.

26   Ibid., 1 & 2 June 1942.

27   The American high command knew the destination was Midway, as the Japanese naval code had secretly been broken.

28   Taggart, *Third Infantry Division*, 6.

29   Wilkinson, "The Way It All Started," 11; Wilkinson diary, 4 June 1942.

30   Wilkinson, "The Way It All Started," 11; Wilkinson diary, 9 and 11 June 1942.

31   Wilkinson diary, 13 June 1942.

32   Ibid., 23 June 1942.

33   Ibid., 18 June 1942.

34   Ibid., 9 June 1942.

35   HQ Co/756th Morning Reports; 6 June 1942.

36   HQ Co/756th Morning Reports, March–June 1942. Sweeting consistently ran the training exercises.

37   Wilkinson diary, 16 June 1942.

38   Ibid., 24 June 1942.

39   B Co/756th Morning Reports, June 1942.

40   Ibid., July 1942.

41   Wilkinson diary, 10 July 1942.

42   Ibid., 21 June 1942.

43   Ibid., 17 June 1942.

44   Ibid., 25 June 1942.

45   HQ Co/756th Morning Reports, August 1942.

46   HQ Co/756th Morning Reports, 1 August 1942. One of the original B Company platoon sergeants—S/Sgt Shields—also transferred to the 743rd Tk Bn (B Co/756th Morning Reports, 8 Aug 1942). According to Redle, (letter 28 June 2009), Shields relished the role of comedian and would entertain others by removing his false teeth, putting a pipe in his mouth, and doing Popeye impressions.

47   "West Point Graduate," *The Wilkes-Barre Record* (Wilkes-Barre, Pennsylvania), 8 June 1933, 24.

48   Tom Treanor, *One Damn Thing After Another* (Garden City, NY: Doubleday, Doran & Company, Inc.), 1944. 258–59; Bernard, "Harry W. Sweeting" memorial; "West Point Graduate," *The Wilkes-Barre Record* (Wilkes-Barre, Pennsylvania), 8 June 1933, 24.

49   S. E. Otto, Ed., *Howitzer* (West Point, NY: United States Corps of Cadets, 1933), 228.

50   Bernard, "Harry W. Sweeting" memorial; "3 Shore Officer Assigned to Posts," *Asbury Park Press* (Asbury Park, New Jersey), 10 August 1933, 1.

51   "Army Post News" *The Baltimore Sun* (Baltimore, Maryland), 25 June 1939, 62; Bernard, "Harry W. Sweeting" memorial.

52   HQ Co/756th Morning Reports, 21 July 1942.

53   Wilkinson, "The Way It All Started," 11.

54   Wilkinson diary, 8–10 August 1942.

55   Ibid., 4 August 1942.

56   "C. M. Wilkinson" (father) obituary, *The Odessa American* (Odessa, Texas), 29 January 1976, 2.

57   Wilkinson diary, 11 August 1942.

58   Ibid., 12 August 1942.

59   Ibid., 14 and 15 August 1942.

60   Ibid., 17 August 1942.

61   Redle "B Company History," 10.

62   Taggart, *Third Infantry Division,* 7; the other two 756th companies are presumed to have participated.

63   Redle "B Company History," 10. Redle letter, 24 June 2002.

64   Redle "B Company History," 10.

65   Taggart, *Third Infantry Division,* 7.

66   Wilkinson diary, 18 August 1942.

67   Taggart, *Third Infantry Division,* 7.

68   Wilkinson diary, 19 August 1942.

69   Redle, "B Company History," 11.

70   Wilkinson, "The Way It All Started," 11.

71   Redle interview, 13 March 2004; Redle letter, 28 June 2009. According to Redle, Shields had been assigned to help protect the American embassy in China at the time and had also witnessed similar Japanese atrocities.

72   Wilkinson diary, 20 August 1942.

73   Ibid., 25 August 1942.

74   Ibid., 24 August 1942.

75   Wilkinson, "The Way It All Started," 11.

76   Wilkinson diary, 28 August 1942.

77   A "problem" was a training exercise designed to mimic wartime conditions according to 2nd Lt Anthony F. Melfi's letter to his wife dated 4 May 1941.

78   Wilkinson diary, 29 August 1942.

79   Ibid., 31 August 1942.

80   Ibid., 1 and 2 September 1942.

81   Ibid., 2 September 1942. (Author's quotes, not Wilkinson's descriptions)

82   Ibid., 3 September 1942.

83   Ibid., 4 September 1942; B Co/756th Morning Reports, August 1942.

84   Wilkinson diary, 5 September 1942.

85   Ibid., 7 September 1942.

86   Wilkinson, "The Way It All Started," 12.

87   Ibid.

88   Wilkinson diary, 10 September 1942.

89   Ibid., 11 September 1942.

90   Ibid., 13 September 1942.
91   Ibid., 12 September 1942.
92   Ibid., 14 September 1942.
93   Wilkinson, "The Way It All Started," 12.
94   Wilkinson diary, 15 September 1942.
95   B Co/756th Morning Reports, August & September 1942; Redle "B Company History," 13.
96   Wilkinson diary, 21 September 1942.
97   Taggart, *Third Infantry Division*, 8.
98   Redle letter, 25 January 2004.
99   Wilkinson, "The Way It All Started," 12.
100 Wilkinson diary, 22 September 1942.
101 Ibid., 23 September 1942.
102 Redle, "B Company History," 12.
103 Wilkinson diary, 24 September 1942.
104 Ibid., 26 September 1942.
105 Ibid., 2 October 1942.
106 Verlag J. Vollert, *Tankograd Technical Manual Series No 6013: U.S. WWII M5 & M5A1 Stuart Light Tanks*, translated and edited by Michael Franz (Erlangen, Germany: Tankograd Publishing, 2008), 4; Zaloga, *M3 & M5 Stuart Light Tank*, 29.
107 Redle, "B Company History," 13. Redle interview, 19 January 2002.
108 Redle interview, 19 January 2002.
109 Taggart, *Third Infantry Division*, 8; Rupert Prohme, *History of the 30th Infantry Regiment World War II* (Washington, D.C.: Infantry Journal Press, 1947), 12.
110 Wilkinson diary, 4 October 1942.
111 Redle, "B Company History," 13.
112 Lewis, personal papers.
113 Wilkinson, "The Way It All Started," 12.
114 Wilkinson diary, 14 October 1942.
115 Ibid., 21 October 1942.
116 Ibid., 16 and 17 October 1942.
117 Wilkinson, "The Way It All Started," 12.
118 Wilkinson diary, 10 November 1942.
119 Redle letter, 24 June 2002.
120 Wilkinson diary, 22 October 1942.
121 Ibid., 23 October and 6 November 1942.
122 Ibid., 10 November 1942.
123 Ibid., 24 October, 13 and 21 November 1942.
124 Ibid., 21 November 1942.
125 Ibid., 3 November 1942.
126 Ibid., 28 and 29 October 1942.
127 Ibid., 13 November 1942. This man, a Pvt Johnson, was transferred to Service Company according to the B Co/756th Morning Reports, 13 November 1942.
128 Wilkinson, "The Way It All Started," 12.
129 Redle letter, 25 January 2004.
130 B Co/756th Morning Reports, 12 November 1942; Wilkinson diary, 9 November 1942; Redle "B Company History," 13. Redle gives Shaw's first name as "Ralph."
131 Redle interview, 16 September 2009.
132 Wilkinson diary, 9 November 1942.
133 Ibid., 14 and 16 November 1942.
134 Ibid., 15 November 1942.
135 B Co/756th Morning Reports, 24 November 1942.
136 Wilkinson diary, 22 November 1942.
137 Ibid., 20 November 1942.

138   Ibid., 27 November 1942; B Co/756th Morning Reports, 27 November 1942.
139   Wilkinson diary, 25 November 1942.
140   Ibid., 28 November 1942.
141   Wilkinson, "The Way It All Started," 13.
142   Wilkinson diary, 29 and 30 November 1942.
143   Ibid., 6 December 1942. First name unknown. Morning Reports did not record first names until mid-1943.
144   Wilkinson, "The Way It All Started," 13.
145   Wilkinson diary, 7 December 1942; B Co/756th Morning Reports, 7 December 1942. Pfc Migliardto and Pvt Saldonis were the accused. Saldonis was arrested on 2 December. Migliardto argued with Shaw but it is unclear exactly why Saldonis was also charged.
146   B Co/756th Morning Reports, 9 December 1942. Migliardto was reduced to Pvt and sent to the stockade. Saldonis returned to duty on 9 December.
147   B Co/756th Morning Reports, 15 December 1942; Wilkinson diary, 10 December 1942.
148   Wilkinson diary, 10 December 1942.
149   Ibid., 2 December 1942.
150   Ibid., 3 and 4 December 1942.
151   Ibid., 11 December 1942.
152   Roy Anderson, phone conversations, 15 May 2003 and 20 June 2009; 756th Association notes to 19–21 September 2002 reunion at Fort Knox, Anderson interview.
153   B Co/756th Morning Reports, 13 January 1943.
154   Wilkinson, "The Way It All Started," 13.
155   Wilkinson diary, 13 January 1943.
156   Ibid.

Chapter 5

1   Wilkinson diary, 14 January 1943.
2   Wilkinson lists Sarno, Alderman, Schmidt, Kremer, Starr, and Holmlund as the six 756th officers in his diary.
3   Wilkinson diary, 15 January 1943.
4   Ibid., 16 and 17 January 1943.
5   B Co/756th Morning Reports, 16 January 1943.
6   Ibid., 14 January 1943.
7   Wilkinson diary, 17 January 1943.
8   Ralph Donley (HQ Co) diary entries from this time period.
9   Ibid.
10   Wilkinson diary, 19 January 1943.
11   Ibid., 18 January 1943.
12   Ibid., 18 and 24 January 1943.
13   Ibid., 24 January 1943.
14   Wilkinson "The Way It All Started," 13.
15   Ibid.
16   Wilkinson diary, 20 and 21 January 1943.
17   B Co/756th Morning Reports, 22 January 1943.
18   Wilkinson diary, 22 January 1943.
19   Ibid., 23 January 1943.
20   Donley diary, 25 January 1943.
21   Ibid.
22   Sadowski's grade as listed in B Co/756th Morning Reports, 25 October 1942; Tirpak's grade as listed in B Co/756th Morning Reports, 2 September 1942.
23   Redle interview, 13 March 2004; Purdue phone conversation, 31 January 2004.
24   Alfreda Sadowski, widow to Ed Sadowski, phone conversation, 25 January 2001 and 12 May 2003; Redle letter, 5 October 2000; Redle interview, 13 March 2004.

25   Wilkinson, "The Way It All Started," 13.
26   B Co/756th Morning Reports, 25 January 1943.
27   Ibid.
28   Wilkinson, "The Way It All Started," 14; Wilkinson diary, 25 January 1943; B Co/756th Morning Reports, 26 January 1943.
29   Donley diary, 26 January 1943.
30   Ibid.
31   B Co/756th Morning Reports, 26 January 1943.
32   Wilkinson, "The Way It All Started," 14.
33   Redle, "B Company History," 15.
34   1930 Census obtained through www.ancestry.com; Warren D. Barton, ed., *Longhorn* (College Station, TX: Texas A&M College, 1939), 65; Francis Ellis (sister to Edwin Y. Arnold), "Holiday Greeting Share Memories, Update Current Events" column, *The Paris News* (Paris, Texas), 12 January 1997, 21.
35   A Co/756th Morning Reports, 8 November 1942.
36   Wilkinson diary, 26 January 1943.
37   C Co/756th Morning Reports, 8 November 1942. 1st Lt Waldron was A Company commander at this time according to A Co/756th Morning Reports, November 1942.
38   Taggart, *Third Infantry Division*, 16–34.
39   C Co/756th Morning Reports, 11 November 1942.
40   A Co/756th Morning Reports, 11 November 1942.
41   Ibid., 10 November 1942; American Battlefield Monuments Commission WWII graves listing at http://www.abmc.gov/; "Soldier's Death Verified; Killed in North Africa," *The Cincinnati Enquirer* (Cincinnati, Ohio), 6 February 1943, 8.
42   A Co/756th Morning Reports, 11 November 1942; The casualty's name appears to be "Goldsberry."
43   Taggart, *Third Infantry Division*, 34.
44   C Co/756th Morning Reports, November 1942.
45   This motor wasn't part of an M5. These were separate generator engines.
46   Edwin B. Olson. Undated war recollections, early 2000s.
47   Olson "War Recollections;" Olson phone conversation 1 October 2007.
48   Olson phone conversation, 1 October 2007.
49   Donley diary, 11 February 2004.
50   Wilkinson diary, 3 February 1943.
51   Ibid., 28 and 29 January 1943.
52   Ibid., 27 January 1943.
53   Ibid., 28 January 1943.
54   Wilkinson, "The Way It All Started," 14.
55   Donley diary, 26 January 1943.
56   Ibid., 5 February 1943; Wilkinson diary, 26 January 1943.
57   Wilkinson diary, 27 January 1943.
58   B Co/756th Morning Reports, 29–31 January 1943.
59   Wilkinson diary, 27 January 1943.
60   Ibid., 30 January 1943.
61   B Co/756th Morning Reports, 29–31 January 1943.
62   Wilkinson diary, 31 January & 1 February 1943.
63   Ibid., 2 February 1943.
64   Redle, "B Company History," 15.
65   Wilkinson diary, 2 February 1943.
66   Donley diary, 4 February 1943.
67   Wilkinson diary, 29 January and 3 February 1943.
68   Ibid., 4 February 1943.
69   Wilkinson, "The Way It All Started," 14.
70   Wilkinson diary, 5 and 6 February 1943.
71   Wilkinson, "The Way It All Started," 14.

72 Wilkinson diary, 11 February 1943.
73 Ibid., 4 & 8 February 1943.
74 Ibid., 11 February 1943.
75 Donley diary, 12 February 1944; Wilkinson diary, 12 February 1943; B Co/756th Morning Reports, 12 February 43.
76 Wilkinson diary, 15–18 February 1943; B Co/756th Morning Reports, February 1943.
77 Wilkinson diary, 13 February 1943.
78 Ibid., 15 February 1943.
79 Ibid., 19 February 1943.
80 HQ Co/756th Morning Reports: 19 February 1943 was the date for Sweeting's promotion.
81 Wilkinson diary, 20 February 1943.
82 Ibid., 21 February 1943.
83 Ibid., 22 February 1943.
84 Ibid.
85 Donley diary, 21 February 1943.
86 Ibid., 23 February 1943.
87 Redle, "B Company History," 15.
88 "Sgt Pennington Overseas" *The Knoxville Journal* (Knoxville, Tennessee), 31 August 1943, 12.
89 Redle letter, 13 March 2004.
90 Donley diary, 23 February 1943; Redle, "B Company History," 15.
91 HQ Co/756th Morning Reports, 24 February 1943.
92 B Co/756th Morning Reports, March 1943; B Co/756th Morning Reports, 24 February 1943.
93 Wilkinson, "The Way It All Started," 14.
94 Wilkinson diary, 23 February 1943.

Chapter 6

1 Wilkinson diary, 23 and 24 February 1943.
2 Donley diary, specifically his post-war handwritten notations near his February 1943 entries.
3 Heinz Guderian, *Achtung - Panzer! The Development of Tank Warfare,* trans. Christopher Duffy (reprint and English Translation, London, UK, Orion Books, Ltd., 1992) 205–06.
4 Brig Gen T. J. Camp, *Tankers in Tunisia* (reprint, Honolulu, Hawaii: University Press of the Pacific, 2004), 24.
5 War Department Training Manuals: "Tank Platoon," FM 17-30, October 22, 1942 and "Tank Company," FM 17-32, 2 August 1942.
6 Redle, "B Company History," 21.
7 B Co/756th Morning Reports, 25 and 26 February 1943.
8 Redle, B Company History," 17.
9 B Co/756th Morning Reports, February 1943.
10 Redle, "B Company History," 17.
11 Wilkinson diary, 26 February 1943.
12 Redle, "B Company History," 22.
13 Donley diary, 26 February 1943.
14 Redle, "B Company History," 17.
15 Ibid.
16 Ibid.
17 Ibid.
18 Ibid.
19 B Co/756th Morning Reports, 27 and 28 February 1943.
20 Redle interview, 19 January 2002.
21 Ibid.
22 Fazendin, *756th at Cassino,* xxxiii.

23   Redle interview, 13 March 2004.
24   Redle interview, 19 January 2002.
25   Donley diary, 1 March 1943; Donley diary, 3 March 1943.
26   Wilkinson, "The Way It All Started," 14.
27   Donley diary, 4 March 1943.
28   Donley diary, 28 February 1943.
29   Redle letter, 5 October 2000.
30   Wilkinson letter, 31 May 2005.
31   Alfred Mancini phone conversation, 4 October 2000; Fazendin, *756th at Cassino*, 23.
32   Wilkinson diary, 7 March 1943.
33   Ibid., 7 and 12 March 1943. This occurred soon after the American disasters at Sidi Bou Zid and the Kasserine Pass. The 3rd Inf and 2nd Armored Divisions were tapped of some 3,400 replacements as a result of those losses. (Taggart, *Third Infantry Division*, 41–42)
34   Taggart, *Third Infantry Division*, 42.
35   Will Lang, "Lucian King Truscott, Jr." *Life* magazine, 2 October 1942, 98: His "rock-crushing" voice was the result of accidentally drinking carbonic acid as a toddler. The incident nearly killed him.
36   Redle, "B Company History," 20; Redle, "B Company Recollections."
37   Redle letter, 25 January 2004.
38   Rabat was the location of the 3rd Inf Div HQ according to Taggart, *Third Infantry Division*, 39.
39   Redle, "B Company History," 19–20.
40   Ibid.
41   Ibid., 20; Redle, "B Company Recollections," 2.
42   Redle, "B Company History," 20–21; Wilkinson diary, 13 March 1943; Wilkinson, "The Way It All Started," 14.
43   Redle, "B Company History," 21.
44   Wilkinson diary, 14 March (a Sunday) 1943.
45   Redle, "B Company Recollections."
46   Wilkinson "The Way It All Started," 14.
47   B Co/756th Morning Reports, 15 March 1943; Wilkinson diary, 14 March 1943.
48   Wilkinson, "The Way It All Started," 15.
49   Ibid.; Wilkinson diary, 11 March 1943.
50   Wilkinson diary, 14 March 1943.
51   Ibid., 15 March 1943.
52   According to the Morning Reports, the three battalion officers selected were Mandel, Rutledge, and Shaw. The B Company enlisted men chosen were Shind, Morris, Crabtree, Merchant, Stone, Addeo, Natalini, and also Migliorato.
53   Redle interview, 15 September 2006.
54   Wilkinson diary, 16 March 1943.
55   Taggart, *Third Infantry Division*, 42; The division's move began 15 March 1943.
56   Wilkinson diary, 21 March 1943; Olson phone conversation, 1 October 2007.
57   B Co/756th Morning Reports, 24 March 1943.
58   Redle, "B Company History," 22.
59   Wilkinson diary, 22 March 1943.
60   Ibid.
61   Wilkinson letter, 18 April 2005.
62   B Co/756th Morning Reports, 26 March 1943.
63   Ibid., 24 March 1943.
64   B Co/756th Morning Reports, 4 April 1943; Redle letter, 25 January 2004; According to Redle, Winlock commanded the 3rd Platoon at this time.
65   B Co/756th Morning Reports, 10 April 1943.
66   HQ Co/756th Morning Reports, 10 April 1943.
67   B Co/756th Morning Reports, 11 April 1943; One officer and nineteen enlisted men departed by motor convoy.

68 Donley diary, 8 and 11 April 1943.
69 B Co/756th Morning Reports, 11 April 1943.
70 Donley diary, 2 April 1943.
71 Redle, "B Company History," 24.
72 Donley, "Recollections," (5 pages), written for the author and dated 8 March 2005.
73 Redle, "B Company Recollections."
74 Donley diary, 13 April 1943.
75 B Co/756th Morning Reports, 4 April 1943.
76 Redle letter, 2 May 2002.
77 B Co/756th Morning Reports, 13 April 1943.
78 HQ Co/756th Morning Reports, 10–12 April 1943; The journey progressed as follows: HQ motor convoy left Port Lyautey at 0700 on 10 April and drove 191 miles to Taza—arriving at 1800. Weather was clear and roads were good. Departed the following day at 0800 and drove 139 miles to Oujda, Algeria, arriving at 1530. Weather was clear and warm. Left Oujda on 12 Apr at 0700 and arrived at St Leu at 1800 after driving 178 miles.
79 HQ Co/756th Morning Reports, 13 April 1943; HQ Co/756th Morning Reports, 14 April 1943.
80 Taggart, *Third Infantry Division*, 42.
81 Donley diary, 14 April 1943; Donley, "Recollections."
82 Fifth Army Invasion Training Center (FAITC), (National Archives, Army Records Group 407, box 2397): G-3 Reports, History, 1943 Training directive.
83 B Co/756th Morning Reports, 13–26 April 1943.
84 Redle, "B Company History," 22.
85 Ibid.
86 Donley diary, 17 April 1943.
87 Donley diary from the period.
88 Taggart, *Third Infantry Division*, 42.
89 White, *Fedala to Berchtesgaden*, 20.
90 Redle, "B Company History," 25.
91 Taggart, *Third Infantry Division*, 42.
92 Donley diary, 27 April 1943.
93 B Co/756th Morning Reports, 27 & 28 April 1943.
94 Ibid., 29 April 1943.
95 White, *Fedala to Berchtesgaden*, 20.
96 Donley diary, 27 April 1943.
97 Ibid., 1–5 May 1943.
98 Ibid., 1 May 1943.

Chapter 7

1 Wilkinson, "The Way It All Started," 15.
2 Ibid.
3 Sidney L. Loveless, ed., *Longhorn* (College Station, TX: Texas A&M College, 1938), 88.
4 Redle interview, 19 January 2002.
5 Wilkinson diary, 24 March 1943.
6 Ibid., 25 March 1943.
7 Ibid., 26 March 1943.
8 Wilkinson, "The Way It All Started," 15.
9 Ibid. Wilkinson diary, 30 March 1943.
10 Matthew Parker, *Monte Cassino: The Hardest-Fought Battle of World War II* (New York, NY: Doubleday, 2004), 63; Arrived in Northern Ireland in early 1942.
11 Wilkinson, "The Way It All Started," 15; *Army Register 1945*, 390: 1929 USMA graduate.
12 Wilkinson diary, 31 March 1943.

13 Ibid., 1 April 1943.

14 Wilkinson, "The Way It All Started," 15.

15 Ibid., 2 April 1943.

16 Ibid., 3 April 1943; Wilkinson diary entry for 8 June 1943 reports Major Langdon transferred from the 751st Tank Battalion to an infantry battalion in the 34th Infantry Division. Lt Col Wendell H. Langdon led the 1st Bn/168th Regiment and was seriously wounded in action on Monte Pantano on 30 November 1943.

17 Ibid., 4 April 1943; Wilkinson ascribes this quote to the French Marshal Lyautey, former colonel administrator of Morocco.

18 Rick Atkinson, *An Army at Dawn: The War in North Africa, 1942–43* (New York, NY: Henry Holt and Company, LLC., 2002), 363.

19 George F. Howe, *Old Ironsides: The Battle History of the 1st Armored Division* (Washington, D.C.: Combat Forces Press, 1957; reprint, Nashville, TN: The Battery Press, 1979), 134–38.

20 "Ami" was a nickname for an American used by German soldiers.

21 Atkinson, *Army at Dawn*, 343; Howe, *Old Ironsides*, 162–64.

22 Taggart, *Third Infantry Division*, 41.

23 Rudolf Böhmler, *Monte Cassino: A German View* (Maximilian Verlag GmbH & Co:1956; reprint, South Yorkshire UK: Pen and Sword Books, 2015), 136–37.

24 Richard F. Wilkinson, *The Breakthrough Battalion: Battles of Company C of the 133rd Infantry Regiment, Tunisia and Italy 1943–1945* (By the author, 2005), 23.

25 Members of the 34th Infantry Division, *The Story of the 34th Infantry Division: Louisiana to Pisa* (MTOUSA: Information and Education Section, 1945), 14.

26 Atkinson, *Army at Dawn*, 468.

27 George F. Howe, *United States Army in World War II Mediterranean Theater of Operations: North Africa: Seizing the Initiative in the West* (Washington, D.C.: Office of the Chief of Military History, Department of the Army, 1957), 578.

28 Lt Col John H. Hougen, *The Story of the Famous 34th Infantry Division* (1949; reprint, Nashville, TN: The Battery Press, 1979), "The First Fondouk" chapter (unnumbered pages); reports receiving artillery fire that "grew in intensity" "almost immediately" after attacking at 0630. However, no hostile fire for first four hours is recorded by Howe, *US Army in WWII Mediterranean*, 581.

29 Atkinson, *Army at Dawn*, 468.

30 Hougen, *34th Infantry Division*, "The First Fondouk"; Atkinson, *Army at Dawn*, 470.

31 Camp, *Tankers in Tunisia*, 54: Hammack account.

32 Atkinson, *Army at Dawn*, 470.

33 Hougen, *34th Infantry Division*, "The Second Fondouk."

34 Ibid.; Atkinson, *Army at Dawn*, 471–72.

35 Wilkinson diary, 5 April 1943.

36 Howe, *US Army in WWII Mediterranean*, 579.

37 Camp, *Tankers in Tunisia*, 54; Hammack account.

38 Ibid., 35.

39 Ibid., 24.

40 Ibid., 23, 41.

41 Donald B. McLean, editor, *Company Officer's Handbook of the German Army* (Wickenburg, AZ: Normount Technical Publications, 1975), 48.

42 Ibid.

43 Camp, *Tankers in Tunisia*, 40.

44 Ibid., 25.

45 Zaloga, *M3 Lee/Grant Medium Tank*, 28.

46 Ibid., 15.

47 Ibid., 14.

48 Wilkinson, *Breakthrough Battalion*, 25.

49 Ibid., 23.

50   Hougen, *34th Infantry Division*, "The Second Fondouk."

51   Wilkinson diary, 9 April 1943.

52   Ibid., 8–10 April 1943; Howe, *US Army in WWII Mediterranean*, 587: The attacking tanks belonged to the 51st Royal Tank Regiment and the troops were from the British 128th Infantry Brigade.

53   Wilkinson diary, 8–10 April 1943.

54   Ibid.; For an excellent first-hand infantry account of this action, read *The Breakthrough Battalion* by Col Richard F. Wilkinson, (unrelated to Charles M. Wilkinson), 23–29.

55   Cheryl Esposito, *The 756th Tank Battalion in the European Theatre* (Privately printed, 1999), 266–67: Oscar Long recollection; Wilkinson, "The Way It All Started," 16.

56   Esposito, *756th in Europe*, 266–67.

57   Wilkinson diary, 10 April 1943; In the 751st Tank Battalion's Commander's Narrative for 30 April 1943, Lt Col Hammack reported a total of 2 officers and 9 men killed with 11 wounded for 9 April 1943. Wilkinson identifies the officer as Lt Williamson. The ABMC website shows a grave site in Tunisia for 2nd Lt John E. Williamson of the 751st Tank Battalion killed in action 10 April 1943. Williamson entered service from New York.

58   Hougen, *34th Infantry Division*, "The Second Fondouk."

59   Ibid.

60   Atkinson, *Army at Dawn*, 475; Buell, *WWII Album*, 316.

61   Wilkinson, "The Way It All Started," 16.

62   Ibid., Wilkinson diary, 14 April 1943.

63   Ibid.

64   Wilkinson, "The Way It All Started," 16.

65   Wilkinson diary, 14 April 1943.

66   Ibid., 15 and16 April 1943. Wilkinson identifies the officer who tried releasing them as a Major Watson.

67   Wilkinson diary, 16 April 1943.

68   United States Army. *752nd Tank Bn* (1945), (PDF version downloaded from Bangor Public Library, World War Regimental Histories. Book 60, http://www.bpl.lib.me.us/), 15–16.

69   Ibid.

70   Wilkinson diary, 17 April 1943. The officer Wilkinson befriended is named as John Burke (no rank given.)

71   Ibid., 23 April 1944: Wilkinson misspelled the town as "Morsoll" in his diary.

72   Macksey, *Tank Tactics*, 17.

73   Wilkinson diary, 23–27 April 1943.

74   Ibid., 28 April 1943.

75   Camp, *Tankers in Tunisia*, 31.

76   Ibid., 32.

77   Ibid., 40, 46.

78   Ibid., 46.

79   Ibid., 36.

80   Ibid., 28.

81   Ibid., 35.

82   Ibid., 28.

83   Ibid., 30.

84   Wilkinson, "The Way It All Started," 17.

85   Taggart, *Third Infantry Division*, 45; Orders were as of noon, 30 April.

86   Ibid.

87   Wilkinson diary 2 May 1943: Wilkinson identifies the officer as "General Eagles." Whether this is Maj Gen William W. Eagles who later commanded the 45th Inf Div, is not clear. It probably was, but the rest of the 45th Inf Div was still training at Camp Picket at the time and would not depart for Oran until later in the month according to Flint Whitlock, *The Rock of Anzio: From Sicily to Dachau: A History of the U.S. 45th Infantry Division* (Boulder, CO: Westview Press, 1998), 31–32. Eagles was assistant division commander of the 3rd Inf Div prior to taking command of the 45th Inf Div in Italy.

88   Wilkinson diary, 5 May 1943.

Chapter 8

1   Lewis, personal papers: "756th HQ attachments" document dated 8 May 1945.

2   The 752nd was part of the 1st Tank Group along with the 751st and 755th Tank Battalions.

3   756th Tank Battalion Unit History for 1943, (National Archives, Army Records Group 407, Boxes 16769–16772).

4   Redle, "B Company History," 26. Donley diary, 12 May 1943.

5   Donley diary, 7 May 1943.

6   Wilkinson diary 8 and 9 May 1943; Donley diary from the time period.

7   Wilkinson diary 9 May 1943.

8   Redle interview, 13 March 2004.

9   Lewis, personal papers: "756th HQ attachments" document dated 8 May 1945; Redle letter, 18 May 2006.

10 Daniel Pompey's enlistment records (National Archives website at www.archives.com) record his year of birth as 1907. Redle remembered Pompey as "about 40."

11 Redle interview, 13 March 2004.

12 Ibid.

13 Redle letter, 18 May 2006.

14 Wilkinson diary, 8–11 May 1943.

15 Ibid., 12 May 1943.

16 Ibid., 9 and 12 May 1943, other B Co NCOs sent were Hogan, Richter, and Colley; John Bierman and Colin Smith, *War Without Hate: The Desert Campaign of 1940–1943* (New York, New York: Penguin Books Ltd., 2004), 406–407. This mass surrender occurred 6–13 May 1943 with over 170,000 prisoners processed by the Allies—nearly double the 100,000 captured at Stalingrad. The Germans wearily called their North African defeat "Tunisgrad."

17 Richter memoirs.

18 Wilkinson diary, 13 May 1943.

19 756th Unit History, 1943, (National Archives, Army Records Group 407, Boxes 16769–16772).

20 Donley diary, 15 May 1943.

21 Redle, "B Company History," 26.

22 Redle interview, 13 March 2004.

23 Perdue phone conversation, 31 January 2004; Redle interview, 13 March 2004; Graffagnini was born in 1919 according to the Social Security Death Index at www.ancestry.com.

24 Redle, "B Company History," 26; Redle, "B Company Recollections."

25 Donley diary from the time period.

26 Redle letter, 25 January 2004; Redle, "B Company Recollections."

27 Donley diary, 16 May 1943.

28 Donley diary, 12 May 1943.

29 Perdue phone conversation, 31 January 2004.

30 Donley diary, 17 May 1943.

31 Redle letter, 28 June 2009.

32 Donley interview, 2005 September 16.

33 Redle letter, 03 January 2001.

34 Esposito, *756th in Europe*, 243–244: Ithel Adlard recollection.

35 Wilkinson diary, 17 and 22 May 1943.

36 Ibid., 26–30, May 1943.

37 Donley diary, 31 May 1943.

38 Wilkinson diary, 1–5 June 1943.

39 Ibid., 5 and 6 June 1943.

40 Donley diary, 6 June 1943. Atabrine was a substitute for Quinine.

41 Redle letter, 28 June 2009.

42 Redle, "B Company History," 27.

43 756th Unit History, 1943; Donley diary, 6–8 June 1943.

44 Wilkinson, "The Way It All Started," 17; Wilkinson diary, 8 June 1943.

45   Lewis, personal papers.
46   Wilkinson diary, 8 June 1943.
47   Ibid., 10 June 1943.
48   Ibid., 9 June 1943.
49   Donley diary, 24 June 1943.
50   Redle, "B Company History," 27.
51   Donley diary, 14 June 1943.
52   Wilkinson letter, 18 April 2005.
53   Redle, "B Company History," 27.
54   Wilkinson diary, 15 June 1943.
55   Redle, "B Company History," 27.
56   Wilkinson diary, 16 March 1943.
57   Perdue phone conversations, 28 December 2001 and 31 January 2004.
58   Wilkinson diary, 5 May 1943.
59   Esposito, *756th in Europe*, 231.
60   Wilkinson diary, 16 June 1943.
61   Ibid., 22 June 1943; The four men were LaDue, Shuder, Osganian, and Guild. B Company Morning Reports are missing for June and July of 1943, so certain details have been lost.
62   Donley diary, 29 June 1943.
63   Ibid., 8 July 1943.
64   Ibid., 2 July 1943.
65   Redle interview, 16 September 2005; Redle phone conversation, 21 July 2003; Redle, "B Company History," 7.
66   Wilkinson diary, 9 July 1943.
67   Donley diary, 10 July 1943; Wilkinson diary, 10 July 1943.
68   Wilkinson diary, 10 July 1943.
69   Lewis personal papers: "756th HQ attachments" document dated 8 May 1945.
70   Wilkinson diary, 13 July 1943.
71   Ibid., 15 July 1943.
72   Mudd, "History 756th," 21.
73   The 70th Tk Bn (Medium), 753rd Tk Bn (Medium) and the 2nd Armored Division were the United States tank units involved.
74   756th Unit History, 1943.
75   Ibid.
76   B Co/756th Morning Reports, 17–20 July 1943: Two officers and seventeen enlisted men from B Company left Magenta, Algeria, at 0600 by motor convoy and arrived at Bizerte on 21 July. They traveled 236 miles the first day and bivouac was in Affreville. On 18 July, four officers and ninety-nine EM left Magenta by rail to arrive on 23 July. Motor convoy traveled 175 miles. On 19 July, convoy left St Onde Maillot and arrived M'Lila, Algeria, after travelling 161 miles. MC goes 164 miles on 20th and arrives at Charimaou, Tunisia. Arrive at Bizerte at 1600 on 21 July after 130 miles.
77   Wilkinson diary, 14–21 July 1943.
78   Ibid., 21 July 1943.
79   Redle, "B Company History," 29–30.
80   Ibid.
81   B Co/756th Morning Reports, 21 July 1943.
82   Ibid., 22–28 July 1943.
83   Perdue phone conversation, 31 January 2004.
84   Wilkinson diary, 25–27 July 1943.
85   B Co/756th Morning Reports, 31 July 1943.
86   Palermo fell on 24 July 1943.
87   Wilkinson diary, 24–26 July 1943.
88   Ibid., 22–24 July 1943.
89   Ibid.
90   Wilkinson diary, 28 July 1943.

91 Ibid., 30–31 July 1943.
92 Redle letter to Teta Fazendin, 1 August 1943.
93 Ibid., Redle letter, 24 June 2002.
94 Wilkinson diary, 4 August 1943.
95 Ibid., 2 August 1943.
96 Wilkinson, "The Way It All Started," 18.
97 Lewis, personal papers: Wilkinson letter to Lewis, 10 August 1975.
98 "Axis Sally" was Mildred Gillar, an American working for the Germans.
99 Wilkinson diary, 7 August 1943.
100 Redle, "B Company History," 31.
101 Wilkinson diary, 10 August 1943. Others who Wilkinson lists were afflicted with malaria at this time were (Capt) Richardson, (Lts) Finn and Nelson, and Dr Easley; B Co/756th Morning Reports, 10 August 1943.
102 Wilkinson diary, 11 August 1943; 756th Unit History, 1943; B Co/756th Morning Reports, 11 August 1943. The location was actually thirteen miles southeast of Ferryville on the Tunis road. The move required thirty-two miles of road travel. Attachment was to the 13th Field Artillery Brigade.
103 Wilkinson diary, 16 August 1943.
104 Ibid., 18 August 1943.
105 Redle, "B Company History," 28.
106 Wilkinson diary, 12 and 15 August 1943; Wilkinson writes Shind "possibly died" in the same incident that killed Crabtree. The author could not locate Isaac Shind on the WWII casualty lists. According to the 1940 census, he appears to have been from Hartford, Connecticut. If this is the same person, Shind survived the war and passed away in Florida in 1977. Edd A. Crabtree is listed as a WWII "death, not battle" by the National Archives.
107 Redle, "B Company History," 31; Wilkinson diary, 19 August 1943.
108 Wilkinson diary, 2 September 1943.
109 Ibid., 20 August 1943.
110 Ibid., 27 August 1943. No first name provided, but he likely was Pvt Richard L. Chapman.
111 Ibid., 26 August 1943.
112 Ibid., 24 August 1943.
113 Ibid., 29 August 1943. Cpl Nusz was with Dolvin on separate duty (SD).
114 Ibid.; B Co/756th Morning Reports, 29 August 1943.
115 Wilkinson diary, 30 August 1943.
116 Wilkinson, "The Way It All Started," 17.
117 Ibid.
118 Ibid., 18.
119 Wilkinson diary, 6 September 1943.
120 Ibid., 6–7 September 1943.
121 Wilkinson, "The Way It All Started," 17.
122 Wilkinson diary, 8 September 1943.
123 Ibid., 9 September 1943.
124 Ibid., 11 September 1943; Wilkinson, "The Way It All Started," 18.
125 Wilkinson diary, 12 September 1943.
126 Wilkinson, "The Way It All Started," 18.
127 Ibid., 19.
128 Redle interview, 13 March 2004. In 1943, $5,000 was equivalent to $75,000 in 2020 dollars—an astounding sum.
129 Fazendin, *756th at Cassino*, xxiv.
130 The other seven were Cpl Anthony L. Notaroberto (maintenance records clerk), Pfc Louis A. Laliberty, and Pvts John F. Bacha, Paul N. Cardullo, Anton E. Fricke, David J. Orris, and Harold R. Stilwell (B Co/756th Morning Reports, 15 September 1943); Richter e-mail, 12 June 2009.
131 B Co/756th Morning Reports, 15 September 1943; Paul Ranspach diary.
132 Wilkinson diary, 15 September 1943.

Chapter 9

1   Ranspach diary, 16 September 1943.
2   Wilkinson diary, 16 September 1943.
3   Martin Blumenson, *Salerno to Cassino* (Washington, D.C.: Center of Military History, U.S. Army, 1993), 82, 84.
4   David A. Redle (son of David D. Redle) email on his father's behalf, 17 July 2014. Redle recalls landing on the beach as the sun went down.
5   B Co/756th Morning Reports, 17 September 1943; Wilkinson diary, 17 September 1943; Ranspach diary, 17 September 1943; The Morning Reports record debarking at 1800, but Wilkinson and Ranspach report debarking at 2200 and 2230 respectively.
6   Wilkinson, "The Way It All Started," 19.
7   Ranspach diary, 17 September 1943.
8   756th Unit History, 1943.
9   Ranspach diary, 17 September 1943.
10 Ibid.
11 Richter memoirs; Richter letter, 12 January 2007.
12 B Co/756th Morning Reports, 17 September 1943.
13 Redle, "B Company History," 30–31; Redle letter, 25 January 2004.
14 Wilkinson diary, 18 September 1943.
15 Redle "B Company History," 31–32.
16 Esposito, *756th in Europe*, 267: Long recollection.
17 Redle "B Company History," 32; Redle letter, 25 January 2004.
18 Wilkinson diary, 18 September 1943; Clyde Guild interview, 15 September 2006; Ranspach diary, 18 September 1943.
19 Redle letter, 25 January 2004.
20 Taggart, *Third Infantry Division*, 80.
21 Lewis personal papers: "756th HQ attachments" document dated 8 May 1945.
22 Redle letter, 9 April 2001; Redle, "B Company History," 33; Redle letter, 25 January 2004.
23 B Co/756th Morning Reports, 19 September 1943; Ranspach diary, 19 September 1943.
24 Ranspach diary, 19 September 1943.
25 Wilkinson diary, 19 September.
26 Redle letter, 25 January 2004.
27 Ibid.
28 B Co/756th Morning Reports, 20 September 1943; Ranspach diary, 20 September 1943.
29 Redle "B Company History," 32.
30 B Co/756th Morning Reports, 20 September 1943; Ranspach diary, 20 September 1943.
31 Redle letter, 25 January 2004.
32 Ranspach diary, 21 September 1943.
33 Perdue phone conversation, 31 January 2004.
34 Ranspach diary, 21 September 1943.
35 Wilkinson diary, 20 and 21 September 1943; Ranspach diary, 21 September 1943.
36 Richter memoirs; Richer letter, 12 January 2007. Their journey was aboard a smaller landing craft with roughly 100 infantrymen, three jeeps, one tank, and a half-track.
37 Ranspach diary, 22 September 1943.
38 B Co/756th Morning Reports, 22 September 43.
39 Ranspach diary, 22 September 1943.
40 Ibid.
41 Sgt Johnny Brown was his name.
42 756th Tank Battalion Commander's Narrative for September 1943, (National Archives, Army Records Group 407, Boxes 16769–16772): Pvt Jones suffered unspecified wounds in the afternoon. Pvt Vasquez suffered severe shrapnel wounds to the back that same evening.
43 756th Commander's Narrative, September 1943.

44 Redle interview, 13 March 2004; Redle letter, 2 May 2002. It is not clear if this incident occurred on this particular night or on another night during the 756th's attachment to the 45th Inf Div.

45 Wilkinson diary, 24 September 1943.

46 756th Commander's Narrative, September 1943.

47 Ibid.

48 B Co/756th Morning Reports, 25 September 1943; Wilkinson diary, 23 September 1943.

49 Ranspach diary, 23 September 1943. The location is identified as "Oliveto" and probably refers to modern day "Ponte Oliveto-Bagni."

50 Ranspach diary, 24 September 1943.

51 Redle, "B Company History," 32; Redle letter, 25 January 2004.

52 Wilkinson diary, 25 September 1943; B Co/756th Morning Reports, 25 September 1943.

53 Ranspach diary, 25 September 1943.

54 Ibid., 26 September 1943. These descriptions are taken directly from Ranspach's diary.

55 Ibid., 27 September 1943.

56 Wilkinson diary, 26 and 27 September 1943.

57 Ranspach diary, 27 September 1943.

58 Ibid., 28 September 1943; Redle letter, 30 October 2000. At this time, Ranspach and Beal were either Pvts or Pfcs. Ranspach was assigned to B Company in June 1943, but the Morning Reports from that month are lost.

59 Ranspach diary, 28 September 1943.

60 Redle letter, 25 January 2004; Redle, "B Company History," 33.

61 Ranspach diary, 29 September 1943.

62 756th Unit History, 1943.

63 B Co/756th Morning Reports, 28 September 1943. Coordinates were 945592 according to the 756th Unit History, 1943.

64 Ranspach diary, 29 September 1943.

65 Wilkinson diary, 28 and 29 September 1943.

66 Ranspach diary, 30 September 1943.

67 B Co/756th Morning Reports, 29 September 1943, records arrival at 2000. They had been assigned to the 204th Military Police Company.

68 Guild interview, 15 September 2006.

69 Ibid.

70 Ranspach diary, 1 October 1943.

71 Ibid., 2 and 3 October 1943.

72 Hougen, 34th Infantry Division, Chapter XIII "The Soft Underbelly."

73 British forces of the X Corps (BR) comprised the 7th Armoured Division (BR) and 46th and 56th Infantry Divisions (BR).

74 Ranspach diary, 5 October 1943.

75 Wilkinson diary, 4 October 1943.

76 Ibid.; Ranspach diary, 4–6 October 1943.

77 Coordinates were 785555 according to the B Co/756th Morning Reports, 7 October 1943.

78 Ranspach diary, 7 October 1943.

79 Coordinates were 523690 according to 756th Unit History, 1943.

80 Ranspach diary, 8 October 1943.

81 Ibid.; Wilkinson diary, 8 October 1943: reports that Nusz had a "very narrow escape" on this trip. This could have been the accident that hurt his back and eventually made him B Company 1st Sgt a few months later.

82 756th Unit History, 1943. Coordinates were 523690 according to the B Co/756th Morning Reports, 8 October 1943.

83 Wilkinson diary, 9 October 1943.

84 Ibid., 10 October 1943.

85 Ranspach diary, 10 October 1943.

86 Ibid., 14 October 1943.

87 Wilkinson diary, 11 to 18 October 1943.

88 Listed as coordinates 370785 in the B Co/756th Morning Reports, 17 October 1943. Miles recorded are "road" mileage.

89 Ranspach diary, 17 October 1943.

90 Ibid.

91 756th Unit History, 1943.

92 Perdue phone conversation, 31 January 2004.

93 Ranspach diary, 18 October 1943. This road is likely the "Via Umberto" road leading south from Caiazzo to the Volturno River.

94 Listed as coordinates 335890 in the B Co/756th Morning Reports, 18 October 1943.

95 Ranspach diary, 18 October 1943.

96 Coordinates listed as 335890 in the 756th Unit History, 1943.

97 Wilkinson diary, 17 and 18 October 1943; Ranspach diary, 18 October 1943.

98 Ranspach diary, 19 October 1943; Wilkinson diary, 19 October 1943.

99 Ranspach diary, 19 and 20 October 1943; Wilkinson diary, 20–24 October 1943.

100 Ranspach diary, 23 October 1943.

101 Wilkinson, "The Way It All Started," 19; Ranspach diary, 22 October 1943; Redle letter, 30 October 2000.

102 Wilkinson, "The Way It All Started," 20; Wilkinson letter to Redle dated 29 June 1998.

103 756th Tank Battalion Unit Journal (Army Records Group 407, Boxes 16769–16772), 1 and 2 November 1943. Coordinates were 267034. Move was made 1 November 1943.

104 B Co/756th Morning Reports, 25 and 29–31 October 1943. Location recorded at 315888, ¾ mile NE of Caiazzo; 756th Tank Battalion Unit History, 1943.

105 Wilkinson diary, 25–29 October 1943; Redle, "B Company History," 33; 756th Unit History, 1943.

106 B Co/756th Morning Reports, 25 October 1943.

107 Redle letter, 25 January 2004.

108 Ranspach diary, 27 October 1943.

109 Wilkinson, "The Way It All Started," 19.

110 Fazendin, 756th at Cassino, 17: Roy L. Johnson recollection.

111 Wilkinson diary, 20–24 October 1943.

112 Ibid., 29 October 1943.

113 Guild interview, 15 September 2006.

114 Wilkinson diary, 29 October 1943.

115 B Co/756th Morning Reports, 1 November 1943.

116 Wilkinson diary, 30 October–1 November 1943.

117 Ranspach diary, 1 November 1943.

118 756th Commander's Narrative, September & October 1943.

119 Wilkinson diary, 30 October 1943; Ranspach diary, 4 November 1943.

120 Wilkinson, "The Way It All Started," 20.

121 Wilkinson diary, 4 November 1943.

122 Ranspach diary, 7 and 8 November 1943.

123 Wilkinson diary, 8–10 November 1943.

124 756th Unit History, 1943.

125 B Co/756th Morning Reports, 12 November 1943.

126 Ranspach diary, 10 November 1943.

127 Redle, "B Company History," 34; Redle, "B Company Recollections."

128 Ranspach diary, 10 November 1943.

129 Redle, "B Company History," 35; Redle, "B Company Recollections."

130 756th Unit History, 1943. Coordinates were 092131.

131 Ibid.; 756th Unit Journal, 11–13 November 1943. Gourley was wounded north of the nearby town of Pozzilli.

132 Lewis, personal papers.

133 Redle interview, 13 March 2004.

134 Wilkinson diary, 11 November 1943.

135 756th Unit Journal, 20–21 November 1943.

136 Wilkinson diary, 14 November 1943; B Co/756th Morning Reports, 14 November 1943.

137 Ranspach diary, 14 November 1943.

138 Ibid.

139 Ibid., 11 November 1943.

140 Ibid., 16 November 1943.

141 Ibid., 15 November 1943.

142 Wilkinson diary, 18 November 1943.

143 Ranspach diary, 18 November 1943.

144 Wilkinson diary, 19 and 20 November 1943; 756th Unit History, 1943; 756th Unit Journal, 17–19 November 1943. Pfc Nicholson died from shrapnel wounds to his left inguinal area.

145 Lewis, personal papers.

146 Wilkinson diary, 20 November 1943; 756th Unit History, 1943.

147 Ibid., 22 November 1943; Ibid.

148 756th Unit Journal, 22 November 1943.

149 Redle, "B Company History," 35–36.

150 Wilkinson diary, 30 November 1943; 756 Unit History, 1943; Redle, "B Company History," 35–36; Fazendin, *756th at Cassino*, xxix.

Chapter 10

1 756th Unit Journal, 4 November 1943.

2 756th Unit History, 1943. Three M8s were turned in on 17 December according to the 756th Unit Journal, 17 December 1943.

3 Ranspach diary, 23 November 1943.

4 Wilkinson diary, 25 November 1943.

5 Ranspach diary, 26 November 1943.

6 Ranspach was selected as company clerk. Chiarelli was selected as platoon sergeant. Sgts Osganian, Grate, and Denton were tank commanders. Small, Bates, Parr, Dyer, and Beal were drivers, and Westle a basic. Nusz was considered for intelligence Tech Sgt, and Demars for mechanic according to Wilkinson's diary for 26 November 1943.

7 Wilkinson diary, 26 & 27 November 1943.

8 Ibid., 30 November 1943; 756th Unit History, 1943; Redle, "B Company History," 36; Ranspach diary, 2 December 1943.

9 Ranspach diary, 30 November and 1 December 1943.

10 Ibid., December 1943.

11 Blumenson, *Salerno to Cassino*, 285.

12 Ibid., 280–84; S/Sgt Richard A. Huff, ed, *The Fighting 36th: A Pictorial History of the Texas Division in Combat* (Austin, Texas: 36th Division Association, 1945), San Pietro section (no numbers); Redle interview, 13 March 2013; The Armor School, *Armor in Mountain Warfare* (Armor School student research report, Officers Advanced Course, Fort Knox, Kentucky: May 1950), 49; Winston G. Ramsey, ed., "The Battle for San Pietro" *After the Battle* Number 18 magazine. 1977, 6–10. Of the sixteen tanks involved, four were destroyed by mines, three by AT fire (tanks 3–5), and the rest became trapped or disabled (threw tracks.)

13 Ranspach diary, 12 December 1943.

14 Wilkinson diary, 15 December 1943.

15 Ibid.; 756th Unit History, 1943.

16 Coordinates were 418766 according to the 756th Unit Journal.

17 B Co Morning Report, 15 December 1943; 756th Unit History, 1943; 756th Unit Journal, December 1943. The battalion was reorganized under T/O&E 17-25 WD, 15 September 1943.

18 Reorganization order dated 9 December 1943 (Field Order #6, "Training Program," signed by Sweeting.)

19 Fazendin, *756th at Cassino*, 13: Redle recollection; Redle letter, 5 October 2000.

20 Wilkinson diary, 16–18, December 1943.

21 756th Unit Journal, 13 December 1943: The thirty-three officers figure includes two warrant officers; 756th Unit Journal, 17 December 1943: The forty-two officers figure includes two warrant officers.

22 756th Unit Journal, 18–19 December 1943.

23 B Co/756th Morning Reports, 15–25 December 1943.

24 General Order (GO) #107, HQ Fifth Army, dated 15 December 1943.

25 Wilkinson diary, 16–18 December 1943.

26 Redle letter, 30 October 2000.

27 Redle letter, 2 May 2002.

28 Redle, "B Company History," 36–37; Redle letter, 30 October 2000; Redle letter, 13 March 2004; Redle letter, 2 May 2002.

29 Redle, "B Company History," 36–37.

30 Wilkinson letter, 20 December 2001; Redle interview, 13 March 2004.

31 Redle, "B Company History," 37.

32 Ibid.

33 Redle, "B Company History," 38; Wilkinson letter, 31 May 2005 letter. Jarvis's name had been anglicized from Luigi Gervasi. He is also remembered for having a great singing voice.

34 Redle, "B Company History," 37.

35 Wilkinson, "They Way It All Started," 19.

36 Redle, "B Company History," 38.

37 Wilkinson diary, 19–20 December 1943.

38 Hunnicutt, *Sherman*, 559.

39 Ibid., 562.

40 Steven J. Zaloga, *Sherman Medium Tank 1942–45* (1978, reprint, Oxford, UK: Osprey Publishing Ltd., 2001), 10; Hunnicutt, *Sherman*, 208; The gun was an M3 model.

41 German tanks relied upon manual cranking or high engine RPMs for turret traverse. In virtually all situations, an M4 equipped with an independent motor traversed faster.

42 Michael Green, *M4 Sherman: Combat and Development History of the Sherman Tank and All Sherman Variants*, (Osceola, Wisconsin: Motorbooks International Publishers & Wholesalers., 1993), 45.

43 Jeffrey Plowman and Perry Rowe, *The Battles for Monte Cassino Then and Now* (Essex: UK, Battle of Britain International Ltd., 2011), 90; Green, *M4 Sherman*, 62.

44 Michael Green and James D. Brown, *M4 Sherman at War* (St Paul, Minnesota: MBI Publishing Co., 2007), 82, 88.

45 The FM Radios were SCR-508 models. The SCR-528 was used for transmitting (installed in the platoon leader and platoon sergeant's tanks), and the SCR-538 receiver was installed in all tanks.

46 Steven J. Zaloga, *US Army Tank Crewman 1941–45, European Theater of Operations 1944–45* (Oxford, UK: Osprey Publishing, Ltd. 2004), 19.

47 318 M4A1 models were sent to the British in September 1941.

48 Zaloga, *Sherman Medium Tank*, 19.

49 Green, *M4 Sherman as War*, 25.

50 Ibid., 27.

51 Peter Chamberlain and Chris Ellis, *The Sherman: An Illustrated History of the M4 Medium Tank* (New York, New York: Arco Publishing Company, Inc., 1978), 76–78.

52 Bob Carruthers, *Panzer IV: The Workhorse of the Panzerwaffe* (South Yorkshire, UK: Pen and Sword Books, Ltd. 2013), 72; Simon & Jonathan Forty, *Survivors: Battlefield Relics of WWII* (New York, NY: Chartwell Books, 2018), 15.

53 Guderian, *Achtung – Panzer!* 208.

54 Alistair Cooke, *Alistair Cooke's America* (New York: Alfred A. Knopf, Inc., 1973), 342. This assurance was made by Goering in a letter to Hitler.

55 A Russian T-34 medium tank was first introduced in 1940, though inferior in quality in many respects to an American M4, it utilized a better high-velocity 76.2mm gun.

56 756th Training Program schedule for 20 December 1943 to 10 January 1944 (undated document included with the 756th Unit Journal, December 1943).

57 "Short arm" was slang for the penis. The U.S. Army had good reason to worry. Statistically speaking, venereal disease cases proved as high of a casualty threat as German artillery.

58 756th Training Program included in Unit Journal, December 1943.

59 Reorganization order dated 9 December 1943 (field order #6, "Training Program" signed by Lt Col Sweeting) and included in the Unit Journal.

60 Wilkinson diary, 21–25 December 1943.

61 Ranspach diary, 26 December 1943.

62 Wilkinson diary, 28 December 1943.

63 Ibid., 27 December 1943. Wilkinson identified these as "panoramic sights." He may have been referring to the gunner's direct view telescopic sight mounted through the gun mantlet on the right side. This was an improvement over a periscopic gun sight.

64 Ibid., 30 December 1943.

65 Ibid., 29 December 1943. This man was Pvt Roy L. Adams. The entry in the A Co/756th Morning Report, 2 January 44, read that Adams was "accidently killed from fall over 40-foot slope between 1800 and 1930, 25 December 43. Cause of death fractured skull."

66 Ibid., 1 and 2 January 1944.

67 756th Unit Journal, 2 January 1943; Donley diary, 1 January 1944.

68 Wilkinson diary, 4 January 1944.

69 Ibid., 5 January 1944.

70 Ibid., 6 January 1944; B/756th Morning Report, 6 January 1944.

71 Wilkinson diary, 6–8 January 1944.

72 Ibid., 7 January 1944.

73 756th Commander's Narrative, January & February 1944, 2, (Army Records Group 407, Boxes 16769–16772).

74 B Co/756th Morning Report, 10 January 1944.

75 Lewis, personal papers: "756th HQ attachments," dated 8 May 1945.

76 The battalion's assault gun platoon, mortar platoon, and the recon officers also went along, according to the 756th Unit Journal, 9 January 1943.

Chapter 11

1 756th Unit Journal, 11 January 1943.

2 Roy Anderson phone conversation, 27 September 2003.

3 756th Unit Journal 11 January 1944: Coordinates were 996118. The B Company Unit Journal for January 1944 (copies obtained from the Dwight D. Eisenhower Library [Abilene, Kansas]: U.S. Army: Unit Records, 1917–50, 756th Tank Battalion, Box 146), records assembling SW of Mignano in 11 January entry.

4 Ranspach Diary, 11 January 1944.

5 Ibid., 13 January 1944; Donley diary, 13 January 1944.

6 This man was 1st Lt Kenneth S. Nelson. According to D Co 17 January 1944 Morning Report, he transferred out sick on 17 January, and 1st Lt Robert F. Kremer took command of D Company thereafter. 2nd Lt Loeb was C Co commander and was promoted to 1st Lt on 16 January 1944 per C Co/756th Morning Report, 26 January 1944.

7 Fazendin, 756th at Cassino, 9–10: Redle recollection; According to 756th Commander's Narrative for January and February 1944, page 2, they were to relieve B Company of the 753rd Tank Battalion; B Co/756th Unit Journal, 12 January 1944.

8 Fazendin, 756th at Cassino, 9: Redle recollection; Wilkinson diary, 10 January 1944; Howe, Old Ironsides, 308–09. Task Force Allen was named after Brig Gen Frank Allen Jr. and built primarily around the 6th Armored Infantry Regiment of the 1st Armored Division. This task force moved into Italy in November 1943.

9 David Hapgood, Monte Cassino (London, UK: Angus and Robertson Publishers, 1984), 3.

10 Harold L. Bond, Return to Cassino: A Memoir of the Fight for Rome (Garden City, New York: Double Day & Company, Inc., 1964), 38–40; Wilkinson, "The Way It All Started," 20.

11 Blumenson, Salerno to Cassino, 310.

12   Ibid., 284–85.

13   Ibid., 286.

14   Lee Caraway Smith, *A River Swift and Deadly: The 36th "Texas" Infantry Division at the Rapido River* (Austin, Texas: Eakin Press, 1989), 18–19.

15   Blumenson, *Salerno to Cassino*, 310.

16   Hougen, *34th Infantry Division,* "Cervaro and Monte Trocchio."

17   Ranspach diary, 12 January 1944.

18   Wilkinson diary, 11 January 1944.

19   756th Commander's Narrative for January and February 1944, 2.

20   Wilkinson diary, 12 January 1944; Wilkinson letter to Redle, 29 June 1998; Huff, *The Fighting 36th*, roster, 33: Lt Hamner was assigned to F Co of the 141st Inf Regt.

21   Blumenson, *Salerno to Cassino*, 310.

22   B Co/756th Unit Journal, 13 January 1944.

23   Fazendin, *756th at Cassino,* 11: Redle recollection.

24   Wilkinson diary, 13 January 1944.

25   Fazendin, *756th at Cassino*, 8–9: Donley recollection, and 7–8, Redle recollection.

26   Ranspach diary, 13 January 1944; 756th Unit Journal, 14 January 1944; C Co/756th Morning Report, 20 January 1944 identifies T/4 Gus T. Markos, DOW 17 January 1944 from anuria, and Cpl Baldemar S. Pantoja and Pfc James F. Feeney as the two others wounded.

27   Ranspach diary, 14 January 1944.

28   B Co/756th Unit Journal, 14 January 1944.

29   Wilkinson diary, 14–15 January 1944; 756 Commander's Narrative for January and February 1944, 3; Ranspach diary, 15 January 1944; B Co/756th Morning Report, 15 January 1944.

30   Lewis, personal papers: Roy Kosanke letter to the 756th Association membership dated 10 December 1987.

31   Dick Offerman (son of Cletus Offerman, B Company/756th Tank Battalion), "My Dad Was A Tanker" biography, letters, and photos (December 2005), 14.

32   Redle letter, 29 April 2003.

33   Wilkinson diary, 16 January 1944; 756 Commander's Narrative, January and February 1944, 3.

34   Fazendin, *756th at Cassino*, 11–12: Redle recollection. This road is the Via Braccio di Croce (Provincial Route 82) between Cervaro and Monte Trocchio on modern maps. Sweeting identifies the location at 905195, which is, indeed, about halfway down this route.

35   Fazendin, *756th at Cassino,* 12: Kosanke recollection.

36   Wilkinson diary, 17–18 January 1944. According to Wilkinson, Gilkerson's tank remained stuck as of 18 January 1944—four days after throwing both tracks. Gilkerson's tank number was #2 (1st Platoon), W-3036580, according to the B Co/756th Unit Journal, 15 January 1944.

37   Wilkinson diary, 16 January 1944; 756th Unit Journal, 16 January 1944.

38   756th Unit Journal, 16 January 1944.

39   Ibid., 17 January 1944.

40   B Co/756th Morning Report, 18 January 1944. All three medium tank companies reported ¾ mile NW of San Pietro as their locations. The 756th Unit Journal gives coordinates of 968159 for A Company; The battalion was located at 961164 according to the Unit Journal, 18 January 1944.

41   Ranspach Diary, 18 January 1944; B Co/756th Unit Journal 18 January 1944.

42   Ibid., 19 January 1944.

43   Hapgood, *Monte Cassino,* 74.

44   Robert Wallace, *The Italian Campaign* (Morristown, New Jersey: Time-Life Books, Inc., 1978), 135.

45   Parker, *Monte Cassino,* xiv.

46   Hapgood, *Monte Cassino,* 9.

47   Ian Gooderson, *Battles in Focus: Cassino 1944* (London, UK: Brassey's, 2003), 66; Hapgood, *Monte Cassino*, 90.

48   The Todt Organization was the name of the National Socialist program for building civilian and military projects.

49   Gooderson, *Cassino 1944*, 67–68; Redle letter, 17 January 2009.

50   Pimlott, *Historical Atlas of World War II*, 42; Gooderson, *Cassino 1944*, 46–56: the British 5th Division and 56th Division operating closer to the coast established small bridgeheads, but these were south of the Liri Valley.

51   Gooderson, *Cassino 1944*, 66.

52   Wilkinson diary, 19 January 1944.

53   Lee McCardell, "Cassino's Defense System Described," *The Baltimore Sun* (Baltimore, Maryland), 1 February 1944, 1.

54   Ranspach diary, 19 January 1944.

55   756th Unit Journal, 19 January 1944; Wilkinson diary, 20 January 1944.

56   Ranspach diary, 20 January 1944.

57   Wilkinson diary, 20 January 1944.

58   Wilkinson, *Breakthrough Battalion*, 59.

59   Redle letter, 17 January 2009.

60   Mudd, "History 756th," 28.

61   756th Commander's Narrative for January and February 1944, 4.

62   Gooderson, *Cassino 1944*, 56–57.

63   Smith, *A River Swift and Deadly*, 37; Blumenson, *Salerno to Cassino*, 329; Wallace, *The Italian Campaign*, 115; Maj Gen Fred L. Walker, "Comments on the Rapido River Crossing, January 1944," Library USA CGSC Ft Levenworth Kansas, 1960, 22.

64   Blumenson, *Salerno to Cassino*, 322.

65   Ibid., 333.

66   Wallace, *The Italian Campaign*, 115–16.

67   Ibid., 16; Gooderson, *Cassino 1944*, 57; Blumenson, *Salerno to Cassino*, 330–35; The 1st Bn/141st attacked on right and managed to place roughly 100 men across initially and the remainder of the battalion a few hours later. The 1st and 3rd Bns/143rd attacked on left and claimed to have most of the 1st Battalion across. However, by 1000, 21 January, the battalion reported these men had been withdrawn. Even to this day, certain details to the debacle remain confused.

68   Redle interview, 13 March 2004.

69   Gooderson, *Cassino 1944*, 59.

70   Redle interview, 13 March 2004.

71   Ibid.

Chapter 12

1   Fazendin, *756th at Cassino*, 42: Lewis recollection.

2   Wilkinson, "The Way It All Started," 20.

3   B Co/756th Morning Reports, 21 January 1944; Wilkinson diary, 21 January 1944; Redle letter, 25 January 2004; Roy Kosanke, "756th Tank Battalion Reunion Book" (756th Tank Battalion Association, late 1980s), 13: Harley was from South Carolina.

4   Fazendin, *756th at Cassino*, 12; Winlock departed 21 January, according to the B Co/756th Morning Reports.

5   756th Unit Journal, 21 January 1944 (1230 entry).

6   756th Commander's Narrative, January & February 1944, 5.

7   Ibid.

8   Peter Caddick-Adams, *Monte Cassino: Ten Armies in Hell*, (New York, NY, Oxford University Press, 2012), 111.

9   Blumenson, *Salerno to Cassino*, 367–68.

10   Dominick Graham, *Cassino: Battle Book No. 16*, (New York, NY: Ballantine Books, Inc., 1970), 47.

11   Fazendin, *756th at Cassino*, 20: Redle recollection. This same hill was also called "Hill 56" by the Allies for unknown reasons—probably from an initial misreading of the "156" elevation mark on the 1:25,000-scale map. The error was repeated consistently in subsequent journals and reports.

12   756th Commander's Narrative, January and February 1944, 6.

13   Ibid., 6.

14　McCardell, Lee. "McCardell Under Fire With Yanks In Final Attacks On Cassino Forts." *The Baltimore Sun* (Baltimore, Maryland), 6 February 1944, 1; McCardell, Lee, "Battle for Cassino Viewed by McCardell," *The Evening Sun* (Baltimore, Maryland), 10 February 1944, 4.

15　The U.S. 3rd Inf Div and British 1st Inf Div comprised the U.S. VI Corps commanded by Maj Gen John P. Lucas.

16　Wilkinson diary, 22 January 1944.

17　Ibid., 23 January 1944.

18　Fazendin, *756th at Cassino*, 70: Deenihan recollection.

19　Ranspach diary, 23 January 1944.

20　756th Unit Journal, 24 January 1944. The attack came at 0045.

21　Ibid., 23 January 1944. The meeting took place at 1900.

22　756th Commander's Narrative, January and February 1944, 7.

23　756th Unit Journal, 23 January 1944 (1900 entry).

24　756 Commander's Narrative, January and February 1944, 7.

25　Treanor, *One Damn Thing*, 258–59.

26　Walker, "Comments on the Rapido River Crossing," 20.

27　Parker, *Monte Cassino*, xv.

28　756th Unit Journal, 24 January 1944, 0900 and 1135.

29　Treanor, *One Damn Thing*, 237; Ranspach diary, 24 January 1944.

30　Treanor, *One Damn Thing*, 237; Lee McCardell, "McCardell Under Fire With Yanks In Final Attacks On Cassino Forts," *The Baltimore Sun* (Baltimore, Maryland), 6 February 1944, 1.

31　Fazendin, *756th at Cassino*, 43: Lewis recollection.

32　"Unit Journal of Cannon Company, 133rd Infantry, January–March 1944," 24 January 1944, transcribed at: http://www.34infdiv.org/history/133cannon/4401.html.

33　Treanor, *One Damn Thing*, 238.

34　Hougen, *34th Infantry Division*, "The 34th Establishes Bridge-Heads."

35　Ken Ford, *Cassino 1944: Breaking the Gustav Line* (Oxford, UK: Osprey Publishing Ltd., 2004), 43.

36　Hougen, *34th Infantry Division*, "The 34th Establishes Bridge-Heads."

37　Based primarily on the disposition map dated 23 January at 1800 hours (231800) by the S-3, 135th Inf Regt and found in the 34th Inf Div G-3 Journal for 24 January 1944, (National Archives, (Army Records Group 407, Boxes 8172 & 8173).

38　Wilkinson, *Breakthrough Battalion*, 59; Blumenson, *Salerno to Cassino*, 369; 133rd Inf Regt S-3 report, 242800 to 251800 January 1944.

39　Treanor, *One Damn Thing*, 238–39.

40　Ibid.

41　34th G-3 Journal, 24 January 1944, and attachments, (National Archives, Army Records Group 407, Boxes 8172 and 8173).

42　Blumenson, *Salerno to Cassino*, 368–70.

43　Gooderson, *Cassino 1944*, 68; Hougen, *34th Infantry Division*, "The 34th Establishes Bridge-Heads."

44　Hougen, *34th Infantry Division*, "The 34th Establishes Bridge-Heads."

45　Wilkinson, *Breakthrough Battalion*, 59.

46　Ibid., 60–63.

47　Masayo Umezawa Duus, *Unlikely Liberators, The Men of the 100th and 442nd*. (English Translation. Honolulu, Hawaii: University of Hawaii Press, 2006), 120.

48　Homer R. Ankrum, *Dogfaces Who Smiled Through Tears*. (Lake Mills, Iowa: Graphic Publishing Company, 1988), 390; Wilkinson, *Breakthrough Battalion*, 59.

49　Duus, *Unlikely Liberators*, 119.

50　756th Unit Journal, 25 January 1944 (0100 and 0345 entries).

51　Fazendin, *756th at Cassino*, 78–79: Collins recollection.

52　756th Unit Journal, 25 January 1944 (0001 and 0345 entries). Location was 886227. The 1944 1:25,000 scale map indicates a field drainage ditch at this location. The engineers apparently used this location to connect routes.

53　756th Commander's Narrative, January and February 1944, 8.

54   Unclear if B Company followed this same route or used another.

55   B Co/756th Unit Journal, 24 January 1944; 756th Unit Journal, 25 January 1944. The battalion CP is listed at 888234—putting them two miles due east of the Monte Villa barracks. On modern maps, the location is along a small ravine between the Via Tora and Via Capo d'Acqua routes.

56   756th Commander's Narrative, January and February 1944, 7.

57   Hougen, *34th Infantry Division*, "The 34th Establishes Bridge-Heads."

58   756th Unit Journal, 25 January 1944 (0500 and 0545 entries).

59   756th Commander's Narrative for January and February 1944, 8.

60   756th Unit Journal, 25 January 1944 (0700 entry).

61   133rd Cannon Co Unit Journal, 25 January 1944.

62   Lee McCardell, "Cassino's Defense System Described," *The Baltimore Sun* (Baltimore, Maryland), 1 February 1944, 1.

63   McCardell, Lee. "Cassino Battle Shifts To Foot of Monastery," *The Baltimore Sun* (Baltimore, Maryland), 9 February 1944, 1.

64   Hougen, *34th Infantry Division*, "The 34th Establishes Bridge-Heads."

65   Wilkinson, *Breakthrough Battalion*, 59.

66   Ankrum, *Dogfaces Who Smiled Through Tears*, 391.

67   Tom Treanor, "Treanor Covers Hell's 100 Acres," *The Los Angeles Times* (Los Angeles, California), 2 February 1944, 1, 4.

68   Wilkinson, B*reakthrough Battalion*, 60.

69   Ibid., 61.

70   Duus, *Unlikely Liberators*, 121.

71   Lee McCardell, "Hawaiian Born Japs (Puka Puka) Led Bold Raid on Cassino," *The Evening Sun* (Baltimore, Maryland), 26 February 1944, 1.

72   Ibid.

73   Blumenson, *Salerno To Cassino*, 369: Reports Ryder ordered 100th Bn to shift to the regiment's far north, but the 34th G-3 Journal and the 133rd Inf Regt S-3 reports do not support this. The 100th Bn actually attacked on the far south.

74   133rd S-3 Report, 241800 to 251800 January 1944.

75   133rd Cannon Co Unit Journal, 25 January 1944.

76   Ibid.

77   Otto, *Howitzer*, 1933, 130.

78   Treanor, *One Damn Thing*, 241. The exact location of Clough's OP was not identified in the Unit Journals. Redle recalls it was across from the barracks and The Pimple, so it is likely one of the farmhouses along the Cassino–Sant' Elia road near the "23" gridline on the 1:25,000 scale map.

79   Unclear whether this was via radio or field phone line.

80   Fazendin, 756th at Cassino, 14–16: Redle recollection.

81   Mudd, "History 756th," 28–29; Gooderson, *Cassino 1944*, 68–69.

82   Redle letter, 25 January 2004; B Co/756th Unit Journal, 24 January 1944.

83   Wilkinson, *Breakthrough Battalion*, 62.

84   Fazendin, *756th at Cassino*, 16–17: Redle recollection.

85   Hougen, *34th Infantry Division*, "The 34th Establishes Bridge-Heads."

86   Treanor, *One Damn Thing*, 239.

87   133rd Cannon Co Unit Journal, 25 January 1944.

88   Wilkinson, *Breakthrough Battalion*, 62.

89   34th Infantry Division, Lessons Learned in Combat, November 7–8 1942–September 1944." Italy, September 1944: Testimony of 1st Lt Jerome L. Fluster, 133rd Inf Regt, 61.

90   Wilkinson, *Breakthrough Battalion*, 61; Hougen, *34th Infantry Division*, "The 34th Establishes Bridge-Heads"; 133rd Inf Regt CP located at 876224 according to the 756th Unit Journal, 25 January 1944 (1015 entry). This location is one mile due east of a Rapido River segment roughly ¼ mile south of the barracks. Modern maps show this is a stone house on the west side of Via San Leonardo Filieri about 200 yards north of the intersection of Via San Pasquale.

91   756th Commander's Narrative, January and February 1944, 8–10.

92   Treanor, *One Damn Thing*, 240; 756th Unit Journal, 25 January 1944 (1015 entry).

93   Redle letter, 5 October 2000

94   Wilkinson, *Breakthrough Battalion*, 59.

95   756th Commander's Narrative for January and February 1944, 10.
      Ibid.

96   Ibid.

97   Ibid., B Company of 16th Armored Engineer Battalion arrived.

98   Ranspach Diary, 25 January 1944; Fazendin, 756th Unit History, 1944, 47; According to the HQ Co 756th
      Morning Reports, 25 January 44, this unfortunate man was Cpl Dean R. Clow.

99   756 Commander's Narrative for January and February 1944, 10–11. B Company of 16th Armored Engineer
      Battalion arrived.

100   Ibid.; 756th Unit Journal, 25 January 1944 (1045 entry).

101   133rd Cannon Co Unit Journal, 25 January 1944.

102   Wilkinson, *Breakthrough Battalion*, 62.

103   133rd Cannon Co Unit Journal, 25 January 1944.

104   B Co/756th Unit Journal, 24 January 1944.

105   Ibid., 25 January 1944; 756th Unit Journal, 25 January 1944 (1500 entry): Road is from "S" to "O" on
      code map.

106   756 S-3 report (34th Inf Div G-3 records), 251800 to 261800 period, January 1944.

107   756th Unit Journal, 25 January 1944 (1630 entry). Location was 864211.

108   Ibid., 1800 entry.

109   The platoon leader involved in this incident may have been S/Sgt Bernard Gaugler.

110   756th Unit Journal, 25 January 1944 (1930 entry).

111   Ibid., 2000 entry; 34th Inf Div G-3 report 261800 to 271800 period, January 1944. The main "corduroy"
      tank trail led to point 861240. The other routes were considered secondary at this early time.

112   133rd Cn Co Unit Journal, 25 January 1944.

113   Fazendin, *756th at Cassino,* 18: Redle recollection.

114   Keynote address by Young O. Kim at 40th Anniversary reunion for the 100th Battalion, July 1982.

115   *U.S. Army Register* 1945, 176.

116   Fazendin, *756th at Cassino,* 18–19: Redle recollection.

117   Gooderson, *Cassino 1944,* 69; Blumenson, *Salerno to Cassino,* 366.

118   Carley Lawrence Marshall 1921 passport application description, U.S. Passport Applications, 1795–1925,
      www.ancestry.com; photo of then Captain Marshall in the article: "CCC Chief" *Guymon Daily News*
      (Guymon, Oklahoma), 23 December 1937, 1.

119   *U.S. Army Register* 1943, 566.

120   Ibid., 566; Marshall 1921 passport description.

121   Hougen, 34th Infantry Division, "Second Fondouk Pass." This battle was witnessed by Captain Wilkinson
      and is described in Chapter 7; "Iowa Outfit Held at Sbiba Against Nazis" *The Des Moines Register* (Des
      Moines, Iowa), 20 August 1943, 1.

122   *U.S. Army Register* 1941, 612.

123   Clough obituary at "Casper Clough, Jr." *Assembly* magazine, USMA, May 1992, Volume L, No.5, 140–41.

124   "442nd Combat team, 100th Inf Battalion, Chapter III: To the Slopes of Monte Cassino," *The Honolulu
      Advertiser* (Honolulu, Hawaii), 4 July 1946, 5.

125   "Casper Clough, Jr." *Assembly* magazine, May 1992, 140–41. Clough later sang many high praises for his
      Nisei troops to several newspapers, calling them "tough and aggressive ... cool, not nervous or flighty ...
      obeying orders implicitly yet they retain initiative of their own," ("Hawaii Battalion Praised by Leader," *The
      Honolulu Advertiser* (Honolulu, Hawaii) 18 August 1944, 1, 8;). "They fight together. One man never leaves
      another holding the bag. They do everything thoroughly and usually accomplish the mission assigned to them.
      They're small but they are tough" ("Puka Battalion form Hawaii Leads Cassino Attack," *Honolulu Star-Bulletin*
      (Honolulu, Hawaii), 29 March 1944, 7.) "They are first class fighters" ("100th Infantry Commander Has
      Praise For Unit," *Honolulu Star-Bulletin* (Honolulu, Hawaii) 8 September 1944, 3.). "Definitely superior
      soldiers, cool and aggressive under fire" (McCardell, Lee. "Hawaiian Born Japs (Puka Puka) Led Bold Raid
      on Cassino." *The Evening Sun* (Baltimore, Maryland), 26 February 1944, 1.) Without question, Clough was
      an officer who cared deeply for his men.

126   Knapp, *Howitzer*, 1939, 130.

127   Duus, *Unlikely Liberators*, 120; Treanor, *One Damn Thing*, 244.

128   Duus, *Unlikely Liberators*, 120.

129   Kim, Keynote address at 40th Anniversary reunion; 34th G-3 Journal, 26 January 1944 (0225 entry).

130   756th Unit Journal, 26 January 1944 (0800 entry). Road is described as running from coordinates 867243 to 852247. Tanks were stuck at 862242. This location is near the bridge.

131   Redle recalls the officer killed was a "Cannon Company captain" but he apparently was not the Cannon Company captain for the 133rd Inf Regt.

132   Duus, *Unlikely Liberators*, 122.

133   133rd Cannon Co Unit Journal, 26 January 1944.

134   34th G-3 report covering 261800 to 271800 period, January 1944.

135   Duus, *Unlikely Liberators*, 122.

136   Treanor, *One Damn Thing*, 241–42.

137   Ibid., 242.

138   Ibid., 242–43.

139   Fazendin, 756th at Cassino, 19: Redle recollection.

140   Treanor, *One Damn Thing*, 243.

141   Ibid.

142   Wilkinson, *Breakthrough Battalion*, 64; 133rd Cn Co Unit Journal, 26 January 1944; 133rd 1st Bn/HQ Co Morning Reports, 27 January 1944.

143   Lewis personal papers: undated letter to Fazendin.

144   Ranspach Diary, 26 January 1944.

145   756th Unit Journal, 26 January 1944 (1410 entry).

146   Ibid., 1030 and 1115 entries.

147   Tom Treanor, "Mine Fields at Rapido Hit Charging Troops," *The Los Angeles Times* (Los Angeles, California) 31 January 1944, 2.

148   756th Unit Journal, 26 January 1944 (1300 entry).

149   Ibid., 1330 entry; 756th S-3 report (34th Inf Div records), 251800 to 261800 period, January 1944.

150   756th Unit Journal, 26 January 1944 (1400 entry).

151   Ibid., 1415 and 1420 entries; Tom Treanor, "The Home Front," *The Los Angeles Times* (Los Angeles, California), 30 January 1944, 2.

152   B Co/756th Unit Journal, 26 January 1944.

153   133rd Cannon Co Unit Journal, 26 January 1944.

154   756th Commander's Narrative, January and February 1944, 11.

155   Ranspach Diary, 26 January 1944; According to the Morning Reports Sv Co/756 27 January 44, the victim was Pvt Envald S. Hindrum. T/5 Earl V. Giesige of Service Company was also lightly wounded in the back the same day but remained on duty. These incidents may have been related.

156   756th Unit Journal, 26 January 1944 (1500 entry).

157   Ibid., 1505 entry.

158   Hougen, *34th Infantry Division*, "The 34th Establishes Bridge-Heads."

159   Captain James A. Luttrell, "The Operations of the 168th Infantry (34th Infantry Division) in the Rapido River Crossing, 28 January – 10 February 1944. (Rome-Arno Campaign) (Personal Experience of a Cannon Company Commander)." The Infantry School, Fort Benning Georgia, Advanced Infantry Officers Course 1948–1949; 12.

160   756th Unit Journal, 26 January 1944 (1245, 1830, and 1920 entries).

161   Ford, *Cassino: Breaking Gustav Line*, 43–44.

162   Gooderson, *Cassino 1944*, 69.

163   756th Unit Journal, 26 January 1944 (2100 entry).

164   Treanor, *One Damn Thing*, 245.

165   Ibid., 246.

166   756th Unit Journal, 26 January 1944 (1830, 1920, and 2020 entries).

167   756th Commander's Narrative, January and February 1944, 10–12.

168   Ibid., 12.

169 Fazendin, *756th at Cassino*, 18: Redle recollection.

170 Ibid.; Mudd, "History 756th," 30.

171 756th Unit Journal, 26 January 1944 (1315 entry). The location of the crossing is at point "H."

172 Wilkinson, *Breakthrough Battalion*, 63.

173 Duus, *Unlikely Liberators*, 120.

174 Ibid., 122.

175 Ibid., 123; United States Army, *Fifth Army History, Part IV, Cassino and Anzio, 16 January 1944–13 March 1944*, (Florence, Italy: L'Impronta Press, 1944?) 53: Reports the 133rd Inf Regt suffered 300 casualties in the two-day attack ending 26 January 1944. Undoubtedly, many of these were Clough's men.

176 B Co/756th Unit Journal, 26 January 1944; Fazendin, *756th at Cassino*, 19: Carl Mras recollection; US World War II Hospital Admission Card Files, 1942–1954 (www.ancestry.com).

177 Ibid., 13–19: Redle recollection.

178 Ibid., 26–32: Wilkinson recollection.

179 Wilkinson, "The Way It All Started," 20–21.

Chapter 13

1 Presumably sixteen tanks lined up, since Redle was not involved. It's unlikely his crew participated without him.

2 34th G-2 Reports, 120026 to 120027 January 1944: Temperature was 35 degrees.

3 Fazendin, *756th at Cassino*, 26–27: Wilkinson recollection.

4 Ibid.; Redle letter, 25 January 2004.

5 Wilkinson, "The Way It All Started," 20.

6 Location is based upon Redle's recollection. His vague description matches the terrain where the 756th HQ CP was established along the ravine near the Via Capo d'Acqua, or it may be a different place.

7 133rd Cannon Co Unit Journal, 27 January 1944.

8 United States Army, *Fifth Army History, Part IV, Cassino and Anzio, 16 January 1944–13 March 1944*, Florence, Italy: L'Impronta Press, 1944, 53.

9 Hougen, *34th Infantry Division*, "The 34th Establishes Bridgeheads." 34th G-3 report, 261800 to 271800 January 1944. Artillery fired from 0630 to 0730 as preparation.

10 756th S-3 report, 271800 to 281800, January 1944: Location provided was 853240; U.S. Army, *Fifth Army History: Part IV*, 53.

11 756th Commander's Narrative, January and February 1944, 12; 1st Lt Belfrad H. Gray, Jr., "The Crossing of the Rapido River and Occupation of Positions Above Cassino, Italy, by Company "I," 168th Infantry (34th Infantry Division) 27 January – 15 February 1944 (Rome-Arno Campaign) (Personal Experience of a Squad Leader," The Infantry School, Fort Benning, Georgia, Advanced Infantry Officers Course 1947–48, 9.

12 Fazendin, *756th at Cassino*, 27: Wilkinson recollection.

13 Hougen, *34th Infantry Division*, "The 34th Establishes Bridgeheads."

14 Camp, *Tankers in Tunisia*, 25.

15 756th Commander's Narrative, January and February 1944, 11–12.

16 Fazendin, *756th at Cassino*, 27: Wilkinson recollection.

17 Ibid., 20: Redle recollection.

18 Redle letter, 5 October 2000.

19 Wilkinson, "The Way It All Started," 20–21.

20 Redle letter, 5 October 2000.

21 Fazendin, *756th at Cassino*, 27: Wilkinson recollection.

22 34th G-3 Journal, 27 January 1944.

23 Fazendin, *756th at Cassino*, 28: Wilkinson recollection.

24 34th G-3 Journal, 27 January 1944, records that elements of A Co/168th Inf Regt were the first infantrymen to cross with the two tanks.

25 34th G-3 Journal, 27 January 1944 (0900 entry).

26 It is unclear why Graffagnini's tank hadn't crossed at this point. One possible reason is that it became mired temporarily.

27 Fazendin, *756th at Cassino*, 32–33: Fazendin's reconstruction of the events; Perdue phone conversation, 31 January 2004. Perdue believes he was assigned to the 1st platoon at the time, but the tank position and Wilkinson's recollection of events makes it more likely he was in the 2nd platoon.

28 Ibid., 28–29: Wilkinson recollection.

29 Sweeting directly relieving Leger is speculative, but Wilkinson would not have had the time nor opportunity to do it himself.

30 B Co/756th Unit Journal, 27 January 1944.

31 Redle interview, 13 March 2004.

32 Wilkinson letter, 31 May 2005.

33 B Co/756th Unit Journal, 27 January 1944, confirms Wilkinson took Sgt Campbell's tank. According to the 1940 Census, Sgt Leland P. Campbell was 25 years old (in 1944) and from Nampa Canyon, Idaho. In Fazendin's book, *756th at Cassino*, 29, Wilkinson mistakenly identifies Osganian as the sergeant, but Osganian transferred to D Company when the battalion reorganized in December 1943.

34 Speculative, but these are likely the instructions Wilkinson gave since his aim was to get as many tanks across the river as quickly as possible.

35 Fazendin, *756th at Cassino*, 29: Wilkinson recollection.

36 Ibid., 33–34: Fazendin's reconstruction of events.

37 Ibid., 13: Redle recollection.

38 756th Commander's Narrative, January and February 1944, 12.

39 Wilkinson, "The Way It All Started," 21.

40 According to the 756th S-3 Report, 271800 to 281800 January 1944, this crossing was accomplished at 0915; The B Co/756th Morning Report, 21 April 1944, under "Record of Events" for 27 January, also reports the crossing occurred at 0915.

41 B Co/756th Unit Journal, 27 January 1944, confirms that Henry, Wilkinson, Cogdill, and Jarvis were the four tank commanders who crossed.

42 Fazendin, *756th at Cassino*, 34: Fazendin reconstruction of events; NARA enlistment records for Joseph Cutrone; Joe Cutrone letter to Dave Redle, 24 September 1989.

43 34th Inf Div "Lessons Learned in Combat," 55: Powers account.

44 Ibid.

45 Fazendin, *756th at Cassino*, 30: Wilkinson recollection.

46 Ranspach diary, 27 January 1944; 34th G-2 reports, 120026 to 120027 January 1944.

47 756th Commander's Narrative for January and February 1944, 12–13; 34th G-3 Journal, 27 January 1944 (1945 and 2045 entries), originally reported five tanks had crossed with 168th with two tanks still across the river that evening. The 34th G-3 Journal, 28 January 1944 (0927 entry), however, corrected the record that only four tanks crossed. The B Co/756th Unit Journal, 27 January 1944, also confirms only four tanks crossed that morning. The tank numbers were as follows: W-3066030 (Campbell/Wilkinson), W-3066400 (Crawford/Henry), W-3010899 (Jarvis), and W-3015622 (Cogdill).

48 Wilkinson, "The Way It All Started," 21; Redle letter, 17 January 2009; 34th Inf Div "Lessons Learned in Combat," 56: Powers account.

49 Redle letter, 17 January 2009.

50 34th G-3 Journal, 27 January 1944 (1035 entry).

51 Ibid.

52 Ibid., 1010 and 1035 entries. The 1010 entry specifically states "4 tanks across just N of barracks. Inf will not jump off until tanks get their job done." The tankers of the 756th have long wondered why the infantry was not more aggressive in following them that day. One reason appears to be that the infantry commanders had unrealistic expectations of what those four tanks could accomplish alone that morning.

53 34th G-3 Journal, 27 January 1944 (1930 entry).

54 133rd Cannon Co Unit Journal, 27 January 1944.

55 I Co/168th and L Co/168th Morning Reports, for 27–31 January 1944.

56 Gray, "Crossing of the Rapido, I Co/168th," 20.

57 Ibid.

58   34th Inf Div "Lessons Learned in Combat," 55: Powers account.

59   168th S-3 Report, 261800 to 271800 January 1944.

60   756th S-3 Report, 271800 to 281800 January 1944. One platoon of tanks reported at 857241 (just to the SE of cemetery) at noon.

61   34th G-3 Journal, 28 January 1944 (1500 entry).

62   34th Inf Div "Lessons Learned in Combat," 55: Powers account.

63   34th G-3 Journal, 27 January 1944 (1930 entry).

64   Ibid., 2010 entry.

65   Pioneer tools included shovels, pickaxes, sledge hammers, cleaning rods, etc.

66   Fazendin, *756th at Cassino*, 23–24: Mancini recollection.

67   "Three More Enlist For Army Service" *Journal and Courier* (Lafayette, Indiana), 23 August 1940, 18.

68   34th Inf Div "Lessons Learned in Combat," 55: Powers account.

69   NARA enlistment record for Randolph H. Perdue.

70   Fazendin, *756th at Cassino*, 34: Fazendin reconstruction; Perdue phone conversation, 31 January 2004. The author is somewhat skeptical that a German soldier would have been operating along the Rapido at this time, but the detail is included since Perdue was reliable with most of his other recollections, and because Fazendin also chose to include it in his book.

71   34th G-3 report, 120027 to 120028 January 1944.

72   Wilkinson, "The Way It All Started," 20–21.

73   Tom Treanor, "Tom Treanor Thumbs Ride Over Rapido" *The Los Angeles Times* (Los Angeles, California), 3 February 1944, 1, 4.

74   34th G-3 Journal, 28 January 1944 (1500 entry).

75   B Co/756th Unit Journal, 27 January 1944, confirms blown track from mine. Wilkinson "The Way It All Started," 21: Redle recalls that Henry gave this instruction to Jarvis, but Wilkinson remembers otherwise; Redle letter, 5 October 2000; Fazendin, *756th at Cassino*, 20–21: Redle recollection; 756th Commander's Narrative, January and February 1944, 12–13; Redle letter, 30 January 2008.

76   756th Commander's Narrative, January and February 1944, 13.

77   Ibid., 13–14.

78   Redle letter, 5 October 2000.

79   34th G-2 Report, 120008 to 120009 February 1944; Gives the 34th HQ OP location as "our OP at 889184" (NE on Mt Trocchio).

80   34th G-3 Journal, 27 January 1944 (1245 entry). Reports Ryder was at this OP when Clark joined him at 1245.

81   Ibid., 0933 and 1127 entries.

82   Ibid., 1155 entry.

83   Ibid., 1125 entry.

84   168th S-3 Report, 261800 to 271800 January 1944.

85   34th G-3 Journal 27 January 1944 (1225 entry): The engineers promised to arrive sometime in the afternoon.

86   Gray, "Crossing of the Rapido, I Co/168th," 23; 34th Inf Div "Lessons Learned in Combat," 60–61: account of Lt Col Robert E. Coffey, commanding 109th Engineer Battalion.

87   34th G-3 Journal, 27 January 1944 (1000 and 1245 entries).

88   Ibid., 1320. This entry also claims I Company had crossed but this is contradicted by 1st Lt. Belfrad Gray's monograph account on page 11. Gray claims I Company failed to cross the river because L Company had halted ahead of them along the far bank.

89   Gooderson, *Cassino 1944*, 69.

90   756th S-3 Report, 271800 to 281800 January 1944. Capt Arnold reports the footbridge position at 860237.

91   Ibid.; 756th S-3 Report, 271800 to 281800 January 1944. Capt Arnold reports the possible crossing point at 863247.

92   Graham, *Cassino*, 41.

93   Ford, *Cassino 1944*, 42; Plowman, *Battles for Cassino*, 76–82; Wallace, *The Italian Campaign*, 134.

94   The German 5th Mountain Division (Wehrmacht) held these heights.

95   Parker, *Monte Cassino*, 125–127; Plowman, *Battles for Cassino*, 80.

96   Hapgood, *Monte Cassino*, 122.

97   E.D. Smith, *The Battles for Monte Cassino* (New York, NY: Charles Scribner & Sons, 1975), 31–32 and 41; Parker, *Monte Cassino*, 128–29; Hapgood, *Monte Cassino*, 121–22.

98   Walker, "Comments on the Rapido River Crossing," 26. In 1962, Walker quantified the casualties this way: "At the end of January 25th, the day of the cessation of fire to permit recovery of our dead and wounded, the 15th Panzer Grenadier Division, which opposed the Rapido crossing, reported having counted 430 American dead and having captured 770 prisoners of war. The 15th Panzer Grenadier Division reported their own casualties for the same period as 64 dead and 179 wounded."

99   Smith, *Battles for Monte Cassino*, 68; Blumenson, *Salerno to Cassino*, 372; Hougen, *34th Infantry Division*, "The French at Belvedere."

100   34th G-3 Journal, 27 January 1944 (1310 and 1915 entries).

101   Wilkinson, "The Way It All Started," 21; Location and time confirmed by the 34th G-3 Journal, 27 January 1944, 1235. 6th Armored Field Artillery observers spotted Wilkinson's tanks moving at this location and contacted 34th G-3 to make sure they were not seeing German tanks.

102   Wilkinson, "The Way It All Started," 21.

103   Ibid., 21.

104   Redle letter, 17 January 2009.

105   Ibid., 30 January 2008.

106   Fazendin, *756th at Cassino*, 31: Wilkinson recollection.

107   Redle letter, 5 October 2000; Redle letter, 4 April 2010.

108   Fazendin, *756th at Cassino*, 31, Wilkinson recollection; Redle letter, 5 Oct 2000.

109   Wilkinson "The Way It All Started" 21: This weapon was either a Faust Patrone 42 or a Panzerfaust 30 model. The author believes this may have been the very first time a German shoulder-fired AT weapon was used against an Allied tank on the Western Front. The weapon is described vaguely in the 34th Inf Div G-2 Intelligence Summary #109, 8 February 44, as a German "Bazooka"—an American term demonstrating unfamiliarity with the German version. Captured and translated instructions on how to fire the weapon were also attached as an addendum. Four days later, a G-2 Report dated 120009 to 120010 February 1944 issued further clarification: "In G-2 Intelligence Summary #109, 8 February 1944, mention was made of the German "Bazooka," but it is the Fistcharge or Faust Patrone #2. The German Bazooka, a sample of which has been sent in from this Hqs, is similar in appearance to ours." The lag time in reporting, the vague language, and the fact a sample was sent to the Fifth Army clearly shows this was a was a new and strange weapon to 34th Inf Div intelligence officers. Gordon L. Rottman, in his book *Panzerfaust and Panzerschreck* (Oxford, UK: Osprey Publishing, 2014, 13–14), claims the Faust Patrone 42 saw only limited field testing in early 1943 on the Eastern Front due to its crude construction and limited range. Either the 34th Inf Div G-2 misidentified the captured weapon, or Faust Patrone 42s eventually saw service in Italy as well. According to Rottman (page 20), the Panzerfaust 30 model was issued in late 1943 and early 1944. In his memoirs, Wilkinson recalled when he first saw the weapon on 27 January 1944 that it "looked like a derby hat on a stick." This roughly describes either model. When asked specifically about the incident in 2014, Redle remembered no U.S. Army weapons demonstrations featuring German "bazookas" prior to Cassino—further indicating it was a weapon unknown to American tankers in January 1944. The B Co/756th Morning Reports, 21 April 1944, "record of events" for 27 January also reports the two tanks were "disabled by bazooka fire." Finally, war correspondent Lee McCardell reports on 15 February 1944: "Nazis have a bazooka ... similar to ours, but of larger and more rugged construction." (McCardell, Lee. "German Stand Below Rome Credited To Reinforcements" *The Baltimore Sun* (Baltimore, Maryland), 15 February 1944, 2.)

110   Redle interview, 13 March 2004; Redle letter, 30 January 2008 to Harry Yeide.

111   Redle letter, 4 April 2010.

112   Wilkinson, "The Way It All Started, 21; IDPF for Paul P. Tirpak. Tirpak was 29 years old with a fiancée back home in Cleveland named Bernadette Koch. Sadly, for many months she wrote letters with faint hopes that Paul's "KIA" status was an administrative error and that he had really been taken prisoner.

113   Fazendin, *756th at Cassino*, 31–32: Wilkinson recollection.

114   Wilkinson, "The Way It All Started," 21.

115   IDPF for John F. Bacha. Bacha was from Cuyahoga Falls, Ohio.

116   Fazendin, *756th at Cassino*, 32: Wilkinson recollection; IDPF file of John F. Bacha: Wilkinson written testimony dated 31 August 1949.

117 Fazendin, *756th at Cassino*, 32: Wilkinson recollection. Buys is misidentified as one of the commanders. The commander was, in fact, Sgt Cogdill.

118 IDPF file for John F. Bacha: testimony of Sgt Clyde F. Cogdill and T/5 Joe K. Wright given 29 February 1944. Both men witnessed Wilkinson's and Henry's tanks get knocked out and the crews captured.

119 Redle letter, 5 October 2000; "Nine Louisianans Prisoners of War" *The Town Talk* (Alexandria, Louisiana), 15 July 1944, 7.

120 Fazendin, *756th at Cassino*, 2: Redle recollection, and 32: Wilkinson recollection; IDPF for Wayne B. Henry; Wilkinson "The Way It All Started," 21.

121 Fazendin, *756th at Cassino*, 21: Redle recollection; 756th Commander's Narrative for January and February 1944, 13.

122 Redle letter, 5 October 2000; Redle letter to Palumbo, 25 November 1986.

123 Wilkinson, "The Way It All Started" 21; Wilkinson recalls that Henry's surviving crew were taken prisoner and brought near his position within moments of his own capture. The U.S. Army Signal Corps photo of Lt Henry's tank taken 8 February 1944 (SC-187910) clearly shows two panzerfaust holes in the front plate. The author has no direct testimony from Henry's crew on the incident, so some speculation is employed on the circumstances surrounding their capture. The 756th Unit Journal for 27 January 1944 (1330 entry), reports both tanks were hit by "bazooka guns"—indicating observers across the river witnessed events as they unfolded. In the 756th Commander's Narrative, January and February 1944, 13, Sweeting places events in following order: "Two tanks were struck by bazooka rockets when Captain Wilkinson lead the tanks in an attack against a concrete pillbox. The crews of these two tanks were captured." The author interprets Sweeting's account to mean the two panzerfaust blasts on Henry's tank directly led to the crew's surrender.

124 Fazendin, *756th at Cassino*, 32, Wilkinson recollection; B Co/756th Morning Reports, 29 January 1944.

125 IDPF file for John F. Bacha: Wilkinson testimony dated 31 Aug 1949.

126 Fazendin, *756th at Cassino*, 32: Wilkinson recollection.

127 IDPF file for John F. Bacha: A letter by Major T. J. Collum dated 16 September 1949 cites Sgt Clyde Cogdill and T/5 Joe Wright testimony given on 29 February 1944. Cogdill and Wright observed Wilkinson's tank firing several rounds into the pillbox at very close range when the turret began smoking. *Four* men then evacuated and ran across the road toward the Italian Barracks. If their testimony is true, one of those four men would have had to have been Bacha. Tragically, the remains of Pvt Bacha were never recovered—even after the war. His dental records were compared with other unknowns from the area, but with negative results. To this day, it remains a complete mystery why Tirpak's body was recovered a few days later and yet Bacha's body was never found. If what Laliberty and Crawford witnessed of Bacha's last minutes are accurate, then both bodies *should* have been recovered from inside the tank. The tank did not burn and Tirpak's IDPF shows no evidence of removal or burial by the Germans. The two most plausible explanations to these discrepancies are: (1) Bacha did not fall back inside the tank but instead fell over upon the ground and his remains were subsequently lost—dispersed, perhaps, by artillery blasts in the days that followed, or (2) Bacha survived—but barely. The Germans evacuated him but he expired while being transported to an aid station further up into the hills. The author believes the latter is the more likely explanation and that Bacha still rests somewhere in an unmarked grave between the barracks and the highlands.

128 B Co/756th Unit Journal, 27 January 1944; Wilkinson, "The Way It All Started." 21. Wilkinson misidentifies Buys, when Cogdill was the actual commander.

129 756th Commander's Narrative, January and February 1944, 13; NARA WWII enlistment record, Clyde F. Cogdill; Entered service at Missoula, Montana, ("Final Day Sees 49 of 52 Accepted, Including Two from Here," *The Missoulian* (Missoula, Montana), 22 March 1941, 1).

130 Fazendin, *756th at Cassino*, 39: Lewis recollection.

131 756th Commander's Narrative, January and February 1944, 14.

132 34th G-3 Journal, 27 January 1944 (1610 entry).

133 Ibid., 1310, 1320, 1410; Locations reported as of 1320: A and B Cos 1st Bn/168th at 858237 and I and L Cos of 3rd Bn/168th at 860243.

134 34th G-3 Journal, 27 January 1944, 1410; Gray, "Crossing of the Rapido, I Co/168th," 11.

135 Gray, "Crossing of the Rapido, I Co/168th," 11.

136 34th G-3 Journal, 27 January 1944, 1410: I and L 3rd Bn/168th are, again, reported across the river, but this is disputed by Gray, "Crossing of the Rapido, I Co/168th," 11–12. Gray does not believe both companies succeeded in crossing the river until the night of 29–30.

137 34th G-3 Journal, 27 January 1944 (1320 entry); S-3 168th map overlay dated 271800 January 1944 shows Cos I & L/168th in positions across the river and northwest of 2nd Bn/168th positions near cemetery.

138 34th G-3 Journal, 27 January 1944 (1430 entry). This happened at 1430.

139 U.S. Army, *Fifth Army History: Part IV*, 54; 34th G-3 Journal, 27 January 1944 (1430 entry); 34th G-3 report, 261800 to 271800, January 1944. The location of the cemetery was at 855242.

140 34th G-3 Journal, 27 January 1944 (1430 entry). Direction where AT gun appeared is speculative, but this is the most likely place.

141 Ibid., 1500.

142 34th G-2 Report, 261201 to 271200 January 1944.

143 34th G-3 Journal, 27 January 1944 (1035, 1055, 1152, 1220, 1405, and 1445 entries): At 1445, the 34th G-3 reported to the air corps liaison officer of a lot of artillery coming from "S Marino." In 34th G-3 Journal 30 January 1944 (2156 and 2223 entries), Gen Butler with 142nd asks for mortar and long-range MG support from 168th in Caira for their own attack on "Marino." The 34th Inf Div G-3 records for 29 January 1944 (1545 entry): Identifies "Marino" at position 852254—which is on the hill NE of Caira located in the middle of what is today a German cemetery.

144 34th G-3 Journal, 27 January 1944 (1515 and 1520 entries).

145 34th G-2 Report, 301201 to 311200 January 1944.

146 756th Commander's Narrative, January and February 1944, 14.

147 Ibid.

148 34th G-3 Journal, 27 January 1944 (1840 entry).

149 Ibid.

150 Ibid., 1830 entry.

151 34th G-3 Report, 261800 to 271800 January 1944.

152 II Corps G-3 Report, 271800 to 281800, January 1944. The 168th's front-line positions reported as 855238–856243–855246.

153 I and L Cos/168th Morning Reports, 27–31 January 1944.

154 Fazendin, *756th at Cassino*, 32: Wilkinson recollection.

155 Wilkinson, "The Way It All Started" 21.

156 Ibid., 22; Fazendin, *756th at Cassino*, 32: Wilkinson recollection.

157 756th Unit Journal, 27 January 1944 (1330 entry). Eighteen total tanks remained bogged.

158 Johannesen was from Marshfield (Coos Harbor), Oregon.

159 Wilkinson letter, 31 May 2005.

160 Fazendin, *756th at Cassino*, 21–22: Redle recollection.

161 Ibid., 22–23: Fazendin reconstruction.

162 Ibid. 35, Fazendin reconstruction; Perdue phone conversation, 31 January 2004.

163 Redle phone conversation, 3 January 2002.

164 Assumed, based upon the circumstances.

165 Fazendin, *756th at Cassino*, 35, Fazendin reconstruction; Perdue phone conversation, 7 January 2004.

166 Ibid., 37, Palumbo recollection.

167 Ibid., 23–24: Mancini recollection.

168 Ibid., 21: Redle recollection; 756th Commander's Narrative for January and February 1944, 13; Redle letter, 5 October 2000; Redle says Jarvis and his crew arrived around 2200; B Co/756th Morning Report, 21 April 1944, "Record of Events" for 27 January reports Jarvis's crew returned "after dusk"; 34th G-3 Journal, 28 January 1944, 1500. B Co/756th Unit Journal, 27 January 1944.

169 Assumed, based upon the circumstances.

170 Fazendin, *756th at Cassino*, 21: Redle recollection.

171 Ibid.

172 756th Commander's Narrative, January and February 1944, 14.

173 Fazendin, *756th at Cassino*, 13: Redle recollection.

174 B Co/756th Unit Journal, 1 February 1944.

175 Fazendin, *756th at Cassino*, 30–31, Fazendin description.

176 Ibid., 24, Redle recollection.

177 Fazendin, *756th at Cassino*, xxxiv.

178 Ibid.

179 Redle letter, 29 April 2003; Redle letter, 3 January 2001.

180 Redle letter, 29 April 2003.

Chapter 14

1 Plowman, *Battles for Cassino*, 83.

2 Steven Thomas Barry, *Battalion Commanders at War: U.S. Army Tactical Leadership in the Mediterranean Theater, 1942–1943* (Lawrence, Kansas: University Press of Kansas, 2013), 180.

3 34th G-3 Journal, 27 January 1944, 1945: A and B Cos/168th at 855238, L Co/168th slightly northeast of cemetery at 856248. I and K Cos/168th across river and will cut south at 854247.

4 34th G-3 Journal, 27 January 1944 (1945 entry).

5 Ibid., 27 January 1944 (2245 entry) and 28 January 1944 (0105 entry).

6 34th G-2 Report, 120027 to 120028 January 1944.

7 Plowman, *Battles for Cassino*, 88.

8 34th G-3 Journal, 27 January 1944, 2045; 34th G-3 Report 120027 to 120028 January 1944: MG positions reported at 857238; II Corps G-3 Report, 271800 to 281800 period, January 1944: 168th line reported as 855238–856243–855246.

9 34th G-2 Report, 120027 to 120028 January 1944.

10 Gray, "Crossing of the Rapido, I Co/168th," 12; 34th G-3 Report, 180027 to 180028 January 1944.

11 Location of crossing attempt was at 867264.

12 34th G-3 Journal, 28 January 1944 (0710 and 0815 entries).

13 Ibid., 0800 entry.

14 Ibid., 0927 entry.

15 Ibid., 27 January 1944 (1840 entry).

16 Treanor, *One Damn Thing*, 246.

17 Fazendin, *756th at Cassino*, 38: Redle recollection.

18 Ibid.

19 756th S-3 report (34th Inf Div records), 251800 to 261800 period, January 1944: San Pietro B-Trains position reported at 961164.

20 Fazendin, *756th at Cassino*, 35: Fazendin reconstruction.

21 Olson phone conversation, 7 December 2007.

22 B Co, 756th Unit Journal, 28 January 1944; B Company handwritten "Yellow Orders," 281400 January, 756th Tank Battalion records, (National Archives, Army Records Group 407, Boxes 16769–16772); B Co/756th Morning Reports, 21 April 1944, "Record of Events" for 27 January 1944.

23 756th Unit Journal, 28 January 1944 (0700 entry).

24 Ibid., 28 January 1944 (1500, and 1700 entries).

25 Treanor, *One Damn Thing*, 246; The engineers were from the 235th Combat Engineers Battalion of the 1108th Engineers group.

26 756th "Yellow Orders," 271600 January 1944.

27 Inferred from Wilkinson's recollections and the fact that the engineers opted to create bypasses to the north and south of the bridge after 27 January 1944.

28 34th Inf Div "Lessons Learned in Combat," 55–56: Powers account.

29 756th "Yellow Orders," 280140 January 1944.

30 Smith, *Battles for Monte Cassino*, 68; Bond, *Return to Cassino*, 69; Probably "Sommerfeld matting"—flexible, reusable wire mesh approximately ten feet wide that was rolled out and secured at the edges with steel stakes.

31 34th G-3 Journal, 27 January 1944 (1520, 1523, and 1528 entries).

32 34th Inf Div "Lessons Learned in Combat," 55: Powers account.

33 756th Unit Journal, 28 January 1944 (1220 entry); Lt Col George M. Davis commanded the 760th at this time. He and Sweeting met at 0115 earlier the same day to coordinate this transfer according to 760th Tank Battalion "Operations in Italy, January 1944" (obtained in PDF form from the CARL, Fort Leavenworth, Kansas) and the 756th Unit Journal 28 January 1944 (0115 entry).

34 756th Unit Journal, 28 January 1944 (1400 entry).
35 Helmuth O. Froeschle, *Our Story of the 760th Tank Battalion, WWII* (Victoria, Canada, Trafford Publishing, 2007), 35; Sawicki, *Tank Battalions of the U.S. Army*, 334.
36 Froeschle, *Our Story of the 760th,* 40–43, 61.
37 Ibid., 152 (photo); Nelson was from Port Richey, Florida according to 760th Tank Battalion "Operations in Italy, May 1944."
38 756th Unit Journal, 28 January 1944 (1800 entry).
39 34th G-3 Journal, 28 January 1944 (1012 entry).
40 Lewis personal papers: undated letter to Fazendin.
41 34th G-3 Journal, 28 January 1944 (2235 entry).
42 Lewis personal papers: undated letter to Fazendin.
43 756th Unit Journal, 28 January 1944, 1900; 34th G-3- Journal, 28 January 1944 (1500 entry).
44 34th G-3 Journal, 28 January 1944 (1500 entry).
45 135th S-3 report, 180027 to 180028 January 1944; 135th S-3 report, 180028 to 180028 January 1944.
46 756th Unit Journal, 28 January 1944 (0925, 0945, 0950, and 1015 entries). Positions fired upon were at 851241 (behind the cemetery) and 850234 (behind the barracks area.)
47 Lewis, personal papers: undated letter to Fazendin. 756th Commander's Narrative for January & February 1944, 15–16.
48 34th G-3 Journal, 28 January 1944 (2040 entry); 34th G-3 Journal, 28 January 1944 (2130 entry).
49 Fazendin, *756th at Cassino*, 58–60, quoting article by Hal Boyle, an AP correspondent in the St. Paul Dispatch dated 2 February 1944.
50 756th Unit Journal, 28 January 1944 (2200 entry).
51 34th G-3 Report, 180027 to 180028 January 1944.
52 These men were Pfc Norval N. Clayton (KIA), Pvt John Rodriguez (SWA) and Cpl Norman S. Lindow, T/5 Otis E. Hyles, Pfc James B. Patty, Pvt Alex P. Reed (all WIA), according to 756th Morning Reports, 28 January 1944.
53 They were Pvt Joseph Czerkas (A Co), Pvt Albert C. Schmall (C Co), both LWA, according to 756th Morning Reports, 28 January 1944.
54 34th G-3 Journal, 28 January 1944 (2235 entry).
55 IDPF file, Wayne B. Henry.
56 34th G-3 Journal, 29 January 1944 (0120, 0300, 0303, 0305, and 0355 entries).
57 Ibid., 0358, 0413 entries. Reports MG at 853237.
58 Gooderson, *Cassino 1944*, 69.
59 34th G-3 Journal, 29 January 1944 (0110 and 0729 entries). Bypasses located just north and south of 861243. Route C located at gridline 261 and Cassino–Sant' Elia road.
60 "Young Combat Engineer Solves Problem that Stumped Generals in Italy Drive." *The Tampa Times* (Tampa, Florida), 2 February 1944, 4.
61 C Co/756th Morning Reports, 29 January 1944. List of casualties: Pfc Clyde M. Long (KIA), Pvt Harvey J. Arrington Jr. (KIA), T/5 Rudolph A. Sharbutt (DOW), T/5 Lewis Paxton (SWA), Sgt Herman C. Kirtley (WIA), T/5 William B. Toler (WIA), 1st Lt David Loeb (WIA), Pvt Bernard L. Cohen (WIA), Pvt Donald G. Isakson (WIA); 756th Unit Journal, 29 January 1944 (0520 entry).
62 C Co/756th Morning Report, 30 January 1944. Perkins was officially given command on 30 January.
63 756th Unit Journal, 29 January 1944 (0520 entry).
64 Lewis personal papers: undated letter to Fazendin.
65 34th G-3 Journal, 29 January 1944 (0610 entry).
66 Ibid., 0606 entry.
67 756th Unit Journal, 29 January 1944 (0600 and 0615 entries).
68 Lewis, personal papers: undated letter to Fazendin.
69 Ibid.
70 Ibid.
71 Lewis does not provide a name for a platoon leader but writes that S/Sgt Harris was in command.
72 Fazendin, *756th at Cassino*, 46–52: Lewis recollection.
73 756th Unit Journal, 29 January 1944 (0630 entry).

74   Ibid., 0600 & 0615 entries.

75   133rd Cannon Co Unit Journal, 29 January 44; Lewis, personal papers: undated letter to Fazendin.

76   Gooderson, *Cassino 1944*, 69.

77   34th G-3 Journal, 29 January 1944 (0617 and 0650 entries); 760th "Operations in Italy, January 1944."

78   34th G-3 Journal, 27 January 1944 (2010 entry); Plowman, *Battles for Cassino*, 88; Blumenson, *Salerno to Cassino*, 372.

79   756th Unit Journal 29 January 1944 (0700 entry).

80   756th S-3 Report, 180028 to 180028 January 1944.

81   34th G-3 Journal, 29 January 1944 (0750 entry).

82   34th Inf Div "Lessons Learned in Combat," 54: Powers account.

83   Treanor, *One Damn Thing*, 246.

84   Lewis misidentified his loader as Pvt Merlin Kudick in Fazendin's book. Lewis had forgotten the man's name after the war and tried to recall his identity in the early '90s by looking through the 756th's KIA list. The IDPF file for Edward J. Dudzinski documents that he was the one killed 29 January 1944 from shell fragment wounds (SFW) to the face. Dudzinski was from Bristol, Connecticut, and married to a woman named Anna.

85   Treanor, *One Damn Thing*, 247: This is presumed to be S/Sgt Ames, as only he, Capt Lewis, and S/Sgt Harris had transmitters. S/Sgt Harris is unlikely to have issued this warning, because his tank was never hit. Had he seen the German SP gun, he would have been able to knock it out.

86   IDPF file, Herman Bayless. S/Sgt Ames and Pfc Frank J. Casper were the only two who evacuated. Cpl William F. McGill, T/4 Bayless, and Pvt Alfred R. Shanahan perished in the resulting fire and their remains were cremated.

87   Lewis personal papers: undated letter to Fazendin, Lewis draft notes; Plowman, *Battles for Cassino*, 88; 756th S-3 Reports, 180028 to 180028 January 44; 756th Unit Journal, 29 January 1944 (0755 entry).

88   Treanor, *One Damn Thing*, 247.

89   Lewis personal papers: undated letter to Fazendin.

90   A Co/756th Morning Reports, 29 January 1944. Four were listed as seriously wounded in action (SWA): S/Sgt Thomas P. Ames, Pvt Vincent P. Ciccarelli, T/4 Leroy Doolittle, and Cpl Nazario Martinez. Seven were listed as wounded in action (WIA): Pfc Frank J. Casper, Capt French G. Lewis, 1st Lt Robert L. Gilman, Cpl Frank H. Linderman, T/4 Earl Hollon, Pfc Ignacio Jimenez, and Pfc Richard F. Makynen.

91   756th Unit History, 1944: GO #29, 34th Inf Div dated 21 April 1944. Hollon was from Quicksand, Kentucky. It is unclear from the citation in which tank he was the driver. Only that it was "knocked out" and he helped his "platoon leader" attend to the other wounded men on 29 January 1944.

92   Lewis personal papers, undated letter to Fazendin. Maj Long letter dated 16 June 1945 "Complete Statement of Services Rendered'; French Lewis received the Silver Star for his actions that day, 756th Unit History, 1944; GO #29 34th Inf Div dated 21 April 1944.

93   Those killed were T/4 Herman Bayless (not recovered), Pvt Edward J. Dudzinski, Sgt Raymond V. Galbraith (not recovered), Cpl William F. McGill, Cpl Joseph J. Olbyk (not recovered), and Pvt Alfred R. Shanahan (not recovered), according to the A Co/756th Morning Reports.

94   *Army Register 1944*, 746: 1937 graduate of USMA.

95   Ankrum, *Dogfaces Who Smiled Through Tears*, 397–98; 756th Unit Journal, 29 January 1944 (0755 and 0800 entries).

96   Ankrum, *Dogfaces Who Smiled Through Tears*, 397.

97   756th Unit Journal, 29 January 1944 (0930 entry): This was probably route "A."

98   Ibid., 0900, 0905, 0910, and 0930 entries.

99   34th G-3 Journal, 29 January 1944 (1045 entry).

100   According to 34th G-3 Journal, 29 January 1944 (0920 entry): The 3rd Bn/168th reported one company at road junction 74 (855248). At 0930, Co A/168th also reported one platoon 200 yards across river just south of 24 grid line.

101   34th G-3 Journal, 29 January 1944 (0854 entry).

102   34th G-3 Journal, 29 January 1944 (0930 and 1110 entries).

103   Ibid., 0930 entry.

104   34th Inf Div "Lessons Learned in Combat," 54: Powers account.

105   34th G-3 Journal, 29 January 1944 (0742 and 1255 entries).

106   756th Unit Journal, 29 January 1944 (1145 entry); 34th G-3 Journal, 29 January 1944 (1150 and 1245 entries).

107   34th G-3 Journal, 29 January 1944 (1255 entry).

108   Ibid., 1415 entry. This happened at 1415.

109   Lewis, personal papers: undated letter to Fazendin.

110   34th G-3 Journal, 29 January 1944 (1623 entry).

111   Ibid., 1425 entry.

112   Ibid., 1455 entry.

113   34th G-3 Journal, 29 January 1944 (1623 entry).

114   "Drawling Alabama Engineer Broke Nazi Line" *Corsicana Daily Sun* (Corsicana, Texas), 2 February 1944, 8. Lynch was from Sapulpa, Oklahoma. Fazendin, *756th at Cassino*, 58–60, quoting news article by Hal Boyle, an AP correspondent story that ran in the *St. Paul Dispatch* dated 2 February 1944. This was a D Co light tank commanded by Lt William H. Newman and driven by T/4 Rene E. Cyr. The other two positions in the tank were taken by Capt Sorrel and another engineer officer named Dallas Lynch.

115   McCardell, "McCardell Under Fire With Yanks," 1.

116   "Capt Walker Byrd Sorrell Outwits the Germans in Italy" *Southern Star* (Newton, Alabama), 3 February 1944, 8; *Tampa Times*, "Young Combat Engineer Solves Problem," 4; "Spectacular Jobs are Routine to Unsung Combat Engineers" *Palladium-Item* (Richmond, Indiana), 12 May 1944, 5.

117   756th Unit Journal, 29 January 1944 (1430 and 1640 entries).

118   Donley interview 16 September 2005. The other two battalion M4s were named "Hellbent" and "Hellfire." There is some ambiguity in Donley's descriptions about exactly where Hellcat crossed, but the river ford is the likely place.

119   Treanor, *One Damn Thing*, 258–59.

120   HQ Co/756th Morning Reports, 1 February 44; Brown was reduced to Pvt from T/5 for unknown reasons on 1 February 1944.

121   Lewis personal papers: undated manning chart for HQ from the early Italian Campaign.

122   Donley obituary.

123   Donley diary, 29 January 1944: letter to Jack Brown attached and undated but written after 1993 as it refers to Fazendin's book.

124   34th G-3 Journal, 29 January 1944 (1623 entry); 760th "Operations in Italy, January 1944."

125   34th G-3 Journal, 29 January 1944 (1632 entry).

126   B Co/756th Unit Journal, 29 January 1944.

127   756th S-3 Report, 180028 to 180028 January 1944.

128   Ankrum, *Dogfaces Who Smiled Through Tears*, 397–98.

129   Fazendin, *756th at Cassino*, 63–64: Treanor account.

130   Treanor, *One Damn Thing*, 250.

131   Donley diary, 29 January 1944, letter to Jack Brown (re: Fazendin's book); Plowman, *Battles for Cassino*, 88.

132   Treanor, *One Damn Thing*, 250; Fazendin, 756th at Cassino, 64.

133   756th Unit Journal, 29 January 1944 (1640, 1655, and 1730 entries); 34th G-3 Journal, 29 January 1944 (1905 entry).

134   Ibid., 29 January 1944 (1730 entry).

135   Treanor, *One Damn Thing*, 248.

136   Identified as SCR-511 radios by Lt Col Powers.

137   34th Inf Div "Lessons Learned in Combat," 56: Powers account.

138   Treanor, *One Damn Thing*, 253.

139   Fazendin, *756th at Cassino*, 44: Lewis recollection; Treanor, *One Damn Thing*, 253: Treanor also seems to have heard this same incident ….

140   Treanor, *One Damn Thing*, 253.

141   Ibid., 249.

142   Ibid., 253.

143   756th S-3 report, 180028 to 180028 January 1944; 34th G-3 Journal, 29 January 1944 (1632 entry).

144   Treanor, *One Damn Thing*, 248.

145 Ibid.

146 34th G-3 Journal, 29 January 1944 (1835 and 1905 entries).

147 34th Inf Div "Lessons Learned in Combat," 55: Powers account.

148 34th G-3 Journal, 29 January 1944 (1930 entry).

149 Ibid., 2053 and 2115 entries.

150 Ibid., 29 January 1944 (1950 and 2026 entries).

151 Froeschle, *Our Story of the 760th,* 87–88: Eugene Gleissner recollection; B Co/756th Morning Report, 23 April 44, Record of events for 29 January.

152 Treanor, *One Damn Thing,* 250.

153 756th Unit Journal, 29 January 1944 (1750 and 1830 entries); Donley diary, 29 January 1944, letter to Jack Brown (re: Fazendin's book).

154 34th G-3 Journal, 29 January 1944 (1930, 1950 and 2026 entries).

155 756th Unit Journal, 29 January 1944 (1850 entry).

156 Gooderson, *Cassino 1944,* 69.

157 Treanor, *One Damn Thing,* 250.

158 34th G-3 Journal, 29 January 1944 (2230 entry).

159 168th S-3 Report, 180029 to 180030 January 1944.

160 756th Unit Journal, 29 January 1944 (2040 entry).

161 34th Inf Div "Lessons Learned in Combat," 56: Powers account; 34th G-3 Journal, 29 January 1944 (2053 and 2115 entries).

162 34th G-3 Journal, 29 January 1944 (2255 entry).

163 34th Inf Div "Lessons Learned in Combat," 55: Powers account.

164 Ibid.

165 Ibid.; This quote is from 34th G-3 Journal, 31 January 1944, 177: "Germans have what is believed the last word in field fortifications, even numbered foxholes."

166 Donley diary, 29 January 1944, letter to Jack Brown (re: Fazendin's book). Donley recalls this conversation took place on the *radio.* Apparently both men were feeling mightily confident.

167 Donley diary, 29 January 1944, letter to Jack Brown (re: Fazendin's book); Treanor, "Treanor Thumbs Ride Over Rapido," 1, 4.

168 Sweeting was awarded the Silver Star for this action: United States War Department, Press Releases and Related Records, 1942–1945 at www.ancestry.com.

169 34th Inf Div "Lessons Learned in Combat," 56: Powers account.

170 34th G-3 Journal, 29 January 1944 (2053 and 2115 entries).

171 756th Unit Journal, 29 January 1944 (1930 and 2040). Location given is 856242.

172 Treanor, *One Damn Thing,* 250–51.

173 34th G-3 Journal, 29 January 1944 (2053 and 2115 entries).

174 B Co/756th Unit Journal, 27 January 1944. Three B Co tanks for the day reported as "not recovered": W-3065879 (bogged), W-3036580 (bogged), W-3010129 (Bogged and burned by enemy action).

175 34th G-2 report, 120003 to 120004 February 1944, PW interrogation report #192.

176 Ibid., 120006 to 120007 February 1944.

177 Redle letter, 17 January 2009.

178 Luttrell, "Operations of the 168th Infantry … Rapido River Crossing" monograph, 20.

179 Smith, *Battles for Monte Cassino,* 67; Parker, *Monte Cassino,* 129.

180 34th G-2 Report, 120006 to 120007 February 1944.

181 Treanor, *One Damn Thing,* 248.

182 Lewis, personal papers: undated letter to Fazendin.

183 Ibid.: Long letter dated 16 June 1945 "Complete Statement of Services Rendered."

184 Ibid., Long recollection.

185 Ibid.: Lewis undated letter to Fazendin, Lewis notes in Fazendin book draft.

186 A Co/756th Morning Reports, 30 January 1944.

187 B Co/756th Morning Reports, 23 April 1944, Record of events for 29 January.

188 Guild interview, 15 September 2006.

189 Redle letter, 29 April 2003.

190 Ibid., 21 January 2002.

Chapter 15

1   Donley diary, 29 January 1944, letter to Jack Brown (re: Fazendin's book). Ordnance replaced the turret and the tank returned to service later.

2   Ibid., 2040 entry.

3   Treanor, *One Damn Thing,* 251.

4   34th G-3 Report, 180029 to 180030 January 1944 and 180030 to 180031 January 1944; 135th S-3 Report, 180029 to 180030 January 1944.

5   Gray, "Crossing of the Rapido, I Co/168th," 12.

6   Ibid.; 168th S-3 Report, 180029 to 180030 January 1944.

7   34th G-3 Journal, 29 January 1944 (2230 entry).

8   Ibid., 30 January 1944 (0440 entry).

9   Message from CG II Corps to CG Fifth Army dated 30/1115, January 1944 (in 34th Inf Div NARA records).

10   34th Inf Div "Lessons Learned in Combat," 55: Powers account; 168th S-3 Report, 180029 to 180030 January 1944.

11   34th G-3 Journal, 30 January 1944 (0300 entry); 34th G-3 Journal 30 January 1944 (0720 entry); Message from CG II Corps to CG Fifth Army dated 301115, January 1944; 168th S-3 Report, 180029 to 180030 January 1944.

12   34th G-3 Journal, 30 January 1944 (0118 entry).

13   Ibid., 0210 entry.

14   Ibid.

15   Ibid; 0315 and 0730 entries.

16   34th Inf Div "Lessons Learned in Combat," 55: Powers account.

17   756th Unit Journal, 30 January 1944 (0500 and 0630 entries).

18   Treanor, *One Damn Thing,* 251.

19   34th Inf Div "Lessons Learned in Combat," 56: Powers account.

20   Treanor, *One Damn Thing,* 251.

21   135th S-3 Report, 180029 to 180030 January 1944.

22   B Co/756th Unit Journal, 29 January 1944.

23   James E. Haspel interview by Pamela G. Patrick, 18 September 1984.

24   Fazendin, *756th at Cassino,* 86.

25   B Co/756th Unit Journal, 30 January 1944; B Co/756th Morning Report, 23 April 1944, "Record of Events" for 30 January 1944.

26   Redle letter, 4 April 2010.

27   Palumbo letter to Redle, 13 November 1986.

28   Some of Gene Palumbo fascinating war recollections are supported by associated primary source material, but others are not. For this work, the author generally chose to include only what could be substantiated. To read all of Gene's reflections, please see his self-published memoirs: Palumbo, Gene. *Load Kick Fire: Fighting with the 756th Tank Battalion, B Company, on the front lines during WWII.* Privately printed by the author, 2012.

29   34th G-3 Journal, 30 January 1944 (0730 entry).

30   Luttrell, "Operations of the 168th Infantry ... Rapido River Crossing," 19.

31   Lt Kerner's first name is unknown.

32   756th Commander's Narrative for January & February 1944, 19–20; Luttrell, "Operations of the 168th Infantry ... Rapido River Crossing," 19.

33   760th "Operations in Italy, January 1944."

34   Ankrum, *Dogfaces Who Smiled Through Tears,* 398.

35   Treanor, *One Damn Thing,* 251.

36   34th G-3 Journal, 30 January 1944 (1010 entry); 34th Div Artillery S-3 Report, 180028 to 180028 January 1944; Treanor, *One Damn Thing,* 251.

37   34th G-3 Journal, 30 January 1944 (1042 entry).

38   Treanor, *One Damn Thing,* 251.

39   Ibid.

40　760th "Operations in Italy, January 1944": The 760th records one man was killed in the tank and the other crewman shot while evacuating was "severely wounded." Names were not provided. The following were 760th casualties for 30 January: Cpl Volandy O. Christian (LWA), Cpl Roy W. Drake (SWA), Pvt Lawrence R. Ash (LWA), Pvt Joe Chavez SWA, and Pvt Thurn J. Wilson (WIA). No one is listed as KIA, so there is some conflict within this report.

41　756th Commander's Narrative for January and February 1944, 19–20; 756th Unit Journal, 30 January 1944 (0845 entry), gives location of both doomed guns at 853245 and 852246. They are identified as "S/P" guns only. These could have been Sturmgeschütz III models.

42　34th G-3 Journal, 30 January 1944 (1020 and 1030 entries). This attack commenced at 0930 after one hour of artillery preparation according to 34th Unit Journal, 30 January 1944 (1110 entry (mislabeled 1010)).

43　Graham, Cassino, 49; Ankrum, Dogfaces Who Smiled Through Tears, 398; 760th "Operations in Italy, February 1944"; 34th G-2 Report, 301201 to 311200 January 1944. Under the command of Oberst Willy Nagel; Treanor, One Damn Thing, 255; 34th Inf Div Report to II Corps, undated but contained with 34th Inf Div G-3 material and labeled with the hour "1545." 756th S-3 Report, 301800 to 311800 January 1944 reports as of 1800, 31 January, 168th had taken prisoner seven officers and 172 enlisted men total in the last 24 hours.

44　Luttrell, "Operations of the 168th Infantry … Rapido River Crossing," 19; Gray, "Crossing of the Rapido, I Co/168th," 14.

45　"Nazis' Cassino Defense System Crumbling" by Hal Boyle, Oakland Tribune (Oakland, California), 1 February 1944, 3.

46　34th G-3 Journal, 30 January 1944 (1135 entry); 756th Unit Journal, 30 January 1944 (1130 entry); 756th Commander's Narrative for January and February 1944, 20; 168th S-3 report, 180029 to 180030 January 1944: Reports town had fallen by 1030.

47　Ankrum, Dogfaces Who Smiled Through Tears, 398.

48　Treanor, "Treanor Thumbs Ride Over the Rapido," 1, 4.

49　34th G-3 Journal, 30 January 1944 (1207 entry).

50　Treanor, One Damn Thing, 255.

51　34th G-3 Journal, 30 January 1944 (1125 entry).

52　Ibid., 1540, Position given was 836246.

53　Ibid., 1502.

54　756th Commander's Narrative for January & February 1944, 19–21.

55　34th G-3 Journal, 30 January 1944 (1010 entry); 34th Artillery S-3 Report, 180028 to 180028 January 1944.

56　34th G-3 Journal, 30 January 1944 (0930 entry).

57　Treanor, One Damn Thing, 255; Boyle, "Nazis' Cassino Defense System Crumbling," 3.

58　Boyle, "Nazis' Cassino Defense System Crumbling," 3.

59　34th G-3 Report, 180029 to 180030 January 1944.

60　Luttrell, "Operations of the 168th Infantry … Rapido River Crossing," 20.

61　34th Inf Div, "Lessons Learned in Combat," 55: Powers account; 34th G-3 Journal, 30 January 1944 (0910, 0918, and 0924 entries).

62　756th Commander's Narrative for January and February 1944, 20.

63　756th Unit Journal, 30 January 1944 (0500 and 0900 entries); Treanor, "Treanor Thumbs Ride Over Rapido," 1, 4: Dolvin's driver was Sgt Lewis Johnson of Fredericks Hall, VA, gunner was Sgt James Overton of Birmingham, Ala, and journalist Tom Treanor rode in the bow gunner position.

64　Treanor, One Damn Thing, 251–52.

65　Palladium-Item, "Spectacular Jobs are Routine to Unsung Combat Engineers," 5; McCardell, "McCardell Under Fire with Yanks," 1.

66　Treanor, One Damn Thing, 252.

67　756th Commander's Narrative for January and February 1944, 20–21; 756th Unit Journal, 30 January 1944, 0500, 1020, 1045 entries. Location of AT was recorded at approximately 857245.

68　Longview Daily News (Longview, Washington), 26 May 2014, 10.

69　Treanor, One Damn Thing, 252; HQ Co/756th Morning Report, 30 January 1944.

70   Stanley Kotarski recalls in Fazendin's original printing of *756th at Cassino,* 82, that Cottonware was killed while unloading the supplies. This detail, however, was mysteriously left out of the reprint version, 68. Treanor, however, wrote that Cottonware was killed at the time of the river crossing.

71   D Co/756th Morning Report, 30 January 1944: Pfc Louis R. Cottonware was killed and Sgt Robert J. Holloway was wounded but remained on duty.

72   HQ Co/756th Morning Report, 30 January 1944.

73   34th Inf Div, "Lessons Learned in Combat," 56–57: Powers account; The radio that Powers used was an SCR-195.

74   Treanor, *One Damn Thing,* 254.

75   Ibid., 252–53.

76   Ibid., 254.

77   Treanor, "Treanor Thumbs Ride Over Rapido," 1, 4.

78   Treanor, *One Damn Thing,* 254–55.

79   Ibid., 254–55.

80   756th Commander's Narrative for January and February 1944, 21.

81   756th Unit Journal, 30 January 1944 (1115 entry).

82   Ibid., 1145 entry.

83   Treanor, *One Damn Thing,* 254–55; Bond, *Return to Cassino,* 33.

84   Redle letter, 25 January 2004. Exact date is unclear when Kremer formally received this promotion, but it was sometime after 17 January 1944.

85   34th Inf Div, "Lessons Learned in Combat," 56–57: Powers account; Powers believed that two M5 lights were hit during these resupply efforts, but this is not reported in the 756th Unit Journal. The 756th Unit Journal does report the loss of one abandoned tank, however.

86   756th Commander's Narrative for January and February 1944, 21; 756th Unit Journal, 30 January 1944 (0500, 1020, and1045 entries); Location of AT was recorded at approximately 857245; 756th Unit Journal, 30 January 1944 (1605, 1620, and 1630 entries); 756th Unit Journal, 30 January 1944 (1545 and 1600 entries).

87   This was probably accomplished during the night as the 760th "Operations in Italy, February 1944" reports that C/Co 760th moved to the 756th bivouac area early in the morning of January 31. The bivouac location is listed at 878222.

88   756th Unit Journal, 30 January 1944 (1820, 1839, 2000, and 2130 entries).

89   Ibid., 31 January 1944 (0900 entry).

90   34th G-3 Journal, 30 January 1944 (2350 entry).

91   Luttrell, "Operations of the 168th Infantry … Rapido River Crossing," 19.

92   II Corps Counterbattery Report, 180028 to 180028 January 1944.

93   34th G-3 Journal, 30 January 1944 (2353 entry).

94   34th Artillery S-3 Report, 180028 to 180028 January 1944.

95   34th G-3 Journal, 30 January 1944, 1855, position given as "85.5 line between 25 and 26 grid squares."

96   Smith, *Battles for Monte Cassino,* 68; Ford, *Cassino: Breaking Gustav Line,* 44.

97   34th G-3 Journal, 30 January 1944 (2108 entry).

98   Ibid., 1855.

99   *The Tampa Bay Times,* "Young Combat Engineer Solves Problem," 4.

100   *Palladium-Item,* "Spectacular Jobs are Routine to Unsung Combat Engineers," 5. The DSC was, in fact, pinned on Captain Sorrell by Maj Gen Keyes in May 1944.

101   Plowman, *Battles for Cassino,* 88.

Chapter 16

1   34th G-3 Journal, 29 January 1944 (0723 entry).

2   Ibid., 30 January 1944 (1540 entry): Position given was 836246; Clifford H. Peek, ed, *Five Years, Five Countries, Five Campaigns: An Account of the One-Hundred-Forty-First Infantry in World War II,* (Munich, Germany: F Bruckmann KG, 1945), 48.

3   34th G-3 Report, 180029 to 180030 January 1944.

4   133rd Cannon Co Unit Journal, 31 January 1944; 34th G-2 Report, 301201 to 311200 January 1944.

5   German term for a common infantryman, foot soldier, or rifleman.

6   34th G-3 Journal, 31 January 1944 (0640 and 0700 entries).

7   Ibid., 0715, 0830 entries; 34th G-3 Report, 180030 to 180031 January 1944.

8   34th G-3 Journal, 31 January 1944 (0945 and 1047 entries).

9   Ibid., 1050 entry.

10 34th G-3 Journal, 31 January 1944 (1225 entry); 756th Commander's Narrative for January & February 1944, 21-22: Specifically, the M5s worked with the 91st Recon Squadron on this patrol.

11 34th G-3 Journal, 31 January 1944 (1015 entry).

12 Ibid., 1120 entry.

13 Ibid., 1040 entry.

14 Ibid., 1400 entry.

15 34th G-3 Journal, 31 January 1944 (2100 entry); 756th Unit Journal, 31 January 1944 (0900, 1100, and 1115 entries).

16 34th G-3 Journal, 31 January 1944 (1225 entry).

17 Ibid., 1625 entry; 756th Unit Journal, 31 January 1944 (1630 entry).

18 756th S-3 Report, 301800 to 311800 January 1944.

19 34th G-3 Journal, 31 January 1944 (2305 entry). Tanks reported at 845265. This position is on the switchback road leading to Terelle.

20 34th G-3 Report, 301800 to 311800 January 1944 and accompanying map; 34th G-3 Journal, 1 February 1944 (0027 entry).

21 34th G-3 Journal, 31 January 1944 (1750 entry). Opposition reported at 833254 and 142nd positions reported at 834270.

22 756th Commander's Narrative for January and February 1944, 21–22: Location was 857234; 34th G-3 Journal, 31 January 1944 (1220 entry); David D. Redle letter, 14 May 2014. Years later, Redle believed Wilkinson's tank was recovered by U.S. forces, but wasn't completely certain.

23 Circumstantial evidence indicates the tank may have belonged to Sgt Norman Fuller. According to the A Co/756th Morning Report, 31 January 1944, Fuller was wounded on this day but remained on duty. Other crewmembers may have also been wounded and one (Pvt Darrell D. Shryer) may have been killed during this incident.

24 756th Commander's Narrative for January and February 1944, 21–22; 756th Unit Journal, 31 January 1944, (1215, 1230, and 1305 entries); 756th S-3 Report, 301800 to 311800 January 1944; Fazendin, *756th at Cassino*, 89–92, Redle recollection.

25 34th G-2 Report, 120031 January to 120001 February 1944.

26 776th Tank Destroyer Battalion Unit Journal, 1 February 1944, (PDF scanned form obtained at: http://tankdestroyer.net/units/battalions700s/274-776th-tank-destroyer-battalion.) Table of Organization No. 18-27, War Department, Washington, D.C., 15 March 1944, Tank Destroyer Gun Company, Tank Destroyer Battalion, Self-Propelled.

27 34th G-3 Journal, 31 January 1944 (1730 entry); 776th Tank Destroyer Bn S-3 Report, 180029 to 180030 January 1944.

28 34th G-3 Journal, 31 January 1944 (1735 entry).

29 756th Commander's Narrative for January and February 1944, 21–22.

30 34th G-3 Journal, 31 January 1944 (1324 entry). 168th positions given for the mid-afternoon of 31 January were 3rd Bn from 844251 to 848245, 2nd Bn from 847242 to 852238, and 1st Bn from 853236 to 858235.

31 34th Inf Div report to II Corps, undated but with 34th G-3 material and labeled with the hour "1545"; 34th G-3 Journal, 31 January 1944 (1415 entry). These patrols were specifically sent to reconnoiter Hill 711, Hill 446, and Hill 382.

32 34th G-3 Journal, 31 January 1944 (1530 entry). The patrol spotting this had gone to Hill 226 at 842245 just to the NW of Hill 213 and reported enemy along trail at 842244 and the group of fifteen at 840245.

33 34th G-3 Journal, 31 January 1944 (1324 entry).

34 133rd HQ "Report on Patrols," 1 February 1944: Patrol leader Lt Brown of L Co reported a dead American from 100th Bn at 862223.

35 133rd HQ "Report on Patrols," 1 February 1944: Patrol leader was Sgt Derby; 34th G-3 Journal, 31 January 1944 (2035 entry).

36 133rd HQ "Report on Patrols," 1 February 1944.

37 133rd HQ "Report on Patrols," 1 February 1944. Reported the vehicle was a "tank" but author could not corroborate any German tank burning. This was likely the American M4 knocked out earlier.

38 Map accompanying 133rd S-3 Report, 180029 to 180030 January 1944; The 133rd Inf Regt was located about a due mile east of the Rapido and northernmost section of Cassino at 873216 according to 133rd HQ "Report on Patrols," dated 31 January 1944.

39 34th G-3 Journal, 31 January 1944 (2028 entry).

40 Ibid., 0330 and 0500 entries.

41 756th S-3 Report, 301800 to 311800 January 1944. Cemetery position given as 854240; Paul Ranspach Diary, 31 January 1944. Lt Czajkowski, Sgts Wunderlich, Smith, and Cogdill (reconstituted 2nd Platoon) arrived 29 January, according to the B Co/756th Unit Journal, 29 January 1944.

42 B Co/756th Unit Journal, 31 January 1944. Lt Redle and Sgt Wunderlich appeared to be commanding two separate tanks at this point. Later, Redle commands Wunderlich's tank. In interviews, Redle, however, always identified Wunderlich as his gunner/tank commander.

43 34th G-3 Journal, 31 January 1944 (1415 entry); B Co/756th Morning Report, 23 April 1944: Record of Events for 31 January 1944.

44 Fazendin, *756th at Cassino*, 131–32. A prisoner captured a few days later on The Pimple knew of this incident and expressed great admiration for the marksmanship skills of the 756th tankers.

45 Henry Sanislow interview, 15 September 2006.

46 Guild interview, 15 September 2006.

47 Redle letter, 1 March 2001.

48 Redle letter to Gene Palumbo dated 25 November 1986.

49 756th Unit Journal, 31 January 1944 (2330 entry).

50 34th G-3 Report, 301800 to 311800 January 1944. The total should have been twenty, but one C Co/760th tank was withdrawn for repairs. Technically, the 2nd platoon from A Co/760th was attached directly to the 133rd Inf Regt according to the 760th Tank Battalion "Operations in Italy, February 1944."

51 133rd S-3 Report, 180029 to 180030 January 1944; 760th Tank Battalion "Operations in Italy, February 1944."

52 B Co/756th Unit Journal, 3 February 1944. Entry states: "Five tanks, commanded by Lt Czajkowski, and consisting of commanders S/Sgt Johannesen, Sgts Buys, Cogdill and Graffagnini came over as reinforcements." However, Czajkowski and Cogdill were already reported across as of 29 January 1944—joining the afternoon attack with Lt Col Sweeting's force. Perhaps this can be explained if Czajkowski and Cogdill returned across the river for repairs. The unit journal does not explain this discrepancy. The date entry may be off two days as well, as Redle recalls Johannesen participated in barracks actions on 1 February.

53 756th Unit Journal, 31 January 1944 (2330 entry).

54 756th Commander's Narrative for January & February 1944, 21–22.

55 Fazendin, *756th at Cassino*, 67.

56 Fazendin, *756th at Cassino*, 68–69, Kotarski recollection. One of the crewmen from the M5 tank was Pfc Stanley J. Kotarski who suffered serious burns to his hands while helping others to safety. Sgt Harrison's crew consisted of Cpl Mike Sudvary (also wounded and evacuated), driver T/5 Overton Bledsoe, Pvt Albert T. Gober (died of wounds), and someone identified by Kotarski years later as "Richards."; Fazendin letter to French Lewis, 10 May (1992?).

57 A Co/756th Morning Report, 31 January 1944: T/5 Albert T. Gober DOW and Pvt Darrell D. Shyrer, KIA.

58 756th Morning Reports for 31 January 1944 list the following as SWA and evacuated: Sgt Howard A. Harrison [A], Cpl Edwin R. Rittenbach [A], Cpl Mike Sudvary Jr. [A], and LWA: Pfc Stanley J. Kotarski [D].

59 Sgt Ithel R. Adlard of the 105mm Assault Gun platoon of HQ company was also injured in action on 31 January 1944. Two others, Sgt Norman C. Fuller [A], Cpl Chester A. Duvinski [A], were wounded but remained on duty.

60 Various photos of Ryder. Plowman, *Battles for Cassino*, 84. *Army Register* 1941, 739. *Army Register* 1945, 811.

61   Treanor, *One Damn Thing*, 246.

62   "Charles W. Ryder, 1915" (West Point obituary): http://apps.westpointaog.org/Memorials/Article/5351/.

63   *Army Register* 1941, 739; *Army Register* 1945, 811.

64   Andrews, Maj Samuel R, "Major General Charles Ryder: The Forging of a World War II Division Commander" (School of Advanced Military Studies, US Army Command and General Staff College, Fort Leavenworth, Kansas), 2014. 1,2; Hougen, *34th Infantry Division*, "General Ryder Leaves the Division" chapter.

65   Andrews, "Major General Charles Ryder," 2.

66   "Charles W. Ryder, 1915" (West Point obituary), http://apps.westpointaog.org/Memorials/Article/5351/.

67   Andrews, "Major General Charles Ryder," 22 and 23.

68   Ibid., 24.

69   Ibid., 28; *Army Register* 1941, 739; *Army Register* 1945, 811, also decorated with Purple Heart, Silver Star, and Bronze Star.

70   Hougen, *34th Infantry Division*, "Days in Ireland and Scotland."

71   Drake, Col Thomas D., "Factual Account of Operations 168th Infantry, 34th Division, from 24 December 1942 to 17 February 1943" After Action Report, 2 April 1945; Andrews, "Major General Charles Ryder," 37.

72   Andrews, "Major General Charles Ryder," 37.

73   Hougen, *34th Infantry Division*, "General Ryder Leaves the Division." Ryder became emotional during his farewell to the division in July 1944 ... although he kept his speech customarily short and to the point, his voice was breaking and he turned away from the men and walked away before his emotions could overtake him.

74   135th S-3 Report, 180031 January to 180001 February 1944; Ankrum, *Dogfaces Who Smiled Through Tears*, 399.

75   Hougen, *34th Infantry Division*, "The Second Phase of Cassino;" Blumenson, *Salerno to Cassino*, 377; Plowman, *Battles for Cassino*, 83; 34th Inf Div Field Order #14 dated 31 January 1944.

76   34th G-3 Journal, 31 January 1944 (1430 entry); 34th G-3 Journal, 1 February 1944 (0705 and 0715 entries).

77   Ibid., 1 February 1944 (0120 entry).

78   34th Inf Div Field Order #14 dated 31 January 1944, Annex #2 "Tank Plan" and separate map; Message from CG II Corps to CG 34th Div, 36th Div and 1 Tank Group dated 31 January 1944.

79   34th G-3 Journal, 31 January 1944 (1550 entry).

80   Ibid., 1 February 1944 (various entries).

81   135th S-3 Report, 180031 January to 180001 February 1944.

82   34th Div Operational Instructions dated 31 January 1944 with a distribution "Same as FO #14."

83   Blumenson, *Salerno to Cassino*, 377.

84   34th G-3 Journal, 1 February 1944 (0835 entry).

85   Hougen, *34th Infantry Division,* "The Second Phase of Cassino"; Graham, *Cassino*, 50; 34th G-3 Journal, 1 February 1944 (1303 entry); 34th G-2 Report, 120031 January to 120001 February 1944.

86   34th G-3 Journal, 1 February 1944 (0855 entry).

87   Gooderson, *Cassino 1944*, 70; Smith, *Battles for Monte Cassino*, 71; Hougen, *34th Infantry Division,* "The Second Phase of Cassino."

88   34th G-3 Journal, 1 February 1944 (0835 entry).

89   756th Unit Journal, 1 February 1944 (0620 and 0720 entries).

90   B Co/756th Morning Report, 23 April 1944, "Record of Events" for 1 February.

91   B Co/756th Unit Journal, 3 February 1944. Reports the 2nd Platoon was up to five tanks (Lt Czajkowski, S/Sgt Johannesen, and Sgts Buys, Codgill, and Graffagnini), so S/Sgt Johannesen had to have joined during the night of 1 February.

92   Fazendin, *756th at Cassino*, 87–88.

93   756th Unit Journal, 1 February 1944 (0720, 0800, and 0830 entries).

94   756th Commander's Narrative for January & February 1944, 22–24.

95   34th G-3 Journal, 1 February 1944, (0840 entry).

96   Ibid., 1150 entry.

97   Ibid., 1026 entry.

98 B Co/756th Morning Report, 23 April 1944, "Record of Events" for 1 February: B Co had been attached directly to the 168th and was released at 0930 that same morning; 756th Commander's Narrative for January and February 1944, 22–24; 756th Unit Journal, 1 February 1944 (1010 and 1040 entries).
99 34th G-3 Journal, 1 February 1944 (0950 entry).
100 34th Div Artillery S-3 Report, 180030 to 180031 January 1944; According to 776th TD Bn S-3 Report, 180031 January to 180001 February 1944, 776th TD Bn C Co platoon positions as of 1200, 1 February, were 1st platoon at 868246, 2nd platoon at 854243 (N of cemetery), 876223. C Co/776th TD Bn was short 2 M-10 (ten of twelve in operation) two were being serviced.
101 34th G-3 Journal, 1 February 1944 (1130 entry).
102 3rd Bn/133rd HQ Co Morning Report, 31 January 1944.
103 *Army Register* 1943, 153; Otto, *Howitzer*, 1933.
104 Joseph L. Galloway and Douglas Pasernak, "The Warrior Class: They Left West Point in 1939, soldier-scholars who made a difference," *U.S. News & World Report* magazine, 5 July 1994, 26–36.
105 Knapp, *Howitzer*, 1939, 127. The term "intermurder" was a grim witticism USMA cadets used to describe their ruthless intramural athletic competitions.
106 Treanor, *One Damn Thing*, 257.
107 133rd S-3 Report, 180031 January to 180001 February 1944; Fraizer's last name was often misspelled "Frazier" in newspaper articles and other primary source documents.
108 133rd S-3 Report, 180031 January to 180001 February 1944. Scant details were provided of exactly what this tank platoon did in the early phase of the attack or even how they got across the river. They likely crossed at the same place the 756th tanks did and crossed the bridge where Lt Henry's tank was positioned—probably once Fraizer's men took the north section of the barracks and drove out the SP gun.
109 34th G-3 Journal, 1 February 1944 (1216 and 1220 entries).
110 34th G-2 Report, 120001 to 120002 February 1944. Location given was 856231.
111 34th G-3 Journal, 1 February 1944 (1545 entry). Movement of the SP gun at this point is conjecture. Somehow those tanks got into the north section. The only way to do so was over the bridge and the only way to cross that bridge was for the SP guns to stop firing at it.
112 34th G-3 Journal, 1 February 1944 (1510 entry); 34th G-3 Journal, 1 February 1944 (1515 entry) 34th G-3 Journal, 1 February 1944 (1610 entry); 133rd S-3 Report, 180031 January to 180001 February 1944; 34th G-3 Report, 180031 January to 180001 February 1944; 756th Unit Journal, 1 February 1944 (1555 entry).
113 B Co/756th Unit Journal, 2 February 1944; 34th G-3 Journal, 1 February 1944 (1625 entry). Position of tanks was 845239; B Co/756th Unit Journal, 2 February 1944.
114 B Co/756th Morning Report, 23 April 1944, "Record of Events" for 2 February. Harley's tank stuck in this draw was not recovered until 19 February according to the B Co/756th Unit Journal, 19 February 1944.
115 756th Commander's Narrative for January and February 1944, 22–24; 756th Unit Journal, 1 February 1944 (1600 entry); Redle letter, 4 April 2010; B Co/756th Morning Report, 23 April 1944, "Record of Events" for 2 February: Records that Redle had two tanks with him at this point.
116 756th Unit Journal, 1 February 1944 (1500 entry): Redle's OP position was at 857238.
117 II Corps Counterbattery Report, 180001 to 180002 February 1944.
118 Location of guns was 857227 according to 34th G-3 Journal, 1 February 1944 (1625 entry).
119 1st Tank Group S-3 Report, 180031 January to 180001 February 1944.
120 34th G-3 Journal, 1 February 1944 (1650 entry).
121 34th G-3 Journal, 1 February 1944 (1625 entry). Artillery fell at location 880240.
122 1st Tank Group S-3 Report, 180031 January to 180001 February 1944.
123 34th G-3 Journal, 1 February 1944 (1715 entry); 756th Unit Journal, 1 February 1944 (1630 entry). Positions of the SP guns were given at 857233 and 857235.
124 756th Unit Journal, 1 February 1944 (1730 entry); 756th Commander's Narrative for January and February 1944, 23–24. When Redle's tanks returned back to Hill 213, they brought along seven German prisoners with them according to B Co/756th Morning Reports, 23 April 1944, "Record of Events" for 2 February.
125 34th G-3 Journal, 1 February 1944 (0955 entry).
126 34th G-2 Reports for 29, 30, and 31 February 1944.
127 34th G-3 Journal, 1 February 1944 (1845 entry).

128   Ibid., 1730 entry. One patrol from F Co ventured out 500 yards south of Hill 445, picked up 11 more PWs and returned; 1845 entry.

129   Plowman, *Battles for Cassino*, 89.

130   34th G-3 Journal, 1 February 1944 (0845 entry). 135th ultimate objective coordinates were 836216.

131   Ibid., 0835 entry: Location was 842205.

132   Ibid., 2040 entry; 34th G-2 Report, 120001 to 120002 February 1944.

133   34th G-3 Journal, 1 February 1944 (1645 entry).

134   135th S-3 Report, 180031 January to 180001 February 1944. Position was 846230.

135   34th G-3 Journal, 1 February 1944 (1730 entry).

136   Ibid., 2115 entry: 240mm artillery units were specifically notified, reported as "90th Lt Div."

137   Ibid., 1800 entry.

138   Ibid., 1905 and 1915 entries; 756th S-3 Report, 180031 January to 180001 February 1944.

139   34th G-3 Journal, 1 February 1944 (1915 entry).

140   756th Unit Journal 1 February 1944 (1735 entry).

141   Ibid., 1740 entry.

142   Ibid., 2000 entry: Location was 859222.

143   34th G-3 Journal, 1 February 1944 (1905 and 1915 entries); Ankrum, *Dogfaces Who Smiled Through Tears*, 399–400.

144   34th G-3 Journal, 1 February 1944 (2020 entry). According to PW from 9th Co/3rd Para Rgt reported in 34th G-2 Report, 120006 to 120007 February 1944, a red flare meant attack, green meant increase range of artillery, and white meant "we have arrived."; 34th G2 Report 120001 to 120002 February 1944.

145   756th Commander's Narrative for January and February 1944, 22–24; Treanor, *One Damn Thing*, 247–48.

146   34th G-3 Journal, 1 February 1944 (2040 entry).

147   Ibid., 2120 entry.

148   34th G-2 Report, 120001 to 120002 February 1944.

149   34th G-3 Journal, 1 February 1944 (2200 entry). There may have been three Sturmgeschützs in the barracks area according to Plowman, *Battles for Cassino*, 89. These were under the command of Oberleutnant Edwin Metzger's 2nd Battery of the 242nd Sturmgeshütz Abteilung Battalion. They retreated to the jail area in Cassino to fight another day. The jail area was controlled by 211st Grenadier Regiment (71st Infantry Division).

150   34th G-2 Report, 120001 to 120002 February 1944. About 120 rounds fell east of the barracks throughout the day. This later concentration lasted from 2200 to midnight.

151   756th Commander's Narrative for January and February 1944, 22–24.

152   34th G-3 Journal, 1 February 1944 (2200 entry).

153   Ibid., 2350 entry; 133rd Inf Regt Commander's Narrative for February 1944 by Col Marshall, (Downloaded from 34th Infantry Division Association at: http://www.34ida.org/history/).

154   Redle letter, 4 April 2010.

155   34th G-3 Report, 180031 January to 180001 February 1944; Graham, *Cassino*, 50.

156   34th G-3 Journal, 1 February 1944 (1755 entry). 142nd positions listed as follows: 3rd Bn at 828278 to 832278, 2nd Bn at 830268 to 826273 as of 1755; 34th G-3 Report, 180031 January to 180001 February 1944, reports that at 1800, 756th light tanks supporting 142nd in reduction of strong points in vicinity 828272.

157   34th G-3 Journal, 1 February 1944 (2125 entry); 34th G-3 Journal, 1 February 1944 (2140 entry): The location recorded is 831255—which put them in a draw about ½-mile west of Caira.

158   756th S-3 Report, 180031 January to 180001 February 1944. As of 1800 that day, locations of these tanks were: 1 Platoon of tanks B Co at 865242 (still on approach to Caira bridge) and 2 Platoons of tanks C Co at 865242 (same place).

159   756th Unit Journal, 1 February 1944 (2300 entry).

160   756th Commander's Narrative for January & February 1944, 22–24. Location of A Co tanks and Sweeting's OP was 869218.

161   Ibid. Locations of C Co/776th TD Bn was 855242 and 875223.

162   Location was 961164.

163   Location was 888234.

164   756th S-3 Report, 180031 January to 180001 February 1944.

165 34th G-3 Journal, 1 February 1944 (2200 entry). D Co tanks were released back to the 756th at this time. Location of D Co tanks were on the ladder road at 855270 as of 1800 according to 756th S-3 Report, 180031 January to 180001 February 1944.

166 34th G-3 Journal, 1 February 1944 (1425 entry).

167 B Co/756th Morning Report, 1 February 1944; B Co/756th Morning Report, 23 April 1944, "Record of Events" for 1 February.

168 HQ Co/756th Morning Report, 1 February 1944.

169 Fazendin, *756th at Cassino*, 79: Collins recollection. One EM was also wounded on 1 February but remained on duty according to D Co/756th Morning Report, 1 February 1944. This man was Pvt Lee P. Barnes, who suffered a LWA minor face wound.

Wilkinson's Odyssey: Part One

1 Wilkinson, "The Way It All Started," 23.

2 Ibid., 24–25.

3 Wilkinson memoir titled "My Experiences in Italy, Part Two," c. 2001.

4 Wilkinson memoir titled "My Experiences in Italy," March 2000.

5 Wilkinson memoir titled "A Guest of the Third Reich," November 2002. The place was, in fact, a movie studio prior to the war.

Index

References to maps are in *italics*.

Adlard, Cpl Ithel R. "Dick," 46, 63, 92, 138
Afrika Korps, 96, 102–12
aircraft, German, 123–4
   ME109, 102, 134–5
   Stukas, 110–11
Alexander, Maj Ralph, 60
Algeria, 93–8, 101–3, 113–21
Allen, Capt Charles, 69
Almaack, USS, 62
American Armor Force, 19–21
Ames, S/Sgt Thomas P., 230–2
amphibious operations, 35, 78–81
   and training, 47–53, 62–4, 97–8
Anderson, Lt Col Glen H., 27
Anderson, T/5 Roy, 117–18
anti-personnel mines, 174, 180–1, 185–6
anti-tank mines (ATs), 16–17
Anzio (Italy), 180–1
Arnold, Capt Edwin "Cotton," 68, 78, 124,
   259, 270
   and bridgehead, 226–7, 229
   and Caira, 250–2
   and Rapido, 178, 197
Arzew (Algeria), 96
Avettant, T/4 Edward A., 214–15
aviation, 4, 7
AWOL (absence without leave), 58, 68–9
Axis Sally, 123–4

Bacha, Pvt John F., 205, 213–15
Badoglio, Pietro, 122, 126
barracks, *see* Rapido River
battleships, 4–5
Beal, Pvt Abe C., 95, 137
Behymer, Cpl Harold M., 259

Belgium, 8
Biles, Sgt Carley W., 248
Bismarck (ship), 23
Bizerte (Tunisia), 121–7
Blackwell, Sgt James H., 52
blitzkrieg ("lightning war"), 7, 10
Boatner, Col Mark M., 209, 215, 217
   and barracks, 256–7, 264
   and bridgehead, 223–4, 233
   and Caira, 246–7, 252
British Army, 110–11
   Eighth, 33, 110, 125, 130, 134, 170–1
   IX Corps, 105
   X Corps, 130–1, 138–9, 172
Brooks, Pvt Merle, 186–7, 193–4, 198
Brown, T/5 Jack, 235, 237, 243
Buchanan, Capt David, 274–5
Butler, Brig Gen Frederic B., 224
Buys, Sgt Roland L., 167, 190, 260

Caira (Italy), 180, 246–53, 255–6
California (CA), *41*, 45–51, 56–9, 62–5
Camp Pickett (VA), 65–70
Campbell, Sgt Leland P., 204, 213
Cardullo, Pvt Paul N., 95
Carleton, Col Don E., 90
Casablanca (Morocco), 69, 74, 76–83, 103
Caucasus, 83
CEF, *see* French Expeditionary Corps
Cervaro (Italy), 165–8
Chaffee, Maj Gen Adna, 6, 8, 17, 19–20, 33
Chamberlain, Neville, 9
Chapman, Maj Warren C. "Buzz," 264–5
Chelif River (Algeria), 115–16
Chiarelli, Sgt Peter, 137
China, 63
Churchill, Winston, 3, 9, 103

civilians, 133–4, 180, 182, 274–5
Clark, Lt Gen Mark W., 130, 172, 175, 210–11, 226
Clough, Maj Casper, Jr., 186–7, 191–4, 198
Cogdill, T/4 Clyde, 70, 235
    and Rapido attack, 205, 209, 212, 214–15, 221
Coleman, Cpl Charles H., 214–15
Colley, Sgt Ray, 117–18, 154
combat leadership, 112–13
compass reading, 119–20
Constantine (Algeria), 113–14
Corbitt, Sgt Mack N., 230–4
Cottonware, Pfc Louis E., 250
Crandall, Capt, 57
Crawford, Sgt Carl T., 28, 46, 196
    and Rapido attack, 200–2, 213–15
Cutrone, Pfc Joseph, 204–5, 208–9, 220
Cyr, T/4 Rene E., 234–5
Czajkowski, 2nd Lt John J., 154, 159–60, 235, 271

Dean, 1st Lt Robert, 60–1
defilade, 86–7
desert warfare, 102–4
Devers, Maj Gen Jacob L., 33
Dewey, Maj George, 192–3
Dick, Pvt Andrew M., 132–3
Division Officers Training Center (DOTC), 15–19, 21–2
Dolvin, 1st Lt Welborn G. "Tom," 42, 44–5, 50, 136
    and barracks, 259, 268, 270
    and Bizerte, 124–7
    and bridgehead, 226, 228, 234–5, 238
    and Caira, 249–51
    and promotion, 51–2, 60, 71
    and Rapido, 195–6
    and Tunisia, 116
Donley, T/4 Ralph, 235, 243
Doolittle, T/4 Leroy "Chief," 232
Dudzinski, Pvt Edward J., 231

Eckerly, Pvt Myron, 83
Egypt, 33, 44, 61, 102–3
espionage, 57

FAITC, see Fifth Army Invasion Training Center

Fazendin, 1st Lt Roger, 39, 57–8, 60–1, 70
    and Algeria, 119–20
    and Bizerte, 122–3, 125
    and Camp Pickett, 66–7, 69
    and Casablanca, 81–2
    and Italy, 141, 143, 146–8
    and Port Lyautey, 89, 93
Fedala (Morocco), 78–80, 84
Fifth Army Invasion Training Center (FAITC), 96–8
Fodor, S/Sgt William, 195–6
Fondouk Pass (Tunisia), 104–10
food, 75, 81–2, 85, 92, 117–18
    and Italy, 139–40, 153–4
Fort Dix (NJ), 70–1
Fort Knox (KY), 15–20, 59–62
Fort Lewis (WA), 25, 26–31, 35–8, 42, 43–4
Fort Ord (CA), 53–9, 62–5
Fraizer, Capt Wayne D., 265–6, 269
France, 3, 5, 6, 8–11, 14
    and Dieppe, 63
    and Paris, 13
    see also French Expeditionary Corps
fratricide, 237
Fredendall, Maj Gen Lloyd, 103–4
French Expeditionary Corps (CEF), 78–9, 81, 210–11, 230, 248–9
    and Caira, 252
    and Port Lyautey, 86, 88–90
French Legionnaires, 94–5

Galbraith, Sgt Raymond, 230–1, 233
German Army:
    15th Panzer Grenadier Dvn, 175
    16th Panzer Dvn, 131
    132nd Grenadier Rgt, 244
    see also Afrika Korps
Germany, 3–11, 14
    and Barbarossa, 33, 44, 61
    and propaganda, 83
Gilkerson, Sgt James H., 122, 168–9
Gilman, 1st Lt Robert L., 227, 230
Gober, Pvt Albert T., 260
Goering, FM Hermann, 158
Gohde, Cpl Henry E., 196
Gourley, 1st Lt Donald, 80–1, 145
Graffagnini, Sgt Charles, 116, 208, 220, 260
Great Britain, 3, 5–6, 8–10, 14, 44
    and Egypt, 102–3

and Tunisia, 83
see also British Army; Royal Navy
Great War, *see* World War I
Greece, 23
Greene, 1st Lt Walter L., 242
Guderian, Col Heinz, 7, 9, 86, 103
    Achtung – Panzer!, 158
Guild, Pvt Clyde W., 138, 141, 143, 242, 259
Gustav Line, 170–1

Hammack, Lt Col Louis A., 101, 106–7
Hamner, 1st Lt Charlie, 166
Hanson, 1st Lt Ralph L., 271
Harley, 2nd Lt Howard M., 178, 187–8, 246,
    259, 265
    and Rapido attack, 200, 203–4
Harris, S/Sgt James "Red," 230–1, 233–4
Harris, USS, 50
Harrison, Sgt Howard, 230–1, 260
Haspel, Sgt James, 46, 204
Henry, 2nd Lt Wayne B., 152–3, 164, 196, 228
    and Rapido attack, 200, 202–3, 205, 209,
    212, 214
Hill 213 (Italy), 180, 183, 190, 195, 201, 207,
    215, 217
    and bridgehead attack, 223–4, 227, 238–9,
    241, 244–6
    and surrender, 249
Hitler, Adolf, 3, 8–9, 104, 158
Hogan, Sgt Jack, 28, 52, 142, 246, 259
    and Algeria, 117–18
    and Camp Pickett, 69
    and Casablanca, 83
    and Port Lyautey, 91–2
    and Rapido attack, 220
    and Tunisia, 109
Hollon, T/4 Earl, 232
Holloway, Sgt Robert J., 250
Hope, Bob, 124
horses, 5, 8, 10, 57
Huffman, Cpl Alexander, 207
Hunter, 2nd Lt Roland V., 120, 122, 230

Italy, 8, 102, 273–5
    and surrender, 125–6, 130–1
    see also Caira; Mignano Gap; Monte
    Cassino; Rapido River; Sicily; Southern
    Italy

Japan, 3–5, 10, 59
    and Pearl Harbor, 36–8, 40
    and the Philippines, 44, 54
Jarvis, Sgt Louis J., 139, 154, 205, 209, 221
Jews, 8
Johannesen, S/Sgt Oric, 220, 260
Jones, Pvt Paul, 39
Juin, Gen Alphonse, 210–11, 230

Kairouan (Tunisia), 105, 110
Kelleher, Pvt, 58–9
Kennedy, Joe, 3–4
Kerner, Lt, 247–8
Keyes, Maj Gen Geoffrey, 172, 191, 228
Keynes, John Maynard, 3
Kim, 1st Lt Young O., 187
King, Cpl Marvin E., 208, 220, 225
Kinsworthy, Pvt Luther, 71
Kosanke, T/4 Roy R., 169
Kremer, 2nd Lt Robert, 45, 71, 84, 251, 256–7
    and Algeria, 96, 120
Krieger, Lt Col Ralph, 133
Kristallnacht ("Night of the Broken Glass"), 8
Kupriance, Pfc Lotka U., 95

LaDue, Pfc Donald E., 138
Laliberty, T/5 Louis A., 87, 92, 204–5, 209,
    212–14
Langdon, Maj Wendell, 102
Langford, Francis, 124
Leger, 2nd Lt William G., 164, 190, 196, 200,
    202–4, 221
Lewis, Sgt Elvis H., 52–3
Lewis, Capt French, 16–17, 19–20, 22, 93
    and bridgehead, 229–33, 241–2
    and Fort Lewis, 27–9, 34–7
    and Mignano, 164
    and Montesano, 39
    and promotion, 61
    and Rapido, 178, 180–2, 188, 193, 195
    and Rapido attack, 200
    and Tunisia, 123
Libya, 44, 102–3
Lierl, Pfc Anthony M., 79
Lindbergh, Charles, 3
Loeb, Lt David, 164, 210, 229
Long, Capt Oscar, 92, 100–2, 108–10, 113,
    124–5

Lucas, Maj Gen John P., 35, 142
Luftwaffe, *see* aircraft, German
Lynch, Lt Dallas, 234

MacFadden, Sgt James, 46, 48
MacLaughlin, Lt Col Severne S., 22, 34, 36, 38, 52
    and beach landings, 53
    and promotion, 60
McNair, Lt Gen Lesley J., 30, 157
McSparron, 1st Lt David, 29, 34, 44–5
Magenta (Algeria), 119–21
malaria, 96, 118, 124–6
Mancini, T/4 Alfred, 90, 93, 95, 154
    and barracks, 259, 265
    and Rapido attack, 207–8, 221
Mandel, Lt Edward, 69
map reading, 119–20
maps:
    California, *41*
    Mignano Gap, *162*
    Monte Cassino, *173, 272*
    North Africa, *73*
    Rapido barracks, *254*
    Rapido River, *177, 189, 218, 240*
    Southern Italy, *129, 149*
    Tunisia, *99*
    United States of America, *12*
    Washington State, *25*
Marin, T/4 Rufus, 204
Marshall, Col Carley L., 188, 191–3, 195, 268, 269
Martinez, Cpl Nazzario, 231–2
Maude, Sgt Glee H., 231–2
Midway, Battle of, 59
Mignano Gap (Italy), 160–1, 163–71
    map, *162*
military police (MPs), 58
Mitchell, Col William "Billy," 4, 59
Mize, T/4 Edward R., 231
Monte Caira (Italy), 171
Monte Cassino (Italy), 145–6, 165, 167, 170–1, 174–5, 185
    and arrival, 295
    map, *173, 272*
Monte Castellone (Italy), 172, 179, 252
    and barracks attack, 258, 260, 262–3, 266–7

Monte Porchia (Italy), 165–6
Monte Trocchio (Italy), 166–7
Montesano (WA), 38–40
Moon, Maj Jacob R., 34, 36–7, 52
Morocco, *see* Casablanca; Port Lyautey
Moseley, Lt Col Eugene L., 192, 195, 212
Moyle, Capt David, 274–5
Mras, T/4 Carl, 186–7, 193, 198, 201
Mulraney, S/Sgt John M., 147
Mussolini, Benito, 3, 122

Naples (Italy), 139–40
Nelson, 1st Lt Frederick L., 226–7, 233–34, 259
Nelson, 1st Lt Kenneth S., 151, 164
Netherlands, the, 8
New York City, 69–70, 72
Newman, Lt William H., 229, 234–5
Nisei (Japanese-American) troops, 186–8, 197, 198
North Africa, 23
    map, *73*
    see also Algeria; Casablanca; Egypt; Port Lyautey; Tunisia
Notoroberto, Cpl Anthony, 153

Offerman, Pvt Cletus, 169
Oliver, Sgt Haskell O., 190
Olson, 2nd Lt Edwin B., 60–1, 68, 93, 159
    and Casablanca, 79–81
    and Rapido attack, 225
operations:
    Barbarossa (1941), 33, 160
    Torch (1942), 81, 103
    Quick (1942), 67
Oran (Algeria), 95–7, 103, 118
Osganian, Pvt Robert, 138

Paestum (Italy), 126, 130–1
Palumbo, Pvt Gene, 220, 225, 246
Paris, 13
partisans, 274
Patten, 1st Lt Moultrie, 146
Patton, Maj Gen George S., Jr., 6, 17, 21, 66, 69
    and Algeria, 118
    and Casablanca, 80–1
    and Port Lyautey, 87

and Tunisia, 104–5
Pearl Harbor, 36–8, 40
Pennington, Sgt Donald L., 84–5, 91
Perdue, T/5 Randolph H., 122, 134–5, 208–9, 220, 225
Perkins, 2nd Lt Gordon E., 229, 259
Petit Port (Algeria), 116–18
Philippines, the, 44, 54
Piedimonte San Germano (Italy), 216–17
Pimple, The, see Hill 213
Poland, 8–11
Pompey, Sgt Daniel, 87, 115–16, 132–3, 147, 259
Port Lyautey (Morocco), 84–94
Powers, Lt Col John L., 233, 236–7, 249–50
President Jackson, USS, 51
Pride, Lt Dale F., 260, 266
prisoners of war (PWs), 110, 167
    and Caira, 248, 255
    and Rapido attack, 214–15, 219, 244
    and Wilkinson, 273–5

radio, 7–8, 123–4, 236–7
Ranspach, Pvt Paul, 137, 141
Rapido River (Italy), 171–2, 174–6, 178–88, 190–9
    and attack, 200–17, 219–22
    and barracks, 246, 254, 255–71
    and bridgehead, 223–39, 241–6
    maps, 177, 218, 240
Reagan, Lt Col Frank A., 49, 264
Redle, 1st Lt David D., 35–7, 70, 71
    and Algeria, 115–16, 120
    and barracks, 246, 258–9, 260, 263, 266, 270
    and bridgehead, 242
    and Fort Ord, 57, 60
    and Italy, 133, 139–43, 147
    and Mignano, 164, 166–8, 169
    and Port Lyautey, 88, 94
    and Rapido, 175–6, 179, 186–8, 191, 193, 198
    and Rapido attack, 200–1, 203, 215, 219–22, 225–6
    and reorganization, 151–3
    and Santa Elena, 72
Reid, Sgt John, 46

Reserve Officer Training Corps (ROTC), 13–14, 16
richochet bursting, 113
Richter, Sgt Art, 40, 94, 95, 116, 151
Rickerson, T/4 Jessie, 202
Robbins, Sgt Ralph, 28, 52
Rommel, Genlt Erwin, 23, 33, 44, 61
    and Egypt, 102–3
    and Tunisia, 83, 104
Roosevelt, Franklin, 4, 14, 34, 75
Royal Navy, 23
Russell, Nell, 101, 125
Russia, see Soviet Union
Ryder, Maj Gen Charles W., 101, 106, 256, 261–2
    and barracks, 262–4, 267–8
    and bridgehead, 224, 229, 239
    and Rapido, 172, 178–9, 183, 191, 197
    and Rapido attack, 210, 217

Sadowski, T/5 Edward J., 77–8
Salerno (Italy), 126–8, 130–5
San Pietro (Italy), 169–70
Santa Elena, USAT, 71–2, 74–7
Sarno, Capt Anthony M. "Doc," 91, 136, 159, 242
Senior, T/5 John "Red," 207–8
Severson, 2nd Lt A. P., 34, 53, 57, 60
Shapiro, Cpl Irving, 91–2
Shaw, 2nd Lt Ralph, 69–70, 81–2, 84, 92
Shew, Pfc Hubert S., 214–15
Shields, Sgt Edward A., 28, 39
Shirley, S/Sgt Gene, 53, 91, 138
Shue, Pvt Bernard, 154, 190
Sicily, 121–2, 124
Smith, Capt Anderson Q., 235, 247–8
Smith, 2nd Lt Foster Carroll "Blanco," 22, 27–9, 42
Smith, Sgt Hamilton A., 88, 139, 167
Solomon Islands, 63
Sorrell, Capt Walker, 227, 229, 234–5, 252–3
Sousse (Tunisia), 110
Southern Italy, 138–9
    and Caiazzo, 142–4
    and Laviano, 136–7
    map, 129, 149
    and Oliveto Citra, 135–6
    and Prata Sannita, 144–7, 150–1

and S'Agata, 152–4, 158–60
and San Martino, 139–40
and Sant'Angelo dei Lombardi, 137–8
and Volturno, 140–2
see also Salerno
Soviet Union, 3, 8–9, 44, 61
and *Barbarossa*, 33
and Caucasus, 83
Spain, 83, 86, 90
Spanish Civil War (1936–39), 18, 32, 58
sport, 115–17
Stalin, Joseph, 3
Sweeting, Lt Col Harry W., 22, 60–1, 69, 76
and Algeria, 115–18
and barracks, 257, 259, 262, 266,
268–70
and Bizerte, 124–7
and bridgehead, 225–7, 229–36, 238–9,
243, 245–6
and Caira, 247, 249–52
and Casablanca, 78, 84
and Italy, 136, 141–4
and Mignano, 166–7, 169, 172
and Port Lyautey, 88–90, 92–93
and Rapido, 178, 181–2, 188, 190–1,
195–7
and Rapido attack, 200–1, 203–4, 207–12,
217, 221
and reorganization, 150–1, 153
and Wilkinson, 53–54, 63–4

Taft, Robert, 3–4
tanks, British: Churchill, 108, 110
tanks, German: Mark IV, 136, 142
tanks, U.S., 5–11, 19–21
and amphibious training, 47–53, 62–4
and desert warfare, 102–3
and history, 17–19
and Italy, 151–2
and maintenance, 59–62, 117
and maneuvers, 86–7
and Rapido River, *189*, 190–1
and training, 29–31, 54, 57–8
tanks, U.S. (models):
Hellcat, 235, 243
M1 "Combat Car," 27, 31–3
M3, 33, 42–4
M3 "Lee" medium, 107, 109

M4, 104, 152–60, 163–4, 168–9, 200–17,
224–5, 251
M5, 66–7, 229, 251, 256
terrain, 86
Terry, Capt Dwight, 27–9, 37, 38, 45
and beach landings, 46, 49–51, 53
and Fort Ord, 57–8
and Montesano, 39–40
and Sweeting, 60
and Wilkinson, 63–5
Texas, USS, 72
Thompson, T/Sgt Morris B., 28, 75, 88,
169, 225
Tirpak, T/5 Paul T., 77–8, 116–17, 134–5,
205, 212–13
Trahan, 1st Lt Leo J., 247–9
Treadwell, 2nd Lt Ray, 54
Treanor, Tom, 194
Truscott, Maj Gen Lucian, 90, 97
Tunisia, 83, 90, 93, 103–13, 121–7
map, *99*

United States of America (USA), 1–6, 10,
23–4, 157–8
U.S. Army, 8, 10–11, 13–19, 26–7
and grades, 279–80
and organization, 281, 286–91
and tanks, 19–21
U.S. Army (units):
Fifth, 125–6, 130, 170–1, 210–11
Seventh, 121
I Armored Corps, 115
II Corps, 103–4, 172
VI Corps, 138, 142–3
1st Armored Dvn, 16, 104, 111–12
3rd Infantry Dvn, 31, 35, 113–14
34th "Red Bull" Infantry Dvn, 101–2,
105–6, 108–9, 141–2, 163–6, 178–9,
216–17, 228–9
36th "Texas" Infantry Dvn, 126, 164–6
45th "Thunderbird" Infantry Dvn, 131,
133, 135–6
82nd Airborne Dvn, 138–9
107th Cavalry Rgt, 57, 59
133rd Infantry Rgt, 107–8, 183–8, 190,
193–7, 244, 258
135th Infantry Rgt, 107–8, 183, 258,
266–7

142nd RCT, 224, 256
157th Rgt, 136–7
168th Rgt, 169, 203, 206–10, 215–16, 223–4, 244–6
194th Tank Btn, 34
751st Tank Btn, 101–2, 107–12
752nd Tank Btn, 111
756th Tank Btn, 21–2
760th Tank Btn, 226–7
776th Tank Destroyer Btn, 257
805th Tank Destroyer Btn, 216
U.S. Navy, 4–5, 47, 59, 62–3, 130–2

Van Voorhis, Col Daniel, 19
vehicles: jeeps, 33
Versailles, Treaty of (1919), 3

Walker, Maj Gen Fred L., 165, 169, 172, 175
war correspondents, 194, 250, 252–3
Ward, Lt Col Robert W., 262, 267
warfare, 4–5
Washington (WA), 25, 26–31, 35–40
weaponry, German: AT guns, 106–7, 109, 112
weaponry, U.S., 5–7, 29, 120–1
    anti-tank mines, 16–17
    machine guns (MGs), 42–3
    and tanks, 18–19, 66–7
    TDs ("Tank Destroyers"), 157
Wilkie, Wendell, 14
Wilkinson, Capt Charles M., 13–17, 19–24, 34
    and Algeria, 101–2, 116, 119–20, 125–6
    and beach landings, 45–51
    and Bizerte, 122–7
    and Camp Pickett, 65–6, 68–9
    and captaincy, 71
    and capture, 273–5
    and Casablanca, 81–4
    and Fort Dix, 70
    and Fort Knox, 59–62
    and Fort Lewis, 26–9, 36–8
    and Fort Ord, 56–9, 62–5
    and Italy, 139–47
    and IX Corps, 42–5
    and Mignano, 164, 166–70, 172, 174
    and Montesano, 39–40
    and Port Lyautey, 87–9, 92–4
    and promotion, 51–5
    and Rapido, 176, 178, 180–1, 195, 197–9
    and Rapido attack, 200–5, 207, 209–15, 219, 221
    and reorganization, 150–3
    and Santa Elena, 72, 74–6
    and training, 159
    and Tunisia, 105–6, 108–13
Winlock, 2nd Lt John, 94, 96, 120, 143, 178
    and Mignano, 164, 168–9
Wolfe, Lt Col Peter T., 49
World War I (1914–18), 2, 5–7, 17–18, 145
Wunderlich, Sgt Eugene, 70, 93, 235

Yugoslavia, 23

Zeilin, USS, 46–8, 50–1